W9-BNF-908

Teachers and the Law

Withdrawn

SIXTH EDITION

Teachers and the Law

Louis Fischer

University of Massachusetts

David Schimmel

University of Massachusetts

Leslie Stellman

Johns Hopkins University

With contributions by Cynthia Kelly

Northwestern University

Boston   New York   San Francisco
Mexico City   Montreal   Toronto   London   Madrid   Munich   Paris
Hong Kong   Singapore   Tokyo   Cape Town   Sydney

Senior Editor: *Arnis E. Burvikovs*
Editorial Assistant: *Christine Lyons*
Marketing Manager: *Tara Whorf*
Editorial Production Service: *Chestnut Hill Enterprises, Inc.*
Electronic Composition: *Omegatype Typography, Inc.*

For related titles and support materials, visit our online catalogue at www.ablongman.com.

Between the time Website information is gathered and published, some sites may have closed. Also, the transcription of URLs can result in typographical errors. The publisher would appreciate notification where these occur so that they may be corrected in subsequent editions.

Library of Congress Cataloging-in-Publication Data

Fischer, Louis
    Teachers and the law/Louis Fischer, David Schimmel, Leslie
Stellman.—6th ed.
        p.   cm.
Includes bibliographical references and index.
    ISBN 0-321-08210-9
    1. Teachers–Legal status, laws, etc.–United States.   2.
Students–Legal status, laws, etc.–United States. I. Schimmel, David.
    II. Stellman, Leslie.   III. Title.
    KF4175.Z9 F55 2003
    344.73'078–dc21

                                                                        2002074577

Printed in the United States of America

10 9 8 7 6 5 4   06 05

CONTENTS

PREFACE

Americans are a litigious people. They have been for a long time; in fact, over a hundred years ago, a French visitor, Alexis de Tocqueville, observed that in the United States all issues become "sooner or later a subject of judicial debate."

Today's schools function in a complex legal environment, and a wide range of legal issues influence the lives of teachers, students, parents, and administrators. In fact, educators ignore the law at their peril, since the U.S. Supreme Court has ruled that teachers and administrators may be held personally liable in money damages for violating students' clearly established constitutional rights.

This book is about teachers and the law that affects them—law established by state and federal statutes, constitutions, and court decisions. The law has little significance unless educators know about it and make the effort to see that it is carried out.

Our purpose in writing this book is not to encourage teachers to litigate. Going to court is expensive—emotionally and financially. Litigation tends to intensify conflict and polarize participants. Our goal is to help resolve educational conflicts without lawyers or courts. How? By helping teachers become *legally literate*—by providing them with information about the law that affects them, how the legal system works, and how that system can work for them in the public school. With this information, teachers can practice "preventive law." This does not mean that they will be their own lawyers, but rather that they will know their legal rights and responsibilities and will be able to educate other members of the school community about the law. Underlying this premise is our belief that unlawful school practices are generally not intentional but result from a misunderstanding about the law. Most school officials are anxious to avoid lawsuits; when teachers can show that a certain policy is illegal, administrators usually prefer to change the policy voluntarily rather than by a court order. We believe also that students' educational experiences improve when all members of the school community behave in a manner consistent with basic constitutional principles, such as due process of law.

Too many teachers view the law with anxiety and fear, as a trap to ensnare any educator who makes an innocent mistake, who disciplines a disruptive student, or who challenges an unreasonable parent. They see themselves as potential victims of a legal system that seems out of control. And they are excessively fearful about being sued. Much of this fear and anxiety is unfounded. It often is based on half-truths, misunderstanding, and misinformation about education law.

Why are so many educators poorly informed about the law that affects them? One reason is that much of this law did not exist when they were students; second, most teachers learned almost nothing about this subject during their education; and third, educators have had little training in applying education law during their professional careers. This book helps to fill that gap. It demystifies the law for teachers by translating professional jargon and legalese into everyday English.

In short, the purpose of this book is to empower teachers to take the law constructively into their own hands, in order to be able to use law as a source of guidance and protection, and to provide them with the knowledge necessary to improve school and class-room rules, to assert their rights, and to bring violations of the law to the attention of administrators and colleagues.

No single volume can address all the issues involving school law; this book covers only issues most central in the daily lives of teachers. It does not, for example, address issues related to the use of school property, school boundaries, school board procedures, and teacher retirement. School law is a broad and burgeoning field, and only some portions of it are directly relevant to the professional roles of most teachers; we focus on those portions.

New to This Edition

Much of the law examined in these pages is neither simple nor unchanging. Many of the cases are as difficult to resolve for lawyers and judges as they are for educators. This is so because cases involving school law often do not address simple conflicts or right against wrong, but rather complex issues encompassing the conflicting interests of teachers, parents, administrators, and students. Moreover, education law is constantly changing. New legislation is passed, regulations are amended, school boards revise their practices, and the Supreme Court denies or supports the constitutionality of particular policies. Because of this diversity and change, our discussion, while as current as we can make it, is intended to be illustrative, not exhaustive. In adding and deleting case references, we have highlighted major cases and legislation of general interest to teachers rather than focus on legal details. Citations to cases are in a form designed to be useful to teachers, rather than in the form used in legal treatises and law review articles. All the cases and legal references have been updated for this edition to provide the most important recent decisions. Specific new features include:

- New court cases from the U.S. Supreme Court as well as from federal and state appeals courts and trial courts.
- A new chapter that highlights controversies likely to be confronted during the beginning of the twenty-first century, including the rights of homosexual teachers and students, control of the Internet, school choice, high stakes testing, AIDS education, condom distribution, equitable school funding, gang clothing, school uniforms, hate speech, compulsory community service, teacher testing, and frivolous lawsuits.

Instructor's Manual

The *Instructor's Manual* to accompany this text includes objectives for each chapter, teaching activities, resources, suggested examination questions, and alternative assessment devices. The *Manual* also includes edited Supreme Court cases affecting education, important federal education laws, and Internet resources for school law. The *Manual* is available from the publisher by writing or accessing this Website:

www.ablongman.com

How This Book Is Organized

This book is divided into two parts. Part I, "The Legal Aspects of Teaching," addresses questions related to teacher contracts, dismissals, tenure, collective bargaining, liability, child abuse, defamation, and copyright laws. Part II, "Teachers' and Students' Rights," explores legal issues related to the scope and limits of personal freedom of expression, religion and conscience, and association; personal appearance, due process, and privacy. This part also includes material on the rights to be free from racial and sexual discrimination and rights related to school records, compulsory schooling, bilingual students, and students with disabilities. Part II concludes with a look at issues of importance for the future.

The book follows a question-and-answer format. Most of the questions and answers are based on reported court cases. By introducing educators to the law through the use of real conflicts, we provide material to which classroom teachers may personally relate. We find that this type of format offers a more lively and effective way for prospective teachers to relate to the law than does a focus on theoretical issues or legal abstractions. At the same time, each chapter—especially in the Summary—goes beyond the outcome of specific cases and identifies the underlying principles that are likely to apply in similar cases in the future.

Books about law typically begin with a description of the legal system and court structure. Since such discussions are often hard to understand in the abstract, we introduce these concepts in the context of an actual case in which a teacher sued her principal, superintendent, and school board for violating her constitutional rights The introductory chapter examines such questions as whether the teacher needed a lawyer, whether she would bring suit in state or federal court, how she would identify the law relevant to her case, and how the case was resolved.

Caution

The law is constantly changing and, although the answers provided here are accurate as of the time of publication, teachers should be aware that they cannot rely on the legal accuracy of this information. If you contemplate legal action, you should first consult with your professional association and/or a knowledgeable lawyer. But since judicial resolution of an educational dispute is often an unhappy, expensive, difficult, and time-consuming process, bringing suit should be the last resort. We hope this book will help you resolve disputes through discussion and negotiation rather than through litigation.

Request to Students and Instructors

We want this book to work for you. By sending us your comments, you can help us improve the next edition. What did you like and find useful? What should be added or eliminated? What was confusing or unclear?

Please send your reactions and suggestions to Louis Fischer or David Schimmel, 265 Hills South, University of Massachusetts, Amherst, MA 01003 (e-mail address:

schimmel@educ.umass.edu) or to Leslie Stellman, 901 Dulaney Valley Rd., Suite 400, Towson, MD 21204 (e-mail: lstellman@hupk.com).

Thanks from each of us.

L. F., D. S., C. K., L. S.

Acknowledgments

We wish to acknowledge and thank those who helped us in creating this edition of the book: Kimberly Steadman, who provided valuable research assistance; and Barbara Morgan, who helped us find relevant cases, statutes, and articles. We also wish to acknowledge the work of Meredith Armstrong, a paralegal in the law offices of Hodes, Ulman, Pessin & Katz, P.A. of Towson, Maryland, who spent untold hours researching and ensuring the accuracy of the case citations found throughout this book.

In addition, we thank to following reviewers for their insightful comments: Brian E. Boettcher, Minnesota State University, Mankato; Max Pierson, Western Illinois University; Susan Bon Reis, Ashland University; and Jerry D. Will, Emporia State University.

Teachers and the Law

1 Teachers and the Legal System

Overview

This chapter is intended to help teachers understand our federal and state court systems, which operate quite differently. We begin with the story of a teacher who was transferred from a high school drama and English position to a similar assignment but in a middle school, all because she produced a controversial play with her high school drama students which resulted in complaints to the school board. We address such issues as: What can teachers do when legal problems arise? What laws apply that affect the manner in which they are treated? When do they need lawyers? When can a teacher's union or association assist them? How can they find legal materials that will help them understand the laws applicable to their problems?

Boring v. The Buncombe County Board of Education[1]

Margaret Boring had been employed since 1979 as an English and drama teacher at the Charles D. Owen High School in Buncombe County, North Carolina. During her years at the school she had "built a national reputation for excellence in teaching drama and directing and producing theater." Plays she produced won numerous awards and many of her students went on with substantial scholarships.

In the fall of 1991, Ms. Boring produced a play in her advanced acting class entitled *Independence,* a drama about a dysfunctional, single-parent family. Characters included a divorced mother and three daughters, one a lesbian, another pregnant with an illegitimate child. The students planned to present the play, under Ms. Boring's direction, in a state competition. After its selection, Ms. Boring informed her principal of her choice, but he did not comment or react. Parents of the actors reviewed advance copies of the script, but registered no complaints. The students then performed *Independence* in a regional competition, where it won numerous awards. After the regional competition but before the state finals, controversy erupted. Another English teacher asked Ms. Boring if her students could observe a scene from the play performed in class, and assured that parental permission slips were obtained, Ms. Boring consented to do so. However, a student in the class who had not obtained a parental permission slip described the scene to his parent, who in turn informed the principal of concerns.

When the principal finally read the script, he forbade Ms. Boring from presenting the play at the state competition without at least deleting certain more controversial scenes.

1

Ms. Boring defied this directive, and the play won second place in the state finals. Despite having received a "superior" evaluation the following spring, Ms. Boring was transferred, at the principal's request, to a middle school where she was assigned to teach introductory drama. Ms. Boring appealed her transfer to the board of education. Following a hearing, the Board denied her appeal and upheld the transfer.

Ms. Boring initially filed her lawsuit in state court, alleging that Board members, the principal, and the superintendent of schools (all called "defendants") violated several of her rights under the state and federal constitutions. She asserted in her lawsuit that the defendants transferred her "in bad faith and with malice...over the ideas expressed in the play" and thus violated her freedom of expression. She claimed that the transfer caused her "emotional distress, personal and professional humiliation...bludgeoned her reputation as an educator, and...caused her to lose professional opportunities."

Because the lawsuit raised issues relating to federal constitutional rights, the Board successfully transferred the case from state court to federal court because the federal courts have principal jurisdiction to resolve questions of this nature. Once in federal court, a judge dismissed her claim without allowing it to go to trial, on the grounds that Ms. Boring's selection of a play for presentation was not an act of constitutionally protected free speech or expression. Thus, the court held that because Ms. Boring was not offering her *own* views, but instead, was presenting a play containing the views of others, she was not engaged in protected speech under the First Amendment. Moreover, the court held, Ms. Boring's transfer did not cause her to lose any income or benefits, and thus it did not constitute an act of retaliation for which the court could grant relief.

Unhappy with this result, Ms. Boring appealed the dismissal of her case to the U.S. Court of Appeals for the Fourth Circuit in Richmond, Virginia, which eventually reversed the lower court decision, and found that Ms. Boring did, in fact, engage in protected speech for which she could not lawfully be punished or retaliated against. The appeals court went on to state that a transfer could be considered an act of retaliation, and sent the case back to the lower court with instructions to allow Ms. Boring to present her case.

What Kinds of Laws Govern Ms. Boring's Situation?

Ms. Boring and all teachers are governed by three main types of laws: statutory law, constitutional law, and common law. *Statutory law* is the law created by legislatures such as Congress; *constitutional law* is law established by court decisions based on the U.S. or state constitution; and *common law* is the law established by other court decisions. In Ms. Boring's case, the appeals court ruled that there were largely constitutional law bases for legal action against the school board. Because Ms. Boring's right of free expression which is guaranteed by the First Amendment of the U.S. Constitution may have been violated by the board of education, she can sue in federal court alleging such violation. In addition, she can charge violations of the common law, such as infliction of emotional distress or breach of contract by virtue of the actions taken against her.

How Would Ms. Boring Decide Whether to Sue in State or Federal Court?

The answer depends on which court has *jurisdiction,* or authority, to consider the dispute. The federal trial courts (called United States district courts) were created under Article III of the U.S. Constitution and given the power to hear only certain types of cases: (1) those cases arising under the U.S. Constitution and/or federal laws, which are called "federal question" cases; (2) cases between citizens of different states where the matter in controversy exceeds $75,000, which are called "diversity" jurisdiction; and (3) cases in which the United States is a party. Cases involving public schools may be "federal question" cases, for they frequently invoke constitutional claims. Students or teachers might claim violations of any provision of the U.S. Constitution listed in Appendix A, such as the due process clause of the Fourteenth Amendment, or violation of any of the civil rights laws listed in Appendix B.

More commonly, education cases involve allegations that a state law, such as a teacher tenure statute or student discipline law, was violated. Students or teachers may also sue alleging violations of state common law, such as those raised by Ms. Boring.

Ms. Boring can sue in state or federal court. When she filed her lawsuit in a North Carolina court, that court could have decided all of her claims, even those involving federal law and the U.S. Constitution. However, the school board exercised its right to "remove," or transfer, the case to federal court because Ms. Boring raised federal questions about her constitutional rights. Once removed, the federal court had discretion to exercise jurisdiction over her state law claims as long as the state and federal claims arose from the same facts. If the federal court decides to rule on the state law claims, it must interpret and apply the appropriate state law. In Ms. Boring's case, the law of North Carolina concerning infliction of emotional distress and breach of contract would apply.

Regardless of which court is chosen by a plaintiff (state or federal) in which to bring a lawsuit, if federal questions are raised in the case, the board of education may, and generally does, remove the case to the federal courts where, it is believed, judges are more eager to dismiss them on pretrial motions rather than sending them to juries, and where the jury pools tend to be more diverse.

How Does Ms. Boring Go About Obtaining Legal Assistance in Her Dispute against the Board?

While Ms. Boring is not required to have a lawyer, she retained one because her case was complicated and required competent legal assistance. An individual has the right to *pro se* representation—that is, to represent one's self—but any person who wishes to file a serious lawsuit in state or federal court should have a lawyer, to provide legal advice, decide which court in which to sue, and to pursue the case through the often complicated legal system.

An effective attorney will represent Ms. Boring's interests in the lawsuit, consult frequently with her, and if a settlement is offered, discuss it with her. Ms. Boring, however, would make the final decision as to whether to settle her case or proceed to trial.

Frequently teachers seeking legal representation turn to their bargaining representative for assistance. In many states the teachers' union employs staff attorneys who will assist those teachers who require legal representation, including in criminal matters where, for instance, teachers are accused of sexual offenses or child abuse. Ms. Boring, for instance, was represented by a law firm retained by the National Education Association, the nation's largest teachers' union.

Are There Other Agencies besides the Courts Which Can Address the Rights of Teachers?

Besides the courts, teachers can turn to a variety of federal and local agencies should they feel that their rights have been violated. For instance, the Civil Rights Act of 1964 created the federal agency known as the Equal Employment Opportunity Commission (EEOC), which has the power to investigate and conciliate charges of employment discrimination based upon race, color, sex, age, national origin, religion, and disability. Many of the states and local governments have their own version of the EEOC with similar authority. In fact, under federal law no discrimination lawsuit may be filed in court unless an employee has first filed a sworn charge with one of these agencies and has received a "right-to-sue" letter from the EEOC.

Besides antidiscrimination agencies, teachers can seek redress for most school-related claims by filing an appeal with their superintendent and, if dissatisfied with the result, with their local board of education. Local boards frequently conduct hearings in order to make decisions regarding the validity of the superintendent's ruling. This is what occurred in the *Boring* case, where the Board upheld the superintendent's decision to transfer Ms. Boring from the high school to the middle school. In some states, decisions of the local boards are appealable by right to the state education authority (often a state board of education or state superintendent), and from there into the courts.

How Did Ms. Boring's Case Proceed?

Ms. Boring's lawyers first filed a *complaint* with the state court. The complaint contained a statement of the basis for the court's jurisdiction (i.e., what law or constitutional provision was violated), the facts upon which she relies to state her claim of such a violation, and what the *plaintiff* seeks (in her case, money damages and an order preventing the superintendent from transferring her to the middle school). The *defendant,* or person sued, has a certain period (usually 30 days) within which to file an *answer;* the answer admits to or denies the allegations contained in the complaint and sets forth the defendant's views about why the plaintiff's claims are legally unfounded. The defendant will often file a *motion to dismiss* with the court, arguing that even if the facts as alleged in the complaint are true, they do not state a valid basis for a lawsuit, also known as a *cause of action.* For instance, in *Boring* the school board asserted that since Ms. Boring was merely transferred between schools with no loss in pay, she had no valid claim of harm. When such a motion is filed, the court must first rule on it before the case can proceed further.

After these initial pleadings are filed, *discovery* begins. This is a process whereby each side finds out information about the other side's case. Discovery is usually prescribed for a limited period set by the court in a pretrial order, and consists largely of *interrogatories* (written questions answered under oath), *depositions* (sworn testimony taken of the parties and witnesses), and *document requests.* In Ms. Boring's case, her lawyer would have sent interrogatories to the school board, and taken depositions of the principal and superintendent of schools to determine the basis for the decision to transfer her. Documents requested would include her evaluations, her contract, and any written complaints about the play she performed made by parents or other teachers.

Prior to trial, there is very often a settlement conference in which the judge or a professional mediator appointed by the court might intervene to urge the parties to negotiate and come to agreement on some issues. If the parties agreed to settle the case (as happens in over 90 percent of all lawsuits filed), the matter would be resolved. If there was no settlement, the case would go to trial.

When Ms. Boring Lost at Trial, Where Did She Appeal?

When Ms. Boring lost in federal district court, she appealed to the next level of federal court, which in her case was the U.S. Court of Appeals for the Fourth Circuit. There are 13 such appeals courts (Figure 1.1), each hearing appeals from the district courts within that geographical circuit. (Figure 1.2). The appeals court decides issues of law and not fact. This court, therefore, will not retry the case but will merely review the trial court record to determine whether the court below made any legal errors in its rulings, or whether the jury's decision is supported by the evidence. To reach its decision, the appeals court will require both parties to submit written briefs setting forth their legal positions regarding each issue being appealed, and it will often hear oral arguments from the attorneys before ruling. The court will then issue a written opinion explaining its decision and reasoning.

If Ms. Boring's lawsuit had stayed in a state trial court, she would also be able to appeal within the North Carolina state court system. Since each state has the power to create its own court system, the systems vary considerably in how they are organized. (Figure 1.3). Most states have trial courts that hear only certain types of cases (e.g., family or probate courts), as well as trial courts that hear all other civil and criminal cases. Most states also have an intermediate appellate court as well as a final appellate court, which in Ms. Boring's case would have been the North Carolina Supreme Court.

Could Ms. Boring's Case End Up Being Heard by the U.S. Supreme Court?

Theoretically, yes, but not likely. Under the U.S. Constitution, the U.S. Supreme Court has the power to consider and decide only limited kinds of cases under its *original jurisdiction,* such as where a state has sued another state, as recently occurred in a dispute over water between Kansas and Colorado. The Constitution gives the Supreme Court discretionary *appellate jurisdiction* over decisions issued by the federal courts of appeal, which means that the Court can pick and choose those cases it wishes to hear, a process known as a *writ of certiorari.*

The Supreme Court also has discretion to review decisions of the highest appeals court of each state, but generally does so only where the issues in controversy involve federal statutory or constitutional questions. For the U.S. Supreme Court to hear a case, four of its nine members must vote to do so, a process known as granting *certiorari.* If, for instance, there is a difference of opinion among the various federal appeals courts, the Supreme Court will often step in and decide such a case. The Supreme Court declines to review far more cases than it hears; if it refuses a petition for *certiorari,* the lower court decision is final.

Could Ms. Boring Avoid Going to Court?

Most lawsuits are settled before going to trial. Ms. Boring might avoid even filing a lawsuit if she chose to resolve her dispute through an alternative dispute resolution (ADR) program. One such ADR option is *mediation,* a process in which adversaries such as Ms. Boring and the school board sit down with a neutral third person to negotiate an agreement that both sides find acceptable. Mediation hearings are informal, and the mediator serves as a facilitator to help the parties clarify the issues and find common ground for agreement. Mediators may make suggestions, but they do not impose a solution. Mediation is commonly used in

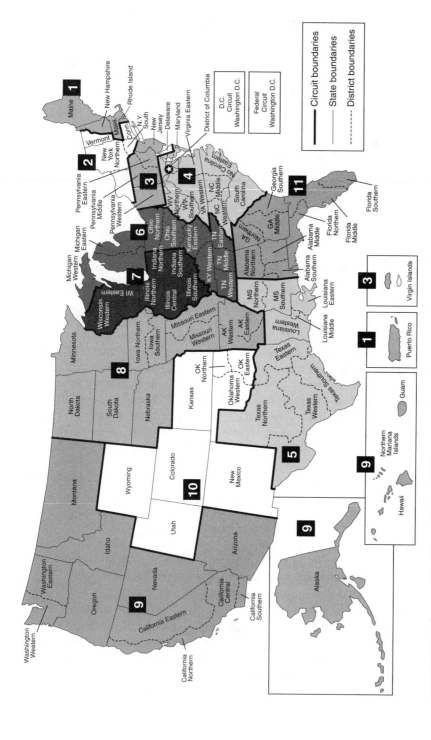

FIGURE 1.1 Geographical boundaries of U.S. courts of appeals and U.S. district courts

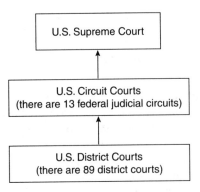

FIGURE 1.2   The federal court system

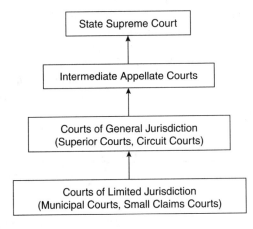

FIGURE 1.3   A typical state court system

family disputes, but the EEOC has launched a pilot program in a number of states where mediation is being used to resolve discrimination claims. Mediators include educators, lawyers, and social workers who are specially trained.

The other basic type of ADR is *arbitration,* which is commonly used to resolve labor-management disputes, including those in school settings. An arbitration hearing is more formal than a mediation hearing. A trained arbitrator, acting as a neutral third party, hears the case, allowing each side to present evidence and witnesses. After each side has made its case, the arbitrator rules for one side or the other. This decision may be either binding or nonbinding (as determined by state law). If the decision is binding, either party can appeal only on procedural grounds or by challenging the arbitrator's neutrality.

Recently the U.S. Supreme Court held that an individual who signed an arbitration agreement with his or her employer could not sue that employer for employment discrimination when the individual lost his or her job, but instead was required to submit the matter to arbitration under the terms of that agreement. Thus, arbitration is taking on a greater role as an alternative means of resolving workplace disputes.

How Could Ms. Boring Find the Law Concerning Teachers and Schools?

Every county has a courthouse that contains a law library. Every law school also has such a library, and most universities and colleges have legal collections as well. In each of these places, a librarian can find cases of interest. The following brief comments introduce some basic legal research materials.

Appellate courts almost always publish their decisions, and teachers who have the citation to a specific case will be able to find it. The decisions of the highest appellate court, the U.S. Supreme Court, can be found in the official reporter, the *United States Reports.* For example, the citation to *Brown* v. *Board of Education of Topeka, Kansas,* 349 U.S. 294 (1955), indicates that the case, decided in 1955, is reported in volume 349 of the *United States Reports* at page 294. Since Supreme Court cases are also reported in several commercial, unofficial publications, the same case may be followed by the notation "75 S.Ct. 753, 99 L.Ed. 1083." This means that the same case also appears in volume 75 of the *Supreme Court Reporter* on page 753 and in volume 99 of the *Lawyers' Edition* on page 1083. The most recent cases decided by the Supreme Court also appear in a loose-leaf volume called *United States Law Week.* An example of such a citation is *Givhan* v. *Western Line Consolidated School District,* originally cited as 47 U.S.L.W. 4102 (January 9, 1979).

Online, one can locate recent decisions of the U.S. Supreme Court at no cost, and in their originally published versions, at *www.supremecourtus.gov.* Just click on the "Opinions" tab, and then go to "Latest Slip Opinions." Similarly, decisions of the federal appeals courts may be found on-line through a free service located at www.findlaw.com. Under "judicial resources," one can locate specific federal appeals courts and even decisions of some of the federal district courts.

Cases decided by the U.S. courts of appeals are reported in the *Federal Reporter.* For example, the cite to the *Boring* case discussed throughout this chapter, *Boring* v. *The Buncombe County Board of Education,* 98 F.3d 1474 (4th Cir. 1996), indicates that this case was decided by the court of appeals for the Fourth Circuit in 1996, and is reported in volume 98 of the *Federal Reporter, Third Series,* on page 1474. Decisions of the federal district courts are reported in the *Federal Supplement* and are similarly cited. For example, *Pyle* v. *South Halley School Committee,* 824 F.Supp. 7 (D. Mass. 1993), a case involving the First Amendment right of students to wear controversial T-shirts to school, indicates that this case was decided by the federal district court for the District of Massachusetts in 1993, and is reported in volume 824 of the *Federal Supplement* on page 7.

Like decisions of the U.S. Supreme Court, state supreme court and state appellate court decisions are often published in more than one set of publications. One set is referred to as the "official reporter," and the other publications are referred to as "unofficial reporters." In New Jersey, for example, the official reporter is *New Jersey Reports* and the unofficial reporter is a regional volume known as the *Atlantic Reporter.* Thus cases decided by the Supreme Court of New Jersey are reported in both publications and a full citation for a case would look like this: *Tibbs* v. *Board of Education,* 59 N.J. 506, 284 A.2d 179 (1971). The "A.2d" indicates that this is the second series of the *Atlantic Reporter.* The original set of the *Atlantic Reporter* is cited as "A."; when a series becomes too long and the volume numbers too large, a second series is begun and cited as "A.2d." (Citations in the endnotes of each chapter in this book refer to the publications to which teachers are most likely to have access, generally "unofficial reporters.")

Teachers may also wish to find a certain state or federal law (statute). Laws passed by the U.S. Congress are referred to as "slip laws," and are cited according to the number of the Congress enacting them and the order of enactment. For example, Public Law No. 94-553, revising the copyright law, was enacted by the 94th Congress, and was the 553rd law passed by Congress and signed by the President. These laws are published in bound volumes called *Statutes at Large.*

Federal laws are also published in the *United States Code* (U.S.C.), which organizes the laws by topic. For example, the copyright laws are grouped together as a "title" (or subject), specifically Title 17. The *United States Code Annotated* (U.S.C.A.) follows the same organizational structure as the U.S. *Code,* but includes "annotations," or summaries, of cases that have interpreted the law.

State laws are compiled in a similar fashion. For example, in Illinois, the public laws are published in order of the General Assembly Session in the *Laws of Illinois.* The laws are organized by subject in both the *Illinois Revised Statutes* and West's *Smith-Hurd Illinois Annotated Statutes.* A summary of the state and federal court reporter system appears as Table 1.1.

Teachers who do not have citations to any specific cases but who wish to find decisions relevant to a particular legal topic must use other legal research tools. First, teachers may wish to gain an overview of a topic by consulting one of the two national legal encyclopedias, *Corpus Juris Secundum* or *American Jurisprudence.* These sources will summarize the law in an area such as sex discrimination and provide citations to cases. Teachers can also consult an annotation, or article, that discusses a certain topic. Annotations are published in the *American Law Reports* (ALR), and can be found by searching a topical index. Turning to the ALR index, for example, under "school teachers," one could find an annotation on "Sexual Conduct as Ground for Dismissal or Revocation of Teaching Certificate" (at 78 ALR3d 19).

All annotations include case citations, but no annotation provides comprehensive coverage of any specific topic. To find every case on a legal issue, a teacher must use a print digest system or a computerized legal research system. Until recently, all researchers relied on the print digest system to find cases. A digest works like an index, with each point of law in a case summarized, arranged by topic, and assigned a key reference number. West Publishing Company's National Reporter System publishes the full text of decisions from all state and federal courts, and also assigns key numbers to the points of law in each of these cases. Using these key numbers, researchers can locate cases from any jurisdiction dealing with these same points of law. An example of this key number system is shown in Figure 1.4, the first page of the *Boring* case. Rather than going to all of the individualized reporters for the various state and federal courts, however, a researcher may turn to West Publishing Company's *Education Law Reporter,* which includes all such cases reported in West's other reporter services, but which focuses exclusively on cases addressing education law. This Reporter also includes periodic research articles on topics of interest in the area of school law.

Today teachers can also find cases by using computerized research systems such as LEXIS or WESTLAW. Both of these systems are available through university and law school

TABLE 1.1   Summary of Court Reporter System

Court	Official Reporter (Citation)	Commercial Reporters (Unofficial Citation)
		Federal Court Reports
U.S. Supreme Court	United States Reports (U.S.)	Supreme Court Reporters (S.Ct.) and Lawyers' Edition (L.Ed.) and United States Law Week (U.S.L.W.)
U.S. Court of Appeals	Slip opinions issued by courts themselves	Federal Reporter (F.2d)
U.S. District Courts	Slip opinions issued by courts themselves	Federal Supplement (F. Supp.)

State Court Reports

Each state has its own official reporter, such as Ohio State Reports for the state of Ohio. In addition, state appellate court cases are published in West's National Reporter system as follows:

Atlantic Reporter (A.2d):
Cases from Maine, New Hampshire, Vermont, Rhode Island, Connecticut, New Jersey, Pennsylvania, Delaware, Maryland, and District of Columbia

North Eastern Reporter (N.E.2d):
Cases from Massachusetts, New York, Ohio, Indiana, and Illinois

North Western Reporter (N.W.2d):
Cases from Michigan, Wisconsin, Iowa, Minnesota, North Dakota, South Dakota, and Nebraska

Pacific Reporter (P.2d):
Cases from Montana, Wyoming, Colorado, Kansas, Oklahoma, New Mexico, Arizona, Utah, Idaho, Washington, Oregon, Nevada, and California

South Eastern Reporter (S.E.2d):
Cases from West Virginia, Virginia, North Carolina, South Carolina, and Georgia

Southern Reporter (So.2d):
Cases from Alabama, Florida, Louisiana, and Mississippi

South Western Reporter (S.W.2d):
Cases from Texas, Missouri, Arkansas, Kentucky, and Tennessee

In addition, West publishes two separate reporters for the two most litigious states:

California: **California Reporter (Cal. Rptr.2d)**

New York: **New York Supplement (N.Y.S.2d)**

libraries, law firms, and some businesses, and both allow access to the full texts of decisions from most state appeals courts and from most federal trial and appellate courts. The systems differ, though, in that LEXIS merely publishes the text of each decision while WESTLAW includes (for cases published in the West reporters) the West key numbers and summaries of points of law. In addition, universities and public libraries may subscribe to other computerized systems such as LawDesk that offer access to the full opinions of court cases.

Margaret BORING, Plaintiff–Appellant,

v.

The BUNCOMBE COUNTY BOARD OF EDUCATION; Charles Johnson, Chairman, Michael Anders; Terry Roberson; Bruce Goforth; Bill Williams; Grace Brazil; Wendell Begley; Dr. J. Frank Yeager, Superintendent; Fred Ivey, Principal, each in his/her individual and official capacity, Defendants–Appellees,

National School Boards Association; North Carolina School Boards Association; Virginia School Boards Association Council Of School Attorneys, Amici Curiae.

No. 95–2593.

United States Court of Appeals,
Fourth Circuit.

Argued March 4, 1997.

Decided Feb. 13, 1998.

High school drama teacher brought action against county board of education and various school officials, alleging that she was transferred to another school in violation of her First Amendment rights. The United

FIGURE 1.4 First page of decision in *Boring* case as it appears in *Federal Reporter* 3d, Volume 136

Reprinted with permission from 136 K3d, Copyright by West Publishing Company.

Many public libraries also subscribe to other computerized database systems that can help teachers find relevant information and names of current cases. For example, InfoTrac is a magazine abstract and full-text database that indexes approximately 400 magazines and newspapers. Teachers can use this database to read more about the legal issues discussed in this text or to follow new developments in the law. And there are many websites that offer information about current trends in school law which are available online at no charge. Be advised, however, that websites change on a daily basis, and are not always a reliable source of accurate information, since anyone can produce a website. Users, therefore, must take care to check the credentials of the source or author. Teachers can rely on information published by reputable and well-known organizations such as the American Library Association (ALA), however, and can visit websites such as the ALA's for information about proposed changes in the copyright act.

Teachers can also visit websites such as the Legal Information Institute established by Cornell Law School (http://www.law.cornell.edu) to access summaries of the law in various topic areas such as copyright, as well as links to key legal authorities including U.S. Supreme Court cases and relevant statutes.

What Actually Happened in Ms. Boring's Case?

The Fourth Circuit Court of Appeals initially ruled in 1996 that Ms. Boring was entitled to prove to the trial court that she was transferred from her high school to middle school assignment in retaliation for the exercise of her constitutional right of free speech. In so ruling, the Court determined that it was too early in the case for the trial court to dismiss her lawsuit, and that as a matter of law, her transfer could be found retaliatory, even if it did not mean a loss of either pay or benefits.

Unfortunately, Ms. Boring's case did not end with this victory before the Court of Appeals. The Buncombe County Board of Education filed a petition for a rehearing of the appeal before all 13 members of the Court of Appeals. This highly infrequent process, known as an *en banc* review, resulted in a narrow, 7-to-6 majority of the 13 judges on the Court of Appeals throwing out the original ruling of the 3-judge panel which had allowed Ms. Boring to try her claims before a jury. Completely repudiating the originally issued appeals court decision, the full court found that production of a school play was inherently part of the school's curriculum, just like the selection of textbooks. The court went on to rule that "the performance of a play under the auspices of a school and which is part of the curriculum of the school is…a legitimate pedagogical concern," over which school authorities have virtually unlimited control. In short, the court ultimately ruled, school officials had final say over "the makeup of the curriculum," including the content of plays performed by the students. Since teachers were deemed without a First Amendment right to "fix the curriculum," Ms. Boring was not, therefore, deprived of her constitutional rights when she was transferred after performing a play to which her principal and superintendent objected.

Ms. Boring's attorneys filed a petition for *certiorari* with the U.S. Supreme Court, which was denied, and the case was thus finally dismissed.

The *Boring* decision represents one of the very rare cases which, once filed, actually proceed to trial, and then the nonprevailing party notes an appeal with the appellate court. The vast majority of lawsuits filed in the U.S. end up settling before trial, largely because both sides quickly come to realize the enormous expense in both time and financial resources in order to proceed to trial. Nonetheless, those lawsuits which find their way all the way into the appellate courts, such as the *Boring* case, often involve significant questions of law or constitutional rights. The body of those cases in the various jurisdictions where court decisions are made have come to define the basic principles of school law. We have tried to capture and summarize those principles in this book.

N O T E S

1. 98 F.3d 1474 (4th Cir. 1996), *rehearing en banc granted and opinion vacated* 136 F.3d 364 (4th Cir. 1998) (*en banc*), *cert. denied* 119 S.Ct. 47 (1999).

PART ONE

The Legal Aspects of Teaching

2 Do I Have a Contract?

Overview

Local school boards have the legal authority to hire teachers, and most school boards have written contracts with their teachers. Local boards also have considerable discretion in deciding to whom they issue a contract so long as they do not violate an individual's statutory or constitutional rights. Under most states' education laws, local boards are supposed to issue contracts only to individuals who have valid teaching certificates. In today's teacher shortage climate contracts are often issued on a provisional basis to teachers who have not yet completed all the requirements of certification.

While local boards and superintendents of schools have the responsibility for ensuring teacher competence, state statutes generally set standards for teacher certification. Such criteria typically include educational requirements, an absence of a criminal background, and in many districts, successful completion of the National Teacher Examination (NTE). The contracts that school boards issue to certified teachers vary widely from district to district, but typically include provisions guaranteeing at least one year's employment provided the teacher does not engage in any act of misconduct, immorality, or other cause for discharge, and identify the teacher's assignment for the year. Many school systems allow these contracts to automatically renew from year to year without being renegotiated, and these basic terms are generally set unilaterally by the state or local boards of education.

In a handful of school districts which have more sophisticated and detailed contracts that result from collective bargaining negotiations, there is often found a provision requiring the school board to recognize the union as the bargaining agent for the teachers; various terms and conditions of employment including wages, salaries, benefits, extra-duty pay scales (such as for coaches) and stipulations regarding assignment, transfer, and promotion procedures, or even class size and the length of the school calendar.

Contract disputes arise in a wide variety of contexts, and their resolution depends on the language and conditions of a particular contract. Teacher contract disputes may also include interpretation of state laws. For example, if a teacher's resignation in the middle of the school year was withdrawn after the superintendent accepted it but before the school board formally acknowledged that acceptance, the court was required to look to state law in order to determine whether the superintendent had the authority to accept it.[1] Because the provisions of school contracts vary tremendously, and because contract disputes can also require interpretation of various state laws, this chapter does not answer questions about individual contracts but rather presents the basic legal principles surrounding the creation and termination of teaching contracts.

Creating a Contract

The *Wilson* Case[2]

On January 20, 1969, Jessie Wilson applied for a position as principal in the District of Columbia summer school program. She later received a form letter advising her that she had been selected for this position. The letter stated that the appointment was subject to full funding of the summer school program and the return of an attached acceptance form within five days. The acceptance form stipulated that the applicant's acceptance was "subject to the approval of the board of education."

Wilson returned the acceptance form within the required time. Before the board approved her appointment, however, the selection criteria for summer positions were revised, and the board decided that Wilson no longer qualified for the position as principal. After the board notified her that it could not approve her appointment, Wilson sued school officials for the loss of income resulting from their withdrawal of the offer of appointment as principal. Wilson argued that a contract was created when the summer school program received full funding and that school officials broke the contract when they refused to hire her.

The District of Columbia Court of Appeals disagreed. The court pointed out that the acceptance form specified the position was subject to approval by the district board of education. (The court also noted that such approval was required by law in the District of Columbia.) Since the board never gave its approval, "no binding contract of employment existed before Ms. Wilson was notified that she did not meet the criteria for appointment." Because no contract was ever created, Wilson did not have a legal right to the position as principal and was not entitled to any money from the board of education for loss of income.

When Is a Contract Created?

As *Wilson* demonstrates, certain requirements must be met before a contract is legally binding on both the teacher and school officials. Like all contracts, a teacher's contract must have: (1) a meeting of the minds of both parties, (2) valid consideration, (3) legal subject matter, (4) competent parties, and (5) definite terms.

In contract law, *a meeting of the minds* refers to mutual assent to the terms of the contract. This mutual agreement is usually reached through the process of offer and acceptance. This requirement was the issue in *Wilson;* the court was asked to decide whether there was a valid offer and acceptance. The court concluded that because the board did not complete proper procedures and did not approve Wilson's contract, there was no meeting of the minds and thus no contract.

Consideration refers to the promises bargained for and exchanged between the parties. To have valid consideration to support a contract, each party must give up something of value, or, in legal terms, "suffer some legal detriment"; that is, the parties to the contract must promise to do something they are not legally obligated to do or must promise to refrain from doing something they are legally privileged to do. In the case of a teaching contract, consideration consists of the exchange of promises between the teacher and the school; the teacher promises to perform certain teaching services, and school officials promise to pay the teacher a certain salary.

Legal subject matter means that the contract cannot require the parties to commit a crime or act against public policy (e.g., an Illinois teacher contracted to have a student murder his principal). *Competent parties* means that the people contracting must be of legal age (generally 18 years of age), and must have the mental capacity to understand the terms of the contract. *Definite terms* means that the contract must be clear enough so that each party knows what is required by it. Like other employment contracts, a teaching contract that does not state either salary or teaching duties is too indefinite to be legally enforced. Thus, an Indiana court ruled that a contract to pay a teacher "good wages" was not valid.[3]

When Does a Contract Become Legally Binding?

As Jessie Wilson discovered, a contract is not valid until the school board approves it. Because school boards act as public bodies, they cannot accept (or ratify) a contract without taking official action. Thus one teacher's contract was not valid when the board of education did not follow the required roll-call procedure in voting on whether to offer her a teaching position.[4] In addition, state law may provide that the school board must ratify a contract before it is legally binding, as in *Wilson*.

Express and Implied Contracts

Does a Contract Have To Be in Writing?

No. Unless state law requires that a teacher's employment contract be in writing, an oral contract that has all the necessary legal requirements is legally binding.

What Is a "Unilateral" Contract, and Can It Be Legally Binding?

A unilateral contract arises from a promise made by one party in exchange for the other party's act or performance.[5] Where, for instance, a school district offered to employ a bus driver, the offer did not solicit a return promise from the driver (and none was given). Because an offer for a unilateral contract is accepted by performance, the school district was not contractually bound until the driver actually commenced performing. Thus, until that point the school district was free to revoke the offer any time prior to acceptance.[6]

Does a Contract Have to Contain All the Relevant Information Regarding the Terms and Conditions of Employment?

Not necessarily. Like other contracts, a teacher's contract includes the provisions of any relevant state laws, such as those concerning teacher tenure and dismissal procedures. The contract also includes (or makes reference to) any rules and regulations adopted by the school board that are in effect at the time the contract is signed. But most teachers' contracts lack much detail, other than dates of employment and salary information.

Can an Employee Handbook Serve as a Basis for Contractual Obligations?

Possibly, provided that the handbook does not contain a disclaimer explicitly denying that it serves as a contract of employment.[7] In such cases, handbooks have been found not to be legally binding contracts.[8] When an employee is working without a formal employment contract, the terms of an employee handbook may be contractually binding. Although some courts reject this idea, the majority of jurisdictions recognize the contract potential of employee handbooks and manuals.[9] An employee handbook creates enforceable contractual rights if the traditional elements of contract formation (offer, acceptance, and consideration) are satisfied.[10] However, courts have consistently held that not every statement made in a personnel handbook or other publication will rise to the level of an enforceable covenant. "General statements of policy are no more than that and do not meet the contractual requirements of an offer."[11] Accordingly, for handbook provisions to rise to the level of contractual commitments they must be specific and clear. The employee must be aware of the policies and believe them to be offered terms of employment; the employee must also continue to work after notification of the handbook terms, thus giving consideration.[12]

How Long Does a Contract Last?

The contract states how long it is to be in effect. Nontenured teachers generally hold their positions under annual contracts. Teachers may also be employed under "continuing contracts," which provide that they will be reemployed unless school officials give notice by a certain date that their contracts will not be renewed. Most states also allow school boards to enter into multiyear employment contracts with teachers.

Can a Teacher Work without a Contract?

A teacher can certainly work without a contract, but by doing so, he or she may have difficulty proving that a certain amount of money is owed as compensation for teaching services. In an Illinois case, for example, the court ruled that tenured teachers did not have to sign contracts.[13] Nevertheless, when a group of tenured teachers refused to sign new contracts, the court held that they should be paid on the basis of the preceding year's salary and should be denied the benefits given to teachers who had signed the new contract. A nontenured teacher who works without a contract will have more difficulty than a tenured teacher in collecting money from school officials. The nontenured teachers may be able to recover the reasonable value of teaching services under a theory of *quantum meruit,* which means that the teacher is compensated for the value of services rendered to the school district.

Breach of Contract

How Can a Contract Be Broken by School Officials?

A contract is binding on both parties, and either party who fails to meet contractual obligations has *breached* (broken) the contract. For example, in one West Virginia case, a teacher who was dismissed due to a lack of need for his services sought a court order reinstating him to his former position. The court rejected the teacher's request, and found no breach of the teacher's contract:

> In the very nature of things, situations frequently arise where competent teachers exceed the demand for their services, and it would be strange indeed if a board of education lacks the power to dispense with the services of teachers who are not needed.... In a case where, in seeking to improve the efficiency of a school, it becomes necessary to dispense with the services of a particular teacher, this Court is not inclined to substitute its judgment for that of the board of education.[14]

School officials can breach a contract if they attempt to change the terms of a contract after it is in effect. In Idaho, for example, three teachers signed regular teachers' contracts which specifically included both their regular salaries in addition to extra-duty assignments such as summer school and working at a youth ranch. Such assignments added 40 paid days to one teacher's school year, for an additional $6,225 above her annual salary of $29,570. Every few years teachers were given contracts containing "change orders" that reflected increases in the base salary, while preserving the extra-duty assignment and pay. In 1995, however, the teachers did not receive the same extra-duty assignments, and were not warned in advance that their assignments were to be eliminated. They filed suit, alleging, among other causes of action, a breach of their contracts. The trial court and, later, the Idaho Supreme Court upheld the teachers' claims, ordering that their extra-duty salaries be restored.[15] As the court concluded, a change in the contract terms could not be implemented without a statutorily-prescribed formal notice and a hearing.[16]

How Can a Teacher Break a Contract?

The same principles that apply to school officials also apply to teachers. A teacher who has signed an employment contract and then refuses to accept the teaching position or abandons the position in midyear has breached the contract.

A teacher who does not abide by its terms also breaches a contract. In Texas, for example, a music teacher was employed by the Mission public schools under a contract that stated that she would not teach anywhere else in Texas during the contract period. Because the teacher left this job to teach music and direct the band in the public schools in Cisco, Texas, the court ruled that she had breached her contract. [17] Similarly, an Arkansas court found that a teacher had breached her employment contract when she took a leave of absence without following the procedure outlined in the school board's regulations.[18]

What Are the Legal Consequences of Breaking a Contract?

When one party breaches a contract, the other party to the contract is entitled to a legal remedy that will compensate for the injury the breaching party has caused. In most situations this remedy will be an award of some amount of money, or *damages*. The specific amount of money to be awarded is determined by the court according to the particular facts in each case.

In general, when a school board breaks an employment contract, the injured teacher is entitled to damages that equal the salary owed under the contract minus an amount of money the teacher actually earned or might have earned had another teaching position been obtained. To understand this rule, it helps to examine a particular case.

In a case in which a teaching contract was breached, the court awarded the teacher, Bertrand Russell, $20,000.[19] To reach this figure, the court engaged in the following analysis: First the court turned to the contract itself to determine how much money Russell would have received if he had been permitted to lecture; under the terms of the contract, the Barnes Foundation had agreed to pay Russell $8,000 a year, or $24,000 for three years. The court then explained that it was up to the Barnes Foundation (the defendant) "to show, in mitigation of this amount, the extent of the plaintiff's [Russell's] earnings or ability to obtain other employment."[20] The evidence showed that during the two years he was teaching for the Barnes Foundation, Russell had earned $2,145.00 and $3,195.68 from other sources, principally his writing and radio addresses. Russell also testified that his earning prospects from these sources for the next three years were slight and that "his advanced age and the drastic curtailment of courses in philosophy in college curricula" made it impossible for him to obtain other employment. Given this evidence, the court found that Russell could expect to earn only $4,000 from outside sources for his teaching activities during the next three years and thus ordered the Barnes Foundation to pay him $20,000 ($24,000–$4,000) as damages for breach of contract.

In suing for breach of contract, a teacher can also collect as damages any other expenses incurred as a result of the school board's action. For example, a Montana teacher collected the value of the living quarters supplied rent-free under her contract after she was wrongfully dismissed.[21] The courts have also held that teachers who are wrongfully discharged can recover expenses that they can show were incurred in seeking another teaching position.[22] Although teachers are generally not awarded money to cover attorneys' fees, such expenses may be awarded as damages under state or federal laws.[23]

The same principles apply when a teacher breaks a contract: School officials are entitled to collect money damages that will cover the school's costs in hiring a replacement. (However, in a time of teacher surplus, when it was relatively easy for school boards to replace teachers, money damages were apt to have been minimal. Today, of course, it is much harder to replace a teacher, particularly in shortage areas such as math and science.) Thus, if a teacher who is under contract quits in the middle of the school year, school officials can sue the teacher for expenses incurred in finding another teacher who can assume the same responsibilities. If the district is forced to pay a higher salary to find a replacement, school officials can sue the leaving teacher for the difference between that teacher's salary and the replacement teacher's salary.

Some employment contracts include provisions that require teachers who break their contracts to pay a specific amount as damages to the school district. In North Dakota, a teacher's contract stated that a teacher who asked to be released from her contract within two weeks before she was scheduled to begin teaching was required to pay damages in the amount of 4 percent of her salary under the contract.[24] These contractual provisions are known as *liquidated damages clauses,* and the courts will enforce them when it is difficult for the parties to a contract to determine the monetary value of a breach of a contract. The courts will not enforce such contractual provisions when they feel that the party who breaks the contract has to pay such a large amount of money that this provision is really a penalty or a punishment for breaching the contract.

In the North Dakota case, six days before she was to begin teaching, Marcia Walker notified her district superintendent that her husband was moving from the area and that she would be unable to meet her contractual obligations. The school district found a replacement before school started but maintained that Ms. Walker was still required to pay damages. Ms. Walker argued that the fixed-damages provision of her contract constituted a penalty and therefore was void under North Dakota law. The court disagreed. Although the court explained that an employer could generally recover only the costs of replacing an employee who breaches a contract, it noted that liquidated-damages provisions were valid when it was difficult to ascertain the exact amount of damages. The court found that teacher replacement was such a situation:

> Thus, when we consider the damages caused by a teacher's breach of an employment contract, we cannot ignore the interruption to the school system and the resultant debilitating effect such interruption has upon the learning process of students in the school system. The possibility that the replacement teacher who was obtained may be less experienced or less qualified and, thus, a less effective instructor must also be considered in the assessment of damages. It would not be possible at the time of contracting to foresee all these elements of damage that may occur. Even if known, it would be extremely difficult to evaluate these damages on a monetary basis.... Such damages are not legally compensable but constitute a public injury which the school district was entitled to consider.[25]

In some states, such as Maryland, the standard form teacher's contract which is dictated by regulations promulgated by the state board of education includes language consenting to the district's right to seek revocation or suspension of a teacher's license as a penalty for breaching that contract by failing to fulfill its terms. For example, in a recent case in that state a teacher who abandoned her position as a first-year kindergarten teacher to accept employment in another school system lost her license to teach, in accordance with the state board of education's governing regulations.[26] However, as prescribed in the cited Maryland regulation, school districts often have discretion to waive these penalties.

When the School Board Breaches a Contract, Must the Teacher Look for Another Teaching Position to Collect Damages?

A teacher who is wrongfully discharged generally has the duty to look for a similar teaching position in order to "mitigate the damages." If the school board can show that other teaching jobs were available, the board can reduce the amount of money owed as damages by the salary the teacher could have earned. Nevertheless, a teacher does not have to accept a job in another locality or a job that is inferior to the denied position. A federal appeal court held, for example, that a principal was not required to mitigate damages by accepting a position as a teacher.[27] Even though the teaching job paid as much as the principalship, the court concluded that the demotion to teacher might cast doubt on the principal's competence as an administrator and affect later career opportunities.

If the school board breaches a contract some time before the teacher is to start working, the teacher is not required to look for another teaching position at once. Instead the teacher has the right to wait until the contract was to begin before looking for another job. In Michigan, for example, the court ruled that a teacher whose contract was wrongfully withdrawn over the summer did not have to abandon her vacation to seek other employment but could notify the school district that she was still prepared to teach. She could wait to look for another job until after school started in the fall.[28]

Can the Court Order a School Board to Rehire a Teacher?

Yes. Although the courts generally do not order people to return to work or to perform certain services, they will do so when an award of money will not adequately compensate the party who has been the victim of a breach of contract. Where a teacher has tenure, for example, the courts can order reinstatement if the teacher has been wrongfully discharged. In one instance, a university failed to follow its own regulations when dismissing a professor, and the court ordered that the professor be reinstated.[29] The court explained: "In view of the uncertainty in measuring damages because of the indefinite duration of the contract and the importance of the status of plaintiffs in the milieu of the college teaching profession it is evident that the remedy of damages at law would not be complete or adequate.... The relief granted herein is appropriate to achieve equity and justice."

The situation for teachers without tenure varies according to the circumstances surrounding the dismissal. If school officials failed to follow proper hearing procedures, for example, the court may merely remand (i.e., send the case back to the board) for a hearing.[30] In other cases, the court may order reinstatement. For example, a federal court ordered the reinstatement of a nontenured teacher when she was improperly dismissed for exercising her constitutional rights under the First Amendment.[31]

Are Other Remedies Available When One Party Breaches a Contract?

Yes. The courts have the power to issue orders, known as *writs of mandamus,* to force school officials to comply with the terms of a contract. When one school board was guilty of racial discrimination in refusing to renew a teacher's employment contract, the court ordered the board to renew the contract. [32] In addition, courts can issue *injunctions* (court orders prohibiting a party from acting in a particular way or compelling a party to take specific action) to require the parties to meet their contractual obligations. For example, a court issued an injunction to prevent a teacher from breaching a contractual provision that prohibited her from teaching music in any other school district in the state.[33] In another case, a court issued an injunction preventing the school board from dismissing a superintendent when the school officials had no legal power to do so.[34]

Are There Other Ways That a Contract Can End?

Yes. Under the doctrine of *impossibility of performance,* a party to a contract is excused from meeting the obligations under that contract if it is impossible to do so. In Washington, for example, a teacher was discharged from his contractual obligation because of his deteriorating eyesight.[35] The court explained that when it is impossible for the teacher to meet contractual duties, the contract to teach is said to be discharged (another term for terminated and no longer legally binding) *by operation of law.* A contract can also be terminated by mutual agreement of the parties. In Kansas, a court held that a teacher's employment contract had been terminated by mutual agreement with the school board after she submitted a letter of resignation and the board voted to accept her resignation.[36] Although there was some question as to whether she had in fact resigned, the court noted that "mutual assent to abandon a contract may be inferred from the conduct of the parties and the attendant circumstances." The court found that there was sufficient evidence to indicate that both the teacher and the school board had intended to end the contract; the court thus concluded that the contract was terminated.

Summary

Where teachers are employed under contracts that outline their rights and responsibilities in employment, the contract becomes effective legally when the following conditions are met: The contract has a legal subject matter; there is a meeting of the minds of both parties; there is valid consideration; the parties are competent; and the contract has definite terms. In addition, school officials must act to officially ratify a teacher's contract.

A contract is binding on both parties; either the teacher or the school officials will be legally liable if obligations under the contract are not met. A school board that breaks a contract to employ a teacher will be required to pay that teacher monetary damages to compensate for loss of salary. In such a situation, however, the teacher has the duty to mitigate these damages by attempting to secure another teaching position. In breach-of-contract situations, the teacher may be entitled to other legal remedies as well, such as reinstatement or an injunction or other order requiring the school board to fulfill its obligations under the contract.

A teacher who breaks a contract will also be liable to the school district. Under traditional contract law principles, the teacher will be liable for the school district's costs in finding a replacement and for any additional salary that might have to be paid. Today, teachers' contracts may describe the specific amount of damages a teacher will have to pay in this situation.

While these legal principles apply in general, state statutes vary. Especially in the area of contract termination, teachers who have questions about specific situations must consult their own state law as well as local board policies for more detailed guidance.

NOTES

1. *Lemlich* v. *Board of Trustees of the Community College of Harford County,* 282 Md. 495, 385 A.2d 1185 (1978).
2. *Board of Education* v. *Wilson,* 290 A.2d 400 (D.C. 1972).
3. *Fairplay School Township* v. *O'Neal,* 26 N.E. 686 (Ind. 1891).
4. *Board of Education* v. *Best,* 39 N.E. 694 (Ohio 1894).
5. *Greene* v. *Oliver Realty, Inc.,* 363 Pa.Super. 534, 526 A.2d 1192 (1987).
6. *Kuhnhoffer* v. *Naperville Community School District,* 758 F.Supp. 468 (N.D. Ill. 1991).
7. *Conkwright* v. *Westinghouse Electric Corp.,* 739 F.Supp. 1066 (D. Md. 1990).
8. *Castiglione* v. *Johns Hopkins Hospital,* 69 Md. App. 325, 517 A.2d 786 (1986).
9. *Toussaint* v. *Blue Cross & Blue Shield of Michigan,* 408 Mich. 579, 292 N.W.2d 880 (1980).
10. *Duldulao* v. *Saint Mary of Nazareth Hospital Center,* 505 N.E.2d 314 (Ill. 1987).
11. *Pine River State Bank* v. *Mettille,* 333 N.W.2d 622 (Minn. 1983).

12. *University of Baltimore* v. *Iz,* 123 Md. App. 135, 716 A.2d 1107 (1998).

13. *Davis* v. *Board of Education of Aurora Public School District No. 131,* 312 N.E.2d 335 (Ill. App. Ct. 1974).

14. *Bates* v. *Board of Education,* 133 W. Va. 225, 55 S.E.2d 777 (1949).

15. *Lowder, Roundy & Winks* v. *Minidoka County Joint School District No. 331,* 979 P.2d 1192 (Idaho 1999).

16. 979 P.2d at 1197.

17. *Mission Independent School District* v. *Diserens,* 188 S.W.2d 568 (Tex. 1945).

18. *Special School District of Fort Smith* v. *Lynch,* 413 S.W.2d 880 (Ark. 1967).

19. *Russell* v. *Barnes Foundation,* 52 F. Supp. 827 (E.D. Pa. 1943).

20. 52 F.Supp. at 829.

21. *Wyatt* v. *School District No. 104, Fergus County,* 417 P.2d 221 (Mont. 1966).

22. *Sams* v. *Board of Commissions of Creek County,* 178 P. 668 (Okla. 1919); *McBeth* v. *Board of Education of DeValls Bluff School District No. 1,* 300 F.Supp. 1270 (E.D. Ark. 1969).

23. *Ward* v. *Kelly,* 515 F.2d 908 (5th Cir. 1975); *Doyal* v. *School Board,* 415 So.2d 791 (Fla. Dist. Ct. App.1982); *Hyde* v. *Wellpinit School District No. 49,* 648 P.2d 892 (Wash. Ct. App. 1982).

24. *Bowbells Public School District No. 14* v. *Walker,* 231 N.W.2d 173 (N.D. 1975).

25. *Id.* At 176.

26. Section 13A.12.05.02 of the Code of Maryland Regulations specifically provides that "[a teaching] certificate may be suspended for not more than 365 days if the certificate holder leaves the employment of a local school system after July 15 without the consent of the local board of education, which may not be unreasonably withheld, and contrary to the provisions of the Regular State Teacher's Contract...."

27. *Williams* v. *Albemarle City Board of Education,* 508 F.2d 1242 (4th Cir. 1974); see also *State ex rel. McGhee* v. *St. John,* 837 S.W.2d 596 (Tenn. 1992).

28. *Farrell* v. *School District,* 56 N.W. 1053 (Mich. 1893).

29. *American Association of University Professors* v. *Bloomfield College,* 346 A.2d 615 (N.J. Super. 1975).

30. *Danroth* v. *Mandaree Public School District No. 36,* 320 N.W.2d 780 (N.D. 1982).

31. *Allen* v. *Autauga County Board of Education,* 685 F.2d 1302 (11th Cir. 1982).

32. *Johnson* v. *Branch,* 364 F.2d 177 (4th Cir. 1966).

33. *Mission Independent School District* v. *Diserens,* 188 S.W.2d 568 (Tex. 1945).

34. *Lemasters* v. *Willman,* 281 S.W.2d 580 (Mo. Ct. App. 1955).

35. *Oneal* v. *Colton Consolidated School District No. 306,* 557 P.2d 11 (Wash. Ct. App. 1976). Of course, the teacher's rights are better defined today under the federal Americans With Disabilities Act, which would prevent discrimination based upon the teacher's visual impairment. Before civil rights laws such as the Americans With Disabilities Act were enacted, teachers were compelled to seek relief under contractual theories such as in the *Oneal* case.

36. *Brinson* v. *School District No. 431,* 576 P.2d 602 (Kan. 1978).

CHAPTER

3 How Secure Is My Employment?

Overview

Teacher tenure laws protect teachers from arbitrary actions by school officials. In the words of the Supreme Court of Pennsylvania:

> Time and again our courts have stated that the purpose of the tenure provisions of the School Code is the maintenance of an adequate and competent teaching staff, free from political or arbitrary interference, whereby capable and competent teachers might feel secure, and more efficiently perform their duty of instruction.[1]

Although some school reform advocates charge that teachers are now adequately protected from arbitrary administrative actions by local collective bargaining agreements and by the U.S. Constitution's due process guarantees, teacher tenure is still the norm. Tenure supporters argue that tenure laws are necessary to protect the state's interest in securing permanency in the teaching force and in creating a uniform system of permanent contracts.[2] Tenure laws can help maintain a good educational system by ensuring the stability and security of satisfactory teachers and by outlining orderly procedures for the dismissal of unsatisfactory teachers.

Teachers who are granted tenure can be dismissed only for a cause set out by law. However, tenured teachers do not have a right either to a particular position in a school district or to indefinite employment. Before tenured teachers can be dismissed, school boards must show cause why they are not fit to teach. Tenured teachers are also entitled to notice of these charges and a hearing in which the board has the burden of proving that there is legal cause for dismissal.

In addition to these state law rights, teachers are given rights under the due process clause of the U.S. Constitution. Regardless of whether a teacher has tenure, the U.S. Supreme Court has held that teachers who have constitutionally protected interests in property or liberty are entitled to notice and a hearing prior to termination.

This chapter examines the state laws and constitutional provisions that define a teacher's right to employment. It explores such topics as how teachers acquire tenure, what rights come with tenure, and what grounds exist for dismissing tenured teachers.

Acquiring Tenure

The *Sindermann* Case[3]

Robert Sindermann was a teacher in the Texas state college system from 1959 to 1969. After teaching for two years at the University of Texas and for four years at San Antonio Junior College, he was employed at Odessa Junior College for four successive years, under a series of one-year contracts.

During the 1968–1969 academic year, Sindermann was elected president of the Texas Junior College Teachers Association and became involved in public disagreements with Odessa Junior College's Board of Regents and administration. In May 1969, Sindermann's one-year employment contract ended, and college officials did not offer him a new contract for the next academic year. They did not provide him with any stated reasons for the nonrenewal of his contract; nor did they allow him a hearing at which he could challenge the nonrenewal. Sindermann brought a suit against the college authorities, arguing that their failure to provide him an opportunity for a hearing violated the Fourteenth Amendment's guarantee of procedural due process.

In considering the teacher's claim that he was entitled to a hearing, the Supreme Court examined his argument that he had a right to continued employment. Sindermann alleged that while the college had no official tenure program, it actually operated a *de facto* tenure program. To support his claim, Sindermann cited the following provision, which had been in the college's official faculty guide for many years:

> Teachers Tenure: Odessa College has no tenure system. The Administration of the College wishes the faculty member to feel that he has permanent tenure as long as his teaching services are satisfactory and as long as he displays a cooperative attitude toward his co-workers and his superiors, and as long as he is happy in his work.[4]

In addition, Sindermann stated, he had relied on guidelines put out by officials of the state college system, which provided that a person employed as a teacher in the system for seven years or more had a form of job tenure.

The Court explained: "A written contract with an explicit provision is clearly evidence of a formal understanding that supports a teacher's claim of entitlement to continued employment unless sufficient cause is shown."[5] However, the Court went on to state that the absence of such a provision would not always foreclose the possibility that a teacher had a "property" interest in reemployment. Although the Court did not decide whether Sindermann was entitled to tenure, it did state that a teacher "who has held his position for a number of years might be able to show, from the circumstances of this service—and from other relevant facts—that he has a legitimate claim of entitlement to job tenure."[6] The Court noted that proof of such a property interest in reemployment would not automatically entitle Sindermann to reinstatement as a teacher. Nevertheless, such proof would obligate college officials to grant a hearing at his request, at which he could be informed of the grounds for his nonretention and could challenge the sufficiency of these grounds.

How Can Teachers Acquire Tenure?

As the Supreme Court explained in *Sindermann,* a teacher may acquire tenure "by custom." In such a situation, a teacher's right to tenure is not formalized in a written contract but is implied from the circumstances of employment. When a teacher can prove an expectancy of continued employment, the teacher has a property interest in job tenure that is protected by the due process clause of the Fourteenth Amendment.

In most situations, however, a teacher's right to tenure is established by state law. Most states have laws that outline the requirements for tenure, and these laws generally require teachers to undergo a period of probationary service before they can become tenured, or "permanent," teachers. In Virginia, for example, a teacher must teach for a probationary period of three years in the same county or city school system before attaining tenure status.[7] Similarly, in Maryland a teacher may acquire tenure status only after his or her contract has been renewed at least two times, although recent legislation allows a district to place a probationary teacher on a third year's probation provided that the teacher demonstrates sufficient promise of future success.[8] During the probationary period, the teacher is employed under a yearly contract and usually can be dismissed by school officials at the end of a contract period for any reason. (See chapter 12 for further discussion of teachers' due process rights.)

To acquire tenured status by law, teachers must comply with the specific requirements of their state's law. In some states, tenure becomes permanent as soon as the teacher completes the required probationary period. In other states, the school board may have to take some positive action for the teacher to achieve tenure.

Whether or not the school board has to take some affirmative step to ensure that a teacher achieves tenure also depends on the nature of the teacher's employment contract. Some teachers are employed under yearly contracts. In such cases, the board must act to renew the contract at the close of the school year before the teacher can be reemployed and thus achieve tenured status. Teachers may also be employed under continuing contracts which are automatically renewed if the school board does not inform them by a certain date that their services will not be needed during the coming year.

There are cases where, despite having met the requirement of being renewed a sufficient number of times, tenure is not achievable where a teacher has failed to meet another precondition for retaining her job. In a Tennessee case, a teacher who had failed on five of six occasions to pass one of the components of the National Teacher Examination (NTE) had her contract rescinded by the local school board. Because she had been granted her contract with a promise of tenure "pending teacher certification," the court found that her failure to meet the precondition that she achieve certification status by passing the NTE entitled the district to rescind its contract and to deny her tenure.[9] Because each state has its own tenure requirements, teachers must consult the statutes and court decisions in their state to determine what specific procedures must be followed.

Can a Teacher Be Awarded Tenure If School Officials Fail to Follow Required Legal Procedures?

It depends on the state. A Kentucky court ruled that a probationary teacher will achieve tenured status if the school board fails to give the teacher proper notice concerning reemployment for the next year.[10] Thus, a Colorado court held that a teacher who did not receive timely notice that her contract would not be renewed was automatically reemployed for a fourth year and entitled to tenured status.[11]

Other courts have interpreted tenure laws strictly. In Tennessee, for example, a court ruled that a probationary teacher who was improperly dismissed because she had not been notified of the decision not to renew her contract in a timely manner, should be rehired, but only under an annual contract.[12] Again the court looked to public policy considerations and concluded that the legislature did not intend that teachers be entitled to tenure as a matter of right after completing their probationary service, but that tenure be granted by an affirmative action of the school board based on the teacher's performance.

How Else Can a Teacher Acquire Tenure?

In addition to a right to tenure under state law, a teacher may also have a right to tenure under an employment contract. The contract may describe in specific terms the teacher's right to continued employment and set out detailed procedures that must be followed before a teacher can be dismissed. For example, a professor at Montana State University achieved "permanent appointment" status under the terms of his employment contract.[13] In this case, university regulations provided that the initial appointment of a professor could be for a limited term, but that "reappointment after three years of service shall be deemed a permanent appointment." After teaching for six years under a series of one-year contracts, the professor claimed permanent appointment status. The court agreed, finding that the university regulations were made part of the professor's contract by language in the contract that stated: "This appointment is subject to the regulations governing tenure printed on the reverse side of this sheet." Among the regulations was one granting permanent appointment after three years of service.

Is There a Condition under Which Tenure Could Be Denied Even Where the Teacher Has Served the Requisite Number of Years?

Yes. For instance, in one Tennessee case a teacher who would have been tenured but for her continued failure to successfully complete all the sections of the National Teacher Examination was denied tenure and her contract was no longer renewed.[14] In many states teachers who lose their certification because, for instance, they did not maintain sufficient continuing education during the course of their certification period in order to maintain their credentials may be stripped of their tenure, and thus would have to become eligible for tenure all over again as if they were beginning teachers.

Can Other School Employees Acquire Tenure?

Most state laws provide that only full-time certificated or professional employees acquire tenure. The definition of exactly which employees are required to have certification can vary from state to state. For instance, some states do not acknowledge tenure beyond that of a classroom teacher, which means that administrators such as principals and department chairpersons do not acquire tenure of title or tenure of position. In a Wyoming case, for example, the court found that a school district was under no obligation to renew the contract of a principal who had also served as a classroom teacher.[15] The court ruled that the principalship position was merely created under an annual contract and was not a tenured position. In addition, the court made clear that the teacher did not lose tenure when he was promoted to principal, and thus, even though he was not reemployed as a principal, he was entitled to be rehired as a classroom teacher. By contrast, some states also grant tenure to administrators in their administrative positions, and even to their specific building assignments.[16]

Similarly, a federal appeals court held that no due process violation occurred when a school district notified physical education teachers who had also served as coaches that they would be reemployed as teachers but not as coaches.[17] The court ruled that the teacher–coaches' due process rights were not violated because coaches were not covered under the state teacher tenure law and therefore they had no property interest in reemployment as coaches.

In Maryland, the state board of education initially ruled that, once appointed a coach a teacher was entitled to demand that the board demonstrate "just cause" before removing the teacher from the coaching position, pursuant to language in the governing collective bargaining agreement that prohibited a teacher from being "reduced in rank" without "just cause."[18] However, in a rare reversal of a previously rendered opinion, the state board of education later concluded that where coaching contracts, like other extra-duty assignments, were for a period of one year only, the non-renewal of such contracts could be terminated without providing any supporting reasons.[19]

Can a State Do Away with Tenure?

Yes. When state law creates a right to tenure, it can usually take this right away. Many teachers' contracts include a provision stating that the teacher's tenure status is subject to change or termination according to any changes in the state law. Even if a teacher's contract does not include such a provision, most courts have ruled that state legislatures have the power to modify their teacher tenure laws, thus possibly depriving a teacher of tenure. In Wisconsin, for instance, the court upheld the legislature's power to repeal the Teachers' Tenure Act.[20] In examining the tenure law, the court concluded that the Teachers' Tenure Act was intended not to create a statutory contract but merely to declare a public policy in favor of tenure. Similarly, a federal appeals court ruled that the Chicago School Reform Act's repeal of principals' tenure was permissible, explaining that tenure was a right created by statute and that a statute is presumed not to create contractual rights.[21]

In the rare situations where the state law creates a contractual right to tenure, the legislature cannot deprive a teacher of tenured status. In an early case the U.S. Supreme Court held that Indiana's teacher tenure law created a contractual right to tenure and that a teacher who had attained tenured status under this law had a continuing contract that could not be broken by a new law passed by the legislature.[22] Thus the Court ruled that the teacher was entitled to maintain her tenured status even though the Indiana legislature had repealed its teacher tenure law.

A provision of the U.S. Constitution which prohibits the states from impeding or breaching contracts[23] has been construed so as to permit school boards nonetheless to violate the terms of collectively bargained contracts in the face of economic exigencies. Thus, for instance, in one case where the Baltimore City board of education imposed a forced teacher furlough due to a budget crisis, the court did not find that the district had unconstitutionally interfered with an existing contract.[24] Similarly, even a tenured teacher may be terminated in the event that the school district lacks sufficient funds or for other financial reasons. In one Illinois case, a tenured professor was terminated because the course he taught was being discontinued in light of declining enrollment. In rejecting a claim that the college had breached the professor's contract and acted inconsistently "with the terms of the policy manual relating to tenure," the courts found that the specific reason for the professor's termination was discontinuation of a particular course of instruction. Thus, the dismissal was upheld.[25] School districts may similarly abolish positions, even if the effect is to discharge tenured teachers.[26]

Can a School Board Do Away with Tenure?

No. A school board in the state of New York decided not to award tenure to two teachers in the district who had fulfilled the necessary requirements under state law, and who had been recommended for tenure by the superintendent of schools. The board's reason for denying tenure was its philosophical objection to the idea of tenure, explaining that tenure currently is "nothing more than guaranteed job security," that "becomes an onerous, lifetime burden on the taxpayers for 20 years."[27] The teachers appealed the board's decision, and a New York trial court ruled that the board acted improperly, noting that although the board was free to negotiate teachers' salaries at the collective bargaining table, it could not withhold tenure purely for "fiscal reasons unrelated to the qualifications of those seeking tenure."[28]

On the other hand, if a teacher is simply not renewed for a second or third year, thus depriving that teacher of tenure, courts have generally concluded that there was an insufficient basis to afford the teacher a full evidentiary hearing—or even, for that matter, a list of reasons for nonrenewal—since nonrenewal of a probationary teacher and consequent denial of tenure does not give rise under *Sindermann* to a Fourteenth Amendment deprivation of a property interest without due process. In one New Jersey case, however, the court rejected the nonrenewal of a school psychologist's contract and the attendant denial of tenure where the teacher's recent illness had prevented her from remaining employed for the full 30-month period before being awarded tenure.[29] In so ruling, the New Jersey Supreme Court held that the use of approved sick leave did not prevent the psychologist from achieving tenure.

Rights of Tenure

What Right Does a Tenured Teacher Have?

A teacher who achieves tenured status has the right to continued employment subject only to dismissal "for cause." Similarly, a nontenured teacher who is terminated during the contract year, rather than simply not renewed at its completion, may invoke the same rights as a tenured teacher to be afforded reasons for the dismissal and a complete evidentiary hearing. The teacher does not have the right to be employed in a particular position, however. School boards retain the authority to transfer and reassign even tenured teachers, provided that they are assigned to comparable positions, the decision to reassign them is in the best interest of the schools, and is neither arbitrary or discriminatory. In one Maryland case, the court held that tenured teachers do not even have the right to an evidentiary hearing in order to challenge what is "merely" a reassignment, regardless of the paucity of reasons to support the decision.[30]

Courts have also ruled that tenured teachers can be reassigned as part of desegregation plans. In cases of school districts under desegregation orders, the courts have stated that school boards could not use tenure laws as an excuse to resist transferring teachers to achieve an appropriate racial balance.[31] (See chapter 14 for a detailed discussion of school desegregation and teachers' rights.)

In addition, the courts have ruled that tenured status does not ensure that a teacher's salary can never be reduced. School boards have the authority to fix teachers' salaries, and they retain the power to reduce them. Any reductions in salary must be applied uniformly to all teachers, and salary schedules cannot be changed in the middle of a school year absent a financial emergency.[32]

Dismissal Procedures

When Can Tenure Be Broken?

School officials can dismiss a tenured teacher only for "cause." Teacher tenure laws generally list specific offenses that constitute legal cause for dismissal, and school officials can dismiss a teacher only for one of these reasons. In Maryland, for instance, the law provides that school boards may dismiss teachers for one of five enumerated reasons: incompetency, misconduct in office, wilful neglect of duty, insubordination, and immorality.[33]

Usually courts have held that tenured teachers can be dismissed only for a cause "which specifically relates to and affects the administration of the office...something of a substantial nature directly affecting the rights and interests of the public...one touching... his performance of his duties, showing he is not a fit or proper person to hold the office."[34] (What constitutes legal cause for dismissal is discussed later in this chapter.) In examining the nature of the offense attributed to a tenured teacher so as to determine if there is sufficient cause to dismiss, there must be a proximate relationship, called "nexus," between the offense and the teacher's fitness for duty. Many negotiated contracts governing teachers' employment contain clauses protecting teachers from being dismissed due to personal lifestyle choices or other activities which are unrelated to their teaching performance.

What Procedures Have to Be Followed Before a Tenured Teacher Can Be Dismissed?

Most states provide for specific procedures before tenured teachers can be dismissed. Typically these statutes require that teachers be given notice of the charges against them and an opportunity for a hearing at which they can respond to those charges. In order to ensure a fair hearing, the following steps ought to be taken to ensure compliance with both constitutional and statutory requirements found in most states' tenure laws:

1. There should be a statement of charges and the basic information upon which those charges are based.
2. If requested, a hearing ought to be held before the school board, a hearing panel, or a hearing officer designated by the school board.
3. Timely written notice of the date, time, and place of the hearing;
4. A hearing in public or, if requested by the teacher, in private;
5. An opportunity to be represented by counsel;
6. An opportunity to call witnesses on the teacher's own behalf;
7. In many (but not all) states, an opportunity to subpoena a person who has made allegations that are used against the teacher as a basis for the termination recommendation;
8. An opportunity to cross-examine witnesses presented against the teacher;

9. Witness testimony should be under oath or affirmation;
10. A record should be made (preferably, by a certified court reporter) of the proceedings, so that they may be reviewed by a higher authority, including the courts;
11. A written decision that contains specific findings of fact, conclusions of law, and grounds upon which the decision is based; and
12. A written statement of the teacher's right to appeal.[35]

The Supreme Court of Nebraska best summarized the minimal due process required before terminating a tenured teacher as requiring that the teacher (1) be advised of the cause or causes for the termination in sufficient detail to fairly enable him or her to prepare a defense; (2) be advised of the names and the nature of the testimony of witnesses who are to testify against the teacher; and (3) be accorded a timely and meaningful opportunity to be heard in his or her own defense (4) before a tribunal that both possesses some academic expertise and has an apparent impartiality toward the charges.[36]

In some states local boards of education have subpoena powers so that teachers may compel the attendance of witnesses, including students, whereas in other states such power does not exist. In all cases, however, minimum due process protects teachers' right to appear with counsel at the hearing, to examine and cross-examine witnesses, and to present a defense to the charges. All testimony is given under oath, and the local or state board of education must pay a reporter to make a written record of the hearing, so that the record may be reviewed by the courts.

Some states also provide that a tenured teacher cannot be dismissed without an opportunity to correct deficiencies that are "remediable." If, following a notice to remedy a deficiency, the teacher does not correct that deficiency within a reasonable period of time, the school district can then move for dismissal. Thus, in an Illinois case, a teacher was found by the court to have been properly dismissed after being frequently evaluated by the principal, assistant principal, and department chair, following which a conference was conducted with the evaluator going over the observation and discussing any deficiencies that were noted. Detailed observations charting the teacher's failure to make improvements were deemed sufficient to support termination based upon incompetency.[37]

When either the state law or local board policy governing dismissal of tenured teachers prescribes a specific procedure, it must be followed exactly. In Maryland, for instance, a school librarian who was terminated for incompetency was reinstated by the courts when it was determined that the superintendent had failed to follow his board's policy which required that an at-risk teacher be first afforded an opportunity to receive assistance, including a professional improvement plan, before being discharged.[38]

In the leading case of *Cleveland Board of Education* v. *Loudermill,* the U.S. Supreme Court further extended due process protections by holding that public employees with constitutionally protected property interests in employment be given "some kind of hearing" *prior* to discharge.[39] The Court stated that the hearing "need not be elaborate" and that "something less than a full evidentiary hearing" would be sufficient, but that the hearing should be designed to determine whether there are reasonable grounds to believe that the charges against an employee are true and support dismissal. Thus the school district must identify the grounds for dismissal and the supporting evidence, and the employee must be given an opportunity to respond before he or she is dismissed. In neither

Roth (see p. 34) nor *Sindermann* did the Court provide any further guidance about the nature of this hearing, such as who should conduct it or whether any other rights apply.

Courts have generally held that it is not a denial of constitutional due process to suspend a tenured teacher without pay during the pendency of the disciplinary proceedings, provided that the hearing is not unduly delayed, or if such suspensions are permitted by the governing teachers' union contract.[40] However, due process violations have been found where the hearing in question lacked impartiality,[41] or where the same school official acted as both prosecutor and hearing officer.[42]

What Notice Must Be Provided to a Tenured Teacher Prior to Dismissal?

The courts have stated that tenured teachers must be given clear statements of the charges against them so that they can answer those charges. Thus a Kentucky court found that a teacher had not been given adequate notice when he was merely informed that he was guilty of "insubordination based upon the fact that you refuse to co-operate with the principal of your school."[43] The court found that this statement was insufficient because it did not inform the teacher of facts on which he could reasonably formulate a defense: "It gives no date of his actions, nor does it indicate in any way the specific nature of his acts."[44] Similarly, because the board had notified her only that her services "had been unsatisfactory and incompetent" over the past year, an Alabama court ruled that a teacher could not be dismissed.[45] The court concluded that "incompetency" is a relative term that may be employed as meaning disqualification, inability, or incapacity.[46] Since the board did not give the teacher any specific information about her "incompetency," she could not be dismissed. However, state courts may vary in the specificity or detail that they consider sufficient. Thus, for example, a Kentucky court ruled that a teacher was provided with sufficient notice when the school board informed her that she would not be reemployed for the following reasons:

1. poor relationship with other teachers
2. lack of cooperation with the principal and the guidance staff,
3. poor attitude and disruptive influence,
4. not in harmony with the educational philosophy of the school, and
5. not in the best interest of the school to award a continuing contract.[47]

These reasons, however, seem to lack the specificity that courts require in many other states. Courts may also be highly critical of a school system which fails to fully inform the teacher of his deficiencies before termination. In a Missouri case, for instance, a tenured teacher who was terminated for incompetency based upon detailed notes taken by her principal which were never previously shown to the teacher was reinstated by the court, which observed that "[t]he school administration knew what the instances of alleged incompetence were as the hearing commenced, but [the teacher] did not. Had she been informed in advance of the specific and particular instances of alleged incompetence with which she would be faced, she could have been prepared to contradict them or to explain them."[48]

Do Teachers without Tenure Have a Right to Notice and a Hearing Prior to Nonrenewal of Their Contracts?

State laws typically do not give nontenured teachers the right to a hearing prior to nonrenewal. In the words of one court, "a school board has unfettered discretion when deciding whether to renew the contract of a probationary teacher."[49] In Maryland, for example, a teacher is not entitled to reasons for his or her nonrenewal, and a hearing is only warranted where the teacher can present facts to prove that the nonrenewal decision was either discriminatory or arbitrary. Some states, however, give nontenured teachers minimal procedural rights. In Illinois, state law requires that a second-year probationary teacher be given notice of the reasons for nonrenewal.[50] In Connecticut, a nontenured teacher must make a special written request in order to receive a statement of the reasons why the board decided not to renew the contract.[51]

A number of states give nontenured teachers additional rights by requiring local districts to conduct formal evaluations of beginning teachers and to develop a plan for improvement if deficiencies are identified. In fourteen of those states, if a school district fails to follow the remediation mandates, the district cannot refuse to renew the teacher's contract because of those teaching deficiencies.[52]

What Constitutional Protections Apply in Cases of Teacher Dismissal?

Regardless of the procedures required under the state law, the U.S. Supreme Court has ruled that teachers are entitled to notice and a hearing if their termination deprives them of *"property"* or *"liberty" interests* under the due process clause of the Fourteenth Amendment to the U.S. Constitution. In *Board of Regents* v. *Roth,*[53] the Court defined these terms: "To have a property interest in a benefit, a person clearly must have more than an abstract need or desire for it. He must have more than a unilateral expectation of it. He must, instead, have a legitimate claim of entitlement to it."[54] The Court went on to explain that property interests are not created by the Constitution. "Rather, they are created and their dimensions are defined by existing rules or understandings that stem from an independent source such as state law—rules or understandings that secure certain benefits and that support claims of entitlement to those benefits."[55] In *Roth,* the teacher involved had been hired under a series of one-year contracts, and the court concluded that he had no such interest in reemployment as to establish a property interest that would entitle him to procedural rights under the Fourteenth Amendment.

Under the reasoning in *Roth,* most nontenured teachers who are employed in a system where there are formal provisions for tenure will rarely be able to establish a property interest. A federal appeals court ruled, for example, that under New Mexico statutes, a school principal who had a one-year contract and whose contract had not been renewed after one year had "no legitimate expectation of reemployment" and thus no property interest.[56] Similarly, an Indiana court ruled, in upholding the nonrenewal of a first-year probationary teacher, that it would not "engraft the statutory provisions for permanent teachers upon the provisions for nonpermanent teachers."[57]

The courts have found a valid property interest to exist in some cases, however. In *Perry* v. *Sindermann,* the U.S. Supreme Court stated that if the customary practices of the institution created a *de facto* tenure system, a teacher would have a property interest in re-employment and would be entitled to due process protection prior to dismissal.[58] Applying *Sindermann* to the public school context, a federal court held that a school district violated the due process rights of a coach and athletic director when it refused to renew his one-year contract.[59] The court found that the coach had a protected property interest in his continued employment when the board had assured him that he would be employed for two years, and when he relied on this promise in leaving a job he had held for ten years. In addition, the court concluded that since the district's action was in breach of contract, the coach was entitled to an award of damages. (This case, which was affirmed by an equally divided U.S. Supreme Court, is especially significant because it allows public school teachers with breach of contract claims to take their cases to either federal or state court.) Other courts have held that when state law recognizes that employee handbooks may form the basis of a contract action, the school employee can rely on the provisions in the employee handbook to bring a claim for deprivation of due process as well as breach of contract. For example, the Colorado Supreme Court held that a school district warehouse foreman could rely on provisions in the employee handbook to state a claim against the district for breach of contract and deprivation of due process.[60]

In *Roth,* the U.S. Supreme Court held that teachers are also entitled to due process protection if their dismissal deprives them of a "liberty" interest under the Fourteenth Amendment. In interpreting this term, the Court included "the right of the individual to contract, to engage in any of the common occupations of life."[61] The Court explained that a violation of this "right" could occur by taking action that would foreclose a teacher's opportunities for employment. The Court stated that a liberty interest would be involved whenever the school board, in declining to rehire a teacher, made a charge that might seriously damage the teacher's standing and associations in the community (e.g., charges such as dishonesty or immorality). In the Court's words: "[W]here a person's good name, reputation, honor, or integrity is at stake because of what the government is doing to him, notice and opportunity to be heard are essential."[62] In a 1976 case, the Supreme Court added the requirement that "stigmatization" could occur only if statements were made publicly about an employee.[63] When a school district publicizes stigmatizing disciplinary charges, however, the employee's liberty interest is implicated and a name-clearing hearing may be required if requested by the teacher. However, courts have ruled that due process does not require a hearing before an employing school district publishes stigmatizing reasons for a teacher's discharge.[64]

In *Roth,* the Court did not find any violation of a liberty interest. The state university had merely refused to renew Roth's one-year teaching contract: university officials did nothing that would have stigmatized Roth so as to reduce his chances of obtaining future employment. In general, the courts have found that a liberty interest is not affected when a teacher who is not rehired is free to seek another job. For example, a court held that a nontenured teacher who was not rehired because of her failure to coordinate her teaching with that of other teachers was not entitled to a hearing, even though her nonretention "unquestionably made [the teacher] less attractive to other employers."[65] Similarly, a court ruled that no liberty interest was involved when a principal described a teacher as "anti-establishment" in a rating report,[66] or when a teacher was dismissed for incompetency and inability to relate well with others.[67] In general, the courts have not required hearings when the charges against teachers have related to their inability to perform. Public charges that have been held to involve a liberty interest and entitle a teacher to a hearing prior to dismissal include allegations of manifest racism,[68] mental illness,[69] fraud,[70] moral unfitness,[71] and a serious drinking problem.[72]

Grounds for Dismissal

What Constitutes Cause for Dismissal?

State laws, local school board policies, and collective bargaining agreements set forth the specific reasons why teachers can be dismissed. In Maryland, for example, the board has the power to fire teachers for "incompetency, willful neglect of duty, immorality, misconduct," and "insubordination."[73] Such grounds for dismissal are common to most states, whose statutes generally prohibit teacher dismissal unless school officials can prove that the teacher's actions violated the state law.

When Can a Teacher Be Fired for Insubordination?

Teachers cannot be dismissed for insubordination unless they deliberately defy school authorities or violate reasonable school rules. For the order to be reasonable, school officials must have the legal authority to issue it. A Kansas teacher who was informed by his principal that he could not be absent yet called in "sick" to attend an interview for another job was terminated for insubordination when his deception was discovered. By absenting himself and willfully disobeying the directions of his superior, the court ruled, the teacher violated his contract and, therefore, was properly terminated.[74]

Some courts have found insubordination in a single incident,[75] while others have concluded that insubordination can only occur when there is a constant or persistent course of conduct.[76] In one New Mexico case a teacher was terminated for insubordination when, during the course of a routine classroom observation, the teacher insisted that the principal leave the classroom, threatening (in front of students) to call the police if he did not and ripping lesson plans out of the principal's hands. The court upheld the dismissal, noting that throughout the incident the principal remained calm and did nothing to provoke such hostile actions by the teacher.[77]

Yet for a rule to be reasonable, it must be clear enough for the teacher to understand. A Kentucky court held that a teacher could not be dismissed for insubordination on the grounds that he refused to "cooperate" with the principal.[78] The court stated that the school board had neither charged the teacher with violating any specific rule nor claimed that the teacher had refused to obey school authorities. Concluding that a charge of noncooperation could be asserted against almost anyone, the court declared that the school board had not proved insubordination.

Finally, teachers cannot be dismissed for failing to follow school rules that violate their constitutional rights. For example, school rules prohibiting teachers from using certain materials in the classroom may interfere with a teacher's right to academic freedom. School rules limiting what teachers can say or write may also violate their First Amendment right of free speech. (Academic freedom and First Amendment rights are discussed in detail in chapter 9.)

In many cases, a teacher's actions speak for themselves. For example, a Utah court found a teacher to be insubordinate when he flatly refused to accept transfer to another school, even though his contract required that he do so.[79] In less obvious cases, courts look at a teacher's pattern of behavior in order to decide whether the teacher is acting willfully. In Washington, a teacher's repeated absences were compounded by his insistence that, due to a lecture commitment overseas, he would absent beyond the date on which he was ordered to return to school. The court upheld his termination for insubordination, observing that the teacher received two letters denying approval of his requested absence and directing him to be present and carry out his assigned duties.[80] The court went on to conclude that the faculty code's prohibition against insubordination was not unconstitutionally vague, but reasonably understood.[81]

When Can a Teacher Be Fired for Incompetency?

An incompetent teacher is one who cannot perform the duties required by the teaching contract. However, a teacher who merely has an "off day" in the classroom cannot be dismissed for incompetency. In order to fire a teacher, school officials generally have to present a number of examples of the teacher's inability to meet contractual responsibilities. School districts in most states, however, are required to work with and attempt to remediate the performance of a poorly performing teacher before terminating the teacher.[82] Whether this requirement is the result of state law or regulation, or whether it is included in a collective bargaining agreement or even the individual teacher's contract, courts tend to strictly enforce this obligation on school boards in any challenge to a subsequent personnel action.[83] Even in states or school districts where remediation is not specifically required, it is not uncommon for state school boards or reviewing courts to impose their own requirement on the local district that the teacher be first afforded remediation before being terminated for incompetence.[84]

A Missouri teacher's termination was reversed and she was reinstated with full back pay by the court when the local board failed to show that it had issued a written warning letter with identified areas for improvement following which the teacher was given sufficient time to correct the identified deficiencies. The court insisted upon a reasonable "curative period" between the warning and the discharge in order to sustain the discharge.[85] In some states, however, remediation is not a legal obligation, and teachers may not be so entitled.[86]

The clearest example of an incompetent teacher is one who lacks knowledge about the subject he or she is supposed to teach. For example, a Louisiana third-grade teacher was dismissed for incompetency when her supervisor "noted many mistakes in her grammar and in her punctuation."[87] A Pennsylvania second-grade teacher was dismissed for incompetency after her supervisors observed that "she showed very little evidence of technical knowledge and skill...that she made errors in the geography lesson; that her spoken English was poor...and that [she] mispronounced words."[88]

Teachers may also be physically unable to teach. However, given the duty of employers under the Americans With Disabilities Act to offer disabled employees "reasonable accommodations" in order to enable them to perform the "essential functions of their job,"[89] a school district should first explore every reasonable and available accommodation to ensure that a disabled teacher may, with or without assistance, be able to continue teaching. Thus, a court held that an Indiana school district could not accuse an individual of poor performance when the district was well aware of the employee's mental disability but made no effort to find out what he needed to enable him to work.[90]

Typical incompetency charges include failure to remedy teaching deficiencies in outline objectives, sequencing subject matter, following lesson plans, and maintaining adequate grades for students.[91] While teachers are rarely found to be incompetent for one reason alone, failure to maintain classroom discipline is one of the most commonly cited problems. Reasoning that even the best-prepared teacher cannot be effective in a chaotic classroom, the courts have emphasized that the inability to maintain discipline is a characteristic of an incompetent teacher. In Indiana, for example, the court found that a teacher had such serious discipline problems that students could not pursue their schoolwork.[92] In a Missouri case, a 43-year veteran teacher was found incompetent, largely by virtue of her inability to control student behavior on the bus during field trips, allowing students to violate the school's dress code, and ignoring students' failure to perform assignments in the classroom.[93]

In an Alabama case, the court upheld the dismissal of a teacher who smoked in front of students, left the classroom unattended, and made sexual remarks to both students and teachers.[94] In a Pennsylvania case, a school psychologist was dismissed because her reports and testing were inadequate, her conduct in conferences unhelpful, and her progress toward improvement imperceptible.[95] A New York teacher was terminated for both misconduct and incompetence when she ignored established procedures for disciplining students despite prior warnings, refused to meet with troubled students' parents, failed to send a student's parents progress reports, did not have her lesson planbooks available as required by school district policy on at least three occasions, and inaccurately graded students.[96]

When Can a Teacher Be Fired for Immoral Conduct?

In the past, teachers were expected to teach morality through their actions, and when teachers violated community norms, they usually resigned quietly or were quickly fired. Teachers have been fired for cheating, lying, talking about sex, using "obscene" language, public drinking, drug use, homosexual conduct, and having a child out of wedlock. Thus what was considered immoral conduct has varied from place to place, and the definition has changed over time.

Today teachers can still be fired for immoral conduct, but in most states such conduct must be linked to a teacher's effectiveness. Sexual misconduct with a student is assuredly an act of immorality which would warrant termination under any state's tenure law.[97] Other acts have been considered "immoral," such as a Pennsylvania teacher who distributed copies of a racist "joke sheet" to his colleagues at school. There, the court agreed with the school district that his behavior served as a poor role model.[98]

A companion to sexual contact but just as appropriate a basis for a finding of "immoral conduct" is a teacher's sexual harassment of students and even other teachers. Where male students accused a tenured faculty member of making sexual advances and offering the students better grades for sexual favors, the court agreed with the school that the teacher unethically exploited students for his own private advantage.[99] A Washington high school math teacher was similarly fired for immorality when the school intercepted a personal, highly seductive note from the teacher soliciting sex from a student with whom he had developed a close personal and trusting relationship.[100] (Chapter 13 further examines the issue of immoral conduct in detail, including the kinds of conduct communities continue to consider immoral for teachers.)

When Can a Teacher Be fired for "Conduct Unbecoming a Teacher?"

Conduct unbecoming a teacher, or "unprofessional conduct" as some states define it, is a broad reason for dismissal that can include a wide variety of actions by teachers. In general, unprofessional conduct refers to any action that violates the rules or ethical code of the teaching profession. Despite the apparent vagueness of this term, courts have ruled that it is a valid ground for dismissing teachers. The following statement by a California court is typical of the reasoning used to support the large amount of discretion school boards have when dismissing teachers: "[T]he teacher is entrusted with the custody of children and their high preparation for useful life. His habits, his speech, his good name, his cleanliness…his associations, all are involved.... How can all of these things be provided for and offenses against them be particularly specified in a single statute?"[101]

Teachers who have attempted to use the classroom for purposes other than teaching have been found guilty of unprofessional conduct. The term has often been interchanged with the expression "irremediable conduct," implying behavior "which has caused significant damage to students, the faculty, or the school and which could not have been corrected even if superiors had given the teacher the statutorily prescribed warning."[102] Where an Illinois teacher, claiming depression and stress, refused to accept her teaching assignment despite repeated written and verbal warnings as to the consequences of her continued behavior, she was deemed properly discharged for "irremediable conduct unbecoming a teacher."[103]

As the term "conduct unbecoming a teacher" suggests, school boards have considerable latitude in this area in imposing discipline on teachers. For example, the New Jersey Supreme Court ruled that a teacher could be convicted of misconduct where she had been acquitted of criminal charges of sexual assault of students, but where the evidence also showed that she had exhibited sexually explicit magazines to her students.[104] Similarly, the Connecticut Supreme Court ruled that a teacher who tampered with the school telephone system could be dismissed even though the teacher had been acquitted of felony charges for eavesdropping.[105]

Are There Other Reasons for Teacher Dismissal?

Yes. Many state laws provide that teachers can be dismissed for "good and just cause," for "willful misconduct," or for "neglect of duty." These catchall phrases give school boards wide discretion, effectively allowing them to dismiss teachers for reasons not specifically listed under state law. Indeed, as a Massachusetts court explained, "good cause includes any ground which is put forward by the [school] committee in good faith and which is not arbitrary, irrational, unreasonable, or irrelevant to the committee's task of building up and maintaining an efficient school system."[106] Using similar reasoning, an Indiana court upheld the dismissal of a teacher–principal who had been dismissed for good and just cause when he failed to cooperate with school officials.[107] The teacher–principal had opposed a plan under which seventh- and eighth-grade students were to be taught by the high school faculty; after the plan had been in operation for a year, he had discontinued it without consulting the superintendent or county officials. In addition, he refused to fill out necessary administrative papers and catalogue the school library as required by the state's Department of Public Instruction. In upholding his dismissal, the court concluded that his actions had a negative effect on his fitness as a teacher–administrator and thus constituted good and just cause for dismissal. In a 1995 case, an Iowa court upheld the dismissal of a tenured ninth-grade English teacher who made sarcastic comments to students, such as telling a student who had submitted a paper about teenage suicide that "he should try it."[108] Based on many such instances, the superintendent believed that the teacher had ceased being an effective role model and could not be counted on to build self-esteem among his students.

The courts have imposed limits on school officials' power to dismiss teachers for "good and just cause." Courts have emphasized that the teacher's action must bear a reasonable relationship to fitness or capacity to discharge the duties of the teaching position. For example, an Ohio court ruled that a teacher could not be fired for hitting another car and leaving the scene of the accident.[109] In interpreting the phrase "good and just cause for dismissal," the court concluded that it must refer to actions as serious as the other grounds for teacher dismissal, including "gross inefficiency or immorality." The court reasoned that the teacher's action in leaving the scene of an accident might adversely reflect upon his character and integrity, but that it was not serious enough to constitute grounds for dismissal. In short, there must be a "nexus" between the offensive conduct and a teacher's primary responsibilities. As another Ohio court observed:

> The private conduct of a man, who is also a teacher, is a proper concern to those who employ him only to the extent that it mars him as a teacher, who is also a man. Where his professional achievement is unaffected, where the school community is placed in no jeopardy, his private acts are his own business and may not be the basis of discipline.[110]

Can a Teacher Be Dismissed for Economic Reasons?

When a student enrollment declines in a school district, teachers may face dismissal on the grounds that a reduction in teaching staff is necessary for financial reasons, a procedure commonly known as *riffing* (which is derived from the acronym "RIF," meaning "reduction in force") or "*excessing*." Such teachers are not dismissed for any adverse behavior that affects their ability to teach. Rather, in a general "reduction in force," both tenured and nontenured teachers may be dismissed in order to accommodate changing staff requirements.

Some state laws specifically provide that tenured teachers can be dismissed for economic reasons. An Alabama law states: "Cancellation of an employment contract with a teacher on continuing service status may be made for incompetency, insubordination, neglect of duty, immorality, justifiable decrease in the number of teaching positions or other good and just cause."[111] Other state laws provide more detailed guidelines about when teachers can be dismissed for economic reasons. For instance, Illinois law provides that when teachers are to be removed as a result of the school board's decision to decrease the number of teachers employed, the board shall dismiss all nontenured teachers before tenured teachers.[112] Tenured teachers are then to be dismissed on the basis of seniority, with those with less seniority being dismissed first, unless an alternative procedure is established in the current collective bargaining agreement.

Even when there is no relevant state law, the courts have held that school officials have the authority to dismiss teachers for economic reasons. A Pennsylvania kindergarten teacher was dismissed when the school board recommended that the entire kindergarten department be abolished "as a matter of good school business administration and instructional efficiency."[113] The legitimate bases for dismissing tenured teachers due to economic or human resources considerations include a decline in interest in a particular department,[114] curricular reorganization, projected losses in student enrollment, and the abolishment of specific teaching positions.

Regardless of the reasons for a reduction-in-force, school boards may not use them for the purpose of discriminating or to circumvent tenure laws. If a court discerns a bad-faith basis for such decision, the teacher may be entitled to reinstatement and back pay.[115]

Summary

Most states have passed tenure laws that give teachers the right to continued employment, subject only to dismissal for "cause." These laws describe the procedures teachers must follow to achieve tenure. They generally include the satisfactory completion of a stated number of years of probationary service (usually ranging from two to three). State legislatures have the power to change or repeal these laws.[116] In addition, the courts have ruled that teachers enjoy tenure of employment and not position, leaving school boards with the authority to reassign and transfer tenured teachers.

State laws, often in conjunction with collective bargaining agreements, describe procedures to be followed before a tenured teacher can be dismissed, as well as specific grounds which must be demonstrated in order to justify terminating a tenured teacher. Courts have interpreted those laws so as to ensure that teachers who are to be terminated have first been given adequate warning of their behavior and its likely consequences, and that proper pretermination steps have been taken where practical. Nontenured teachers are entitled to constitutional protections when they can demonstrate that they have been deprived of a liberty interest or a property interest, the latter of which is far more difficult to demonstrate as compared with tenured teachers, who have such interest in continued employment and therefore are always entitled to due process protections prior to dismissal.

NOTES

1. *Smith* v. *School District of Township of Darby,* 130 A.2d 661 (Pa. 1957).
2. *Board of Trustees of Hamilton Heights School Corporation* v. *Landry,* 560 N.E.2d 102 (Ind. Ct. App. 1st Dist. 1990).
3. *Perry* v. *Sindermann,* 408 U.S. 593 (1972).
4. *Id.* at 600.
5. *Id.* at 601.
6. *Id.* at 603.
7. VA. CODE ANN. § 22.1-303 (Michie 1985).
8. MD. ANN. CODE, Education Article Section 6-202(b) (Michie 1999).
9. *Cooper* v. *Norris,* 2000 WL 173209 (Tenn. Ct. App. 2001).
10. *Harrodsburg Board of Education* v. *Powell,* 792 S.W.2d 376 (Ky. Ct. App. 1990).
11. *Day* v. *Prowers County School District RE-1,* 725 P.2d 14 (Colo. Ct. App. 1986).
12. *Snell* v. *Brothers,* 527 S.W.2d 114 (Tenn. 1975).
13. *State ex rel. Keeney* v. *Ayers,* 92 P.2d 306 (Mont. 1939).

14. *Cooper* v. *Norris,* 2000 WL 173209 (Tenn. Ct. App. 2001).

15. *Spurlock* v. *Board of Trustees,* 699 P.2d 270 (Wyo. 1985).

16. For a detailed discussion of the basis for the repeal of New York legislation that had formerly granted building tenure to New York City principals, see J. Fernandez, *Tales Out of Schools: Joseph Fernandez's Crusade to Rescue American Education* (New York: Little Brown & Co., 1993).

17. *Smith* v. *Board of Education of Urbana School District No. 116,* 708 F.2d 258 (7th Cir. 1983).

18. *Regala* v. *Board of Education of Charles County,* 5 Op. MSDE 319 (1989).

19. *Education Association of St. Mary's County & Thomas Murray* v. *Board of Education St. Mary's County,* 7 Op. MSDE 683 (1997).

20. *State ex rel. McKenna* v. *District No. 8,* 10 N.W.2d 155 (Wis. 1943).

21. *Pittman* v. *Chicago Board of Education,* 64 F.3d 1098 (7th Cir. 1995).

22. *Indiana ex rel. Anderson* v. *Brand,* 303 U.S. 95 (1938).

23. U.S. CONST., art. I, § 10, cl. 1.

24. *Baltimore Teachers Union* v. *Mayor of Baltimore,* 6 F.3d 1012 (4th Cir. 1993).

25. *Rymer* v. *Kendall College,* 64 Ill. App. 3d 355, 380 N.E.2d 1089 (Ill. App. Ct. 1978).

26. *Gross* v. *Board of Education of the Elmsford Union Free School District,* 78 N.Y.2d 13, 574 N.E.2d 438, 571 N.Y.S.2d 200 (1991).

27. *Conetta* v. *Board of Education of Patchogue,* 629 N.Y.S.2d 640 (N.Y. Sup. Ct., 1995).

28. *Id.,* at 642.

29. *Kletzkin* v. *Board of Education of the Borough of Spotswood,* 136 N.J. 275, 642 A.2d 993 (1994).

30. *Hurl* v. *Board of Education of Howard County,* 107 Md. App. 269, 667 A.2d 970 (1995).

31. For example, *United States* v. *Board of Education of City of Bessemer,* 396 F.2d 44 (5th Cir. 1968).

32. *Compton Community College Federation of Teachers* v. *Compton Community College District,* 211 Cal. Rptr. 231 (Cal. Ct. App. 2d Dist. 1985).

33. *Annotated Code of Maryland,* Education Article § 6-202(a) (Michie 1999).

34. *State ex rel. Richardson* v. *Board of Regents,* 261 P.2d 515 (Nev. 1953).

35. *Source:* E. M. Bridges and B. Groves (1984). *Managing the Incompetent Teacher* (Eugene, OR: ERIC Clearinghouse on Educational Management, 1984). For an excellent discussion of the dynamics of terminating tenured teachers, see H. Andrews, *Teachers Can Be Fired! The Quest for Quality* (Chicago: Catfeet Press, 1995).

36. *Eshom* v. *Board of Education of School District No. 54, Thayer and Nuckolls Counties, Nebraska,* 219 Neb. 467, 364 N.W.2d 7 (1985).

37. *DeBernard* v. *Illinois State Board of Education,* 527 N.E.2d 616 (Ill. App. Ct. 1988).

38. *Board of Education of Baltimore County* v. *Ballard,* 67 Md. App. 235, 507 A.2d 192 (1986).

39. 470 U.S. 532 (1985).

40. *Jerry* v. *Board of Education, Syracuse City School District,* 35 N.Y.S.2d 534, 541 (N.Y. Ct. App. 1974). See also *Barry* v. *Barchi,* 443 U.S. 55 (1979) (holding that an indefinite postponement of a license suspension hearing is violative of due process).

41. *Keith* v. *Community School District of Wilton,* 262 N.W.2d 249 (Iowa 1978), where Board chose not to call any witnesses, choosing instead to rely upon its collective recollection of the facts.

42. *Board of Education* v. *Lockhart,* 687 P.2d 1306 (Colo. 1984).

43. *Osborne* v. *Bullitt County Board of Education,* 415 S.W.2d 607 (Ky. Ct. App. 1967).

44. *Id.* at 609–610.

45. *County Board of Education of Clarke County* v. *Oliver,* 116 So.2d 566 (Ala. 1959).

46. *Id.* at 567.

47. *Sparks* v. *Board of Education of Ashland Independent School District,* 549 S.W.2d 323 (Ky. Ct. App. 1977).

48. *Jefferson Consolidated School District C-123* v. *Carden,* 772 S.W.2d 753 (Mo. Ct. App. 1989).

49. *Johnson* v. *Independent School District No. 281,* 479 N.W.2d 392 (Minn. Ct. App. 1991).

50. *Id.*

51. CONN. GEN. STAT. ANN. § 10-151 (West 1996).

52. Those states are: Arkansas, Delaware, Idaho, Indiana, Kentucky, Louisiana, Michigan, Nebraska, New York, Ohio, Oklahoma, Pennsylvania, Texas, and West Virginia. M. Simpson, "The Rights of Nontenured Teachers," Conference Paper, Education Law Association, Albuquerque, NM, November 16, 2001.

53. 408 U.S. 564 (1972).

54. *Id.* at 577.

55. *Id.*

56. *Cole* v. *Ruidoso Municipal Schools,* 947 F.2d 903 (10th Cir. 1991).

57. *Tishey* v. *Board of School Trustees of North Newton School Corporation,* 575 N.E.2d 1018 (Ct. App. Ind. 1991).

58. 408 U.S. 564 (1972).

59. *Vail* v. *Board of Education of Paris Union School District No. 95,* 706 F.2d 1435 (7th Cir. 1983).

60. *Adams County School District No. 50* v. *Dickey,* 791 P.2d 688 (Colo. 1990); see also *Thomas* v. *Ward,* 529 F.2d 916 (4th Cir. 1975); *Patkus* v. *Sangamon-Cass Consortium,* 769 F.2d 1251 (7th Cir., 1985).

61. 408 U.S. at 572.

62. *Id.* at 573 (quoting *Wisconsin* v. *Constantineau,* 400 U.S. 433 (1971).

63. *Bishop* v. *Wood,* 426 U.S. 341 (1976).

64. *Rankin* v. *Independent School District No. I-3,* 876 F.2d 838 (10th Cir. 1989).

65. *Shirck* v. *Thomas,* 486 F.2d 691 (7th Cir. 1973).

66. *Lipp* v. *Board of Education of City of Chicago,* 470 F.2d 802 (7th Cir. 1972).

67. *Hayes* v. *Phoenix-Talent School District,* 893 F.2d 235 (9th Cir. 1990).

68. *Wellner* v. *Minnesota State Junior College Board,* 487 F.2d 153 (8th Cir. 1973).

69. *Lombard* v. *Board of Education of City of New York,* 502 F.2d 631 (2d Cir. 1974).

70. *Huntley* v. *North Carolina State Board of Education,* 493 F.2d 1016 (4th Cir. 1974).

71. *McGhee* v. *Draper,* 564 F.2d 902 (10th Cir. 1977); *Vanelli* v. *Reynolds School District No. 7,* 667 F.2d 773 (9th Cir. 1982).

72. *Dennis* v. *S & S Consolidated Rural High School District,* 577 F.2d 338 (5th Cir. 1978).

73. MD. ANNOT. CODE, Education Article §6-202(b).

74. *Gaylord* v. *Board of Education, Unified School District No. 218, Morton County, Kansas,* 14 Kan App. 2d 462, 794 P.2d 307 (1990); see also *Leaming* v. *Unified School District No. 214,* 242 Kan. 743, 750 P.2d 1041 (1988).

75. *Crump* v. *Bd. of Education,* 79 N.C. App. 372, 339 S.E.2d 483, *review denied* 317 N.C. 333 (1986).

76. *Sims* v. *Bd. of Trustees, Holly Springs,* 414 So. 2d 431 (Miss. 1982).

77. *Kleinberg* v. *Board of Education of the Albuquerque Public Schools,* 107 N.M. 38, 751 P.2d 722 (1988).

78. *Osborne* v. *Bullitt County Board of Education,* 415 S.W.2d 607 (Ky. Ct. App. 1967); see also *Werblo* v. *Board of School Trustees of the Hamilton Heights School Corp., et al.,* 519 N.E.2d 185 (Ind. Ct. App. 1988).

79. *Brough* v. *Board of Education of Millard County School District,* 460 P.2d 336 (Utah 1969).

80. *Stastny* v. *Board of Trustees of Central Washington University,* 32 Wash. App. 239, 647 P.2d 496 (1982).

81. *Id.* at 252-253, 647 P.2d at 505.

82. See, for example, ILL. REV. STAT. 1985, ch. 122, par. 34-85; *McCrackin* v. *Elko County School District,* 103 Nev. 655, 77 P.2d 1373 (1987).

83. *Naylor* v. *Cardinal Local School District Board of Education,* 69 Ohio St. 3d 162, 630 N.E.2d 725 (1994).

84. One Missouri court referred to this as the "required good faith effort to give the teacher a chance to remedy defects." *Iven* v. *Hazelwood School District,* 710 S.W.2d 462 (Mo. Ct. App. 1986).

85. *In the Matter of Mary Selby* v. *North Callaway Board of Education,* 777 S.W.2d 275 (Mo. Ct. App. 1989).

86. For instance, Minnesota Stat. §§125.12, subd. 13 and 125.17 (1988) explicitly exempt such requirements with respect to teachers employed by certain sized cities. *See In re Proposed Termination of James E. Johnson's Teaching Contract with Independent School District Number 79,* 451 N.W.2d 343 (Minn. Ct. App. 1990).

87. *Singleton* v. *Iberville Parish School Board,* 136 So.2d 809, 811 (La. Ct. App. 1961).

88. *Appeal of Mulhollen,* 39 A.2d 283 (Pa. Super. Ct. 1944); see also *Beck* v. *James,* 793 S.W.2d 416 (Mo. Ct. App. 1990).

89. 42 U.S.C. §12112 (2000).

90. *Bultemeyer* v. *Fort Wayne Community Schools,* 100 F.3d 1281 (7th Cir. 1996).

91. *DeBernard* v. *Illinois State Board of Education,* 172 Ill. App. 3d 938, 527 N.E.2d 616 (1988);

92. *Biggs.* v. *School City of Mt. Vernon,* 90 N.E. 105 (Ind. Ct. App. 1909).

93. *Jefferson Consolidated School District C-123* v. *Carden,* 772 S.W.2d 753 (Mo. Ct. App. 1989).

94. *Bradshaw* v. *Alabama State Tenure Commission,* 520 So.2d 541 (Ala. Civ. App. 1988).

95. *Grant* v. *Board of School Directors,* 471 A.2d 1292 (Pa. Commw. Ct. 1984).

96. *Jackson* v. *Sobol,* 170 A.D.2d 718, 565 N.Y.S.2d 612 (App. Div. 3d Dep't. 1991).

97. *Strain* v. *Rapid City School Board for Rapid City Area School District,* 447 N.W.2d 332 (S.D. 1989).

98. *Reitmeyer* v. *Unemployment Compensation Board of Review,* 602 A.2d 505 (Pa. Commw. Ct. 1992).

99. *Korf* v. *Ball State University Board of Trustees,* 726 F.2d 1222 (7th Cir. 1984).

100. *Sauter* v. *Mount Vernon School District No. 320,* 58 Wash. App. 121, 791 P.2d 549 (1990).

101. *Goldsmith* v. *Board of Education of Sacramento City High School District No. 66,* 225 P. 783 (Cal. Dist. Ct. App. 1924); see also *Wishart* v. *McDonald,* 500 F.2d 1110 (1st Cir. 1974).

102. *Gilliland* v. *Board of Education of Pleasant View Consolidated School District No. 622,* 67 Ill. 2d 143, 153, 365 N.E.2d 322, 326 (1977).

103. *Board of Education of the City of Chicago* v. *Harris,* 218 Ill. App. 3d 1017, 578 N.E.2d 1244 (1991).

104. *State* v. *Parker,* 592 A.2d 228 (N.J. 1991).

105. *Rado* v. *Board of Education of Borough of Naugatuck,* 583 A.2d 102 (Conn. 1990).

106. *Rinaldo* v. *School Commission,* 1 N.E.2d 37, 38 (Mass. 1936).

107. *Stiver* v. *State,* 1 N.E.2d 1006 (Ind. 1936).

108. *Sheldon Community School District Board of Directors* v. *Lundblad,* 528 N.W.2d 593 (Iowa 1995).

109. *Hale* v. *Board of Education, City of Lancaster,* 234 N.E.2d 583 (Ohio 1968).

110. *Jarvella* v. *Willoughby-Eastlake City School District,* 12 Ohio Misc. 288, 291, 233 N.E.2d 143, 146 (1967).

111. ALA. CODE § 16-24-8 (1985).

112. 105 ILCS 5/24-12 (1992 State Bar Edition)

113. *Ehret* v. *Kulpmont Borough School District,* 5 A.2d 188 (Pa. 1939).

114. *Taxman* v. *Board of Education of Township of Piscataway,* 91 F.3d 1547 (3rd Cir. 1996). Under New Jersey law, tenured teachers could only be laid off after nontenured teachers, whereafter seniority would determine who would remain. N.J. Stat. Ann. §18A:28-10.

115. See *Genco* v. *Bristol Borough School District,* 423 A.2d 36 (Pa. Commw. Ct. 1980); *Buchheit* v. *Hamilton City Board of Education,* 473 N.E.2d 61 (Ohio Ct. App. 1984).

116. For instance, Colorado's legislature eliminated teacher tenure with the enactment of the Teacher Employment Compensation Act of 1990. COLO. REV. STAT. § 22-63-203. Besides eliminating the word "tenure" from the law, this Colorado statute added "unsatisfactory performance" to the grounds for teacher dismissal. COLO. REV. STAT. § 22-63-301.

4 How Does Collective Bargaining Affect Me?

Overview

The American labor union movement began in response to poor working conditions in industry but has now spread to include workers employed in the public sector. While private sector labor union membership has dramatically declined over the past 25 years as a percentage of the total workforce,[1] it has concomitantly increased dramatically in the public sector, including among teachers. Today, over 80 percent of all public school teachers belong to or are represented either by the National Education Association (NEA), which has over two million members, or the American Federation of Teachers (AFT), which has approximately half a million members. While the NEA began as a professional organization largely consisting of school administrators, it has swiftly grown to be the largest and one of the most politically powerful of the public sector unions in the United States. The AFT, founded in New York City, focused from the start upon organizing teachers in urban school systems, and adheres to traditional labor union policies and objectives, including the improvement of wages, hours, and working conditions for its members.

About two thirds of the states have passed laws outlining school boards' responsibilities in collective bargaining with these groups. This chapter examines the impact of these laws and the relevant court cases that have considered such questions as: Does a teacher have a right to join a union? Can a teacher be forced to join a union? What is collective bargaining? What duties does a union have to perform for its members? Are teachers allowed to go on strike?

The Right to Organize

The *Norwalk Teachers' Association* Case[2]

Do Teachers Have the Right to Organize?

In 1946, all but 2 of the 300 teachers in the Norwalk, Connecticut, school system were members of the Norwalk Teachers' Association (NTA). In April of that year, a dispute broke out between the NTA and the board of education of the city of Norwalk concerning teachers' salaries. After protracted negotiations, 230 NTA members rejected their employment contracts and refused to return to their teaching duties. After further negotiations, the NTA and the board of education entered into a contract that gave the NTA the exclusive right to represent Norwalk teachers in collective bargaining over teachers' working conditions. The contract also established a grievance procedure and a salary schedule.

Even with a contract negotiated, the NTA and the board of education continued to disagree about its interpretation and about a number of state education laws that seemed to be inconsistent with the contract's provisions. Fearful of another teachers' strike, the NTA went to court to ask for an order declaring the rights of both parties to the contract. Specifically, the NTA wanted answers to the following questions:

1. Is it permitted to the plaintiff (NTA) under our laws to organize itself as a labor union for the purpose of demanding and receiving recognition and collective bargaining?
2. May the plaintiff (NTA) engage in concerted action such as a strike, work stoppage, or collective refusal to enter upon duties?

In a decision that was to be followed by courts in other states, the Connecticut court ruled that the teachers did have the right to organize a labor union. The court noted that the laws in Connecticut were completely silent on the subject of teacher unions. After pointing out that "union organization in industry is now the rule rather than the exception," the court upheld the teachers' right to organize a labor union: "In the absence of prohibitory statute or regulation, no good reason appears why public employees should not organize as a labor union." The court warned that the NTA did not have unlimited bargaining rights, however; teacher associations could organize and bargain collectively only "for the pay and working conditions which it may be in the power of the board of education to grant." The NTA's salary demands, for example, had to be subject to the board's taxation power.

Turning to the second question, the court held that the teachers had no right to strike. In reaching its decision, the court explained: "It should be the aim of every employee of the government to do his or her part to make it function as efficiently and economically as possible. The drastic remedy of the organized strike to enforce the demands of unions of government employees is in direct contravention of this principle." The court stated that government employees occupy a different status from those who work in private enterprise because they "serve the public welfare," and it concluded that allowing teachers to strike would "deny the authority of government and contravene the public welfare."

Do All Teachers Have a Right to Join a Union and Engage in Collective Bargaining?

Teachers have a constitutional right to join a union. Whether they have a right to engage in collective bargaining depends on state law. In 1951, the time *Norwalk* was decided, none of the states had passed laws permitting boards of education to engage in collective bargaining with teacher organizations, and the courts had to resolve questions that arose in this area. Today, over forty states have passed laws guaranteeing that public employees have a right to engage in collective bargaining. These laws generally provide that public school teachers have the right to organize and join employee labor organizations, and that they can select representatives to bargain with their employer about "wages, hours, and other terms and conditions of employment."

The state laws vary considerably. Some states merely require boards of education to "meet and confer" with teacher organizations. In states with these general statutes, it is up to the courts to resolve any disputes concerning the proper subjects of collective bargaining.

Other state laws are much more detailed and require boards of education to meet with the teachers' organizations to negotiate specific topics. Such laws usually include more detailed procedures for resolving negotiating impasses that may arise during the bargaining process. The California law, for example, provides that the board and the teachers' representative must negotiate health and welfare benefits, leave, transfer and reassignment policies, safety conditions, class size, evaluation procedures, grievance procedures, and the layoff of probationary certificated school district employees.[3]

Teachers' Rights

How Are Collective Bargaining Laws Enforced?

To enforce collective bargaining and other laws affecting public employees, many states have established labor relations boards. These boards attempt to ensure that both school officials and teachers' organizations comply with the law. For example, Illinois law provides that either party to collective bargaining negotiations can complain to the state's educational labor relations board if either party fails to negotiate or to bargain in good faith.[4]

Are There Any Federal Laws Concerning Teachers' Unions?

There is no federal law that specifically regulates collective bargaining for teachers.[5] In 1978, Congress passed comprehensive legislation establishing and regulating collective bargaining rights for federal employees, and teachers who are employed in any educational institutions owned and operated by the federal government are covered by this law.[6] The vast majority of public school teachers, however, are employed by local school districts and must look to state laws for protection.

Is There a Constitutional Right to Organize?

Yes. In addition to state laws giving teachers the right to join unions, the courts have ruled that the U.S. Constitution gives teachers the right to organize. In Illinois, two probationary teachers were dismissed because of their work for the American Federation of Teachers. A federal appeals court ruled that "teachers have the right of free association, and unjustified interference with teachers' associational freedom violates the due process clause of the Fourteenth Amendment."[7] Another federal court ruled that a school board violated teachers' rights of association and free speech when the board refused to appoint teachers to supervisory positions unless they resigned from the teachers' association.[8] (For a detailed discussion of teachers' rights of association, see chapter 11.)

Is There a Constitutional Right to Bargain?

No. Most states have statutes that provide for collective bargaining for teachers, but in the absence of such laws, teachers do not have a constitutional right to bargain collectively. This issue was confronted in 1974 when the North Carolina legislature passed a law abolishing collective bargaining between public employees and any state or city agency. The state education association sued to have the law declared unconstitutional, but a federal court ruled that there was no such constitutional right.[9] "The Constitution," wrote the court, does not require that the government "be compelled to talk to or contract" with any organizatio

Although the teachers' union "may someday persuade state government of the asserted value of collective bargaining agreements," this is a political and not a judicial matter. While the First Amendment protects the right of teachers to associate and advocate, it does not guarantee that their advocacy will be effective or that government bodies must bargain with them.

Who Decides Who Will Represent Teachers in the Collective Bargaining Process?

State laws that provide for collective bargaining for teachers generally also establish a procedure to decide who will represent the teachers in negotiations with the school board. Typically the laws state that the board must bargain with the organization that a majority of teachers in the district (or other "bargaining unit") designates as the exclusive representative. This organization is usually elected.

In addition, state laws usually define who the union will represent as part of the bargaining unit. This unit, or group of teachers, may include all teachers in a city or school district or all teachers under the same salary schedule. Decisions about the size of such a unit and whether it is appropriate for a particular group of teachers to be represented by only one union are often made by the state's employment relations board. State laws also determine whether supervisory employees such as principals may be allowed in the same unit as nonsupervisory employees such as teachers. Some statutes prohibit supervisors from participation in the same unit they supervise; other states are silent on this issue. Finally, some states prohibit superintendents from participation in a bargaining unit with teachers.

Do All Teachers Have to Join the Employee Organization Selected as the Exclusive Bargaining Representative?

No. Public employees cannot be forced to join a union as a condition of their employment (the so-called *union shop,* or *closed shop*). Some state laws have explicitly recognized this right. In California, for example, the law provides that although public employees have the right to join a union, they also have the right "to refuse to join or participate in the activities of employee organizations. "[10]

In addition, the U.S. Supreme Court has ruled that the First Amendment gives teachers who are not union members the right to make public comments about matters that are the subject of collective bargaining negotiations. In *Madison Joint School District* v. *Wisconsin Employment Relations Commission,* Holmquist, a nonunion teacher, attended a public meeting of the board of education and spoke against a topic the union was supporting in collective bargaining negotiations.[11] The union filed a complaint with the state's employment relations board, claiming that the board of education had violated its duty under Wisconsin law to negotiate only with the teachers' exclusive collective bargaining representative when it permitted Holmquist to speak at the board meeting.

The Court, however, ruled that the First Amendment's guarantee of freedom of speech gave Holmquist the right to express his views:

> Holmquist did not seek to bargain or offer to enter into any bargain with the board, nor does it appear that he was authorized by any other teachers to enter into any agreement on their behalf.... Moreover, the school board meeting at which Holmquist was permitted to speak

was open to the public. He addressed the school board not merely as one of its employees but also as a concerned citizen, seeking to express his views on an important decision of his government.

The Court explained that according to its decision in *Pickering* v. *Board of Education* (see chapter 9 for a detailed discussion of this case), teachers cannot be "compelled to relinquish the First Amendment rights they would otherwise enjoy as citizens to comment on matters of public interest in connection with the operation of the public schools in which they work," and it concluded that "the mere expression of an opinion about a matter subject to collective bargaining, whether or not the speaker is a member of the bargaining unit, poses no genuine threat to the policy of exclusive representation that Wisconsin has adopted."

Can Teachers Who Are Not Union Members be Required to Pay Fees to a Union?

Yes. Over half of the states have passed laws that permit "agency-shop," or "fair share," arrangements under which employees who are not members of a union can be required to pay fees to a union as a condition of their employment. Although such agreements are not likely to be upheld in the absence of such a state law, the U.S. Supreme Court has ruled that they are constitutional. In *Abood* v. *Detroit Board of Education,* a group of teachers challenged the validity of an agency-shop clause in a collective bargaining agreement between the Detroit Board of Education and the Detroit Federation of Teachers.[12] Michigan law authorized a provision whereby every teacher who had not become a union member within 60 days of hire had to pay the union an amount equal to the regular dues or face discharge. The nonunion teachers stated that they were opposed to collective bargaining and that they did not approve of a number of the union's political activities unrelated to collective bargaining. They asked the Court to declare the agency-shop clause unconstitutional, arguing that it deprived them of their right to freedom of association protected by the First and Fourteenth Amendments.

The Supreme Court ruled that the agency-shop clause was constitutional. The Court noted that such arrangements had previously been upheld in labor relations in the private sector on the grounds that since the union's collective bargaining activities benefited all employees, all employees should help defray the union's expenses in these negotiations. The Court explained that a "union-shop arrangement has been thought to distribute fairly the cost of these activities among those who benefit, and it counteracts the incentive that employees might otherwise have to become 'free riders'—to refuse to contribute to the union while obtaining benefits of union representation that necessarily accrue to all employees." The Court concluded that this reasoning also made agency-shop arrangements valid for public employees:

> Public employees are not basically different from private employees; on the whole, they have the same sort of skills, the same needs, and seek the same advantages.... The very real differences between exclusive-agent collective bargaining in the public and private sectors are not such as to work any greater infringement upon the First Amendment interests of public employees.

Although the Supreme Court has upheld agency-shop provisions, states are still free to prohibit agency shops, and some do. For example, the Vermont Supreme Court has ruled that an agency fee is prohibited under the state law that ensures that teachers have the right not to join a union.[13]

Can Teachers Be Required to Support Union Political Activities?

No. In *Abood,* the U.S. Supreme Court ruled that it was a violation of the First Amendment to require a public employee to be forced to pay dues to support a union's political activities. The Court did not attempt to define which union activities (e.g., political lobbying) need not be supported financially. Instead, the Court merely noted that there would be "difficult problems in drawing lines between collective-bargaining activities, for which contributions may be compelled, and ideological activities unrelated to collective bargaining, for which such compulsion is prohibited."

The U.S. Supreme Court provided further guidance in a 1984 case.[14] The Court was asked to decide whether a union's nonpolitical publications, conventions, and social activities incidental to meetings were sufficiently related to collective bargaining as to allow the union to charge these activities to nonunion members under an agency-shop provision, The Court said yes, reasoning that these activities were all germane to the union's work in the area of collective bargaining. The Court also found, however, that the union could not charge objecting employees for litigation expenses not involving the negotiation of agreements or settlement of grievances, nor charge for general organizing efforts.

In a 1986 case, U.S. Supreme Court gave additional protection to nonunion members who are required to pay fees under an agency-shop agreement.[15] The Court held that procedural safeguards are necessary to protect nonmembers from being compelled to subsidize political or ideological activities not germane to the collective bargaining process. Specifically, the Court ruled that the First Amendment requires that the union must provide the following: an adequate explanation of the agency fee, a reasonably prompt opportunity to challenge the amount of the fee before an impartial decision maker, and an escrow for the amounts reasonably in dispute while such challenges are pending.

In a 1991 case, the U.S. Supreme Court issued a splintered decision upholding agency-shop agreements for the university community.[16] In *Lehnert* v. *Ferris Faculty Association,* six faculty members at Ferris State College in Big Rapids, Michigan, brought suit against the faculty union, claiming that the union's collection of a $284 service fee from nonmembers violated their First and Fourteenth Amendment rights. Of the $284, $24.80 went to the local union, $211.20 to the state affiliate, and $48 to the national affiliate (i.e., the National Education Association). The faculty members objected to being charged for lobbying activities that did not concern their (local) collective bargaining agreement and for activities not undertaken directly on behalf of the bargaining unit to which they belonged.

While the Court explained that the decisions in this area proscribe a case-by-case analysis, prior cases did set forth several "guidelines" to use in determining which activities a union may consistently charge to dissenting employees: (1) activities germane to collective bargaining activity, (2) the activities justified by the government's interest in labor peace, and (3) activities that do not significantly burden free speech. Applying these guidelines, the Court found that the union could not charge for legislative lobbying, reasoning that lobbying activities did not necessarily promote labor peace and would further interfere with First Amendment interests of objecting employees. On the other hand, the Court concluded that the union could charge nonmembers for activities beyond local labor negotiations. The Court explained that the essence of union affiliation is the notion that the parent could bring its resources to bear when needed by the local; thus local unions could charge nonmembers for the cost of state and national affiliate activities, even if those activities were not performed for the direct benefit of the employees' bargaining unit. Examining the specific expenditures involved, the Court ruled that the union could charge nonmembers for some expenses of a union publication, for convention expenses, and for expenses related to preparations for a possible strike. The union could not charge for public relations expenses to "enhance the reputation of the teaching profession," for litigation expenses not related to the local bargaining unit, or for the cost of an education program to affect the outcome of ballot issues.

The Ninth Circuit Court of Appeals applied the principles outlined in these cases in a 1993 challenge to a dispute between employee union and non-member agency fee payers.[17] The union had instituted a procedure whereby it deducted the full union dues from agency fee payers' paychecks in September and paid a rebate to objecting fee payers in December. Declaring that "there's no such thing as a free lunch,"[18] the court held that this deduction-escrow-refund procedure was permissible. The court found that this procedure was necessary for the union to be able to identify all agency fee payers at the beginning of each school year, and that the refund schedule was reasonably prompt.

What Are the Union's Legal Responsibilities as the Exclusive Collective Bargaining Representative for Teachers?

The employee organization that acts as the exclusive bargaining agent also has the legal duty to represent all teachers in that bargaining unit. This *duty of fair representation* prohibits the union from discriminating against any of its members in the negotiation and administration of collective bargaining agreements. In addition, the union must represent the interests of all members of the bargaining unit—even those who are not union members—in the negotiation process. The duty of fair representation requires the union to be honest and fair but does not deprive it of discretion in deciding how to negotiate with the school board or how to handle teachers' grievances. Unless a union is acting out of a political, racial, or other "bad-faith" reason, it is not a violation of this duty for the union to take a position that some members oppose, or to decide to settle a grievance. For example, a New York court ruled that a union did not breach its duty of fair representation for 35 special education teachers when it permitted the school district to modify the collective bargaining agreement to provide a salary differential for another group of special education teachers.[19] The court reasoned that there was a rational basis for differentiating between teachers who taught severely handicapped children and those who taught only the mildly handicapped.

The union also has the obligation to bargain with the school board in *good faith*. This requires the union to meet at reasonable times to negotiate with the school board and to make a sincere effort to reach an agreement on the topics under discussion. Good faith does *not* require that the union reach an agreement with the school board, but it does mean that the union cannot merely go through the motions of meeting with school officials. The union must consider and respond to the board's proposals. Examples of bad-faith bargaining include refusing to bargain with the designated representative or refusing to participate in mediation required by the terms of the contract or state law.

Can a Union Have Exclusive Access to School Mail Facilities?

Yes. In 1983, the U.S. Supreme Court ruled that there was no violation of teachers' First or Fourteenth Amendment rights when an Indiana school board agreed to limit access to teacher mailboxes to the union designated as the exclusive bargaining representative.[20] The Court reasoned that the school mailboxes did not constitute a public forum and therefore could be limited to official school business. The Court emphasized that rival union groups could still communicate with the teachers via other methods (such as bulletin boards). (For a detailed discussion of teachers' First Amendment rights, including the rights of nonunion members to criticize union policy, see chapter 9.) State laws, however, may still give rival unions greater protection and prohibit exclusive access to school mail facilities.

What Legal Responsibilities Does the School Board Have in the Bargaining Process?

The school board has the same legal duty to bargain in good faith as the union does. In addition, state law may impose certain responsibilities on the school board to inform the public about the nature of the collective bargaining process. Many states have passed "open public meeting laws," which require school boards to inform the public about educational policy decisions.

Can the School Board Bypass the Union and Make Salary Agreements with Individual Teachers?

No. The school board must bargain exclusively with the teachers' designated representative over wages, hours, and other terms and conditions of employment. It was an *unfair labor practice* (a legal term for violation of the law by a union or employer) for a school district to enter into individual arrangements with certain teachers and to agree to pay them different retirement benefits than the other teachers who were union members.[21] Even if the teachers initiated these changes, the school board's agreement was not permissible because it denied the union its statutory right to bargain collectively for the benefit of all member teachers.

Contract Negotiations

What Happens During Collective Bargaining?

The bargaining process can begin when either (1) the teachers' union or the school board drafts a contract proposal or (2) there is an exchange of initial proposals between the teachers' union and the school board. (If either the union or the board submits an initial proposal, the other party will submit a counterproposal.) In either situation, after the two sides have exchanged the preliminary statements that describe their positions, they proceed to the discussion table. Each side usually appoints one spokesperson, and bargaining sessions are held to discuss each of the proposed contracts' provisions. The bargaining sessions involve a complicated process of give and take through which each side must evaluate the other side's demands and decide on which issues to compromise. The steps in the negotiating process vary depending on the tactics adopted by the two parties.

What Do the Union and the School Board Bargain About?

State laws determine what the union and board can bargain about, and these laws vary widely. A majority of the states require unions and school boards to bargain about "wages, hours, and other terms and conditions of employment." Other states require that the bargaining be restricted to specific mandatory subjects, such as insurance, fringe benefits, or sick leave.

When the law is not specific, the courts have had to decide the mandatory subjects for collective bargaining. Usually courts have held that topics "directly" or "significantly" related to the teachers' working conditions are mandatory subjects (e.g., salaries, sick leave, and seniority). Topics that concern educational policies that only indirectly affect working conditions and that the board must control in order to manage the schools effectively are not within the scope of bargaining (e.g., curriculum content and hiring policies).

In applying these general rules, the courts look at each individual case in light of whatever state statute may apply. As might be expected, different courts have reached different conclusions. In North Dakota, the state's supreme court has held that there are only five mandatory subjects: salary, hours, formulation of an agreement, binding arbitration, and interpretation of an existing agreement.[22] All other subjects are permissive. The Alaska Supreme Court has ruled that salaries, fringe benefits, number of hours worked, and the amount of leave time are mandatory subjects for negotiation, whereas class size, pupil-teacher ratio, school calendar, and teacher representation on school board advisory committees are not.[23] The Supreme Court of Wisconsin has held that the length of the school calendar is a mandatory subject of bargaining whereas class size is not.[24] On the other hand, the Supreme Court of Connecticut has found that the length of the school calendar is not a mandatory subject, whereas class size is.[25] Courts have also differed on whether evaluation procedures[26] and student discipline procedures[27] are mandatory subjects of bargaining.

Are There Other Limitations on the Scope of Collective Bargaining?

Yes. First, the parties cannot enter into any contractual negotiations that are in violation of constitutional law. For example, nonunion teachers have the right to make comments at public meetings on issues subject to collective bargaining negotiations, and so the union and school board cannot agree to a contract that prohibits such activity (see discussion in chapter 9). Similarly, the parties must abide by existing state and federal laws. If state laws establish certain certification requirements for teachers, the collective bargaining contract cannot set up conflicting standards. Finally, the collective bargaining contract must recognize any rights that exist under other contracts currently in effect.

What Happens If the Union and the School Board Cannot Agree on a Contract?

State procedures vary when the union and the school board have reached an impasse in their negotiations. States with laws that merely require the school board to "meet and confer" with the union do not have any procedures for resolving a deadlock in negotiations. A majority of states, however, do make some provision for this situation. The most common process is mediation, in which the parties meet with a neutral third person (or persons) who attempts to resolve their differences through discussion and by proposing compromise provisions. The mediator merely functions as a facilitator and has no legal power to force the parties to accept these suggestions.

If the parties reject the mediator's recommendations, the next step is usually fact finding. The fact-finding process involves a more formal discussion, during which each party again presents its position and supporting facts. The fact-finding body (a panel of people usually trained as arbitrators) then issues its recommendations. Unlike mediation, fact-finding recommendations are generally made public, thus placing additional pressure on the parties to come to an agreement. If the parties are still at an impasse, state law may require the union and the school board to submit to arbitration. At this point, the parties agree to abide by an impartial arbitrator's decision.

What Does a Collective Bargaining Contract Include?

Every collective bargaining contract is different, reflecting the concerns of teachers and school officials in diverse districts. The provisions described below, however, are generally part of all collective bargaining contracts:

1. *Preamble:* Identifies the parties to the contract and the period for which the contract will be in effect.
2. *Recognition Clause:* identifies the union/association as the exclusive representative of the teachers in a defined bargaining unit. A typical recognition clause might state: "The Board of Trustees of Smalltown School District hereby recognizes the Smalltown Community Education Association as the exclusive representative of all teachers employed by the Smalltown Community Schools Corporation."
3. *Maintenance Clause:* provides that no changes in wages, hours, and other terms and conditions of employment that are not covered in the contract, but that are mandatory subjects of bargaining, shall be made without the union's agreement.
4. *Grievance Procedure:* defines "grievance" and describes the steps to be followed if a grievance is filed. A grievance may be defined as "a claim by a teacher or by the union that there has been a violation, a misapplication, or a misinterpretation of the agreement"; a grievance may also be defined more broadly to mean "a claim by a teacher or the union that there has been a violation, a misapplication, or a misinterpretation of any policy or administrative decision affecting employees of the school district." The procedure usually defines the steps that must be taken and the time limits that apply. It may include provisions for arbitration.
5. *Teachers' Rights Clause:* provides that teachers have the right to organize for the purpose of collective negotiations and prohibits discrimination against teachers regardless of membership or nonmembership in any employee organization.
6. *Teacher Organizations' Rights Clause:* outlines union/association rights to communicate with members, including the right to use bulletin board space, place mail in teachers' mailboxes, schedule meetings with teachers, and have access to certain school board documents.

7. *Representation Clause:* describes the procedure to be followed if the school board or any employee organization wishes to challenge the union/association status as the exclusive bargaining agent.

8. *Management Rights Clause:* provides that the school board does not "waive any rights or powers granted under the laws of the state." This provision merely affirms what is already the law, that school boards cannot be required to bargain away their rights to establish educational policy.

9. *Terms of the Agreement:* describes the specific contract provisions concerning teachers' employment; it generally includes provisions concerning salaries, sick leave, pregnancy leave, other leaves of absence, insurance, vacations, transfer policy and procedures, and teaching days and hours.

Strikes

Do Teachers Have the Right to Strike?

Although teachers have no constitutional right to strike, about half of the states have passed laws that give teachers a limited right to strike. Generally, these laws provide that teachers in a union/association are allowed to strike only after they have complied with the state's procedures for impasse resolution, and after they have notified the school board of their intent to strike. In Illinois, for example, a comprehensive law regulating educational labor relations gives educational employees the right to strike when each of the following conditions is met:

1. They are represented by an exclusive bargaining representative.
2. Mediation has been used without success.
3. At least five days have elapsed after a notice of intent to strike has been given by the exclusive bargaining representative to the educational employer, the regional superintendent, and the Illinois Educational Labor Relations Board.
4. The collective bargaining agreement between the educational employer and educational employees, if any, has expired.
5. The employer and the exclusive bargaining representative have not mutually submitted the unresolved issues to arbitration.[28]

As is the case in other states, the Illinois law also provides that if an employer believes that a strike is a clear and present danger to the health or safety of the public, the employer can ask a court for appropriate relief (such as an injunction to prohibit the strike).

What Penalties Can Be Imposed on Teachers Who Engage in an Illegal Strike?

Some state laws describe penalties that may be imposed on teachers or organization officials who engage in an illegal strike. For example, Indiana law states that a striking teachers' union/association loses its dues deduction privilege for one year; in addition, teachers will not be paid for any school day missed as the result of a strike.[29] Nevada law provides that school officials can impose any of the following sanctions on teachers who engage in a strike:

1. dismiss, suspend, or demote all or any employees who participate in such strike or violation;
2. cancel the contracts of employment of all or any employees who participate in such strike or violation; and
3. withhold all or any part of the salaries or wages that would otherwise accrue to all or any employees who participate in such strike or violation.[30]

Florida law provides that a teachers' organization can be liable for damages that the school district may have suffered due to the strike and can also be fined up to $20,000 for each day of the strike.[31] Oklahoma law states that a teachers' union that engages in a strike will cease to be recognized as the representative of the teachers and that the school district is then relieved of any duty to bargain.[32]

In addition to the sanctions described in state laws, courts have ruled that school boards have certain options available in strike situations. School officials can ask the courts to issue an injunction to prohibit the strike. The union, its officers, and members can be held in contempt and fined or jailed if they remain on strike in violation of a court order to return to work.[33] The courts have ruled that the school board can fire teachers who engage in an illegal strike. In a Wisconsin case, teachers went out on strike while the school board and the teachers' association were negotiating over the terms of the new contract.[34] After sending letters to the striking teachers informing them that the strike was illegal, school officials scheduled disciplinary hearings for each striking teacher. The teachers then appeared before the school board, asking that they be treated as a group in any disciplinary proceedings. The board voted to fire all the teachers, and the Wisconsin Supreme Court upheld the board's decision.

Finally, the courts have ruled that school boards can impose economic sanctions on teachers who go on strike. A New York court upheld the constitutionality of a state law that allowed the board to make payroll deductions in the amount of twice the daily rate of pay for each day a teacher was on strike.[35] Similarly, a Florida court ruled that a school board had the authority under state law to require each striking teacher to pay $100 to the board as a condition of reemployment.[36]

In 1991, an Indiana appellate court ruled that an elementary school student could not maintain an action for damages she allegedly sustained when her teachers participated in an illegal strike.[37] The student claimed that she was deprived of educational instruction for a period of five days and that she also suffered emotional distress because of the teachers' actions. The court found that Indiana law explicitly provides that only a school corporation can maintain an action against striking teachers. Courts in other states have allowed private suits stemming from public employee strikes, however, on the ground that the public is the real party injured when a union breaches its contract with the public school employer.

Summary

Over the past 30 years, collective bargaining in the public schools has become a common practice. Most states have passed laws that give teachers the right to join employee organizations, and the majority of teachers are union/association members. In addition, the courts have held that teachers have a constitutional right to organize as part of their right of free association.

Most state laws outline procedures for teachers to follow when selecting an organization as their exclusive bargaining agent in contract negotiations with the school board. The laws vary widely from state to state but generally require school boards to bargain with teacher organizations about "wages, hours, and other terms and conditions of employment." Most states also describe the procedure to be followed when there is an impasse in collective bargaining negotiations.

Despite the support for collective bargaining in education, there are limits on teachers' rights. Teachers do not have the constitutional right to bargain with school boards, and about half of the states prohibit all strikes by teachers. The trend today, however, is for states to give teachers a limited right to strike. In situations where state law prohibits strikes or teachers fail to meet the specified conditions for a strike, the courts have upheld the school board's right to dismiss striking teachers. In addition, the courts have issued injunctions against teachers who engage in illegal strikes and have upheld the board's authority to impose economic sanctions on striking teachers.

NOTES

1. From a peak of 35.5 percent of the total nonpublic work force in 1945, labor union representation of such workers has dropped below 13 percent.
2. *Norwalk Teachers' Association* v. *Board of Education,* 83 A.2d 482 (Conn. 1951).
3. CAL. GOVT. CODE § 3543.2[a] (West 1997).
4. 115 ILCS 5/15 (1993 State Bar Edition).
5. The National Labor Relations Act of 1935 and the Taft-Hartley Act of 1977 regulate labor-management relations in private industry but do not apply to public employees, and the U.S. Supreme Court has ruled that the National Labor Relations Act does not cover teachers in church-related schools. *NLRB* v. *Catholic Bishop of Chicago,* 440 U.S. 490 (1979). The Supreme Court has let stand a Ninth Circuit Court of Appeals decision, however, that held that the NLRA does cover nonteaching staff at parochial schools. *National Labor Relations Board* v. *Hanna Boys Center,* 940 F.2d 1295 (9th Cir. 1991).
6. Federal Service Labor-Management Relations Statute, 5 U.S.C. § 7101 (1997). Teachers covered by this law include individuals who are employed overseas at schools run by the U.S. Department of Defense or at schools on Indian reservations run by the Bureau of Indian Affairs.
7. *McLaughlin* v. *Tilendis,* 398 F.2d 287 (7th Cir. 1968).
8. *Lake Park Education Association* v. *Board of Education of Lake Park,* 526 F.Supp. 710 (N.D. Ill. 1981).
9. *Winston-Salem/Forsyth County Unit of the North Carolina Association of Educators* v. *Phillips,* 381 F.Supp. 644 (M.D. N.C. 1974).
10. CAL. GOVT. CODE § 3543 (West 1997).
11. 429 U.S. 167 (1976).
12. 431 U.S. 209 (1977).
13. *Weissenstein* v. *Burlington Board of School Commissions,* 543 A.2d 691 (Vt. 1988).
14. *Ellis* v. *Brotherhood of Railway Clerks,* 466 U.S. 435 (1984).
15. *Chicago Teachers Union, Local No. 1* v. *Hudson,* 475 U.S. 292 (1986).
16. *Lehnert* v. *Ferris Faculty Association,* 500 U.S. 507 (1991).
17. *Grunwald et al.* v. *San Bernardino City Unified School District,* 994 F.2d 1370 (9th Cir. 1993).
18. *Id.* at 1372.
19. *Litman* v. *Board of Education* of New York, 565 N.Y.S.2d 93 (N.Y. App. Div. 1991).
20. *Perry Education Association* v. *Perry Local Education Association,* 460, U.S. 37 (1983).

21. *Board of Education* v. *Illinois Educational Labor Relations Board,* 620 N.E.2d 418 (Ill. App. Ct. 1993).

22. *Fargo Education Association* v. *Fargo Public School District,* 291 N.W.2d 267 (N.D. 1980).

23. *Kenai Peninsula Borough School District* v. *Kenai Peninsula Education Association,* 572 P.2d 416 (Alaska 1977).

24. *Beloit Education Association* v. *Wisconsin Employment Relations Commission,* 242 N.W.2d 231 (Wis. 1976).

25. *West Hartford Education Association* v. *DeCourcy,* 295 A.2d 526 (Conn. 1972).

26. Holding yes: *Board of Education* v. *Fair Lawn Education Association,* 417 A.2d 76 (N.J. Super. Ct. App. Div. 1980); *Northeast Community School District* v. *Public Employment Relations Board,* 408 N.W.2d 46 (Iowa 1987). Holding no: *Springfield Education Association* v. *Springfield School District,* 621 P.2d 547 (Or. 1980); *Wethersfield Board of Education* v. *Connecticut State Board of Labor Relations,* 519 A.2d 41 (Conn. 1986); *Alton Community Unified School District No. 11* v. *Illinois Educational Labor Relations Board,* 567 N.E.2d 671 (Ill. App. Ct. 1991).

27. Holding yes: *Sutherlin Education Association* v. *Sutherlin School District,* 548 P.2d 204 (Or. Ct. App. 1976). Holding no: *Beloit Education Association* v. *Employment Relation Commission,* 242 NW.2d 231 (Wis. 1976).

28. 115 ILCS 5/13 (1993 State Bar Edition).

29. IND. CODE ANN. § 20-7.5-1-14.

30. NEV. REV. STAT. § 288.260 (1995).

31. FLA. STAT. ANN. § 447.507 (West 1997).

32. OKLA. STAT. ANN. tit. 70, § 509.8 (West 1989).

33. *In re Block,* 236 A.2 (1589 (N.J. 1967).

34. *Hortonville Education Association* v. *Hortonville Joint School District,* 225 N.W.2d 658 (Wis. 1975). This case also raised the question of whether the school board violated the teachers' due process rights by both engaging in collective bargaining as agent for the school district and holding discharge hearings for striking teachers. The Wisconsin Supreme Court found a due process violation but the U.S. Supreme Court reversed the decision.

35. *Lawson* v. *Board of Education,* 307 N.Y.S.2d 333 (N.Y. Sup. Ct. 1970).

36. *National Education Association, Inc.* v. *Lee County Board of Public Instruction,* 299 F.Supp. 834 (M.D. Fla. 1969).

37. *Coons* v. *Kaiser,* 567 N.E.2d 851 (Ind. Ct. App. 1991).

5 When Am I Liable?

Overview

Historically, the courts have ruled that school districts and school board members acting in good faith within their prescribed authority could not be liable for injuries to students or teachers that were a result of errors of judgment. This doctrine of *tort immunity* was based on the idea that public funds designated for schooling should not be paid to private individuals for noneducational purposes. In recent years, the courts have carved out some exceptions to this doctrine, and state statutes have modified its scope.

School board members have been liable as individuals, though, when they exceeded their authority, and teachers have always been liable for injuries to others caused by their own negligence. The law requires teachers to perform as a reasonably prudent person, and when a teacher's actions fall below the standard of care, the teacher will be liable for the resulting injury.

Student Injuries

Under the common law, teachers have a mandatory duty to supervise students under their control. Individual teachers can be held liable for damages to an injured student if the student can prove four things: (1) the teacher had a duty to be careful not to injure the student and to protect the student from being injured, (2) the teacher failed to use due care, (3) the teacher's carelessness caused the injury, and (4) the student sustained provable damages. Usually in cases of student injury, it is easy to prove that the teacher had a duty to be careful toward his or her students and that the injuries resulted in monetary damages. Sometimes there is a question about what precisely caused the injury. In most cases, the critical question is whether the teacher violated his or her duty of due care and therefore was negligent.

The *Sheehan* Case[1]

When Is a Teacher Negligent?

If a teacher fails to exercise *reasonable care* to protect his or her students from injury, the teacher is negligent. Such negligence was involved in the case of Margaret Sheehan, an eighth-grade student at St. Peter's Catholic School who was injured one morning during recess. The injury occurred when a teacher took Margaret and 19 other girls to an athletic field where a group of eighth-grade boys were playing baseball. The teacher told the girls to sit on a log on the third-base line and then she returned to the school. About five minutes after the teacher left, some of the boys waiting their turn to bat began throwing pebbles at the girls. Although the girls protested, the pebble throwing continued for several minutes, until Margaret was seriously injured by a pebble that struck her eye. Margaret's parents sued for damages on her behalf. They alleged that the school and the teacher were negligent in failing to supervise the children's recess. The evidence indicated that the teacher was absent from the athletic area from the time she brought the girls there until after the accident.

After both sides presented their case, the judge instructed the jury on the law to be applied. "It is the duty of a school," said the judge, "to use ordinary care and to protect its students from injury resulting from the conduct of other students under circumstances where such conduct would reasonably have been foreseen and could have been prevented by the use of ordinary care." The jury found that it was reasonable to foresee that a student might be hurt as a result of failure to supervise an athletic area. It therefore decided that the school was negligent. The school appealed on the grounds that there was no past proof that this activity was dangerous or that supervision would have prevented the accident. But the Supreme Court of Minnesota ruled in Margaret's favor. It noted that children have a "known proclivity to act impulsively without thought of the possibilities of danger." It is precisely this lack of mature judgment that makes supervision so vital. "The mere presence of the hand of authority," wrote the court, "normally is effective to curb this youthful exuberance and to protect the children against their own folly."

This does not mean that a teacher is expected to anticipate every situation in which one child may suddenly injure another. The law does not expect a teacher to prevent an unforeseen injury that could happen quickly without warning. But this was not such a case. Here, the girls protested when the pebble throwing began, and the boys continued throwing for several minutes before Margaret was injured. Under these circumstances, the jury concluded that a teacher using reasonable care would have put a stop to this activity and would have prevented the injury. The teacher therefore was negligent in leaving the athletic field unsupervised.

The legal principles to be applied in cases of alleged negligence are clear: Teachers have a duty to exercise reasonable care not to injure their students and to prevent them from being injured. *Reasonable care* is the degree of care a teacher of ordinary prudence would have used under like circumstances. The circumstances considered would include the same maturity and experience of the students, and the extent of danger involved. For example, a school board was found liable when a six-year-old student using the monkey bars swung onto a tether ball pole and was injured when she slid over a screw that protruded approximately 1.5 inches out of the pole.[2] The court noted that the injury occurred at 8:30 A.M., when there were between 160 and 180 children in the schoolyard under the supervision of one teacher. The teacher's duties that morning included supervising school bus unloading, patrolling the playground, and overseeing students in the school basement, a situation that made her supervisory functions "totally inadequate and virtually impossible." The court also found that the school board was negligent in placing the tether ball pole so close to the monkey bars, providing a natural incentive for a young child to try to slide down the pole.

When circumstances are more dangerous, as they could be in shop or physical education classes, a teacher would be expected to exercise greater care. Failure to be more careful when dangers are greater—to provide careful instructions, clear warnings, and close supervision—would constitute negligence. For example, a shop instructor was found guilty of negligence when one student injured another during the operation of a drill press.[3] The student's improper operation of the press caused the drill bit to deflect and strike the assisting student in the temple, which resulted in lacerations and a skull fracture. Although the student was told to wait for the teacher's assistance, the court found the teacher negligent in giving the student the drill bit before the teacher was ready to supervise him. The court further found the teacher liable for failing to warn the students of the dangers involved in assisting one another and for leaving the students unsupervised in a room of operational shop equipment. Neither the school district nor the junior high school teacher was liable, however, when a sixth-grade student was injured in a wrestling match in a required physical education class.[4] Here, the court found that the teacher exercised the appropriate degree of care by teaching the rules of wrestling, demonstrating wrestling maneuvers, matching students according to height, weight, and size, and closely supervising the students.

The concept of *duty of care* was applied in a Maryland case to hold two high school counselors liable for failing to attempt to prevent a student's suicide.[5] In that case, the father of a 13-year-old student sued the counselors when his daughter consummated a murder-suicide pact with another 13-year-old girl. He alleged that his daughter had told several friends she intended to kill herself and that the friends had told the two counselors. The counselors questioned his daughter, but when she denied making any suicide threat, they did nothing further. The father claimed that had the counselors notified him of his daughter's intent, he could have intervened to prevent the suicide. The court agreed, holding that there is a duty to attempt to prevent an adolescent's suicide by reasonable means, including, in this case, warning the parent. In imposing this duty the court emphasized the significance of the underlying public policy issue: "when the risk of death to a child is balanced against the burden sought to be imposed on the counselors, the scales tip overwhelmingly in favor of duty."[6]

Are Teachers Required to Supervise Their Students at All Times?

Not always. According to a Minnesota court, there is generally "no requirement of constant supervision of all the movements of the pupils at all times."[7] However, a teacher would have a duty to provide constant supervision under dangerous conditions, especially among young children.

The *Mancha* Case[8]

In Chicago, two teachers organized a field trip to the city's natural history museum for about 50 students, 12 to 15 years of age. At the museum, the students were allowed to view the exhibits without direct supervision. When Roberto Mancha was away from the teachers, he was beaten by several boys not connected with the school. Roberto's parents sued, charging that the teachers who organized the trip were negligent in not supervising their students and in failing to foresee and guard against Roberto's injury.

In discussing this charge, an Illinois court observed that hindsight makes every event foreseeable. However, according to the court, a teacher's duty does not depend only on foreseeability. Judges should also consider the likelihood of the injury, the magnitude of the burden of guarding against it, and the consequences of placing that burden on teachers. The court regarded the risk that a 12-year-old boy would be assaulted in the museum as "minimal." The burden of constantly supervising children in cases such as this would be extremely heavy and would discourage teachers from planning many useful extracurricular activities. The court pointed out that even a game of hopscotch could suddenly break into a fight resulting in serious injury. It also would be practically impossible to require a teacher to watch each student at all times. Moreover, the judge noted that the museum in this case had been a "great educational enterprise," not a place of danger. Under these circumstances, the court ruled that the teachers did not have a duty to anticipate an assault or directly supervise the entire museum trip.

Similarly, a California district was not held liable when a 12-year-old student was fatally injured playing a dangerous skateboard game at an elementary school playground at approximately 5:30 P.M.[9] The student's parents sued the school for negligent supervision and for maintaining grounds that were not locked. The court said that schools do *not* have a duty to supervise the grounds at all times. On the contrary, the duty of supervision is limited to school-related or encouraged functions and activities that take place during school hours. "To require round-the-clock supervision or prison-tight security for school premises," wrote the court, "would impose too great a financial burden on the schools."

On the other hand, the judge in *Mancha* acknowledged that constant supervision would be required on some field trips (e.g., where dangerous machinery is used or where there is reason to believe an assault might occur). Similarly, it might be reasonable to require teachers to provide close supervision for students working with dangerous equipment in school. This was the ruling in an Indiana case in which Tom Peters, a ninth-grade student, lost four fingers while working with a circular saw in an industrial arts class.[10] Peters was cutting wood, one of the saw guards was broken, and his teacher was supervising another class in an adjacent room. A state appeals court found it reasonable to hold the school liable for the damage to Peters because he was allowed to use improperly guarded machinery without the personal supervision of the teacher.

Can a Teacher's Duty of Supervision Extend Beyond School Hours?

Yes. While teachers are not ordinarily liable for students' acts after school, they can be held liable if they assign or initiate dangerous activities. In a Louisiana case, for example, the court found a science teacher to be liable when a 13-year-old was injured building a model volcano in his home as part of a class science project.[11] The court found that the teacher was negligent in conducting a classroom volcano demonstration and then allowing the student to take his own volcano project home without determining exactly what chemical substances the student had used or whether the project was dangerous to himself or others.

Can Teachers Be Held Liable If a Student Injures Another Student or a Teacher?

Yes. If a teacher knows or should know that a student is likely to harm another student or a teacher, the teacher has an obligation to try to prevent the injury. In a representative case from

New York, a student who had a record of misbehavior transferred to another junior high school, where she assaulted Josette Ferraro.[12] The court noted that during her three months at the school, the student had assaulted other students on three occasions and was "a source of constant quarrelling and aggressive behavior toward other students as well as teachers." On the day of the assault, a substitute teacher was in charge of Josette's class. The court found the school to be negligent in not informing the substitute teacher about Josette's tendency to misbehave, noting that had it done so, steps might have been taken to prevent the assault, such as requiring the unruly student to sit in a seat directly in front of the teacher.

Neither the school board nor the wrestling coach were liable, however, when a student member of the wrestling team, after losing a match, threw a chair that injured a spectator.[13] The court held that there was no pattern of violence on the part of the student that would have put the faculty or school board on notice of the student's propensity to act inappropriately.

Can Teachers Be Held Liable If a Classroom Aide Injures a Student?

Not if the teacher exercises ordinary care in supervising the aide. In a Georgia case, for example, a parent sued a special education teacher after the classroom aide severely beat her child while the child and the aide were in the bathroom.[14] The court found that there was no evidence that the teacher knew that the aide was beating the student or that she could have foreseen such an action. Furthermore, there was no showing that any amount of additional supervision could have prevented such an injury. The court therefore dismissed the claim against the teacher.

If Teachers Are Careless, Are They Automatically Liable for Damages?

No. To recover damages, injured students must prove more than that the teacher was careless; they must also show that the teacher's failure to use due care was the cause of the injury. For example, Wilmer Nash, an elementary school student from Louisiana, was waiting for the school bus to take him home. He was playing with a girl when another girl struck him in the eye with a stick, the injury leading to partial blindness. Wilmer's parents sued the school.

The court noted that the school is required to provide supervision while students are waiting for the school bus and that it failed to do so at the time Wilmer was injured.[15] Nevertheless, the court did not find the school or the teachers liable because Wilmer was not able to prove that careful supervision would have prevented the injury. "How," asked the judge, "could any teacher anticipate a situation where one child, while teasing another child, would be struck in the eye with a stick by a third child?" Even if educators can anticipate that accidents like this sometimes happen, there was no evidence that this injury could have been prevented if a teacher had been present. "As is often the case," concluded the judge, "accidents such as this involving school children at play happen so quickly that unless there was direct supervision of every child (which we recognize as being impossible), the accident can be said to be almost impossible to prevent." Thus the court did not find the school liable for damages because Wilmer failed to show a causal connection between the absence of supervision and his accident.

In New York City, Alan Kaufman was critically injured when he jumped for a basketball and bumped heads with another student. Kaufman's father sued, alleging that the school failed to supervise the game properly. But the court ruled in favor of the school.[16]

According to the court, even if there was an absence of supervision and even if "such absence constituted negligence, still under the circumstances, such lack of supervision was not the proximate cause of the accident." The presence of a teacher would not have prevented the boys from bumping their heads during the basketball game. "That," wrote the court, "is one of the natural and normal possible consequences or occurrences in a game of this sort which cannot be prevented no matter how adequate the supervision."

Are There Special Liability Standards for Substitute Teachers and Student Teachers?

No. Substitute teachers and student teachers are held to the same duties of care as full-time teachers and would be liable for foreseeable injuries that are caused by their negligent acts. A substitute teacher was found liable, for example, when she failed to supervise a shop class adequately and one student sexually assaulted another student behind a portable chalkboard in the classroom.[17] The court found that the teacher breached her duty of reasonable supervision when she was absent from the classroom for some or all of the ten minutes during which the assault took place. The court further noted that there had been an even greater duty of supervision here because of a unique combination of factors, including an oversize classroom, the presence of dangerous machinery, and the intermingling of regular and emotionally and mentally handicapped students.

However, a substitute or student teacher would not be liable for damages resulting from a student's unforeseeable behavior. For example, a New York court ruled that neither a teacher's aide nor the school district was liable when a sixth-grade student was injured because a classmate pulled his chair out from under him as he went to sit down.[18] The court explained that even though there was only one aide supervising two classrooms, there had been no reason to expect any behavioral problems with such an arrangement, and the injury was the result of an unexpected prank that could not have been anticipated or prevented.

Defenses against Liability

Injured students who sue teachers and administrations for damages may encounter the defenses of contributory or comparative negligence, assumption of risk, or governmental immunity.

What Is Contributory Negligence?

If a student's own negligence contributed to the injury, the law in a few states would consider the student guilty of *contributory negligence.* Under the common-law doctrine of contributory negligence, a plaintiff cannot recover damages if the plaintiff's own negligence was in any way a cause of the injury. Unless the injured student was very young, this would usually prevent the student from recovering damages against a negligent teacher. This principle is illustrated in the 1979 case of a 17-year-old high school student named Jodeen Miles.[19] Jodeen was working on her senior project in Shop II when she attempted to remove a piece of wood from an operating machine with her hands, contrary to safe practice. As a result, she severed two fingers and sued her instructor for negligent supervision.

Evidence indicated that the teacher had demonstrated the safe use of power tools, had assigned a safety booklet for students to read, had given a safety exam, and had watched Jodeen operate the machine safely. Although there was some question about whether the teacher was negligent in not directly supervising her at the time of the injury, the court ruled that Jodeen was negligent in failing to use the ordinary care that a student of her age and maturity "would have used under like circumstances." Thus, the court dismissed Jodeen's claim and concluded that her contributory negligence was the "proximate cause of the injuries she sustained in this unfortunate accident."

Another court reached a similar finding after a high school sophomore was injured in a science class when a beaker of burning alcohol spilled on him.[20] The accident occurred when Ronald Rixmann and two of his friends lit some heated alcohol on a table during an experiment, although they had been warned not to place any flame near alcohol. Evidence indicated that the teacher was negligent in the way he attempted to put out the fire, but the court ruled that the student was also negligent and that his negligence was a substantial factor contributing to his injuries.

Does a Student's Negligence Always Prevent Recovery?

No. The younger the student, the more difficult it is to prove contributory negligence. In most states, courts hold that very young children, typically those under seven years of age, are incapable of contributory negligence. This means that even if the carelessness of such students contributed to their injury, this fact would not prevent them from recovering damages from a negligent teacher. For older children, usually those between 7 and 14, there is often a "rebuttable presumption" that they are incapable of contributory negligence.[21] With sufficient evidence concerning their intelligence, maturity, and the circumstances of the case, this presumption can be rebutted and the court can find them negligent and bar any recovery.

The most significant factor allowing negligent students to recover damages has been the trend toward adoption of *comparative negligence* statutes. In the majority of states, a student's contributory negligence does not completely prevent the student from recovering damages from a negligent teacher.[22] Instead, comparative negligence laws permit the judge or jury to compare the relative negligence of the plaintiff and the defendant in causing the injury and to make an appropriate damage award. Thus, where the plaintiff (student) was also responsible for causing the injury, the student would be entitled to only a portion of the normally awarded damages. For example, in a Louisiana case involving a 9-year-old girl who broke her leg jumping off a merry-go-round, the court compared the negligence of the student with that of the school board.[23] It found both the school board negligent in the supervision of the student and the child negligent in jumping off the merry-go-round. Since the student was equally responsible for causing the injury, the court reduced the amount of compensation awarded to her by 50 percent. In many states, however, comparative negligence laws bar recovery if the plaintiff's negligence is equal to or greater than that of the defendant.[24]

When Does a Student Assume the Risk of Being Injured?

The doctrine of assumption of risk has been recognized as a defense against liability in activities such as competitive sports. It is based on the theory that people who know and appreciate the danger involved in an activity and voluntarily engage in it willingly expose themselves to certain predictable risks. This doctrine is illustrated by a New York case where a student teacher was injured while participating in a donkey basketball game.[25] The court ruled that she could not recover damages for her injuries from either the school district or the company that provided the donkeys because she admitted that she had been informed of the risk of injury and had voluntarily participated in the game.

On the other hand, an 11-year-old student who sustained mouth injuries in a floor hockey game did not assume the risk of his injuries.[26] The court held that the assumption of risk was not a viable defense when the student's lack of experience, lack of information, and tender age impaired his appreciation of the dangers involved in floor hockey.

Can Teachers Use Governmental Immunity As a Defense Against Negligence?

No. Governmental immunity is a common-law theory which holds that since the state and its agencies are sovereign, they cannot be sued without their consent and should not be held liable for the negligence of their employees. Some courts justify this practice on the grounds that public funds raised for schooling should not be legally diverted for noneducational purposes. In recent years, however, this doctrine has been widely condemned by legal writers, and an increasing number of state courts or legislatures have abolished governmental immunity. In other states that support the concept, the courts or legislatures have found that the purchase of liability insurance eliminates the defense to the extent of the insurance coverage, or they have created exceptions to the doctrine (e.g., holding schools liable for nonessential activities, such as leasing a portion of the premises). Even in states where this doctrine still can prevent negligence suits against school districts, students may sue individual teachers, who can be held personally liable for their negligence.

Recently, some states have passed statutes that offer teachers or administrators some level of immunity, and some states have passed laws providing absolute immunity to teachers acting within the scope of their authority. For example, a Michigan court interpreting such a statute found that a school superintendent was not liable when a second-grade student hung himself after viewing a film in class about a nineteenth-century amputee who had also hung himself.[27] The court held that the superintendent was acting within the scope of his authority in allowing a film about mental health issues to be shown in a second-grade class, and therefore was immune from liability under Michigan law.

The 2002 No Child Left Behind Act contains a provision known as the Paul D. Coverdell Teacher Protection Act, which immunizes from liability any teacher who "was acting within the scope of the teacher's employment or responsibilities to a school," or where the actions of the teacher were "carried out in…furtherance of efforts to control, discipline, expel, or suspend a student or maintain order or control in the classroom or school."[28] This new law goes on to prevent teachers from being liable for punitive damages "in an action brought for harm based on the act or omission of a teacher acting within the scope of the teacher's employment…unless the claimant establishes by clear and convincing evidence that the harm was proximately caused by an act or omission of such teacher that constitutes willful or criminal misconduct, or a conscious, flagrant indifference to the rights or safety of the individual harmed."[29] Thus, for the first time, a federal law was enacted for the express purpose of preventing teachers from being sued for acts arising out of the normal course of their jobs, including imposing discipline on students.

Does a "Waiver" or "Release" Prevent an Injured Student from Suing?

Generally not. Most courts that have addressed the issue[30] have found that such releases are invalid on public policy grounds. For example, the Washington Supreme Court held that a school district could not require parents to sign forms absolving the school of liability for sports accidents.[31] Because athletics are "part and parcel" of the educational program, the court stated, the district is obliged to participate in the dangers inherent in such programs. Other courts have held that minors are not bound by releases executed by their parents.[32]

Even where releases are not illegal, judges are usually extremely strict in interpreting them and, in practice, schools are generally unsuccessful in using waivers to prohibit negligence suits. This point was illustrated by a New York case in which a student, Bruce Gross, sued a parachute training school.[33] After breaking his leg when he landed on his first jump, Gross charged that the school was negligent in failing to instruct him properly. The school tried to block the suit on the grounds that Gross signed a responsibility release that said he would "waive any and all claims" he may have against the school "for any personal injuries…that I may sustain or which may arise out of my learning, practice or actually jumping out of an aircraft."

Despite this release, the court allowed Gross to sue. According to the judge, such releases are "closely scrutinized and strictly construed" by the courts and will be enforced only when the limits of liability are "precisely defined" and any omissions plainly noted. Since the release did not contain any specific provision which waived any claim for the defendant's failure to instruct plaintiff properly, it did not release the school from negligence arising out of improper instruction.

In the few cases where releases have been upheld, parents or guardians have generally failed to disclose important information that schools should have known about a student. For example, a court upheld a release where a parent had signed a form giving permission for his son to use the swimming pool but did not inform school officials that the student could not swim.[34]

Other Types of Liability

Are Teachers Liable If They Fail to Report Child Abuse?

Yes. Every state plus all U.S. territories require that teachers, along with administrators and counselors, report known or suspected cases of child abuse or neglect, and those who fail to do so are subject to penalties under the law. Every state also protects reporting individuals by granting civil or criminal immunity from any liability from their reports, provided that the reports were made in "good faith" or "without malice." (See chapter 6 for an in-depth discussion of this topic.)

Can Schools Be Held Liable If Students or Employees with AIDS Are in Attendance?

That depends on the facts of the particular situation. The legal principle related to negligence would apply to a situation where acquired immunodeficiency syndrome (AIDS) was present just as to other situations. Understandably, some parents as well as educators are deeply concerned about this issue in light of its seriousness.

Most states and school districts have created policies to guide schools threatened with the virus. The concerns are equally serious for children and adults who have AIDS and are thus vulnerable to various diseases as they are for those who are in danger of getting the virus from infected children or adults. There are important constitutional issues related to privacy, equal protection, and due process involved in how schools handle this matter, but the protection of the community also weighs heavily on educators as they formulate and administer policies.

Typically these guidelines follow recommendations issued by the Centers for Disease Control and the American Academy of Pediatrics. As of 1991, these groups recommend that most school-age children infected with the human immunodeficiency virus (HIV) be allowed to attend school without restrictions and with the approval of the child's physician. Infected students who pose an increased risk to others in school, such as those who lack control of body secretions, who display behavior such as biting, or who have open skin sores that cannot be covered, may require a more restricted school environment. Confidential school records should be maintained, and the number of personnel aware of the child's condition should be kept to a minimum. It is generally recommended that anyone with the virus not handle food and that school personnel be trained to deal appropriately with blood or other body fluids that might be spilled in school. It is also recommended that school districts create medical teams to examine students and/or employees who have the virus to determine whether their continued school attendance is likely to endanger others.

Schools that adopt policies reflecting current research and apply them with care are not likely to find themselves liable in a civil suit for money damages. Schools may be liable, however, if they totally exclude students or teachers with AIDS. In 1987, the U.S. Supreme Court held that a teacher's rights were violated when she was fired after testing positive for contagious tuberculosis.[35] In its decision, which can be applied to many illnesses, the Court found that Section 504 of the 1973 Rehabilitation Act required that the teacher's case be studied to determine whether she could be accommodated safely in her employment position. The courts have ruled that students with AIDS are also protected against discrimination by Section 504 of this act and that schools cannot exclude students who pose a minimal health risk to others.[36] Students and teachers infected with HIV, even in its asymptomatic stage, are also protected from discrimination under the Americans With Disabilities Act.[37] If school officials believe that a child with AIDS needs placement outside of the regular classroom, Section 504 requires an evaluation and placement process to determine the appropriate educational setting. (For discussion of the rights of handicapped students, see chapter 16.) To make appropriate placement decisions, schools should consult guidelines issued by the Centers for Disease Control and the U.S. Department of Education.[38]

Can Schools Be Held Liable for Failure to Maintain a Safe Environment?

With school crime increasing, students and teachers who are injured on school premises often sue the school district for failure to maintain a safe environment. A number of courts have held that a special relationship exists between educators and students because students are required to attend school and their care is entrusted to school officials. Under this theory, the courts have held schools liable for student injuries that are reasonably foreseeable. For example, a Florida court held that a school distinct was liable when a high school student was attacked and beaten by other students on school premises.[39] The student was beaten outside the cafeteria while using the phone after a junior varsity football practice. The court found that the school was negligent in not providing for any supervision of the cafeteria area and that student misbehavior was a foreseeable result of such a lack of supervision.

Some courts have also applied this theory to hold schools liable when students are injured by nonstudents. In a California case, the court found the school district liable when a student member of the wrestling team was assaulted by a nonstudent in an unsupervised restroom in the high school.[40] The court found it reasonable that attacks were likely to occur in an unsupervised restroom. Similarly, an Oregon court held that a school district was liable for the rape of a 15-year-old high school student when a woman delivering newspapers to the school 15 days before had also been sexually assaulted on the same school property.[41] Where the injuries to a student are not foreseeable, the school district will not be held liable. For example, a school will not be liable for a violent student's attack upon another student unless the school had knowledge about the aggressor's behavior that would have made the attack reasonably foreseeable.[42]

Can Schools Be Held Liable for Educational Malpractice?

Probably not. Some students have brought legal actions alleging that schools should be held liable for negligent teaching that injures a student intellectually or psychologically, just as physicians and lawyers are liable to their patients and clients when they are negligent. In few of the cases have the students prevailed, however. In the first such case, filed in California in 1976, a high school graduate who could read only at the fifth-grade level sued the school district for failing to provide him with adequate instruction in basic skills.[43] The court analyzed the law of negligence and concluded that the suit should have been dismissed for the following reasons: (1) There were no clear standards to determine whether the school had been negligent, (2) there was no way to determine that a teacher's negligence was the proximate cause of the student's injury, and (3) it would impose too great a financial burden on schools to hold them to an actionable duty of care in the discharge of their academic functions. Many other courts have followed this decision, refusing on public policy grounds to second-guess the professional judgments of educators in selecting programs for particular students.[44]

In one case, however, a state court recognized a claim for educational malpractice based on negligent placement of a special education student.[45] In this case, a student was diagnosed as mentally retarded and placed in a segregated classroom. After the child's foster mother noticed a worsening of her daughter's behavior, she filed suit alleging that the school had negligently misplaced the child. The Montana Supreme Court agreed. The court concluded that the school owed a duty of care in testing and placing special education students under the Montana State Constitution and administrative statutes and that the school had breached its duty in this case.

Using a different legal theory, parents were also successful in another case challenging their child's placement. In a Maryland case, parents were allowed to bring an action against school officials for intentionally and maliciously injuring their child by furnishing false information regarding the student's learning disability, altering school records to cover up their actions, and demeaning the child.[46] The court explained that "where an individual engaged in the educational process is shown to have willfully and maliciously injured a child entrusted to his care, such outrageous conduct really outweighs any public policy considerations which would otherwise preclude liability to authorize recovery." The significance of this decision is quite limited, however, because few parents will be able to prove that educators were acting maliciously and intentionally when a student was injured as a result of an inappropriate educational placement.

Can Schools Be Held Liable for Negligent Hiring or Retention of Unfit Employees?

Yes. Under this common-law theory, employers can be liable to employees or to third persons when they are negligent in hiring or retaining employees whom they know or should have known are unfit and who put others at unreasonable risk of harm. While some courts have found that school districts are immune from this type of liability,[47] others have found schools to be liable when it can be shown that the employee was predisposed to commit a wrong and that this wrong was reasonably foreseeable. As one court explained in a case where the school board and superintendent were found negligent in the retention of a teacher who sexually abused a student, a "school board has a common-law duty to protect others from the result of negligent hiring, supervision, or retention, which duty is identical to the duty upon private employers who hire, retain or supervise employees whose negligent or intentional acts in positions of employment can foreseeably cause injuries to third parties."[48]

School districts will not be liable, however, if they had no reason to know that an employee was unfit. For example, in a 1990 North Carolina case the court found that the board of education was not liable to a student for hiring and retaining a principal who allegedly assaulted her.[49] Although the principal had earlier resigned from another school after being accused of sexually assaulting a student, there was no evidence that school officials knew or reasonably should have known of any pedophilic tendencies. The principal had resigned from his previous position officially for "health reasons," and none of the people contacted as references mentioned the alleged sexual assault. Instead, they had described him as "one of the most promising men in education" and noted that the system had "lost a very valuable educator."

Students have also brought such actions under a federal law known as Section 1983, claiming that school officials violated students' right to liberty in situations where teachers were hired who later injured students, especially in cases of sexual abuse. (These claims, sometimes referred to as constitutional torts, are discussed later in this chapter.)

Can Schools Be Held Liable for Emotional Injuries Suffered by Students?

Yes. Although such cases are rare, teachers have been found liable. In a Louisiana, a physical education teacher was found to be liable for a kindergarten student's emotional injuries after the teacher pretended that he had hanged the student's two friends.[50] Following this incident, the student developed a variety of psychological problems that medical experts identified as caused by the stress from viewing his "dead" friends. The school district was required to pay the parents $117,658 in damages to cover the costs of psychotherapy for the mental anguish suffered by the child.

Can Schools Be Held Liable for Negligence When Teachers Are Injured?

Yes, but such cases are rare. When teachers suffer injuries in the course of their employment, they will generally be compensated under state laws providing for workers' compensation benefits. Such injuries are compensated by administrative review boards without regard to a school board's negligence. For example, the injuries suffered by a teacher in Texas who was sexually assaulted by a student were covered by workers' compensation, precluding her from suing the school for common-law damages.[51] Similarly, a Louisiana teacher was entitled to workers' compensation benefits when she was hit by a falling door in the school auditorium while participating in a girls' fashion show.[52]

A second reason that negligence lawsuits are rare is that they may be barred by governmental immunity. Under the common law, governmental agencies cannot be held liable for their tortuous actions. and some states still apply this theory to protect school districts from liability. For example, a Tennessee state court held that a school board was immune from liability when a school principal left a door unlocked and an intruder later entered the school building through this door and assaulted a teacher.[53] The court held that in deciding to leave the door unlocked, the principal was exercising discretion in implementing a governmental policy, an act that should not be second-guessed by the courts. Using a similar legal theory a New York court refused to hold a school board liable when a high school assistant principal was sexually assaulted in an unlocked room by an armed assailant.[54]

Some courts have carved out exceptions to governmental immunity, however, and found school boards liable. In one New York case, the court found the school board negligent in failing to take reasonable measures to protect a teacher from injury.[55] The teacher had taken her students into the schoolyard and was injured when a metal object was hurled toward her from the adjoining property. The evidence showed that although this teacher taught at this school only two days a week and had no knowledge about the danger in the schoolyard, other teachers had reported prior incidents to a school administrator. The school board claimed immunity, but the court disagreed, holding that the school board's liability here arose not from performing a governmental function, but from a breach of its duty as a landlord. Just as any landlord, the court reasoned, the board had a duty to issue warnings or take other action (such as locking the doors from inside) with respect to known and foreseeable dangers. Similarly, in a more recent New York case the court awarded $1,075,000 in damages to a school psychologist who was raped and sodomized in her office in a school annex building.[56] The court ruled that the board could be held liable even when performing a governmental function if there was also a special duty owed the plaintiff. In this case, the court found that the teacher had relied on express assurances by the school board that security measures had been taken for her protection. Since the teacher reasonably relied on these assurances, the school board owed her a special duty and could be liable for the damages resulting from its negligence in not providing adequate protection.

Can Parents Be Held Liable When Teachers Are Injured by Students?

Yes, said the Supreme Court of Wisconsin in a novel case involving a fourth-grade student where the teacher sustained a neck injury when he violently pulled her hair.[57] The student, Jason, had been diagnosed with attention deficit hyperactivity disorder, and doctors had prescribed Dexedrine for him. After eight months, however, Jason's parents decided to discontinue the medication. They did not consult with Jason's doctors, nor did they tell anyone at school that the medication had been discontinued and that Jason's disruptive behavior might return.

The court found that the parents had a duty to exercise reasonable control over their child to prevent the risk of injury to others, and that the parents breached that duty in this case. The court explained that the parents had the right to discontinue their son's medication but then had the responsibility of working with the school to develop a new plan to manage Jason's behavior.

The court recognized that its decision would have important public policy implications, but did not believe that it would "open a flood gate of new litigation" or that it would "force parents to medicate their children against their will."[58] Rather, the court felt that its decision was necessary to clarify the law at a time when teachers face dangers in the classroom from increasing numbers of students exhibiting emotional or behavioral problems.

Where parents do not have any knowledge of a child's propensity to engage in conduct that might injure others, they will not be held liable. For example, in a New York case, parents were not liable when a high school teacher was injured trying to break up a fight between their daughter Tracy and her sister.[59] Tracy had never engaged in such behavior before, and since the parents had no reason to anticipate such actions, they were not held responsible.

Can School Districts and School Officials Be Held Liable for Violating a Student's Constitutional Rights?

Yes. Public school districts and school officials who violate students' constitutional rights can be liable for damages under a federal statute, commonly referred to as Section 1983, that allows a suit against any person who, "under color of any statute, ordinance, regulation, custom or usage of any State or Territory or the District of Columbia, subjects, or causes to be subjected, any citizen of the United States or any other person within the jurisdiction thereof to the deprivation of any rights, privileges, or immunities secured by the Constitution" and laws.[60]

The U.S. Supreme Court has ruled that local governmental units such as school districts are "persons" and can be held liable under Section 1983 for violations of students' and teachers' constitutional rights.[61] The Court has also ruled, however, that local governmental units such as school districts cannot be liable under this law for the mere negligence of their employees, but are liable only when employees with authority act under an official policy, practice, or custom that shows deliberate indifference to an individual's constitutional rights.[62] As the Supreme Court explained, a local governmental unit is not vicariously liable under Section 1983 for the constitutional torts of its agents; it is liable only when it can be fairly said that the governmental unit "itself is the wrongdoer."[63] Thus, a school district was not liable in a case where a middle school student sued the school district, supervisory officials, and a bus driver after being beaten by other students on a school bus, alleging that the district deprived him of liberty because its instructions to bus drivers regarding the prevention of violence were inadequate.[64] The Fifth Circuit held that the school district was not liable because the student did not prove pervasiveness of violence or a preexisting pattern of student fights on buses which warranted an official response. Thus, there was no actionable official policy or custom. In another case where a student sued a school district for failure to supervise its employees, the court held that a single isolated incident by a teacher does not establish an official policy or practice sufficient to establish Section 1983 liability.[65]

School officials such as board members and administrators acting under color of state law can also be held liable under Section 1983 for violations of an individual's constitutional rights. These individual employees can raise a defense that is not available to school districts, however. In the case of *Wood* v. *Strickland,* two Arkansas students were unlawfully suspended without due process.[66] The U.S. Supreme Court ruled that school officials had qualified immunity (and were not liable for money damages) unless the officials "knew or reasonably should have known that the action they took within their sphere of official responsibility would violate the constitutional rights of the students affected."[67] Thus, school officials are protected for good-faith actions taken to fulfill their official duties.

The actions of officials are determined to be in good faith using only an objective standard. A 1982 Supreme Court case held that public officials "generally are shielded from liability for civil damages insofar as their conduct does not violate clearly established statutory or constitutional rights of which a reasonable person would have known."[68]

Since the Supreme Court has not explained what constitutes "clearly established" law, the circuit courts have had to decide how a reasonable public official would know that the action that he or she is about to undertake would violate an established constitutional right. Generally clearly established law is found through an examination of the decisions of the courts with controlling jurisdiction for the geographical area involved: the U.S. Supreme Court, the U.S. court of appeals, the local U.S. distinct court, and the highest state court. For example, when middle school students in Virginia sued school officials alleging that general searches of students violated their constitutional rights under the Fourth Amendment, a federal district court held that the officials were entitled to qualified immunity.[69] The court found that the legal rules applicable to this situation were not "clearly established" at the time the officials acted because the specific legal issue involved had not been addressed by the U.S. Supreme Court, the U.S. Court of Appeals for the Fourth Circuit, or the Supreme Court of Virginia. The court concluded: "while the defendants must certainly be charged with knowledge that the Fourth Amendment protects students' legitimate privacy interests, plaintiffs have not shown to the requisite level of specificity that the defendants should have known that the actions taken in this case would violate those interests."

In cases where an issue has not been dealt with by the courts with controlling jurisdiction, however, most circuit courts will examine decisions from other circuits to determine whether there is a substantial consensus on the issue. In one such case where there was no Seventh Circuit precedent, the Seventh Circuit Court of Appeals ruled that three other circuit court decisions in a relatively short period of time were sufficient to establish the existence of a constitutional right.[70] In sum, school board members and administrators should carefully monitor federal constitutional decisions not only of the courts that have jurisdiction over them, but also in other federal circuits, to keep apprised of current constitutional standards.

Can School Officials or Teachers Be Held Liable Under Section 1983 for Abuse of Students by Teachers or Other Students?

The U.S. Supreme Court has established that Section 1983 liability may be imposed upon the state for the actions of third parties who deprive individuals of life, liberty, or property only when the state has a special relationship with that individual.[71] The Court determined that state officials have such a "special relationship" with prison inmates and institutionalized mental patients.[72] On the basis of these decisions, students who have been victims of abuse by teachers and other students have brought actions in federal court alleging that the state has a special relationship with students in public schools and that schools are liable for violations of the due process rights of students whose liberty interests are violated when they are physically abused in school.

Several courts of appeals have held that public school students have a constitutionally protected interest to be free from violations of bodily integrity by school employees.[73] In one such case, the Ninth Circuit held that a school principal could be liable for violating a high school student's right to bodily integrity when he slapped the student and grabbed his neck.[74] The court stated that "no reasonable principal could think it constitutional to intentionally punch, slap, grab, and slam students into lockers."

A majority of federal courts, however, have dismissed such lawsuits. Most courts have concluded that school districts have no duty to protect students from abuse from teachers,[75] while others have found that school officials are not acting with the required level of deliberate indifference when students are abused by teachers.[76] A Sixth Circuit case, for example, held that neither the school board, superintendent, or principal could be held liable under Section 1983 when a high school teacher sexually abused a 14-year-old female high school student.[77] Although the court concluded that the student's constitutional right to bodily integrity was violated, it found that the school district's failure to act did not amount to a custom (or policy) of deliberate indifference. The court concluded, "Although the facts of this case are tragic and we are deeply disturbed by Davis's [the teacher's] sexual abuse of Doe [the student],…the Due Process Clause does not impose an affirmative constitutional duty on the school board to assume the responsibility of protecting its students against the unconstitutional acts of its employees."[78]

The courts are even less likely to hold school officials or teachers liable under Section 1983 in cases where students are injured by other students or nonstudents. For example, a federal court held that the school district was not liable under Section 1983 when an eighth-grade girl was sexually assaulted by a male student.[79] The girl had reported the boy's threat that he was going to rape her to her teacher, but the court concluded that there was no special relationship between the student and the school that would give rise to an affirmative duty on the part of the school to protect the student. The Fifth Circuit reached a similar conclusion in a case where an 18-year-old student was killed by random gunfire in a high school parking lot.[80] The court held that no special relationship exists between a district and its pupils during a school-sponsored dance and that even if there were such a duty to protect these students, none of the alleged facts indicated a deliberate indifference to those dangers.

Although school officials are not likely to be held liable for violating students' rights under the due process clause, the possibility still exists that school officials could be liable under Section 1983 for violating students' rights under the equal protection clause. The Seventh Circuit Court of Appeals in 1996 ruled in favor of a gay male student on the basis of this theory.[81] In this case, the student alleged that he suffered ongoing sexual harassment beginning in seventh grade and continuing until he withdrew from school during the eleventh grade. Among other things, he was called "faggot" and "queer" and assaulted on numerous occasions. In one such incident, two students held him to the floor and performed a "mock rape" on him; in another incident he was kicked in the stomach for 5 to 10 minutes, causing him to suffer internal bleeding. Although the court found no due process violation, it ruled that school officials were liable for discriminating against the student on the basis of his sexual orientation, a violation of the equal protection clause. The court explained that homosexuals are a "definable minority" protected from discrimination both under the U.S. Constitution and under Wisconsin law, and that he was treated differently on the basis of his sexual orientation when school officials permitted other students to assault him. Other cases alleging Section 1983 violations on the basis of denial of equal protection of the law will undoubtedly arise, and will require the U.S. Supreme Court to clarify this issue.

Can School Officials Be Liable Under Title IX for the Wrongful Acts of Students and Teachers?

Yes, if the officials are aware of the wrongful acts, which must be sufficiently severe, and act with deliberate indifference. Title IX provides that "no person shall, on the basis of sex, be excluded from participation in, be denied the benefits of, or be subjected to discrimination under any educational program or activity" receiving federal funding.[82] In 1999, the Supreme Court held that a private right of action existed under Title IX against school board members for allowing student-on-student sexual harassment.[83] In this case, a fifth-grade female student endured several months of harassing comments and conduct from a male classmate. Despite complaints made to teachers, no action, such as changing classroom seating, was taken. In upholding the right to sue school officials under Title IX, the Court held that the school board could be liable if shown to have acted with deliberate indifference to known acts of harassment that were so severe, pervasive, and objectively offensive that it barred the victimized student's access to an educational opportunity. (Title IX is discussed in more detail in chapter 15.)

Damages

What Kinds of Damages Are Awarded by the Courts?

Courts can award several kinds of damages. The most common is an award for *compensatory damages.* The purpose of this award is to compensate injured persons for their actual losses—for their medical expenses, lost salary, court costs, and other expenses incurred as a result of the defendant's negligence. Damages can be awarded for monetary, physical, or psychological injury. *Exemplary* or *punitive damages* are awarded where defendants have shown malice, fraud, or reckless disregard for an injured person's safety or constitutional rights. The purpose of this award is to punish the defendants for their wrongful actions and to deter similar actions in the future. *Nominal damages* are a small symbolic award (e.g., $1), where the plaintiff has been wronged but has not been able to show actual damages.

When a Student's Rights Are Violated, How Will the Amount of Damages Be Determined?

In 1978, the U.S. Supreme Court answered this question in *Carey* v. *Piphus,* a case involving two Chicago students who were suspended for 20 days without due process.[84] Their lawyer introduced no evidence to show that they had suffered any actual damages because of their suspension, but he argued that they should receive substantial damages simply because they had been deprived of their constitutional rights.

The Court disagreed. It ruled that when a student is deprived of his or her constitutional rights, the amount of damages should depend on the circumstances of the case. A student should be awarded substantial sums for two reasons: (1) as punitive damages to deter or punish school officials who intentionally deprive the student of his or her rights, or (2) as compensatory damages for actual injury which can include "mental and emotional distress" as well as financial loss. When the violation is unintentional and no actual injury is shown, the student is entitled only to the award of a nominal sum of money.

In a similar case, several Puerto Rican college students sued for damages when they were unlawfully suspended for up to 12 days.[85] They were unable to prove an actual injury such as "delay in meeting academic requirements or significant harm to plaintiff's reputation in the community or medically cognizable psychological distress." Nor were they able to show that their suspension was caused by school officials acting in bad faith or trying to harass them. Rather, the evidence indicated that the improper suspension "was nothing more than an isolated error in the administration of university discipline." Under these circumstances, the court refused to award compensatory damages for "general mental distress." Instead, the appeals court felt that the appropriate award was to grant the students nominal damages plus the costs of their attorneys' fees.

Since its pronouncements in *Carey,* the Supreme Court has amplified its remarks concerning the appropriate assessment of damages. In *Memphis Community School District* v. *Stachura,* an action arising from the unwarranted discharge of a teacher, the Court cited *Carey* in support of its holding that the abstract value of a constitutional right could not serve as a basis for an award of compensatory damages in an action arising under Section 1983.[86] In accordance with its conclusion that damages in a Section 1983 action are ordinarily determined by common-law tort principles, the Court further reaffirmed that compensatory damages might include not only verified pecuniary losses, but also payment for such subjective consequences as impairment of reputation, personal humiliation, and mental anguish and suffering. Finally, the Court observed that punitive damages in an action of this sort would be appropriate only to punish willful or malicious conduct on the part of the defendant or to deter others from similar conduct in the future.

Can Teachers Be Awarded Damages If Their Constitutional Rights Are Violated?

Yes. The same legal principles that were described for students determine whether a teacher can bring an action under Section 1983 and, if successful, what damages can be awarded. A 1978 federal court decision illustrated these principles in the case of a Texas teacher.[87] Jerry Burnaman was a competent, dedicated, well-qualified educator who had taught successfully in the Bay City schools for more than a decade. A new principal and superintendent (the latter considered an expert in school law) were then brought in to "shake up the school system and make substantial changes." Among the changes they wanted to make was to demote or remove Burnaman. They did this through a two-step process: They gave him the first unfavorable recommendation he had ever received, and they then recommended that his year-to-year contract not be renewed. Burnaman requested a hearing in mid-April to refute the negative recommendation, but the administration delayed the hearing until late August, after which his discharge was upheld. (During this time he had further angered the administration by testifying in favor of another educator who had been fired.) As a result of these events, Burnaman sued the principal, the superintendent, and the school board, charging that they had violated his constitutional rights.

A federal judge agreed. The court found that the principal's negative evaluation was "inaccurate, nonfactual, grossly unfair," and not prepared in accordance with school policy requiring the use of objective evaluation standards. The court also found that in the evaluation the principal made statements he knew or should have known were inaccurate. The judge concluded that Burnaman's discharge violated his due process rights, was in retaliation for statements he had made that were protected by the First Amendment, and damaged his professional reputation. Therefore the jury granted him several awards: (1) compensatory damages of $16,440 for loss of wages and $17,000 "for mental anguish accompanying the termination of his employment," (2) exemplary damages of $25,000 against the superintendent and principal for acting with malice and intentionally depriving him of his constitutional rights, and (3) fees for his attorneys, which were incurred unnecessarily because of the "school board's unreasonable and obdurate obstinance."

Are Students or Teachers Who Bring Successful Civil Rights Lawsuits Entitled to Recover Their Attorneys' Fees?

Yes. Federal law provides that in Section 1983 lawsuits, the court "may allow the prevailing party, other than the United States, a reasonable attorney's fee as part of the costs."[88] This law is intended to encourage lawyers to represent civil rights plaintiffs who may otherwise be unable to afford to hire lawyers, and courts have used it to award attorneys' fees in cases where students and teachers prevailed in lawsuits alleging violations of their rights.

The U.S. Supreme Court has had to interpret what is meant by the term "prevailing party." Plaintiffs who were prevailing parties are entitled to attorneys' fees if they achieved success on any significant issue in the case.[89] However, plaintiffs who were awarded only nominal damages, such as $1 when merely identifying a violation of a civil right which did not change the relationship between the parties, are still prevailing parties but were not entitled to attorneys' fees.[90] In addition, when defendants voluntarily change their conduct after plaintiffs file suit but before trial, the plaintiffs cannot be considered to be prevailing parties entitled to attorneys' fees even if they win their case.[91] The Court has not decided, though, whether plaintiffs who win injunctions or other types of relief in federal court can recover attorneys' fees.

Defendants (usually school districts in cases brought by teachers or students) may also be awarded attorneys' fees, but only upon a finding that the plaintiff's action was frivolous, unreasonable, or without foundation.[92] Such awards are made to discourage plaintiffs from bringing groundless lawsuits which burden the courts. For example, a federal court ruled that a defendant school district was entitled to an award of attorneys' fees in the amount of $60,000 where a high school student's mother brought a clearly frivolous claim that the student's civil rights were violated when she was not admitted to the National Honor Society.[93]

Summary

To hold a teacher liable for a student's injury, the student must prove the following:

The teacher owed a duty of care to the student. Teachers can be held liable only when they are legally responsible for students' care, such as during school hours or school-sponsored field trips. Ordinarily teachers are not liable for students' afterschool or off-premises injuries. Teachers also have a duty to report child abuse and neglect.

The teacher was negligent. Teachers have a duty to exercise reasonable care not to injure their students and to prevent them from being injured. *Reasonable care* is that degree of care that a reasonable prudent teacher would have exercised under the circumstances. The circumstances considered by the courts include the age, maturity, and experience of the students and the extent of danger involved. When conditions are more dangerous (e.g., in wood-shop, a chemistry lab, or a boxing class), a reasonable teacher would be expected to be more careful—to provide closer supervision, clear warnings, and careful instructions. If teachers do not use reasonable care, there is a breach of duty and they are negligent.

The teacher's negligence was the cause of the student's injury. To recover damages against a teacher, a student must be able to show that it was the teacher's negligence that caused the injury. Suits for educational malpractice have not generally been allowed because the courts have not been able to determine which of a myriad of factors actually caused a student to fail academically. In addition, the doctrines of *contributory negligence* or *comparative negligence* may identify the student as the total or partial cause of the injury, thus eliminating or reducing the amount of damages that can be recovered against a teacher.

The student was actually damaged by the teacher's negligence. Students must be able to show actual damages in order to recover from a teacher's negligence. Such damages can include monetary loss, such as medical expenses, or psychological injury. In addition, in certain cases where a teacher has acted with malice or fraud, the court has awarded punitive damages to deter future such actions.

In recent years, courts have also held school officials personally liable for damages if they violate the clearly established constitutional rights of students or teachers. Such awards could include compensatory damages for actual financial, physical, or psychological injuries, exemplary or punitive damages for intentional violations, or nominal damages where the violation is not intentional and no actual injuries are proven.

N O T E S

1. *Sheehan* v. *St. Peter's Catholic School,* 188 N.W.2d 868 (Minn. 1971).
2. *Gibbons* v. *Orleans Parish School Board,* 391 So.2d 976 (La. App. 1980).
3. *Roberts* v. *Robertson County Board of Education,* 692 S.W.2d 863 (Tenn. 1985).
4. *Toller* v. *Plainfield School District No. 202,* 582 N.W.2d 237 (Ill. App. 1991).
5. *Eisel* v. *Board of Education of Montgomery County,* 597 A.2d 447 (Md. 1991).
6. *Id.* at 455.
7. *Sheehan* v. *St. Peter's Catholic School,* 188 N.W.2d 868 (Minn. 1971).
8. *Mancha* v. *Field Museum of Natural History,* 283 N.E.2d 899 (Ill. App. 1972).
9. *Bartell* v. *Palos Verdes Peninsula School District,* 147 Cal. Rptr. 898 (App. 1978).
10. *South Ripley Community School Corp.* v. *Peters,* 396 N.E.2d 144 (Ind. App. 1979).
11. *Simmons* v. *Beauregard Parish School Board,* 315 So.2d 883 (La. App. 1975).

12. *Ferraro* v. *Board of Education of the City of New York,* 212 N.Y.S.2d 615 (N.Y App. Term. 1961).

13. *Oast* v. *Lafeyette Parish School Board,* 591 So.2d 1257 (La. App. 1975).

14. *Allen* v. *Crawford,* 438 S.E.2d 178 (Ga. App. 1993).

15. *Nash* v. *Rapides Parish School Board,* 188 So.2d 508 (La. App. 1966).

16. *Kaufman* v. *City of New York,* 214 N.Y.S.2d 767 (N.Y. Sup. Ct. 1961).

17. *Collins* v. *School Board of Broward County,* 471 So.2d 560 (Fla.. App. 1985).

18. *Tomlinson* v. *Board of Education,* 583 N.Y.S.2d 664 (N.Y. App. Div. 1992).

19. *Miles* v. *School District No. 138 of Cheyenne County,* 281 N.W.2d 396 (Neb. 1979).

20. *Rixmann* v. *Somerset Public Schools,* 266 N.W.2d 326 (Wis. 1978).

21. See, for example, *Berman* v. *Philadelphia Board of Education,* 456 A.2d 545 (Pa. Super. 1983).

22. As of 2001, 44 states have adopted some form of comparative negligence.

23. *Rollins* v. *Concordia Parish School Board,* 465 So.2d 213 (La. App. 1985).

24. Prosser & Keeton on the Law of Torts 471, note 30 (West 1988); 57B AM. JUR.2d *Negligence* § 1140 (1989).

25. *Arbegast* v. *Board of Education of South New Berlin Central School District,* 480 N.E.2d 365 (N.Y. 1985).

26. *Berman* v. *Philadelphia Board of Education,* 456 A.2d 545 (Pa. Super. 1983).

27. *Nalepa* v. *Plymouth-Canton Community School District,* 525 N.W.2d 897 (Mich. App. 1994).

28. *Downing* v. *Brown,* 935 S.W.2d 112 (Tex. 1996).

29. 745 ILCS 10/2-202 (West 1993).

30. See, for example, *Porumbiansky* v. *Emory University,* 275 S.E.2d 163 (Ga. App. 1980); *Whittington* v. *Sowela Technical Institute,* 438 So.2d 236 (La. App. 1983).

31. *Wagenblast* v. *Odessa School District,* 758 P.2d 968 (Wash. 1988).

32. See, for example, *Alexander* v. *Kendall Central School District,* 634 N.Y.S.2d 318 (N.Y. App. Div. 1995).

33. *Goss* v. *Sweet,* 400 N.E.2d 306 (N.Y. 1979).

34. *Powell* v. *Orleans Parish School Board,* 354 So.2d 299 (La. App. 1978).

35. *School Board of Nassau County, Florida* v. *Arline,* 480 U.S. 273 (1987).

36. *Doe* v. *Dolton Elementary School District No. 148,* 694 F. Supp. 440 (N.D. Ill. 1988); *Phipps* v. *Saddleback Valley Unified School District,* 251 Cal. Rptr. 720 (App. 1988).

37. *Bragdon* v. *Abbott,* 524 U.S. 624 (1998).

38. *Someone at School Has AIDS* (Alexandria VA: National Association of State Boards of Education, 1989); *Placement of School Children with AIDS* (Washington, DC: U.S. Department of Education Office for Civil Rights).

39. *Broward County School Board* v. *Ruiz,* 493 So.2d 474 (Fla. App. 1986).

40. *Leger* v. *Stockton Unified School District,* 249 Cal. Rptr. 688 (App. 1988).

41. *Fazzolari* v. *Portland School District No. 1J,* 734 P.2d 1326 (Or. 1987).

42. *McLoughlin* v. *Holy Cross High School,* 521 N.Y.S.2d 744 (App. Div. 1987).

43. *Peter W.* v. *San Francisco Unified School District,* 131 Cal. Rptr. 854 (App. 1976).

44. *Hoffman* v. *Board of Education of the City of New York,* 400 N.E.2d 317 (N.Y. 1979); *D.S.W.* v. *Fairbanks North Star Borough School District,* 628 P.2d 554 (Alaska 1981); *Tubell* v. *Dade County Public Schools,* 419 So.2d 388 (Fla. App. 1982); *Silano* v. *Tirozzi,* 651 F. Supp. 1021 (D. Conn. 1987); *Rich* v. *Kentucky Country Day, Inc.,* 793 S.W.2d 832 (Ky. App. 1990); *Poe* v. *Hamilton,* 565 N.E.2d 887 (Ohio App. 1990); *Norris* v. *Board of Education,* 797 F. Supp. 1452 (S.D. Ind. 1992); *Helbig* v. *City of New York,* 597 N.Y.S.2d 585 (Sup. 1993).

45. *B. M.* v. *State of Montana,* 649 P.2d 425 (Mont. 1982).

46. *Hunter* v. *Board of Education of Montgomery County,* 425 A.2d 681 (Md. Ct. Spec. App. 1981).

47. *Willoughby* v. *Lehrbass,* 388 N.W.2d 688 (Mich. App. 1986); *Kimpton* v. *School District of New Lisbon,* 405 N.W.2d 740 (Wis. Ct. App. 1987); *Garcia* v. *Albuquerque Public School Board of Education,* 622 P.2d 699 (N.M. App. 1980).

48. *School Board of Orange County* v. *Coffey,* 524 So.2d 1052 (Fla. App. 1988).

49. *Medlin* v. *Bass,* 398 S.E.2d 460 (N.C. 1990); see also *Godar* v. *Edwards,* 588 N.W.2d 701 (Iowa 1999).

50. *Spears ex rel. Spears* v. *Jefferson Parish School Board,* 646 So.2d 1104 (La. App. 5th Div. 1994).

51. *Simpson* v. *State,* 998 S.W.2d 304 (Tex. App.-Austin 1999).

52. *Maurice* v. *Orleans Parish School Board,* 295 So.2d 184 (La. App. 4th Div. 1974).

53. *Doe* v. *Board of Education of Memphis,* 799 S.W.2d 246 (Tenn. App. 1990).

54. *Porterfield* v. *City of New York,* 573 N.Y.S.2d 681 (N.Y. App. Div. 1991).

55. *Rubino* v. *City of New York,* 498 N.Y.S.2d 831 (N.Y. App. Div. 1st Dept. 1986).

56. *Carole A.* v. *City of New York,* 565 N.Y.S.2d 169 (N.Y. App. Div. 2d Dept. 1991).

57. *Nieuwendorp* v. *American Family Insurance Co.,* 529 N.W.2d 594 (Wis. 1995).

58. *Id.* at 602.

59. *Armour* v. *England,* 619 N.Y.S.2d 807 (N.Y. App. Div. 1994).

60. 42 U.S.C. § 1983 (West 1994).

61. *Monell* v. *Department of Social Services of the City of New York,* 436 U.S. 658 (1978).

62. *Collins* v. *City of Harker Heights,* 503 U.S. 115 (1992).

63. *Id.* at 1067.

64. *Lopez* v. *Houston Independent School District,* 817 F.2d 351 (5th Cir. 1987).

65. *De Falco* v. *Deer Lake School District,* 663 F. Supp. 1108 (W.D. Pa. 1987).

66. *Wood* v. *Strickland,* 420 U.S. 308 (1975).

67. *Id.* at 322.

68. *Harlow* v. *Fitzgerald,* 457 U.S. 800 (1982).

69. *Burnham* v. *West,* 681 F. Supp. 1160 (E.D. Va. 1987).

70. *Cleveland-Perdue* v. *Brutsche,* 881 F.2d 427 (7th Cir. 1989).

71. *DeShaney* v. *Winnebago County Department of Social Services,* 489 U.S. 189 (1989).

72. *Estelle* v. *Gamble,* 429 U.S. 97 (1976); *Youngberg v. Romeo,* 457 U.S. 307 (1982).

73. See, for example, *Doe* v. *Taylor Independent School District,* 15 F.3d 443 (5th Cir. 1994); *Stoneking* v. *Bradford Area School District,* 882 F.2d 720 (3d Cir. 1989).

74. *P. B.* v. *Koch,* 96 F.3d 1298 (9th Cir. 1996).

75. *J. O.* v. *Alton Community Unit School District No. 11,* 909 F.2d 267 (7th Cir. 1990).

76. *Thelma D.* v. *Board of Education,* 934 F.2d 929 (8th Cir. 1991).

77. *Doe* v. *Claiborne County, Tennessee,* 103 F.3d 495 (6th Cir. 1996).

78. *Id.* at 510.

79. *B. M. H.* v. *School Board,* 833 F. Supp. 560 (E.D. Va. 1993).

80. *Leffall* v. *Dallas Independent School District,* 28 F.3d 521 (5th Cir. 1994).

81. *Nabozny* v. *Podlesny,* 92 F.3d 446 (7th Cir. 1996).

82. 20 U.S.C. § 16811(a) (West 2000).

83. *Davis* v. *Monroe County Board of Education,* 526 U.S. 629 (1999).

84. *Carey* v. *Piphus,* 435 U.S. 247 (1978).

85. *Perez* v. *Rodriguez Bou,* 575 F.2d 21 (1st Cir. 1978).

86. *Memphis Community School District* v. *Stachura,* 477 U.S. 299 (1986).

87. *Burnaman* v. *Bay City Independent School District,* 445 F. Supp. 927 (S.D. Tex. 1978).

88. 42 U.S.C. § 1988 (West 1994).

89. *Texas State Teachers Association* v. *Garland Independent School District,* 489 U.S. 782 (1989).

90. *Farrar* v. *Hobby,* 506 U.S. 103 (1992).

91. *Buckhannon Board & Care Home, Inc.* v. *West Virginia Department of Health & Human Resources,* 532 U.S. 598, 121 S. Ct. 1835 (2001).

92. *Christianburg Garment Co.* v. *Equal Employment Opportunity Commission,* 434 U.S. 412 (1978).

93. *Dangler ex rel. Dangler* v. *Yorktown Central Schools,* 777 F. Supp. 1175 (S.D. N.Y. 1991); see also *Munson* v. *Milwaukee Board of School Directors,* 969 F.2d 266 (7th Cir. 1992).

6 What Constitutes Slander and Libel?

Overview

The law of civil defamation makes it unlawful for one person to make a false statement of fact that tends to harm another person's reputation. Statements are defamatory if they tend to expose another person to hatred, shame, disgrace, contempt, or ridicule. When such statements are spoken, they are called slander; when written, they are called libel. Because defamation law is concerned with reputation, a statement can be defamatory only if it is communicated to a third person. For example, if a principal writes a defamatory letter to a teacher, no libel is involved unless someone besides the teacher sees the letter.

This chapter examines how the courts have applied these principles in cases involving teachers. It addresses such questions as: Can a teacher who ridicules students be found guilty of slander? Can a teacher who writes negative comments in a student's permanent file be guilty of libel? Can a teacher sue a principal for slander for making critical remarks about his or her teaching techniques? Can students sue teachers for giving them low grades? What constitutional considerations apply in cases of libel or slander?

Defamatory Statements about Teachers

The Pitka Case:[1] How Can Teachers Be Libeled?

Elizabeth Pitka, a schoolteacher in North Pole, Alaska, a small community not far from Fairbanks, resigned from her position, but a few days later withdrew the resignation with the consent of the North Pole School Board. A few months later, she wrote to the board saying that she intended to resign "effective in thirty days from this date." Before the thirty days had expired, she received a letter advising her that the board had voted "to relieve you of your duties as head teacher and teacher." After she ignored a school board letter to stay off school property, she was arrested for disturbing the peace. That evening, the Fairbanks newspaper carried a front-page article describing Pitka's difficulties with the school board. The headline read: "North Pole Teacher Fights Board," with a subheading that stated, "Territorial Police Called to Expel Fired Schoolmarm, Dispute at Outlying Community Finds Teacher Defying School Board: She Is Arrested for Disorderly Conduct." Pitka claimed that these words were false and defamatory and sued the newspaper for libel.

The Supreme Court of Alaska ruled that the newspaper headline was libelous on its face (or libelous per se). The court explained that "for a publication to be libelous per se the words used must be so unambiguous as to be reasonably susceptible of only one interpretation—that is, one which has a natural tendency to injure another's reputation [footnote omitted]. If the publication on its face shows that it is of that type, then the judge has the right to tell the jury that the words are defamatory." Examining the specific language in the newspaper headline, the court concluded that it was libelous per se: "A statement that a school teacher was engaged in a 'fight' with her employer, that she was 'fired,' that the police were called to expel her, and that she was arrested for disorderly conduct, would have a natural tendency to diminish the esteem in which she was held and to result in a lack of confidence in her professional competency."

The Supreme Court of Alaska also ruled, however, that the newspaper company should have had the opportunity to raise the defense that the statements in the headline were true. The court explained that under the common law, truth is an absolute defense and would constitute a complete justification for the statements. Whether the teacher was involved in an actual "fight" with the school board and whether she had actually been "fired" were questions of fact that ought to have been submitted to the jury for their decision. If the jury found that the statements were true, the newspaper would not be liable.

Is Truth Always an Absolute Defense to a Defamation Action?

No. This rule, relied on by the court in *Pitka,* was the standard under the English common law and was followed by the overwhelming majority of jurisdictions in the United States. About a dozen states, however, have modified this common-law rule by either statute or judicial decision. In some states, truth is a defense unless the defamation was published with "malicious motives"; in others there is a requirement of a "justifiable purpose."[2]

What Kinds of Statements Are Defamatory?

As the court pointed out in *Pitka,* some statements are automatically assumed to be defamatory. Historically, words have been held to be clearly defamatory on their face if they: (1) impute a criminal offense; (2) impute a loathsome disease (e.g., venereal disease); (3) disparage professional competency (as in *Pitka*); or (4) impute lack of chastity or morality (e.g., a charge of incest or child abuse).

Statements that do not fall into one of these four categories also can be defamatory. Such statements are not defamatory on their face, however, but require additional information to show that they injured someone's reputation. For example, a New York school principal sued a newspaper publisher for an article that appeared months after the principal had transferred from one school to another school.[3] The article stated that at the school where the principal had formerly taught, a new principal had "brought harmony out of chaos," the "teachers would do anything in the world for him," and from 150 to 200 boys "used to come late to school and now the average is not more that seven or eight." Although these statements were not defamatory on their face, the former principal argued that anyone who knew he had previously been in charge of the school would interpret these statements to mean that he had lacked administrative ability.

The court did not agree that these additional facts made the statement libelous. The court concluded that no particular charge was made against the former principal, and there was no reason for readers to assume that the charges of chaos and disharmony referred to him. In addition, the court stated that there was no reason to assume that the principal was responsible for the tardiness of the boys. "He may have materially improved conditions during his administration of the school, and the parents or guardians of the pupils may have been responsible for their tardiness."

Courts in some states treat slander and libel differently. Reasoning that written statements are more likely to cause harm because they are permanent, some courts have not required that a written statement fall into one of the four categories listed above in order to be found defamatory on its face. In these states, any written words that expose a person to hatred, ridicule, or abuse are defamatory on their face; spoken words are actionable on their face only if they fall into one of the four listed categories.

Statements that are clearly understood as being satire or humor and that are not understood to state actual facts about a person are not defamatory.[4] For example, a New Jersey court found that a teacher could not bring a defamation action against the high school student whose yearbook contained a picture with a caption suggesting that the teacher was engaged in a sexual relationship with another faculty member.[5] Similarly a California court ruled that a student's statement in the high school newspaper that a teacher was a "babbler" was not defamatory.[6] The court reasoned that readers of the article would have understood that the word was being used as an exaggeration and not as a statement of actual fact about the teacher.

What Is the Significance of Finding That a Statement Is Defamatory on Its Face?

If a statement is defamatory on its face, the law assumes that an individual's reputation has been injured. An individual who can prove that such a statement was made falsely will be awarded damages automatically. This individual is not required to show how he or she was injured by the false statements. The amount of the damages can vary, however, according to whether or not the statements were made maliciously.

If the false statements are not defamatory on their face, the injured party can collect monetary damages only by showing that he or she was directly harmed in some way by these statements. Examples of such harm could include physical or mental illness or loss of salary.

What Are Examples of Statements About Teachers That Have Been Found to Be Defamatory on Their Face?

The courts have ruled that any statements that falsely disparage a teacher's professional competence are defamatory on their face. In an early Ohio case,[7] for example, the court found the following statement about a teacher, made by the president of the board of education, was defamatory on its face: "He is not a fit person to teach in any school. He is no good as a teacher.... He plays for dances and then goes to sleep in the school room during school hours." In addition, courts have held all of the following charges defamatory on their face: a statement before the school board that a teacher was so "intoxicated at the public dinner at Bundick's creek...that it was necessary that [he] be brought to the table,"[8] and a teacher's statement that a principal allowed students to "pet" in the hallways without taking any disciplinary action.[9] In addition, statements falsely charging teachers with criminal activity have been held to be defamatory on their face, as when an Indiana newspaper printed an article headlined "A School Child Killed in Pike County by a Teacher,"[10] and when television reports accused a teacher of directing other students to assault another student.[11]

    • To be defamatory the false statements must relate to the teacher's professional performance. For example, an Iowa court ruled that a letter from a finance company to a school superintendent stating that a teacher in his district owed money on a debt was not defamatory on its face.[12] In so ruling, the court concluded that a mere statement regarding unpaid debts did not necessarily reflect negatively on either professional ability or qualifications: "The statements allegedly made of plaintiff [teacher] do not impute insolvency or that plaintiff has failed to pay the debt from dishonest motives and from a desire to defraud the creditor. They do not relate to her profession."

    A Colorado court recently ruled, however, that even where statements were made in an employment context, it was not slander per se to falsely accuse a high school teacher of homosexual conduct.[13] The court noted that although cases in various jurisdictions have reached different conclusions in deciding whether statements falsely accusing a person of being a homosexual constitute slander per se, the trend today is to limit the per se category of slander "to those instances in which the defamatory remark is apparent from the publication itself without reference to intrinsic facts."[14] The court reasoned that since sexual activities between consenting adults of the same sex were no longer illegal in Colorado, and since there was no evidence to show that homosexuals were exposed to public contempt, there was no reason to classify the statements as slanderous per se.

When an Individual Is Slandered or Libeled, How Is the Amount of Damages Determined?

The amount of damages awarded to the plaintiff will vary according to how seriously the jury feels the plaintiff's reputation has been harmed. In making a decision, the jury can consider such factors as the plaintiff's general character and reputation in the community, the nature of the statements made, and the number of people who heard or read these statements. Quantifying damage to reputation is obviously a difficult task, and the size of the awards varies considerably.

    For example, a judge awarded a teacher $9,000, which included damages for counseling bills, medication, and mental suffering, in her libel action against a student's parents.[15] A principal and vice principal in West Virginia were each awarded $7,000 after the school superintendent charged them with willful neglect of duty at a meeting of the county board of education.[16]

    In addition to injury to reputation, damage awards may include compensation for mental or physical injury or for other financial losses suffered as a result of defamatory statements. A District of Columbia jury awarded an attorney $15,000 in damages to compensate him for mental anguish and the business he lost after one of his clients was falsely informed that he had acted fraudulently in the past, practiced bigotry, and should be sued for malpractice.[17]

    Finally, if the defendant has acted maliciously or with reckless disregard for the truth, the jury can award punitive damages to punish the defendant and to deter such further behavior. In Georgia, for example, the court awarded $900,000 to a former university student after the head of the chemistry department falsely accused him of forging paychecks.[18] The award of punitive damages was based on the fact that the university professor made defamatory remarks about the student to many people not involved in the criminal investigation and that he continued to claim that the student was guilty long after the university investigation had disclosed that the discrepancy in the accounts had been caused by an embezzler in the professor's department. A New York court awarded $300,000 in punitive damages to a school district's chief negotiator when the faculty association falsely stated during contract negotiations that he had made a racial slur.[19]

Can Teachers Sue Other Educators, Including Their Superiors, for Defamatory Statements Made in Letters of Recommendation or on Evaluation Forms?

The courts have ruled that supervisors, such as principals and assistant central office department directors, generally have what is known as *qualified privilege* to comment on matters concerning the operation of the school. Under this qualified privilege school administrators will not be liable for defamatory statements even if false if administrators are under a duty to comment and are acting in good faith. This privilege extends to comments made in letters of recommendation.

For example, a Wisconsin court ruled that a school superintendent could not be sued for libel when he wrote a negative letter of recommendation about a teacher formerly employed as a speech therapist in his school district.[20] The teacher, Hett, had applied for a job at another school and had listed the superintendent as a reference. In writing a letter in reply to a request for information, the superintendent made the following statements: "I, personally, feel that Mr. Hett does not belong in the teaching field. He has a rather odd personality and it is rather difficult for him to gain the confidence of his fellow workers and the boys and girls with whom he works." The court ruled that the superintendent's statements were made in good faith and as part of his official responsibilities, and thus Hett could not sue him for libel: "The background of the relationship of Hett and Ploetz [the superintendent] satisfactorily demonstrates the latter's negative recommendation was grounded on the record and not upon malice. Ploetz was not an intermeddler; he had a proper interest in connection with the letter he wrote."

In a 1991 case, a federal court ruled under Kansas law that school officials had a qualified privilege to disclose information relating to child abuse charges against a teacher to a limited number of persons who were assessing her conduct for purposes of retention.[21]

School officials can lose this qualified privilege if they act in bad faith or without regard for whether the statements are true. For example, the president of a Texas commercial college wrote a letter to a student's prospective employer stating incorrectly that the student "was arrested and put in jail for stealing a typewriter."[22] Evidence showed that the president later discovered that this charge was false but he did not correct it because he wanted the job filled by a graduate of the college. The court ruled that his statements in the letter were not privileged.

In very infrequent situations, courts have ruled that school officials' statements are *absolutely privileged* and an administrator in such cases cannot be found liable for defamation even where he or she acted maliciously or in bad faith. For example, a Missouri teacher sued a school superintendent for slander, claiming that in response to her request for the reasons she was not being reemployed, she was defamed when he falsely stated at a school board meeting: "that plaintiff [teacher] had disobeyed school rules and regulations; that plaintiff was insubordinate; and that plaintiff was insufficient and inadequate with her students."[23] In reaching its decision, the court first noted that whether a statement is subject to an absolute or a qualified privilege depends on "the occasion or circumstances surrounding the utterance of the alleged slander." The court concluded that the superintendent's statements were absolutely privileged because they were made in response to the teacher's request. "[T]he publication of false and defamatory matter of another is *absolutely* privileged if the other consents thereto." When the teacher asked the superintendent why she was not to be reemployed the following school year, the superintendent was "absolutely protected in his explanation" and was not liable for slander. Similarly, a Pennsylvania court held that an absolute privilege protected a school board director who, in a letter to a newspaper editor, accused a district business manager of misconduct and malfeasance in the handling of a $13.5 million school renovation project.[24]

Courts have also held that statements made by public officials during judicial, legislative, or official executive proceedings are absolutely privileged. For example, statements by a school principal reporting student accusations of a teacher's sexual misconduct made before a state credentials committee were absolutely privileged despite a confidentiality agreement between the teacher and the school district.[25] Where school officials have made comments about teachers as part of their administrative duties, some courts have ruled that these statements are also absolutely privileged. An Illinois court dismissed a suit for slander against a superintendent of schools who made statements to the board of education that a teacher's performance in the classroom was poor, that he had done poorly in certain college courses, and that he had left his classroom unattended.[26] The court explained that "all communications, either verbal or written, passing between public officials pertaining to their duties and in the conduct of public business are of necessity absolutely privileged and such matters cannot be made the basis of recovery in a suit at law." Finding that the superintendent was carrying out an official duty when making these comments, the court dismissed the suit against him.

In general, then, statements by school officials are subject to a qualified privilege when they are made in good faith and about matters concerning school administration. School officials are not liable for defamatory statements that fall under this qualified privilege even if such statements turn out to be false. School officials are liable if they act maliciously or with reckless disregard for the truth of their statements, or if their statements concern matters outside the scope of their official duties.

Some statements by school officials, however, are held to be absolutely privileged; in those situations, school officials can never be held liable for defamatory statements. An absolute privilege in some states can extend to statements that the other party invites or to which the other party consents, as well as statements made in the course of judicial, legislative, or administrative proceedings, including school board hearings.

Defamatory Statements about Students

Can Students Sue Teachers for Written Statements in Students' Files?

The Family Educational Rights and Privacy Act of 1974 guarantees students' rights to privacy in their educational records.[27] In general, it provides that in schools receiving federal funds, students and their parents must have access to permanent school records. This right becomes the student's exclusively when she or he becomes 18 years old or is attending an institution of postsecondary education. Under the act, teachers can make notes about students for their own personal use. As long as a teacher does not show these notes to any person except a substitute teacher, students and their parents have no right to see them. In addition, the act provides that students can give up their rights to have access to certain papers. (See chapter 17 for a more detailed discussion of this act.)

Teachers can be sued for defamatory statements published in students' permanent records, however. In an early case in Oklahoma, a teacher was found to have libeled a student after he made a note in the school register that the student was "ruined by tobacco and whisky."[28] To avoid being sued for defamation, teachers should be careful to describe accurately relevant, observable behavior rather than make derogatory remarks about students. Courts generally have held that teachers are protected by a qualified privilege when they act in good faith in recording comments about students, and they will not be liable for statements about students unless the statements are made with malicious intent.

Can Teachers Be Sued for Making Negative Comments About Students in Classrooms or in the Teachers' Lounge?

If teachers knowingly spread false gossip that harms a student's reputation, they can be found to have slandered the student. Nevertheless, some court decisions suggest that a teacher's statements are subject to a qualified privilege if they are made as part of the teacher's professional responsibilities. For example, a Georgia court held that a college president's statements charging a student with theft were conditionally privileged when made during an investigation of the crime.[29] The president had accused the student of theft during a meeting with the student and the college chaplain. The court ruled that such statements were conditionally privileged because the were made by the president as part of his official responsibility to "inquire into and regulate the behavior of members of the student body." Invoking the concept of *in loco parentis* as support, the Court concluded that:

> This case cannot be justly decided if the fact that it involves the relationship, standards and duties of a college faculty and the students is lost sight of. Does a father slander his child when he accuses it of wrong in the presence of its mother? The parent-child relationship very closely parallels that of a college faculty and students in matters of discipline, discovering misconduct and punishing therefore. Any legal restraint of either parent or faculty in the reasonable discharge of duty, not only would not be beneficial to the child or student but might well be disastrous to them.[30]

Following this reasoning, a teacher's statements may be conditionally privileged if they are made as part of the disciplinary process or of the teacher's administrative responsibilities.

Can Students Sue Teachers for Negative Statements Made in Letters of Recommendation?

The Family Educational Rights and Privacy Act provides that a student can waive the right to see such letters if the student, upon request, is notified of the names of all persons making such recommendations and if the recommendations are used solely for the purpose for which they were specifically intended. If students gain access to these letters, however, teachers can be sued for any defamatory statements they may have made. The same general principles outlined regarding administrators' liability in suits by teachers apply here: A teacher's statements about a student will be at least conditionally privileged when a student lists a teacher as a reference and the teacher responds to such a request for information about the student's competence and character. Thus, unless a teacher acts maliciously by making statements the teacher knows are untrue, the teacher will not be liable for any negative statements made in such letters.

Can Students Sue Teachers for Giving Them Low Grades?

Low grades certainly may expose students to shame or ridicule, but the courts have not found that giving low grades is libelous. The courts have reasoned that they do not have the expertise to evaluate the accuracy of a teacher's grading decision and will not intervene in grading unless it can be shown that school officials acted in bad faith.

This philosophy was illustrated in an early Massachusetts case where the court ruled that it was not proper for a jury even to examine the question whether a high school student had been properly dismissed for failure to attain an adequate standard of scholarship.[31] The court explained: "So long as the school committee acts in good faith, their conduct in formulating and applying standards and making decisions touching this matter is not subject to review by any other tribunal.... It is an educational question, the final determination of which is vested by law in the public officers charged with the performance of that important duty." In effect, this position prohibits any libel suit by students because the courts refuse to consider the "truth" or "falsity" of the grade.

A federal district court in Vermont applied the same reasoning in a more recent case in which a medical student sued the state college of medicine, claiming that he should not have been dismissed for failing to attain a proper standard of scholarship.[32] The court explained:

> The reason for this rule is that in matters of scholarship. the school authorities are uniquely qualified by training and experience to judge the qualifications of a student, and efficiency of instruction depends in no small degree upon the school faculty's freedom from interference from other noneducational tribunals. It is only when the school authorities abuse this discretion that a court may interfere with their decision.[33]

Public Officials

Do Any Constitutional Considerations Apply in Slander or Libel Cases?

Yes. In *New York Times* v. *Sullivan,* the U.S. Supreme Court ruled that the First Amendment's guarantees of freedom of speech and press require that public officials cannot be awarded damages for libel or slander unless they can prove that such statements were made with actual malice.[34] "Actual malice" means that the defendant made the libelous or slanderous statements either knowing that they were false or with a reckless disregard for the truth of the statements. Thus, the Court ruled that the First and Fourteenth Amendments require that public officials must meet a higher standard of proof in defamation suits. The Court first noted that the First Amendment embodies "a profound national commitment to the principle that debate on public issues should be uninhibited, robust, and wide-open, and that it may well include repellent, caustic, and sometimes unpleasantly sharp attacks on government and public officials." A rule that would require a critic of official conduct to guarantee the truth of all factual assertions or risk a suit for defamation would be inconsistent with this principle: it would make people afraid to voice their criticism, thus dampening the rigor and limiting the variety of political debate. The Court therefore protected individuals who criticized public officials in holding that such individuals would not be liable for defamation unless they acted with "actual malice."

Can Teachers, Students, or Administrators Be Considered Public Officials?

Yes. The *New York Times* standard would apply to any teacher, student, or administrator serving as a duly elected public official. For example, an elected or appointed member of a board of education would be considered a public official.[35] Similarly, a Maryland court ruled that a high school principal constituted a public official, as well, and thus, a newspaper which ranked county principals by purported competence could not successfully be sued due to the alleged injury to the principal's reputation.[36] In that case, the local newspaper had published an article entitled "Our High School Principals: How Good Are They?" When Dunn, a principal, was given an "unsuited" rating in the article, he brought a libel action against the newspaper. On the grounds that his suitability for the position was a "matter of public or general interest or concern," the court ruled that the *New York Times* standard applied.

Whether teachers or school officials will be considered public officials varies from state to state. The U.S. Supreme Court has not yet decided this issue, and courts have reached different conclusions depending on the role of the educator. The courts that have held that principals are public officials reason that principals have significant governmental power over public education and that public debate about their actions should be encouraged.[37] The courts that hold that principals are not public officials reason that the principal's relationship with the conduct of government is too remote "to justify exposing these individuals to a qualifiedly privileged assault upon his or her reputation."[38] State courts are divided on the status of teachers, but the trend is to hold that they are not public officials.[39]

Does the New York Times *Standard Apply to All Defamatory Statements Made about Public Officials?*

No. The *New York Times* standard applies only when the defamatory statements relate to "official conduct." In a New York case, the court held that this standard applied in a libel suit brought by a member of a board of education when a newspaper made charges that she was pressing her son's math teacher to raise his grade.[40] While conceding that she was a public official, the school board member argued that the *New York Times* standard should not apply because the defamatory statements concerned private rather than official conduct. The court agreed that the *New York Times* rule would not apply to statements about conduct as a private citizen and a mother. However, since these charges stated that she had used the power of her office for personal gain, the court found that they related to her duties as a public official and that the newspaper would not be liable unless she could show that the statements were made with actual malice.

Can the New York Times *Standard Be Applied to Others Besides Public Officials?*

Yes. The U.S. Supreme Court has extended the *New York Times* standard to public figures. A "public figure" is one who either (1) achieves general fame or notoriety in the community or (2) "voluntarily injects himself or is drawn into a particular controversy and thereby becomes a public figure for a limited range of issues."[41]

Depending on the circumstances, administrators, teachers, and students could all qualify as public figures. For example, a Texas court held that a university professor was a public figure after he led an anti–Vietnam War demonstration "which aroused a considerable amount of interest and comment in the city of El Paso."[42] Similarly, a New York court concluded that a school district's superintendent of buildings and grounds was a public figure in the context of a controversy over his appointment.[43]

Does the New York Times *Standard Apply to Statements of Opinion As Well As of Fact?*

Yes, according to a 1990 U.S. Supreme Court decision,[44] in which a high school wrestling coach sued a newspaper after it published an editorial stating, among other things, that the coach had "apparently" lied under oath in a judicial proceeding. The newspaper's publishers argued that this statement was not a fact but purely an opinion and therefore not subject to a libel action. The U.S. Supreme Court resolved the controversy by making clear that there is no wholesale defamation exemption for anything that might be labeled "opinion." Expressions of opinion may often imply an association of objective fact. The Court then identified the factors that must be examined to determine whether a statement does imply "actual facts about an individual": the type of language used, the meaning of the statement in context, whether the statement is verifiable, and the broader social circumstances in which the statement was made. In this case, the Court found that a reasonable fact finder could conclude that the statements in the editorial implied that the coach perjured himself, and that the contention that he committed perjury was sufficiently factual to be susceptible of being proved true or false. The Court therefore ruled that the coach could maintain his libel action, and it remanded the case to the Ohio court to decide whether he had been defamed.

Do Constitutional Principles Apply to Damage Awards?

Yes. The U.S. Supreme Court has held that the First Amendment restricted the damages that a private individual could obtain from a publisher for a libel that involved a matter of public concern.[45] The Court stated that in these circumstances the First Amendment prohibited awards of presumed and punitive damages for false and defamatory statements unless the plaintiff showed *actual malice.*

To prove actual malice, the plaintiff must make the same showing necessary to meet the so-called *New York Times* test, described above. That is, it must be shown that the defendant made the objectionable statements either with knowledge that they were false or with reckless disregard of whether or not they were false. In attempting to meet this test, the plaintiff is allowed to inquire into the defendant's state of mind at the time the statements were made and to gather other evidence to show that the defendant knew the statements were false when he or she made them.[46]

A black high school principal did not prove actual malice when he sued a black citizens' group that published a pamphlet criticizing his supervision of the school.[47] The pamphlet called the principal "an Uncle Tom, a traitor to his race, a stooge, a stool pigeon, an informer and a betrayer of his people." Although the defendants testified that it was their intention to have the principal removed from his position at the school, the court ruled that this ill will did not constitute actual malice. Since the principal offered no evidence that the defendants knew the statements were false or that they were made with reckless disregard for whether they were false, he did not meet his burden of proving actual malice, and the suit was dismissed.

In a 1985 case, the U.S. Supreme Court found that a credit report that had been circulated to five subscribers was not a public matter but was "speech solely in the individual interest of the speaker and its specific business audience," and thus concluded that "speech on matters of purely private concern is of less First Amendment concern."[48] The Court ruled that awards for presumed and punitive damages could be made in such cases even in the absence of a showing "actual malice."

Summary

Both teachers and administrators who make false statements that harm teachers' and students' reputations are liable for defamation. A written comment in a student's school record can lead to a libel suit. A gossip session in the teachers' lounge can support a charge of slander.

In many situations, however, teachers and administrators are protected in making statements about other teachers' and students' character and ability. The courts have ruled that educators who are acting in good faith have a qualified privilege to comment on matters that are within their scope of authority. For example, an educator can explain to a parent why a student was disciplined without being liable for defamation. Even if these statements turn out to be false, the teacher is not liable for defamation unless found to be acting maliciously knowing that these statements were false when he or she made them or from some improper purpose (e.g., lying to the parent because of personal animosity toward the student). This conditional or qualified privilege also protects teachers and administrators who write negative evaluations or letters of recommendation.

In some situations, the courts have also ruled that educators' statements are absolutely privileged and that the individuals cannot be held liable even if their comments were made maliciously. An absolute privilege has been applied in many states, for example, where an administrator who testifies before a board of education hearing as to the reasons for a teacher's dismissal.

Teachers can also sue individuals who defame them. When teachers are falsely charged with matters relating to their professional competence, they can collect damages to compensate for injury to their reputation. If such statements are clearly related to a teacher's professional competence (e.g., a charge of brutality against students), the courts automatically assume that a teacher has been injured and is entitled to some amount of damages. In other situations, a teacher may have to prove that the comments actually did harm his or her reputation in order to be awarded damages. In addition to collecting damages for injury to reputation, teachers can also be awarded monetary damages to compensate them for mental or physical injury or financial loss. Punitive damages can be awarded when false statements are made maliciously.

Teachers and administrators found to be either public officials or public figures have a higher burden of proof in defamation suits. In *New York Times* v. *Sullivan,* the U.S. Supreme Court ruled that public officials and public figures can be awarded damages for libel or slander only if they can prove that the defendant made defamatory statements with actual malice. To prove actual malice, the plaintiff must show that the defendant made the statement either knowing that it was false or with reckless disregard for whether it was true or false.

NOTES

1. *Fairbanks Publishing Co.* v. *Pitka,* 376 P.2d 190 (Alaska 1962).
2. B. Dill, *The Journalist's Handbook on Libel and Privacy 5–3* (New York: Free Press, 1986).
3. *Barringer* v. *Sun Printing and Publishing Association,* 145 N.Y.S. 776 (N.Y. App. Div. 1914).
4. *Hustler Magazine, Inc.* v. *Falwell,* 485 U.S. 46 (1988).
5. *Salek* v. *Passaic Collegiate School,* 605 A.2d 276 (N.J. Sup. Ct. App. Div. 1992).
6. *Moyer* v. *Amador Valley Joint Union High School District,* 275 Cal. Rptr. 494 (Ct. App. 1990).
7. *Mulcahy* v. *Deitrick,* 176 N.E. 481, 482 (Ohio Ct. App. 1931).
8. *Ford* v. *Jeane,* 106 So. 558 (La. 1925).
9. *Larive* v. *Willitt,* 315 P.2d 732 (Cal. Ct. App. 1957).
10. *Doan* v. *Kelley,* 23 N.E. 266 (Ind. 1890); see also *Joseph* v. *Elam,* 709 S.W.2d 517 (Mo. Ct. App. 1986).
11. *Snitowski* v. *NBC Subsidiary (WMAQ-TV), Inc.,* 696 N.E.2d 761 (Ill. App. 1 Dist. 1998).
12. *Ragland* v. *Household Finance Corp.,* 119 N.W.2d 788 (Iowa 1963).
13. *Hayes* v. *Smith,* 832 P.2d 1022 (Colo. Ct. App. 1991).
14. *Id.,* at 1024.
15. *Beckham* v. *Durant,* 387 S.E.2d 701 (S.C. Ct. App. 1989).
16. *Chambers* v. *Smith,* 198 S.E.2d 806 (W. Va. 1973).
17. *Collins* v. *Brown,* 268 F. Supp. 198 (D.D.C. 1967).
18. *Melton* v. *Bow,* 247 S.E.2d 100 (Ga. 1978).
19. *O'Neil* v. *Peekskill Faculty Association Local No. 2916,* 549 N.Y.S.2d 41 (App. Div. 2d Dept. 1989).
20. *Hett* v. *Ploetz,* 121 N.W.2d 270 (Wis. 1963).
21. *Ginwright* v. *Unified School District No. 457,* 756 F.Supp. 1458 (D. Kan. 1991).
22. *Lattimore* v. *Tyler Commercial College,* 24 S.W.2d 361, 362 (Tex. Ct. App. 1930).
23. *Williams* v. *School District of Springfield R-12,* 447 S.W.2d 256, 257 (Mo. 1969).
24. *Matta* v. *Burton,* 721 A.2d 1164 (Pa. Cmwlth. 1998).
25. *Picton* v. *Anderson Union High School,* 57 Cap. Rptr. 2d 829 (Cal. App. 3 Dist. 1996).
26. *McLaughlin* v. *Tilendis,* 253 N.E.2d 85 (Ill. Ct. App. 1969).
27. 20 U.S.C. § 1232(g) (West 1978 and Supp. 1985).
28. *Dawkins* v. *Billingsley,* 172 P. 69 (Okla. 1918).
29. *Davidson* v. *Walter,* 91 S.E.2d 520 (Ga. Ct. App. 1956).
30. *Walter* v. *Davidson,* 104 S.E.2d 113 (Ga. 1958).
31. *Barnard* v. *Inhabitants of Shelburne,* 102 N.E. 1095, 1096 (Mass. 1913).
32. *Connelly* v. *University of Vermont and State Agricultural College,* 244 F. Supp. 156 (D. Vt. 1965).
33. *Id.*
34. *New York Times Co.* v. *Sullivan,* 376 U.S. 254 (1964).
35. *Cabin* v. *Community Newspapers, Inc.,* 270 N.Y.S.2d 913 (N.Y. Sup. Ct. 1966) (elected officials); *Henry* v. *Collins,* 380 U.S. 356 (1965) (appointed officials).
36. *Kapiloff* v. *Dunn,* 343 A.2d 251 (Md. Ct. Spec. App. 1974).

37. See *Johnson* v. *Robbinsdale Independent School District, No. 281,* 827 F. Supp. 1439 (D. Minn. 1993) (elementary school principal is a public official); *Reaves* v. *Foster,* 200 So.2d 453 (Miss. 1967) (high school principal is a public official); *Jee* v. *New York Post Co., Inc.,* 671 N.Y.S.2d 920 (N.Y. Sup. Ct. 1998) (same).

38. *East Canton Education Association* v. *McIntosh,* 709 N.E.2d 468 (Ohio 1999).

39. *Poe* v. *San Antonio Express News Corp.,* 590 S.W.2d 537 (Tex. Civ. App.1979); *McCutcheon* v. *Moran,* 425 N.E.2d 1130 (Ill. Ct. App. 1981); *True* v. *Ladner,* 513 A.2d 257 (Me. 1986); *Richmond Newspapers, Inc.* v. *Lipscomb,* 362 S.E.2d 32 (Va. 1987); *Nodar* v. *Galbreath,* 462 So.2d 803 (Fla. 1984). But see *Elstrom* v. *Independent School District No. 270,* 533 N.W.2d 51 (Minn. App. 1995); *Gallman* v. *Carnes,* 497 S.W.2d 47 (Ark. 1973); *Johnston* v. *Corinthian Television Corp.,* 583 P.2d 1101 (Okla. 1978).

40. *Cabin* v. *Community Newspapers, Inc.,* 270 N.Y.S.2d 913 (N.Y. Sup. Ct. 1966).

41. *Gertz* v. *Robert Welch, Inc.,* 418 U.S. 323 (1974).

42. *El Paso Times, Inc.* v. *Trexler,* 447 S.W.2d 403, 404 (Tex. 1969).

43. *DiBernardo* v. *Tonawanda Publishing Corp.,* 499 N.Y.S.2d 553 (N.Y. App. Div. 4th Dept. 1986).

44. *Milkovich* v. *Lorain Journal Co.,* 497 U.S. 1 (1990).

45. *Gertz* v. *Robert Welch, Inc.,* 418 U.S. 323 (1974).

46. *Sas Jaworsky* v. *Padfield,* 211 So.2d 122 (La. Ct. App. 1968).

47. *Reaves* v. *Foster,* 200 So.2d 453 (Miss. 1967).

48. *Dun & Bradstreet, Inc.* v. *Greenmoss Builders, Inc.,* 472 U.S. 749 (1985).

7 How Should I Deal with Child Abuse and Neglect?

Overview

Scholarly accounts of the history of childhood reveal that children have been subjected to various abuses throughout the ages. Some historians trace such abuse back to biblical references, others to Greek and Roman antiquity.[1] There is ample historical evidence that during every age, children have been grossly mistreated, abused, often whipped, sacrificed, burned, disfigured, and killed. In Western law, they were often treated as chattel, completely at the disposal of their owners.

In recent years, the public has become aware and concerned about this type of behavior.

No reliable statistics exist, however, on the extent of child abuse and neglect because of inconsistencies in definitions of abuse and neglect, variations in reporting laws from state to state, and different methods of data collection. Nonetheless, it has been estimated that each year close to one and a half million cases of child abuse and neglect are reported to child welfare agencies.[2]

Various professionals are legally responsible for reporting suspected cases of child abuse. Are teachers, therapists, and counselors among them? If yes, to whom do they report and how? What are the obligations and liabilities involved in such reporting? And what is child abuse? These are some questions considered in this chapter.

Child Abuse and Neglect

What Is Child Abuse?

No single, authoritative definition of "child abuse" exists. The National Committee for the Prevention of Child Abuse defines it as a nonaccidental injury or a pattern of injuries to a child for which there is no "reasonable" explanation. For our purposes, this definition is too vague. We will look at how the term is defined in federal and state laws.

In 1974, Congress enacted the National Child Abuse Prevention and Treatment Act, which defines child abuse and neglect as:

Physical or mental injury, sexual abuse or exploitation, negligent treatment, or maltreatment of a child under the age of eighteen or the age specified by the child protection law of the state in question, by a person who is responsible for the child's welfare, under circumstances which indicate that the child's health or welfare is harmed or threatened thereby.

Because child abuse is not a federal crime, the federal law did no more than make money available to the states that met its reporting guidelines and other qualifications, and set reporting standards. The act also provided help to local agencies concerned with child abuse and neglect and established a central registry that lists substantiated cases of child abuse.

In the Child Abuse Prevention, Adoption, and Family Services Act of 1988, Congress buttressed the federal involvement in this area by appropriating $48 million through 1991. The act also created the position of a permanent director and professional staff for the National Center on Child Abuse and Neglect, an advisory board, and an interagency task force. The center provides technical assistance and conducts research on the causes, prevention, and treatment of child abuse and neglect.[3]

Congress further strengthened the federal role in this area as it amended the law in 1992, 1994, and most recently in the Child Abuse Prevention and Treatment Act Amendments of 1996. The 1996 amendments substantially raise the amounts of money Congress may appropriate for various aspects of the program. In addition to a national advisory board on abuse and neglect, the act now supports research and assistance activities and provides for demonstration or service projects. Furthermore, the act provides funds for prevention and emergency programs as well as for investigations and prosecution of abusers.[4]

Because child abuse is a state crime, state definitions are important. Although state statutory definitions vary, the following two from Alaska and Vermont are typical:

> Child abuse or neglect means the physical injury or neglect, sexual abuse, sexual exploitation, or maltreatment of a child under the age of eighteen by a person who is responsible for the child's welfare under circumstances which indicate that the child's health or welfare is harmed or threatened.[5]
>
> "Abused or neglected child" means a child whose physical or mental health or welfare is harmed or threatened with harm by acts or omissions of his parent or other person responsible for his welfare.[6]

Although state laws vary, they all use a combination of two or more of the following elements in defining abuse and neglect: (1) physical injury, (2) mental or emotional injury, (3) sexual molestation or exploitation.[7]

Is Distinguishing between Abuse and Neglect Important?

No. Whereas some states define them as a single concept, others have separate definitions for them. In 1977, the U.S. Department of Health, Education, and Welfare created the Model Child Protection Act with Commentary, which states that the reporter is not required to know or to be certain whether it is abuse or neglect to which a child has been subjected. State laws are similar to this act in not requiring a person to know whether it is abuse or neglect that is being reported.[8]

> The time and effort spent in trying to distinguish between abuse and neglect serves no useful purpose. A child may suffer serious or permanent harm and even death as a result of

neglect. Therefore, the same reasons that justify the mandatory reporting of abuse require the mandatory reporting of child neglect.[9]

State Reporting Requirements

Which States Require Reporting of Child Abuse and Neglect?

All of them do if the abuse or neglect results in physical injury. The states that do not require the reporting of emotional or mental injury are Georgia, Indiana, Iowa, Maryland, Minnesota, Oregon, and Wisconsin. Today all states include sexual abuse and exploitation in their definition of child abuse. This came about after Congress broadened its definition of sexual abuse in the Federal Child Abuse and Prevention Act of 1984 to include sexual exploitation.[10] In order to receive federal funds, all states had to enact laws consistent with the Act. Therefore, educators must check with appropriate state agencies to keep up-to-date with the law in their respective states. Because state laws change rapidly, the reader should contact the American Bar Association's National Legal Center on Child Advocacy and Protection, 1800 M Street, N.W., Washington, D.C. 20036, (202) 662-1000 for up-to-date information.

How Certain Must I Be That Abuse or Neglect Is Taking Place Before Reporting It?

No state requires that you be absolutely certain before you file a report that abuse is taking place. It is sufficient that you have "reason to believe" or "reasonable cause to believe or suspect" that a child is subject to abuse or neglect. As in many other areas of the law, the standard applied is what the reasonable person would believe under similar circumstances. Because abuse seldom occurs in front of witnesses, and because the protection of children is the main purpose of reporting laws, the reporters are not held to unduly rigorous standards as long as they act in good faith. In fact, some states require one to report even when he or she "observes the child being subjected to conditions or circumstances which would reasonably result in child abuse or neglect."[11]

Symptoms of Abuse and Neglect

What Symptoms Should Alert Me to Child Abuse and Neglect?

There are various symptoms that should alert educators that some form of abuse or neglect is taking place. Educators in general and counselors in particular are trained observers of children. Through formal education and their work experience, they have become sensitive to the range of normal behavior expected of children in their school and classes and are quick to notice deviations or exceptional behavior. They often observe the same children day after day over long periods of time; thus they are in a key position to notice signs of abuse or neglect. With a little training that focuses on the most common symptoms, they can become the most reliable reporters of such damage or danger to children.

Table 7.1 lists the most common indicators of abuse or neglect. It is neither exhaustive nor definitive. Not all indicators are included, nor is the presence of a single indicator

TABLE 7.1 Physical and Behavioral Indicators of Child Abuse and Neglect (CA/N)

Type of CA/N	Physical Indicators	Behavioral Indicators
Physical abuse	Unexplained bruises and welts: —on face, lips, mouth —on torso, back, buttocks, thighs —in various stages of healing —clustered, forming regular patterns —reflecting shape of article used to inflict (electric cord, belt buckle) —on several different surface areas —regularly appearing after absence, weekend, or vacation Unexplained burns: —cigar, cigarette burns, especially on soles, palms, back, or buttocks —immersion burns (socklike, glovelike, doughnut shaped on buttocks or genitalia) —patterned like electric burner, iron, etc. —rope burns on arms, legs, neck, or torso Unexplained fractures: —to skull, nose, facial structure —in various stages of healing —multiple or spiral fractures Unexplained lacerations or abrasions: —to mouth, lips, gums, eyes —to external genitalia	Wary of adult contacts Apprehensive when other children cry Behavioral extremes: —aggressiveness, or —withdrawal Frightened of parents Afraid to go home Reporting injury by parents
Physical neglect	Consistent hunger, poor hygiene, inappropriate dress Consistent lack of supervision, especially in dangerous activities or long periods Unattended physical problems or medical needs Abandonment	Begging, stealing food Extended stays at school (early arrival and late departure) Constant fatigue, listlessness, or falling asleep in class Alcohol or drug abuse Delinquency (e.g., thefts) Stating there is no caretaker
Sexual abuse	Difficulty in walking or sitting Torn, stained, or bloody underclothing Pain or itching in genital area Bruises or bleeding in external genitalia, vaginal, or anal area Venereal disease, especially in preteens Pregnancy	Unwilling to change for gym or participate in physical education class Withdrawal, fantasy, or infantile behavior Bizarre, sophisticated, or unusual sexual behavior or knowledge Poor peer relationships Delinquent or runaway Reporting sexual assault by caretaker

(continued)

TABLE 7.1   Continued

Type of CA/N	Physical Indicators	Behavioral Indicators
Emotional maltreatment	Speech disorders Lagging in physical development Failure to thrive	Habit disorders (sucking, biting, rocking, etc.) Conduct disorders (antisocial, destructive, etc.) Neurotic traits (sleep disorders, inhibition of play) Psychoneurotic reactions (hysteria, obsession, compulsion, phobias, hypochondria) Behavior extremes: —compliant, passive —aggressive, demanding Overly adaptive behavior: —inappropriately adult —inappropriately infant Developmental lags (mental, emotional) Attempted suicide

Source: D. D. Broadhurst, *The Educator's Role in the Prevention and Treatment of Child Abuse and Neglect* (Washington, D.C.: National Center on Child Abuse and Neglect, U.S. Department of Health, Education, and Welfare, Pub. No. 79-30172, 1979).

an assurance that abuse or neglect exists. These are, rather, some of the major indicators that should alert one to the possibility that abuse or neglect is taking place and should be investigated. Clearly, if several indicators are present, or if they occur repeatedly, the probability of maltreatment is greater.

Even in the absence of the specific symptoms or indicators listed in Table 7.1, educators might recognize some general signs of abuse and neglect or both. These can be either academic or psychological clues. Sudden changes in academic performance or sudden loss of interest in schoolwork should alert the observer to the possibility of mistreatment of a student. Studies indicate that there is a significant relationship between child abuse and/or neglect and learning difficulties. Delayed language and motor development is found in a high proportion of such children. Also the emotional stress placed on families with special-needs children can bring on abuse or neglect. Educators experienced with special-needs children know that family neglect may lead to failure to provide the child with a hearing aid or glasses, which in turn impedes academic progress. Similarly, sudden changes in a child's emotional tone may be a clue to abuse or neglect. A previously outgoing, happy child who becomes angry, withdrawn, or sullen may be signaling serious changes in the child's home life. Children who are very passive and uncommunicative should alert us to the possibility that problems exist in the life of the family. Clearly, there is not a one-to-one correlation between academic problems and abuse or neglect, but alert and knowledgeable educators can gather clues from a variety of sources in the process of identifying problems in their schools.

All these signs are only indicators that should alert reasonable educators to the *possibility* of abuse or neglect. They do not *prove* that abuse or neglect exists. Through conversations with the parents or with the child, further clues may be gathered that will confirm suspicions of abuse or neglect or that will provide other satisfactory explanations for the child's condition.[12] Some states, however, expressly prohibit teachers from investigation, requiring them to report suspected abuse to law enforcement authorities.

Reporting Child Abuse and Neglect

Do Laws Require Educators to Report Child Abuse and Neglect?

Yes. Some state statutes explicitly name "school counselors" among the mandatory reporters of child abuse or neglect. Others include among them "educators," "other school personnel," or "employees or officials of any public or private school." Still others have catchall provisions that require reporting by "any person" who works with children and has "reasonable cause to believe" that abuse or neglect is going on. Such general requirements would clearly include teachers, therapists, and counselors who work with children.

Allegations of child abuse are serious because they can damage an individual's reputation and career. Therefore, it is proper and common to conduct an investigation before making a report.[13] A school employee who suspects that child abuse is occurring often alerts the principal or superintendent, who then reports it to the relevant authorities. This is quite appropriate. However, if the superior officer does not make the report, the employee should.[14]

Can Educators Be Registered as Suspected Child Abusers?

Yes, in states that require that a register of cases be maintained. At times, inconsistencies exist between the disciplinary policies and practices of a school and the criteria used by social service agencies as to what is excessive punishment and sufficient to constitute child abuse. For example, in a case from Arkansas an assistant principal paddled a child such that the bruises remained visible for at least 24 hours.[15] The court held that the assistant principal's name should not be placed on the child abuse registry because there was no proof of excessive paddling. Thus, the employee was entitled to have his name expunged from the state abuse registry.

Whether the employee succeeds in expunging his or her name from the state registry may depend on the state in which the action occurred and more likely on the facts of the case. A 1994 case in Illinois held that no liberty interest was implicated by having one's name placed on the list.[16] Similarly, Arkansas held that the name can remain on the list for the statutorily required three-year period, even if the report of child abuse was unsubstantiated.[17] However, the trend of court decisions recognizes that being placed on such a list implicates one's liberty interest safeguarded by the Fourteenth Amendment and is thus protected by due process, and allegations of abuse must be proven by a *preponderance* of evidence, not merely *credible evidence*.[18] This was the *Cavaretta* case in Illinois, where a junior high school physical education teacher was alleged to have fondled and tickled a 14-year-old female student. Although the state statutes specified the timelines within which hearings and appeals must be held, the Department of Child and Family Services grossly exceeded those timelines.

The court of appeals recognized that being placed on a registry of abusers is a serious stigma that is likely to damage one's reputation and one's professional career, and therefore implicates the liberty interest. The 598 days it took to complete the appeal process was excessive and thus a denial of due process.

Is the Reporter of Child Abuse or Neglect Protected from Lawsuits?

Yes. Every state provides immunity by law from civil suit and criminal prosecution that might arise from the reporting of suspected child abuse or neglect. Such immunity applies to all mandatory or permissible reporters who act "in good faith." In many states, good faith is presumed; therefore the person suing the reporter has the burden to prove that the reporter acted in bad faith. *Clearly, any educator, therapist, or counselor who acts in good faith and is mandated by law to report suspected cases of abuse or neglect is immune from suit.*

To be eligible for federal funds under the Child Abuse Prevention, Adoption, and Family Services Act, states must grant immunity to reporters. All states have complied with this requirement. The expressed intent of immunity legislation is to encourage reporting without fear of civil or criminal liability.

Should Counselors Violate Privileged Communication by Reporting Suspected Cases of Abuse or Neglect?

Yes. In fact they must. First, most states deny such privilege to counselors in any legal proceeding. Second, as a matter of public policy it is more important to require the reporting than to respect the privilege. Finally, because counselors and teachers are among those who must report, *the legal requirement of reporting overrides any claim to privilege or confidential communication.*

Do Religious Beliefs Provide Exemption from Liability for Child Abuse?

Yes, in most states, although this matter continues to be controversial. Because some religions believe in nonmedical spiritual healing, most states provide special laws pertaining to them. Typical is the Missouri statute, which makes the following provision:

> A child who does not receive specific medical treatment by reason of the legitimate practice of the religious belief of said child's parents, guardians, or others legally responsible for said child, for that reason alone, shall not be considered to be an abused or neglected child.[19]

Although 44 states have similar statutes, some of them explicitly authorize courts to order medical treatment when the child's health requires it. Furthermore, courts may have such power even without explicit statutory authorization.[20]

The Mechanics of Reporting Child Abuse and Neglect

Is There a Penalty for Failure to Report Suspected Child Abuse or Neglect?

Yes; in all but five states (Idaho, Illinois, Mississippi, Montana, and Wyoming) mandated reporters are criminally liable for failure to report a suspected case of child abuse or neglect. Failure to report is a misdemeanor in most states. The penalty might range from a jail sentence of 5 to 30 days and/or a fine of $10 to $100 to a year in jail and a fine of $1,000.

However, there are no *reported* cases of a criminal prosecution for failure to report a case of child abuse or neglect. Why? Because state laws usually require a "knowing" or "willful" failure to report. It is extremely difficult to prove, beyond all reasonable doubt, that someone "knowingly" or "willfully" failed to report; therefore cases are not prosecuted. Perhaps a more likely route of enforcement is the threat of civil liability (liability in money damages).

Some states have enacted laws that impose civil liability for failure to report. However, different state laws require differing degrees of proof. For example, in Arkansas, Colorado, Iowa, and New York, proof of willful misconduct is required, whereas Michigan and Montana use a lesser standard for establishing liability, namely the standard of negligence.[21] Various scholars believe that civil liability for not reporting will be the trend of the future and will help increase the number of abuse and neglect cases reported.[22]

At this writing, there are no reported cases imposing civil liability on teachers or counselors for failure to report, but with the increase in the number of states imposing such liability by statute, such cases are likely to arise. Currently the best-known cases seeking money damages for failure to report child abuse and neglect have been filed against physicians and hospitals. The landmark case of *Landeros* v. *Flood* established the principle that a physician could be held liable in money damages for failure to report a case of child abuse.[23] Reasoning by analogy, courts could hold educators, including counselors, liable for money damages for violating their mandated duty to report. Such liability will be all the more possible in states that explicitly impose liability by statute, such as Michigan and Montana.

There are cases, however, where counselors or psychologists have been disciplined for failure to report promptly a suspected case of child abuse. One controversial case arose in Illinois, where Dr. Rosario C. Pesce, a tenured teacher school psychologist, was suspended without pay for five days and demoted from "school psychologist" to "school psychologist for the behavior disorders program." The state law required school psychologists to report *immediately* suspected cases of abuse or neglect. When information first came to Pesce about the probability of abuse, he consulted with his attorney and a psychologist and chose not to report for 10 days, at which time he became more certain of the actual abuse. The facts indicated probable sexual involvement of the student with his male teacher as well as threats of suicide. When Pesce challenged the administrative action, claiming it violated his constitutional right to due process as well as his federal right to confidentiality, the U.S. district court and the court of appeals ruled against him.[24]

How Do I Report Child Abuse or Neglect?

Each state statute that mandates reporting of child abuse or neglect specifies the procedures reporters are required to follow. Most states require an oral report, within a reasonable period of time (twenty-four to seventy-two hours, although some allow up to seven days), followed by a more detailed written report. Some states have set up 24-hour toll-free "hotlines" to facilitate reporting.

Most states require that the reporter include in the report, if known, the name and address of the child, the nature and extent of the injury or condition observed, and the reporter's name and address. The reporting form often has a general request for "any other information that the person making the report believes may be helpful in establishing the cause of the injury…and protecting the child." Some states and some school districts provide a reporting form to facilitate the writing of reports. The absence of such forms, however, does not excuse one from reporting; any piece of paper may be used as long as the required information is provided.

Is a Social Service Agency Liable for Failure to Protect the Child After the Abuse Has Been Reported?

No, ruled a divided U.S. Supreme Court in the 1989 *DeShaney* case.[25] Joshua DeShaney was repeatedly beaten by his father to the point of abuse from the time he was one year old until the age of four, when he was admitted to the hospital in a life-threatening coma. After brain surgery, he was expected to live as a profoundly retarded person. His father was convicted of child abuse.

Suit was filed in a federal court on behalf of Joshua and his mother, alleging that the county department of social services deprived him of "his liberty without due process of law" by failing to intervene to protect him after the department knew or should have known of the risk of violence at his father's hands. Although the Supreme Court acknowledged that "the facts of this case are undeniably tragic" and that the social service worker was fully cognizant of the brutality of the beatings and did not intervene except to take notes, the majority of six justices held that the Fourteenth Amendment was not violated. The purpose of the amendment, according to the majority, is to protect people from the state and not from each other or from private actors. Thus, the social worker or the department of social services was under no duty to protect Joshua. If there is to be such duty placed on them, reasoned the Court, the state legislature has to create the obligation; it is not for the courts to impose it. A minority of three justices disagreed. They would have held that once the state intervened and the department of social services moved in to document and report the abuse, a duty was created to protect Joshua.

Summary

Although child abuse and neglect is an age-old pattern of behavior, it has become a matter of concern to the public only in recent decades. California, in 1962, was the first state to require by law the reporting of child abuse. By 1964, 20 states had followed suit. Today, all states, the District of Columbia, Puerto Rico, the Virgin Islands, and American Samoa have such laws.

Laws, however much they may help, do not prevent child abuse and neglect from occurring. During recent years, over one million such cases per year have been brought to the attention of the National Center on Child Abuse and Neglect. This is probably only the tip of the iceberg, for it is generally believed that a large number of child abuse and neglect cases never get reported.

Teachers, among others, are mandated by law to report cases of suspected or known abuse. One who has reasonable grounds to suspect that abuse or neglect is occurring is required by law to report under penalty of a fine, a jail term, or both. Furthermore, a suit for money damages may be filed against one who fails to report. States are increasingly enacting laws imposing liability for failure to report on those mandated to file child abuse reports. State laws also grant immunity for those who are mandated to report; thus individuals need not fear lawsuits for invasion of privacy, defamation, or some other cause of action.

Federal funds are available to states that meet certain requirements for reporting cases of abuse or neglect. The ultimate purpose of all these laws, federal and state, is to increase the reporting of children in danger of abuse or neglect and to provide more comprehensive services for those children and their families. Counselors and educators are in key positions to assist in these efforts, and they are legally required to do so.

NOTES

1. M. R. Friedman, *Unequal and Inadequate Protection Under the Law: State Child Abuse Statutes,* 50 Geo. Wash. L. Rev. 234-274 (1982).

2. See generally U.S. Department of Health and Human Services, *Study Findings, Child Maltreatment 1998* (Washington, D.C.: Report by the National Center on Child Abuse and Neglect, 1998).

3. For more information, see Child Abuse Prevention, Adoption, and Family Services Act of 1988, Pub. L. No. 100-294, §§101-401, 42 U.S.C. § 5101.

4. Pub. L. No. 102-295 (1992); and see *Child Maltreatment 1998, id.,* for more recent legislation.

5. ALASKA STAT. ch. 17, § 47.17.010.

6. VT. STAT. ANN. tit. 13, §§ 1351-1356 (Supp. 1981–1982).

7. B. G. Fraser, *A Glance at the Past, A Gaze at the Present, A Glimpse at the Future: A Critical Analysis of the Development of Child Abuse Reporting Statutes,* 54 CHI.-KENT L. REV. 641, 643 (1978).

8. U.S. Department of Health, Education and Welfare Child Abuse & Neglect, State Reporting Laws (Washington, D.C.: special report from the National Center on Child Abuse and Neglect, DHHS Pub. No. (OHDS) 80-30265, 1977), at 3.

9. *Id.* at 5.

10. Protection of Children Against Sexual Exploitation Act of 1977, 18 U.S.C. 2251, as amended in 1984.

11. Such laws are found in Arkansas, Colorado, Idaho, Maine, Utah, West Virginia, American Samoa, and the Virgin Islands. See *supra* note 8, at 3.

12. For an excellent guide to the use of such clues and interviews, see *supra* note 8 at 20-27.

13. *Phillips* v. *Behnke,* 531 NW.2d 619 (Wis. Ct. App. 1995).

14. *Id.* at 622.

15. *Arkansas Department of Human Services* v. *Caldwell,* 832 SW.2d 510 (Ark. Ct. App. 1992).

16. *Lewis* v. *Department of Children and Family Services,* 1994 270265 (N.D. Ill. 1994).

17. *Arkansas Department of Human Services* v. *Heath,* 848 SW.2d 927 (Ark. 1993).

18. *Cavarretta* v. *Department of Children and Family Services,* 660 N.E.2d 250, (Ill. App. Ct. 2d Dist. 1996).

19. MO. REV. STAT. § 210.115(3) (Supp. 1979).

20. See, e.g., *In re Sampson,* 278 N.E.2d 918 (Ct. of Appeals of New York 1972). For a list of states granting religious immunity as well as modified immunity, see *supra* note 8, at 15.

21. J. Aaron, *Civil Liability for Teachers' Negligent Failure to Report Suspected Child, Abuse,* 28 WAYNE L. REV. 183-213 (1981).

22. *Id.*

23. *Landeros* v. *Flood,* 551 P.2d 389 (Cal. 1976).

24. *Pesce* v. *J. Sterling Morton High School,* 830 F.2d 789 (7th Cir. 1987).

25. *DeShaney* v. *Winnebago County Department of Social Services,* 489 U.S. 189 (1989).

8 How Does Copyright Law Affect Me?

Overview

Copyright law gives authors and artists the right to own their creative works. Under principles of state law adopted from the law in England, authors have the right to publish their writings first. In addition to this common-law "right of first publication," federal law also provides protection, giving authors the exclusive right to control who can make copies of their work. A comprehensive law that became effective on January 1, 1978 describes the procedures that must be followed to obtain a federal copyright.[1] This chapter describes that law, answering such questions as: What materials can be copyrighted? How long does a copyright last? Can teachers copyright their own teaching materials? Can teachers make photocopies of published materials without violating copyright laws? What are the penalties for violating copyright laws?

Introduction to Copyright Law

Copyright law is a branch of property law which protects the creative works of authors. For the purposes of copyright law, "authors" are not only the individuals who produce written works, but also those who produce musical, dramatic, or other pictorial or graphic works. Almost any type of original work can be copyrighted; the only exceptions are inventions that deal with machines, which are covered by patent law, and symbols used to identify businesses, which are covered by trademark law.

The purpose of a copyright is to give the author the right to establish ownership of a creative work and to prevent anyone else from copying it or using it in any other way without the author's permission. A copyright gives the author the exclusive right to reproduce copies, prepare derivative works, distribute copies, and publicly display the copyrighted work. It also gives the author the power to transfer these rights to others.

Our current law can be traced to Renaissance Italy when the Italian city-states gave authors and architects exclusive rights over their works, and to sixteenth-century England, when the law protected the printer but not the author. In the United States, a copyright clause was included in the U.S. Constitution, giving Congress the enumerated power to pass laws "[t]o promote the progress of science and useful arts, by securing for limited times to authors and inventors the exclusive right to their respective writings and discoveries."[2] The first federal copyright law was passed in 1790.

In addition to this federal legislation, there is a common law of copyright. Common law refers to the rules of law that developed over time from decisions made by courts in individual cases in the various states. Prior to 1978, this common law of copyright existed along with various revisions of the federal copyright statute. On January 1, 1978, a new copyright law[3] went into effect that is so comprehensive as to supersede most rules under the common law. This chapter examines this federal law. Because so many works currently in existence were created prior to 1978, a brief discussion of the common law is also included.

Materials Covered by Copyright

The *Williams* Case[4]

Do Teachers Have a Copyright on Their Own Materials?

Operating a business known as Class Notes, Edwin Weisser published and sold outlines and notes from various courses at the University of California at Los Angeles (UCLA). Weisser obtained these materials by paying UCLA students to attend classes and turn over copies of their notes to him. In 1965, Weisser paid Karen Allen to attend Dr. Williams' class in Anthropology I and provide him with typed copies of notes from the lectures. After Allen delivered her notes, Weisser put a copyright notice on them in the name of Class Notes and sold them to other students. When Williams discovered that notes from his lectures were being offered for sale by Class Notes, he sued Weisser. Williams claimed that the lecture notes were his property and that they were protected by a common-law copyright. He asked the court to prohibit Weisser from publishing the notes and to award him a sum of money as damages.

The California court agreed with Williams. First, the court found that the lectures were indeed protected by a common-law copyright. Weisser argued that the lectures were "merely lightly embellished and thinly disguised paraphrases of the works of others, both as to form and content...[and were] wholly in the public domain." The court, however, found that the lectures were created by Williams and were therefore covered by the common-law copyright law that gave the author the first right to publish the notes.

The court also rejected Weisser's argument that Williams lost his common-law copyright protection when he delivered his lectures. The court recognized that an author loses a copyright under common law after the materials have been made generally available but concluded that Williams was not making "general" publication when he delivered his lectures:

> [W]here the persons present at a lecture are not the general public, but a limited class of the public selected and admitted for the sole and special purpose of receiving individual instruction, they rightly make any use they can of the lecture, to the extent of taking it down in shorthand, for their own information and improvement, but cannot publish it.

Finally, the court considered whether the university owned the copyright on Williams' lecture notes. The court noted that while the common law gives the copyright to the creator of an intellectual or artistic work, employers own the copyright on materials their employees produce as part of their job. Under this doctrine of "work for hire," the employer owns the copyright only when the materials are created as part of the employee's duties and when the employer has control over the employee's work product. In the case of a university professor, the court concluded that this doctrine did not apply and that Williams owned the copyright on his lectures. As the court explained:

> A university's obligation to its students is to make the subject matter covered by a course available for study by various methods, including classroom presentation.... As far as the teacher is concerned, neither the record in this case nor any custom known to us suggests that the university can prescribe his way of expressing the ideas he puts before his students.

Finding that Weisser had indeed violated Williams' common-law copyright in his lecture notes, the court ordered Weisser to pay him $1,500 as damages.

What Material Can Be Covered by a Copyright?

As the court explained in *Williams,* a common-law copyright protects all intellectual products including writings, drawings, photographs and musical scores, before publication. A copyright does not cover everything, however. The basic rule of copyright is that expression is protected but that ideas are not. A teacher can copyright his or her lecture notes in a math class, for example, but no one can copyright a mathematical formula.

In determining what constitutes "publication," the courts have held that a common-law copyright applies up to the point of *general* publication. Thus the common law protected Williams' limited publication of his lecture notes. The common law did not protect another university employee, however, who submitted a grant proposal through the university administration to the government. The court in that case stated that a limited publication is one directed "to a definitely selected group and for a limited purpose and without the right of diffusion, reproduction, distribution, or sale,"[5] and that the university employee had engaged in a general publication when the grant proposal was so widely distributed.

The Copyright Act of 1976 supersedes this common-law protection, providing that federal copyright law covers all works that are "fixed in any tangible medium of expression."[6] Federal copyright therefore applies as soon as an author uses a pen or a typewriter to put ideas on paper, or as soon as an artist puts paint on a canvas. In addition, federal law covers such other "fixed" works as sound recordings and computer programs. In fact, almost the only creative works not covered by federal copyright law are extemporaneous performances, such as dances or musical compositions. In those situations, state law still applies to protect the creator's ownership of the artistic product.

What Is the Significance of Having a Copyright under Federal Law?

Any author who has a federal copyright has, in effect, a monopoly on the materials created; the author has the right to control how the materials are to be distributed to the general public. Under the copyright act, the copyright owner has the exclusive right to reproduce the work, prepare derivative works, distribute copies by sale or other transfer, and display the work publicly. Under this law, copying includes fixing a work in any form through which it can be "perceived, reproduced, or otherwise communicated, either directly or with the aid of a machine or device"[7] and therefore includes copying a work on paper or onto a magnetic tape or other recording device. Protection under federal copyright law enables the copyright owner to go to federal court to sue anyone who reproduces, distributes, or displays copies of the owner's work without permission.

How Can I Obtain a Copyright?

Federal law gives authors and artists the right to own their creative works as soon as they are "fixed" in a tangible form.

Under the Copyright Act of 1976, an author or artist was required to put a copyright "notice" on all copies of the work. The notice had to include the following:

1. the symbol © or the words "copyright" or "Copr.,"
2. the year of first publication of the work, and
3. the name of the owner of the copyright.[8]

The notice also had to be placed in such manner and location as to give reasonable notice of the claim of copyright.[9] While failure to affix a notice did not destroy a copyright, it meant that anyone who used the materials before the notice was given would not be liable for damages and could only be enjoined from further infringing use.[10]

In 1988 this law changed when Congress passed the Berne Convention Implementation Act, which made the United States a party to the Convention for the Protection of Literary and Artistic Works. The Berne Convention has been in effect for over 100 years and over 100 other countries participate. Our participation made it easier to have access to courts in other countries to enforce copyright violations. Since March 1, 1989, when the act went into effect, authors and artists are no longer required to place a copyright notice on their works. Affixing such a notice, however, prohibits anyone from raising a defense that they "innocently" infringed a copyright and thus are not liable for the full amount of actual or statutory damages.[11]

An author who wishes to be fully protected must register the copyright and deposit two copies of the work along with a nominal fee with the copyright office within three months after the work is published.[12] An author who does not register a copyright will not be able to maintain a suit against anyone who makes unauthorized copies. Registration and deposit are also necessary before a court can take certain actions against those who violate a copyright.

When a Copyright Notice Is Required, Is a Copyright Lost If the Author Does Not Follow These Procedures?

For works produced prior to March 1, 1989, that are required to have a copyright, the law provides that a copyright is not lost when an author omits the copyright notice from only a "relatively small number"[13] of copies distributed to the public. In addition, the act states that even an author who distributes copies without a copyright notice will retain the copyright if the author registers the work with the copyright office within five years of publication and if a "reasonable effort"[14] is made to add the copyright notice to all copies distributed to the public after the omission was discovered. The courts have held that what constitutes a "reasonable effort" is a question of fact, depending on the circumstances.[15]

How Long Does a Copyright Last?

The "right of first publication" that existed under common law existed indefinitely. Federal law now states that all works created on or after January 1, 1978, have copyrights that last until 50 years after the death of the author. If there is more than one author, the 50-year term begins only after the death of the last surviving author.[16]

Can an Author Sell a Copyright?

Yes. Federal law provides that the owner of a copyright can transfer this right to someone else. Merely transferring the physical object itself is not sufficient to transfer the copyright; the copyright owner must clearly state in writing that he or she is giving someone else the right to make copies of the work. After such transfer is made, federal law gives the new copyright owner the power to sue for violation of the exclusive right to make and distribute copies of the original work.

Who Owns the Copyright When There Is More than One Author?

When two or more authors collaborate on a "joint work," they will both (all) own a right to the entire work. Although the authors can agree among themselves to any other type of division of rights to the work, the law gives each of them the right to transfer his or her interest in the work without asking permission from any of the others.

In many cases, it is easy to determine what is a joint work. As the federal copyright law provides, a joint work is a work "prepared by two or more authors with the intention that their contributions be merged into inseparable or interdependent parts of a unitary whole."[17] When two authors write a book together, the work is clearly a joint work. A question can arise, however, when a work is not "inseparable or interdependent," as in the case of an author and a photographer who collaborate on a picture book. In such a case, whether the work is a joint work will depend on the intent of the author and the photographer when each made his or her contribution.

Does an Employee Own a Copyright on Works Produced on the Job?

Teachers and many other employees produce original works while they are employed. Teachers may create lesson plans, books, and other teaching materials that they wish to copyright. Under a rule known as "work made for hire," however, the author of the work is considered to be the employer; the employee who actually created the work does not own the copyright. Thus the copyright to any materials that a teacher produces within the scope of his or her employment is owned by the school district (or other employer).

In 1989, the U.S. Supreme Court decided a case that provided additional guidance as to what constitutes a "work prepared by an employee within the scope of his or her employment."[18] In that case, the Community for Creative Non-Violence (CCNV), an organization dedicated to eliminating homelessness, decided to sponsor a Christmas display that would dramatize the plight of the homeless. One of CCNV's trustees contacted James Earl Reid, a sculptor, and Reid agreed to sculpt three human beings along with a shopping cart. CCNV hired others to produce additional parts of the display, including the pedestal. Neither CCNV nor Reid discussed who would own the copyright, but when Reid later objected to

CCNV's plan to take the sculpture on tour, Reid and CCNV both filed applications for copyright registration. CCNV claimed that Reid was their "employee" because CCNV had conceived of and directed the project and that the sculpture was a work made for hire.

The U.S. Supreme Court disagreed. The Court looked at the history behind the copyright act and concluded that Congress had intended to adopt the common-law distinction between employees and independent contractors. Under these common-law principles, one partner's right to control the manner and means by which the product is accomplished is only one of the factors to consider, others include:

> the skill required; the source of the instrumentalities and tools: the location of the work; the duration of the relationship between the parties; whether the hiring party has the right to assign additional projects to the hired party; the extent of the hired party's discretion over when and how long to work; the method of payment; the hired party's role in hiring paying assistants; whether the work is part of the regular business of the hiring party; whether the hiring party is in business; the provision of employee benefits; and the tax treatment of the hired party. No one of these factors is determinative.[19]

Applying these factors, the Court held that Reid was not an employee of CCNV but an independent contractor. Although CCNV directed Reid's work, all other factors weighed against finding an employment relationship (Reid supplied his own tools, worked in his own studio, was retained for a short period of time, and had absolute freedom to decide when and how long to work). The Court left open the question of whether CCNV could be considered a joint author of the sculpture; if so, CCNV and Reid would be co-owners of the copyright in the work.

Under the reasoning of this case, a teacher who acts as an "independent contractor" can obtain a copyright. A reading teacher, for example, might agree to produce materials for the school district. If the district relies on the teacher's expertise, specially compensates the teacher for this project, requests that the teacher use his or her own equipment and resources, and otherwise gives the teacher complete freedom as to how to structure the materials, the teacher could be considered an independent contractor and not subject to the work-for-hire doctrine. A teacher could also avoid the application of this doctrine by signing a contract with the employer limiting the employer's rights in two ways. First, the contract could specify that certain types of activities, such as any materials presented at national professional meetings, will not be considered within the scope of employment. Second, the contract could give the teacher rights other than ownership of the copyright. For example, under such terms, the employer, which still owns the copyright, could give the teacher the right to reproduce or distribute curriculum materials.

How Does Copyright Law Apply to Works Appearing on the Internet?

Courts have applied the basic doctrines of copyright law to protect works appearing on and distributed by the internet. In 2001, for example, the Ninth Circuit held that a file sharing program distributed by the Napster Corporation which allowed users to share and download "free" digitized music files over the Internet infringed upon music industry's and artists' copyrights. The court granted injunctive relief[20] requiring the corporation to ensure copyrighted music was no longer being distributed using its program. For teachers, the implications are obvious: students may not be encouraged in the classroom to utilize infringing forms of technology.

Congress has also modified copyright statutes to make the rules concerning enforcement of copyrights on the Internet easier. One recent statutory change gives Internet service providers a safe harbor from infringing material posted by others on websites hosted by those service providers if the service providers do not edit the material on the sites and provide warnings against the posting of copyrighted material without permission.[21] The statute also provides a legal process under which Internet service providers will reveal the identity of a user who posts material which infringes a copyright.

Fair Use

Is It Ever Possible to Make Copies of an Author's Copyrighted Work without First Securing Permission?

Yes. Under a doctrine known as "fair use," courts have ruled that it is in the public interest to allow certain uses of copyrighted materials. Generally, it is not a violation of a copyright to use the "idea" or "system" developed by an author. Although an author has a monopoly on the particular form of expression created, the author has no exclusive right to control dissemination of the theory developed. Another author can quote Einstein's theory of relativity, for example, without violating any copyright held by Einstein. In addition, the courts have held that it is a fair use of copyrighted material to make copies in news reporting, criticism, or scholarly research. For example, a scholar who as part of doing research copies a short quotation from an earlier writer in the field does not violate the copyright laws.

What Is "Fair Use"?

The doctrine of fair use is an exception to the general rules of copyright law that allows use of copyrighted material in a reasonable manner without the user's securing the copyright owner's consent. The doctrine is designed to balance the exclusive rights of the copyright owner against the public's interest in dissemination of information of universal concern. When determining whether a particular use of copyrighted material is fair use, courts consider the purpose of the fair use doctrine[22] and the following statutory criteria:

1. the purpose and character of the use, including whether such use is of a commercial nature or is for nonprofit educational purpose.
2. the nature of the copyrighted work;
3. the amount and substantiality of the portion used in relation to the copyrighted work as a whole;
4. the effect of the use upon the potential market for or value of the copyrighted work.[23]

An example of what the U.S. Supreme Court considered not to be fair use occurred in a case where Harper & Row had been given the exclusive right to license prepublication excerpts of President Ford's memoirs.[24] Harper & Row agreed to let *Time* magazine publish a 7,000-word excerpt from the memoirs, but, shortly before the excerpt was to appear in *Time,* an unauthorized source sent a copy of the manuscript to the *Nation.* The *Nation* then published a 2,950-word article, using between 300 and 400 words of the copyrighted material. As a result, *Time* decided not to publish its scheduled article and refused to pay the $12,500 it still owed Harper & Row.

The Supreme Court examined the four factors listed in the federal law defining fair use and held that the *Nation*'s use was not fair. First, the Court found the fact that the subject matter was new was not determinative: the *Nation* was publishing for commercial purposes and timed to exploit the headline value of its infringement. Second, even though the nature of the work was fact and not fiction, the *Nation*'s publication went far beyond what was necessary to disseminate the facts. Third, although the quotes from the copyrighted material were only a small portion of the total, they constituted the essence of Ford's distinctive expression. The Court also looked at the fourth factor, the effect of the use on the potential market, and stated that this factor is undoubtedly "the single most important element of fair use." The Court found that *Time*'s cancellation of its projected serialization and its refusal to pay the $12,500 owed to Harper & Row were the direct effect of the infringement and that this case presented "clear-cut evidence of actual damage." Finally, the Court went on to clarify the burden of proof in this area, explaining that once a copyright holder establishes a causal connection between the infringement and loss of revenue, the burden shifts to the infringer to show that the damage would have occurred had there been no infringement of the copyright. To negate a claim of fair use, it is necessary only to show that if the challenged use should become widespread, it would adversely affect the potential market for the copyrighted work.

In contrast, a New York court found that it was fair use for a physician to present a medical syllabus at a nuclear medicine review course.[25] The physician was a collaborator and joint author with another physician, who had previously served as a resident under him and who had presented the same syllabus at another conference two years earlier. After concluding that the physicians were joint authors and thus each entitled to license work without the other's consent, the court went on to explain that even if they were not joint authors such a publication would be fair use. The court reached its conclusion by applying the factors described above in Harper & Row as follows: (1) the use was entirely noncommercial and for nonprofit educational purposes (the physician neither profited nor stood to profit from any publication); (2) the nature of the work was factual and scientific in nature and already published by the plaintiff; (3) the entire syllabus was copied, and the content virtually in its entirety had been published by both authors; (4) the use of the syllabus would not impair its market value, and dissemination of results and research at any institution would in all likelihood only increase the "marketability" of a paper emanating from that department.

Are There Any Fair Use Exceptions for Teachers?

Although members of Congress did not agree on standards for educational copying, they did endorse guidelines developed by the Ad Hoc Committee of Educational Institutions and Organizations on Copyright Law Revision, the Author's League of America, Inc., and the Association of American Publishers, Inc. These guidelines are included in the official comments on the statute[26] and list a number of specific exceptions for teachers. First, teachers are permitted to make *single* copies of the following copyrighted works for their own use in scholarly research or classroom preparation:

1. a chapter from a book;
2. an article from a periodical or newspaper;
3. a short story, short essay, or short poem;
4. a chart, graph, diagram, drawing, cartoon, or picture from a book, newspaper, or periodical.

In addition, a teacher can make multiple copies of the following copyrighted works for use in the classroom (with the number of copies not to exceed one copy per student in the class), provided that copying meets certain tests of brevity, spontaneity, and cumulative effect and that each copy includes a notice of copyright. The definition of *brevity* is as follows:

1. a complete poem, if it is less than 250 words and printed on not more than two pages;
2. an excerpt from a longer poem, if it is not more that 250 words;
3. a complete article, story. or essay if it is less than 2,500 words;
4. an excerpt from a prose work, if it is less than 1,000 words or 10 percent of the work, whichever is less;
5. one chart, diagram. cartoon, or picture per book or periodical.

The definition of *spontaneity* is as follows:

1. the copying is at the instance and inspiration of the individual teacher, and,
2. the inspiration and decision to use the work and the moment of its use for maximum teaching effectiveness are so close in time that it would be unreasonable to expect a timely reply to a request for permission.

To meet the test of *cumulative effect:*

1. the copying of the material is for only one course in the school in which the copies are made;
2. not more than one short poem, article, story, essay; or two excerpts are copied from the same author, or more than three from the same collective work or periodical volume during one class term;
3. there are not more than nine instances of such multiple copying for one course during one class term.[27]

In addition, teachers cannot make copies of "consumable" materials, such as workbooks or answer sheets to standardized tests. Finally teachers are prohibited from making a copy of works to take the place of an anthology.

In addition to the exceptions for copying, the Act also exempts certain public performances. For example, the performance of a copyrighted dramatic work by students and teachers in the classroom is not a copyright violation. If students give a "public performance" of a copyrighted work, however, they will be protected from copyright violation only when there is no admission charge and no compensation paid to any performer or promoter. Even when students perform without pay, if the school charges admission to the performance, the copyright owner has the right to prohibit the performance by giving proper notice.[28]

Teachers who do not follow these guidelines can be held liable for copyright infringement. In a 1983 case, for example, a teacher was held liable for damages when she prepared a booklet entitled "Cake Decorating Learning Activity Package" (LAP) for use in her food service career classes.[29] The teacher admitted copying 11 of the 24 in her LAP from a copyrighted book entitled *Cake Decorating Made Easy,* written by a former home economics teacher, and admitted putting 15 copies of the LAP on file so that they would be available to her students over a three-year period. The court found that the teacher's copying did not meet the guidelines for making multiple classroom copies because neither the tests for "brevity" nor "spontaneity" were met, nor did any copy include a notice of copyright.

Are There Any "Fair Use" Exceptions for Libraries?

Yes. These federal copyright law exceptions apply only in cases where the following standards are met:

1. the library is making a reproduction without any purpose of commercial advantage,
2. the library collection is open to the public,
3. the library reproduces no more than one copy of a work,
4. the reproduction includes a notice of copyright.[30]

A library complying with these requirements is permitted to make copies in the following situations:

1. to preserve in facsimile form an unpublished work currently in the library or for another library (such as putting a copy of a doctoral dissertation on microfiche);
2. to replace in facsimile form a published work that is damaged, lost, or stolen if the library has, after reasonable effort, determined that an unused replacement cannot be obtained at a fair price;
3. in response to a request by a user or by another library on behalf of a user. (This exemption applies only if the copy becomes the property of the user, the library has no reason to believe that it will be used for purposes other than private study or research, and the library displays a copyright warning notice.)

In addition, the law provides that a library shall not be liable for copyright infringement by its patrons where it displays on its copying equipment a notice that the making of a copy may be subject to the copyright law.[31]

Is It Fair Use to Copy Computer Software for Educational Purposes?

No. Computer programs are eligible for copyright.[32] Neither the federal copyright law nor guidelines mentioned above apply to copying computer software, and such copying is not fair use. The federal law was amended in 1980, however, to provide that the owner of a copy of a copyrighted program does not infringe the copyright if the "new copy or adaptation is created as an essential step in the utilization of the program in conjunction with a machine" or if the new copy or adaptation is for archival (backup) purposes only.[33] Thus teachers who load a copyrighted program onto a classroom terminal or make a backup copy of a program are not infringing a copyright, but a teacher who makes copies of software for students or who uses the original program in one terminal while a student uses the backup copy is.

Because it is so easy to copy computer software,[34] schools must be especially careful to educate students and teachers about illegal copying.[35] In 1992, the U.S. Departments of Justice and Education jointly issued a report calling on the nation's schools to expand their teaching of the ethical use of computers.[36] Educational institutions that do not do so may be the subject of lawsuits. In 1991, for example, the Software Publishers Association filed suit against the University of Oregon, charging their continuing-education center with illegally copying computer programs onto 60 computers. The case was later settled out of court with the university agreeing to pay $130,000 for software copyright infringement.[37]

Schools can also protect themselves by entering into contractual agreements with software companies (site licenses). For example, local districts can negotiate with software suppliers for reasonably priced copies of educational software that can be downloaded onto an in-school network system. School districts can also negotiate for rights to duplicate from the purchased copy only the number of copies needed to service the number of teachers or computers in a particular school.

Is It Fair Use to Videotape for Educational Purposes?

The federal law allows only libraries or archives to tape an audiovisual news program.[38] As in the case of educational photocopy, the original law did not include specific rules for educational videotaping. To deal with this issue, in 1979 the House Judiciary Committee formed a committee of representatives of educational organizations, copyright proprietors, and creative guilds and unions to develop appropriate guidelines.[39] The committee submitted guidelines that applied to off-air recording by nonprofit educational institutions. In general, these guidelines provide that nonprofit educational institutions may videotape copyrighted television programs broadcast to the general public but may keep the tape for only 45 days (unless they obtain a license). At the end of 45 days, the tape must be erased or destroyed. During the first 10 consecutive school days after taping, teachers may use the tapes for instructional purposes, but they may repeat such use only once for purposes of instructional reinforcement. After this 10-day period, the tape may be used only for purposes of evaluating its educational usefulness.

There have been a number of court cases involving the question of whether videotaping constitutes fair use. In a New York case, a federal district court found that a nonprofit educational service agency was guilty of copyright violations.[40] The service agency had routinely copied all daytime programs broadcast by the local public television station, as well as some evening programs on commercial stations, and had maintained a library of 4,300 videotapes that were available for distribution to teachers at over 100 schools. The court stated that the "massive and systematic videotape copying"[41] and the highly sophisticated methods used by defendants could not be considered fair use.

In 1984, the U.S. Supreme Court decided a videotaping case that, while not directly involving education, establishes a standard for fair use in videotaping.[42] The issue in the case was whether Sony Corporation's sale of videotaping equipment to the general public constituted an infringement of copyright. The Court held that private home-use "time-shifting" was permissible, finding little harm to the television market where viewers merely changed the time that they saw a freely available television program. The Court did not endorse taping of programs for use outside the home, however, and educators who wish to use off-air recordings in the classroom are advised to follow the guidelines discussed above. In situations not covered by the guidelines, such as taping of a cable program, the legality of the teacher's actions will still be analyzed under the doctrine of fair use. Although no court has yet considered the question, the best case for such a fair use exception would seem to be one where the program taped is not commercially available either for rental or purchase, and the teacher's classroom use therefore does not affect the producer's market value.

Is It Fair Use to Copy Excerpts from Books, Compile Them into Course Packets, and Sell Them to College Students?

In a 1991 case, *Basic Books, Inc.* v. *Kinko's,* a federal district court said no.[43] Kinko's was sued by major publishing houses for copyright infringement when Kinko's copied excerpts from books without getting permission from the publishers and sold the copies for a profit. Kinko's admitted that it sold the materials to college students in the form of course packets (which Kinko's called anthologies) but defended its actions on a number of grounds. First, Kinko's argued that its use of the excerpts in the anthologies was fair use. The court examined the four factors listed in the copyright act and ruled for the publishers. First, the court noted that Kinko's use was commercial and that it was a mere repackaging, adding nothing to the original, thus weighing against the defendant. The second factor, the nature of the copyrighted work, was a factor weighing in favor of the defendant because the copyrighted works were factual and the scope of fair use is greater with respect to factual than nonfactual works. Third, the court examined the amount and substantiality of the portion used. Here, the court found that in almost ever case, Kinko's copied at least an entire chapter of a plaintiff's book, and it concluded that the portions copied were critical parts, meant to stand alone as a complete representation of a concept. This factor also then weighed against Kinko's. The fourth factor, market effect, also failed the defendant. The court noted that Kinko's had 900 stores nationwide, with a potential for widespread copyright infringement. Finally, the court mentioned that this case presented an important additional factor: the fact that Kinko's had effectively created a new nationwide business by usurping the plaintiffs' copyrights and profits. The court concluded that "this cannot be sustained by this court as its result is complete frustration of the intent of the copyright law."

The court then went on to analyze whether Kinko's publication of anthologies was protected as educational copying under the classroom guidelines. The court explained that it was examining the guidelines because, even though Kinko's was not a teacher or part of an educational institution, the court found the circumstance of copying for college students to be particularly compelling. However, the court concluded that even if Kinko's copying had warranted review under the classroom guidelines, it was excessive and in violation of the guidelines' requirements. The court awarded the plaintiffs injunctive relief as well as statutory damages of $510,000 and attorneys' fees and costs.

How Can I Get Permission to Photocopy or Videotape in Cases Where There Is No Fair Use Exception?

Teachers who believe that their photocopying or videotaping goes beyond fair use should get written permission to copy or tape from the copyright owner. In requesting permission. the teacher should specify: the exact material to be copied, the number of copies, and the proposed use of these materials.

Copyright Violation

Are All Schools Liable for Damages When Charged with Copyright Violations?

It depends upon whether the school district is considered as an agency of the state government. After a number of federal courts[44] had held that states and their agents were immune from suit under the Eleventh Amendment, Congress amended the copyright law to abrogate immunity.[45] However, in 1999 the Supreme Court, ruling on a similar immunity statute for patents, held that Congress lacked the power to abrogate state immunity.[46] One federal circuit has ruled that the statute abrogating state immunity from copyright violations is also invalid.[47] However, in most states local boards of education are not considered as state agencies, and so they are indeed liable for damages under copyright infringement laws.

What Are the Penalties for Violating a Copyright?

The Copyright Act of 1976 provides that the owner of a copyright can sue anyone who "infringes" his or her exclusive right to control the distribution of literary or artistic property.[48]

In a suit for copyright infringement, a court has the power to issue an injunction to prevent people from making or distributing further copies of a work. A court may also impound all copies claimed to have been made in violation of the owner's copyright. If the court later finds that there has been a copyright violation, it can order that all illegal copies be destroyed or otherwise disposed of. The copyright act also states that the copyright owner can collect either one of the following monetary awards:

1. any actual damages the copyright owner has sustained, as well as any profits the copyright infringer has made; or
2. an amount of money to be determined by the court, which can range from $500 to $20,000 for an infringement of any one work. If the court finds that the infringer acted willfully: the court can increase the award to $100,000; if the infringer was unaware that he or she was violating someone else's copyright, the court can award as little as $200.[49]

Criminal sanctions are levied against infringers if the infringement was willful and for purposes of commercial advantage or private financial gain.[50] The copyright act also makes certain noninfringements criminal acts, including placing a copyright notice that a person knows to be false on an article,[51] and removing or altering, with fraudulent intent, any notice of copyright on a copy of the copyrighted work.[52]

However, even when the copyright owner cannot show that he or she was damaged in any specific uses (e.g., through a loss of sales of the work), the court can still make a monetary award. For example, one author's copyright was violated when two commercial book companies published and sold copies of his book without his permission.[53] Although both publishing companies lost money on the book, and the author could not show that he had suffered any damages, the court still awarded the author 10 cents for every copy that was sold. In addition, as the copyright act allows, the court made an award to cover the costs of the author's attorneys' fees in bringing the suit.

Summary

Copyright law gives authors property rights in their work. Under the common law they have the right of first publication. Once authors publish or distribute a creative work, however, this protection under the common law is lost and the authors must look to federal law to protect their right to control distribution of the work. Federal law protects all literary and artistic works from the moment that they are "fixed" in some form, whether in writing or on a computer disk.

To establish a copyright under federal law, an author or artist merely places the proper copyright notice on all copies of the work. To fully protect his or her rights, the copyright owner must also register and deposit copies of the work with the Copyright Office. Federal law provides various remedies for copyright infringement, including the owner's right to monetary damages and criminal sanctions against the perpetrator in cases of willful infringement. However, exceptions to the copyright laws enable so-called "fair use," which includes noncommercial, educational purposes.

NOTES

1. Copyright Act of 1976, 17 U.S.C. §§ 101–1010.
2. U.S. Const., Art. I, § 8, cl. 8.
3. See 17 U.S.C. §§ 101–1010.
4. *Williams* v. *Weisser,* 78 Cal. Rptr. 542 (Ct. App. 1969).
5. *White* v. *Kimmel,* 193 F.2d 744, 746 (9th Cir. 1952).
6. 17 U.S.C. § 102.
7. 17 U.S.C. § 101.
8. 17 U.S.C. § 401(a) & (b).
9. 17 U.S.C. § 401(c).
10. 17 U.S.C. § 405(b).
11. 17 U.S.C. § 401(d).
12. For information on how to register, see the U.S. Copyright Office website at http://www.loc.gov/copyright/.
13. 17 U.S.C. § 405(a)(1).
14. 17 U.S.C. § 405(a)(2).
15. *Princess Fabrics, Inc.* v. *CHF, Inc.,* 922 F.2d 99 (2nd Cir. 1990).
16. 17 U.S.C. § 302.
17. 17 U.S.C. § 101.
18. *Community for Creative Non-Violence* v. *Reid,* 490 U.S. 730 (1989).

19. *Id.* at 751–52.

20. *A&M Records* v. *Napster, Inc.*, 239 F.3d 1004 (9th Cir. 2001).

21. 17 U.S.C. § 512.

22. *Educational Testing Service* v. *Stanley H. Kaplan Educational Center, Inc.*, 965 F. Supp. 731 (D. Md. 1997).

23. 17 U.S.C. § 107.

24. *Harper & Row Publishers, Inc.* v. *Nation Enterprises*, 471 U.S. 539 (1985).

25. *Weissmann* v. *Freeman*, 684 F. Supp. 1284 (S.D. N.Y. 1988), *aff'd in part and rev'd in part*, 868 F.2d 1313 (2nd Cir. 1989); *see also Arica Institute, Inc.* v. *Palmer*, 761 F. Supp. 1056 (S.D. N.Y. 1991).

26. Notes of Committee on the Judiciary, H.R. No. 94-1476, 94th Cong., 201 Sess. 68–70 (1976).

27. Numbers 2 and 3 of the cumulative effect test do not apply to current news periodicals and newspapers.

28. 17 U.S.C. § 110(4)(b).

29. *Marcus* v. *Rowley*, 695 F.2d 1171 (9th Cir. 1983).

30. 17 U.S.C. § 108.

31. 17 U.S.C. § 108(f)(1).

32. 17 U.S.C. §§ 102(a), 117. Copyright protection extends to nonliteral aspects of a computer program. *Lotus Development Corp.* v. *Borland International, Inc.*, 831 F. Supp. 223 (D. Mass. 1993); *Digital Communications Associates, Inc.* v. *Softklone Distributing Corp.*, 659 F. Supp. 449 (N.D. Ga. 1987).

33. 17 U.S.C. § 117.

34. The software industry estimates that $2.4 billion worth of their products—almost half of their total sales of $5.7 billion—were stolen in 1990 in the United States and Canada. *Chicago Daily Law Bulletin*, July 28, 1992, at 3.

35. For a model school district software policy, see John Soma & Dwight Pringle, *Computer Software in the Public Schools*, 28 ED. LAW REP. 315, 323–24 (1985).

36. Chicago Daily Law Bulletin, July 28, 1992, at 3.

37. *Workplace Expectations, Computerworld*, Oct. 31, 1991, at 31.

38. 17 U.S.C. § 108(f)(3).

39. Guidelines for Off-Air Recording of Broadcast Programming for Educational Purposes, 97 *Cong. Rec.* § E4751 daily ed. (Oct. 14, 1981).

40. *Encyclopedia Britannica Educational Corp.* v. *Crooks*, 542 F. Supp. 1156 (W.D. N.Y. 1982).

41. *Id.* at 1181.

42. *Sony Corp. of America* v. *Universal City Studios, Inc.*, 464 U.S. 417 (1984).

43. *Basic Books, Inc.* v. *Kinko's Graphics Corp.*, 758 F. Supp. 1522 (S.D. N.Y. 1991).

44. *Richard Anderson Photography* v. *Radford University*, 633 F. Supp. 1154 (W.D. Va. 1986), *aff'd in part and rev'd in part; Richard Anderson Photography* v. *Brown*, 852 F.2d 114 (4th Cir. 1988); *BV Engineering* v. *University of California, Los Angeles*, 858 F.2d 1394 (4th Cir. 1988).

45. 17 U.S.C. § 511(a) (1991).

46. *Florida Prepaid Secondary Education Expense Board* v. *College Savings Bank*, 119 S.Ct. 2199 (1999).

47. *Rodriguez* v. *Texas Commission on the Arts*, 199 F.3d 279 (5th Cir. 2000).

48. 17 U.S.C. § 501(b).

49. 17 U.S.C. § 504.

50. 17 U.S.C. § 506(a).

51. 17 U.S.C. § 506(c).

52. 17 U.S.C. § 506(a).

53. *Robinson* v. *Bantam Books, Inc.*, 339 F. Supp. 150 (S.D. N.Y. 1972).

PART TWO

Teachers' and Students' Rights

CHAPTER

9

When Can Schools Restrict Freedom of Expression?

Overview

During the first half of the 20th century, the Bill of Rights was rarely referred to when teachers or students challenged the constitutionality of school rules. Courts generally used the *reasonableness* test to judge school policies. If there was any reasonable relationship between the rule and some educational purpose, the rule would be upheld even if most judges believed it was unwise, unnecessary, or restricted freedom of expression. Judges felt that school boards should have wide discretion and that courts should not substitute their judgment for that of school officials, who were presumed to be experts in educational matters.

Then, in 1969, the U.S. Supreme Court handed down a historic decision that challenged the reasonableness test. In *Tinker* v. *Des Moines* (discussed later in this chapter), the Court ruled that neither teachers nor students lose their constitutional rights to freedom of expression when they enter the public schools. Of course, the fact that the Constitution now applies to schooling does not mean that teachers and students can say or write anything they wish. When conflicts arise between the rights of teachers or students and the authority of school administrators, it is the job of the courts to balance the legitimate rights in conflict and determine when to protect and when to limit freedom of expression. In resolving these conflicts, the courts establish legal principles that apply to similar cases. On the basis of these cases and principles, this chapter explains when the Constitution protects teachers' freedom to criticize school policy and to use controversial methods and materials, and when students' freedom of speech and of the press are protected.

In this chapter and throughout Part II, we have not separated teachers' and students' rights but have put related issues concerning both in the same chapter.

Criticizing School Policy or Personnel

Does the First Amendment Apply to Public Schools?

Yes. Although the First Amendment originally prohibited only the federal government from abridging freedom of expression, the U.S. Supreme Court has interpreted the Fourteenth Amendment (which prohibits *states* from depriving citizens of life, liberty, or property without due process) to incorporate the provisions of the First Amendment. As a result, neither the federal nor the state governments (including their public schools) can abridge freedom of speech or of the press. As the Supreme Court has written: "The Fourteenth Amendment…protects the citizen against the state itself and all its creatures—Boards of Education not excepted. These have…important…discretionary functions, but none that they may not perform within the limits of the Bill of Rights."[1]

Pickering v. *Board of Education*[2]

An employee of a private business who is discharged for publicly "blasting" the boss has no constitutional right to be reemployed, since the First Amendment applies only to government action. Should a public school teacher have more freedom than an employee in private industry? Or should a teacher have a duty of loyalty to superiors, an obligation to go through prescribed channels before making criticism public, and a greater responsibility than the average citizen to speak carefully and accurately about educational matters? If a teacher fails to exercise this responsibility, what disciplinary actions can a school board take? These are the questions examined in the Pickering case.

Marvin Pickering was a high school teacher from Will County, Illinois, who published a long, sarcastic letter in the local newspaper about the way his superintendent and school board raised and spent school funds. Pickering's letter detailed his objection to the "excessive" athletic expenditures by school officials, who were then allegedly unable to pay teachers' salaries. He also wrote that "taxpayers were really taken to the cleaners" by those who built one of the local schools. And he criticized the "totalitarianism teachers live in" at the high school.

Angered by the letter, the board of education charged that it contained false and misleading statements, "damaged the professional reputations" of school administrators and the board, and was "detrimental to the efficient operation and administration of the schools." Pickering argued that his letter should be protected by his right of free speech, but the Illinois courts ruled against him. Since Pickering held a position as teacher, the state supreme court wrote that he "is no more entitled to harm the schools by speech than by incompetency."

Pickering still believed his letter was protected by the First Amendment, so he appealed to the U.S. Supreme Court. On behalf of the Court, Justice Thurgood Marshall wrote that the problem in this case is "to arrive at a balance between the interests of the teacher, as citizen, in commenting upon matters of public concern, and the interests of the state, as an employer, in promoting the efficiency of the public services it performs through its employees." The Court's examination of the issues in this case are outlined in the questions and answers that follow.

Can a Teacher Be Dismissed for Publicly Criticizing School Policy?

Not usually. The Court found that Pickering's letter consisted mainly of criticism of the school board's allocation of funds and of both the board's and the superintendent's method of informing (or not informing) the taxpayers of the reasons why additional funds were sought. Since such statements were not directed toward people Pickering normally worked with, they raised no question of maintaining discipline by immediate superiors or harmony among co-workers. Pickering's relationships with the board and superintendent, wrote the

Court, "are not the kind of close working relationships for which it can persuasively be claimed that personal loyalty and confidence are necessary." Thus the Court "unequivocally" rejected the board's position that critical public comments by a teacher on matters of public concern may furnish grounds for dismissal.

The question whether a school system requires additional funds is a matter of legitimate public concern. On such an issue, wrote the Court,

> free and open debate is vital to informed decision making by the electorate. Teachers are, as a class, the members of a community most likely to have informed and definite opinions as to how funds allocated to the operation of the schools should be spent. Accordingly, it is essential that they be able to speak out freely on such questions without fear of retaliatory dismissal.

Can a Teacher Be Dismissed for Making Public Statements That Are Not Accurate?

Pickering's inaccurate statements consisted mainly of exaggerated cost claims for the athletic program, the erroneous suggestion that teachers had not been paid on occasion, and a false statement regarding the cost of transporting athletes. The Court found no evidence that these inaccurate statements were intentional or that they damaged the professional reputations of the board and the superintendent. In fact, wrote the Court, "Pickering's letter was greeted by everyone but its main target, the board, with massive apathy."

According to Justice Marshall, the accusation that administrators are spending too much money on athletics cannot be regarded as "detrimental to the district's schools." Such an accusation, wrote the Court, reflects "a difference of opinion between Pickering and the board as to the preferable manner of operating the school system, a difference of opinion that clearly concerns an issue of general public interest."

In sum, Pickering unintentionally made several incorrect statements on current issues that were critical of his employer but did not impede his teaching or interfere with the regular operation of the schools. The Court therefore concluded that "absent proof of false statements knowingly or recklessly made by him, a teacher's exercise of his right to speak on issues of public importance may not furnish the basis for his dismissal from public employment."

Can a Teacher Be Transferred for Publicly Criticizing a School Program?

It depends on the circumstances. The decision in *Pickering* protected a teacher from being fired, but what about a teacher who is simply transferred with no loss of pay or status? In Arizona, a teacher and guidance counselor publicly opposed the way Mexican American children were placed in classes for the mentally retarded, because they were tested in English rather than Spanish. After the teacher suggested that parents could sue to stop this practice, she was transferred to a wealthy school with very few Mexican American children. She felt the transfer violated her rights, and a federal appeals court agreed.[3] The court acknowledged that she had no right initially to be assigned to work with Mexican American children, but once she was given such an assignment, officials could not constitutionally transfer her because of her public criticism. The court concluded that the school's interest in being free from criticism "cannot outweigh the right of a sincere educational counselor to speak out against a policy she believes to be both harmful and unlawful."

In a related Virginia case, a teacher was disciplined because he published a controversial, satirical letter in the high school newspaper about male chauvinism and sex discrimination in physical education classes.[4] In defending the teacher, the judge quoted a U.S. Supreme Court opinion that "the public expression of ideas may not be prohibited merely because the ideas are themselves offensive." The judge concluded that the teacher's "use of satire to comment on a matter of public concern" did not deprive him of First Amendment protection.

Can a School Board Ever Restrict Teachers' Rights to Publicize Their Views?

Yes. In *Pickering,* Justice Marshall wrote: "It is possible to conceive of some positions in public employment in which the need for confidentiality is so great that even completely correct public statements might furnish a permissible ground for dismissal." For example, unprofessional disclosures within the school may not be protected. Thus an Ohio guidance counselor was disciplined for telling a school secretary that two of the students she was counseling were homosexual. In supporting the disciplinary action, an appeals court wrote that this disclosure "was a serious breach of confidence which reflected seriously on the [counselor's] judgment and qualifications" and were "sufficient reason to suspend or reassign her."[5]

In New Jersey, the president of a local teachers' association was dismissed as a result of a speech she gave at an orientation for new teachers. In her speech she described the district as a "snakepit for young teachers" and characterized the superintendent as a "villain" who was "intimately embroiled" in local politics. A state appeals court ruled that her speech was not protected by the First Amendment, that free speech does "not endow a teacher …with a license to vilify superiors publicly."[6] Unlike the case with *Pickering,* the court found that this teacher did not speak directly about issues of public concern "but distorted them into a vehicle to bring scorn and abuse" on the school administration.

An Alabama case involving James Swilley, a teacher who disseminated to the news media charges about a local principal's negligence, led to a different result.[7] The school board reprimanded the teacher because he refused to wait until the board's investigation was complete before publicizing his allegations. Swilley then charged the board with violating his freedom of speech. The court ruled in favor of Swilley because it held that his charge about the principal's negligent conduct was not a "petty personal attack" or a private personnel issue. Rather it was a matter of important public concern about "the physical safety and wellbeing of our school children" and, therefore, was protected by the First Amendment.

Can Teachers Be Disciplined for Publicly Criticizing Their Immediate Superiors?

This would depend on the circumstances. In *Picketing,* Justice Marshall wrote that "certain forms of public criticism of the superior by the subordinate would seriously undermine the effectiveness of the working relationship between them" and thus justify appropriate discipline. In an Alaska case, for example, the court upheld the dismissal of two teachers for publishing an "open letter" to the school board that contained a series of false charges against their immediate superior.[8] Unlike Pickering's letter, these false allegations "were not consistent with good faith and were made in reckless disregard of the truth." (For a discussion of teacher liability for slander and libel, see chapter 7.)

On the other hand, a federal court protected Haywood Lusk, a Texas teacher, after his critical statements received wide media coverage and seriously injured his relationship with his principal.[9] The teacher was dismissed after he testified before the school board and city council that his principal and co-workers were "mentally and sociologically unqualified to deal with modern, complex, multiracial student bodies." He also charged that students in his school "learn to disobey authority, run, lie, cheat and steal" in order to survive. In rejecting Lusk's dismissal, a federal court wrote that his criticism concerned "matters of vital interest to every citizen of Dallas" and that they were properly brought to the attention "of the governing bodies who had the power to act" on them. In this case, the court concluded that "society's interest in information concerning the operation of its schools far outweighs any strain on the teacher–principal relationship."

Can Teachers Always Be Punished If Their Statements Cause Disruption in the School?

Not necessarily. It depends on the facts of the case. In Arkansas, Bob Bowman, an assistant football coach, publicly criticized the head coach, Jimmy Walker, for using excessive corporal punishment. The criticism led to extensive press coverage, intense public debate, and "turmoil in the community." As a result, Walker apologized and kept his job. Bowman, however, was transferred to a less desirable school; he sued, claiming that the transfer violated his rights.

In this case, the court balanced the interests of the teacher against the interests of the school board by considering several factors: (1) the need for harmony in the schools; (2) whether the criticism injured the working relationships; (3) the time, manner, place, and context of the speech; (4) the degree of public interest involved; and (5) the effect of the speech on the teacher's ability to work effectively.[10]

The judge noted that two of the factors clearly favored the school board: Bowman's speech (1) contributed to turmoil in the community, and (2) destroyed his working relationship with Coach Walker. On the other hand, several factors favored Bowman: (1) There was intense public interest in the physical mistreatment of students, (2) Bowman's comments were made at school board meetings and other appropriate places, and (3) there was no evidence that the controversy affected Bowman's ability to work with students—only that Walker refused to work with him. After weighing these competing factors, the court ruled that Bowman's speech was protected. "In our minds," wrote Judge Ross, "the public's need to know whether children are being mistreated in school outweighs the other legitimate concerns of the government."

Would Pickering Always Protect Teachers Who Make Unintentional False Public Statements?

Generally, but not always. In Hartford, Connecticut, for example, a tenured high school teacher was dismissed for distributing leaflets that contained a number of false statements about her principal.[11] Prepared by a radical student group at a time of racial tension, the leaflets charged the principal with imposing a "reign of terror" at the school and falsely alleged that he had refused to reinstate a militant student despite a court order and had used "military riot gas" against demonstrating students at another school. The teacher testified that she did not know the charges were false. However, a federal court ruled that her distribution of these leaflets was not protected by the First Amendment because their basic purpose was to cause dissension, and they contained serious, damaging, and incorrect accusations that had an immediate and harmful impact on the school.

Is Private Criticism Protected?

It depends on the circumstances. Bessie Givhan, an English teacher, was dismissed after a series of private encounters with her principal. The principal alleged that Givhan made "petty and unreasonable demands" in an "insulting, loud, and hostile" manner. The trial court found that her demands were not petty or unreasonable, since they involved practices she felt were racially discriminatory. But a court of appeals ruled for the school on the grounds that private complaints were not protected by the Constitution. The U.S. Supreme Court disagreed and extended the *Pickering* ruling to apply to private as well as public criticism.[12]

The Court rejected the notion that the First Amendment does not protect criticism of a principal simply because of the close working relationship between principal and teacher. The Court emphasized that freedom of speech is not lost when a teacher "arranges to communicate privately with his employer rather than to spread his views before the public." On the other hand, a teacher's criticism might not be protected when it specifically impedes classroom duties or the operation of the schools. In regard to personal confrontations between an educator and an immediate superior, the Court noted that judges may also consider the "manner, time, and place" of confrontations when balancing the rights in conflict.

In another federal case, the court ruled that a tenured teacher, Evelyn Anderson, could be dismissed for telling her black principal and assistant principal, "I hate all black folks."[13] Unlike in the *Pickering* case, Anderson's remarks created tension between the teacher and her principals, they caused an adverse reaction among co-workers, and they "cast serious doubt on her judgment and general competence as a teacher" in a school district where most students were black. Under these circumstances, the court ruled that the school board's interest in maintaining an efficient system and in employing effective teachers outweighed Anderson's free speech interest and, therefore, that her dismissal was not unconstitutional.

Can Teachers Be Required to Go Through the Chain of Command?

Not about matters of public concern. In Oregon, for example, a coach was suspended for mailing a letter about the athletic program directly to the school board and not sending it through proper channels. In ruling against the administration, the judge barred the enforcement of "any policy which prohibits direct communication by teachers on matters of public concern with the members of the District School Board."[14]

Similarly, in Arkansas, the contracts of several teachers were not renewed because they wrote to the state department of education complaining of a colleague's deficiencies in implementing the special education law. The district said the teachers' letter should not be protected because it was merely an "internal grievance over employment" and made the school "look bad." But a federal judge ruled for the teachers who, he wrote, "were exercising their rights as citizens regarding a matter of public concern with respect to the quality of education and observance of federal policy" regarding handicapped children.[15]

Are Personal Complaints Protected by the First Amendment?

No. In 1983, the U.S. Supreme Court ruled in *Connick* v. *Myers* that "when a public employee speaks not as a citizen upon matters of public concern, but instead as an employee upon matters only of personal interest…a federal court is not the appropriate forum in which to review the wisdom" of the public agency's personnel decision.[16]

When Are Teachers' Statements Matters of Public Concern?

According to *Connick,* when they relate to "any matter of political, social, or other concern to the community." Whether a statement is a matter of public concern also depends on its content, form, and context. Thus, a federal court protected a South Carolina teacher who was fired for a disrespectful letter to the editor criticizing school board members who "had the gall" to request reimbursement for a "luxurious" convention "vacation" and another letter criticizing some of her colleagues for being oblivious to school problems. Although her public criticism angered her principal and most of her fellow teachers, she was reinstated by the court because the superintendent used extraordinary measures to discredit her on the basis of her criticisms that "unquestionably addressed matters of public concern."[17]

Similarly, a federal court protected New Jersey teacher, Arthur Wichert, who publicly criticized his school board's transfer of another teacher as a "ridiculous, stupid and obvious political move."[18] Because of this statement to a reporter, Wichert was charged with insubordination and "unbecoming conduct" for his "reckless," "false," and "misleading" statements. But the court ruled that such statements are matters of public concern when they seek "to bring light on actual or potential wrongdoing…by government officials." What distinguishes a democratic from a totalitarian state, wrote the judge, "is the freedom to speak and criticize the government…without fear of government retaliation."

In a Utah case, high school teacher Wendy Weaver was not reappointed as a volleyball coach because of her out-of-school disclosure that she was a lesbian. A federal court ruled that "in Utah at least" the topic of sexual orientation is a matter of public concern, and therefore Weaver's comments about this topic "off the job," cannot be restricted unless they adversely affect the school.[19] And another federal judge has noted that critical speech is not unprotected just because it is "bluntly worded and directed at specific government officials."[20]

When Are Teachers' Comments Not Considered Matters of Public Concern?

The following cases illustrate when courts have ruled that a teacher's statements have not been protected by the First Amendment.

In Illinois, a federal appeals court wrote that a series of "sarcastic, unprofessional, and insulting" memoranda to school officials were not protected because the teacher was not speaking as a citizen concerned with problems facing the school district, but was expressing "his own private disagreement with policies and procedures which he had either failed to apply or refused to follow."[21]

In Washington, D.C., a court did not protect a teacher's letters about overcrowding in her classroom, which she claimed was a safety hazard.[22] The court explained that if the reason for the letters was the teacher's personal interests, a passing reference to safety "will not transform a private employee grievance into a matter of public concern." And a federal appeals court ruled against a coach who was not rehired after a controversial newspaper interview about his termination.[23] According to the court, a teacher's personal grievance does not become a matter of public concern simply because there is a story about it in the newspaper.

In Pittsburgh, a high school teacher alleged that she lost her coaching position in retaliation for a faculty newsletter she published that included a discussion of staff problems such as "undue stress" and "low esteem." A federal appeals court ruled that the teacher's statements "did not comment on any broad social or policy issue" but "solely on employee morale." The judges concluded: "We see no meaningful distinction between these statements and those found unprotected in *Connick*."[24]

After Ohio track coach Bob Schul was warned not to suggest caffeine to his athletes, he was fired for recommending that one of his runners "consume a cola, because the caffeine would help his body function properly during an upcoming race." Schul argued that his remarks about caffeine constituted protected speech. However, a federal court disagreed. In this 2000 decision, the court concluded that Schul "spoke not as a citizen advocating the use of caffeine generally, but as a high school coach discussing a matter of personal concern."[25]

In sum, these cases illustrate that (1) all courts recognize that matters of public concern are protected by the First Amendment; (2) judges do not always agree about what matters concern the public; and (3) courts have granted school boards the right to control teachers' speech that is related to their personal interests.

Are All Personnel Matters Excluded from First Amendment Protection?

Not necessarily. Most personnel issues are considered matters of private, not public, concern. However, a North Carolina case concerning teacher Edwin Piver illustrates when controversial statements about a personnel controversy were protected by the courts. After Piver spoke in favor of renewing his principal's contract at a school board meeting and later urged the board to reverse its nonrenewal decision, he was transferred to a less desirable assignment. The board argued that the dispute was not protected by the First Amendment because it was an internal personnel matter. But a federal appeals court disagreed.[26] Piver's speech to the board was protected because there is community interest in "frank and open discussion of agenda items at public meetings." Furthermore, Piver had "particular expertise" concerning his principal's performance, and "the public has a need to hear from those who know" about the performance of public officials.

How Do Courts Rule When Some of a Teacher's Speech Is Protected and Some Is Not?

In these complex situations, the courts follow a four-step analysis. This process was illustrated by a case from Peoria, Illinois, involving Terry Knapp, a tenured high school teacher and coach who was reprimanded, relieved of his coaching duties, and transferred because of his repeated complaints to his principal and school board.[27] His complaints concerned his classroom assignment, his evaluations, the district's grievance procedure, the inequitable mileage allowance for coaches, and the inadequate liability insurance for coaches and parents who drove athletes to games.

The first step in the court's analysis was to decide whether Knapp's complaints involved matters of public concern. The appeals court ruled that some did and some did not. According to Judge Coffey, classroom assignments and evaluations "are clearly personal matters relating solely to Knapp's employment." Therefore the teacher's complaints about these issues are simply disagreements with "internal decisions made by his immediate superiors" and are not protected by the First Amendment.

The court ruled differently about Knapp's other complaints. The teacher's criticism of inequitable mileage allowances, wrote the judge, "enlightened the public" about the unequal expenditures and "involves not only Knapp but all of the coaches." The complaints about inadequate liability insurance also are about a matter of public concern in "today's litigious society." And the grievance procedure was an issue about which the school board requested teacher comments and was of concern to taxpayers who have a financial interest in the settlement of school disputes.

Since the court found that some of the teacher's complaints involved matters of public concern, the second step was to apply the *Pickering* test—balancing Knapp's interest as a citizen in discussing public issues against the board's interest as an employer in promoting efficiency. Since Knapp's complaints did not interfere with his teaching, did not cause disruption or destroy morale, and were directed at policies rather than individuals, the court ruled that the teacher's right to discuss public matters outweighed the interests of the administration and were protected by the First Amendment.

The third step was to ask whether Knapp's protected speech was a "substantial or motivating factor" in the board's action against him. Since the evidence indicated it was, the final issue to be decided was whether the board would have reached the same decision "even in the absence of the protected conduct." The evidence indicated it would not. Therefore Knapp was awarded compensatory damages and reassigned to his teaching and coaching jobs.

When Does the "Pickering *Balance Test*" Favor Teachers?

Here are two cases where courts ruled that the teacher's right to discuss matters of public concern outweighed the school's interest in efficiency.

In Rhode Island, an art teacher videotaped health and safety hazards in her high school. When the principal ordered her to stop, she went to court. Although health and safety issues are matters of public concern, the principal argued that the balance of interests should favor the school since the videotaping caused disruption, negative publicity and a resulting lack of confidence in the school. However, the court ruled that First Amendment rights cannot be conditioned on whether the image of the school is adversely affected. Otherwise, a teacher's free speech rights would almost always be denied since "the government rarely challenges an employee's right to speak where the speech is complimentary."[28] According to the court, the proper reaction of the school is to respond to the teacher's criticism, not to silence her. The judge concluded that he would "not consider negative publicity as a factor in the *Pickering* balance test" and ruled that administrators could not prohibit release of the videotapes.

In a recent New Jersey case, teacher Elizabeth Carlino went to court after she was fired as the field hockey coach for posting a sign in front of her home criticizing her principal as a poor role model for punishing her son for drinking alcohol on a senior class trip when the principal also had been drinking on the trip. The judge wrote that Carlino "spoke as a parent and as a citizen" and not as an employee when she criticized the principal and that his ability to serve as a role model is a matter of public concern.[29] The principal argued that Carlino's insulting, disrespectful, and "extremely disruptive" conduct should outweigh her free speech rights. However, the judge concluded that Carlino's criticism did not impede her ability to coach and that any injury the principal might have suffered does not outweigh "Carlino's interest in expressing her concern" about the principal's behavior while chaperoning the trip.

When Are Teachers' Public Comments Not Protected?

When judges consider the time, place, manner, context, and consequences of a teacher's expression and conclude that the school's interest outweighs the teacher's.

This was illustrated by the case of Robert Hennessy, a senior in the teacher certification program at Salem State College. For his student teaching practicum, he was assigned to an elementary school where he aggressively expressed his views against abortion to another teacher, stormed out of class during a parent's art presentation which he termed "disgusting," and, in a meeting with the principal, condemned the curriculum and explained that he was "more interested in pleasing God" than in pleasing her.[30] As a result of these and other incidents, the school terminated his practicum, and Hennessy claimed that he was unconstitutionally punished for his protected speech. In a 1999 decision, a federal appeals court wrote that where "an apprentice teacher elects a mode of communication—audible denigration and visible petulance in the learning environment, in front of other students—that plainly conflicts with the school's legitimate interest...the constitutional balance tips sharply in the employer's favor." The court concluded that the school's interest "in preserving a collegial atmosphere, harmonious relations among teachers and respect for the curriculum while in the classroom outweighed [Hennessy's] interest in proselytizing for his chosen cause."

In a recent Illinois case, Chicago teacher George Schmidt was fired for publishing several standardized copyrighted tests in a newspaper he edited in order "to stir public debate" about the testing he opposed. Schmidt argued that a teacher may not be dismissed for speaking on issues of public importance. The court acknowledged that "creating public awareness of potentially ineffective educational tests is an admirable goal."[31] However, the judge ruled that this goal "fails to convert [Schmidt's] copyright violations to conduct protected by the First Amendment." The judge concluded that "the Board's interest in efficiently promoting its educational mission outweighs Schmidt's interest in commenting on the tests" by publishing them.

In a 2000 decision, Jeffry Newton, a Virginia high school English teacher, was ordered to remove the 1998–1999 banned books pamphlets he posted outside his classroom door. The pamphlets listed and described banned books that ranged from *Catcher in the Rye* and *The Firm* to the *Joy of Gay Sex*. A federal court acknowledged that a discussion of censorship is "a matter of important public policy."[32] But the judge ruled that the posting of material on classroom doors is an extension of the curriculum, the curriculum is the responsibility of school officials, and "teachers may not claim constitutional rights in order to take control of the curriculum."

Do Teachers Have the Right to Circulate Controversial Petitions on School Premises?

According to a 1975 California Supreme Court decision, they do.[33] In Los Angeles, the school board prohibited the circulation of a teachers' union petition to public officials protesting cutbacks in education funds and calling for an overhaul of the tax structure. The board prohibited the petition because it was controversial and would cause teachers to take opposing political positions, thereby creating discord. However, the liberal California court defended the right of teachers to petition for a redress of grievances.

The court pointed out that "tolerance of the unrest intrinsic to the expression of controversial ideas is constitutionally required even in the school." According to the court: "It cannot seriously be argued that school officials may demand a teaching faculty composed …of thinking individuals sworn never to share their ideas with one another for fear they may disagree." The court concluded: "Absent a showing of a clear and substantial threat to order and efficiency in the school, such proposed First Amendment activity should not be stifled."

What About Political Speech?

The First Amendment protects teachers' rights to participate in political activity as citizens in the community. Teachers may put political stickers on their cars that are parked at school, and they probably can wear political buttons on their clothing in class. However, they must be careful not to try to persuade students to adopt their personal political views. Furthermore, teachers may be prohibited from using school time to engage in partisan politics. Thus a 1997 federal decision upheld a school policy that prohibited political activity by employees on school grounds during school hours.[34]

When Discussing a Contract at an Open Meeting, Can a School Board Prohibit Nonunion Members from Speaking?

No. During contract negotiations in Madison, Wisconsin, a nonunion teacher was allowed to address the school board concerning a controversial contract provision, over the objection of the union. The union claimed the teacher's statements constituted unauthorized negotiations. But the U.S. Supreme Court disagreed.[35] The Court wrote: "When the State has opened a forum for direct citizen involvement, it is difficult to find justification for excluding teachers…who are most vitally concerned." Whatever its duties as an employer, when a school board sits in public meetings to hear the views of citizens, it cannot be required to discriminate against speakers who are not members of the union. (For a discussion of other collective bargaining issues, see chapter 4.)

Are Teachers at Private Schools That Receive State Funds Protected by the First Amendment?

No. This was the ruling of the U.S. Supreme Court in a case concerning teachers who were dismissed from a private school for publicly opposing policies of the administration and publishing a letter protesting the school's picketing policy.[36] Although the state paid over

90 percent of the school's budget, the Court ruled that the acts of the school in dismissing the teachers did not become acts of the government because the government did not influence those actions. Thus the First Amendment did not apply to this case because the discharge of the teachers was not a state action.

Do Whistleblower Statutes Protect Teachers?

Yes. More than 40 states have whistleblower laws.[37] Generally, they cover teachers and other public employees who in good faith report a violation of law. Many also cover employees who report gross waste of public funds, or specific dangers to public health, safety, or welfare. These statutes protect teachers who make such reports against discharge, coercion, or discrimination and thus supplement rights protected by the First Amendment. The statutes also specify how whistleblowers can obtain legal protection and what remedies are available to whistleblowers who have suffered reprisals.

Are School Employees Protected against Retaliation If They Complain about Illegal Actions?

Yes, if their state has a whistleblower law. In Texas, school cafeteria workers were fired after they complained to their superintendent that they were required to "volunteer" to work without pay preparing meals for school board meetings. They sued and won under the Texas Whistleblower Act, which prohibits government bodies such as school boards from suspending or discriminating against an employee "who reports a violation of law to an appropriate law enforcement authority." The court concluded that requiring school employees to work without pay was illegal, that the superintendent was the appropriate authority to whom to report, and that his firing of the employees was therefore illegal.[38]

In a 2001 case in which Sacramento school employees were demoted for accusing a deputy superintendent of illegally using federal funds, an appeals court ruled that the public's interest in learning about illegal conduct by public officials outweighs a state employer's interest in avoiding workplace disturbance. The court concluded that a government employer "cannot justify retaliation against whistleblowers as a legitimate means of avoiding the disruption that necessarily accompanies such exposure."[39]

In a related Maine case, a probationary special education teacher claimed that her contract was not renewed because she alleged at a school board meeting that the middle school was violating special education laws. To prevail under the state's Whistleblower Protection Act, the teacher must prove that (1) she was engaged in activity protected by the act, (2) was "the subject of adverse employment action," and (3) there was a "causal link between the protected activity" and her nonrenewal. Since the school "presented persuasive evidence"[40] that the reasons for the teacher's nonrenewal were not connected to her allegations at the board meeting, the court ruled in favor of the school.

Controversial Issues and Academic Freedom

What Is Academic Freedom?

Academic freedom includes the right of teachers to speak freely about their subjects, to experiment with new ideas, and to select appropriate teaching materials and methods. Courts have held that academic freedom is based on the First Amendment and is fundamental to our democratic society. It protects a teacher's right to evaluate and criticize existing values and practices in order to allow for political, social, economic, and scientific progress. Academic freedom is not absolute, and courts balance it against competing educational values.

Does Academic Freedom Protect the Assignment of Controversial Materials?

Earlier cases ruled that it does if the material is relevant to the subject, is appropriate to the age and maturity of the students, and does not cause disruption. In Montgomery, Alabama, Marilyn Parducci assigned her eleventh-grade class a satire by Kurt Vonnegut, Jr., entitled "Welcome to the Monkey House." The next day her principal and associate superintendent advised her not to teach the story which they described as "literary garbage" that condoned "the killing off of elderly people and free sex." Parducci considered the story a good literary piece and believed she had a professional obligation to teach it. Because she refused the advice of her principal and assigned "disruptive" material, she was dismissed. Parducci felt her dismissal violated her right to academic freedom.

A federal trial court agreed.[41] In considering the case, Judge Johnson first summarized the constitutional principles involved. The U.S. Supreme Court, he wrote, "has on numerous occasions" emphasized that academic freedom—the right to teach, to evaluate, and to experiment with new ideas—is "fundamental to a democratic society." On the other hand, academic freedom, like all other constitutional rights, is not absolute and must be balanced against competing interests. According to Judge Johnson, school officials cannot restrict First Amendment rights unless they first demonstrate that "the forbidden conduct would *materially* and *substantially* interfere" with school discipline. Applying these principles to this case, the court found that the school board "failed to show either that the assignment was inappropriate reading for high school juniors or that it created a significant disruption to the educational process." Therefore this liberal decision held that Parducci's dismissal "constituted an unwarranted invasion of her First Amendment right to academic freedom."

In Ipswich, Massachusetts, Robert Keefe, the head of the high school English department, assigned his senior class an article from the *Atlantic Monthly* magazine which discussed dissent, protest, and revolt. Entitled "The Young and the Old," the article contained the word "motherfucker" a number of times. Several parents found the word offensive and protested to the school committee. Members of the committee asked Keefe if he would agree not to use the word again in class, but Keefe refused to agree, was dismissed, and went to court.

The judge found the article "scholarly, thoughtful, and thought provoking."[42] If it raised the concept of incest, wrote the judge, "it was not to suggest it but to condemn it," for the word was used "as a superlative of opprobrium." The court also noted that no proper study of the article could avoid considering the word. Under these circumstances, the judge doubted that quoting a "dirty" word in current use would shock these high school seniors or that they needed to be protected from such exposure. This 1969 appeals court decision concluded that the sensibilities of offended parents "are not the full measure of what is proper in education."

Parducci and *Keefe* reflect the views of those courts that place a high value on academic freedom. But these decisions do not mean that teachers have the right to use any language in the classroom. Even the *Keefe* case acknowledged that some regulation of classroom speech "is inherent in every provision of public education." Thus, a judge's decision about whether offensive language can be prohibited might depend on the specific situation—the age of the students, the word used, its relevance to the curriculum, the purpose of its use, and whether teachers know of its prohibition.

Since there is no Supreme Court decision about the scope and limits of academic freedom in public schools, court decisions vary, and a few judges believe that academic freedom does not apply to public schools. In Colorado, for example, a federal appeals court upheld a reprimand against a social studies teacher, John Miles, for discussing a rumor about "two students making out on the tennis courts" to illustrate his belief that the quality of education is declining. In rejecting the teacher's claim that his remarks were protected by the First Amendment, the court wrote that "case law does not support Miles' position that a secondary teacher has a constitutional right to academic freedom."[43]

Can a School Board Require or Prohibit the Use of Textbooks?

Yes. School boards usually have the authority to select or eliminate texts, even if teachers disagree with the board's decision. In Colorado, for example, a board approved a broad, diverse list of 1,285 books for use in elective high school literature courses; however, the board banned from the list ten books that teachers had used. The teachers argued that this prohibition violated their rights. A federal appeals court disagreed.[44]

The court recognized that teachers do have "rights to freedom of expression in the classroom" and "cannot be made to simply read from a script prepared or approved by the board." In addition, the board probably cannot "prohibit mention of these books in class" or their brief discussion. State law, however, gives control of instruction to local school boards. Since these boards can eliminate an elective course completely, they can eliminate certain books from being assigned if their decisions are not arbitrary. The court distinguished this case from *Parducci,* since in that case the "school authorities acted in the absence of a general policy" and "after the fact." Thus when teachers and school boards have a legitimate disagreement about what texts to use, the boards have the ultimate authority to make these decisions in elective as well as in required courses.

Are Curricular Disputes Matters of Public Concern?

Recent decisions indicate that courts do not consider disagreements between teachers and school officials about curricular and curricular-related issues to be matters of public concern. In North Carolina, for example, Margaret Boring, an award-winning high school teacher, challenged her transfer for failing to follow the school's "controversial materials policy" in producing the play *Independence.* She claimed that her transfer was an unconstitutional retaliation for the unpopular views in the play. However, a sharply divided appeals court ruled that the selection of a play is a curricular issue, not a matter of public concern. The court noted that academic freedom "has never conferred upon teachers the control of public school curricula." The majority concluded that this case is "nothing more than an ordinary employment dispute" and therefore dose not involve a teacher's First Amendment rights.[45] (See chapter 1.)

Can Schools Remove Literary Classics from the Curriculum?

Yes. In Florida, a school board removed Aristophanes' *Lysistrata* and Chaucer's *The Miller's Tale* from the curriculum of an optional high school humanities course because of their "sexuality and excessively vulgar language." A federal appeals court ruled that the board's action was not unconstitutional because it was reasonably related to legitimate educational concerns about the "exceptional sexual explicitness" in these books.[46]

This case illustrates the difference between what courts think is unlawful and unwise. The judges emphasized that they did "not endorse the Board's decision"; they ruled only that the books' removal was not unconstitutional. In fact, the judges wrote: "We seriously question how young persons just below the age of majority can be harmed by these masterpieces of Western Literature." (Library book censorship is discussed later in this chapter.)

Can School Boards Reject Texts for Any Reason?

No. A California decision explained that a school board's discretion to remove books must be exercised in a constitutional manner.[47] Thus, a board's decision would be impermissible if it were based (1) "upon disagreement with the constitutionally protected ideas contained in the books" or (2) "upon the board's desire to impose upon the students a religious [or political] orthodoxy." Similarly, a federal appeals court held that a Minnesota school board could not constitutionally ban *The Lottery* from its American Literature course because a majority of the board "object to the film's religious and ideological content and wish to prevent the ideas contained in the material from being expressed in the school."[48] Furthermore, decisions cannot be based on a desire to promote a particular religious viewpoint by prohibiting texts that teach evolution or by requiring texts that teach "creation science."[49]

Nor do boards have the discretion to reject texts based on racially discriminatory motives. Thus, a federal court ruled that a decision to reject a controversial history book by a Mississippi textbook selection committee based on "an intent to perpetuate ideas of segregation and discrimination" was unconstitutional.[50]

Can Social Studies Teachers Be Prohibited from Discussing Controversial Issues?

It would probably be unconstitutional for a school official to order teachers of civics, history, or current events not to discuss any controversial questions. This was the ruling of a federal court in a case that arose in Stafford, Texas.[51] Parents objected to the way Henry Sterzing, a civics teacher, taught a unit on race relations and to his response to a question that indicated he did not oppose interracial marriage. As a result, the principal and the school board told him to teach his course "within the text and not discuss controversial issues." After Sterzing replied that it was impossible to teach current events to high school seniors and avoid controversial questions, he was dismissed for insubordination. But the court ruled that he could not be fired for discussing controversial issues. The judge acknowledged that a teacher has a duty to be "fair and objective in presenting his personally held opinions" and to ensure that different views are presented. In this case, however, the court held that Sterzing's classroom methods were "conducted within the ambit of professional standards" and that his statements in class neither interfered with discipline nor subjected students to unfair indoctrination.

In a related case, another Texas teacher, Janet Cooper, got into trouble for using a controversial "sunshine simulation" to teach about American history after the Civil War. The technique, which involved role playing by high school students to recreate the historic time, evoked strong feelings about racial issues. As a result, a number of parents complained to the school board, and Cooper was advised "not to discuss Blacks in American History." Because of her use of the simulation, Cooper's contract was not renewed. She argued that her classroom discussions were protected by the First Amendment, and a federal appeals court agreed, reinstated Cooper, and awarded her back pay and attorneys' fees.[52]

In a third Texas case, a high school psychology teacher in a conservative community was fired for using a masculinity survey from *Psychology Today*. A federal district court ruled that the school violated her constitutional right "to engage in a teaching method of her choosing even though the subject matter may be controversial" without showing that this method caused substantial disruption or that there was a clear, prior prohibition against it.[53]

On the other hand, teachers have no right to promote views in school that contradict the curriculum. This was illustrated by the 2000 case of Robert Downs, a Los Angeles high school teacher who wanted to post material in opposition to the school's bulletin boards that promoted tolerance during Gay and Lesbian Awareness Month. A federal appeals court ruled that a school may not only advocate tolerance but also may prohibit contrary speech by its teachers. The court concluded: "Just as a school can prohibit a teacher from posting racist material" during Black History Month, "it may prohibit [Downs] from posting intolerant materials during Gay and Lesbian Awareness Month."[54]

Do Teachers Have the Right to Preach Their Religious Beliefs in School?

No. In New York, an art teacher was dismissed for recruiting students for her religious organization under the guise of guidance and for using classroom facilities during school time to preach about her religion. Since the teacher failed to stop discussing her beliefs in school, a state court ruled that her actions were not protected.[55]

Similarly, a biology teacher, who claimed he had a right to present his creationist beliefs to students during lunch and class breaks, was not supported by a federal court.[56] Instead the judge ruled that teachers may be instructed not to discuss religion with students during the school day and to refer a student's religious questions to his or her parents or clergy. According to the appeals court, the school's "interest in avoiding an Establishment Clause violation trumps [the teacher's] right to free speech" since the likelihood of students "equating his views with those of the school is substantial."

Does Academic Freedom Allow Teachers to Disregard the Text and Syllabus?

No. A federal court considered this question when a biology teacher was not rehired because he overemphasized sex in his health course.[57] The teacher explained that his students "wanted sex education and mental health emphasized," and he agreed to "only touch on the other topics covered by the assigned text and course syllabus." In rejecting the teacher's contention that his First Amendment rights had been violated, the court ruled that he had no constitutional right "to override the...judgment of his superiors and fellow faculty members as to the proper content of the required health course." The court concluded that academic freedom is not "a license for uncontrolled expression at variance with established curricular content."

In a related case, a federal appeals court held that a history teacher had no right to substitute his own reading list for the school's official list without seeking administrative approval as required by school policy. As the court noted, "The First Amendment has never required school districts to abdicate control over public school curricula."[58] And, in a California case concerning a biology teacher who objected to teaching evolution, a federal judge wrote: "If every teacher…omitted those topics which are different from beliefs they hold, a curriculum…would be useless."[59]

Can Teachers Be Punished for Discussing Topics or Distributing Materials That Are Not Relevant?

Yes. Academic freedom does not protect materials, discussions, or comments that are not relevant to the assigned subject. A federal case from Cook County, Illinois, illustrated this point when it upheld the dismissal of three eighth-grade teachers for distributing movie brochures about the 1969 rock festival Woodstock.[60] The brochures contained pictures, articles, and poems that included positive views on drugs, sexual freedom, and vulgar language. The three teachers taught French, industrial arts, and language arts. The brochures were distributed to any student who wanted them ("to promote rapport"), but the teachers did not related the brochures to what the students were studying. In addition to being irrelevant, the court found that the brochures were inappropriate for eighth-grade students and promoted a viewpoint on drug use that was contrary to what state law required students to be taught about the "harmful effects of narcotics."

Are a Teacher's Controversial Responses to Students' Questions Protected?

They might be if they relate to a matter of public concern even if they are not related to the teacher's specialization. This was the ruling in a 1995 case involving Lari Scruggs, a Virginia high school math teacher who responded with negative comments to two students who asked her views on interracial dating in study hall.[61] As a result, the school did not rehire Scruggs because: (1) her only job was to teach math, and (2) her comments were "potentially disruptive." But a federal judge disagreed. The teacher's responsibility in study hall, wrote the judge, "is to guide students in their studies" and to "respond as best she could" to student questions. According to the judge,

> …if a question involves math, so much the better. But if the question involves an important social issue…the teacher need not remain silent, or as [the school's] counsel suggested, refer the student to a guidance counselor. Rather, the teacher has the right, and perhaps the duty, to respond…. I do not believe a public school teacher, when asked by a student for guidance on important social issues of the day, must stand mute.

Regarding the school's concern about "potential disruption," the judge noted that there was none. He concluded that "the negative reaction of a few people to the speech is insufficient" to overcome the teacher's "strong First Amendment interest in speaking on social issues of concern to the community."

Can Teachers Be Punished If Their Use of Approved Materials Causes Substantial Disruption in the Community?

No. In Michigan, the teaching of an approved unit on human reproduction in a seventh-grade life science class led to an uproar in the community. It also resulted in widely publicized charges against the teacher that were false, his suspension without a fair hearing, and a large jury verdict in his favor. An appeals court said that the school board's actions were irresponsible, violated the teacher's academic freedom, and injured his professional career. However, the court ruled that the citizen who organized the protests against the teacher's course should not be held liable, since her charges to the school board were protected by her First Amendment right to petition the government.[62]

Can a Teacher Be Punished for Showing an R-Rated Film to Students?

Probably, although it may depend on the students, the movie, and how it is shown. An example of how not to do it is provided by the case of Jacqueline Fowler, a tenured Kentucky teacher, who was fired for showing an R-rated film, *Pink Floyd—The Wall,* to students in grades 9 through 11. The movie was shown at the request of students on the "noninstructional" last day of school while Fowler was completing grade cards. She had not seen the film, did not discuss it with the class, but asked one of the students to "edit out" any parts that were unsuitable for viewing in school. He attempted to do this by holding a 8½ × 11-inch file folder in front of the 25-inch screen.

Fowler argued that the film contained "important, socially valuable messages." But a federal appeals court held that showing the film was not a constitutionally protected educational activity.[63] The judge concluded that by introducing a "controversial and sexually explicit movie into a classroom of adolescents without preview, preparation, or discussion," Fowler "abdicated her function as an educator" and demonstrated a "blatant lack of judgment" that constituted "conduct unbecoming a teacher."

In a related Louisiana case, a teacher was suspended for showing *Boss,* a PG-rated film which depicts racial stereotypes in reverse and repeatedly uses the word "nigger." The teacher said he showed the movie to stop his black students from using the racial slur; but because the film was not discussed or related to the curriculum, the court upheld the suspension for "neglect of duty and incompetence."[64]

Is a Teacher's Offensive Out-of-class Language protected?

Sometimes. In a New York case, teacher Christie Rothschild was not rehired because of her participation in a private, experimental videotape film that included extensive vulgar language and scenes administrators found offensive. (The actors had been given permission to make the film in school during nonschool hours.) A federal district court ruled that Rothschild's First Amendment rights were violated because the content of the film was the reason she was not rehired, and there was no evidence that her participation "damaged the effective functioning" of the school.[65]

On the other hand, a Pennsylvania decision upheld the dismissal of a sixth-grade teacher for distributing copies of racist "jokes" in school to a coworker that contained "vicious and scurrilous" statements against people of African descent.[66] The court concluded that the teacher's distribution of racist material at school "was a horrible example for his students" and "disregarded standards of behavior the school had a right to expect."

Teaching Methods

Can a Teacher Be Punished for Using a Controversial Method That Is Not Clearly Prohibited?

Not usually. If a teacher does not know that a certain method is prohibited, it would probably be a violation of due process for the teacher to be punished for using that method unless it had no recognized educational purpose. (The concept of due process for teachers is discussed more fully in chapter 12.)

In Lawrence, Massachusetts, an 11th-grade English teacher, Roger Mailloux, was discussing a novel about conservative customs in rural Kentucky when a student said that the custom of seating boys and girls on opposite sides of the classroom was ridiculous. Mailloux said that some current attitudes are just as ridiculous. As an example, he introduced the subject of taboo words and wrote the word "fuck" on the blackboard. He then "asked the class in general for an explanation. After a couple of minutes, a boy volunteered the word meant 'sexual intercourse.' Plaintiff [Mailloux], without using the word orally, said: 'We have two words, sexual intercourse, and this word on the board; one is accepted by society, the other is not accepted. It is a taboo word.'" After a few minutes of discussion, Mailloux went on to other matters.

As a result of this incident, Mailloux was dismissed and took his case to court. The court found that Mailloux's method did not disturb the students, that the topic of taboo words was relevant to the subject, and that the word "fuck" was relevant to the topic of taboo words.[67] ("Its impact," wrote the judge, "effectively illustrates how taboo words function.") The court also found that educational experts were in conflict about Mailloux's method: Some thought the way he used the word was appropriate; others did not.

With these facts in mind, the judge discussed the law in such cases. The *Keefe* case, wrote the court, upheld two kinds of academic freedom: the "substantive" right of a teacher to choose a teaching method that serves a "demonstrated" educational purpose, and the "procedural" right of a teacher not to be discharged for the use of a teaching method not prohibited by clear regulation. This procedural protection is afforded a teacher because he or she is engaged in the exercise of "vital First Amendment rights" and should not be required to "guess what conduct or utterance may lose him his position." Since Mailloux did not know that his conduct was prohibited, the court ruled that it was a violation of due process for the school committee to discharge him.

In a controversial California case, Eileen Olicker, a reading teacher, was dismissed for distributing students' writings containing vulgar descriptions of sexual organs and the sex act. The material was written as part of a class assignment for poor readers, who were told that they could write about anything they chose and that their stories would be shared with the class. Olicker was dismissed after a student she had disciplined left a copy of the material in the principal's box a month after the incident. In a 2–1 decision, a state appeals court ruled in Olicker's favor.[68] The court noted that she had been an unusually sensitive, dedicated, and effective teacher and that this one incident did not cause "any disruption or impairment of discipline." Moreover, two experts testified that Olicker's method of having students write about subjects that interested them was "a sound educational approach," although they would not have reproduced the materials. The majority concluded that teachers should not be disciplined "merely because they made a reasonable, good faith, professional judgment in the course of their employment with which higher authorities later disagreed."

In a Massachusetts case, a federal appeals court explained that a school may restrict a teacher's classroom activities if two conditions are met. First, the restriction must be "reasonably related to a legitimate pedagogical concern." According to the court, this will depend on "the age and sophistication of the students, the relationship between teaching method and valid educational objective and the context and manner of the presentation."[69] Second, the school must have notified the teacher about what conduct was prohibited. The court explained that a school is not entitled to punish teachers for speech that it never prohibited because few subjects lack controversy and "if teachers must fear retaliation for every utterance, they will fear teaching." However, the court did not hold that schools must "expressly prohibit every imaginable inappropriate conduct," since such a requirement would be an "impossible and undesirable burden." Rather, the question is: Was it reasonable for the teacher to know that her method was prohibited?

When Are Controversial Methods Not Protected?

When methods are inappropriate for the age and maturity of the students, when they are not supported by any significant professional opinion, or when they are prohibited by reasonable school policy, they are not protected by academic freedom. The following cases indicate when and why courts were unwilling to protect controversial methods.

Allen Celestine, a fifth-grade teacher from Louisiana, became increasingly concerned about the vulgar language used by his students. Therefore when two girls in his class used the word "fuck," he required them to write it 1,000 times. As a result, he was dismissed for incompetence. Celestine claimed that his academic freedom should protect his choice of punishment, but no educational experts defended Celestine's method, and a state court ruled against him.[70] It wrote that the First Amendment does not entitle a teacher to require young students to use vulgar words, "particularly when no academic or educational purpose can possibly be served."

Frances Ahern, a high school economics teacher, attended a summer institute that led her to change her teaching methods and allow students to determine course topics and materials. She also began spending substantial time discussing classroom rules and school conflicts. The principal directed her to stop discussing school politics, to teach economics, and to use more conventional teaching methods. Ahern ignored the warning and argued that she had the freedom to select her own teaching methods. But a federal appeals court ruled that the U.S. Constitution does not give a teacher the right to use methods that violate valid administrative requirements.[71]

In a Pennsylvania case, teacher Earl Bradley was told to stop using his "Learnball teaching technique," which included a sports format and team competition in class. The teacher was fired after he continued to use the technique, advocated its use in other classes, and publicly criticized the "Pittsburgh school regime." While the court acknowledged that teachers have a First Amendment right to advocate controversial teaching methods and to criticize school officials, it ruled that Bradley had "no constitutional right to use Learnball in the classroom."[72]

Cecilia Lacks, a high school drama teacher from Missouri, was fired for allowing her students to use frequent and "*extreme* profanity" in plays they wrote, performed, and videotaped.[73] Lacks didn't censor the profanity because she used a "student-centered method" designed to help students "find their own voices." Furthermore, Lacks thought the profanity prohibition applied only to student behavior and not to students' creative assignments. But a federal appeals court upheld her dismissal because the school had a legitimate academic interest in prohibiting profanity in students' writing, the policy against profanity was clear, Lacks knew the policy, and she knew the contents of the plays before they were performed.

Can Schools Impose an Inflexible Grading Policy on Teachers?

The answer may depend on the facts of the case and the rigidity of the policy. In Minnesota, a math teacher, who had received negative evaluations, objected to the specific instructions he was given about how to teach and grade. A state court approved the detailed instructions about teaching but not about grading.[74]

In view of the parental complaints about the teacher, the state court ruled that specific directions to change his teaching methods did not violate his academic freedom. However, the court labeled as "inappropriate" the directive that the teacher's grade distribution "not deviate by more than two percent from distributions in other similar classes." Such a "rigid, numerical grading standard," wrote the court, "appears to us to potentially interfere with a teacher's legitimate need for classroom flexibility."

Can a Teacher Be Punished for Failing to Submit Lesson Plans?

Yes. In New York State, Richard Meyer, a tenured high school science teacher, was fined $8,000 for repeatedly "failing to provide comprehensive weekly lesson plans." According to the court, the teacher's lesson plans "were seriously deficient despite repeated counseling directives" made to him over an extended period.[75] The court also ruled that the penalty was not excessive, since "formal lesson plans play a vital role" in effective teaching and the teacher "virtually ignored" the instructions of his superiors and showed a "cavalier attitude about this problem."

Does Academic Freedom Protect a Teacher's Assignments?

According to the New York commissioner of education it does. In Albany County, the school board tried to dismiss teacher Janet Morgan for insubordination because she refused (on grounds of academic freedom) to rescind an assignment she had given and refused to turn over her lesson plan and grade book. The assignment required students to write an essay expressing their opinion about the firing of a television sports commentator and about an editorial Morgan had written.

In a liberal opinion, upheld in a 1992 New York appeals court decision, the commissioner of education ruled that "the district's directives which attempted to interfere with the teacher's right to give the homework assignment or assign a grade constitute an unreasonable intrusion into the teacher's academic freedom."[76] The commissioner wrote that the assignment was "consistent with a teacher's role in eliciting student opinion and providing assignments which strengthen analytic skills." However, the commissioner also ruled that the school district had "final authority to review and assign grades" and therefore did not violate Morgan's academic freedom by requesting her lesson plans and grade book.

Is It Legal for a School to Refuse to Rehire a Teacher Because of Disagreement Over Teaching Methods and Philosophy?

Probably. For example, Phyllis Hetrick was not rehired as an English instructor at a college in Kentucky. The college expected instructors "to teach on a basic level, to stress fundamentals, and to follow conventional teaching patterns." Hetrick emphasized student freedom and choice and failed to cover the material she had been told to teach. The issue in this case, wrote a federal court, is not which educational philosophy has greater merit but whether a school "has the right to require some conformity" to its educational philosophy and whether it may decline to hire a teacher whose methods are not conducive "to the achievement of the academic goals they espoused."[77] In ruling for the administration, the court wrote that academic freedom "does not encompass the right of a nontenured teacher to have her teaching methods insulated from review."

On the other hand, a Colorado court ruled in favor of a teacher who was not rehired because she allowed two articles to be published in the school newspaper that the principal felt "portrayed the school in a negative light," and because she refused to publish a retraction and advised her students of their right to refuse as well. In a liberal opinion holding that all of her conduct was protected by the First Amendment, the state court noted that academic freedom "includes a teacher's interest in choosing a particular pedagogical method for a course" if "the teaching method serves a demonstrable educational purpose."[78] Moreover the court found that it was part of the teacher's responsibility in her school newspaper course "to teach her students about the legal concepts applicable to journalism."

Is Academic Freedom the Same in Public Schools and in Colleges?

No. The scope of this freedom is broader in colleges and universities than in public schools. In *Mailloux v. Kiley*, Judge Wyzanski explained that this is so because in secondary schools

> the faculty does not have the independent traditions, the broad discretion as to teaching methods, nor usually the intellectual qualifications, of university professors....Some teachers and most students have limited intellectual and emotional maturity.... While secondary schools are not rigid disciplinary institutions, neither are they open forums in which mature adults, already habituated to social restraints, exchange ideas on a level of parity. Moreover...a secondary school student, unlike most college students, is usually required to attend school classes and may have no choice as to his teacher.[79]

Students and Free Speech

The *Wooster* Case[80]

Earl Wooster was expelled from a California high school because he refused to apologize for a controversial speech he made during a school assembly. The speech was critical of the Fresno School Board for "compelling" students to use "unsafe" facilities, and it included caustic comments about some of the board's policies. School officials called Wooster's talk a "breach of school discipline" that was intended to discredit the board in the eyes of the students. A state court agreed and wrote that Wooster's refusal to apologize not only "accentuated his misconduct" but also "made it necessary' to expel him to maintain school discipline.

Wooster was decided in 1915. Wooster's lawyer did not even raise the possibility that his client's speech might be protected by the U.S. Constitution. How would the case be decided today? Even if students have freedom of speech in public schools, can't schools restrict that freedom? Can administrators, for example, limit student speech if they fear it will lead to disruption or if they know it will offend other students? Some of these questions are confronted by the U.S. Supreme Court in the following controversy.

The *Tinker* Case[81]

Does Freedom of Speech Apply to Students in the Classroom?

In 1965, when the debate over American involvement in the Vietnam War was becoming heated, a group of students in Des Moines, Iowa, decided to publicize their antiwar views by wearing black armbands. On learning of the plan, principals of the Des Moines schools established a policy prohibiting armbands in order to prevent any possible disturbance. Although they knew about the policy, several students wore armbands to school, refused to remove them, and were suspended. A federal judge ruled that the anti-armband policy was reasonable, but the students appealed their case to the U.S. Supreme Court, which considered it a conflict between their rights and the rules of the school.

First, the Court outlined the legal principles to be applied. While it recognized that school officials must have authority to control student conduct, it held that neither students nor teachers "shed their constitutional rights to freedom of speech or expression at the schoolhouse gate." To support this ruling, Justice Fortas noted that since school boards "are educating the young for citizenship," they should scrupulously protect the "constitutional freedoms of the individual, if we are not to strangle the free mind at its source and teach youth to discount important principles of our government as mere platitudes."

Concerning this case, the Court wrote that the First Amendment protects symbolic speech as well as pure speech. The wearing of an armband to express certain views is the kind of symbolic act protected by that amendment. After reviewing the facts, the Court found "no evidence whatsoever" that wearing armbands interfered "with the school's work or with the rights of other students to be secure or to be left alone." School officials might have honestly feared that the armbands would lead to a disturbance, but the Court said that this fear was not sufficient to violate student rights. "In our system," wrote the Court, "undifferentiated fear or apprehension of disturbance is not enough to overcome the right to freedom of expression."

While the Court recognized that free speech in the schools may cause problems, it noted that

> any word spoken in class, in the lunchroom or on the campus that deviates from the views of another person may start an argument or cause a disturbance. But our Constitution says we must take this risk; and our history says that it is this sort of hazardous freedom—this kind of openness—that is the basis of our national strength and of the independence and vigor of Americans who grow up and live in this relatively permissive, often disputatious society.

In a provocative comment about education and freedom, the Court wrote:

> In our system, state operated schools may not be enclaves of totalitarianism.... Students in schools as well as out of school are possessed of fundamental rights which the State must respect, just as they themselves must respect their obligations to the State. In our system, students may not be regarded as closed-circuit recipients of only that which the State chooses to communicate.

In sum, *Tinker* held that school officials cannot prohibit a particular opinion merely "to avoid the discomfort and unpleasantness that always accompany an unpopular viewpoint." On the contrary, unless there is evidence that the forbidden expression would "materially and substantially" interfere with the work of the school or the rights of others, such a prohibition is unconstitutional.

Does Tinker *Apply Only to the Classroom?*

No. The Court ruled that the principles of this case are not confined to the curriculum or to classroom hours. On the contrary, a student's right to freedom of expression applies equally "in the cafeteria, or on the playing field" and in other school activities.

Does Tinker *Apply to Elementary Students?*

The answer is uncertain, since few courts have discussed this issue. In a 1996 Florida case that did, the judges could not agree. In that federal appeals court decision concerning a student's attempt to hand out invitations to a religious meeting, Judge Manion commented that "it is unlikely that *Tinker* and its progeny apply to public elementary" students. Manion also wrote that "age is a critical factor in student speech cases" and the U.S. Supreme Court "has not suggested that fourth-graders have the free expression rights of high school students."[82] But two concurring judges disassociated themselves from Manion's comments. Thus, Judge Rovner flatly stated: "I disagree with the suggestion that the standard articulated in *Tinker* is unlikely to apply to grammar school students."

In a related Indiana case, the principal of the Lost Creek Elementary School prevented student Chelsie Baxter from wearing T-shirts that read: "Unfair Grades," "racism," and "I Hate Lost Creek." Relying on *Tinker,* Chelsie's parents sued the principal, alleging that their daughter had a clearly established right to wear the shirts to protest various school policies. The principal argued that Chelsie's rights were not "clearly established," and therefore he should not be held personally liable for violating them. A federal appeals court agreed that despite *Tinker,* the extent of Chelsie's free speech rights is unclear.[83] This is because Chelsie was "at least several years younger" than the youngest student in *Tinker,* because "age *is* a relevant factor" in assessing elementary students' rights, and because there is a "dearth of case law" on this issue. Thus, further litigation is required to determine whether *Tinker* applies to elementary students and, if so, to what extent.

Can Schools Legally Limit Student Expression or Symbolic Speech?

Yes. There are limits to all constitutional rights. In *Tinker,* the Court stated that any student conduct that "materially disrupts classwork or involves substantial disorder or invasion of the rights of others is, of course, not immunized by the Constitutional guarantee of freedom of speech." Thus a federal appeals court upheld the rule of a Cleveland high school forbidding all buttons and badges because the wearing of some symbols had led to fighting between black students and white students.[84] Evidence indicated that if all symbols were permitted, racial tensions would be intensified and the educational process would be "significantly and substantially disrupted."

Must Officials Wait Until a Disruption Has Occurred Before Acting?

No. In a case involving a student demonstration inside a high school, a federal judge ruled that the First Amendment does not require school officials to wait until actual disruption takes place before they act.[85] The judge explained that an official may take reasonable action to restrict student expression when there is significant evidence that there is a "reasonable likelihood of substantial disorder."

After a variety of conflicts between black and white students in a Kansas high school, the district adopted a Racial Harassment Policy that prohibited students from wearing or possessing items that denote "Black Power, Confederate flags," or any hate group. Pursuant to this policy, T. W. was suspended for three days for drawing a Confederate flag during math class. T. W. argued that the school violated his rights since his drawing caused no disruption. However, a 2000 decision by a federal appeals court upheld the suspension. The court noted that the Racial Harassment Policy was clearly in response to more than a desire to avoid the unpleasantness that always accompanies an unpopular view. According to the court, "the history of racial tension in the district made...concerns about future substantial disruptions from possession of Confederate flag symbols at school reasonable."[86] The fact that the student's conduct did not cause disruption does not mean that schools cannot act to prevent problems before they occur. Thus, educators can restrict student expression when they have "a reasonable basis for forecasting disruption" from that expression.

Another 2000 decision in a related Florida case illustrates how a few judges seem to be limiting *Tinker*'s holding. The case concerned Wayne Denno, who was suspended for displaying a small Confederate flag while discussing the Civil War with friends during lunch because the principal considered the flag a racist symbol. Since there was no history of racial tension at the school and no rule prohibiting Denno's conduct, which caused no disruption, he sued the principal for violating his rights. But a divided appeals court ruled that it was not unlawful for administrators to balance *Tinker*'s substantial disruption test with the Supreme Court's more flexible standard in *Bethel v. Fraser* (discussed on p. 149) that allows educators to consider "the school's interest in teaching students the boundaries of socially appropriate behavior."[87] Since, according to the majority there is some doubt whether *Tinker*'s disruption test or *Fraser*'s reasonableness test should apply in this case, the court declined to rule that the principal violated Denno's clearly established constitutional rights.[88] In a thoughtful dissenting opinion, Judge Forrester reviewed the relevant precedents, and explained why *Fraser* should not apply in this case and why *Tinker* clearly established that Denno should not have been punished since his quiet flag display caused no disruption.

Can Officials Always Restrict Symbols that Might Lead to Disruption?

Not in a Texas case where officials prohibited armbands because they expected those who opposed the armbands to cause disruption.[89] Since no one thought the armband wearers would cause trouble, the court ruled that the expectation of disruption by others was not enough to suspend the students' right of symbolic speech. What more was required? To justify the school's action, administrators should make an effort to bring leaders of different student factions together to agree on mutual respect for each other's constitutional rights. If actions such as these had been tried and failed, this failure would have justified restricting the armbands.

Can Administrators Change a School's Symbol Against the Wishes of Most Students?

Yes. For years, the symbol of Virginia's Fairfax High School Rebels was "Johnny Reb." The principal eliminated the symbol after receiving complaints that it offended black students, and he allowed students to choose a new symbol unrelated to the Confederacy. But many students protested the elimination of their traditional symbol and claimed that the principal unconstitutionally censored their expression. However, a federal judge disagreed.[90] He explained that educators might have to tolerate students' symbolic speech but have no obligation to sponsor it. Since a school symbol "bears the stamp of approval" of the institution, administrators "are free to disassociate the school from such a symbol" because of the educational concerns that prompted the principal's decision.

Can Demonstrations Be Prohibited Near the School?

If they interfere with schoolwork, they can. The U.S. Supreme Court upheld the conviction of a high school student who violated a law prohibiting demonstrations on or near school grounds that disturbed classes.[91] In upholding the law, Justice Marshall noted that the constitutionality of a restriction may depend on what is being regulated and where. Making a speech in a public park might be protected, while making the same speech in a public library might not be. "The crucial question," wrote the Court, "is whether the manner of expression is basically incompatible with the normal activity of a particular place at a particular time." Just as *Tinker* made clear that free speech is not off limits in the schools, so Justice Marshall emphasized that "the public sidewalk adjacent to school grounds may not be declared off-limits for expressive activity" that is not disruptive. Thus, a federal judge ruled that a school policy broadly prohibiting "distribution of any materials" on a public sidewalk in front of an Illinois high school violated the First Amendment rights of a citizen who wanted to peacefully pass out Bibles there.[92]

Are "Fighting Words" Protected?

No. In a Pennsylvania case, a high school senior was punished when he loudly commented to a friend off campus as his teacher passed by that he was "a prick."[93] The court said that the student's conduct involved an invasion of the right of the teacher "to be free from being loudly insulted in a public place." The judge concluded that the use of "fighting words—those which by their very utterance inflict injury"—is not protected by the constitutional guarantee of freedom of speech. Similarly, a federal court recently ruled that students also can be punished for using fighting words against other students.[94] According to the judge, schools may forbid the use of language "that incenses students to fight, either physically or verbally."

In a related California decision, a high school student argued that her angry statement about shooting someone was not a threat but a protected "figure of speech."[95] The appeals court ruled against the student and explained that the test to determine whether a statement constitutes a threat that is not protected by the First Amendment is "whether a reasonable person would foresee that the statement would be interpreted" by those addressed "as a serious expression of intent to harm." The court commented: "Given the level of violence pervasive in public schools today, it is no wonder that [the teacher] felt threatened."

Can School Officials Punish Lewd and Offensive Speech?

Yes. The U.S. Supreme Court has held that school officials have broad authority to punish students for using "offensively lewd and indecent speech" in school-sponsored educational activities. The case arose in Bethel, Washington, when a high school senior, Matthew Fraser, gave a nominating speech at a school assembly that referred to his candidate by using "an elaborate, graphic, and explicit sexual metaphor."[96] The Court ruled that such speech could be punished even if it was not legally obscene and did not cause substantial disruption. Furthermore, *Fraser* held that school officials have discretion to determine "what manner of speech" is vulgar and offensive in classrooms and assemblies. However, the *Fraser* decision does not apply to speech about political, religious, educational, or other controversial public policy issues that is not indecent. Such speech is still protected by the First Amendment unless it causes substantial disruption or interferes with the rights of others.[97]

In a related 1996 decision, Emily Heller, an Indiana high school student, was suspended for using the "f-word" in response to another student who used the word first.[98] Administrators charged Emily with violating the school's rule prohibiting "obscene language." But Emily argued that the school violated her free speech rights, since she didn't start the name-calling exchange and, unlike *Fraser,* it did not occur as part of an academic activity. A federal judge ruled against Emily, explaining that *Fraser* could be extended to allow schools to suppress speech that is "obscene or plainly offensive without a showing that such speech occurred during a school-sponsored event."[99] The judge added that Emily's punishment for using offensive and vulgar language was justified even though she was returning words originally directed at her.

In a 2000 decision from South Dakota, a student said "shit" talking to herself in the school office after learning she had missed her bus home. Her profanity was overheard by the school secretary and resulted in the student receiving an in-school suspension in accord with school rules. The judge acknowledged that the profanity caused no disruption and that a student's purely personal speech is entitled to a higher degree of protection than school-sponsored speech. Nevertheless, the court upheld the punishment since the student knew the rule and clearly violated it. However, the judge seemed troubled by the punishment in this case, commented on the "mindlessness of some zero tolerance rules," and noted that not all rule or law breakers should always be punished.[100]

Can Schools Restrict Messages on T-Shirts?

It may depend on how judges view the message and what precedents they apply. When Ohio school administrators prohibited Nicholas Boroff from wearing Marilyn Manson T-shirts, he and his mother went to court. They argued that, since the T-shirts caused no disruption, the prohibition violated Nicholas's First Amendment rights. But a divided federal appeals court disagreed. According to this 2000 decision, "the standard for reviewing the suppression of vulgar or plainly offensive speech is governed by *Fraser*," not *Tinker*. The school argued that Manson T-shirts were offensive because the band promotes violence, illegal drug use, and other "destructive conduct and demoralizing values that are contrary to the educational mission of the school."[101] The majority concluded that, under *Fraser*, these were sufficient reasons to uphold the school's action.

In a dissenting opinion, Judge Gilman wrote that the majority apparently reads *Fraser* as "essentially overruling *Tinker*," by allowing school officials to forbid "whatever student speech they consider 'offensive'…as long as their decision does not appear 'manifestly unreasonable.'" In contrast, Gilman argued that *Tinker* forbids schools from prohibiting T-shirts simply because the shirts convey messages with which they disagree. (For more on controversial T-shirts, see chapter 19.)

A related case concerned Adam Smith, a fifth-grade student from Georgia who exchanged charges with a teacher's aide about being a racist and a liar. A few days later, Adam came to school wearing a shirt his mother designed, which read "KIDS HAVE CIVIL RIGHTS TOO" on the front and "EVEN ADULTS LIE" on the back. Based on a series of disputes with the principal, Adam was suspended for defiant conduct. However, Adam and his mother alleged that he was punished for wearing his "civil rights" shirt in violation of *Tinker*. In a 2000 decision, a federal court ruled that this case was not like *Tinker* because the shirt was not the primary reason for his suspension, but was one of a series of acts of defiance.[102] Thus, schools will not be prohibited from punishing a student for improper behavior simply because the student is wearing a protected message on a T-shirt.

Can Schools Ban Controversial Political Buttons as "Inherently Disruptive"?

Probably not. In Oregon, two high school students were suspended for wearing antiscab buttons to protest the hiring of new teachers to replace those on strike. Some buttons read "Scabs" with a line through it and "Scab we will never forget." The school argued that *Fraser* gave administrators discretion to disassociate the school from the students' message and to determine what speech was disruptive. The trial court agreed that the slogans were "inherently disruptive." However, a federal appeals court disagreed and held that the principles of *Tinker*, not *Fraser*, should be applied.[103] In a case such as this involving political speech, "courts have a First Amendment responsibility to insure that robust rhetoric …is not suppressed by prudish failures to distinguish the vigorous from the vulgar."[104] Since there was no evidence that the buttons caused disruption, the appeals court ruled that they could not be considered activities "which inherently distract students."

Can a Student Be Punished for Making "Discourteous" Remarks at a School Assembly?

Yes, according to some federal judges. In Tennessee, Dean Poling, a candidate for president of his high school council, gave a speech that included "discourteous" statements about the administration and the vice principal. As a result, he was disqualified as a candidate, and he went to court.

A majority of the judges ruled against Poling.[105] Although they acknowledged that the school administration may have overreacted to the speech (which contained no vulgar language), the court wrote that such a "judgment call is best left to the locally elected school board, not to a distant, life-tenured judiciary." Since the election assembly was a school-sponsored educational activity, the actions of the administration should be upheld if related to "legitimate pedagogical concerns." According to the majority, "the art of stating one's views…without unnecessarily hurting the feelings of others surely has a legitimate place in any high school curriculum."

In a strong dissenting opinion, Judge Merritt wrote: "If the school administration can silence a student criticizing it for being narrow-minded and authoritarian, how can students engage in political dialogue with their educators about their education?"

Can States Make It a Crime to Insult Teachers?

Probably not. Courts in Kentucky and Washington have held that statutes that made it a crime for anyone to "insult or abuse any teacher in the public schools" were unconstitutionally vague and overbroad and, consequently, in violation of the First Amendment.[106] These decisions do not mean that schools cannot punish students for insulting and abusing teachers; they mean only that criminal statutes that apply to all citizens and restrict speech must be more precise and narrow in scope.

Can a Student Be Required to Pledge Allegiance?

No. Closely related to the right to speak is the right to remain silent—especially in relation to matters of conscience. (A discussion of students' rights under freedom of conscience can be found in chapter 10.)

Thus a federal appeals court ruled in favor of a New Jersey student who refused to stand during a recitation of the Pledge of Allegiance.[107] The judge wrote that the state cannot require a student to engage in "implicit expression" by standing at attention while the flag is being saluted. A requirement that students engage in a form of symbolic speech is unconstitutional and interferes with the students' right "not to participate" in the flag ceremony.

Can Schools Remove Controversial Books from a School Library?

The answer depends on the facts of the case. After obtaining a list of "objectionable" books from a conservative parents' organization, a New York school board removed 10 books from their school libraries because they were considered "anti-American, anti-Christian, anti-Semitic and just plain filthy." But a group of students and parents claimed that the board's action was unconstitutional, and a majority of the U.S. Supreme Court in *Board of Education, Island Trees Union Free School District No. 26* v. *Pico* agreed.[108] In *Pico,* Justice Brennan emphasized that students' First Amendment rights are applicable to the school library and that a school board's discretion "may not be exercised in a narrowly partisan or political manner," because "our Constitution does not permit the official suppression of ideas." If board members "intended by their removal decision" to deny students "access to ideas" with which the board disagreed and if this intent was "the decisive factor" in the board's decision, then the board's action was unconstitutional. On the other hand, Justice Brennan indicated several legitimate motivations for removing library books, including pervasive vulgarity, educational suitability, "good taste," "relevance," and "appropriateness to age and grade level." In sum, to avoid violating the First Amendment, "boards may not remove books from school library shelves simply because they dislike the ideas contained in those books." Rather they should establish and follow constitutional criteria and reasonable procedures before removing controversial material.[109] (The related issue of a student's right to hear controversial speakers is considered in chapter 11.)

A 1995 Kansas case illustrates how *Pico* has been applied to other school library controversies.[110] The case concerned the award-winning novel *Annie on My Mind,* which depicts a romantic relationship between two high school girls. The controversy erupted after local newspapers gave extensive publicity to the fact that the book was donated to the schools by the Gay and Lesbian Alliance Against Discrimination. As a result, some protesters burned copies of the book on the steps of the school district office. Because of the "turmoil created in the media" regarding *Annie,* Superintendent Ron Wimmer decided to remove all copies from the school libraries. Although school board members never discussed the book's merits, they voted to support Wimmer after being advised by the board's lawyer that if they removed the book because of its educational suitability, their decision would be legal. Board members testified that because of *Annie*'s "glorification of the gay lifestyle" and its conflict with the district's "traditional family values," it was "educationally unsuitable." The judge, however, concluded that the board's "actual motivation" for removing *Annie* was the members' "personal disapproval" of its ideas. This conclusion was based on two factors: First, the district "ignored its own guidelines and criteria established for the reconsideration of library materials." Second, board members who said their removal vote was based on educational suitability really meant they disagreed with the book's ideas; and, wrote the judge, their "invocation of 'educational suitability' does nothing to counterbalance the overwhelming evidence of viewpoint discrimination." Therefore, the judge ruled that the removal of *Annie* violated the First Amendment, and he ordered the book returned to the school libraries.

Under some state laws, judges have gone further than the U.S. Supreme Court in protecting students' and teachers' First Amendment rights. Thus a California appeals court ruled that a school district could not remove five books from a high school library because they were not "socially acceptable" and contained offensive language.[111] The court's liberal majority concluded that under California law the board did not have the authority to remove these books from the school library on the basis of "their perceived offensive content."

Do Students Have a Right to Academic Freedom?

No. Although students may choose courses, curriculum materials, teachers, and schools in some school districts, this is a matter of local discretion and not a constitutional right. Courts have not ruled that students have a right to determine courses, texts, or teaching methods. In a Wisconsin case, for example, a school board refused to allow its history teachers to show *Schindler's List,* a film about the Holocaust, because it was R-rated.[112] After gathering 400 student signatures protesting the decision, a high school student, Ben Borger, argued that the board violated his First Amendment rights by prohibiting the movie based on an outside organization rating without viewing it and thus restricting his access to important ideas. But a judge disagreed, emphasizing that this case was different from *Pico,* since the board here did not attempt to prohibit access to ideas about the Holocaust. Instead, Borger was trying "to force the school board to *add*" new materials to the curriculum. Since the school had a legitimate nonideological explanation for banning all R-rated films (to exclude "too much violence, nudity or 'hard' language"), the board's decision was reasonable. And "reasonableness," concluded the judge, is all that is necessary for "a constitutional exercise of school board discretion." Similarly, a federal appeals court held that students have no constitutional right to challenge a school board's decision to eliminate a popular course or to remove certain books from the curriculum.[113]

Do Students Have a Right to Remove "Racist" Books from the Curriculum?

Not because they are alleged to be racist. In Tempe, Arizona, a ninth-grade student and her mother asked a federal court to remove *The Adventures of Huckleberry Finn* from the high school's required reading list since it used the "insulting and racially derogatory term 'nigger'" over 200 times. The appeals court acknowledged that "books can hurt and that words can hurt—particularly racist epithets."[114] However, Judge Reinhardt wrote that courts may not ban books based on their content. Such action would severely restrict students' right to receive material and violate their First Amendment freedoms. Schools may be sued for racist policies, but not because assigned books are alleged to be racist. According to the court, permitting suits such as this "could have a significant chilling effect on a school district's willingness to assign books with themes, characters...or words that might offend." The function of books, wrote the judge, "is to stimulate thought, to explore ideas, to engender intellectual exchanges. Bad ideas should be countered with good ones, not banned by the courts."

Can Teachers Prohibit Students from Writing Papers on Religious Topics?

Teachers have discretion to decide what topics students may or may not write about. This was the ruling of a federal appeals court that upheld the decision of Dana Ramsey, a junior high school teacher from Tennessee, to refuse to accept a research paper entitled, "The Life of Jesus Christ" and gave her student, Brittany Settle, a zero for refusing to write on another topic.[115] Brittany's parents argued that Ramsey had violated their daughter's right to freedom of speech. But the court disagreed and wrote that teachers must be given "broad leeway" to determine the nature of the curriculum, and judges should not "overrule the teacher's view that the student should learn to write research papers beginning with a topic other than their own theology."[116]

Student Publications

Can Schools Regulate Student Publications?

The answer depends on whether the publication is sponsored by the school as part of the curriculum. If it is, educators have substantial control over its contents and style. However, underground student newspapers that are written and published off campus are protected by the First Amendment according to the principles of the *Tinker* decision. The following cases examine the scope and limits of school authority to regulate different types of student publications.

The *Hazelwood* Case[117]

Can Educators Control Publications Sponsored by the School?

Yes. The U.S. Supreme Court explained the scope of such control in a case that arose in Missouri's Hazelwood High School. The controversy concerned two stories that were deleted by principal Robert Reynolds from *Spectrum,* a newspaper published by the Journalism II class. The first described three students' experiences with pregnancy. Although the article used false names, Reynolds was concerned that the students still might be identifiable and that references to sexuality were inappropriate for younger students. Reynolds objected to the second article, about divorce, because one student complained about her father's behavior without giving the father an opportunity to respond.

Staff members of the *Spectrum* charged that the principal violated their First Amendment rights, but a majority of the Supreme Court disagreed. The Court ruled that educators can exercise substantial control over school-sponsored activities such as student publications or plays and other expressive activities that students, parents, and the public "might reasonably perceive to bear the imprimatur of the school…whether or not they occur in a traditional classroom setting."

Can Educators Regulate the Contents of School-Sponsored Publications or Plays Even If They Do Not Cause Disruption?

Yes. This is because the school, as publisher of a newspaper or producer of a play, may "refuse to lend its name and resources" to student expression that does not meet its "high standards." Thus, wrote the Supreme Court, educators have broad discretion to prohibit articles that are "ungrammatical, poorly written, inadequately researched, biased or prejudiced, vulgar or profane, or unsuitable for immature audiences." Furthermore, schools may refuse to sponsor student expression that may "advocate drug or alcohol use, irresponsible sex" or a controversial political position. The Court held that educators do not violate the First Amendment by "exercising editorial control over the style and content of student speech in school-sponsored expressive activities so long as their actions are reasonably related to legitimate pedagogical concerns." Thus, in *Hazelwood,* the Court ruled that the principal acted reasonably in removing the articles about pregnancy and divorce because of concern about protecting student anonymity and the privacy interests of the father, as well as protecting younger students from the "frank talk" about sex.

In a recent related case, members of a Missouri high school marching band sued their superintendent, Bernard DuBray, for violating their First Amendment rights by prohibiting them from performing the song "White Rabbit" by Jefferson Airplane.[118] Because he believed the lyrics to the song referred to using drugs, DuBray concluded that playing the song "would send a message inconsistent with the District's strong anti-drug policy." While the judge acknowledged that playing "White Rabbit" constitutes protected speech, he noted that *Hazelwood* allows officials to regulate student expression in school-sponsored activities when their actions are related to legitimate educational concerns. Therefore, this 1999 decision concluded that DuBray was "undoubtedly" authorized to restrict the band's performance of a song that might "reasonably be perceived" to advocate or tolerate drug use.

Are There Limits to Administrative Control Over School-Sponsored Publications or Plays?

Yes. According to the Court, educators do not have unlimited discretion "to censor a school-sponsored publication" or theatrical production. Such censorship would violate the U.S. Constitution if it had "no valid educational purpose" or was "unreasonable." In a New Jersey case, for example, a principal censored Brian Desilets's reviews about *Mississippi Burning* and *Rain Man* in his junior high school newspaper because they were R-rated films.[119] The reviews contained nothing that was vulgar or offensive. Nevertheless, school officials claimed that their censorship was based on legitimate educational concerns because R-rated movies could pose a "danger to student health." But they offered no evidence to support their claim. In ruling for the student, Judge Keefe wrote that a school's assertion that censorship is "justified by pedagogical concerns does not make it so." The judge added that "curtailment of cherished First Amendment rights mandates careful analysis of the reasons given…to determine if there is any valid educational purpose to support the censorship." Since the censorship in this case had nothing to do with the reviews' style or content (only the subject matter), the court ruled that the school violated Brian's constitutional rights.[120]

Does Hazelwood Require Educators to Control the Contents of School-Sponsored Publications?

No. *Hazelwood* ruled only that schools *may* control school-sponsored publications. Such regulation is not required. In fact, some state laws limit broad administrative control over school-supported student publications.

In California, for example, the Education Code states that "students of the public school shall have the right to exercise freedom of speech and of the press…in official publications…supported financially by the school."[121] Thus in a case concerning an allegedly defamatory article in a faculty-supervised school newspaper, a California judge wrote: "The broad power to censor expression in school-sponsored publications for pedagogical purposes recognized in [*Hazelwood v.*] *Kuhlmeier* is not available to this state's educators."[122] The judge noted that administrators "may censor expression from official school publications which…contain actionable defamation, but not as a matter of taste or pedagogy." Similarly, a Massachusetts law protects the right of students "to write, publish, and disseminate their views" in the public schools "provided that such right shall not cause any disruption."[123] In addition, Colorado law protects freedom of expression and prohibits prior restraint in student publications "whether or not such publication is school sponsored."[124] Iowa has a similar law.[125]

These state laws, however, do not eliminate all educational control. Thus, a California appeals court upheld the right of school officials to censor profanity in a proposed student script in a high school film arts class.[126] Students argued that profanity made the film more realistic. But the court upheld the censorship because the California law that protected student freedom of expression included an exception allowing faculty "to maintain professional standards of English."

Does Hazelwood *Allow Schools to Censor School-Sponsored Publications that Are Not Part of the Curriculum?*

Courts are in conflict about this question. In one controversial opinion, a divided federal appeals court upheld the decisions of Nevada principals who refused to print an advertisement by Planned Parenthood not only in the school newspaper and yearbook, which were part of the curriculum, but also in the school athletic programs, which were not.[127] According to the majority, schools retain the right to disapprove of ads that might carry a school-sponsored message to readers and put their imprimatur on one side of a controversial issue.

In a recent decision by the same appeals court, a California businessman sued a local high school for refusing to post his advertisement of the Ten Commandments on its baseball field fence along with other commercial ads. Using the "reasonableness" analysis, the court ruled that the school did not have to open the fence to advertisements regarding personal, political, and religious beliefs, and concerns regarding disruption are legitimate reasons for restricting ads on controversial topics.[128]

In a related Massachusetts case, a parent sued public high school officials after the student editors of the school newspaper refused his advertisement promoting sexual abstinence. The parent argued that the students' decision was a government action that violated his First Amendment rights since the paper has a faculty advisor and receives financial support from the school. But the court ruled that school funding and teacher advice did not transform the students' independent editorial judgment into state action.[129]

In New York a federal court interpreted *Hazelwood* narrowly in a case concerning a controversial student-written op-ed piece in a school-sponsored noncurricular newspaper.[130] The school argued that its authority to control the curriculum should include extra-curricular and co-curricular activities. But the court disagreed and refused to interpret *Hazelwood* broadly because it "opens the door to significant curtailment of cherished First Amendment rights." The court concluded that "educators may exercise greater editorial control over what students write for class than what they voluntarily submit to an extracurricular, albeit school-funded publication."

Does Hazelwood *Apply to a Student's Research and Classroom Report?*

It might. In a 1991 federal decision, a fifth-grade student, Diana Duran, claimed that her free speech rights were violated when she was prevented from distributing a survey and making an oral report on God.[131] (She gave her report only to her teacher.) Both the survey and report were related to an assignment on "The Power of _____." The trial court extended the reasoning of *Hazelwood* to apply to the decision of Diana's teacher. Thus the judge ruled that the restrictions on Diana's speech "were reasonably related to legitimate pedagogical concerns" about the impact on young students of teacher involvement with religious subjects, and about the "substantial risk" that Diana's views would be erroneously attributed to the school. The judge concluded that he need not decide whether the teacher's judgment was "right," only whether her "concern was reasonable."

Underground Publications

Does Hazelwood *Apply to Student Publications That Are Not Sponsored by the School?*

No. *Hazelwood* does not give educators control over the style and content of "underground" student periodicals that are published without school sponsorship or support and are not part of the curriculum. Instead, *Tinker* governs underground publications, which usually cannot be restricted unless they are libelous or obscene or are likely to cause substantial disruption or interfere with the rights of others.

Can an Underground Newspaper Be Banned for Discussing Controversial or Unpopular Topics?

No. In a case involving a high school underground paper, a federal appeals court wrote: "It should be axiomatic at this point in our nation's history that in a democracy 'controversy' is, as a matter of constitutional law, never sufficient in and of itself to stifle the views of any citizen."[132] The controversial subjects in the student publication included a statement about the injustice of current drug laws and an offer of information about birth control, venereal disease, and drug counseling. The court seemed surprised that an educational institution "would boggle at controversy" to such an extent that it would restrict a student publication merely because it urged students to become informed about these widely discussed and significant issues. The court commented that "our recollection of the learning process is that the purpose of education is to spread, not to stifle, ideas and views. Ideas must be freed from despotic dispensation by all men, be they robed as academicians or judges or citizen members of a board of education."[133]

Can an Underground Publication Be Prohibited from Criticizing School Officials?

No. In a Texas case, school officials defended their ban of a student newspaper because of its "negative attitude" and its criticism of the administration.[134] In rejecting this defense, the court explained that "aversion to criticism" is not a constitutional justification for restricting student expression. The First Amendment, wrote the court, protects freedom of the press precisely because those regulated "should have the right and even the responsibility" of commenting upon the actions of their regulators.

In a related Illinois case, a student was suspended for writing an editorial in an underground paper that criticized the senior dean. The court acknowledged that the editorial reflected a "disrespectful and tasteless attitude toward authority." Nevertheless, it ruled that schools cannot punish students merely because they express feelings that officials do not want to confront.[135]

Can an Underground Newspaper Be Prohibited from Criticizing School Policies?

No. Mere criticism of school rules and policies is not enough to allow officials to ban student publications or to punish the writers. To support such action, officials would have to show that the publications caused or would probably cause substantial and material disruption.

In the Illinois case mentioned in the previous question, the student editorial had strongly criticized some school procedures as "utterly idiotic and asinine" and called the school's detention policy "despicable and disgusting." The court ruled that these comments did not justify suspending the student responsible for the editorial. Moreover, the court noted that "prudent criticism" by high school students may be socially valuable because they possess a unique perspective on matters of school policy.

Distribution Policies

Do Schools Have Any Control over the Distribution of Underground Publications?

Yes. Officials can enforce reasonable regulations concerning the time, place, and manner in which student publications are distributed, but the rules cannot be so restrictive that they prevent the distribution of student views. This means that administrators could probably not prohibit all "in-school" distribution or distribution "while any class is being conducted," since such rules are broader than necessary for safety or to prevent disruption of school activities.[136] Examples of appropriate restrictions might include prohibiting distribution in laboratories, on stairways, or in narrow corridors and establishing rules aimed at minimizing litter on campus. In Colorado, for example, a federal court ruled that the ban on hallway distribution did not violate student freedom of expression, since distribution was allowed in other school locations and since the ban applied equally to all students, was designed to maintain order, and was not based on the viewpoint of the publication.[137]

When Can Schools Restrict the Content of Underground Publications?

School officials may restrict the distribution of material that is libelous, obscene, or substantially disruptive. Officials cannot restrict an underground publication simply on the basis of their "fear," "intuition," or "belief" that it will cause disruption; their judgment must be supported by significant facts and evidence.

Libel is a false written statement that injures a person's reputation. A person who is libeled can sue for damages. If the person is a public figure, he or she must prove that the writer knew or should have known that the statement was untrue. Writing falsely that the principal stole $1,000 would probably be libelous; an editorial alleging that "some teachers" in a school district are incompetent probably is not. (For more on libel, see chapter 7.)

Is a Publication Legally Obscene If It Contains Offensive, Vulgar, or "Dirty" Language?

No. Many parents and teachers equate obscenity with offensive four-letter words, but this is not what lawyers and judges mean. To be legally obscene, material must violate three tests developed by the U.S. Supreme Court: (1) It must appeal to the prurient or lustful interest of minors; (2) it must describe sexual conduct in a way that is "patently offensive" to community standards, *and* (3) taken as a whole, it "must lack serious literary, artistic, political or scientific value."[138]

Parents, teachers, and administrators may be offended by student use of profanity in their writing; however, most controversial articles about social, political, or educational issues in underground newspapers, even though they may use offensive language, do not violate the three-part Supreme Court test. However, judges are less likely to protect student publications that contain vulgar, offensive language and more likely to protect those that deal with controversial political ideas.

Can Schools Ban Distribution of Publications That Promote a Particular Religious Belief?

No. Schools cannot restrict the distribution of materials by students because of the subject matter or because other students would think they were school-sponsored. This was the ruling of a federal appeals court in an Illinois case involving a Wauconda Junior High School student who was prohibited from distributing a church publication.[139] Concerning a policy that banned the distribution of all religious material at elementary and junior high schools, Judge Easterbrook wrote: "No arm of government may discriminate against religious speech when speech on other subjects is permitted in the same place." The school revised its policy to prohibit distribution of religious material that students might mistakenly believe was "endorsed by the school." The court, however, rejected the notion that "the best defense against misunderstandings is censorship." Far better, wrote the judge, is to teach students about the First Amendment, "about the difference between private and public action, about why we tolerate divergent views." The court ruled that students may hand out literature even if other students "misunderstand its provenance." According to the judge, "Schools may explain that they do not endorse speech by permitting it. If pupils do not comprehend so simple a lesson, then one wonders whether the Wauconda schools can teach anything at all."

In a related Colorado case, students who were suspended for giving out a Christian newspaper challenged a policy prohibiting distribution of "material that proselytizes a particular religious or political belief."[140] Administrators argued that *Hazelwood* allowed them to prohibit distribution of such controversial publications. But the judge disagreed and explained:"Because students have a right to engage in political and religious speech," school policies that ban such publications "do not advance any legitimate government interest." Instead, by preventing students from discussing issues they feel are important, the policy "cripples them as contributing citizens," inhibits their individual development, and "defeat[s] the very purpose of public education in secondary schools."

Are Policies That Require Administrative Approval of Underground Publications Unconstitutional?

A few courts believe they are. Their position is illustrated by a case that arose when five students at Washington's Lindbergh High School distributed 350 copies of an underground student newspaper, *Bad Astra,* at a senior class barbecue.[141] The paper, which was printed off campus, included a mock teacher evaluation poll and articles that were critical of administrative policy. The students were censured for violating a rule that required all student-written material to be submitted to the administration for approval before distribution on school property. However, the Ninth Circuit Court of Appeals held the rule unconstitutional. According to the court, "student distribution of non-school-sponsored material under the Supreme Court's decisions in *Tinker* and *Hazelwood* cannot be subjected to regulation on the basis of undifferentiated fears of possible disturbances or embarrassment."[142]

Courts are in conflict about this issue, and most hold that prior review policies are not unconstitutional.[143] For example, the Eighth Circuit Court of Appeals considered a Minnesota high school's guidelines requiring administrative review before the distribution of "unofficial written material on school premises."[144] Students who wanted to distribute an underground paper, *Tour de Farce,* claimed that the guidelines violated their rights. However, the court ruled that the school's policy is "not unconstitutional merely because it asserts a right of prior review." Furthermore, the court approved the guidelines that prohibit material that is obscene, libelous, or disruptive or is "pervasively indecent or vulgar." Nevertheless, the judge reminded school officials that "criticism of established policies, even in vigorous or abrasive terms, is not to be equated with disruptiveness." Similarly, a 1996 federal decision upheld an Indiana school policy that required students to give their principal a copy of material they wanted to distribute 48 hours in advance.[145] The court ruled that the policy was not an "impermissible prior restraint" because it did not give administrators discretion to prohibit distribution based on content and was mainly used to regulate the time, place, and manner of distribution.

What Procedures and Standards Are Necessary Before Schools Can Require Prior Review of Student Publications?

Some courts have held prior review procedures to be unconstitutional because they lacked either clear standards or due process safeguards. In a Maryland case, for example, a federal appeals court wrote that rules requiring prior review "must contain narrow, objective, and reasonable standards" by which the material will be judged.[146] Such standards are required so that those who enforce the rules are not given "impermissible power to judge the material on an ad hoc and subjective basis." The court wrote that legal terms such as "libelous" or "obscene" used without explanation "are not sufficiently precise or understandable by high school students and administrators untutored in the law" to be acceptable criteria of what is prohibited. Therefore, prior review policies must contain "precise criteria sufficiently spelling out what is forbidden" so that students may clearly know what they may or may not write.

In another federal case, an appeals court declared a Texas school's prior review requirement unconstitutional because it lacked due process safeguards.[147] There was no provision for an appeal if the principal prohibited distribution, nor did the rules state how long the principal could take to make a decision. Delays in reviewing newspapers, wrote the court, "carry the inherent danger that the exercise of speech might be chilled altogether during the period of its importance." Therefore, the court held that any requirement for screening student publications before distribution must clearly state (1) how students are to submit proposed materials to the administration, (2) a brief period of time during which the administration must make its decision, (3) a clear and reasonable method of appeal, and (4) a brief time during which the appeal must be decided. Due process should also provide for some kind of informal hearing for the students affected. Because the regulations challenged in this case violated the students' constitutional rights, the court commented that "it would be well if those entrusted to administer the teaching of American history and government to our students began their efforts by practicing the document on which that history and government are based."

In 1996, however, a divided federal appeals court upheld an elementary school's prior restraint policy even through it contained no procedural safeguards and no time limit within which a decision had to be made.[148] The court explained that because schools are "not courts or administrative tribunals," judges should not impose "rigid deadlines or intricate procedures" that restrict reasonable administrative discretion.

Can Administrators Suppress Student Publications without Written Guidelines?

Sometimes. In a New York high school, for example, the principal seized all copies of a student newspaper because of a "threatening" letter falsely attributed to the lacrosse team and a "libelous" letter about the vice president of the student government. The student editors claimed that the principal could not legally suppress their paper because there were no specific school policies giving him that authority. A federal court disagreed, however.[149]

The judge acknowledged that suppression of a publication by school officials must be "scrutinized more carefully" in the absence of guidelines. Nevertheless, Judge Pratt ruled that school officials have the power to prevent distribution within the school of material that is "libelous, obscene,...likely to create substantial disorder or which invades the rights of others," even if the school has no written policies on the subject.

Can Schools Ban the Sale of Underground Publications on Campus?

Probably not. An Indiana case held that a rule prohibiting the sale of all publications except those benefiting the school was unconstitutional.[150] School officials had argued that newspaper sales and other commercial activities are "unnecessary distractions" that are "inherently disruptive." The judge acknowledged that administrators have a legitimate interest in limiting commercial activities on campus by nonstudents, but he pointed out that the reason the students sold the newspaper in this case was only to raise the money needed to publish their paper. The court noted that administrators have ample authority to regulate the time, place, and manner of newspaper sales to maintain order and avoid littering or interference with others without restricting First Amendment rights. In a related California case, the state supreme court wrote: "We fail to see how the *sale* of newspapers on the school premises will necessarily disrupt the work and discipline of the school whereas their distribution free of charge will not."[151]

Can Schools Prohibit the Distribution of Material Not Written by a Student or a School Employee?

Probably not. In the Indiana case mentioned in the previous question, the court wrote that such a rule would prohibit use of materials by all sorts of people "whose views might be thought by the students to be worthy of circulation."[152] And the judge indicated that he had "no doubt" that such a rule violated the students' First Amendment rights.

On the other hand, a federal appeals court upheld an Illinois school policy prohibiting students from distributing more than ten copies of materials prepared by nonstudents.[153] The judge wrote that the policy served a reasonable educational purpose because "learning how to express thoughts in your own words is an essential component of education."[154] Since the school allowed the distribution of ten copies of materials for students who didn't want to "undertake the labor of exposition" and since the policy was educational, "not arbitrary or whimsical," the court ruled it was not unconstitutional.

Can Schools Prohibit the Distribution of Anonymous Articles?

Not according to one federal judge who noted that historically anonymous publications have been an important vehicle for criticizing oppressive practices and laws and that anonymous student publications can perform a similar function in schools. "Without anonymity," wrote the judge, "fear of reprisal may deter peaceful discussion of controversial but important school rules and policies."[155] The problem with this prohibition, the court explained, is That it is not limited to potentially libelous, obscene, or disruptive material but applies equally to thoughtful, responsible criticism.

Can Administrators Ban the Distribution of Underground Newspapers That Encourage Drug Use?

Yes. In a Maryland case, a federal appeals court upheld the authority of a high school principal to seize an "underground" publication because it contained an advertisement for a waterpipe used to smoke marijuana and hashish.[156] Student publishers of the non-school-sponsored newspaper claimed that the seizure violated their rights because the ad would not substantially disrupt school activities. The court rejected this argument, however.

Substantial disruption, wrote the judge, "is merely one justification for school authorities to restrain distribution," not the "sole justification." The judge noted that "advertisements encouraging the use of drugs" can endanger students' health. Therefore the court ruled that the First Amendment rights of students "must yield to the superior interest of the school" in prohibiting the distribution of publications "that encourage actions which endanger the health or safety of students."

Can Schools Regulate Off-Campus Publications?

Not according to judge Irving Kaufman.[157] The case concerned several high school students from a small, rural New York community who produced *Hard Times,* a satirical publication addressed to the school community. The language in the publication was considered "indecent," but it was not legally obscene. *Hard Times* was written, sold, and printed off campus, but when the president of the local school board learned about the publication, she urged administrative action. As a result, the school penalized the student publishers, and they took their case to court.

According to the court: "We may not permit school administrators to seek approval of the community-at-large by punishing students for expression that took place off school property. Nor may courts endorse such punishment be cause the populace would approve." Despite the good intentions of school officials, Judge Kaufman said they must be restrained in moving against student expression since they act "as both a prosecutor and a judge" and because their desire to preserve decorum gives them "a vested interest in suppressing controversy." Therefore the First Amendment "forbids public school administrators and teachers from regulating the material to which a child is exposed after he leaves school each afternoon."

Can Teachers Sue Students for Verbal Attacks?

In rare cases of outrageous student publications, where teachers are threatened with violence, the students could be sued for money damages for "the intentional infliction of emotional distress." This was the ruling in a 2000 Florida case where two high school seniors wrote and distributed a publication entitled "Low Life," which attacked a teacher with vulgar, abusive, and racist language and threatened to rape her and her children. Because the students' conduct was so outrageous, the court concluded that "justice, reason, and common sense compel a remedy for the revilement inflicted upon the teacher."[158] (Suits for defamation are discussed in chapter 6.)

Summary

For most of the 20th century, the U.S. Constitution did not protect students or teachers when they spoke out on controversial issues. In 1969, however, the U.S. Supreme Court ruled that neither teachers nor students lose their right to freedom of expression when they enter the public schools. But freedom of expression, like most constitutional rights, is not absolute; it can be limited when it conflicts with other basic values.

To decide when a teacher's controversial out-of-class statements are protected, judges usually balance "the interests of the teacher, as citizen, in commenting on matters of public concern and the interests of the state, as employer, in promoting the efficiency of the schools." In the *Pickering* case, the Court emphasized that voters should be able to hear the informed opinions of teachers about public educational issues and that teachers should not be punished merely for expressing their views on controversial topics. If teachers' statements are constitutionally protected, they cannot be reprimanded, transferred, or otherwise disciplined for making them. On the other hand, courts have held that the First Amendment does not protect a teacher's false and reckless accusations, statements to the press about a personnel matter under investigation, scornful and abusive personal attacks on school officials, repeated criticism of teaching assignments and evaluations, or public disclosure of confidential information. Furthermore, the Supreme Court ruled that if a teacher speaks, not as a citizen about matters of public concern but as an employee about matters of personal interest, such views are not protected. Because judges have differing notions of what constitutes "a matter of public concern," and because they weigh the rights of the teachers and the interests of the schools differently, the outcome of a close case may vary from one court to another.

When teachers allege that they are unconstitutionally punished because of their statements, court decisions suggest a four-step analysis. (1) Do the statements involve matters of public concern? If so, (2) does the teacher's right to discuss public matters outweigh the school's interest in promoting efficiency? If the court answers these questions in the affirmative, the teacher's statements would be protected by the First Amendment. But before judges order schools to rescind the punishment, they also ask: (3) Was the teacher's speech a substantial or motivating factor in the action against him or her? If so, (4) did the administration prove that it would have taken the same action even in the absence of the protected conduct? If not, courts should find the punishment unconstitutional and perhaps award damages.

In deciding whether to protect controversial teaching methods and materials, many courts use a "balancing test," a case-by-case inquiry that balances the teacher's right to academic freedom against the legitimate interests of the community. When judging academic freedom cases, courts give special consideration to the following factors: whether the controversial language or publication was relevant to the curriculum, whether it was appropriate to the age and maturity of the students, the quality of the teaching material and its effect on the students. According to most courts, even when schools can prohibit certain methods or materials, teachers should not be disciplined for using them unless the teachers know in advance that they are prohibited.

In recent years, an increasing number of courts have articulated a narrower view of academic freedom. According to this view, school restrictions on a teacher's methods and materials are constitutional if they are "reasonably related to legitimate pedagogical concerns."[159] Such an approach gives schools and judges wide discretion to determine what is reasonable and what are legitimate educational concerns. But these courts also usually require advance notice of what is not allowed.

In sum, teachers have less First Amendment protection in the classroom than outside the school. Nevertheless, teachers who are punished for using controversial materials that are relevant and nondisruptive will probably be protected by most courts if such materials were not clearly prohibited. Academic freedom, however, does not give teachers the right to refuse to use required texts or to ignore the established curriculum; nor does it protect incompetent teaching or religious or political indoctrination.[160]

Courts now recognize that the First Amendment applies to students as well as teachers. In *Tinker*, the Supreme Court held that it is unconstitutional to restrict student expression unless it would "materially and substantially interfere" with school activities or the rights of others. Schools can restrict symbolic expression when such symbols have caused material disruption in the past or when there is evidence that they would probably cause substantial disorder. Although officials may not suppress student access to ideas for political or religious reasons, they may remove library books that are pervasively vulgar or educationally unsuitable. Furthermore, the Supreme Court has ruled that students can be punished for using "vulgar and offensive" language in classes, assemblies, and other educational activities. Also, fighting words and obscene language can be prohibited anywhere on campus.

In the *Hazelwood* case, the Supreme Court held that educators had broad discretion to regulate the style and content of student expression in curriculum-related publications or plays. As a result, courts will probably uphold any regulation of school-sponsored publications, plays, or other curruculum-related activities if the regulation is "reasonable," unless state laws more broadly protect student freedom of expression. *Hazelwood*, however, does not allow schools to control the contents of "underground" student periodicals that are written and published off campus without school support. Instead, *Tinker* governs such publications, which usually cannot be restricted unless they are libelous or obscene or are likely to cause substantial disruption or interfere with the rights of others. Thus, underground student newspapers cannot be censored by school officials because they discuss unpopular or controversial topics or criticize administrators, teachers, or school policies.

Schools have the right to establish reasonable rules regulating the time, place, and manner for distributing all student publications. Moreover, most courts allow schools to screen student publications prior to distribution if they have issued clear, objective standards and have procedural safeguards for the review process. And one court has ruled that even without written policies, officials can suppress a student publication that is libelous, obscene, or likely to create substantial disorder.

NOTES

1. *West Virginia State Bd. of Educ.* v. *Barnette,* 319 U.S. 624 (1943).
2. *Pickering* v. *Board of Education,* 391 U.S. 563 (1968). For a more recent application of *Pickering,* see *Anderson* v. *Central Point School District No. 6,* 746 F.2d 505 (9th Cir. 1984).
3. *Bernasconi* v. *Tempe Elementary School District No. 3,* 548 F.2d 857 (9th Cir. 1977).
4. *Seemuller* v. *Fairfax County School Board,* 878 F.2d 1578 (4th Cir. 1989).
5. *Rowland* v. *Mad River Local School District, Montgomery County,* 730 F.2d 444 (6th Cir. 1984). See thoughtful dissenting opinion by Justice Brennan, *Id.* For other aspects of this case, see chapter 13.
6. *Pietrunti* v. *Board of Education of Brick Township,* 319 A.2d 262 (N.J. 1974).
7. *Swilley* v. *Alexander,* 629 F.2d 1018 (5th Cir. 1980).
8. *Watts* v. *Seward School Board,* 454 P.2d 732 (Alaska 1969).
9. *Lusk* v. *Estes,* 361 F.Supp. 653 (N.D. Tex. 1973).
10. *Bowman* v. *Pulaski County Special School District,* 723 F.2d 640 (8th Cir. 1983).
11. *Gilbertson* v. *McAlister,* 403 F.Supp. 1 (D. Conn. 1975).
12. *Givhan* v. *Western Line Consolidated School District,* 439 U.S. 410 (1979); see also *Ayers* v. *Western Line Consolidated School District,* 691 F.2d 766 (5th Cir. 1982).
13. *Anderson* v. *Evans,* 660 F.2d 153 (6th Cir. 1981).
14. *Anderson* v. *Central Point School District No. 6,* 746 F.2d 505 (9th Cir. 1984).
15. *Southside Public Schools* v. *Hill,* 827 F.2d 270 (8th Cir. 1987).
16. 461 U.S. 138 (1983).
17. *Hall* v. *Marion School District No. 2,* 860 F.Supp. 278 (D. S.C. 1993). The measures included placing a threatening ad in a local newspaper and hiring a photographer to try to catch her "in a clear act of insubordination."
18. *Wichert* v. *Walter,* 606 F.Supp. 1516 (D. N.J. 1985).
19. *Weaver* v. *Nebo School District,* 29 F.Supp.2d 1279 (D. Utah 1998).
20. *Lewis* v. *Harrison School District No. 1,* 805 F.2d 310 (8th Cir. 1986).
21. *Hesse* v. *Board of Education of Township High School District No. 211,* 848 F.2d 748 (7th Cir. 1988).
22. *Ifill* v. *District of Columbia,* 665 A.2d 185 (D.C. 1995).
23. *Vukadinovich* v. *Bartels,* 853 F.2d 1387 (7th Cir. 1988).
24. *Sanguigni* v. *Pittsburgh Board of Public Education,* 968 F.2d 393 (3rd Cir. 1992).
25. *Schul* v. *Sherard,* 102 F.Supp.2d 877 (S.D. Ohio 2000).
26. *Piver* v. *Pender County Board of Education,* 835 F.2d 1076 (4th Cir. 1987).
27. *Knapp* v. *Whitaker,* 757 F.2d 827 (7th Cir. 1985). For a more recent case, see *Green* v. *Maine School Adminstrative District #77,* 52 F. Supp. 2d 98 (D.Me. 1999).
28. *Cirelli* v. *Town of Johnston School District,* 897 F.Supp. 663 (D.R.J. 1995).
29. *Carlino* v. *Gloucester City High School,* 57 F.Supp.2d 1 (D.N.J. 1999).
30. *Hennessy* v. *City of Melrose,* 194 F.3d 237 (1st Cir. 1999).
31. *Chicago School Reform Board of Trustees* v. *Substance, Inc.,* 79 F.Supp.2d 919 (N.D.Ill. 2000).

32. *Newton* v. *Slye,* 116 F.Supp.2d 677 (W.D.Va. 2000).

33. *Los Angeles Teachers Union* v. *Los Angeles City Board of Education,* 455 P.2d 827 (Cal. 1969).

34. *Coover* v. *Saucon Valley School District,* 955 F.Supp. 392 (E.D. Pa. 1997).

35. *City of Madison Joint School District No. 8* v. *Wisconsin Employment Relations Commission,* 429 U.S. 167 (1976).

36. *Rendell-Baker* v. *Kohn,* 457 U.S. 830 (1982).

37. States with whistleblower statutes include Arkansas, Arizona, California, Colorado, Connecticut, Delaware, Florida, Georgia, Hawaii, Illinois, Indiana, Iowa, Kansas, Kentucky, Louisiana, Maine, Maryland, Massachusetts, Michigan, Minnesota, Mississippi, Montana, Nevada, New Hampshire, New Jersey, New Mexico, New York, North Carolina, North Dakota, Ohio, Oklahoma, Oregon, Pennsylvania, Rhode Island, South Carolina, South Dakota, Tennessee, Texas, Utah, Washington, West Virginia, Wisconsin, and Wyoming. [This list is based on Tim Barnett, *Overview of State Whistleblower Protection Statutes, 43 Labor L.J.* 440 (1992); LEXIS/NEXIS Research Software (August 1997)]. In addition, many federal statutes (e.g., those governing workplace safety and minimum wages, and prohibiting discrimination) include antiretaliation provisions.

38. *Knowlton* v. *Greenwood Independent School District,* 957 F.2d 1172 (5th Cir. 1992).

39. *Keyser* v. *Sacramento City Unified School District,* 238 F.3d 1132 (9th Cir. 2001).

40. *Wytrwal* v. *Mowles,* 886 F.Supp. 128 (D.Me. 1995).

41. *Parducci* v. *Rutland,* 316 F.Supp. 352 (M.D. Ala. 1970).

42. *Keefe* v. *Geanakos,* 418 F.2d 359 (1st Cir. 1969).

43. *Miles* v. *Denver Public Schools,* 944 F.2d 773 (10th Cir. 1991).

44. *Cary* v. *Board of Education, Adams-Arapahoe School District,* 598 F.2d 535 (10th Cir. 1979).

45. *Boring* v. *Buncombe County Board of Education,* 136 F.3d 364 (4th Cir. 1998). Also, see the strong dissenting opinion by Judge Diana Motz, Id. at 375.

46. *Virgil* v. *School Board of Columbia County, Florida,* 862 F.2d 1517 (11th Cir. 1989).

47. *McCarthy* v. *Fletcher,* 254 Cal. Rptr. 714 (Cal. Ct. App. 1989).

48. *Pratt* v. *Independent School District No. 831, Forest Lake,* 670 F.2d 771 (8th Cir. 1982).

49. *Epperson* v. *Arkansas,* 393 U.S. 97 (1968).

50. *Loewen* v. *Turnipseed,* 488 F.Supp. 1138 (N.D. Miss. 1980).

51. *Sterzing* v. *Fort Bend Independent School District,* 376 F.Supp. 657 (S.D. Tex. 1972).

52. *Kingsville Independent School District* v. *Cooper,* 611 F.2d 1109 (5th Cir. 1980).

53. *Dean* v. *Timpson Independent School District,* 486 F.Supp. 302 (E.D. Tex. 1979).

54. *Downs* v. *Los Angeles Unified School District,* 228 F.3d 1003 (9th Cir. 2000).

55. *La Rocca* v. *Board of Education of Rye City School District,* 406 N.Y.S.2d 348 (N.Y. App. Div. 1978).

56. *Peloza* v. *Capistrano Unified School District,* 782 F.Supp. 1412 (C.D. Cal. 1992).

57. *Clark* v. *Holmes,* 474 F.2d 928 (7th Cir. 1972).

58. *Kirkland* v. *Northside Independent School District,* 890 F.2d 794 (5th Cir. 1989).

59. *Peloza, supra* note 56.

60. *Brubaker* v. *Board of Education, School District No. 149, Cook County, Illinois,* 502 F.2d 973 (7th Cir. 1974).

61. *Scruggs* v. *Keen,* 900 F.Supp. 821 (W.D. Va. 1995).

62. *Stachura* v. *Truszkowski,* 763 F.2d 211 (6th Cir. 1985), *Memphis Community School District* v. *Stachura,* 477 U.S. 299 (1986).

63. *Fowler* v. *Board of Education of Lincoln County, Kentucky,* 819 F.2d 657 (6th Cir. 1987).

64. *Spurger* v. *Rapides Parish School Board,* 628 So.2d 1317 (La. Ct. App. 3d Cir. 1993).

65. *Rothschild* v. *Board of Education of the City of Buffalo,* 778 F.Supp. 642 (W.D. N.Y. 1991).

66. *Reitmeyer* v. *Unemployment Compensation Board of Review,* 602 A.2d 505 (Pa. Commw. 1992).

67. *Mailloux* v. *Kiley,* 323 F.Supp. 1387 (D. Mass. 1971).

68. *Oakland Unified School District* v. *Olicker,* 102 Cal. Rptr. 421 (Cal. Ct. App. 1972).

69. *Ward* v. *Hickey,* 996 F.2d 448 (1st Cir. 1993).

70. *Celestine* v. *Lafayette Parish School Board,* 284 So.2d 650 (La. 1973).

71. *Ahern* v. *Board of Education of School District of Grand Island,* 456 F.2d 399 (8th Cir. 1972).

72. *Bradley* v. *Pittsburgh Board of Education*, 913 F.2d 1064 (3d Cir. 1990). For a similar, more recent decision, see *Murray* v. *Pittsburgh Board of Public Education*, 919 F.Supp. 838 (W.D. Pa. 1996).

73. *Lacks* v. *Ferguson Reorganized School District R2*, 147 F.3d 718 (8th Cir. 1998). The plays included words such as "fuck," "shit," "bitch," and "nigger" and were used more than 150 times in about 40 minutes. *Id.* at 719.

74. *In re Proposed Termination of Johnson's Teaching Contract*, 451 N.W.2d 343 (Minn. Ct. App. 1990).

75. *Meyer* v. *Board of Education of Charlotte Valley Central School District*, 581 N.Y.S.2d 920 (App. Div. 3d Dept. 1992).

76. *Malverne Union Free School District* v. *Sobol*, 586 N.Y.S.2d 673 (App. Div. 3d Dept. 1992).

77. *Hetrick* v. *Martin*, 480 F.2d 705 (6th Cir. 1973).

78. *Watson* v. *Eagle County School District*, 797 P.2d 768 (Colo. Ct. App. 1990)

79. 323 F.Supp. 1387 (D. Mass. 1971).

80. *Wooster* v. *Sunderland*, 148 P. 959 RE-50 (Cal. Ct. App. 1915).

81. *Tinker* v. *Des Moines Independent School District*, 393 U.S. 503 (1969).

82. *Muller by Muller* v. *Jefferson Lighthouse School*, 98 F.3d 1530 (7th Cir. 1996). Judge Manion also wrote: "The 'marketplace of ideas,' an important theme in high school student expression cases, is a less appropriate description of an elementary school, where children are just beginning to acquire the means of expression." *Id.* at 1538.

83. *Baxter by Baxter* v. *Vigo County School Corporation*, 26 F.3d 728 (7th Cir. 1994).

84. *Guzick* v. *Drebus*, 431 F.2d 594 (6th Cir. 1970).

85. *Karp* v. *Becken*, 477 F.2d 171 (9th Cir. 1973).

86. *West* v. *Derby Unified School District No. 260*, 206 F.3d 1358 (10th Cir. 2000).

87. *Denno ex rel. Denno* v. *School Board of Volusia County, Florida*, 218 F.3d 1267 (11th Cir. 2000).

88. The majority also quoted with approval this judicial comment: "Since *Tinker,* however, the Supreme Court has cast some doubt on the extent to which students retain free speech rights in the school setting." *Baxter* v. *Vigo County School Corporation*, 26 F.3d 728 (7th Cir. 1994).

89. *Butts* v. *Dallas Independent School District*, 436 F.2d 728 (5th Cir. 1971).

90. *Crosby* v. *Holsinger*, 852 F.2d 801 (4th Cir. 1988).

91. *Grayned* v. *City of Rockford*, 408 U.S. 104 (1972).

92. *Bacon* v. *Bradley-Bourbonnais High School District No. 307*, 707 F.Supp. 1005 (C.D. Ill. 1989).

93. *Fenton* v. *Stear*, 423 F.Supp. 767 (W.D. Pa. 1976).

94. *Heller* v. *Hodgin*, 928 F.Supp. 789 (S.D. Ind. 1996).

95. *Lovell* v. *Poway Unified School District*, 90 F.3d 367 (9th Cir. 1996).

96. *Bethel School District No. 403* v. *Fraser*, 478 U.S. 675 (1986). The following excerpts are illustrative of Fraser's six-sentence nominating speech: "I know a man who is firm—he's firm in his pants…his character is firm…he's a man who takes his point and pounds it in.…He doesn't attack things in spurts—he drives hard, pushing and pushing until finally he succeeds. Jeff is a man who will go to the very end—even the climax, for each and every one of you.…"

97. For more information on this topic, see D. Schimmel, *Lewd Language Not Protected: Bethel* v. *Fraser*, 33 EDUC. L. REP. 999 (1986).

98. *Heller* v. *Hodgin*, 928 F.Supp. 789 (S.D. Ind. 1996). Emily shouted that she was not a "white ass fucking bitch" after another student called her one. *Id.* at 792.

99. *Id.* at 798 (quoting *Chandler* v. *McMinnville School District*, 978 F.2d 524 (9th Cir. 1992)).

100. *Anderson* v. *Milbank School District 25–41*, 197 F.R.D. 682 (D.S.D. 2000).

101. *Boroff* v. *Van Wert City Board of Education*, 220 F.3d 465 (6th Cir. 2000).

102. *Smith ex rel. Lanham* v. *Greene County School District*, 100 F. Supp.2d 1354 (M.D.Ga. 2000).

103. *Chandler* v. *McMinnville School District*, 978 F.2d 524 (9th Cir. 1992).

104. *Id.* at 531 (quoting *Thomas* v. *Board of Education*, 607 F.2d 1043, 1057 (2d Cir. 1979)).

105. *Poling* v. *Murphy*, 872 F.2d 757 (6th Cir. 1989).

106. *Commonwealth* v. *Ashcraft*, 691 S.W.2d 229 (Ky. Ct. App. 1985), *State* v. *Reyes*, 700 P.2d 1155 (Wash. 1985). A related Georgia law provides that persons other than students who "insult or abuse school teachers in the presence of pupils" in a public school or school bus may be guilty of a misdemeanor if they are asked to leave the school or bus and fail to do so. GA. CODE ANN. § 20-2-1182 (1993).

107. *Lipp* v. *Morris,* 579 F.2d 834 (3d Cir. 1978).

108. 457 U.S. 853 (1982).

109. For more on this topic, see David Schimmel, *The Limits of School Board Discretion: Board of Education* v. *Pico, 6 Educ. L. Rep.* 285 (1983).

110. *Case* v. *Unified School District No. 233,* 908 F.Supp. 864 (D. Kan. 1995).

111. *Wexner* v. *Anderson Union High School District,* 258 Cal. Rptr. 26 (Cal. Ct. App. 1989).

112. *Borger* v. *Bisciglia,* 888 F.Supp. 97 (E.D. Wis. 1995).

113. *Zykan* v. *Warsaw Community School Corporation,* 631 F.2d 1300 (7th Cir. 1980).

114. *Monteiro* v. *Tempe Union High School District,* 158 F.3D 1022 (9th Cir. 1998).

115. *Settle* v. *Dickson County School Board,* 53 F.3d 152 (6th Cir. 1995). In justifying her action, Ramsey claimed that the law prohibits dealing with religious issues in the classroom. In a concurring opinion, Judge Batchelder responded: "Ms. Ramsey was dead wrong in her view that…a paper of a religious nature is impermissible in the public schools. Had the assignment been to write a paper of opinion, and had Ms. Ramsey rejected the paper on the grounds of its religious content alone, Brittany's freedom of speech truly would have been violated." *Id.* at 159.

116. *Id.* at 156.

117. *Hazelwood School District* v. *Kuhlmeier,* 484 U.S. 260 (1988).

118. *McCann* v. *Fort Zumwalt School District,* 50 F.Supp.2d 918 (E.D.Mo. 1999).

119. *Desilets ex rel. Desilets* v. *Clearview Regional Board of Education,* 630 A.2d 333 (N.J. Super. App. Div. 1993).

120. On appeal, the New Jersey Supreme Court also supported the student, and noted that the school's educational policy applied here was vague, inconsistent, and often ignored. It concluded that the school violated Brien's "expressional rights" because it "failed to establish a legitimate educational policy" concerning the publication of challenged materials. *Desilets ex rel. Desilets* v. *Clearview Regional Board of Education,* 647 A.2d 150 (N.J. 1994).

121. Cal. Ed. Code § 48907.

122. *Leeb* v. *DeLong,* 243 Cal. Rptr. 494 (Cal. Ct. App. 1988).

123. Mass. Gen. L. ch. 71, § 82 (1989).

124. Colo. Rev. Stat. § 22-1-120(1) (1990).

125. Iowa CODE § 280-22 (1989).

126. *Lopez* v. *Tulare Joint Union High School District Board of Trustees,* 40 Cal. Rptr. 2d 762 (Cal. Ct. App. 5th Dist. 1995). The film dialogue included words such as "shit," "bitch," and "fuck."

127. *Planned Parenthood* v. *Clark County School District,* 941 F.2d 817 (9th Cir. 1991).

128. *Diloreto* v. *Downey Unified School District Board of Education,* 196 F.3d 958 (9th Cir. 1999).

129. *Yeo* v. *Town of Lexington,* 131 F.3d 241 (1st Cir. 1997).

130. *Romano* v. *Harrington,* 725 F.Supp. 687 (E.D. N.Y. 1989).

131. *Duran* v. *Nitsche,* 780 F.Supp. 1048 (E.D. Pa. 1991).

132. *Shanley* v. *Northeast Independent School District,* 462 F.2d 960 (5th Cir. 1972).

133. *Id.*

134. *Id.*

135. *Scoville* v. *Board of Education of Joliet Township,* 425 F.2d 10 (7th Cir. 1970).

136. *Jacobs* v. *Board of School Commissioners,* 490 F.2d 601 (7th Cir. 1973).

137. *Hemry* v. *School Board of Colorado Springs,* 760 F.Supp. 856 (D. Colo. 1991).

138. *Miller* v. *California,* 413 U.S. 15 (1973).

139. *Hedges* v. *Wauconda Community Unit School District No. 118,* 9 F.3d 1295 (7th Cir. 1993).

140. *Rivera* v. *East Otero School District R-1,* 721 F.Supp. 1189 (D. Colo. 1989).

141. *Burch* v. *Barker,* 861 F.2d 1149 (9th Cir. 1988).

142. An earlier federal appeals court ruled that schools cannot request that all student publications be submitted for approval before distribution. *Fujishima* v. *Board of Education,* 460 F.2d 1355 (7th Cir. 1972).

143. For example, the Second Circuit allowed broad prior review in *Eisner* v. *Stamford Board of Education,* 440 F.2d 803 (1971), and the Fifth Circuit held that a policy of prior review was not unconstitutional "per se" in *Shanley, supra* note 133. Similarly, the First Circuit in *Riseman* v. *School Committee of Quincy,* 439 F.2d 148 (1971), and the Fourth Circuit in *Baughman* v. *Freienmuth* 478 F.2d 1345 (1973), indicated that a narrowly drawn set of prior review guidelines would be constitutional.

144. *Bystrom* v. *Fridley High School Independent School District No. 14,* 822 F.2d 747 (8th Cir. 1987).

145. *Harless* v. *Darr,* 937 F.Supp. 1351 (S.D. Ind. 1996).

146. *Baughman* v. *Freienmuth,* 478 F.2d 1345 (4th Cir. 1973).

147. *Shanley, supra* note 133.

148. *Muller* v. *Jefferson Lighthouse School,* 98 F.3d 1530 (7th Cir. 1996). Concurring, Judge Rovner "disagreed with the majority" about the absence of a time limit and wrote that "a regulation containing no limitation whatsoever on the review period would not pass constitutional muster." *Id.* at 1547.

149. *Frasca* v. *Andrews,* 463 F.Supp. 1043 (E.D. N.Y. 1979).

150. *Jacobs* v. *Board of School Commissioners,* 490 F.2d 601 (7th Cir. 1973).

151. *Bright* v. *Los Angeles Unified School District,* 134 Cal. Rptr. 639 (Cal. 1976).

152. *Jacobs, supra* note 150.

153. *Hedges* v. *Wauconda Community Unit School District* 118, 9 F.3d 1295 (7th Cir. 1993).

154. *Id.* at 1302.

155. *Jacobs, supra* note 150.

156. *Williams* v. *Spencer,* 622 F.2d 1200 (4th Cir. 1980).

157. *Nims* v. *Harrison,* 768 So.2d 1198 (Fla.App. 1 Dist.2000).

158. *Thomas* v. *Board of Education, Granville Central School District,* 607 F.2d 1043 (2d Cir. 1979).

159. For more on this topic, see E. Edmund Ruetter, Jr., *Academic Freedom Advisory: Be Wary of the Long Arm of* Kuhlmeier, 89 EDUC. L. REP. 347 (1994).

160. For more on this topic, see Jennifer Turner-Egner, *Teachers' Discretion in Selecting Instructional Materials and Methods,* 53 EDUC. L. REP. 365 (1989).

10 When Can Schools Limit Religious Freedom?

Overview

Controversies concerning the appropriate place, if any, of religion in the public schools have occurred periodically since the early days of the Republic. Although the First Amendment states that "Congress shall make no law respecting an establishment of religion, or prohibiting the free exercise thereof," the interpretation of these general provisions and their application to public schools have been problematic. Religion tends to be so important in the lives of people, and so surrounded by powerful emotions, that many want to use the schools to maintain and spread their religious beliefs at the same time that others insist on the complete exclusion of religion from public schools.

Some of the most bitter controversies that have embroiled America's schools have involved religion. This chapter addresses only those questions concerning religion and public education that are of greatest relevance to teachers and students. For example, must teachers and students salute the flag or follow the curriculum if doing so violates their religious beliefs? Are prayers permitted in the public schools? What about silent meditation? Are students exempt from compulsory schooling or from certain courses in the curriculum on religious grounds? Can voluntary student religious groups meet in school facilities before or after school? Can creationism be taught in public schools? Can vouchers be used in religious schools?

Teachers' Freedom of Conscience

In recent decades, although public attention has focused on issues related to religion and public education, the attention of the courts and media has been primarily on students: their right and/or obligation to read the Bible in school, to pray, to salute the flag, to be exempted from objectionable parts of the curriculum, and other issues. But teachers, too have religious beliefs and commitments. There are important differences between teachers and students, the most salient being that teachers are adults and are paid employees hired to accomplish certain objectives for the community, while students are minors and are compelled by law to attend school. Should these differences lead to different applications of the U.S. Constitution for teachers and for students? We must look to court cases for the answers.

Can Teachers Be Excused from Saluting the Flag?

Yes, if their objections are based on either religion or conscience. When a New York high school art teacher refused to participate in the daily flag ceremony, she was dismissed from her job. A federal appeals court upheld her right not to participate in such a ceremony and the U.S. Supreme Court denied a request to review the decision, allowing the ruling of the lower court to stand.[1] The nonparticipating teacher stood silently and respectfully while another instructor conducted the program. The teacher's objections were held to be a matter of conscience and not necessarily disloyal. In the words of the court, "we ought not impugn the loyalty of a citizen...merely for refusing to pledge allegiance, any more than we ought necessarily to praise the loyalty of a citizen who without conviction or meaning, and with mental reservation, recites the pledge by rote each morning."

What If State Law Requires a Daily Pledge of Allegiance?

State law requiring a Pledge of Allegiance is superseded by the First Amendment of the Constitution. Many states mandate daily flag salutes and other patriotic exercises. For example, a Massachusetts law passed in 1977 provides that "each teacher at the commencement of the first class of each day in all public schools shall lead the class in a group recitation of the Pledge of Allegiance to the Flag." The state supreme court advised the governor that the law violated the First Amendment rights of teachers.[2] The court based its opinion on the U.S. Supreme Court ruling in the *Barnette* case (discussed later in this chapter), indicating that the reasons used to excuse students from saluting the flag apply equally to teachers. According to the Massachusetts court, "any attempt by a governmental authority to induce belief in an ideological conviction by forcing an individual to identify himself with that conviction through compelled expression of it is prohibited by the First Amendment."

Can a Teacher Refuse to Follow the Curriculum If the Refusal Is Based on Religious Objections?

No. This question was raised in the Chicago public schools when Joethelia Palmer, a probationary kindergarten teacher and a member of Jehovah's Witnesses, informed her principal that because of her religion she would not be able "to teach any subjects having to do with love of country, the flag or other patriotic matters in the prescribed curriculum." For example, she considered it "to be promoting idolatry...to teach...about President Lincoln and why we observe his birthday." School officials insisted that these matters were part of the regular curriculum; although *she* did not have to salute the flag, provisions should be made for students to do so. Moreover, students were to follow the prescribed curriculum, which included holiday observances, songs, and patriotic exercises.

The Seventh Circuit Court of Appeals ruled in favor of the school board, and the U.S. Supreme Court upheld the ruling.[3] The court commented that "the First Amendment was not a teacher license for uncontrolled expression at variance with established curricular content." Furthermore, "there is a compelling state interest in the choice and adherence to a suitable curriculum for the benefit of our young citizens and society." While Palmer's right to her beliefs must be respected, she has no "right to require others to submit to her views and to forgo a portion of their education they would otherwise be entitled to enjoy."

Are Teachers Who Belong to Jehovah's Witnesses Unqualified to Teach in Public Schools?

Not necessarily. Their qualifications depend on their willingness to provide the prescribed curriculum for children in their classes. For example, Bein, a New York kindergarten teacher, told the parents of her students that she could no longer lead certain activities or participate in certain projects because these were "religiously oriented" according to her newly acquired faith of Jehovah's Witnesses. She could not decorate the classroom for holidays, coordinate gift exchange during the Christmas season, sing "Happy Birthday," or recite the Pledge of Allegiance. When some parents and school officials wanted to dismiss her, the teacher insisted that she was competent to teach and that the First Amendment protected her from participating in activities forbidden by her religion. The important difference between this case and the one discussed above was that Bein made arrangements to provide the children with all the curricular activities she could not conduct. With the cooperation of parents, older students, and other teachers, all activities specified in the curriculum were conducted. Thus Bein's religious views were not imposed on the children, and the school's objectives in connection with patriotic exercises and holiday celebrations were satisfied. The New York State Commissioner of Education ruled in Bein's favor and held that her dismissal violated the religious freedom provisions of the First Amendment.[4]

Religious Holidays

Can Teachers Take Religious Holiday Leaves?

Yes, if they don't take too many leaves. State laws or local district policies usually allow teachers to be absent from school for the major holidays of recognized religions. Nevertheless, problems have arisen over questions of pay for religious holidays as well as over the taking of an excessive number of days off for religious reasons.

Must Schools Pay Teachers for Religious Holiday Leaves?

No. Payment for religious holiday leaves is within the discretion of the local school district. This question arose in California when a high school teacher requested a "personal necessity leave" to observe Rosh Hashanah, a Jewish holiday. Like many other states, California provides a certain number of paid days a year for "personal necessity leave" for teachers. It is up to local school authorities to adopt rules controlling the use of such leaves.

The teacher claimed that under the First Amendment she had a right to a leave for a major religious holiday and that it should be a paid leave under the personal necessity leave policy of the state and the district. The court ruled against her, holding that it was within the discretion of the school board to decide when to consider a leave a personal necessity.[5] If courts imposed such a rule on schools, said the court, "the results would be chaotic. Every school teacher belonging to every sect, whether a legitimate religious group or not, would forthwith be entitled to six days of paid holidays. It appears reasonable, therefore, to limit the definition of personal necessity in a way which allows for effective supervision."

A federal appeals court reached the same conclusion when a teacher brought suit under Title VII, which requires reasonable accommodation to religious beliefs.[6] The teacher claimed that a school policy that allowed only two days "special leave" violated the First Amendment. The court, holding that the policy was reasonable, ruled that school districts are not required to enact policies so broad as to accommodate religious preference. The loss of a day's pay for time not worked does not amount to a significant infringement on First Amendment rights and "does not constitute substantial pressure on a teacher to modify his or her behavior."

The Second Circuit Court of Appeals ruled in favor of a teacher who wanted to use paid leave time to observe religious holidays that fell on school days. In this case, Ronald Philbrook, a member of the Worldwide Church of God in Connecticut, wanted to use six school days for religious observance. The collective bargaining contract between the school board and the teachers granted only three days paid leave for religious purposes and specified that personal business leave must be used for secular purposes. When Philbrook challenged this arrangement and lost at the district court level, he appealed. On appeal, the circuit court, interpreting Title VII,[7] held that an employer must make reasonable accommodations to employees' religious needs, unless such accommodations will cause "undue hardship on the conduct of the employer's business." On appeal, the U.S. Supreme Court held that Title VII is satisfied when the employer demonstrates that it has offered a reasonable accommodation to the employee, and that unpaid leave for religious observances is a reasonable accommodation unless paid leave is provided for all purposes except religious ones.[8]

Can Teachers Take Unpaid Religious Holidays at Will?

Within limits, teachers' freedom of religion will be protected even if the number of special holidays taken seems excessive to some school officials. This issue arose in California, and the judges were closely divided in their attempts to balance the rights of the individual to the free exercise of his or her religion and the legitimate interest of the state to provide effective schooling for all children.[9] Byars was a competent teacher employed by his school district in 1969. He joined the Worldwide Church of God in 1971 and requested certain days off for religious holidays. Despite the fact that his request was denied, between 1971 and 1975 he was absent from work for 31 days to observe religious holidays. School officials notified him in 1973 that his absences were not approved and that if he continued them, he would be dismissed for "persistent failure to abide by the rules of the District." Byars, insisting that he had a constitutional right to practice his religion, continued to observe the religious holidays of his church and missed more classes. When the school board dismissed him, Byars went to court.

The school board claimed that continuity of instruction was very important and that the repeated use of substitutes would diminish the educational benefits of the students. The court ruled in favor of the board, recognizing the clash of interests between the individual and society, the court observed: "While the free exercise clause prevents any governmental regulation of religious beliefs, in this case we are concerned not with…[the teacher's] beliefs but only with his practice in leaving his teaching duties for the purpose of religious observances while under contract with the district."

Nevertheless, the Supreme Court of California, by a vote of 4–3, ruled in favor of the teacher. The court based its ruling on the California Constitution's provision protecting freedom of religion. The court was influenced by the fact that the total number of days

Byars was absent was approximately the same as the mandatory number of paid leave days provided for teachers by the state. Thus the majority held that this teacher's religious beliefs must be accommodated, despite the inconvenience and disruption it might entail for the schools.[10] The U.S. Supreme Court dismissed an appeal "for want of a substantial federal question."

In a related case also involving a member of the Worldwide Church of God, plaintiff H. claimed that she was not hired because of religious discrimination. The facts indicated that her attendance would have been quite unpredictable because it would be influenced by "the moon and stars," according to her religious beliefs. The court ruled in favor of the school board and held that it may choose not to hire a person on the basis of nondiscriminatory reasons, such as a preference for teachers without attendance problems.[11] Thus school boards have some discretion when considering the religious practice of teachers in the process of hiring.

Can Teachers Wear Distinctively Religious Clothing in Public Schools?

Probably not, although there is no uniform law on this question applicable to the entire nation. Objections have arisen to Catholic nuns teaching in religious garb. When there was no evidence that the nuns injected religious views into their teaching, some courts did not prohibit them from wearing their religious clothing.[12] An earlier case forbade nuns even from teaching in public schools, on the grounds that their lives are dedicated to religion and their constant presence in the classroom violates the "establishment clause" of the First Amendment.[13] The First Amendment begins with the provision that "Congress shall make no law respecting an establishment of religion, or prohibiting the free exercise thereof...." The general meaning of the "establishment clause" is that the government and all its policies and employees will remain neutral with respect to religion, neither favoring nor disparaging it. The specific meaning of the clause can only be derived from a case-by-case analysis of court decisions.

There are no recent cases on this issue, but it is probable that today nuns or ministers may teach secular subjects in public schools *if they do not wear religious garb or other sectarian symbols.* The fact that they may contribute their earnings to a church is their own personal and private business.[14] This principle would apply with equal force to members of, say, the Hare Krishna sect, as well as to more traditional religions.

When the issue of teaching in religious clothing has arisen, most states have passed laws against the practice or forbidden it by administrative regulation. Such laws and regulations have been upheld by the courts.[15] A majority of educators and judges today hold the view that the wearing of religious garb introduces a sectarian influence that should not be present in the public schools. Such clothing also gives the impression, particularly to less mature students, that the school supports the particular religion. In sum, the teacher's religious *beliefs* are always protected; *actions* based on religious beliefs may be limited when a compelling state interest is at stake.

A 1991 district court decision interpreted a Pennsylvania law prohibiting the wearing of religious "garb."[16] In this instance, the headcover worn did not "indicate the wearer's religious affiliation even though she wore the colorful scarf for religious reasons, as a Muslim." Therefore, ruled the court, contrary to earlier cases, the organization had to accommodate the employee's religious belief or practice, unless it would result in demonstrable "undue hardship" to the organization.

Students' Freedom of Conscience

In an oft-quoted statement, Justice Jackson spoke for the majority of the U.S. Supreme Court when he wrote in *West Virginia* v. *Barnette:*

> If there is any fixed star in our constitutional constellation, it is that no official, high or petty, can prescribe what shall be orthodox in politics, nationalism, religion, or other matters of opinion or force citizens to confess by word or act their faith therein. If there are any circumstances which permit an exception, they do not now occur to us.[17]

As this quote suggests, certain social issues or conflicts are never completely resolved; they are perennial. The specific substance of the issues may change over time, but the general substance and form remain the same. They relate to two basic principles of the First Amendment, one of which guarantees the free *exercise* of religion while the other orders government officials not to *establish* any religion. But what do these principles mean in the daily lives of students in public schools?

Must Students Salute the Flag?

No, not if they have deeply felt objections to such an act. However, most schools still require children to recite the Pledge of Allegiance at the start of each school day by virtue of state law or by policy of the school board. In the 1940s, children of the Jehovah's Witnesses faith refused to participate in the official pledge and offered instead to recite their own religious pledge. When school officials insisted on their reciting the official pledge, the students went to court. Their refusal eventually led to the Supreme Court's ruling in *Barnette* in favor of the children.[18] In the words of the Court: "We think the action of the local authorities in compelling the flag salute and pledge transcends constitutional limitations on their power and invades the sphere of intellect and spirit which it is the purpose of the First Amendment to reserve from all official control."

The Court overruled an earlier case that did not consider saluting the flag a significant enough religious act to merit constitutional protection. Many people, perhaps most, do not consider flag salutes or other patriotic exercises religious activities, therefore they cannot understand why anyone should have religious objections to them. Nevertheless, the Court held that school administrators or other officials may not determine for a religious group whether such activities are allowed or proscribed by their religion. There is to be no official orthodoxy under the Constitution. Majority vote, or the vote of a legislature, cannot resolve this question, said the Court:

> The very purpose of a Bill of Rights was to withdraw certain subjects from the vicissitudes of political controversy, to place them beyond the reach of majorities and officials and to establish them as legal principles to be applied by the courts. One's right to life, liberty, and

property, to free speech, a free press, freedom of worship and assembly, and other fundamental rights may not be submitted to vote; they depend on the outcome of no elections.

The majority of the Court considered freedom of religion a *fundamental* or *preferred freedom.* Such freedoms can be abridged only if the state shows it has a *compelling* need to do so. This is in contrast to *ordinary freedoms,* such as the freedom to drive a car, which can be restricted or regulated if the government has some legitimate reason to do so (e.g., to reduce pollution or congestion). There was no compelling state interest requiring Jehovah's Witnesses to salute the flag because no major public interest was threatened by their refusal; thus their fundamental religious freedom prevailed. There have been instances of religious freedom being outweighed by a powerful public interest, however. For example, mandatory polio immunization of all school children has been upheld, despite the religious objections of some parents.

Does a State Law That Requires the Daily Recitation of the Pledge of Allegiance Violate the Establishment Clause?

It does not, ruled a federal district court in an Illinois case where an atheist father and his son challenged the daily recitation requirement. The court found that the purpose of the Pledge was secular, namely to instill patriotism and "knowledge of American ideals in elementary school students." Furthermore, unless all students are required to recite the Pledge, there is no violation of the free exercise clause either. On appeal, the Seventh Circuit Court of Appeals upheld the Illinois law requiring the recitation of the Pledge in public schools.[19] The court held that the phrase "under God" did not make the Pledge a prayer; thus there was no violation of the establishment clause. The court considered it important that individual students were not compelled to recite the Pledge. Furthermore, since the government has the right to set the curriculum in its schools, those who cannot accept the result may "select private education at their own expense."

Is Religion the Only Basis for Not Saluting the Flag?

No. Some students object to saluting the flag as a matter of conscience. Courts have held that a sincerely held conscientious objection to the flag salute receives the same protection from the U.S. Constitution as an objection based on religious beliefs.

A student at Coral Gables High School in Florida had a deeply felt objection to the flag salute and did not even want to stand while the salute was being conducted. A board policy allowed him not to participate but required that nonparticipating students stand quietly during the salute. The student claimed that such a requirement violated his right of free speech, and a federal district court upheld this contention.[20] The court noted that "standing is an integral portion of the pledge ceremony and is no less a gesture of acceptance and respect than is the salute or the utterance of the words of allegiance."

A federal appeals court ruled similarly in the case of a New York honors student, president of his class, who refused to pledge allegiance to the flag because he believed "that there [isn't] liberty and justice for all in the United States." The school board offered the student the option of leaving the room or of standing silently. The student wished instead to remain seated. The court, citing *West Virginia* v. *Barnette,* held that the state may not compel students to affirm their loyalty "by word or act." In this case, the act of standing was itself part of the pledge and a gesture of respect similar to the salute. "Therefore, the alternative offered plaintiff of standing in silence is an act that cannot be compelled over his deeply held convictions. It can no more be required than the pledge itself."[21]

In a similar case, New York students challenged the rule that nonparticipating students must leave the room and wait in the hall.[22] They considered such treatment a punishment for the exercise of a constitutional right. The New York court agreed with the students and upheld their right not to participate in the flag salute for reasons of conscience, as well as their right to remain quietly in the room. What if the refusal becomes contagious and other students also refuse to salute the flag? The New York case noted that "the First Amendment protects successful dissent as well as ineffective protest."

Can Public Schools Start the Day with Prayers?

No. Historically, many public schools began each day with a required prayer, Bible reading, or both. In 1959, Pennsylvania enacted a law requiring daily Bible reading in the schools but exempting children who had written requests for exemption from their parents. The Schempp children, who were Unitarians, challenged the law. Their case eventually reached the U.S. Supreme Court, which ruled in their favor.[23]

The Court held that state-required Bible reading or prayer violates the establishment clause of the First Amendment when it is part of the curriculum in schools children are required to attend: "They [prayers] are held in the school buildings under the supervision and with the participation of teachers employed in those schools…such as opening exercises in a religious ceremony." The fact that students may be excused from the exercises does not change the fact that schools, which are arms of the state, are involved.

Although these principles were established in law more than thirty years ago, violations still occur today. Such violations are illustrated in a 1996 case from Mississippi.[24] A mother sued on behalf of herself and her school-age children, alleging several different violations of the establishment clause. Evidence in this case showed that schoolwide prayers and Bible readings were conducted after announcements, in a kindergarten through grade twelve school. Such a practice, indicated the court, would not be allowed even under the Equal Access Act, because all students were captives to the intercom prayers and the act applies only to voluntary meetings. Furthermore, the act applies only to secondary schools, therefore it cannot be used to justify the practice in a school of kindergarten through grade twelve.

Classroom prayers and religiously oriented Bible classes were also struck down pursuant to the *Lemon* test (discussed later in this chapter). While this case breaks no new legal ground, it does illustrate the persistence of the issue and the tenacity of some people to insert religion into various aspects of our public schools.

Can There Be Prayers at Graduation Ceremonies?

The answer might depend on who schedules or arranges the invocation or benediction and whether it is completely secular or contains references to a deity or other religious symbols. While prayers, invocations, and benedictions have long been a part of public school graduation ceremonies, during recent years several lawsuits challenged these practices.

Courts have reached conflicting results in these cases, and the U.S. Supreme Court had not ruled on the matter until 1992 in *Lee* v. *Weisman.*

Invocations and benedictions at graduation exercises can serve a "solemnizing" function. As Justice O'Connor said in 1983, some governmental acknowledgment of religion, as in legislative prayers, "In God We Trust" on coins, and opening court sessions with "God save the United States and this honorable court" serve "the legitimate secular purpose of solemnizing public occasions, expressing confidence in the future, and encouraging the recognition of what is worthy of appreciation in society." Ceremonial invocations and benedictions serve such purposes, and the public nature of the occasion and the usual presence of parents act as buffers against religious coercion. Thus such ceremonials do not violate the First Amendment unless the language used in them is unacceptable. Such language was found in the *Stein* case in Michigan, where the language of Christian theology and prayer was employed, including the name of Jesus as the Savior. The appeals court held this to be inconsistent with America's "civil religion" and a violation of the establishment clause.

A novel situation found its way to the federal courts in the *Guidry* v. *Broussard* in which Angela Guidry was scheduled to deliver a valedictorian speech at graduation exercises in Sam Houston High School in Moss Bluff, Louisiana.[25] Following the practice of previewing such speeches, the principal found Angela's speech to be a thoroughly Christian, personal statement of the importance of God, the Bible, and Jesus in her life and she urged all other students to "…give your heart and your life to Him so you can live forever in Heaven with Him." When the principal requested the deletion of all personal religious beliefs from the speech and she refused to do so, her speech was deleted from the graduation proceedings.

Angela went to court claiming that her freedom of speech was restricted because of its content. In the final analysis the federal district court ruled in favor of the school administration, holding that the primary effect of permitting the speech would have been to communicate "a message of governmental endorsement…of religion." Even if there were no actual support or endorsement by the school, concluded the court, there is the danger of public perception of such endorsement; therefore the principal's action was a reasonable attempt to avoid such appearances.

In light of the widespread concern about this issue, and in view of conflicting lower court decisions, the U.S. Supreme Court handed down a decision on graduation prayers in 1992, in *Lee* v. *Weisman.*[26] In sum, the court ruled that a school-sponsored religious invocation or benediction at graduation ceremonies is unconstitutional. The complexity of this issue can be inferred from the fact that the Court split five to four in striking down an invocation and benediction by a clergyman, and that four different opinions were written by the Justices to explain their interpretation of the establishment clause.

Writing for the majority, Justice Kennedy explained that even though attendance was voluntary and the invocation nondenominational, there are sufficient elements of "psychological coercion" present in such situations to place the government in a position of supporting religion in violation of the establishment clause. In the words of Justice Kennedy:

> …Everyone knows that in our society and in our culture high school graduation is one of life's most significant occasions…attendance may not be required by official decree, yet it

is apparent that a student is not free to absent herself from the graduation exercise in any real sense of the term "voluntary," for absence would require forfeiture of those intangible benefits which have motivated the student through youth and all her high schools years."[27]

Because, in this case, the school principal selected the clergyman to give the invocation and gave him directions for the content of the prayer, clearly a governmental official was involved in promoting religion in violation of the First Amendment.

Justices Blackmun and Souter each wrote concurring opinions, emphasizing the doctrine of separation of church and state and forbidding aid to all religions, respectively. Justice Scalia, however, wrote a scathing dissent, criticizing particularly the majority's reliance on psychological coercion as a criterion, which, in his opinion, is a "boundlessly manipulable" criterion.[28]

Lee v. *Weisman* leaves many questions unanswered. For example, what if a student committee selects the clergy and provides directions for the emphasis of the invocation? One circuit court of appeals upheld a policy that permitted high school seniors to choose student volunteers to deliver nonsectarian, nonproselytizing invocations at their graduation ceremonies.[29] What if parents are in control of the event even though it is a high school graduation? These and other questions are likely to find their way to the courts as our culture continues to search for the proper interpretations of the establishments and free exercise clauses of the First Amendment.

Are Invocations at School Athletic Events Constitutional?

Not according to a 1989 federal appeals court decision.[30] The case concerned Doug Jager, a member of a Georgia high school marching band, who objected to invocations before home football games. The invocations had been organized by local Protestant ministers and frequently closed with the words "in Jesus' name, we pray." The court found this practice unconstitutional.

Because of the controversy surrounding the clergy-led invocations, the school then proposed an "equal access plan," which involved the random selection of invocation speakers from among student, parent, or school staff volunteers. The school argued that the purpose of the plan was to provide "inspirational speeches about sportsmanship, safety and the values of team-work and competition." However, a federal appeals court found that the school could have achieved all of these purposes by providing "wholly secular" inspirational speeches and that the school's real purpose was to provide invocations "that publicly express support for Protestant Christianity." These invocations, ruled the court, "violate the Establishment Clause of the First Amendment." In a related case, the Fifth Circuit Court of Appeals declared unconstitutional a long-standing practice of team prayer, led by teachers and coaches at girls' junior high school basketball games in Duncanville, Texas.[31]

The Santa Fe Independent School District authorized students to vote whether "invocations" should be delivered before each home football game and a second election to select a spokesperson to deliver the invocation. Mormon and Catholic students, alumni, and parents filed suit, claiming a violation of the Establishment Clause of the First Amendment. The District Court ruled to permit non-sectarian, non-proselytizing prayers. The Fifth Circuit Court and then, on appeal, the Supreme Court held that the policy permitting such student-led and student-initiated prayer at football games violates the Establishment Clause.[32]

Since the school conducted the elections, its involvement makes it clear that the pre-game prayers bear "the imprint of the state and put school-age children who objected in an untenable position." The policy states that the purpose of the message was to "solemnize the event"; thus, it clearly has a religious purpose. The court examined the history of the policy, the total environment in which the "invocations" were to be delivered, and the perceptions of students as well as independent observers. From all this, the majority concluded that the purpose of the policy was "to preserve a popular 'state-sponsored religious practice.'"

Chief Justice Rehnquist dissented, together with Justices Scalia and Thomas. Their main disagreement was based on the fact that the policy was declared unconstitutional before it had been put into practice. While they claimed that the policy might be implemented in the future in a way consistent with the Constitution, the majority, however, struck down the policy since it had an unconstitutional purpose, according to *Lemon* v. *Kurtzman* (see below).

Must Religion Be Completely Excluded from Schools?

The U.S. Supreme Court never mandated such exclusion. In fact, *Schempp,* (see Note 33) which declared prayers and Bible reading unconstitutional, made it clear that studying *about* religion is perfectly legitimate, whether it be through comparative religion; the history of religion; art, music and religion; or other approaches.[33] Religious exercises, rituals, and celebrations, however, are against the law, whether compulsory or voluntary.

In 1971 the Supreme Court came up with some guiding principles to be used in First Amendment cases involving the establishment clause. In *Lemon* v. *Kurtzman,*[34] the Court applied the so-called "tripartite test" that has lasted for over three decades. *Lemon* involved two appeals about the constitutionality of Pennsylvania and Rhode Island statutes providing state aid to church-related schools. The Pennsylvania statute provided public funds to reimburse private schools for teachers' salaries, textbooks, and instructional materials in specified secular subjects. Rhode Island adopted a statute under which the state paid a 15 percent annual supplement to teachers in nonpublic elementary schools.

The Court declared these statutes unconstitutional by applying the following tests: First, the statute must have a secular legislative purpose; second, its principal or primary effect must be one that neither advances nor inhibits religion; and finally, the statute must not foster an excessive government entanglement with religion. Applying these tests, the Court concluded that to administer such public aid to the programs of parochial schools would inevitably lead to excessive entanglement between government authorities and religious schools.

In 1981, the Supreme Court in a 5–4 decision declared unconstitutional a Kentucky statute that required posting a copy of the Ten Commandments, purchased with private contributions, on the wall of each classroom in the public schools of the state.[35] The Court applied its three-part *Lemon* test noted above and concluded that it served a religious rather than a secular purpose.[36]

Similarly, when a high school senior objected to a picture of Jesus Christ, which had hung in the hallways of Bloomingdale High School for about 30 years, as a violation of the establishment clause, the court agreed with him and ordered the picture covered, pending appeal. The federal district found that the two- by three-foot portrait of Jesus Christ prominently displayed in the public school hallway next to the principal's office violated the establishment clause of the First Amendment. On appeal, the Sixth Circuit Court of Appeals affirmed this decision. It held that the display of the picture of Jesus Christ in a public school hallway violated all three prongs of the *Lemon* test and therefore the establishment clause. Furthermore, when the school claimed that the case was now moot because the student had graduated, the appeals court disagreed. The court held that the portrait affects both students and nonstudents who visit the school. Any member of the public who visited the school for any event and "took the portrait as a serious insult to her religious sensibilities" suffered an injury, therefore the case was not moot.[37]

Certain school practices and a school board policy related to Christmas programs in public schools were challenged in Sioux Falls, South Dakota, in 1979. In short, the courts ruled that schools may teach about religion as a significant aspect of our culture and our history.[38] Religious ceremonies must not be performed in schools "under the guise of 'study,'" yet the performance of religious art, literature, or music does not necessarily invalidate the activity if the primary purpose served is secular and not religious. Schools should be sensitive to the "religious beliefs and disbeliefs of their constituents and should attempt to avoid conflict," according to the court, "but they need not and should not sacrifice the quality of the students' education."

Christmas programs in schools have led to controversies and lawsuits in many communities. "Balancing" Christmas celebrations with Hanukkah celebrations does not resolve the legal problem, for if one such activity violates the establishment clause of the First Amendment, a double violation is not the right remedy. Whether or not some children or parents object to the practice is not the key issue. *Religious* celebrations have no place in public schools, although teaching *about* religion is acceptable. Thus the challenge to educators is how to incorporate such activities into school programs in ways consistent with their educational mission while deemphasizing or eliminating their religious flavor. Recent Supreme Court cases related to the display of nativity scenes, along with other Christmas and patriotic symbols, would support this analysis.[39] One of these cases dealt with a display in the Pittsburgh County Courthouse that was exclusively religious; in the other, in the City-County Building one block away stood a display that contained a huge decorated Christmas tree, a large menorah (a Hanukkah candelabrum), and a large sign from the mayor, "Salute to Liberty," with an additional message from the mayor.

In the final analysis, the Supreme Court in a 5–4 decision struck down the first display and upheld the second one. According to the majority, the "principal and primary effect" of displaying the creche is to advance religion and thus violate the establishment clause. A divided majority upheld the other display as one that sends "a message of pluralism and freedom to choose one's own beliefs" along with support for patriotism. Thus the overall impression created is secular and not religious. The strong dissenting opinions of four justices indicates that the Court is seriously divided on this issue and that we can anticipate further cases that might revise the three-prong test that developed in *Lemon.*

Cases related to prayers in school, Bible reading, prayers at graduation ceremonies, and athletic events continue to arise despite the fact that they have been repeatedly declared unconstitutional by the Supreme Court and by many lower courts. A dramatic example of this is the *Chandler* case in Alabama, decided in November, 1997.[40] The facts of this case show that prayers were conducted by a teacher and his son in the classroom, there were prayers over the intercom, at student assemblies and athletic events, and Gideon Bibles were repeatedly distributed at school.

School officials even raised questions about the authority of federal judges over matters like religion in public school. They proposed that only elected officials could make decisions over such matters. The district court made it very clear that the school practices were unconstitutional and issued an injunction forbidding their continuation.

Can Students Receive Religious Instruction During School Hours?

Yes. The instruction must take place away from school, however, not on school grounds, and must be conducted by teachers or religious figures independent of the school and not paid by the school. This "released time" religious education is used in some communities in the country, and the U.S. Supreme Court has ruled that the arrangement does not violate the U.S. Constitution.[41]

A very different situation arose in Lubbock, Texas, where pursuant to school board policy students could gather before or after school hours, under school supervision, for voluntary moral, religious, or ethical activities led by students. When the policy and practice were challenged, the court of appeals[42] also applied the three-pronged *Lemon* test:

1. Does the policy or practice have a secular purpose?
2. Is the primary effect of the policy or practice one that neither advances nor inhibits religion?
3. Does the policy or practice avoid an excessive entanglement with religion?

To satisfy the Constitution, the answer must be in the affirmative for *each* of these questions. In *Lubbock,* the policy and practice failed on all three grounds. The facts showed that the purpose was clearly to advance religion and that its primary effect would do the same. Furthermore, school supervision of the activities is precisely the kind of entanglement that is impermissible under constitutional precedents.

The *Lemon* test, however, is undergoing reexamination by the Court. This fact is clear from a careful reading of *Wallace* v. *Jaffree,* a 1985 case that declared an Alabama statute providing for silent prayer in schools unconstitutional.[43] The Court ruled that the statute violated the establishment clause because it had no secular purpose and was a government "endorsement" of prayer. However, a strong dissent by Justice Rehnquist indicates his readiness to abandon the *Lemon* test and the idea of "separation of church and state." His views, along with those of Justices Thomas, Scalia, and Kennedy, gleaned from several cases, seem to indicate that the Court is moving toward "accommodation" between church and state, a position different from a view previously dominant and embodied in the *Lemon* test. A clear, authoritative statement of the new doctrine evolving is yet to be announced.

Are Silent Meditations Allowed?

Maybe. It depends on the wording of the statute or policy and the intentions behind it.

Massachusetts passed a law that required public schools to observe a minute of silence "for meditation or prayer." The law was challenged by students and parents who claimed that it was a violation of the establishment clause of the First Amendment. The word "or" saved the law from being declared unconstitutional, however. According to the court, meditation refers to a silent reflection on any subject, religious or secular.[44] Thus, since meditation can be on a secular subject, and the law used the disjunctive "or," there is no necessary prayer involved—only a moment of silence.

Other cases have reached different conclusions. A Louisiana statute, in addition to its provision for silent meditation, authorized teachers to ask students whether they wished to pray. If no students chose to pray, the teacher was permitted to pray for a period of up to five minutes. Although there was no compulsion for students to participate or even to be present, the courts ruled the statute unconstitutional.[45] The federal appeals court held that the principles of *Schempp* applied and that the voluntary nature of the activity is "no defense to a claim of unconstitutionality under the Establishment Clause."

In Alabama, three students challenged a state law that provided for a silent prayer and that permitted teachers to lead their classes in prayer. The district court recognized that the Alabama statute violated the establishment clause as construed by the Supreme Court. Nevertheless, the district court ruled "that the United States Supreme Court has erred." On appeal, the Supreme Court held that the district court was obligated to follow precedents established by the Supreme Court and that the state statute was unconstitutional.[46] In their written opinions, the majority of the Justices indicated that a period of meditation, provided for a secular purpose, would be constitutionally acceptable; whether it is necessary to legislate such a period of silence or whether it is educationally desirable is not for courts to decide.

A variation on this issue arose in New Mexico, where a statute authorized school boards to permit one minute of silence at the beginning of the school day. The schools claimed that the purpose of the statute was to enhance discipline and instill "intellectual composure" in the students. Furthermore, the schools claimed that "meditation," as used by the statute, indicated a neutral purpose. The district court considered the statutory language, statements of its legislative sponsors, and the historical context in which is was enacted and concluded that the legislative purpose was nonsecular, that is, "to establish prayer in public schools."[47]

In light of the foregoing cases, Massachusetts changed its law in 1985 and completely excluded any mention of prayer in its new legislation. The new law reads:

> At the commencement of the first class each day in all grades in all public schools the teacher in charge of the room in which each such class is held shall announce that a period of silence not to exceed one minute in duration shall be observed for personal thoughts, and during any such period, silence shall be maintained and no other activity engaged in.[48]

In a 1997 case, the Eleventh Circuit Court of Appeals upheld Georgia's Moment of Quiet Reflection in Schools Act, which requires that "[i]n each public school classroom, the teacher in charge shall, at the opening of school upon every school day, conduct a brief period of quiet reflection for not more than 60 seconds with the participation of all the pupils therein assembled."[49] Brian B. Bown, a high school teacher, objected to the law and refused to cooperate with the minute of silence. He believed that the law violated the establishment clause of the First Amendment as indicated in the legislative history of the act. Bown was suspended and then terminated from his teaching position. When he went to court, the district court ruled against him and so did the court of appeals. The appeals court applied the three-prong *Lemon* test and found that the act satisfied each prong. Thus, while various cases have raised some doubts about the continued viability of the *Lemon* test, it has continued to be used with no new test or standard having been created by a majority of the Supreme Court.

Is Transcendental Meditation Allowed in Schools?

No, it is not, ruled a federal court in New Jersey after schools introduced a course in Transcendental Meditation (TM), claiming that it would reduce stress and produce a variety of beneficial physical effects. Some parents believed that TM was a religion and, as such, had no place in public schools. Although there was conflicting testimony on whether or not the course was religious, the judge ruled that it was.[50] A *mantra,* a special word repeated regularly by the meditating person, and a special textbook were assigned to each student at an out-of-school religious ceremony. In the estimate of the judge, the goals of TM may have been secular, but the means used were religious and therefore violated the First Amendment.

Must Children Attend Public Schools?

Children and their parents may choose among several alternatives that include public schools, private religious or secular schools, or private military schools. (See chapter 18 for a detailed discussion of schooling and parents' rights.) The U.S. Supreme Court established this principle in 1925 when an Oregon law that required every child between the ages of 8 and 16 to attend public schools was challenged by a Catholic religious order. The Court ruled in favor of the religious order.[51]

The Court recognized the right of states to require that all children of certain ages attend school and the right of states to provide reasonable regulations for all schools, public and private, related to school buildings, teachers, and the curriculum. Nevertheless, to require that all educating be done in public schools was considered arbitrary and unreasonable. In a famous quote, the Court warned against the standardization of children and recognized the parents' right to guide and nurture the young:

> The fundamental theory of liberty upon which all governments in this Union repose excludes any general power of the state to standardize its children by forcing them to accept instruction from public teachers only. The child is not the mere creature of the state; those who nurture him and direct his destiny have the right, coupled with the high duty, to recognize and prepare him for additional obligations.[52]

Can Vouchers Be Used at Either Public or Parochial Schools?

The answer depends on the wording of the law or policy that created the voucher plan as well as the laws of the particular state where the plan was created and was to be applied. In 1998, the Supreme Court of Wisconsin ruled in *Jackson* v. *Benson* that taxpayer-funded vouchers could be used in Milwaukee at either public or private schools, secular or religious.[53]

The Milwaukee Parental Choice Plan (MPCP) provided publicly funded vouchers for children from low-income families to attend private schools. The law provided a provision enabling students to "opt out" of religious activities and it also forbade racial discrimination. While the state lower courts ruled that the program violates Wisconsin law, the state supreme court, in a split vote (4–2), held that it violated neither the federal Constitution nor the state law. The Court examined the sequence of U.S. Supreme Court cases on the evolving laws related to the Establishment Clause and, applying the three-prong test of *Lemon* v. *Kurtzman,* declared the voucher plan constitutional. The U.S. Supreme Court declined to review the case.

In 1999, the Supreme Court of Ohio ruled on a voucher program of Cleveland, upholding it in part and striking down certain provisions of it as violative of state law. Its analysis of the Establishment Clause challenge was similar to the Milwaukee case, and the Ohio court also found no violation of the federal Constitution in voucher-plan funds being used in parochial schools.[54]

When the Supreme Court of Ohio found some problems with the state statute, the Ohio legislature re-enacted the law with some changes.[55] Opponents of the voucher plan filed suit in federal court challenging the new law claiming that the tuition grants for low-income parents who wished to send their children to religious schools violated the Establishment Clause. The Supreme Court, in a 5–4 decision, ruled the plan constitutional, for it was neutral with respect to religion. Individual recipients of funds could choose secular or religious schools, public or private (*New York Times,* June 28, 2002).

May a State Exclude Religious Schools from a State-Funded Program That Subsidizes Parents' Choice of Private Schools?

Yes, it may, ruled the Supreme Court of Maine in the 1999 case of *Bagley* v. *Raymond School Dept.*[56] The State of Maine had a law that provided public funds to parents in communities that had no secondary schools. These funds could be used to pay tuition at public schools in other districts that accept the students or to private schools, secular or religious. In 1981, concerned that providing public funds for tuition in religious schools would violate the Establishment Clause, in the opinion of the Maine attorney general, the legislature passed an Amendment excluding religious schools from receiving the state tuition funds. Parents of Catholic children challenged the law as a violation of the First and Fourteenth Amendments, that is, violating the Establishment Clause, the Free Exercise Clause, and the Equal Protection Clause.

The Supreme Court of Maine rejected each of these claims. The court noted that parents are free to seek a religious education for their children and the "Free Exercise Clause does not mandate that the State subsidize a person's constitutional right to send their (sic) children to church-related schools." Similarly, the court quickly rejected the claim of Establishment Clause violation, since the gist of that clause is to prohibit the government from supporting or advancing religion and "from forcing religion, even in subtle ways, on those who choose not to accept it." Finally, applying the strict scrutiny test, the court found no violation of the Equal Protection Clause; thus it held the law to be constitutional.

Can Children Attend Church School at Home?

They can only if the "home school" qualifies under the requirements of the particular state. (See chapter 18 for a detailed discussion of home schooling.) In most states this would mean that the parents or other adults teaching the children would have to be qualified in the eyes of the court and would have to present an acceptable educational program for the children. That a school claims to be a religious school does not exempt it from reasonable state regulation.

A court in Florida ruled on a case involving a church "school" in a home where the mother was the only teacher.[57] The parents claimed that their religious beliefs forbade "race mixing as practiced in the public schools" as "sinful." The mother was not certified to teach, nor did she meet state regulations for private tutors, and the church to which they claimed to belong was not a regularly established church in Florida. Thus the court held that the home arrangement was unacceptable and the children had to attend either the local public school or some acceptable private school. (However, as chapter 18 explains, very few states require that parents who instruct their own children be certified teachers.)

Can Children Avoid School Attendance Altogether for Religious Reasons?

In general, they cannot, although special circumstances may lead to some exemptions. A child who lives in a state that requires school attendance must attend *some* acceptable school during the years of compulsory education. What if the family has religious objections? This question was raised by some Amish children in Wisconsin, and the U.S. Supreme Court provided some exceptions to this general rule.[58] Wisconsin required school attendance until the age of 16. The Amish believed that the curriculum of the high school, particularly its emphasis on intellectual and scientific achievement, competition, worldly success, and social life, was inconsistent with their religious beliefs. They accepted the need for basic literacy but were convinced that schooling beyond the eighth grade would destroy their close-knit rural, religion-centered way of life. They insisted that after eighth grade, their youth should learn the skills relevant to the Amish way of life on their farms and in their homes. The state, on the other hand, insisted that the compulsory laws applied to all children, without exception.

After reviewing all the evidence and arguments, the Court exempted the Amish children from high school attendance. The Court was impressed by the fact that this religion-based, self-sufficient community has existed successfully for over 200 years. In effect, the Amish way of life was an "alternative to formal secondary school education" and enabled the Amish to live peacefully and to fulfill successfully their economic, social, and political responsibilities without becoming burdens on the larger society. After balancing the interests of the state against the Amish interest in the preservation and practice of their religion, the Court reached a decision on behalf of religious freedom. As the Court recognized, the case involved "the fundamental interest of parents, as contrasted with that of the State, to guide the religious future and education of their children," and the primary role of parents in the upbringing of their children "is now established beyond debate as an enduring American tradition."

Courts are unlikely to extend the ruling regarding the Amish to other religious groups that object to school attendance. The Court made it clear that the long history of the Amish religious way of life was important to its decision and that groups "claiming to have recently discovered some 'progressive'" or other enlightened way of rearing children for a modern life will not qualify for similar exemption. Since the law is always growing and changing, only time will tell whether some other groups will find ways to successfully challenge state compulsory education laws.

An attempt by other parents in Wisconsin illustrates this point. When the Kasuboski parents did not send their eight children to public schools, they claimed an exemption for religious reasons. They were members of the Basic Bible Church and alleged that the schools' teaching of racial equity, humanism, and "one-world government," together with the influence of communists and Jews, was offensive to their religion. Evidence showed that the particular church was not opposed to education and that some of its members sent their children to public schools. The court ruled that the Kasuboski children could not be exempted because their parents' objection was based on philosophic and ideological grounds and not religious ones.[59] The Amish case could not be used as a precedent by them. "A personal, philosophic choice by parents, rather than a religious choice, does not rise to the level of a First Amendment claim of religious expression." (A related question appears on p. 390.)

Can Students Be Exempted from Certain Courses for Religious Reasons?

That depends on the state law. Religious objections have been raised by parents and students to various parts of the curriculum. The most often heard objection is to sex education courses, whether labeled family life education, human development, human sexuality, or some other title. The course itself does not violate freedom of religion, ruled a California court, particularly if the state law permits children to be excused from participating in such classes.[60] Schools usually make such courses voluntary, but the New Jersey Commissioner of Education ruled that even a required course on family living in which some sex education was included does not violate freedom of religion.[61]

Courts have long protected students who have genuine religious objections from participating in dancing.[62] Similarly, courts would uphold a student's religious objection to watching movies in schools or playing with cards, even if such activities were part of the curriculum. A federal appeals court also ruled in favor of a high school student who objected to Reserve Officer Training Corps (ROTC) training on grounds of religious freedom.[63] In his high school, ROTC was part of a required physical education course, and the court held that the student need not "choose between following his religious beliefs and forfeiting his diploma, on the one hand, and abandoning his religious beliefs and receiving his diploma on the other hand."

In 1985, a federal circuit court ruled on a case involving a parent's request to remove a book from the curriculum on the grounds that it violated her religious beliefs.[64] Cassie Grove, a sophomore, and her mother claimed that *The Learning Tree* by Gordon Parks offended their religious views and advanced secular humanism, thus violating both religious clauses of the First Amendment. The court inquired into: (1) the extent of the burden upon the free exercise of religion, (2) the existence of a compelling state interest to justify that burden, and (3) the extent to which accommodating the student would impede the state's objectives. Since the student was assigned an alternative book and could absent herself during discussions of *The Learning Tree,* the burden on her was minimal. At the same time, the state's compelling interest in providing a well-rounded education would be critically impeded by accommodating the plaintiff's wishes, for by the same logic the schools should eliminate everything objectionable to any other religious views. In the court's opinion, doing this would "leave public education in shreds." The court also found that the book served a secular educational function because it shared a working-class black family's perspective of racism. Thus its use did not constitute establishment of religion or of antireligion.

In *Mozert* v. *Hawkins County Public Schools,* a federal district court in Tennessee ruled that students may "opt out" of reading books objectionable to their religion. The case involved fundamentalist Christian families who objected to stories such as the *Wizard of Oz, Rumpelstiltskin, Macbeth,* and the Holt Rinehart & Winston series. They objected to materials that expose children to feminism, witchcraft, pacifism, vegetarianism, and situational ethics.

In 1987, the Sixth Circuit Court of Appeals reversed this decision.[65] Although the appeals court was unanimous in reversing the lower court, the judges each had different reasons for their conclusions. The basic conflict in the *Mozert* case is between students' right to free exercise of religion on the one hand and the state's compelling interest in educating children on the other. In all likelihood, public schools can expect students to participate in the required parts of the curriculum if they can show those parts essential to achieving some compelling state interest, such as competence in the 3R's and in citizenship. This is particularly the case if there are no easily applied practical alternatives to achieving the same educational objectives.

Parents brought suit against school officials of the Bedford Central School District in New York, alleging violation of their and their children's First Amendment rights.[66] The schools, in their social studies curriculum, had students study various aspects of the culture of India, including learning about Ganesha, a Hindu god. As a follow-up, the students, third graders, were assigned the task of building a replica of Ganesha out of clay. Students also learned to play a very complex math game using cards with a variety of graphic illustrations of zombies, vampires, a unicorn, etc. The game was called "Magic: The Gathering." Students could also make "Worry Dolls," or purchase them at the school store. The program also included Earth Day activities, including prayers to Mother Earth and a liturgy to the Earth as if it were the creator, allegedly derived from American Indian culture.

These practices, among others, were challenged as violations of the Establishment Clause on behalf of Catholic children and as violations of the Catholic religion as worship of graven images. The court ruled unconstitutional the requirement of constructing a model of Ganesha the Hindu god, who is worshiped today by a large number of people in India as well as the reliance on Worry Dolls, which have the power of taking one's worries away. This shows the school's preference of superstition over religion. The other aspects of the curriculum do not violate the Constitution, even if they are objectionable to Catholicism or some other religion.

Do Fantasy Stories in Children's Literature Encourage a Religion of Paganism?

Several cases have so alleged, claiming a violation of the establishment clause as well as the free exercise clause.[67] The latest of these challenged the *Impressions* series by Holt Publishing Company, where the plaintiffs alleged that the series encourages the religions of Wicca, satanism, and witchcraft, as well as interfering with the free exercise of religion.

The district court ruled against the parents in *Fleischfresser* v. *Directors of School District No. 200* in Wheaton, Illinois, and the federal appeals court agreed.[68] The court reasoned that the series, which included fiction and fantasy by well-known authors, helped "...expand

funds in parochial schools in Louisiana. The funds were allocated under Chapter 2 of Title I of the Elementary and Secondary Act of 1965 (ESEA). Under the Act, local educational agencies lend materials and equipment, such as books, computer software and hardware, etc., to public and private schools to implement "secular, neutral, and nonideological programs." The plaintiffs claimed that the allocation of these funds to parochial schools violated the Establishment Clause of the First Amendment. While lower courts agreed with the plaintiffs, a divided Supreme Court upheld the program.

Justice Thomas, writing for a plurality, concluded that lending materials on a neutral basis to all schools does not violate the *Lemon* test and does not lead to indoctrination if the aid is allocated in a way that neither favors nor disfavors religion. Justice Souter wrote a lengthy dissent, accusing, in a detailed analysis, the majority with misinterpreting earlier rulings of the Court. He was joined by Justices Stevens and Ginsburg.

Can Public School District Boundaries Be So Drawn as to Exclude All but Members of One Religion?

No, doing so violates the establishment clause, ruled the U.S. Supreme Court in *Kiryas Joel I*.[77] In this case, New York enacted special legislation to create a school district specifically to serve the needs of the Satmar Ha-sidim, practitioners of a strict form of Judaism. Members of this group speak only Yiddish, segregate the sexes outside the home, dress in distinctive ways, and have separate private religious schools for boys and girls. Since these schools offered no distinctive services for handicapped children, the surrounding public school system offered these services on site at the Yiddish school for girls. This arrangement stopped in 1985 when the Supreme Court declared such services on site to be unconstitutional.[78] When these special-needs children were forced to attend public schools, most parents withdrew them from school, citing "the panic, fear and trauma [the children] suffered in leaving their own community and being with people whose ways were so different." Ultimately, this situation led to special legislation under which a special school was created to serve the needs of the handicapped children. The main question is whether or not such a law violates the establishment clause.

The Supreme Court in *Kiryas Joel I*, in a fragmented decision, ruled the arrangement to be unconstitutional. The majority held that it constituted impermissible aid to religion and that the special needs of the handicapped should have been attended to in some other way. Justice O'Connor suggested another legislative approach that might alleviate the constitutional problem: legislation that would be of general applicability rather than tailored to the needs of Kiryas Joel, so other groups in other areas of the state might fall under it.

A few days after the Supreme Court struck down the first arrangement, the New York legislature enacted a new law to achieve the same goal. This law was challenged and struck down in 1996 as an obvious subterfuge.[79] As the court noted, "...the Constitution 'nullifies sophisticated as well as simple-minded modes' of infringing on constitutional protections." In other words, one cannot do indirectly what cannot be accomplished directly.[80]

Can Student Religious Groups Use School Facilities?

Yes they can pursuant to the Equal Access Act (EAA),[81] passed by Congress in 1984, which provides that it shall be unlawful for any public secondary school that is receiving federal funds and that has a limited open forum[82] to deny equal access to, or discriminate against, any students who wish to conduct a meeting in that forum. The act applies to "non-instructional time," that is, before or after regular school hours. The student group must be voluntary and student-initiated. The school or its employees may not sponsor the meetings and employees may be present only as nonparticipants. Such meetings may not interfere with the conduct of educational activities, and persons not associated with the school may not direct, conduct, control, or regularly attend such meetings.

The Equal Access Act was challenged in several cases, raising questions about its constitutionality as violative of the establishment clause. This issue was settled in 1990 in the *Board of Education of the Westside Community Schools* v. *Mergens,* in which the U.S. Supreme Court ruled that there was no establishment clause violation when student-initiated religious meetings were held in public schools during noninstructional time.[83] Since the high school in *Mergens* allowed at least one noncurriculum group use of its facilities (a chess club), access could not be denied to the student religious group. According to the Court, "...there is a crucial difference between *governmental* speech endorsing religion, which the establishment clause forbids, and *private* speech endorsing religion, which the free speech and free exercise clauses protect."

In California, a San Diego high school denied a religious club the right to meet during lunch like other clubs.[84] The school has a "limited open forum" which allows non-curricular clubs to meet during noninstructional time. The Equal Access Act defines this as the time "before actual classroom instruction begins or after classroom instruction ends." The school argued that denying the student religious club the right to meet at lunch doesn't violate the act since it doesn't fit the act's definition of noninstructional time. But the court ruled that, at this school, lunchtime was noninstructional time since there are no classes during lunch hour, which is therefore after instruction ends in the morning and before it begins in the afternoon. The court noted the limitations of its ruling—that the school could still prohibit religious groups from meeting at lunch time if it made its prohibition "neutral, so that all noncurricular-related groups are barred from meeting at lunch." The court concluded that the school "wrongfully discriminated" against the religious group by denying them equal access.

The Supreme Court ruled on a related case in 2001 in *Good News Club* v. *Milford Central School.*[85] Under New York law, the school district created a policy authorizing residents to use its buildings after school for, "among other things, (1) instruction in education, learning, or the arts and (2) social, civic, recreational, and entertainment uses pertaining to the community welfare." Two residents, sponsors of the Good News Club, a private Christian Organization for children ages 6 to 12, requested to use the building for the club's weekly after-school meetings. The children were to sing songs, hear Bible lessons, memorize scripture, and pray. The school administration denied their request, claiming the proposed use was for religious worship prohibited by the community-use policy. The district court and the Second Circuit Court of Appeals ruled in favor of the school district, but the Supreme Court reversed their rulings.

All parties agreed that the school created a limited open forum under the laws of New York. Under such a law, the state may be justified "in reserving (its forum) for certain groups or for the discussion of certain topics." However, the restrictions the state imposes must not discriminate against speech on the basis of viewpoint, and must be reasonable in light of the purpose served by the forum.

Writing for the majority, Justice Thomas concluded that morals and character can be taught using religious stories, songs, and materials as well as through various other means and methods. Thus, citing earlier Supreme Court cases, the Justice wrote that "…speech discussing otherwise permissible subjects cannot be excluded from a limited public forum on the ground that the subject is discussed from a religious viewpoint." Such exclusion "constitutes impermissible viewpoint discrimination."

The school district also claimed that the elementary school age children would get the impression that the school is endorsing the club and feel coerced to participate. The Court rejected this argument since the children could attend club meetings only with parental permission. If anything, said Justice Thomas, allowing the club to meet on school grounds, after school hours, would show neutrality toward a broad range of groups without regard to their religion. Justices Stevens, Souter, and Ginsburg wrote dissenting opinions asserting that the meetings of the Good News Club were not only to develop morals and character, but primarily "for an evangelical service of worship calling children to commit themselves in an act of Christian conversion."

Can a Student Group Organized Under the Equal Access Act Require a Religious Qualification for its Leadership?

This question was decided in 1996 by the Second Circuit Court of Appeals in a case that arose in Roslyn, New York.[86] Emily Hsu and other students wanted to form a Bible club and requested permission to do so from the high school principal. After lengthy delays by the administrators and the school board, the students submitted their proposed constitution for the club. The proposed club, to be named "Walking on Water," would be open to all students, would focus on Christian fellowship, and would praise God and sing "inspirational music which exalts the Lord Jesus Christ." It would have five officers: president, vice-president, secretary, music coordinator, and activities coordinator, all of whom must be "professed Christians either through baptism or confirmation."

School administrators objected to the provision requiring all officers to be professed Christians and offered recognition only if all students could become members of the club and be eligible for office without regard to creed or religion. The students believed that the possibility of non-Christian officers "would influence the form and content of the Club and influence speech at the Club meetings." They filed suit, claiming violation of the Equal Access Act, the Religious Freedom Restoration Act, the free exercise clause, the establishment clause, the free speech clause, the equal protection clause, the due process clause, the right to free association, and various provisions of the New York State Constitution.

The district court ruled against the students based on a school board policy of nondiscrimination against any student on the basis of creed or religion. On appeal, the court focused on Hsu's statutory claim, which was consistent with the general judicial practice of avoiding constitutional questions whenever a case can be decided on statutory grounds. In the final analysis, based on the Equal Access Act, the court concluded that the religious qualification for the president, vice-president, and music coordinator of the club were defensible because "their duties consist of leading Christian prayers and devotions and safeguarding the 'spiritual content' of the meetings." Religious qualification for the other officers was disallowed.

Can Public Schools Provide Sign-Language Interpreters for Deaf Students Attending Religious Schools?

Yes, ruled a divided U.S. Supreme Court (5–4) in 1993.[87] The case involved a Roman Catholic school student, deaf since birth, who requested that a public school district in Tucson, Arizona, provide him with a sign language interpreter pursuant to the Individuals with Disabilities Education Act (IDEA). The school district and the lower courts considered such provision to violate the establishment clause of the First Amendment, but the majority of the Supreme Court disagreed.

Justice Rehnquist, writing for the majority, indicated that the government program involved in this case distributes benefits neutrally to all children qualified as disabled under the IDEA without regard to the sectarian-nonsectarian nature of the school the child attends. Furthermore, the interpreter merely transmits the information presented to the class as a whole, unlike a teacher or counselor who would help shape the substance of the student's education. Therefore the establishment clause is not violated.

Can Public Schools Deny the Use of Their Facilities to Religious Groups?

It depends on the circumstances. The U.S. Supreme Court ruled in 1993 on a case that arose in the state of New York, whose law authorizes local school boards to regulate the after-hours use of school property.[88] The rules allow the use of school facilities for social, civic, and recreational purposes but not for religious purposes. When Lamb's Chapel, an evangelical church, requested the afterhours use of school facilities to show a film series emphasizing family values from a Christian point of view, it was denied permission. The church went to court, claiming that its right to freedom of expression was violated because permission was denied on the basis of the content of its expression.

The Supreme Court ruled unanimously in favor of the church. The court found that the school created a limited open forum when it allowed its facilities to be used by outside groups for civic or social purposes. Clearly, a film series on child rearing and family values falls within those purposes, and the church's film series was excluded solely because it dealt with the subject from a religious standpoint. It is settled law, ruled the Court that "...the First Amendment forbids the government to regulate speech in ways that favor some viewpoints or ideas at the expense of others."

An interesting legal issue remains to be addressed by the Court. Since many state constitutions provide for a stricter standard of separation of church and state than does the federal Constitution, there is a question whether the state constitutions should prevail over the Equal Access Act or whether the supremacy clause of the Constitution dictates that the federal law supersedes the states' constitutions. The two district courts that addressed this question reached opposite conclusions. In an Idaho case, the court held that the EAA, which was enacted pursuant to the Constitution, preempted the state constitutional provisions in conflict with it, and the court ordered school officials to follow the EAA.[89] In Washington, however, the district court ruled that the supremacy clause did not prohibit the state constitution from limiting the application of the EAA.[90] In the final analysis, the Supreme Court will be called on to resolve these conflicting interpretations.

In a recent case, a public school in New York denied the use of its facilities for religious worship when requested by the Full Gospel Tabernacle.[91] The school district, in its refusal, relied on a state statute (N.Y. Educ. Law § 414) and the Board of Education policy that prohibits the use of school facilities for religious worship services. The plaintiff alleged the law violates the First and Fourteenth Amendments to the U.S. Constitution, particularly since, on two previous occasions, other churches were allowed to use the facilities for religious services.

The District Court ruled against the plaintiffs. It explained that the law of New York created limited open forum in the school and specifically excluded uses for religious services. The two prior uses were allowed due to clerical administrative errors, which have been corrected, and, since the corrections, no such permits have been issued and requests for them have been denied. Thus, the court upheld the state law excluding the use of school facilities for religious services and the U.S. Court of Appeals, Second Circuit, affirmed its decision.

Does the Religious Freedom Restoration Act Violate the Principle of Federalism?

This issue was raised in Bourne, Texas, where a city ordinance that created historic districts prevented a church from expanding its meeting and worship facilities. The church claimed that the ordinance violated the Religious Freedom Restoration Act (RFRA), while the city challenged the constitutionality of the act as usurping the prerogatives of the judicial system.[92] The RFRA, enacted by Congress in 1993,[93] mandated that any law that would substantially burden religion, even if the law or rule is of general applicability, must be "...in furtherance of a compelling governmental interest...and is the least restrictive means of furthering that compelling governmental interest." The district court held the RFRA invalid as an infringement on the authority of the judiciary. The court of appeals reversed this decision and the U.S. Supreme Court accepted the case for review.

In June, 1997, the Court declared the act unconstitutional because it violates the separation of powers provision of the Constitution. In the act, Congress specifies the standard courts must use in considering the legality of certain laws or policies and this is, according to the Court, a prerogative of the judicial branch of the government.

Much controversy followed the Court's ruling, and some members of Congress immediately announced that they will introduce new legislation to strengthen religious freedom. Others claimed that the First Amendment is sufficient as it is to protect freedom of religion.

Can Students Distribute Religious Literature at School?

That depends on whether the *Tinker* test or the "forum analysis" is used by the court to reach a decision (see chapter 9). The *Tinker* test would favor the students as long as there was no substantial or material disruption of schooling. On the other hand, the forum analysis used in *Hazelwood* v. *Kuhlmeier* gives school authorities much broader powers to determine whether the student activity is inconsistent with the school's educational purposes.

This issue arose in Illinois, where students wanted to distribute religious literature at school. The students argued that the forum analysis applies only to outsiders seeking access to school property and not to students, who already have access to the property. While the District Court rejected this argument, the Seventh Circuit Court of Appeals ruled in favor of the students. The judge noted that it is unreasonable and arbitrary to prohibit students from distributing material prepared by others which the students want to adopt as their own.[94]

Can Bibles Be Distributed in Public Schools?

No. Representatives of Gideon International had been distributing Bibles in the public schools of Rensselaer, Indiana, for many years. When the father of a fifth-grade student challenged this practice as a violation of the establishment clause, the court[95] declared the practice unconstitutional under the principles articulated in both *Lemon* v. *Kurtzman* and *Lee* v. *Weisman.* The school argued that prohibiting the distribution of the Bible violated the Gideons' right of free speech. The appeals court noted that the First Amendment guarantee of free speech does not automatically trump the First Amendment prohibition on state-sponsored religious activity. In fact, noted the court, the reverse is true in public schools. The U.S. Supreme Court, without comment, refused to hear the case on appeal.[96]

By contrast, a federal district court in West Virginia allowed community members to place Bibles on unattended tables in public schools. The court protected this practice under the free speech guarantee of the First Amendment.[97] Because the school had a limited open forum, restricting religious speech, which the Bibles represented, would have been a content-based restriction and therefore unconstitutional. The court also ordered the school board to place large, easily readable signs next to the Bibles, disclaiming any approval or disapproval of these displayed materials.

Can "Creationism" Be Taught in Public Schools?

It could probably be taught in social studies classes as describing a belief held by certain segments of the population. However, state laws that require the teaching of "creationism" or "scientific creationism" in courses that also teach the theory of evolution have been declared unconstitutional. The leading case declaring such laws to be efforts to advance religion was *McLean* v. *Arkansas Board of Education* decided in 1982.[98]

Later cases reached similar conclusions, and the majority of the Supreme Court declared the Louisiana Creationism Act unconstitutional because it lacked a clear secular purpose.[99] The federal appeals court had reasoned: "The Act's intended effect is to discredit evolution by counterbalancing its teaching at every turn with the teaching of creationism, a religious belief." While the majority of the Court agreed with the appeals court, declaring the Louisiana law unconstitutional, Chief Justice Rehnquist along with Justice Scalia would uphold it if it had *any* secular purpose.

A variation on the "creationism controversy" arose in the Capistrano Unified School District in California, where the school district required teaching about evolution in a biology class. When a teacher objected, claiming that "evolutionism" and "secular humanism" were religions for purposes of the First Amendment, the Ninth Circuit Court of Appeals disagreed, ruling that the district may require John E. Peloza, the teacher, to teach the theory of evolution but not creationism in his biology classes.[100]

Peloza also alleged a violation of his rights of free speech by not allowing him to discuss his religious views in his classes or anytime in or out of class while students are required to be on campus. He claimed that evolutionism and creationism are both religions. Both the district court and the Ninth Circuit Court of Appeals ruled against him, holding, based on earlier Supreme Court decisions, that evolutionism is not a religion but a scientific theory, unlike creationism. Furthermore, Peloza was not wrongly restricted in his right to free speech because the school district may abridge a teacher's free speech rights in order to avoid a violation of the establishment clause.

The school board of Tangipahoa Parish Public Schools in Louisiana adopted a resolution that required teachers to read a disclaimer in elementary or secondary school classes before they teach about the scientific theory of evolution.[101] The disclaimer was to recognize that the theory of evolution was "to inform the students of the scientific concept and not intended to influence or dissuade the Biblical version of Creation or any other concept." When parents challenged the disclaimer, the District Court held that it constituted an establishment of religion in violation of the First Amendment. In 2000, the court of appeals held that the disclaimer was an endorsement of religion and violated the second prong of the *Lemon* test, that is, its primary effect is to advance religion.

Can a School Board Adopt a Policy Prohibiting Dancing at School?

Yes, if the policy or rule mentions no religious reasons for the prohibition and if public discussion by the board of education offers no reasons or only secular reasons for it. So held the Eighth Circuit Court of Appeals, reversing a district court in a Missouri case.[102] Although it was clear that the rule was consistent with a "vocal segment" of the community and with private beliefs of board members, on its face it was not based on religion. Thus the court held that the *Lemon* test was satisfied and any remedy lies in the ballot box.

Can Students Be Exempt from Required Immunization Contrary to Their Religion Beliefs?

Yes, ruled a district court in New York, in 2002. When the Liverpool School District denied registration for kindergarten for Kelly Turner who wanted an exemption to the state's mandatory immunization law which violated her religious beliefs, she filed suit in federal court. Liverpool claimed that a religious exemption would violate the establishment clause. Applying the *Lemon* test, the district court rejected Liverpool's argument.[103]

Summary

Throughout the history of public schooling, disagreements concerning the appropriate relationship between religion and public education have resulted in spirited controversies that have had to be resolved by our courts. Although controversies still abound, there are some guiding principles for the conduct of daily schooling.

It is clear today that teachers and students may be exempt from saluting the flag if they have objections based on either religion or conscience. Teachers or students so exempted may remain in the classroom and sit or stand respectfully while others participate in the ceremony. Teachers may not, however, refuse to follow a curriculum properly adopted by a school board, even though they may have personal religious objections to it. If parts of the curriculum are objectionable to them, they must provide acceptable alternative ways for the students to learn the materials.

Teachers may take personal leave for religious holidays, but it is up to the local school district whether to pay them for such leaves. When school officials consider such leaves excessive and thus an interference with the continuity of instruction, provisions of the state or federal law must be consulted. A teacher who brought suit under Title VII of the Civil Rights Act of 1964 prevailed in a case where a federal appeals court required school boards to make reasonable accommodations to the teacher's religion as long as no undue hardship accrues to the employer. But another appeals court ruled to the contrary in a similar case under Title VII. The Supreme Court held that while Title VII requires reasonable accommodation by the employer, the accommodation need not be the one preferred by the teacher.

Courts have ruled that prayers or Bible reading must be excluded from public schools as violations of the establishment clause of the First Amendment. This is the case whether such practices are mandatory or voluntary and whether led by faculty or students. Studying *about* religion is legal, however, and so is released-time religious instruction as long as it takes place away from school facilities and does not involve school personnel or other support from the schools. Provisions for a period for silent meditation or prayer may or may not violate the Constitution, depending on the wording of the statute or policy as well as the intent behind its creation. If it is clear from the legislative history that its intent is to further religion, courts will strike it down as violative of the establishment clause of the First Amendment. A court ruled similarly on the inclusion of Transcendental Meditation in the curriculum. On the other hand, a simple provision of a brief period of silence at the start of the school day is likely to be upheld. Outside groups may display Bibles on tables outside classrooms where students may voluntarily read them or ignore them.

The right of high school students to form voluntary student-initiated and student-led prayer groups that meet on school property outside regular school hours was upheld by the Supreme Court in 1990.

Students have the right to attend either private or public schools, and state compulsory attendance laws may be satisfied by attendance at religious or secular schools. In at least one case, some students were exempt from attending school beyond the eighth grade when they could show that the high school curriculum would violate their religious beliefs and religiously based way of life. Other attempts at "home schooling" based on religious grounds succeeded only if the state requirements for such alternatives were satisfied. State law may also specify whether students may be exempted from certain parts of the curriculum. For example, courses related to sex education are often made elective, though some courts have upheld their inclusion in the curriculum even when they were required. Students have been exempted from participating in ancillary parts of curriculum such as dancing in physical education classes if they could show genuine religious objections to the activities. The use of vouchers in religious schools has been upheld by the Supreme Court of Wisconsin, while prohibited by state law in Maine. A case that arose in Cleveland is currently before the Supreme Court.

Thus, while controversies still abound surrounding the issue of religion and public education, careful examination shows that both students and teachers have made significant gains in asserting their right to free exercise of religion on the one hand and being free from the states' efforts to use the schools to "establish" religion on the other. It is likely that with changes in the Supreme Court, we may expect new interpretations of the First Amendment's clauses related to religion.

NOTES

1. *Russo* v. *Central School District No. 1,* 469 F.2d 623 (2d Cir. 1972), *cert. denied,* 411 U.S. 932 (1973).
2. *Opinions of the Justices to the Governor,* 363 N.E.2d 251 (Mass. 1977).
3. *Palmer* v. *Board of Education of City of Chicago,* 603 F.2d 1271 (7th Cir. 1979), *cert. denied,* 44 U.S. 1026 (1980).
4. *Matter of Bein,* 15 EDUC. DEP. REP. 407 N.Y. Comm'r Dec. No. 9226 (1976).
5. *California Teachers Association* v. *Board of Trustees,* 138 Cal. Rptr. 817 (Ct. App. 1977).
6. *Pinkster* v. *Joint District No. 283,* 735 F.2d 388 (10th Cir. 1984).
7. 42 U.S.C. § 2000e(i) (n.d.).
8. *Philbrook* v. *Ansonia Board of Education,* 479 U.S. 60 (1986).
9. *Rankins* v. *Commission on Professional Competence of Ducor Union School District,* 142 Cal. Rptr. 101 (Ct. App. 1977).
10. *Rankins* v. *Commission on Professional Competence of Ducor Union School District,* 154 Cal. Rptr. 907 (Cal. 1979), *appeal dismissed,* 100 S.Ct. 515 (1979).
11. *Williams* v. *Van Buren School District,* 742 F.2d 1458 (6th Cir. 1984).
12. *Rawlings* v. *Butler,* 290 S.W.2d 801 (Ky. 1956); *New Haven* v. *Torrington,* 43 A.2d 455 (Conn. 1945).
13. *Harfst* v. *Hoegen,* 163 S.W.2d 609 (Mo. 1942).
14. *Gerhardt* v. *Heidt,* 267 N.W. 127 (N.D. 1936).
15. *Commonwealth* v. *Herr,* 78 A. 68 (Pa. 1910); *Zellers* v. *Huff,* 236 P.2d 949 (N.M. 1951).
16. *Equal Employment Opportunity Commission* v. *Reads,* 759 F.Supp. 1150 (E.D. Pa. 1991).
17. 319 U.S. 624, 642 (1943).
18. *Id.*
19. *Sherman* v. *Community Consolidated School District No. 21,* 980 F.2d 437 (7th Cir. 1992).
20. *Banks* v. *Board of Public Instruction of Dade County,* 314 F.Supp. 285 (S.D. Fla. 1970).
21. *Goetz* v. *Ansell,* 477 F.2d 636 (2d Cir. 1973); the same result was reached in *Lipp* v. *Morris,* 579 F.2d 834, 836 (3d Cir. 1978).
22. *Frain* v. *Barron,* 307 F.Supp. 27 (E.D. N.Y. 1969).
23. *Abington School District* v. *Schempp,* 374 U.S. 203 (1963).
24. *Herdahl* v. *Pontotoc County School District,* 933 F.Supp. 582 (N.D. Miss. 1996).
25. 897 F.2d 181 (5th Cir. 1990).
26. 112 S.Ct. 2649 (1992).
27. *Id.* at 2659.
28. For a systematic analysis of *Lee* v. *Weisman,* see David Schimmel, *Graduation Prayers Flunk Coercion Text: An Analysis of* Lee v. Weisman," 76 EDUC. L. REP. 913 (1992).
29. *Jones et al.* v. *Clear Creek Independent School District,* 977 F.2d 963 (5th Cir. 1992).
30. *Jager* v. *Douglas County School District,* 862 F.2d 824 (11th Cir. 1989).
31. *Doe* v. *Duncanville Independent School District,* 994 F.2d 160 (5th Cir. 1993).
32. *Santa Fe Indep. Sch. Dist.* v. *Doe,* 530 U.S. 290 (2000).
33. *School District of Abington Township, Pennsylvania, et al.* v. *Schempp et al.,* 374 U.S. 203 (1963).
34. 403 U.S. 602 (1971).
35. *Stone* v. *Grabam,* 449 U.S. 39 (1981).
36. *Washegesic* v. *Bloomingdale Public Schools,* 813 F.Supp. 559 (W.D. Mich. 1993).
37. *Washegesic* v. *Bloomingdale High School,* 33 F.3d 679 (6th Cir. 1994), *cert. denied,* 115 S.Ct. 1822 (1995).
38. *Florey* v. *Sioux Falls School District, No. 49–5,* 619 F.2d 1311 (8th Cir. 1980), *cert. denied,* 449 U.S. 897 (1980).
39. *County of Allegheny* v. *American Civil Liberties Union Greater Pittsburgh Chapter,* 492 U.S. 573 (1989).
40. *Chandler et al.* v. *Fob James et al.,* ev 96-D-169N (D.C.M.D. Alabama, 1997).
41. *Board of Education of Kiryas Joel Village School District* v. *Grumet,* 114 S.Ct. 2481 (1994).
42. *Lubbock Civil Liberties Union* v. *Lubbock Independent School District,* 669 F.2d 1038 (5th Cir. 1984).
43. 427 U.S. 38 (1985).

44. *Gaines* v. *Anderson*, 421 F.Supp. 337 (D. Mass. 1976).

45. *Karen B.* v. *Treen*, 653 F.2d 897 (5th Cir. 1981), *aff'd on appeal*, 455 U.S. 913 (1982).

46. *Jaffree et al.* v. *Board of School Commissioners of Mobile County*, 459 U.S. 1314 (1983).

47. *Duffy* v. *Las Cruces Public Schools*, 557 F.Supp. 1013 (D. N.M. 1983); see also *May* v. *Cooperman*, 572 F.Supp. 1561 (D. N.J. 1983).

48. Mass. Gen. L. Ch. 690 (1985).

49. *Bown* v. *Gwinnett County School District*, 112 F.3d 1464 (11th Cir. 1997).

50. *Malnak* v. *Yogi*, 440 F.Supp. 1284 (D. N.J. 1977), *aff'd*, 592 F.2d 197 (3d Cir. 1979).

51. *Pierce* v. *Society of Sisters*, 268 U.S. 510 (1925).

52. *Id.* at 535.

53. *Jackson* v. *Benson*, 578 N.W.2d 602 (Wis. 1998).

54. *Simmons-Harris* v. *Goff*, 711 N.E.2d 203 (Ohio 1999).

55. *Zelman* v. *Simmon-Harris*, 234 F.3d 945 (6th Cir. 2000).

56. *Bagley* v. *Raymond School Dept.*, 728 A.2d 127 (Me. 1999).

57. *T.A.F. and E.M.E.* v. *Duval County*, 237 So.2d 15 (Fla. 1973).

58. *Wisconsin* v. *Yoder*, 406 U.S. 205 (1972).

59. *State* v. *Kasuboski*, 275 N.W.2d 101 (Wis. Ct. App. 1978).

60. *Citizens for Parental Rights* v. *San Mateo City Board of Education*, 124 Cal. Rptr. 68 (Ct. App. 1975).

61. *"J.B." and "B.B." as Guardians and Natural Parents of "P.B." and "J.B."* v. *Dumont Board of Education*, Dec. of N.J. Comm'r of Education (1977).

62. *Hardwick* v. *Board of Trustees*, 54 Cal. App. 696 (1921).

63. *Spence* v. *Bailey*, 465 F.2d 797 (6th Cir. 1972).

64. *Grove* v. *Mead School District No. 354*, 753 F.2d 1528 (9th Cir. 1985).

65. 827 F.2d 1058 (6th Cir. 1987), *cert. denied*, 108 S.Ct. 1029 (1988).

66. *Altman* v. *Bedford Cent. School Dist.*, 45 F.Supp.2d 368 (S.D.N.Y. 1999).

67. For a comprehensive view and analysis of these cases, see Frances R. A. Patterson, *Challenges to Public School Reading Textbooks*, 106 Educ. L. Rep. 1 (1996).

68. 15 F.3d 680 (7th Cir. 1994).

69. *Settle* v. *Dickson County School Board*, 53 F.3d 152 (6th Cir. 1995).

70. *Id.* at 155.

71. *Bangor Baptist Church* v. *State of Maine, Department of Educational and Cultural Services*, 549 F.Supp. 1208 (D. Maine 1982).

72. Ohio Rev. Code ch. 4112 (1985).

73. *Dayton Christian Schools* v. *Ohio Civil Rights Commission*, 477 U.S. 619 (1986).

74. *Pulido* v. *Cavazos*, 934 F.2d 912 (8th Cir. 1991).

75. *Agostini* v. *Felton* 118 S.Ct. 40 (1997).

76. *Mitchell* v. *Helms*, 120 S.Ct. 2530 (2000).

77. *Board of Education of Kiryas Joel* v. *Grumet*, 114 S.Ct. 2481 (1994).

78. *Aguilar* v. *Felton*, 473 U.S. 402 (1985).

79. *Grumet* v. *Cuomo*, 647 N.Y.S.2d 565 (App. Div. 3d Dept. 1996).

80. The U.S. Supreme Court issued a stay of the New York decision pending a decision on a petition for certiorary (*Grumet* v. *Pataki*, 527 U.S. 1019, 1999).

81. Pub. L. No. 98-377, § 801 et seq., (codified at 20 U.S.C. § 4071 et seq.).

82. A school has a limited open forum if non-curriculum-related student groups, such as a chess club or a scuba diving club, may meet on school premises during noninstructional time.

83. 496 U.S. 226 (1990); see also 20 U.S.C. § 4071 (1988).

84. *Ceniceros* v. *Bd. of Trustees of San Diego School Dist.*, 106 F.3d 878 (9th Cir. 1997). For an alternative view, see the dissenting opinion of Judge Lay, *Id.* at 883.

85. *Good News Club* v. *Milford Cent. School*, 121 S.Ct. 2093 (2001).

86. *Hsu* v. *Roslyn Union Free School District No. 3*, 85 F.3d 839 (2d Cir. 1996).

87. *Larry Zobrest, et ux; et al.* v. *Catalina Foothills School District*, 509 U.S. 1 (1993), 61 U.S.L.W. 4641 (June 18, 1993).

88. *Lamb's Chapel* v. *Center Moriches School District*, 508 U.S. 384 (1993), 61 U.S.L.W. 4549 (June 7, 1993).

89. *Hooppock* v. *Twin Falls School District,* 772 F.Supp. 1160 (D. Idaho 1991).
90. *Garnett* v. *Renton School District,* 772 F.Supp. 531 (W.D. Wash. 1991).
91. *Full Gospel Tabernacle* v. *Community School Dist.,* 979 F.Supp. 214 (S.D.N.Y. 1997); aff'd 164 F.3d 829 (2nd Cir. 1999).
92. *City of Bourne* v. *Flores,* 521 U.S. 507 (1997).
93. 42 U.S.C. § 2000bb (1993).
94. *Hedges* v. *Waueonda Community School District* No. 118, 9 F.3rd 1295 (7th Cir. 1993).
95. *Berger* v. *Rensselaer Central School Corporation,* 982 F.2d 1160 (7th Cir. 1993).
96. *Rensselaer Cent. Sch. Corp.* v. *Berger,* 508 U.S. 911 (1993).
97. *Peck* v. *Upshur County Board of Education,* 941 F.Supp. 1478 (N.D. W. Va. 1996).
98. 529 F.Supp. 1255 (E.D. Ark. 1982).
99. *Edwards* v. *Aquillard,* 482 U.S. 578 (1987).
100. *Pelazo* v. *Capistrano Unified School District,* 37 F.3d 517 (9th Cir. 1994), *cert. denied,* 115 S.Ct. 2640 (1995).
101. *Freiler* v. *Tangipahoa Parish Bd. of Educ.,* 195 F.3d 337 (5th Cir. 1999).
102. *Clayton by Clayton* v. *Place,* 889 F.2d 192 (8th Cir. 1989).
103. *Turner* v. *Liverpool Central School,* 2002 WL 214965 (N.D.N.Y.) Feb. 11, 2002.

11 When Can Schools Limit Freedom of Association?

Overview

Citizens often judge teachers and students by the company they keep and the organizations they join. In the past, teachers have been fired for being members of groups considered subversive or even for being active in partisan politics. Students have been prohibited from organizing controversial groups on campus if their aims conflicted with the goals of the school or the mores of their community. Some teachers and students believed that they were victims of guilt by association and that restrictions on their organizational activity violated their freedom of association. However, many school administrators argue that teachers and students are in a special category and that their associational freedom should not be as broad as the freedom of other citizens.

On the other hand, increasing numbers of teachers and students are rejecting the notion that their rights should be less or their obligations more than those of other people. Teachers object to being penalized for failure to sign loyalty oaths, for membership in unpopular or controversial organizations, or for participating in partisan politics. Students want to be able to organize social, religious, or political groups in school and to organize demonstrations and hear controversial speakers.

The scope and limits of teachers' and students' freedom of association is the focus of this chapter. The court cases discussed indicate how judges have been resolving conflicts on these issues.

Student Organizations

Does the Equal Access Act Protect Controversial Student Organizations?

Partly. Congress passed the Equal Access Act in 1984 to prohibit any public secondary school that has a "limited open forum" from discriminating against or denying equal access to any student group "on the basis of the religious, political, philosophical or other content" of their views. A school is considered to have a limited open forum if it permits "one or more noncurriculum related student groups to meet on school premises during noninstructional time."[1] However, the act does not limit the authority of administrators to prohibit all extracurricular organizations or permit only curriculum-related groups which schools can then control.

Are Student Religious Groups Entitled to Recognition?

Yes, if they are not school sponsored. As noted above, the Equal Access Act prohibits schools from discriminating against student religious groups. Although some lawyers believed this act violated the establishment clause, in *Board of Education* v. *Mergens,* the U.S. Supreme Court upheld the act and ruled that student religious clubs can meet on the same basis as other extracurricular activities. In *Mergens,* a Nebraska high school had denied students permission to form a Christian club.[2] The Court ruled that the denial violated the Equal Access Act because the school recognized other noncurriculum-related student groups, such as the chess and scuba diving clubs. The Court also held that permitting religious clubs to meet is not an endorsement of religion by the school. "We think," wrote Justice O'Connor, "that secondary school students are mature enough...to understand that a school does not endorse or support student speech that it merely permits...."

In a related decision, a Washington high school refused to recognize a religious club because a state law prohibited religious groups from meeting on school property.[3] The students claimed that their rights under the Equal Access Act were violated, and a federal appeals court agreed. The court explained that when state and federal laws clash, the federal law prevails. The court concluded that states "can be more protective of individual rights than the federal Constitution. However, states cannot abridge rights granted by federal law." (For more on this topic, see chapter 10.)

Must Schools Recognize a Gay/Straight Alliance Club?

Such a club must be treated like any other student group seeking school recognition and cannot be discriminated against because of its viewpoint.

In 1999, Anthony Colin and a friend decided to form a Gay/Straight Alliance (GSA) club at El Modena High School in Orange, California. In accord with school policy, the students applied for recognition as a noncurricular group to "promote tolerance by providing a safe forum for discussion of issues related to sexual orientation and homophobia." According to the group's mission statement, "this is not a sexual issue," it is about "promoting respect for all students." Instead of approving the application as she did for 38 other student groups, the principal asked the students to delete references to "gay" and "sexual orientation" and to change the club's name to something "more appropriate" such as Tolerance for All. The students refused and the school board rejected the club's application. According to one board member, asking us to approve the GSA "is asking us to legitimize sin." The students went to court, alleging that the board violated the Equal Access Act (EAA).[4]

In a 2000 decision, Judge Carter noted that "there are about six hundred gay–straight alliance clubs at high schools across the country," and this is only the fourth suit on this issue. The judge then placed this case in the context of the First Amendment's "ban on official censorship" that "does not permit educators to act as 'thought police.'" As Justice Kennedy pointed out in a previous Supreme Court case, one of the consequences of the Equal Access Act "is that clubs of a most controversial character might have access to the student life of high schools that in the past have given recognition only to clubs of a more conventional kind."[5] Moreover, Judge Carter wrote that, in passing the EAA, Congress did not pass an "Access for All Students Except Gay Students Act, because to do so would be unconstitutional."

The school argued that the GSA was not protected since it is related to the curriculum which deals with human sexuality. But, according to the court, so long as the school allows any noncurricular group to meet, it cannot prohibit the GSA from having equal access even if its meetings do relate to the curriculum. In view of the school's limited open forum, it can only prohibit groups that would "materially and substantially" interfere with school activities. And, wrote Judge Carter, the school will not be able to show that "students discussing homophobia and acceptance of all students regardless of sexual orientation somehow serves as a major disruption to the education of students." The court also rejected the school's requirement that the group change its name to something less "divisive." "A group's speech and association rights," wrote the court, "are implicated in the name it chooses for itself" and the school's suggested alternative names "would attack the very core reasons for having the club."

Until the late 1990s, it was unclear whether schools would be required to recognize gay student clubs since there were no reported decisions on the issue, and some administrators argued that schools should be able to restrict such clubs on the grounds that the EAA does not protect groups that interfere with the school's responsibility "to protect the well-being of students." However, the trend of judicial decision now requires high schools to permit Gay–Straight Alliances to have access to school facilities like all other student clubs.

Furthermore, some educators are calling on schools to do more—to develop affirmative policies to protect homosexual students from harassment and to teach tolerance of alternative lifestyles. In 1993, for example, the Massachusetts Board of Education approved the first state policy prohibiting discrimination against homosexual students, and the state now allocates funds to encourage schools to provide counseling and to establish gay/straight alliances. In 2001, over 150 Massachusetts public high schools received grants from the State Department of Education to support activities of their Safe Schools Program for Gay and Lesbian Youth.[6] In contrast, Alabama law requires sex education classes to teach that "homosexuality is not a lifestyle acceptable to the general public and that homosexual conduct is a criminal offense."[7]

When Can Schools Deny Access to Student Groups?

When the school prohibits all student clubs or when the club is noncurricular and the school only permits curriculum-related groups.

To avoid the requirements of the Equal Access Act, the Salt Lake City School Board adopted a policy prohibiting any student group "not directly related to the curriculum to organize or meet on school property." Based on this policy, school officials denied access to the noncurricular Gay–Straight Alliance. The GSA students alleged that the school discriminated against them by permitting access to groups such as the Future Business Leaders of America (FBLA) and the National Honor Society (NHS) that the school considered "curricular" when in fact they engaged in many noncurricular activities.

In a 1999 decision, a federal court discussed what constitutes a curricular group. The court wrote that a group is deemed curricular if it "directly relates to the curriculum" and "if the subject matter of the group is actually taught or will soon be taught in a regularly offered course" or "concerns the body of courses as a whole."[8] The judge found that the FBLA was related to the Applied Technology curriculum and the NHS related to the curriculum as a whole. Admittedly, these groups also engaged in substantial social, fund-raising, and community service activities. But, according to the judge, that does not mean they are not curriculum-related. A literature club, he explained, may devote considerable time raising money for a trip to a Shakespeare festival without becoming noncurricular. Since the school only approved curricular groups, it did not trigger the equal access guarantees of the EAA. Therefore, the school did not violate the GSA's rights by denying it access since it was admittedly a noncurricular group.

Some courts may require a closer and more direct relationship between school courses and a club to consider it curricular. This was what happened when a judge ruled that a Key Club was noncurricular even though the school argued that its food drives were "directly related to the high school's History and Humanities classes, which teach a unit on homelessness, hunger and poverty."[9] The controversy erupted when a New Jersey administrator turned down a student's proposed Bible Club as noncurricular because of the school's policy that only approved clubs that were directly related to its courses. The student claimed that the approved Key Club was noncurricular and therefore the exclusion of the Bible Club violated the EAA. Judge Nygaard agreed. According to the judge, for a club to be curricular-related, it must do more than relate "in some marginal way" to something taught; rather, "the *subject matter* of the student group must be taught in class." The judge concluded that "the subject matter of the Key Club is *not* poverty and homelessness" but community service and fundraising, and "a few isolated club activities" cannot turn a noncurricular student group into a curricular one. Since the judge found that the Key Club was noncurricular, this triggered the EAA and required the school to give equal access to the Bible Club.

What If a Gay/Straight Group Seeks Access as a Curriculum-Related Club?

This is what occurred in a 2000 case from Salt Lake City when the PRISM (People Recognizing Important Social Movements) club sought approval as a curriculum-related group at East High School. PRISM's application stated:

> We want to talk about democracy, civil rights, equality, discrimination and diversity.... The club will serve as a prism through which historical and current events, institutions, and culture can be viewed in terms of the impact, experience and contributions of gays and lesbians.... That dialogue is directly related to many of the topics covered in the U.S. History, American Government, and Sociology courses at East High.[10]

School officials did not approve the club as curriculum-related because its subject matter "narrows to...the experience and contributions of gays and lesbians." In response, the students showed to the court's satisfaction that their club's goals were directly related to 13 of the course objectives in sociology, U.S. history, and government. Concerning the school's argument that PRISM's focus was "too narrow," the court agreed that "PRISM narrows the subject matter of courses to which it claims a relation." But the evidence indicated that the school's "no narrowing" policy had never been applied to other approved clubs—all of which focus on some course objectives and not others. Therefore, the court ruled that the school violated the students' First Amendment rights by applying its policy in an unconstitutional manner.

Does the Equal Access Act Apply to Elementary Schools?

No, only to secondary schools. Thus courts look to constitutional principles and state law rather than to the Equal Access Act when resolving conflicts about religious clubs in elementary schools. Such a conflict arose in Ohio when a teacher-sponsored religious club was denied permission to meet immediately after school but was allowed to meet at 6:30 P.M. In view of the teacher's sponsorship, the court reasoned that allowing the club to meet at 3:45 P.M. created a danger that the elementary students would view the club as school-sponsored, but permitting the club to meet at 6:30 P.M. broke the link between the school day and the religious activity.[11] It also accommodated the interests of club members, the principles of the establishment clause, and Ohio state law, which allows religious groups to use school buildings.

Is Freedom of Association a Right of Public School Students?

While courts have broadly protected freedom of association among teachers and other adults, its application to students in the public schools has been narrower. Thus a federal court upheld a Minnesota high school rule that permitted student athletes to be punished for "attending parties where alcohol and/or illegal drugs…are present."[12] A student who had her athletic letter revoked for merely attending such an off-campus party claimed that the policy violated her constitutional right to freedom of association. The court ruled that the student's "desire to associate socially with her peers at parties" is not a form of association entitled to constitutional protection. The judge concluded: "Disciplining of a student for attending a party at which alcohol is consumed by minors is a reasonable means of deterring alcohol consumption among students, a goal which is not only legitimate, but highly compelling."

Can Secret Societies Be Prohibited in Public Schools?

Yes. As early as 1909, the California legislature declared it unlawful for any public school student to become a member of any secret society or club. In defending this legislation, a state court wrote that such groups "tend to engender an undemocratic spirit of caste" and "to promote cliques" among students.[13] The judge noted that "regulations have recently been adopted by boards of education in many cities of the country" to curb the negative effects of secret organizations, and "courts have uniformly held valid reasonable rules adapted by school authorities to prevent the establishment" of such groups. This decision was written in 1912, and it is still the prevailing legal opinion on the subject.

Can Schools Prohibit Students from Belonging to Fraternities, Sororities, and Other Undemocratic Organizations?

Yes. Although adults cannot be prohibited from joining undemocratic groups, courts have held that such prohibitions can apply to high school students "in their formative years." A California case concerned a former high school sorority that had given up its secret ritual, handshake, and Greek letter name and reorganized itself into the Manana Club. Despite these changes, the Sacramento School Board prohibited the Manana Club and other undemocratic organizations. One of the club members went to court and argued that the club was not secret and that its objectives were "literature, charity, and democracy." But a California appeals court found that the club had different purposes than its stated objectives and upheld the school regulations.[14]

The court said that schools had authority to restrict student social organizations that try to create a membership composed of the "socially elite" by "self-perpetuation, rushing, [and] pledging." The Manana Club's rules provided that only 20 girls from the Sacramento schools could be rushed each semester, and new members were chosen by a secret process. Thus the court concluded that the purpose of this organization is "not to foster democracy (as the Manana constitution preaches) but to frustrate democracy (as the Manana Club by its admitted activities practices)."[15]

Do Many States Have Legislation Outlawing Undemocratic High School Organizations, and Have Such Laws Been Upheld?

Yes to both questions. Although such legislation might seem inconsistent with the principles of the *Tinker* decision and the Equal Access Act, statutes in about 25 states have outlawed high school fraternities, sororities, and organizations such as the Manana Club, and numerous cases over the past 60 years have upheld such legislation against attack. The following states have legislation similar to California's, which makes it unlawful for any public school student to join "any fraternity, sorority or secret club": Arkansas, Colorado, Florida, Illinois, Indiana, Iowa, Kansas, Louisiana, Maine, Massachusetts (optional with local board), Michigan, Minnesota, Mississippi, Montana, Nebraska, New Jersey, Ohio, Oklahoma, Oregon, Pennsylvania, Rhode Island, Texas (limited), Vermont, Virginia, and Washington. In addition, Maryland, Missouri, and New York (optional with local school board) prohibit public schools from setting up secret organizations.[16]

Does Recognition of an Organization Imply Approval of Its Goals or Programs?

No. The purpose of recognition is to enable school officials to be informed about the purposes and activities of an organization, to ensure that student groups understand and are willing to comply with reasonable school rules, and to establish procedures for governing the time, place, and manner in which groups may conduct their activities. If school officials used the term "registered" (rather than "recognized") student organizations, they might lessen the tendency of many parents and educators to erroneously believe that recognition implies approval.

Can Schools Regulate or Restrict Student Organizations?

Yes. Administrators can require student groups to obey a variety of reasonable regulations governing the equitable and responsible use of school facilities. Groups that fail to comply with such regulations can be disciplined and barred from campus. Moreover, the U.S. Supreme Court ruled that school officials would be justified in refusing to recognize a proposed organization if there was evidence that the group was likely to be a disruptive influence and break "reasonable rules, interrupt classes, or substantially interfere" with other students' rights.[17]

Demonstrations and Protests

Do Students Have a Right to Demonstrate on Campus?

Yes. School officials probably could not issue a total prohibition against all demonstrations anywhere on campus without violating students' First Amendment rights. Yet administrators clearly have the authority to protect safety, property, and normal school operations by placing reasonable, nondiscriminatory restrictions on the time, place, and manner of proposed demonstrations.

In Pennsylvania, a group of high school students were suspended for participating in a sit-in demonstration, although they attempted to conduct their protest in a peaceful and orderly fashion. The evidence indicated that some demonstrators were noisy and skipped classes and that the demonstration made it necessary to relocate other students. Therefore, despite the students' peaceful intentions, the judge ruled against them because their protest substantially interfered with the educational process.[18] However, the court noted that the demonstration was not illegal merely because it was held in school, because other students gathered to watch, or because school administrators were distracted from their regular duties. (Related questions appear in chapter 9.)

Do Peace Groups Have a Right to Recruit in Public Schools?

They probably do if branches of the U.S. Armed Forces are allowed to recruit there. In Chicago, the board of education allowed military recruiters to disseminate literature, advertise in the school papers and on bulletin boards, and counsel students concerning careers in the armed services. However, the board denied a peace group the opportunity to distribute information and counsel students about "conscientious objection and legal alternatives to the draft" because they feared the group would use the schools "to propagandize their views on...the evils of war." But the group sued and won. According to the court, this is an issue of "equal access" to discuss a subject the board already approved when it allowed military recruiters into the schools.[19] If military representatives are allowed to discuss military careers, then the peace group should be allowed an equal opportunity to discuss alternative careers. Otherwise the schools would be officially discriminating against a particular point of view.

Similarly, a federal court in Georgia ruled that a local antiwar group should not be denied the same access as military recruiters and therefore should be allowed "to present peace-oriented educational and career opportunities to Atlanta public school students."[20] In addition, the court held that schools cannot prohibit accurate information that discourages students from entering the military. However, the court ruled that exhortations simply denouncing a military career can be banned. On a related issue, a federal court in Pennsylvania held that a school was not required to make its facilities available to a student group for an antinuclear rally open to the public where such facilities have not been generally open.[21]

Can Controversial Speakers Be Prohibited from Public Schools?

Sometimes, but not simply because they are controversial. In a Maine case, a school board, after several bomb threats, cancelled the observance of Tolerance Day and the appearance of a homosexual speaker. The speaker and the program organizers alleged that the school violated their First Amendment rights. However, a state court upheld the board's action for two reasons: First, the board's motive was to prevent substantial disruption, not to restrict discussion of controversial ideas; second, because Tolerance Day was to be part of the required school curriculum, the board had the discretion to change the program as long as it did not restrict discussion of homosexuality, prejudice, or other issues of concern.[22]

On the other hand, a 1996 federal decision ruled that the Denver School Board could not prohibit a controversial community organization from using a school auditorium for an after-school youth forum.[23] Board policy had permitted a variety of community groups to use their facilities when school was not in session. But the board denied permission for the youth forum because the forum was "not in the best interest of the school" since some of the speakers were associated with a student walkout a few weeks before. The judge ruled that the "best interests" standard was unconstitutional because it gave the board "unfettered discretion" to impose an unlawful "prior restraint of expression." Prohibiting the forum also constituted unconstitutional viewpoint discrimination by the government because there was no evidence that the speakers would promote unlawful action.

Can Schools Bar All Outside Political Speakers?

No. A case confronting this issue arose in Oregon when a high school teacher invited a variety of political speakers, including a communist, to his class.[24] Before the communist was to speak, the school board banned "all political speakers" from the high school. The ban was ruled unconstitutional by a federal court.

The judge wrote that schools might exclude all speakers, unqualified speakers, or speakers who would cause disruption, but officials could not bar only "outside political speakers," nor could they contend that "political subjects are inappropriate in a high school curriculum." On the contrary, the court noted that political subjects are frequently discussed in schools and such discussions are often "required by law."

The judge acknowledged the problem faced by school officials in a community in which many people equate communism with "violence, deception and imperialism." He observed, however, that schools would eliminate much of their curriculum if they teach only about "pacifist, honest, and nonexpansionist societies." "I am firmly convinced," concluded the judge, "that a course designed to teach students that a free and democratic society is superior to those in which freedoms are sharply curtailed will fail entirely if it fails to teach one important lesson: that the power of the state is never so great that it can silence a man or woman simply because there are those who disagree."

Can Administrators Refuse to Hire a Teacher Who Participated in Disruptions at Another School?

Yes. Bruce Franklin, a Marxist English scholar, had his appointment rejected by the University of Colorado because of his participation in disruptions at Stanford University. Franklin argued that he never violated any criminal statutes. But a federal judge noted that schools need not tolerate political conduct "substantially disrupting school discipline even though that conduct was perhaps not unlawful."[25] The judge emphasized that he was not ruling against Franklin because of his political beliefs or his associations with radical political groups. Rather he was doing so because (1) there was "clear and convincing" evidence that Franklin's conduct at Stanford "materially and substantially interfered with university activities," and (2) this was a reasonable basis on which to conclude that he posed a "substantial threat of material disruption" at the University of Colorado.

Can Schools Prohibit Suspended Teachers from Associating with Students?

Under some circumstances, they can. In West Virginia, for example, a high school basketball coach was suspended for beating a student and, during the suspension, was prohibited "from any professional association with public school students." The coach claimed that this prohibition violated his constitutional right of association. But a federal court disagreed.[26] It ruled that the administration had a compelling interest in seeing that the effectiveness of the coach's replacement was not undermined. According to the court, "the specter of a former authority figure competing with his replacement for the affection and respect of the students justified the restrictions imposed."

Teachers and Partisan Politics

Can a Teacher Elected to Public Office Be Required to Resign?

Yes. Professor Mary Jane Galer was elected to the Georgia House of Delegates and requested an unpaid leave of absence. Because a state statute prohibited members of the legislature from being employed by a state agency, Galer's request was denied. She argued that the statute was unconstitutional because it restricted her right to hold office. The Georgia Supreme Court ruled that the law was a reasonable restriction on her rights because it furthered an important governmental interest.[27] Its purpose was to prevent "the obvious conflict of interests inherent in situations where an individual serves concurrently in two of the branches of state government." Thus the court ruled that Galer may be employed by her state college or by the legislature, but not by both. Although many schools grant leaves of absence to faculty members appointed or elected to political office, *Galer* indicates that they are under no constitutional obligation to do so.

Can a Teacher Be Prohibited from Running for Political Office?

Courts are split on this issue. Some hold that it is reasonable to require a teacher to resign before campaigning for public office; others feel that a general prohibition against running for any office is unconstitutional. In resolving this issue, one judge might focus on whether the prohibition is overly broad; another judge might consider whether campaigning would interfere with the teacher's duties or whether the office is highly political or nonpartisan.

In Florida, for example, a law professor was dismissed after he filed to run for circuit judge because he violated a university rule prohibiting employees from engaging in "a political campaign for public office." The professor argued that the rule was unconstitutional, but a Florida court held that it was reasonable because:

1. the demands on the time and energies of a candidate in a "warmly contested" political campaign would necessarily affect his efficiency as a teacher;
2. campaigning can bring political influences to bear on the students that might affect them detrimentally; and
3. the potential political involvement of a state university, which depends on public support from all political elements, is a major consideration supporting the reasonableness of the prohibition against teachers running for office.[28]

On the other hand, an Oregon court ruled that a state law prohibiting public employees from running for *any* political office was unconstitutional.[29] The court recognized that the state could bar some of its employees from campaigning for some offices to promote an efficient public service. This law, however, went much further than necessary, broadly restricting the First Amendment right of political expression. The court noted that "a revolution has occurred in the law relative to the state's power to limit federal First Amendment rights. Thirty years ago the statutes now under consideration would have been held to be constitutional." In this case, however, the court concluded that it cannot be demonstrated "that the good of the public service requires all of the prohibitions of the present statute."

In a related Kentucky case, a state court ruled that requiring mandatory leaves for all teachers who become candidates for any part-time public office violated their equal protection rights, since the requirement did not apply to teachers engaged in other time-consuming activities.[30]

Can Teachers Be Penalized Because of Their Political Opposition to a Superintendent or School Board Member?

No. Nathaniel Martin was a teacher and guidance counselor in Claiborne County, Mississippi, for 11 years. After he supported a recall petition against three board members and opposed the election of the superintendent, Martin was told he would not be rehired "because of a reduction in force in the area of his employment." But the Mississippi Supreme Court concluded that the school's explanation was a pretext because there was no evidence of a funding shortage, no evidence that Martin was incompetent, and no evidence that the counseling needs would be less in the future than they had been in the past.[31] According to the court, "where a teacher has engaged in constitutionally protected activity, and where the superintendent's reason for non-reemployment is shown to be false or a sham," the teacher is entitled to reinstatement. In a similar Texas case, a federal judge went further and held several members of the school board personally liable for damages because their failure to rehire two teachers based on their political associations was done "in disregard of the teachers' clearly established constitutional rights."[32]

What if a teacher is not fired but only reassigned (with less salary) because of his support for an unsuccessful school board candidate? Is this still an infringement of his First Amendment rights? A federal appeals court ruled that it was.[33] In this Oklahoma case, the court held that a teacher has a constitutional right to support any school board candidate and that retaliation in the form of "altered employment conditions instead of termination" is nevertheless an "unconstitutional infringement" of that right.

In a recent related Chicago case, Charlotte Klug was transferred from dean of freshmen at a vocational school to teacher at an elementary school. She claimed that this violated her right to freedom of association with "her group" that wanted to promote educational improvement and opposed an "old guard" that did not want to change and wanted to get rid of her. According to a federal court, in the Seventh Circuit public employees are protected from an adverse employment decision based on their freedom of association "only when the associational conduct relates to a matter of public concern."[34] After reviewing Klug's complaint, which was "replete with allegations of bickering," the judge concluded that in this case "the association seems much more devoted to petty office politics than to matters of public concern," and he dismissed Klug's case.

Can Political Affiliation Be Considered in the Hiring of Teachers?

While such consideration may violate some state laws and may be unwise, it apparently would not be unconstitutional. In a Puerto Rican case, a teacher claimed she was not rehired because of her political activity. Although a federal court found no evidence to support her claim, it noted a distinction between hiring and rehiring decisions.[35] A school could not refuse to rehire a teacher because of her party membership; however, the court wrote that a "hiring system which took into account potential employees' political affiliations was not in violation of any constitutional right." As another federal court explained: "Hiring policies based solely on political affiliation" violate the First Amendment, "but elected officials may weight political factors such as party allegiance along with other factors in making subjective hiring judgments."[36]

Can Teachers Be Prohibited from Participating in Partisan Politics?

Probably. Since the U.S. Supreme Court has upheld the Hatch Act, which prevents federal employees from being active in partisan politics, it is likely that school districts could impose similar restrictions on their teachers. The purpose of the Hatch Act is to reduce the hazards to fair and impartial government, prevent political parties from using public employees for political campaigns, and prohibit selection of government employees on the basis of political performance. Yet the act does not bar all political activities. Employees are allowed to vote and contribute funds, to express their opinions on political subjects and candidates, to display political stickers and badges, and to participate in nonpartisan elections. Many school districts allow greater political freedom for their teachers. But a 1973 U.S. Supreme Court ruling concerning federal employees indicates that Hatch Act-type restrictions on teachers probably would not violate the U.S. Constitution although they may violate some state constitutions.[37]

In a related case, the West Virginia Supreme Court upheld a state law prohibiting membership in county boards of education by officials of any political party.[38] A local Republican party official claimed the law violated equal protection and First Amendment principles. The court disagreed and concluded that the law was designed "to keep partisan politics from influencing the decisions of local school boards" and was less restrictive than the Hatch Act, which was upheld by the U.S. Supreme Court.

In a 1992 decision, teachers challenged a Kentucky statute that prohibited them from the "management activities" of any school board campaign and forbade board candidates from soliciting contributions or services from school employees.[39] The teachers argued that the law restricted their rights and that the prohibition concerning political "activities" was unconstitutionally vague. A majority of the Kentucky Supreme Court agreed that the word "activities" was too "broad and vague." However, the court upheld the remainder of the political restrictions because of the compelling state interest in keeping the public schools free of political influence.

Can Teachers Be Prohibited from Participating in All Political Activity Except Voting?

No, ruled a federal court in Texas.[40] The court acknowledged that school boards can protect their educational system from undue political activity that may "materially and substantially interfere" with their schools. But a broad ban on *all* political activity went too far and violated the teacher's constitutional rights. This prohibition, wrote the judge, threatens popular government, not only "because it injures the individuals muzzled, but also because of its harmful effect on the community" in depriving it of the political participation of its teachers.

Can Teachers Be Barred from Political Activity on Campus During Off-Duty Hours?

No. This question was answered in a 1996 federal court decision after a Pennsylvania school board prohibited its employees from engaging in any political activity on school property in order to stop off-duty teachers from soliciting votes at polling places in public schools.[41] The board said its policy was intended to diminish "disruption in the educational process" and to protect voters "from undue influence at polling places" by teachers. Also, evidence indicated that board members were "annoyed about teachers advocating the election of rival board candidates."

The court ruled that none of these reasons justified the board's restrictions of teachers' First Amendment rights. On the contrary, teachers have a strong interest in participating in political activities, including the distribution of information about opposition candidates. "The very essence of free political speech," wrote Judge Waldman, "is the right to criticize an existing regime and voice support for alternatives." With respect to school board elections, Judge Waldman wrote that teachers are in "a unique position to provide the public with information and informed opinions on matters affecting educational quality" and other controversial issues facing the board.

Oaths of Loyalty

What Are the Goals of Loyalty Oaths?

Oaths of allegiance for state officials typically include a pledge of loyalty to the federal and state constitutions, and some, as discussed below, require much more. The goals of loyalty oaths for teachers have varied according to the times and the legislatures that enacted them. In the 1950s, when half the states passed such oaths, their focus was to ensure that teachers were loyal to the U.S. form of government and that schools were free from the influence of subversive teachers. In upholding a New Jersey loyalty oath, a judge noted, "A teacher who is bereft of the essential quality of loyalty and devotion to his government and the fundamentals of our democratic society is lacking in a basic qualification for teaching."[42] While educators have debated whether these oaths are a good way to ensure loyal teachers, courts have considered whether they are constitutional.

Can Teachers Be Required to Swear That They Will Promote "Respect for the Flag," "Reverence for Law and Order," and "Undivided Allegiance" to the Government?

No. The state of Washington required its teachers to swear to the above until the U.S. Supreme Court declared the oath unconstitutionally vague, ambiguous, and overly broad.[43] The Court wondered about the institutions for which teachers are expected to "promote respect." Does the oath prevent teachers from criticizing their state's judicial system, the Supreme Court, or the FBI? Would teachers who refused to say the Pledge of Allegiance because of religious beliefs be charged with breaking their promise to promote respect for the flag? "It would not be unreasonable," wrote Justice White, "for the serious-minded oath taker to conclude that he should dispense with lectures voicing far-reaching criticism of any old or new [government] policy" lest he be accused of violating his oath to "promote undivided allegiance" to the U.S. government. The result of these uncertainties is that teachers who are conscientious about their "solemn oath" and sensitive to the dangers posed by the oath's indefinite language can avoid risk "only by restricting their conduct to that which is unquestionably safe." Free speech, wrote the Court, "may not be so inhibited."

Can Teachers be Required to Swear That They Are Not Subversive?

No. In two related cases, the U.S. Supreme Court held that "negative" oaths that prohibit "subversive activities" are unconstitutional. In the first case, the Court noted that it was not clear what "subversive" activity includes.[44] In the second case, a Maryland loyalty oath law provided for the discharge of subversive persons and called for perjury action against those who violated the oath.[45] The Court wrote that "the continuing surveillance which this type of law places on teachers is hostile to academic freedom," and its "overbreadth" makes possible "oppressive or capricious applications as regimes change."

Can Teachers Be Required to Swear That They Will Uphold the Federal and State Constitutions?

Yes. A group of Denver teachers argued that such an oath was unconstitutional, but a federal district court disagreed.[46] According to the court, the oath is simply a recognition of our system of constitutional law. It is not overly broad and is not an improper invasion of a teacher's freedom of expression. On the contrary, the judge wrote that "support for the constitutions and laws of the nation and state does not call for blind subservience." This oath, explained the court, has roots as deep as the U.S. Constitution, which requires that the President swear to uphold it.

In a 1995 New Jersey case, a prospective teacher objected to part of a state loyalty oath requiring that he "bear true faith and allegiance" to the federal and state constitutions and governments. The teacher claimed that the oath infringed his "right to express dissent against the government." In upholding the oath, a state court wrote that the teacher's dilemma "is much more personal than realistic" since his constitutional right to dissent "is fully protected by law" and the "teacher's loyalty oath does not diminish these rights."[47]

Is an Oath That Teachers Will "Faithfully Perform" Their Duties Constitutional?

Yes. Again, Denver teachers argued that this oath was unconstitutionally vague, and again the district court disagreed.[48] It held that a state can reasonably ask teachers in public schools to subscribe to professional competence and dedication. "It is certain," wrote the court, "that there is no right to be unfaithful in the performance of duties."

Is a Loyalty Oath Unconstitutional If It Applies to Teachers and Not to Other State Employees?

No. Teachers claimed that such an oath deprived them of equal protection by arbitrarily requiring educators but not all state employees to take it. The court replied that an oath to uphold the federal and state constitutions is "an almost universal requirement of all public officials, including lawyers and judges, and it cannot be truthfully said that teachers are being picked on."[49] As long as the oath is reasonable as applied to teachers, who work in an influential area, there is no constitutional requirement that it be applied to all public employees.

Can Teachers Be Required to Swear to "Oppose the Overthrow" of the Government by Any "Illegal or Unconstitutional Method"?

Yes. Opponents of this Massachusetts oath said it raised the specter of "vague, undefinable responsibilities actively to combat a potential overthrow of the government." U.S. Supreme Court Chief Justice Burger rejected such "literal notions." On behalf of the Court, he wrote that the purpose of the oath was not to create specific responsibilities but "to assure that those in positions of public trust were willing to commit themselves to live by the constitutional process of our system" and not to use illegal force to change it.[50]

Political and Social Affiliations

Is Freedom of Association a Constitutional Right?

Yes. Although freedom of association is not directly mentioned in the U.S. Constitution, the Supreme Court has held that right to be "implicit" in the freedoms of speech, assembly, and petition. "Among the rights protected by the First Amendment," wrote Justice Lewis Powell, "is the right of individuals to associate to further their personal beliefs.[51]

Can a Teacher Be Fired for Belonging to a Communist, Nazi, or Revolutionary Organization?

No. A teacher cannot be punished merely for being a member of such an organization. This was the ruling of the U.S. Supreme Court in the case of a New York instructor Harry Keyishian.[52] When Keyishian refused to sign a certificate stating he was not a communist, his contract was not renewed. Administrators explained that to preserve our democracy, it was reasonable not to employ teachers who belonged to subversive organizations.

The U.S. Supreme Court disagreed. On behalf of the Court, Justice Brennan wrote:

> Under our traditions, beliefs are personal and not a matter of mere association, and men in adhering to a political party or other organization do not subscribe unqualifiedly to all of its platforms or asserted principles. A law which applies to membership, without the specific intent to further the illegal aims of the organization, infringes unnecessarily on protected freedoms. It rests on the doctrine of guilt by association which has no place here.

The Court believed that the New York law would "cast a pall of orthodoxy over the classroom," encourage suspicion and distrust, and restrict academic freedom in the schools. Thus it would have a damaging effect on educators and the nation. "Teachers and students," wrote Justice Brennan, "must always remain free to inquire, to study, and to evaluate, to gain new maturity and understanding; otherwise our civilization will stagnate and die." According to the Court, those who join an organization but do not share its unlawful purposes and do not participate in its unlawful activities pose no threat, either as citizens or as teachers. Therefore mere membership in the communist party or any other subversive organization, without a specific intent to further the unlawful aims of the organization, is not a constitutional basis for excluding an individual from his or her teaching position.

Does Keyishian *Automatically Void State Laws Prohibiting Membership in Subversive Organizations?*

No. When the U.S. Supreme Court declares a state law unconstitutional, similar statutes in other states are not automatically voided. They remain "on the books" and are sometimes enforced unless the state legislature repeals them or a court specifically holds that they are unconstitutional. This was the situation in Arkansas when a professor who taught his course from a Marxist perspective and advocated "revolutionary change" was fired under a state law that prohibited any "member of a Nazi, Fascist, or Communist" organization from being employed by the state. The Supreme Court of Arkansas reluctantly ruled that the law was unconstitutional.[53] After considering *Keyishian* and related decisions of the U.S. Supreme Court, the Arkansas court indicated that it had "no choice but to follow these decisions of the Court which is the final arbiter when constitutional interpretation is in dispute." In a subsequent federal case, the court upheld the professor's right to inform his students of his Marxist views; however, the court did not indicate whether the same expression by a high school teacher would also be protected.[54]

A similar situation occurred in California in 1980 when Marvin Schmid applied for a teaching position and was required to sign a non-communist loyalty oath pursuant to state law. Most school districts realized the requirement was unconstitutional and did not enforce it. Schmid's district, however, said it had to enforce the law, so the teacher went to court. The state judge ruled that the law was clearly "repugnant to both the United States and California constitutions," and he ordered the state to inform all schools of its unconstitutionality and to prohibit its enforcement.[55]

Do Teachers Have a Right to Advocate, Organize, and Join a Union?

Yes. According to the federal courts, the First Amendment protects the right of teachers to promote and organize a union. It also protects the rights of teachers' associations "to engage in advocacy on behalf of their members."[56] This protection is illustrated by an Illinois case in which three teachers were dismissed because of their union activities. The school board claimed the dismissals were required by economic necessity. But a state court ruled in favor of the teachers because they had been leaders of a recent unionization campaign, had greater seniority than teachers who were retained, and showed there was no economic necessity for their dismissals.[57] (For more on teachers' unions and collective bargaining, see chapter 4.)

On the other hand, the Mississippi Supreme Court upheld a school board's decision not to reemploy the president of the local teachers' association, mostly because of her insubordination and partly because of her criticism of the administration.[58] The court did not reinstate the teacher because her insubordination was a "substantial and credible" reason for her nonemployment and because the district would have taken the same action even if she had not participated in the union activity. (For more on the scope and limits of teacher freedom of expression, see chapter 9.)

Can Teachers Be Prohibited from Sending Their Children to Private, Segregated Schools?

The answer depends on the circumstances. In the *1975 Cook* v. *Hudson* case, a federal appeals court supported such a prohibition.[59] The case involved several Mississippi teachers who were not rehired when they sent their children to private, segregated academies in violation of school board policy designed to ensure faculty support for desegregation. The court upheld the policy because of the importance of desegregation and because of evidence that students in desegregated classes are "likely to perceive rejection…from a teacher whose own children attend a nearby racially segregated school."

In two subsequent cases, federal appeals courts have given greater weight to the rights of teachers. In a 1983 Mississippi case, the federal appeals court ruled that a school employee's interest in controlling the education of her child "takes precedence over the school board's interests" unless the enrollment of her son in a private school "materially and substantially interfered with the operation" of the public schools.[60] In a 1984 Alabama case, a federal appeals court ruled that two tenured teachers who wanted to send their children to a virtually all-white Christian academy should be exempt from the school board policy prohibiting employees from sending their children to private schools.[61] The court distinguished this controversy from the 1975 *Cook* case on two grounds: First, in *Cook*, "the sole reason" why the teachers enrolled their children in private school was to avoid desegregation, while in this case segregation was not "the motivating factor" behind the teachers' decision; second, enrollment in the private academy is not "a serious threat to integration of the public schools."

Can a New School Board Refuse to Reappoint Teachers Because of Their Association with Former Board Members?

No. In a small Texas school district, two political factions were vying for control of the school board. A teacher, Troy Burris, was friendly with members of the old board, whose policies he supported, and with the superintendent, who recommended him for reappointment. When a new board that was hostile to the superintendent and the old board was elected, it refused to approve the reappointment of Burris. The teacher claimed that the new board's action was based on his friendship with the old board and violated his First Amendment freedom of association. Although a school board may refuse to renew a teacher's contract for any legitimate reason, a federal appeals court ruled that it may not do so simply in retaliation for his support for and association with members of the former board.[62]

In a similar Alabama case, Robin Milligan's contract as a teacher's aide was not renewed because of her close association with school board member Thedford Watson. Milligan's termination was apparently used as a "bargaining chip" to get Watson to change his vote on a controversial issue. When Watson refused, Milligan's contract was not renewed. The board argued that since Milligan was a probationary teacher, she could be nonrenewed for any reason. But the court ruled that her nonrenewal cannot be based on the exercise of her constitutional right to freedom of association, which "includes the right to simply meet with others."[63] When determining whether a teacher has been fired for exercising his or her constitutional right of association, the teacher must show that the association was a motivating factor in the board's decision and that it would not have reached the same decision absent the protected conduct.

Can Teachers Be Denied Employment Because the People They Married Are Controversial or Because of Their Divorce?

No, ruled a federal court in the case of a middle school teacher who was denied a job because her husband was a controversial civil rights leader who helped organize a local school boycott.[64] The court concluded that the teacher could not be punished "because she elected to become the wife" of a civil rights activist. Similarly, a federal appeals court ruled that a school cannot refuse to rehire a teacher on the basis of her divorce because "matters involving marriage and family relationships involve privacy rights that are constitutionally protected."[65]

In a related Massachusetts case, an elementary teacher who had received a "superlative" evaluation was not rehired because she lived with and intended to marry a man who had been charged with rape and abuse of his child. The teacher alleged that the school's action violated her right to intimate association. The judge acknowledged that the outer limits of the right of association are not clear and that some associations such as those "with dancers in a dance hall" are not protected.[66] Nevertheless, he ruled that in this case the teacher has "a constitutional right to associate intimately without fear that the government will use her association when making decisions concerning her employment." According to the judge, this right includes the teacher's decision to cohabit with a man, "to raise a family with him, [and] to be seen with him in public."

Nevertheless, there are limits to a teacher's freedom of association in this area. These limits were confronted by a South Carolina teacher whose contract was not renewed because of his serious personal problems with his wife. On several occasions, she had assaulted him with a bottle or a knife, and once she burst into his classroom and threatened his life. A federal court noted that school officials in this case were faced with a "potentially explosive and dangerous" domestic conflict that had disrupted school activities.[67] The court denied that a teacher's right to marry whom he wishes gives him the right "to engage in domestic altercations in the classroom of a public high school."

Can a Teacher Be Prohibited from Marrying an Administrator?

Yes, or the board might transfer or dismiss an administrator for marrying a teacher. Either action might be legitimate to avoid conflicts of interest. Thus a Minnesota school board did not renew a high school principal's contract when he married a physical education teacher in violation of a board policy prohibiting administrator–teacher marriages. The principal claimed that this violated his constitutional rights. The court ruled, however, that the policy "does not deny people the right to marry; it only prohibits the employment of married couples in administrator–teacher situations."[68] The purpose of the rule, wrote the court, is "a laudatory one—preventing conflicts of interest and favoritism." Situations where such conflicts might occur include teacher evaluation and recommendations, classroom and extracurricular assignments, disagreements among teachers, and school resource allocations. Therefore, because the interest of the state in avoiding such conflicts is strong and the impact of the policy on marriage itself is "so attenuated," the court upheld the board's policy.

Similarly, a New York court ruled that a school district could transfer a teacher who married her assistant principal.[69] Because district policy prohibited any employee supervising a "near relative" and because the assistant principal supervised his wife, the court held that the transfer was a reasonable action to avoid the "perception of favoritism on the part of other members of the teaching faculty."

Can Laws Prohibit School Boards from Employing Relatives of Members?

Yes. In Virginia, for example, the state's Conflict of Interests Act not only prohibits boards from employing immediate relatives of members but also prohibits the hiring of a son- or daughter-in-law or a brother- or sister-in-law of a member. The Supreme Court of Virginia explained that the purpose of the law is to "engender confidence" in school boards and to eliminate situations in which the judgment of a board member will be influenced in hiring decisions "based on a familial relationship."[70,71]

Can Laws Allow School Boards to Hire Relatives of Members?

Yes. State conflict-of-interest statutes vary. As noted in the previous question, Virginia law prohibits school boards from hiring relatives of members without exception. But in other states, such as Arizona and Wyoming, a conflict of interest does not automatically disqualify a person from becoming a teacher. If a conflict occurs, Wyoming law requires that the board member concerned must (1) disclose the interest, (2) be absent during consideration of the matter, and (3) not attempt to influence the board's decision. Failure to do so will result in nullification of the decision and will subject the board member to criminal prosecution.[72] Whether the approach of Virginia or Wyoming better protects the public interest and the interests of those involved continues to be debated.

Can Teachers Be Prohibited from Being School Board Members?

Teachers can be prohibited from serving on school boards in districts where they work. In Wyoming, for example, teacher Ray Haskins was elected to the school board in the district where he had taught for 15 years. Board members charged that the two positions were incompatible, since Haskins as a board member would have "power and authority over himself as teacher, over other teachers, and over administrative personnel," who, in turn, had power over Haskins as a teacher. The court ruled that even if citizens have a right to hold public office, the common law has imposed "reasonable restrictions on those rights" in the public interest. The court concluded that the positions of teacher and board member in the same district are "incompatible and inconsistent."[73]

Is a Policy Unconstitutional If It Prohibits Spouses from Working in the Same School?

Probably not. This question arose in Ohio when Suzanne Montgomery was transferred after she married another teacher in her school. She was transferred because of an antinepotism policy that prevented spouses from working together on the same campus. Montgomery claimed the policy was unreasonable and violated her constitutional freedom of association, which protects "intimate human relationships" from undue intrusion by the government.

In discussing Montgomery's case, a federal appeals court explained that if a government action or policy is a "direct and substantial interference with the right of marriage," the policy will be struck down unless it serves an "important state interest."[74] But where there is no substantial interference with marriage, the policy will be upheld unless there is no rational basis for it. Here, the court first ruled that Montgomery's lateral transfer to a nearby school (with no loss of pay, benefits, or change of responsibilities) was not a substantial interference with her marriage. Second, the court held that the antinepotism policy was reasonably related to the educational goal of preventing such problems as "disruption of staff 'collegiality,' the lessening of productivity of spouses who work together, and the disruption of the educational program when spouses separate or divorce." Judge Boggs acknowledged that none of these justifications "is overwhelming," but he added "they do not have to be." They "merely have to be rational."[75]

However, a federal appeals court ruled that a Kentucky school superintendent went too far when he refused to rehire Mary Jo Adkins, a school secretary who was married to the principal, to punish her because of the superintendent's conflict with her husband.[76] Although Adkins had no right to continued employment, the court wrote that "she had a liberty interest in not being denied employment for exercising her First Amendment right to freedom of association" which is violated if she is terminated not because of her work but solely because of her marriage.[77] While many districts have antinepotism policies that prohibit principals from supervising their spouses, the Kentucky district had no such policy. And in this case, where school officials initially approved Adkins being a secretary for her husband, the court did not allow the superintendent to terminate her simply because of a dispute concerning her husband.

In a related Mississippi case, a court ruled that an individual could not be prohibited from serving in the state legislature and voting on education laws simply because his wife was a public school teacher.[78] According to the court, indirect, remote, insubstantial conflicts of interest should not be prohibited where the "interest is so small" that it "could not reasonably be expected to influence his judgment."

Can Teachers Be Prohibited from Promoting Political Candidates in Class?

Yes. An early California case provides an example of an educator who was punished for such behavior.[79] In 1922, a Sacramento teacher named Goldsmith suggested to his students that their parents support one of the candidates for school superintendent. According to Goldsmith, his candidate "would be more helpful to our department than a lady, and we need more men in our schools." As a result of these comments, the administration suspended him for "unprofessional conduct," and a state court supported this action. Similarly, teachers today can be prohibited from promoting candidates for any political office in class.

Can Teachers Wear Political Buttons, Badges, or Armbands to Class?

Yes, as long as such symbols do not interfere with a teacher's classroom performance and are not an attempt to proselytize or indoctrinate students. A case in point occurred when a New York English teacher, Charles James, refused to stop wearing an armband to class to protest the Vietnam War. As a result he was dismissed for presenting only one point of view on a controversial public issue. A federal appeals court ruled in James's favor.[80] The court noted that teachers do not "shed their constitutional rights to freedom of speech or expression at the schoolhouse gate" unless they cause substantial disruption.

On the other hand, since students may be a captive audience, there must be some restraint on the free expression of a teacher's view. Thus if a teacher tries to persuade students that they should adopt the teacher's values, it is reasonable "to expect the state to protect impressionable children from such dogmatism." In James's case, however, the wearing of an armband did not interfere with his teaching, was not coercive, and was not an attempt to indoctrinate his students.

Can Teachers Be Prohibited from Encouraging or Participating in Demonstrations?

No. Such a broad prohibition would violate a teacher's constitutional rights. This was the ruling of a federal court in Alabama, where the legislature barred raises to any teacher who "participates in, encourages or condones…any extracurricular demonstration."[81] The court acknowledged that a state may punish a teacher who disrupts schooling. Under the legislature's vague policy, however, teachers can be punished for encouraging a peaceful demonstration. According to the court, this policy is a "comprehensive interference with associational freedom which goes far beyond what might be justified in the protection of the state's legitimate interest."

Summary

In past decades, the U.S. Supreme Court had been critical of teacher loyalty oaths because they tended to inhibit the exercise of First Amendment freedoms. Negative oaths (e.g., swearing that one does not belong to any subversive organization) and oaths that were "overbroad" and ambiguous were usually struck down—especially when there were statutory procedures to "police" the oath and punish violators. Nevertheless, two kinds of oaths have been consistently upheld: (1) loyalty oaths drawn with precision and prohibiting clearly unlawful conduct, and (2) positive employment oaths affirming support for the state and federal constitutions or pledging to uphold professional standards.

Teachers cannot be dismissed simply because they are members of a revolutionary or subversive organization unless the organization has conducted illegal activities that they have supported. Similarly, teachers cannot be penalized because they associate with union organizers, political extremists, or unsuccessful school board candidates, or because their spouse engages in controversial activities unless competent evidence indicates that such behavior impairs the teacher's effectiveness. It is unclear whether teachers can be prohibited from sending their children to private, segregated schools. However, to protect against conflicts of interest, laws may prohibit teachers from being members of school boards, school boards from employing relatives of board members, and administrators from supervising relatives.

In recent years, teachers' organizations have become powerful political machines, and individual teachers are no longer prohibited from engaging in all political activity.

Today's teachers cannot be punished merely for wearing political symbols, for supporting particular candidates, or for participating in political demonstrations. On the other hand, they have no right to campaign for candidates in school, to indoctrinate students, or to urge disruptive political action. While in some districts teachers may run for and hold partisan political office, this is not a constitutional right; this usually depends on state legislation or local policy.

Although adults have the right to join secret and undemocratic organizations, courts have refused to grant this right to public school students. Statutes in over twenty states have outlawed high school fraternities, sororities, and similar groups that choose their members in an undemocratic manner. Numerous cases during the past 60 years have upheld such laws against charges of unconstitutionality.

When school officials refuse, without justification, to recognize a proposed student organization, such action violates the students' constitutional rights of association. This means that if administrators deny recognition to a student group, they bear a "heavy burden" to demonstrate the appropriateness of their action. Furthermore, the Equal Access Act prohibits discrimination against student groups because of the religious, philosophic, or political content of their speech. In addition, schools must provide equal access to Gay/Straight Alliance Clubs. On the other hand, schools may issue reasonable rules concerning the time, place, and manner in which student groups must conduct their activities, and they may deny recognition to groups that do not follow such rules.

When schools provide a forum for outside speakers, they must give equal time to opposing views and may not discriminate among proposed speakers or censor their ideas. Moreover, public schools may not discriminate against political speakers or all candidates for public office or prohibit views with which most students, teachers, or parents disagree. However, student groups can be required to request approval of school officials before inviting an outside speaker. If a request is denied, there should be a fair and prompt hearing.

N O T E S

1. 20 U.S.C.A. § 4071(a) and (b) (2000).
2. *Board of Education of Westside Community Schools* v. *Mergens,* 496 U.S. 226 (1990).
3. *Garnett* v. *Renton School District No. 403,* 987 F.2d 641 (9th Cir. 1993).
4. *Colin* v. *Orange Unified School District,* 83 F.Supp. 2d 1135 (C.D. Cal. 2000).
5. *Mergens* at 259.
6. In 2001, about $400,000 was allocated to high schools to support their work. Interview with the Tim Hack, program supervisor, Safe Schools Program for Gay & Lesbian youth, Massachusetts, Department of Education, November 19, 2001.
7. Code of Alabama § 16-40A-2(c)(8).
8. *East High Gay/Straight Alliance* v. *Board of Education of Salt Lake City School District,* 81 F.Supp.2d 1166 (D.Utah 1999).
9. *Pope* v. *East Brunswick Board of Education,* 12 F.3d 1244 (3rd. Cir. 1993).
10. *East High School Prism Club* v. *Seidel,* 95 F.Supp.2d 1239 (D. Utah 2000).
11. *Quappe* v. *Endry,* 772 F.Supp. 1004 (S.D. Ohio 1991).
12. *Bush* v. *Dassel-Cakato Board of Education,* 745 F.Supp. 562 (D. Minn. 1990).
13. *Bradford* v. *Board of Education,* 121 P. 929 (Cal. 1912).
14. *Robinson* v. *Sacramento City Unified School District,* 53 Cal. Rptr. 781 (Ct. App. 1966).
15. *Id. Robinson* apparently still reflects prevailing law. 10 A.L.R.3d 384–409 (Supp. 1997).

16. *State Legal Standards for the Provision of Public Education* 32 (Washington, DC: National Institute of Education, 1978).

17. *Healy* v. *James,* 408 U.S. 169 (1972).

18. *Gebert* v. *Hoffman,* 336 F.Supp. 694 (E.D. Pa. 1972). For a more restrictive decision, see *Sword* v. *Fox,* 446 F.2d 1091 (4th Cir. 1971).

19. *Clergy and Laity Concerned* v. *Chicago Board of Education,* 586 F.Supp. 1408 (N.D. Ill. 1984).

20. *Searcey* v. *Crim,* 681 F.Supp. 821 (N.D. Ga. 1988).

21. *Student Coalition for Peace* v. *Lower Merton School District Board of School Directors,* 618 F.Supp. 53 (D.C. Pa. 1985). On appeal, the court ruled that the Equal Access Act of 1984 would apply to this case "only if a limited open forum existed after the Act became law." 776 F.2d431 (3d Cir. 1985).

22. *Solmitz* v. *Maine School Administrative District No. 59,* 495 A.2d 812 (Me. 1985).

23. *Local Organizing Committee, Million Man March* v. *Cook,* 922 F.Supp. 1494 (D. Colo. 1996).

24. *Wilson* v. *Chancellor,* 418 F.Supp. 1358 (D.Or. 1976).

25. *Franklin* v. *Atkins,* 409 F.Supp. 439 (D. Colo. 1976), 562 F.2d 1188 (10th Cir. 1977).

26. *Cook* v. *Board of Education for Logan County,* 671 F.Supp. 1110 (S.D. W.Va. 1987).

27. *Galer* v. *Board of Regents of the University System,* 236 S.E.2d 617 (Ga. 1977).

28. *Jones* v. *Board of Control,* 131 So.2d 713 (Fla. 1961).

29. *Minielly* v. *State,* 411 P.2d 69 (Or. 1966).

30. *Allen* v. *Board of Education,* 584 S.W.2d 408 (Ky. Ct. App. 1979).

31. *Claiborne County Board of Education* v. *Martin,* 500 So.2d 981 (Miss. 1986).

32. *Guerra* v. *Roma Independent School District,* 444 F.Supp. 812 (S.D. Tex. 1977).

33. *Childers* v. *Independent School District No. 1 of Bryan County, Oklahoma,* 676 F.2d 1338 (10th Cir. 1982).

34. *Klug* v. *Chicago School Reform Board of Trustees,* 197 F.3d 853 (7th Cir. 1999).

35. *Saquebo* v. *Roque,* 716 F.Supp. 709 (D. P.R. 1989).

36. *Avery* v. *Jennings,* 786 F.2d 233 (6th Cir. 1986).

37. *U.S. Civil Service Commission* v. *National Association of Letter Carriers, AFL-CIO,* 413 U.S. 548 (1973).

38. *Carpenter* v. *Cobb,* 387 S.E.2d 858 (W.Va. 1989).

39. *State Board for Elementary and Secondary Education* v. *Howard,* 834 S.W.2d 657 (Ky. 1992).

40. *Montgomery* v. *White,* 320 F.Supp. 303 (E.D. Tex. 1969).

41. *Castle* v. *Colonial School District,* 933 F.Supp. 458 (E.D. Pa. 1996).

42. As quoted in R. R. Hamilton, *Legal Rights and Liabilities of Teachers* 84 (Laramie, WY: School Law Publications, 1956).

43. *Baggett* v. *Bullitt,* 377 U.S. 360 (1964).

44. *Id.*

45. *Whitehill* v. *Elkins,* 389 U.S. 54 (1967).

46. *Ohlson* v. *Phillips,* 304 F.Supp. 1152 (D. Colo. 1969).

47. *Gough* v. *State of New Jersey,* 667 A.2d 1057 (N.J.Super.A.D. 1995).

48. *Ohlson* v. *Phillips, Id.*

49. *Id.*

50. *Cole* v. *Richardson,* 405 U.S. 676 (1972).

51. *Healy* v. *James,* 408 U.S. 169 (1972).

52. *Keyishian* v. *Board of Regents of New York,* 385 U.S. 589 (1967).

53. *Cooper* v. *Henslee,* 522 S.W.2d 391 (Ark. 1975).

54. *Cooper* v. *Ross,* 472 F.Supp. 802 (E.D.Ark. 1979). The focus of the state court decision was the constitutionality of the Arkansas statute. The federal case concerned whether the university violated the professor's First Amendment rights by not reappointing him.

55. *Schmid* v. *Lovette,* 201 Cal. Rptr. 424 (Ct. App. 1st Dist. 1984).

56. *Missouri National Education Association* v. *New Madrid County R-1 Enlarged School District,* 810 F.2d 164 (8th Cir. 1987).

57. *Temple* v. *Board of Education of School District No. 94,* 548 N.E.2d 640 (Ill.App. Ct. 1st Dist. 1989).

58. *Board of Trustees* v. *Gates,* 461 So.2d 730 (Miss. 1984).

59. 511 F.2d 744 (5th Cir. 1975).

60. *Brantley* v. *Surles*, 718 F.2d 1354 (5th Cir. 1983).

61. *Stough* v. *Crenshaw County Board of Education*, 744 F.2d 1479 (11th Cir. 1984).

62. *Burris* v. *Willis Independent School District, Inc.*, 713 F.2d 1087 (5th Cir. 1983).

63. *Milligan* v. *Albertville City Board of Education*, 628 So.2d 625 (Ala. Civ. App. 1993).

64. *Randle* v. *Indianola Municipal Separate School District*, 373 F.Supp 766 (N.D. Miss. 1974).

65. *Littlejohn* v. *Rose*, 768 F.2d 765 (6th Cir. 1985).

66. *LaSota* v. *Town of Topsfield*, 979 F.Supp. 45 (D.Mass. 1997).

67. *Mescia* v. *Berry*, 406 F.Supp. 1181 (D. S.C. 1974).

68. *Keckeisen* v. *Independent School District No. 612*, 509 F.2d 1062 (8th Cir. 1975).

69. *Solomon* v. *Quinones*, 531 N.Y.S.2d 349 (N.Y. App. Div. 1988).

70. *Williams* v. *Augusta County School Board*, 445 S.E.2d 118 (Va. 1994). The law includes an exception if a teacher was hired before the relative became a board member.

71. Similarly, Missippi law prohibits school boards from entering into any contract in which a school board member has a direct or indirect interest *Smith* v. *Dorsey*, 530 So.2d 5 (Miss. 1988).

72. *Coyne* v. *State ex rel. Thomas*, 595 P.2d 970 (Wyo. 1979).

73. *Haskins* v. *State ex. rel. Harrington*, 516 P.2d 1171 (Wyo. 1973).

74. *Montgomery* v. *Carr*, 848 F.Supp. 770 (S.D. Ohio 1993).

75. *Id.* at 1130–31.

76. *Adkins* v. *Board of Education of Magoffin County, Kentucky*, 982 F.2d 952 (6th Cir. 1993).

77. *Id.* at 955.

78. *Frazier* v. *State by and through Pittman*, 504 So.2d 675 (Miss. 1987).

79. *Goldsmith* v. *Board of Education*, 225 P. 783 (Cal. 1924).

80. *James* v. *Board of Education of Central District No. 1*, 461 F.2d 566 (2d Cir. 1972).

81. *Alabama Education Association* v. *Wallace*, 362 F.Supp. 682 (M.D. Ala. 1973).

12 What Are My Rights under Due Process?

Overview

It is commonly accepted among lawyers that a right without adequate procedures to protect and enforce it is no right at all. This point was recognized by the framers of the U.S. Constitution when they inserted the right to due process of law in both the Fifth and Fourteenth Amendments. This chapter focuses on the Fourteenth Amendment, for public schools are agencies of the state, and the amendment provides that no "State shall deprive any person of life, liberty, or property, without due process of law." Courts have held that actions of school officials and board members are state actions and therefore the Fourteenth Amendment applies to them.

Due process may be thought of in ordinary language as "fair process," an attempt to secure justice in official actions. Most people gain their impression of due process from television's presentation of criminal cases. This chapter centers around civil cases, where individuals find themselves in conflict with school officials concerning their jobs or some restrictions related to their work or schooling. In these matters, due process requires that governmental action not be arbitrary, unreasonable, or discriminatory and that fair procedures be followed by officials before they carry out any action depriving anyone of "life, liberty, or property."

Due Process for Teachers

When Is Official Action Arbitrary or Unreasonable?

Like many other concepts used to govern human affairs, terms such as "arbitrary," "discriminatory," and "unreasonable" are not easily and simply defined. Their legal meanings become clearer as we look at the ways courts have used and interpreted them. Various cases have held, for example, that it is arbitrary to dismiss teachers for membership in a controversial or even subversive organization. Since many members of such organizations are innocent of any wrongdoing and may not even be aware of the organization's purposes and activities, it is arbitrary to classify such members with those who knowingly participate in illegal activities.[1] Thus some classifications are arbitrary while others are reasonable. It is reasonable to classify people according to age for purposes such as voting, driving a car, and running for the Senate, but it is unreasonable to use age classification for access to food or medical care. It has been held reasonable to classify males and females separately for military services but arbitrary to classify them separately for purposes of voting or being school administrators.

Furthermore, as we will see in chapter 19, some courts consider it arbitrary to regulate teachers' or students' hair length while others consider such policies reasonable. What is arbitrary or discriminatory is not always clear or simple. Courts tend to apply a three-step test to determine whether a law or policy is arbitrary: (1) They ask whether there is a legitimate social goal or objective to be attained by the law or policy, (2) they seek a rational connection between the objective and the means created to achieve it, and (3) they look for alternative and less restrictive ways of achieving the desired goal.

A further concern of courts when examining laws and policies under the due process clause is vagueness. If a law or policy is so vague that a reasonable person of ordinary intelligence cannot be guided by it, it is said to violate due process. Such policies often occur in schools that attempt to control the grooming of teachers and students and are not sufficiently specific in their stated policies or rules. For example, a requirement that "teachers must dress in good taste" would be void because it is too vague. To say that the principal will be the judge of what is in good taste does not cure the defect, for it gives arbitrary power to the principal and thus violates due process.

Many lawsuits filed under other provisions of the Constitution also allege that certain policies or laws that involve racial, sexual, or other discrimination, or that abridge one's liberty, are in violation of the due process clause because they are unreasonable, arbitrary, or vague.[2] We now turn to questions related to fair procedures, questions that most educators think about when the right to due process is mentioned.

Can Local Communities Attach Any Condition They Wish to the Privilege of Teaching?

No. Moreover, teaching can no longer be thought of as merely a privilege. Historically, the issue of whether teaching was a right or a privilege was important because various conditions could be attached to the granting of a privilege but rights could not be so restricted. Today, it is clear that while no one has a right to public employment, unconstitutional conditions cannot be attached to a public job. For example, as a condition for teaching in its schools, a community cannot require that teachers be members of a certain religion or that they vote for candidates of a specific political party. As the U.S. Supreme Court has said: "We need not pause to consider whether an abstract right to public employment exists. It is sufficient to say that constitutional protection does extend to the public servant whose exclusion pursuant to a statute is patently arbitrary or discriminatory."[3]

Is There a Distinction between Tenured and Probationary Teachers in the Right to Due Process?

Yes. This distinction was established and explained in chapter 3. Since the Fourteenth Amendment applies only if one is being deprived of "life, liberty, or property," the teacher who claims a denial of due process because job security is threatened must show a deprivation of one of these rights.

Tenured teachers have a reasonable expectancy that their position will be continuous. Such expectation of a "continuous contract" is the meaning of tenure, and courts have held that this is a sufficient "property" right to warrant the protection of the due process clause.

Probationary teachers have no continuous contract and therefore cannot make a claim to a property right on that basis. Other grounds may permit them to claim the protection of the due process clause, however.

The *Roth* Case[4]

When David Roth, a nontenured assistant professor at a public institution, was informed that he would not be rehired for the upcoming academic year, he went to court.[5] He claimed that he was never given a notice or a hearing regarding any reasons for the nonrenewal of his contract. This, he alleged, violated his constitutional rights by depriving him of his "liberty" and "property" without due process of law.

The U.S. Supreme Court disagreed with Roth. The Court distinguished a probationary teacher from a tenured teacher and held that only the tenured teacher had a reasonable expectancy of continuous employment, which created a property interest meriting due process protection. The probationary teacher has a property interest only for the duration of the contract. Thus, if the probationary teacher is dismissed *during* the year of the contract, then notice, a hearing, and reasons for dismissal are required. There is an important difference, however, between a dismissal during the term of the contract and a mere nonrenewal. Since the teacher does not have a right to a renewal of the contract, its nonrenewal violates no rights. That is the very meaning of the probationary period.

The Court then turned to the claim that the teacher's "liberty" interest was diminished. There are conceivable circumstances, reasoned the Court, where even a probationary teacher would have a right to a hearing. This would be the case if the employing school made negative statements about the teacher that seriously damaged possibilities for future employment. According to the Court, if in connection with the nonrenewal, the school damaged the teacher's "good name, reputation, honor or integrity...a notice and an opportunity to be heard are essential."

Unless local law requires it, schools are under no legal obligation to give reasons for not renewing the contract of a probationary teacher. If they give such reasons and allege incompetence, racism, sexism, mental or moral unfitness, fraud, or other damaging reasons, the teacher has a right to notice and a hearing where the validity of these charges can be examined and refuted.[6]

In sum, the Supreme Court has ruled that important distinctions exist between tenured and probationary teachers related to the right to due process. In the ordinary case of the nonrenewal of a contract of a probationary teacher, there is no constitutional right to due process, for no property right is being violated. Under special circumstances, where the teacher's reputation is stigmatized by charges made by school officials, the teacher's liberty interest is implicated, and proper procedures must be followed to provide an opportunity for the teacher to refute those charges.

Some states or local school districts expand these due process rights to provide for minimal due process even for probationary teachers, although typically nothing more than a statement of the reasons for nonrenewal is required.

Tenured teachers can also claim a right to due process before the school district might take some action that could be stigmatizing. Such was the effort in a Texas case in 1996, where a teacher, in addition to his regular duties, had a supplemental assignment as an assistant athletic coach.[7] When reassigned from his supplemental duties, he claimed that this was stigmatizing so as to trigger a Fourteenth Amendment liberty interest protected by due process. The federal district court ruled against him, holding that the teacher had no protected property interest in the supplemental coaching position, therefore the reassignment was not stigmatizing so as to damage any liberty interest. Thus there was no violation of his right to due process.

Does a Tenured Teacher Have a Right to an Explanation When His Position Is Eliminated?

Yes, he does, ruled a federal district court in Illinois in the *Chandler* case. Without explanation, the school board informed Chandler, a physical education teacher for 22 years, that his position was eliminated. When Chandler claimed that the termination violated procedural due process, the court agreed. He may have been terminated because "…of an unlawful reduction in the high school's physical education requirements, or he may have been unlawfully discriminated against because of his age or race." In this 2000 decision, the court noted that Chandler should not be left to hypothesize about why he was terminated.[8]

Does a Teacher Have a Right to a Hearing Prior to a Reassignment?

That depends on the situation. A school district has broad discretion in assigning teachers to different schools if the reassignment is based on sound educational reasons and the needs of the district; if the reassignment is for *disciplinary* reasons, a prior due process hearing is warranted.

The Eighth Circuit Court of Appeals so ruled in a case involving Larry Winegar, an industrial arts teacher in Des Moines, Iowa.[9] Winegar, a tenured teacher with an impeccable 19-year teaching record, became involved in an altercation with a student. After the student hit him in the chest, Winegar fell backward and hit his head. The teacher, allegedly in self-defense, kicked the student "in the groin or upper thigh" and slapped him across the face. Pursuant to reports and investigations, it was concluded that there was a likelihood of abuse, and Winegar was suspended for four days and transferred to another school.

When Winegar filed suit claiming a deprivation of property in violation of the due process clause, the circuit court agreed. The court recognized that a tenured teacher has an important property right in his job as well as in the particular assignment where he could reasonably expect to continue in the absence of the disciplinary action. Such an important property right cannot be taken away without careful due process. Winegar was involved in *investigations* but not in a *hearing* where he could challenge and cross-examine witnesses. The court emphasized the difference between an investigation and a hearing. Furthermore, because there was an initial and a subsequent suspension, the teacher had a right to a meaningful opportunity to be heard *after* the initial suspension as well as *before*. Thus, when a tenured teacher's good name, reputation, honor, or integrity is at stake, the court recognized a right to meaningful pre- and postdeprivation hearings guaranteed by the Fourteenth Amendment. This is a much greater protection than that afforded to probationary teachers.

A very different case based on reassignment arose recently in Connecticut.[10] A tenured seventh-grade language arts teacher was suspended for alleged inefficiency and incompetence. During her suspension, she received full salary, benefits, and seniority. An impartial hearing panel found no basis to terminate her. The following year, she was transferred to the high school to teach math and writing classes for which she was certified. She filed suit, claiming her right to due process was violated.

In a 2000 decision, the court ruled that she had no entitlement to remain in her position as a seventh grade language arts teacher. Thus, the reassignment did not deprive her of a property interest. Furthermore, although her suspension may have caused her embarrassment or humiliation, it didn't stigmatize her or cause any other deprivation. Therefore, she didn't prove a violation of her constitutionally protected liberty interest. In sum, the school district's actions were not so arbitrary or oppressive as to shock the conscience and violate substantive due process.

Can Schools Refuse to Rehire Probationary Teachers for Any Reason?

No. School officials do not have unlimited discretion not to renew the contract of probationary teachers. The U.S. Supreme Court in *Roth* said that only in the ordinary case of nonrenewal of a probationary teacher's contract is there no constitutional right to due process. Stigmatizing reasons for nonrenewal give rise to sufficient due process rights to enable teachers to clear their names.

Due process rights must also be granted if the probationary teacher's nonrenewal relates to some constitutionally protected activity (e.g., exercise of the right to free speech or union organizing). This principle was applied in the case of two teachers in the Miami-Dade County, Florida, Junior College. When the Board of Public Instruction of Dade County denied them tenure by refusing to hire them for a fourth year, the teachers claimed that the board's action was in retaliation for their union-organizing activities and also because one of them supported in her classroom some "new demands for campus freedom." A federal appeals court wrote:

> …unpersuasive is the argument that since there is no constitutional right to public employment, school officials only allowed these teachers' contracts to expire…. The right sought to be vindicated is *not* a contractual one, nor could it be since no right to reemployment existed. What is at stake is the vindication of constitutional rights—the right not to be punished by the state or to suffer retaliation at its hand because a public employee persists in the exercise of First Amendment rights.

The judge quoted from leading Supreme Court cases to support his position: "To state that a person does not have a constitutional right to government employment is only to say that he must comply with reasonable, lawful, and nondiscriminatory terms laid down by the proper authorities."[11] Furthermore, "constitutional protection does extend to the public servant whose exclusion pursuant to a statute is patently arbitrary or discriminatory."[12] Other cases have reaffirmed these principles. For example, three Missouri teachers found their jobs in jeopardy because they had been active in the Missouri branch of the National Education Association and had spoken out against the school board at public meetings regarding salary increases. The court ordered their reinstatement because it found that their terminations were motivated by their exercise of First Amendment rights.[13] In West Virginia, the court reinstated three teachers and awarded them back pay when it found that their transfers or dismissals were in retaliation for political activities on behalf of a school board candidate.[14] The West Virginia court said that "the law, applicable to the merits of this case is clear: A non-policy-making, nonconfidential government employee may not be discharged from a job that he or she is satisfactorily performing upon the sole ground of his political beliefs or activities."

Thus, if a probationary teacher presents evidence to indicate that nonrenewal is in retaliation for the exercise of a constitutional right, due process must be available to determine whether the nonrenewal is so motivated. If the facts indicate that the sole motivation for nonrenewal was a constitutionally protected activity, the termination will not stand. If there are mixed reasons for nonrenewal, the outcome may be different.

The *Mt. Healthy* Case[15]

Doyle, a public school teacher in Ohio, went to court to challenge the action of the school board not to reappoint him. Doyle was very active in the teachers' association and, in fact, had served as its president. During his presidency, but not directly connected with his role in the association, he had gotten into an altercation with another teacher, which led to a one-day suspension for both teachers. He had also gotten into arguments with cafeteria employees over the amount of spaghetti served him, had referred to students as "sons of bitches," and had made obscene gestures at two girls in the cafeteria who disobeyed him. In his capacity as president of the teachers' association, he had called the local radio station and made critical remarks about his principal's memorandum concerning a dress code for teachers and how such a code might influence public support of a bond issue.

Doyle contended that he had a constitutional right to communicate with the radio station and that his exercise of such a right played a "substantial" part in the board's decision not to renew his contract. The district court agreed with Doyle and ordered his reinstatement with back pay. After the court of appeals affirmed this decision, the case went to the U.S. Supreme Court.

The Supreme Court, upholding the constitutional rights of probationary teachers, said that "Doyle's claims under the First and Fourth Amendments are not defeated by the fact that he did not have tenure." He might establish a claim to reinstatement if the decision not to rehire him was based on his exercise of a constitutional right. Nevertheless, the Court asked whether other legitimate grounds, independent of any First Amendment rights, were involved in not extending tenure to Doyle. If there were such grounds, the fact that the school board included some impermissible grounds in its decision would not save the teacher's job.

The Court tried to balance the rights of the individual probationary teacher with the important social interest in conducting effective and efficient public schools. If the individual can show that the protected activity was a "substantial factor" or a "motivating factor" in the board's decision not to renew the contract, the board may still show by a preponderance of evidence that the teacher would not have been reemployed even in the absence of the protected conduct. Thus the Supreme Court sent the case back to the lower courts to determine in the light of these principles.

Various lower courts have applied the *Mt. Healthy* test. For example, a Louisiana teacher challenged the nonrenewal of his contract, claiming that his freedom of expression was violated by this action. Although the teacher could show that "his constitutionally protected conduct was a motivating factor in the board's decision," the court ruled that the principal's negative evaluations were sufficient for the board to reach the same conclusion.[16] By contrast, a Texas court ruled on behalf of teachers who showed that the only credible explanation for the nonrenewal of their contracts was their political activities on behalf of opponents of three recently elected board members.[17] (A related question appears in chapter 11.)

What Is Procedural Due Process?

In the final analysis, the legal concept of procedural due process refers to fair procedures. There is no single, technical definition for this concept; its basic elements must be applied and interpreted in light of the unique circumstances of each case. As a general rule, fairness would require that before a teacher is deprived of any substantial liberty or property interest, there ought to be adequate notice and a hearing before an impartial tribunal where the teacher's side of the conflict is presented. A sense of fairness also includes the right to be represented by a lawyer or a friend, to present evidence and to cross-examine witnesses, to receive a written copy of the findings and conclusions, and to have an opportunity to appeal. In addition to the constitutional right to due process, most states also have statutes that establish procedures for the termination of teachers.

School board policies must also be followed, but they do not have the same force as state laws. For example, a probationary teacher in Wyoming was terminated without being evaluated four times during the year, which was the school's policy. The teacher claimed that her right to due process was violated because the school board did not follow its own policies. However, the state court ruled that she had no property interest in the position and thus was not entitled to a statement of reasons for the nonrenewal; she was entitled only to a notice of nonrenewal by March 15 as prescribed by state law.[18]

Is a School Board a Fair Tribunal for the Hearing?

Yes, according to various court decisions. Although it would seem that the board represents the administration and the community in conflict with the individual teacher who is being dismissed or whose contract is not being renewed, the U.S. Supreme Court ruled that this fact alone does not disqualify the board as a decision maker if the hearing is otherwise fair.[19] At a typical school board hearing, strict legal procedures need not be used, for these are administrative hearings and not court proceedings. Technical rules of evidence do not apply, but the proceedings must be orderly.[20]

An interesting case arose concerning the "appearance of impropriety" of a hearing panel in 1992 in the state of New York. A high school teacher, dismissed for insubordination, appealed her termination. A member of the hearing panel that made the determination to dismiss her requested and was given an additional stipend by the school board. This payment created an impression of impropriety. The New York appeals court held that even the appearance of impropriety was sufficient to violate the teacher's right to an impartial hearing.[21]

Must State Laws Be Strictly Followed?

Yes, in states that have enacted statutes to govern nonrenewals or dismissals. For example, a probationary teacher in Ohio claimed that her notice of nonrenewal was late and that therefore she was entitled to reemployment for the ensuing year. The facts showed that she was aware that the board had not renewed her contract and that she was not available to receive the notice when attempts were made to deliver it at her home. Nevertheless, the Ohio

Supreme Court ruled in her favor because she did not purposely avoid receiving the notice, and the school board had not exerted the necessary efforts to comply with the requirements of the statute.[22]

Questions also arise concerning the adequacy of the substance of the notice. For example, Alabama law requires adequate notice that specifies the grounds for the administrative action. When one principal wrote a letter to a teacher stating: "You have not done well enough for me to recommend that you come back next year," the state's supreme court ruled that the state statute was not satisfied by this letter.[23] Some states require two notices, one that specifies the deficiencies at a specified time prior to the later notice of dismissal charges. The purpose of the earlier notice is to give the teacher time to overcome the specified deficiencies. When a dismissed tenured teacher in Missouri challenged the adequacy of both notices, the court ruled for the school board.[24] The court recognized the dilemma of the board as follows: "If the board sets forth the charges…at length and in detail including a recital of incidents to support the charges, it is contended that new and different charges have been made. If it states them in a cryptic way, it is contended that they are not set forth with particularity."

Is Due Process Always Satisfied by Following State Law?

In *Cleveland Board of Education* v. *Loudermill,* a 1985 case that arose in Cleveland, the U.S. Supreme Court clarified some aspects of the due process protections to be accorded to tenured state employees under the Fourteenth Amendment.[25] While the plaintiff, Loudermill, was a security guard, under the wording of the state law he could be fired only "for cause," and thus his situation is analogous to that of tenured teachers.

According to the Court, following procedures specified by the state law may not be sufficient to satisfy the constitutional requirements of due process. The U.S. Constitution requires "notice and an opportunity to respond. The opportunity to present reasons, either in person or in writing, why proposed action should not be taken is a fundamental due process requirement. The tenured public employee is entitled to oral or written notice of the charges against him, an explanation of the employer's evidence, and an opportunity to present his side of the story." In this case, when Loudermill received a hearing only after he was dismissed, he went to court. In the final appeal, the Supreme Court ruled in his favor, holding that since a tenured employee has a property right to continued employment, he has a right to a hearing *prior* to being terminated.

Does Verbal Harassment Violate Due Process?

Probably not. An interesting case was decided by the First Circuit Court of Appeals in 1991.[26] A teacher charged that her supervisor, among other things, berated her in the presence of her students; ordered her in "a crass and gross tone" to admit a student she had previously excluded from the class; in calls to her co-workers defamed her, "creating an uncomfortable environment for her to work"; and in an oral evaluation, which the supervisor refused to put into writing, called her a poor teacher. The teacher claimed she became ill as a result of such harassment and sued, claiming a violation of her substantive due process rights under the U.S. Constitution. There was no claim of loss of employment, benefits, or responsibilities.

The court ruled against the teacher, finding that the Constitution does not protect one against risks to emotional health resulting from a supervisor's verbal harassment. While substantive due process protects one against action that is "egregiously unacceptable, outrageous or conscience-shocking," wrote the court, it is not enough that the action violates "some fastidious squeamishness or private sentimentalism." Nor did the court consider the supervisor's verbal indignities "sufficiently close to the rack and the screw or egregiously unacceptable or outrageous." (We wonder whether a simpler action for defamation might have succeeded rather than a claim of constitutional violation, which might be much more difficult to establish.)

Can a State Require Drug Testing for Teachers?

Only in exceptional circumstances, ruled a district court in a Georgia case.[27] The case involved a challenge to a Georgia law requiring applicants for public school positions to take urine tests for the presence of illegal drugs. The court held that the statute violates the Fourth Amendment. However, it held that the state could require such tests if it could show that it had special interests to protect that necessarily outweighed the individual's right to privacy.

A different result was reached in 1998 by the 6th Circuit Court in a case that arose in Knox County, Tennessee.[28] There, the county school system adopted a "Drug-Free Workplace Substance Abuse Policy" which, among other provisions, called for "suspicionless drug testing for all individuals who apply for, transfer to, or are promoted to, 'safety sensitive' positions within the Knox County School System, including teaching positions...." This policy was challenged by the Knox County Education Association as a violation of the Fourth Amendment's prohibition against unreasonable searches and seizures. When the district court enjoined the board from implementing and enforcing the policy, the board appealed.

The appeals court clearly recognized that urine testing for drugs is a "search" that cannot be an arbitrary and unwarranted governmental intrusion into an individual's privacy. At the same time, the Fourth Amendment does not prohibit "all searches and seizures, but only those that are unreasonable." Thus, the constitutionality of the search is decided by applying a balancing test, weighing the individual's interest in privacy against the state's interest in such testing.

The court examined the four leading Supreme Court cases related to drug testing. Among these, the court relied most heavily on *Von Raab*,[29] where suspicionless searches of customs agents were upheld, since customs agents are in critical positions to prevent illegal drugs from entering the country. They might be particularly susceptible to drug use or to bribery. The national interest in self-protection outweighs the agents' interest in privacy. Similarly, the court reasoned that teachers occupy "a singularly critical and unique role in our society in that for a great portion of a child's life they occupy a position of immense direct influence on a child, with a potential for both good and bad." The laws of the State of Tennessee also specify that "teachers shall serve in an *in loco parentis* capacity and are charged with the responsibility 'to secure order and to protect students from harm while in their custody.'" This unique role of the teachers, together with their duty, is sufficient, the court said, "to overcome the presumption against suspicionless testing."

The appeals court was careful to describe the procedures used to ensure the privacy of the urine testing itself, the confidentiality of the results, and medical reviews of positive results to determine if they were caused by legally prescribed medicine. On appeal, the Supreme Court denied review of the case.

An unusual case related to a "search" involving a teacher arose when drug-sniffing dogs alerted to a teacher's car through an open window during a campuswide "drug lockdown." School board policy required the taking of a drug test within two hours of such a suspicion. The teacher was terminated when she refused to take a drug test after marijuana was allegedly found in her car in the school parking lot. She took the test, after two days, at her attorney's advice.

The court found that the school policy requiring an employee's consent or a search warrant to search an employee's personal property at school did not apply to a search of the teacher's car.

The search, according to the court, provided a reasonable suspicion regarding the teacher's drug use. At that point, the policy was triggered requiring drug testing within two hours. Her refusal to take the test justified the discharge, according to the 11th Circuit Court. The teacher requested review by the Supreme Court.[30]

Does a Teacher Have a Duty to Disarm a Student?

Not necessarily, ruled the West Virginia Supreme Court in a case involving a sixth-grade teacher dismissed for "willfully neglecting his duties."[31] This charge was based on his failure to confiscate a gun which a student brought to class. The teacher conducted the class in a calm manner so as not to upset the student. Later, when the principal tried to take the loaded gun, the student aimed at the principal and ran away. The West Virginia Supreme Court held for the teacher, ruling the dismissal to be "arbitrary since evidence was insufficient to support charges of teacher's willful neglect of duty."

Is One Punishment Enough?

Generally speaking, yes. A teacher was given a letter of reprimand for using vulgar terms in class. Subsequently, a new superintendent sent a second letter of reprimand and filed unprofessional conduct charges with the state professional practices commission. The commission ruled that the teacher had been punished enough. Nevertheless, on the superintendent's recommendation, the teacher was terminated the following spring, even though her evaluations for years had been satisfactory. The South Dakota Supreme Court as well as the trial court ordered her reinstatement with back pay, holding the administrative action arbitrary, capricious, and an abuse of discretion.[32]

Can a State Require Teachers to Share in the Cost of a Panel Used in a Due Process Hearing?

No, ruled the Tenth Circuit Court of Appeals in a case involving an Oklahoma statute.[33] Under the statute, panel members and the hearing judge were to be paid certain sums and there was no way of predicting how long the hearings would last or what the size of the transcript would be. The court held that because the tenured teacher had a right to due process, a cost-sharing requirement imposed an impermissible burden on that right. The court applied the strict scrutiny test and found no compelling state interest to justify the requirement. *Strict scrutiny* is a stringent standard applied by courts when a person's important constitutional right is restricted or denied by official action. Such a standard is satisfied only if the state can show it has a compelling interest in applying the restriction. A lesser standard is the "rational basis test" under which the state only needs to show a reasonable connection between its policy or action and a legitimate goal or purpose.

Due Process for Students

Many of the oppressive features of schooling have been challenged and to some extent changed with the increasing application of constitutional rights to life in school. One area of dramatic change, mandated by important decisions of the U.S. Supreme Court and further implemented by various decisions of lower courts, is the right of students to due process of law in school-related controversies. This section explores this topic as well as other aspects of discipline, including corporal punishment and "search and seizure" in schools.

What Is the Current Status of the Doctrine of In Loco Parentis?

In loco parentis is not as strong as it once was, but it is still often invoked by the courts. It means "in place of the parents" and has been used historically to justify the power and authority of school officials over students at school or while traveling to and from school. Although the doctrine gave substantial authority to school officials in years past, many courts and legislatures have limited its applicability. When parents, for example, notify schools not to use corporal punishment on their children, it is odd to justify such punishment with an appeal to *in loco parentis.* As more courts have recognized that constitutional rights apply to students and schools, the *in loco parentis* doctrine has been weakened, though not completely eradicated.

Must Schools Follow Due Process in Cases of Short Suspension?

Yes. However, the legal requirements are not onerous or unduly demanding if the disciplinary violation is a minor one. The U.S. Supreme Court addressed this issue in *Goss* v. *Lopez.*[34] Dwight Lopez and several other students were suspended from school in Columbus, Ohio, during the 1970–1971 academic year without receiving a hearing. Some were suspended for documented acts of violence, but others, Dwight among them, were suspended even though they claimed to be innocent bystanders of demonstrations or disturbances. Moreover, they were never informed of what they were accused of doing. The students, who were suspended for up to 10 days without a hearing, went to court and claimed that their right to due process was violated. When the federal district court agreed with them, the administrators appealed to the U.S. Supreme Court. In a 5–4 opinion, the Court ruled in favor of the students and discussed several issues of importance to students, teachers, and administrators.

The Court reiterated the key principle of *Tinker,* that "young people do not 'shed their constitutional rights' at the schoolhouse door." Justice White, writing for the majority, indicated that the U.S. Constitution does not require states to establish schools, but once they do, students have a property right in them, which may not be withdrawn without "fundamentally fair procedures." Clearly, said the Court, the Constitution protects students in cases of expulsion from the public schools. Furthermore, some degree of due process is required even in cases of short-term suspension.

A suspension for up to 10 days is not so minor a punishment that it may be imposed "in complete disregard of the Due Process Clause," wrote Justice White. Such exclusion from school is a serious event in the life of the child, and it becomes even more serious if the misconduct is recorded in the student's file. Such a record is likely to damage the student's standing with teachers and "interfere with later opportunities for higher education and employment." Thus it is clear that the law requires schools to respect students' constitutional right to due process in both serious and minor disciplinary matters that might lead to either expulsion or suspension from school.

What Process Is Due in Minor Disciplinary Cases?

The seriousness of the possible penalty influences the extent and thoroughness of the due process requirement. Since due process is a flexible concept and not a fixed set of requirements, some minimal but fair procedures will satisfy the courts in cases that might lead to short-term suspension. As a minimum, students facing suspension "must be given some kind of notice and afforded some kind of hearing."

Notice of the charges may be oral or written, and a student who denies the charges must be given "an explanation of the evidence the authorities have and an opportunity to present his side of the story." The central concern of the U.S. Supreme Court is that there be at least "rudimentary precautions against unfair or mistaken findings of misconduct and arbitrary expulsion from school." Thus the Court does not turn schools into courtrooms and does not place unreasonable burdens on educators faced with disciplinary problems. Most schools had followed such fair procedures long before *Goss*.

What Process Is Due in Serious Cases?

Serious disciplinary cases, by contrast, may require extensive and thorough procedures. "Serious cases" are those that might lead to long-term suspension or expulsion. Since such actions are likely to have important consequences on students' educational and even occupational life, their property interests are in serious jeopardy, and meticulous procedures are required.

Cases involving serious disciplinary violations call for a written notice specifying the charges, the time and place of the hearing, and a description of procedures to be followed at the hearing. Students should know what evidence will be used against them, the names of witnesses who will testify, and the substance of witnesses' testimony. Students usually have the right to cross-examine witnesses, as well as to present witnesses and evidence on their own behalf. A written or taped record of the proceeding should be available to students, together with the findings and recommendation of the group conducting the hearing (usually the school board). The right of appeal should also be clearly stated.[35] Although the *Dixon* case, from which these requirements were taken, involved college students, courts, including the Supreme Court, have referred to *Dixon* with approval in various cases involving high school students.

Do Courts Always Allow the Cross-Examination of Witnesses?

There are conflicting cases on the right to confront and cross-examine accusing witnesses. Even the U.S. Supreme Court has said that a "full-dress judicial hearing, with the right to cross-examine witnesses" may not always be required. A Connecticut case ruled that confrontation and cross-examination may be dispensed with if extenuating circumstances or persuasive evidence reveals that the accusing witnesses will be inhibited to a significant degree or fearful for their personal safety because of probable revenge or retaliation.[36] A Kansas court ruled similarly.[37] In another expulsion case, however, a New Jersey court required that the accusing witnesses be available for cross-examination.[38] The witnesses' fear of physical reprisal was no justification for depriving the accused of the right to confront and examine witnesses, ruled the court. It is a community obligation to protect such witnesses against retaliation.

In a 1996 case that arose at George Washington Junior High School in Montgomery County, Alabama, a student was suspended and later expelled for possessing marijuana.[39] One student and several adults testified at the hearings, while other students submitted written testimony but would not appear to testify in person. The district court, in upholding the suspension and expulsion, quoted several sources while concluding that a student has no constitutional right to cross-examine witnesses at an expulsion hearing. The student did cross-examine witnesses who appeared at the hearing, but could not examine those who submitted written testimony. Thus, the weight of evidence seems to be that students have no constitutional right to cross-examine witnesses, particularly student witnesses against them. In fact, some courts hold that they do not even have the right to know the identities of accusing students.[40]

Several cases have held that hearsay evidence may be used in school disciplinary hearings, unlike in courts of law. Thus, in a Wisconsin case, a student whose ring was stolen did not testify at the expulsion hearing of the accused student.[41] The court reviewed *Goss* as well as other relevant cases and rejected technical legal rules of evidence, proclaiming: "[A] student's right to due process is satisfied even though some of the testimony presented was hearsay given by members of the school staff."

Do Students Have a Right to Have Lawyers Represent Them?

There is no generally applicable answer to this question. Clearly there is no right to representation in connection with short-term suspensions. According to the U.S. Supreme Court in *Goss,* "further formalizing the suspension process and escalating its formality and adversary nature may not only make it too costly as a regular disciplinary tool but also destroy its effectiveness as part of the teaching process." On the other hand, courts have held that lawyers might attend serious disciplinary hearings to observe the procedures and give assistance to the student. This happened, for example, when a senior in a New York high school was accused of cheating on a state Regents Examination. Since this is an important exam in New York, and since a charge of cheating could lead to very serious consequences, the state court upheld the student's right to be assisted by counsel.[42] A case involving a college student came to the same conclusion.[43]

Do "Miranda Rights" Apply to School Situations?

No. In 1966 the U.S. Supreme Court held in *Miranda* v. *Arizona* that the Fifth Amendment privilege against self-incrimination applies to those under questioning while in official custody related to a criminal investigation.[44] This means that persons deprived of their freedom of action in any significant way must be informed of their right to remain silent, that anything they say may be used against them, and that they have a right to the assistance of a lawyer. Such rules, however, do not apply when school officials detain students for questioning[45]—they have no right even to have their parents present. Since the *Miranda* rule derives from the Fifth Amendment provision that a person shall not be "compelled in a criminal case to be a witness against himself," and since public school disciplinary proceedings and inquiries are not criminal proceedings, *Miranda* does not apply.

A different conclusion was reached by the Supreme Court of Pennsylvania in 2002. When a classroom was vandalized, a school police officer questioned R.H., a student, about the event without giving him the Miranda warnings. After R.H. admitted the break-in and vandalism, he was charged with several crimes in juvenile court. R.H. claimed his Fifth Amendment rights were violated and his admissions made to the police should be excluded. The court concluded that the school police officers were "law enforcement officers" for purposes of the Fifth Amendment and therefore were required to issue Miranda warnings. The court ordered all statements made by R.H. to the police excluded.[46]

Are There Disciplinary Situations Where Due Process Is Not a Prerequisite?

Yes. In two situations teachers or school administrators may proceed without first observing any formalities of due process. The first involves the myriad of trivial disciplinary matters routinely experienced in schools. For minor infractions of rules or nonperformance of required tasks, students are given a variety of "punishments," ranging from brief detentions to extra work, verbal chastisement, being sent to the principal's office, and so forth. The legal maxim *de minimis non court lex* (the law does not deal with trifles) is applicable to these situations, and schools ought to rely on their knowledge of pedagogical principles to deal with such matters. For example, a federal court in Maine held that a student placed on "school probation" after returning from disciplinary expulsion was not denied any liberty or property interest, and so due process was inapplicable.[47]

The second exception involves emergencies in which educators must act quickly to preserve the safety of persons or property. The U.S. Supreme Court recognized in *Goss* that emergencies occur in school that would make notice and hearing prior to action impracticable because the situation presents danger to persons or property. In such situations, the only legal requirement is that fair procedures be followed "as soon as practicable after removal of the danger or disruption."

At least one federal appeals court also held that participation in interscholastic athletics is not a property interest protected by the due process clause.[48] The case involved a 17-year-old student who claimed that the interscholastic league rule that made him ineligible to participate in high school football when he moved from one town to another denied him his constitutional rights. The court was concerned that to escalate to "constitutional magnitude" a youth's desire to play high school football would trivialize the Constitution. A 1996 Massachusetts case also held that exclusion from the soccer team is not a "property or liberty" interest protected by due process.[49] This is the case, ruled the court, even where suspension from athletic participation is also linked to suspension from school.

Could the Punishment Violate Due Process?

Yes. Due process requires fair procedures on one hand and fairness in punishment on the other. That is, the punishment must not be so excessive as to be arbitrary and grossly unfair. For example, when two students who vandalized a school were suspended pending an investigation, and their suspension turned into an expulsion for the balance of the school year, the court ruled that the school officials violated both *procedural* and *substantive* due process.[50] Fair procedures were violated because there was neither an expulsion hearing nor a notice of the charges against the students. Substantive due process rights were violated because school officials never determined when the suspension would end, which was unfair to the students. This case suggests that care must be exercised in the use of indefinite suspension when a case is investigated, lest it turn into a *de facto* expulsion and thus violate due process.

Is There a Due Process Requirement for Guidance Conferences?

No. Under ordinary circumstances, a guidance conference is not considered a disciplinary proceeding. For example, guidance conferences related to the appropriate placement of a student or concerning progress in scheduled courses are not disciplinary matters. Absent special circumstances, the student is not being deprived of liberty or property; therefore there is no constitutional right to due process. In special circumstances, such right is granted by statute (e.g., in the case of exceptional or bilingual students). By state statute or local policy, it is always possible to expand the due process rights of students beyond those granted by the Constitution. Our discussion has focused on the interpretation of the constitutional provisions that apply to all public schools. Nevertheless, as in all other controversies, the importance of state law and local policy must not be underestimated.

Can Schools Create General Rules to Govern Student Behavior?

Yes, as long as such rules are sufficiently clear to guide student behavior. For example, a rule requiring students to be in their assigned homeroom and in their seat at the time the school bell rings at 8:30 A.M. is a legally valid general rule. It is clear and unambiguous. By contrast, consider a rule that required students "to dress in good taste" and avoid "extremes in style." Under this rule a student in Arcata, California, was suspended because he had long hair. The student and his parents went to court seeking reinstatement and claimed that the rule was so vague that it violated his right to due process. The California Supreme Court agreed with the student and found that the rule was void because it was too vague.[51] The court said that "a law violates due process if it is so vague and standardless that it leaves the public uncertain as to the conduct it prohibits or leaves judges or jurors free to decide, without any legally fixed standards, what is prohibited and what is not in each case."

Similarly, a school rule that is too broad will not stand up in court. The written regulations of a school in Texas gave the principal power to make rules "in the best interest of the school." When the principal acted under this regulation and expelled two students for publishing an underground newspaper, the students went to court, claiming the rule to be vague and overly broad.[52] The court agreed with the students and said that "school rules probably need not be as narrow as criminal statutes, but if school officials contemplate severe punishment they must do so on the basis of a rule which is drawn so as to reasonably inform the student what specific conduct is proscribed."

When a principal has the power to do anything "in the best interest of the school," there are no clear or objective standards by which students can guide their behavior. The rule may even cover constitutionally protected activities, such as freedom of speech and of the press. Therefore the rule is unconstitutional.

An interesting case was decided in Hawaii in 2000. James P. and friends allegedly drank alcohol at his home before attending a school luau. The next day, he was allowed to participate in a state cross-country championship. Two days later, he and his friends were questioned in the principal's office. James denied drinking and claimed he merely provided his friends' glasses. The school had a zero tolerance policy under which suspension could be imposed for up to 92 days.

James' father signed an agreement to a five-day suspension, fearing further disciplinary action if he refused. James was prohibited from athletic participation for the remainder of the school year, not allowed to make up work missed, and required to attend a drug and alcohol counseling program. He and his parents sued, claiming violation of his due process rights.

The court held that the school had no evidence that the student possessed alcohol while attending school, even if he did drink prior to a school event. Being intoxicated at a school function was not covered by the statute and it was ambiguous whether "possession" of alcohol could mean "present within the body." Thus, due process was violated and all punishment rescinded. The court protected the student's property interest in education and liberty interest in his reputation.[53]

Have Due Process Requirements Turned Classrooms and Schools into Courtrooms?

No. When the U.S. Supreme Court ruled in *Goss* that even short-term suspensions require some modicum of due process, a hue and cry arose across the land. School administrators, parents, and teachers were upset, fearing that the decision would force school officials to consult lawyers before they could take any disciplinary measures. These fears were grossly exaggerated. Careful reading of *Goss* and other cases indicates that the legal requirements are not excessive and that there is no need for lawyers to be at the side of administrators or teachers. Conscientious educators used fair procedures long before these cases went to court, and their procedures amply satisfy the law.

On the other hand, oppressive, authoritarian procedures that do not respect students' rights to know why they are being disciplined and do not provide opportunities for students to present their defense in a fair way are crumbling as a result of the application of the U.S. Constitution to the schools. In sum, one may think of the right to due process as applying to student disciplinary matters on a continuum represented as follows:

May Act without Due Process:	*Some Modicum of Due Process Is Necessary:*	*Extensive, Careful Due Process Is Required:*
Trivial or minor matters; or emergencies (which must be followed by due process as soon as possible).	Disciplinary matters that may lead to short-term suspensions of one to ten days or to entry on the student's record.	Disciplinary matters that may result in long-term suspension or expulsion or in a significant penalty (e.g., a short suspension during final exams).

Thus, the more serious the possible penalty, the more formal the procedure due.

Corporal Punishment

Is Reasonable Corporal Punishment Unconstitutional?

No. The U.S. Constitution is silent on this matter, as it is silent on education in general. Thus courts have held that education is a function of state governments (under the reserved powers of the Tenth Amendment to the Constitution) and that states may further delegate power over schooling to local governments. As of 2001, 27 states and the District of Columbia prohibit the use of corporal punishment: Alaska, California, Connecticut, Hawaii, Illinois, Iowa, Maine, Maryland, Massachusetts, Michigan, Minnesota, Montana, Nebraska, Nevada, New Hampshire, New Jersey, New York, North Dakota, Oregon, Rhode Island, South Dakota, Utah, Vermont, Virginia, Washington, West Virginia, and Wisconsin. Some of these states prohibit corporal punishment by law, others (e.g., New York, New Hampshire, and Utah), by regulation of the state board or department of education, or by action of every local school board (as in Rhode Island), while in South Dakota it is banned by law rescinding authorization to use it.[54] Efforts are also being made in other states to outlaw the use of such punishment. Furthermore, many local communities outlaw the practice where the state law does not forbid it. Some school districts that allow corporal punishment restrict its administration in various ways, in which case the restrictions must be followed. The most common restriction is that an administrator is the only person authorized to spank students and then only in the presence of an adult witness. In any event, it is clear that ordinary corporal punishment does not violate the Constitution.

Can a Supervisor Forbid Teachers' Use of Corporal Punishment?

Not if the state law and district policy allow it. Such a case arose in Colorado when a middle school teacher struck two students who struck her while interrupting her classroom.[55] She was dismissed for "insubordination, neglect of duty, and other good and just cause." On appeal, the court overruled the board order of termination with back pay and benefits. The court noted that, although her supervisor ordered her "not to ever physically touch a child for disciplinary reasons," this order cannot override the district's own policy giving her such authority. The supervisor's order was unreasonable in light of such district policy, and the teacher cannot be insubordinate violating such an order. Similarly, since the teacher responded to the classroom incident in a manner authorized by district policy, her actions cannot be characterized as "failure to carry out her obligations and responsibilities." Finally, there was no evidence indicating "other good and just cause" to adversely affect her teaching.

Is Excessive Corporal Punishment Unconstitutional?

It might be, depending on the severity of the punishment. In Dade County, Florida, James Ingraham and Roosevelt Andrews, junior high school students, were severely paddled during the 1970–1971 school year. In fact, James was so harshly beaten that the resulting hematoma required medical attention, and he missed 11 days of school. The paddling Roosevelt received included being struck on his arms, depriving him the use of an arm for a week.

At the time of the paddling, Dade County schools used corporal punishment as one means of maintaining discipline. Simultaneously, a Florida law forbade punishment that was "degrading or unduly severe" or that took place prior to consultation with the principal or the teacher in charge of the school. The students filed suit against several school administrators and claimed that the severe beatings they received constituted cruel and unusual punishment. The district court, the court of appeals, and finally the U.S. Supreme Court all ruled that the beating, although excessive and unreasonable, did not violate the Eighth Amendment, which prohibits cruel and unusual punishment.[56]

Does that mean that the U.S. Supreme Court recommends physical punishment of students or condones excessive punishment? Not at all. Whether school children and youth ought to be physically punished is not a legal matter; it is a policy question for educators to decide with appropriate consideration of psychological, developmental, and other factors. Even when such punishment is allowed, it must remain within reasonable limits. To be "reasonable," punishment must relate to an educational purpose and not be merely an expression of a teacher's anger, frustration, or malice. The severity of the punishment should relate to the gravity of the offense and should consider the ability of the student to bear it. Therefore the size, age, sex, and physical and emotional condition of the child must be considered. Excessive punishment is unreasonable, and the law has always provided ways for legal redress against it. Students may sue the perpetrators for money damages for the suffering endured as well as seek an indictment for assault and battery. The Supreme Court has ruled that these traditional remedies are sufficient to deter educators and minimize abuse. The Court examined the history of the Eighth Amendment and concluded that it was never intended to apply to schools but was created to control the punishment of criminals who are incarcerated in closed institutions. The very "openness of the public school and its supervision by the community afford significant safeguards against the kind of abuse from which the Eighth Amendment protects the prisoner."

In a Pennsylvania case, a 36-year-old, 6-foot tall, 210-pound school principal paddled a 45-pound first-grade boy four times during the same day, with a total of 60 to 70 swats.[57] The parents had previously signed a consent form for paddling their child, who was hyperactive and on medication for behavioral problems. Since the incident, the boy had psychological counseling, cried during the night, had nightmares, and had trouble sleeping. The jury decided that he had suffered "extreme pain" within the meaning of the state statute, which defined assault as "…attempts to cause or intentionally, knowingly, or recklessly causes bodily injury (substantial pain) to another." The principal was fined $500, given a suspended jail sentence, 12 months' probation, and 150 hours of community work. This is one of the few cases in which parents were successful in bringing suit against school employees for excessive and unreasonable corporal punishment. Note, however, that the suit was based on state law and not on the U.S. Constitution.

Teachers can also lose their jobs for violating state laws or school board policies related to corporal punishment. Courts in Texas,[58] Michigan,[59] Pennsylvania,[60] and other states have upheld dismissals of teachers who violated such laws and policies.

In what many consider a bizarre case, a student in Texas brought suit against two athletic coaches for the use of excessive force in discipline.[61] The two coaches called the 14-year-old junior high student into their office, where one of them held his head in a headlock and threatened to kill him if his grades did not improve. They told him they would hang him and placed what the student thought was a gun against his head. The coaches denied all these allegations, but testimonies by the student, one coach, and the superintendent were sufficient to cause the state appeals court to deny summary judgment and ordered that the trial proceed.

A high school principal was not protected by qualified immunity when he used excessive force against three male students. The first student said, "Yeah, Heil Hitler," referring to a quarterback at a football game who always wanted to have his way. Koch, the high school principal, mistakenly assumed the comments were directed at him. He hit the student across the mouth, grabbed him by the neck, and squeezed sufficiently to cause purple bruises that lasted a couple of days. The student received emergency treatment, Advil, and ice packs. On two other occasions, the principal gave similar rough treatments to students. The school board placed him on probation for one year and the courts denied him qualified immunity, holding that the students had a clearly established liberty interest to be free from arbitrary corporal punishment.[62]

Must Due Process Be Used Before Corporal Punishment Is Administered?

In reference to *Ingraham* v. *Wright,* the U.S. Supreme Court ruled that existing remedies would suffice and the addition of procedural safeguards while protecting student rights "would entail a significant intrusion into an area of primary educational responsibility." Thus the question of whether to have corporal punishment is for legislatures and local school boards to decide. Courts will intrude only when the punishment is excessive and unreasonable.

This issue surfaced again in 1995 in Mississippi, where the mother of a young child claimed that paddling her son violated due process. A federal district court dismissed the case in a brief opinion consistent with the U.S. Supreme Court, ruling that the student's due process rights were "not violated by the administration of corporal punishment if the state affords him adequate post-punishment remedies."[63] In other words, the remedy, if any, lies in a suit under state law for excessive use of force, if the facts so indicate.

A different issue was raised and decided in 1980 by the U.S. Court of Appeals for the Fourth Circuit when it ruled that excessive corporal punishment in a public school might be a violation of "constitutional rights given protection under the rubric of substantive due process."[64] The court spoke of "the right to be free of state intrusions into realms of personal privacy and bodily security through means so brutal, demeaning, and harmful as literally to shock the conscience of a court. The existence of this right to ultimate bodily security—the most fundamental aspect of personal privacy—is unmistakably established in our constitutional decisions as an attribute of the ordered liberty that is the concern of substantive due process."

In this case it was alleged that a young girl was so severely paddled in school that she was badly bruised and required 10 days' hospitalization and treatment "of traumatic injury to the soft tissue of the left hip and thigh and…the left buttock," with possible injuries to her lower back and spine. The court held that the student's substantive due process rights were violated if the evidence showed that "the force applied caused injury so severe, was so disproportionate to the need presented and was so inspired by malice or sadism rather than a merely careless or unwise excess of zeal that it amounted to a brutal and inhumane abuse of official power literally shocking to the conscience."

In an important New Mexico case, the Tenth Circuit Court of Appeals came to the same conclusion in 1987.[65] There, nine-year-old Teresa Garcia was excessively beaten on two separate occasions with a split wooden paddle. On the first occasion a teacher held her upside down by the ankles while Theresa Miera, the principal, beat her repeatedly "on the front of her leg between the knee and the waist." Teresa bled, and she had welts on her leg and a two-inch cut that left a permanent scar. The second beating, about a month later, caused severe bruises on her buttocks, shocking a physician who treated her and causing a nurse to say that if Teresa had received this type of injury at home, the nurse "would have called [the police department's] Protective Services," reporting child abuse.

The court ruled that this type of excessive beating is so brutal and offensive to human dignity as to shock the conscience, and that the excessive punishment violated Teresa's constitutional right to substantive due process. The court identified three levels of corporal punishment: "Punishments that do not exceed the traditional common law standard of reasonableness are not actionable; punishments that exceed the common law standard without adequate state remedies violate procedural due process rights; and finally, punishments that are so grossly excessive as to be shocking to the conscience violate substantive due process rights, without regard to the adequacy of state remedies."

There is a developing trend among federal appeals courts to hold grossly excessive corporal punishment violative of substantive due process. The Fifth Circuit ruled otherwise in *Ingraham;* but since the time of *Ingraham,* both the Fourth and Tenth Circuits ruled in favor of protecting students' rights and the Supreme Court has declined to overrule them.

Thus, while corporal punishment does not necessarily require prior procedural due process, and while it does not violate the Eighth Amendment prohibition against cruel and unusual punishment, excessive punishment might violate the substantive due process rights embodied in the Fourteenth Amendment.

Although it does not involve corporal punishment, a very different case arose in 1992 to illustrate the substantive due process rights of students.[66] A 14-year-old female student brought suit against her teacher, principal, superintendent, and school district. She claimed a violation of her due process and equal protection rights by a teacher who had sexually molested her and by the principal and superintendent, who had failed to protect her. The Fifth Circuit Court of Appeals held that the principal and superintendent had an affirmative constitutional duty to protect the student from the teacher's actions and that the teacher's sexual molestation violated the student's firmly established constitutional rights to substantive due process. (See also chapter 15.)

Can Parents Prohibit the Use of Corporal Punishment?

In general, no. If a state allows corporal punishment, parental objection to the practice will not necessarily prevail. The U.S. Supreme Court so ruled in a North Carolina case in which a sixth-grade boy was spanked for violating a school rule against throwing balls at specified times.[67] Virginia Baker had requested that her son not be spanked or paddled, for she opposed such practices in principle. While the law of North Carolina allowed the use of force reasonably necessary "to restrain or correct pupils and to maintain order," Baker claimed the law was unconstitutional because it allowed such punishment over parental objections. Although recognizing the parents' basic right to supervise the upbringing of children, the Court also considered the "legitimate and substantial interest" of the state "in maintaining order and discipline in the public schools." In the final analysis, since both professional and popular opinion are split on the question of corporal punishment, the Court refused to allow "the wishes of a parent to restrict school officials' discretion in deciding the methods to be used in…maintaining discipline."

Some states have passed laws that provide for prior written parental approval before a student may be spanked. At times, local school districts create their own policies regulating this matter. In the absence of state legislation or local regulation, it is clear that schools do not have to get parental approval to use corporal punishment, and, in fact, may use it over the objections of parents. As a general rule, school discipline is a local matter, and school boards may adopt reasonable rules and regulations to conduct their schools efficiently. The authority of school personnel, in the conduct of the ordinary affairs of the school, derives in part from state law and in part from remaining vestiges of the doctrine of *in loco parentis* introduced earlier in this chapter.

Can Students Be Disciplined for Conduct Outside School?

Yes, if the rule they violate is reasonably connected to the operation of the school. A Texas court so ruled, upholding the suspension of a student for drinking vodka on school grounds, violating a known school rule.[68] If the alleged wrong took place away from the school and the school grounds, school officials should allow the civil authorities to handle the matter.[69] However, when a student's conduct gets him or her in trouble with the civil authorities, that fact does not preclude the schools from applying appropriate disciplinary measures if the behavior is connected to the school. Punishment by both school and outside authorities does not constitute double jeopardy, which is a technical legal concept that applies to criminal proceedings. School disciplinary matters are not criminal proceedings.

In a California case, a high school student was expelled for using a stun gun during a fight with another student.[70] The county board of education ruled that the district lacked jurisdiction because the fight occurred at another school district and was thus unrelated to the offending student's school activity or attendance. On appeal, however, the court ruled against the student and rejected the interpretation of the state code that would limit prohibited conduct to the student's school or the school's activities. Such narrow interpretation, according to the court, would not promote a safe and orderly educational environment.

Students who consumed alcohol while on a field trip to Busch Gardens were banned from participating in graduation exercises as punishment. They sued and so did their parents, claiming they suffered emotional distress as a result of not being able to attend their children's graduation. Another student sued for emotional distress when he was accidentally left at Busch Gardens and had to return by taxi to the hotel where they were staying.[71]

The mother of one of the students sued when she lost her position as a field hockey coach in retaliation for posting a sign in front of her house questioning the fitness of the principal to punish the students for drinking alcohol when he himself drank on the trip. She claimed her free speech rights were violated. (This topic is discussed in chapter 9).

The court ruled against the students for violating the school's "no alcohol" rule. They received notice of the charges and an opportunity to explain their side of the story; thus, their right to due process was not violated. The claims of the stranded student and the parents were dismissed as frivolous; their attorney was fined $500 for filing a frivolous claim and ordered to attend two courses in continuing legal education. The coach/mother's suit against the board for retaliation was allowed to continue.

Can Schools Lower Grades or Withhold Diplomas as Disciplinary Measures?

Courts are divided on this issue. In the past, schools often withheld diplomas as punishment and teachers often lowered students' grades for misbehaving in class. The trend among educators is to assign separate grades for academic work and for behavior, or "citizenship." As a general rule, the law does not intrude into disputes over grading policies or practices; these are matters for educators to decide. Nevertheless, if a student can show that a grade was lowered for disciplinary reasons or that the teacher acted out of prejudice or malice, the courts will listen and help. The burden of proof is on the student to establish that the reasons for the low grade were illegitimate and not related to the quality of the work. This is a difficult burden of proof, and there are no cases reported wherein a student below the college level has succeeded in such a suit.

Diplomas should not be withheld as punishment for an alleged violation of a school rule. The reason for this principle is that the diploma is a symbol and recognition of academic accomplishment and not a reward for good behavior. Misbehavior should be faced directly through disciplinary procedures, not indirectly through the withholding of a symbol of academic accomplishment.

Although there are few cases on point, there are some that have upheld school officials' right to reduce a student's grade in addition to imposing a penalty, such as suspension from school. In a case involving two high school seniors in Texas who were suspended for three days and given zeros for the three days' graded schoolwork for consuming alcohol on school grounds, the court upheld both school punishments.[72] The court ruled that the punishments did not injure either the property or liberty rights of the students and thus did not violate their due process rights.

By contrast, a Pennsylvania court struck down a policy that provided for a reduction in grades in all classes by two percentage points for each day of suspension.[73] When an 11th-grade student on a field trip to New York drank a glass of wine while with friends in a restaurant, she was suspended for five days and expelled from the cheerleading squad and the National Honor Society. When the student and her parents challenged the grade reduction policy, the court struck it down. According to the court, the reduction of the grade would misrepresent academic achievement and such misrepresentation would be both improper and illegal. Similarly, in a case where previously earned credit was taken away from students for failure to make up excessive absences, the court ruled that the loss of credit is disciplinary in nature and thus students are entitled to due process prior to the punishment.[74]

In the absence of state statutes controlling the imposition of what some consider a double penalty, courts are likely to respect the discretion of school officials and will not substitute their judgment for those of educators. However, if the penalty is severe, the courts will scrutinize official action to ensure that both procedural and substantive due process rights were respected.

Is It Unconstitutional for Schools to Require Passing Grades as a Precondition for Participating in Extracurricular Activities?

No, ruled the Texas Supreme Court.[75] The so-called "no pass, no play" rule required that students wishing to participate in extracurricular activities, including sports, earn grades no lower than 70 on a scale of 100 in an academic class. When the rule was challenged by students as a violation of the equal protection and due process clauses of the Fourteenth Amendment, the district court ruled in their favor; the state supreme court reversed that ruling.

The highest court of Texas held that participation in extracurricular activities is not a fundamental right akin to student speech or religion. Furthermore, the rule does not burden an inherently suspect class of students, such as a racial, ethnic, or religious group. Therefore, applying the rational basis test, the court found the rule to be reasonably related to a legitimate state objective by providing an incentive for students to keep up their performance in academic subjects.

School Searches

Can School Officials Search Student Lockers?

Yes, if they have reasonable grounds to suspect that something illegal or dangerous is in the locker. In recent years, students have objected to locker searches on the grounds that since they were unauthorized, searches without a warrant violate the Fourth Amendment right against illegal search and seizure.

The *Overton* Case[76]

In a high school in New York, police showed the vice principal a search warrant and, with his help, searched the lockers of two students. They found four marijuana cigarettes in Carlos Overton's locker. When the search warrant turned out to be defective, Carlos claimed that the entire search was illegal and therefore the evidence obtained could not be used in court. The police and the school claimed that the vice principal gave consent for the search; therefore, since no unauthorized search took place, the evidence found could be used. The court ruled against Carlos and upheld the validity of the search and the use of the evidence. The court held that students had exclusive use of the lockers vis-á-vis other students but not in relation to school authorities. School officials have the locker combinations, and if they have reason to suspect that something illegal or dangerous is in a locker, they have a right to inspect it. In fact, the New York court went further and said that "not only have the school authorities the right to inspect but the right becomes a duty when suspicion arises that something of an illegal nature may be secreted there."

In typical situations away from school, law enforcement officials need "probable cause" to secure a search warrant to search a person's home, a rented locker, or even an occupied telephone booth. Schools, however, are special environments where school officials have the duty and responsibility for the safety, health, and learning of children. Therefore courts apply less demanding standards to searches conducted by school personnel than by law enforcement officials.

New Jersey v. T.L.O.[77]

Because of conflicting decisions handed down by lower courts, the U.S. Supreme Court rendered an opinion in January 1985 related to the authority of school officials to search students for contraband.

The facts were that a teacher, upon entering the girls' restroom, found T.L.O. and another student holding lighted cigarettes. Since school rules forbade smoking there, the girls were escorted to the assistant vice principal's office. When questioned, T.L.O. denied smoking. At the request of the official, she opened her purse, where, in addition to cigarettes, there was drug paraphernalia and evidence that she had sold drugs. After examining the purse, the assistant vice principal summoned T.L.O.'s mother and the police.

A divided Supreme Court said school searches are justified "when there are reasonable grounds for suspecting that the search will turn up evidence that the student has violated or is violating either the law or the rules of the school." The Court rejected the Fourth Amendment requirement of probable cause as inapplicable to school students. Instead, expressing confidence that educators will behave "according to the dictates of reason and common sense," Justice White, writing for the majority, said that the proper standard for searches by educators is "reasonableness, under all the circumstances." Reasonableness "involves a twofold inquiry: first, one must consider 'whether the...action was justified at its inception';...second, one must determine whether the search as actually conducted was 'reasonably related in scope to the circumstances which justified the interference in the first place.'"

Justice White concluded that the initial search for the cigarettes was reasonable, since finding cigarettes in the purse "would both corroborate the report that she had been smoking and undermine the credibility of her defense to the charge of smoking." When drug paraphernalia was plainly visible in the purse, the second search for marijuana was also considered reasonable by the Court. The Court also explicitly rejected the applicability of the *in loco parentis* doctrine, which would hold that because the school's authority is the same as that of the parents, it is not subject to the Fourth Amendment. Since school authorities are state agents for purposes of constitutional law, they are exercising public rather than parental authority when conducting searches of students.

While the Court was divided in its analysis, educators can be guided by the standard applied by the Court. However, several issues related to school searches remain unresolved. As Justice White indicated, the Supreme Court has not yet ruled on:

1. the search of lockers, desks, and other storage areas provided by schools, and what standards should be used for searching such areas;
2. searches by educators at the request of law enforcement officials;
3. whether "individualized suspicion" is an essential part of the standard of reasonableness; and
4. whether the "exclusionary rule applies to the fruits of unlawful searches conducted by school authorities."

The Court as a whole has not yet resolved issues related to the use of search dogs, or the standards to be used for searching student automobiles. It is quite probable that these and other issues will be addressed as more cases percolate up through our appellate courts.

Courts below the U.S. Supreme Court level have applied the *T.L.O.* principles to a variety of cases. For example, the Court of Appeals of Alaska ruled on a case involving the search of student's car by school officials.[78] In this case, a teacher in a library noticed a student with glassy eyes, face flushed, behaving in a way that led the teacher to suspect the student was under the influence of alcohol. When the "safety/security home school coordinator" was called, he escorted the student into the storeroom for a talk. The student bumped into large objects and swayed as he walked, his speech was slurred, and there was an odor of alcohol on him. In the assistant principal's office, school officials suspected a combination of alcohol and drug use during the lunch hour, and after discussion the student gave them his car keys and signed a form consenting to the search of his car.

When cocaine was found in the ashtray of the car, the student wanted the judge to exclude the evidence, claiming the search to be illegal. The court, following *T.L.O.*, ruled that the search was proper in its inception and its scope. However, the court held that the consent form was void because it was not freely given by the intoxicated student, but that under the circumstances the school officials had reasonable grounds to suspect drug use and, particularly because the student's car was improperly parked in the parking lot, it was reasonable to search the car as well.

By contrast, a Pennsylvania court declared invalid a locker search by school officials that produced some marijuana cigarettes in a jacket pocket.[79] In this case, the student was observed getting a pack of cigarettes out of his locker and giving one of the cigarettes to another student. The assistant principal took the cigarette and the pack away and then searched the locker. The court, applying the *T.L.O.* standard, found (1) that students do have a reasonable expectancy of privacy in their jacket that they take to school, which expectation they do not lose by placing the jacket in the school locker, and (2) that once the school officials seized the cigarette and the pack, they had no reasonable basis to suspect that there would be more in the locker. Catching the juvenile with cigarettes "formed a pretext for a search for drugs" in violation of the Fourteenth Amendment.

An interesting case arose in Michigan, where a school security guard apprehended a female student ducking behind a parked car in the school parking lot during class time.[80] When she emptied her purse after being ordered to do so, it was found to contain several "readmittance slips" that the student should not have had. A further search of the student for drugs was ordered by the vice principal. In a suit by the student, the court held that her constitutional rights were violated. The court reasoned that *T.L.O.* does not justify the search just because *some* school rule or law was violated by the student. The administrator must show that the "student's conduct creates a reasonable suspicion that a specific rule or law has been violated and that a search could reasonably be expected to produce evidence of that violation." Courts have also held consistently that the *T.L.O.* test of reasonable suspicion applies to locker searches.[81] Some courts have ruled that there is no expectation of privacy in lockers owned by the school if schools have the combinations and a notice of likely inspection is in the student handbook.

Variations on school-related searches are legion. For example, after receiving reports of stolen items, the vice principal interviewed several students and focused her attention on four who were alone in the locker room at the time of the theft. Although she did invite the police liaison officer to be present in the building to accompany her, she conducted the investigation independently. After the vice principal found some of the stolen items, the police officer participated in the search by "patting down" a girl. The federal appeals court upheld the search by the vice principal as justified by reasonable suspicion based on the information she received.[82] The court distinguished between a search conducted "with" the police present and "at the request (behest)" of law enforcement personnel. The *T.L.O.* standard applies in the former and a warrant requirement in the latter.

In a different type of case, the principal searched a student's hotel room for alcohol during a school-sponsored field trip. The district court applied the *T.L.O.* analysis but limited itself to *T.L.O.* as it applies to in-school searches. The federal appeals court found the *T.L.O.* standard relevant but went further and applied the *in loco parentis* doctrine as well and held the search to be reasonable.[83]

Thus school officials must be careful in following the guiding principles laid down by the Supreme Court in *New Jersey* v. *T.L.O.* and the *in loco parentis* doctrine, which may further complicate search and seizure cases, particularly on field trips. Some courts no longer apply the *in loco parentis* doctrine while others do, particularly in school-sponsored after-school activities. In such situations, courts are likely to give school authorities more leeway to search under suspicious circumstances.

Are Strip Searches Illegal?

Usually. There are important differences between searching lockers, which are school property, and searching students' clothes, which are not. Because clothing or body searches entail a greater invasion of privacy, courts have imposed high standards of protection against such searches. For example, a 17-year-old student was subjected to a body search when he was observed entering a bathroom with a fellow student twice within the same hour and leaving within a few seconds. For months he had been suspected of dealing in drugs. The search revealed illegal drugs, yet the Court of Appeals of New York excluded the evidence and ruled the search unconstitutional.[84] Though the court recognized the widespread use of drugs and the need to protect the school environment, it held that even these considerations did "not permit random, causeless searches" that might result in "psychological damage to sensitive children" and expose them to serious consequences, such as possible criminal convictions.

An extreme example is that of a school that conducted a strip search of an entire fifth-grade class over a report of $3 missing from a student's coat pocket. The search, which was conducted with boys and girls separated, was fruitless. The court considered the school's action excessive and thus illegal.[85]

As when other student rights are violated, courts may award money damages for illegal and unauthorized searches. For example, $7,500 in damages was awarded to a student in connection with a strip search a federal appeals court found to be illegal.[86] The Second Circuit Court of Appeals indicated that "reasonable suspicion" might suffice to search students' lockers, but for highly invasive searches, such as body or strip searches, a higher standard is required (i.e., "probable cause"). The distinction between these two standards is not entirely clear, but in law they are significantly different. "Probable cause" is also the standard used by law enforcement officials when they request a search warrant from a court.

The *Williams* Case[87]

The Sixth Circuit Court of Appeals, however, purportedly applying the *T.L.O.* standards, upheld a student strip search in 1991. The case involved Angela Lee Williams, an above-average 10th-grade student in Mayfield, Kentucky, active in extracurricular activities, whom no one considered a discipline problem. School officials learned from various students that Rush was being inhaled by some students in school, including Angela. Rush is a volatile substance purchasable over the counter; its possession is legal, but its inhalation is illegal under Kentucky law.

After several days of investigation, school officials searched Angela's locker, purse, and books in vain. Then the female principal, in her office and in the presence of a female secretary (consistent with school policy), had Angela empty her pockets and remove her T-shirt. She pulled on Angela's brassiere elastic to see if anything would fall out. The assistant principal then had Angela put her T-shirt on and drop her blue jeans to her knees. She looked for suspicious bulges and pulled on elastic waist and leg bands, although these facts are in contention. After Angela pulled up her jeans, she was asked to remove her shoes and socks. No drugs were found during the search.

Angela sued all the school officials and the board of education, claiming violations of her Fourth Amendment right to be free of unreasonable searches and seizures, defamation, battery, and intentional infliction of emotional stress. She also sued the board of education under 42 U.S.C.A. § 1983 for allowing the violation of her constitutional rights by its employees and agents. Both the district court and the court of appeals ruled in favor of the school's right to search, applying the criteria set forth in *T.L.O.* While *T.L.O.* did not directly address strip searches, these courts, invoking *T.L.O.* as their authority, concluded that the search was reasonable in light of all the circumstances and that its scope was not excessive. Addressing the question of intrusiveness, the district court even noted that the strip inspection of Angela avoided any necessity for touching and, even if there might have been some "incidental touching" in tugging on the elastic of the undergarments, this was no more intrusive than a "visual scrutiny of the intensity necessary to disclose the evidence she sought."

Other recent cases involving the strip search of students reached conflicting results. While there are states, such as Oklahoma, that by statute forbid student strip searches without a warrant, most cases are decided on the basis of federal and state constitutions. The *Williams* case used the less demanding "reasonable cause" criterion of *T.L.O.* and upheld the search, yet some commentators claim that the Sixth Circuit Court of Appeals focused on school safety issues rather than on students' rights.[88] When analyzing strip search cases, courts consider the object of the search important. Drugs or dangerous weapons are more likely to justify an intensive search than are allegations of lost or stolen money.

Similarly, the Seventh Circuit upheld the strip search of a 16-year-old boy, applying the *T.L.O.* test, balancing the privacy interest of students against the schools' need to maintain order and a drug-free environment.[89] Since the administrators had reason to suspect the student was "crotching" drugs, the court found the administrators' belief that a strip search was the least intrusive method of searching the student to be not unreasonable.

By contrast, the Supreme Court of Appeals of West Virginia declared unreasonable a warrantless strip search of a student, in whose underpants were found the missing $100 that he had taken from a teacher's purse.[90] The court contrasted the stealing of money to the presence of drugs and found that the stealing of money involved relatively slight danger to others and thus cannot justify a highly invasive search. (Therefore, in a criminal proceeding, the evidence was inadmissible.) A warrantless strip search in school might be justified, according to this court, only if necessary to ensure the safety of other students.

A missing $7 led to the strip search of two eight-year-old second-grade students in Alabama. The Eleventh Circuit Court of Appeals ruled in 1996 against the teachers who conducted the search, indicating that the *T.L.O* criteria do not justify such an intrusive search for a small amount of money[91] The court hypothesized a continuum: at one extreme placing dangerous weapons and drugs; in the middle, large amounts of money or valuables; and at the other extreme, small amounts of money, less valuable items, and "nondangerous contraband." The latter, according to the court, would never justify strip searches. The dissent argued that the teachers should have been granted qualified immunity because the law related to this type of search was not clear and certain at the time the controversy arose and thus they cannot be held personally liable. The majority of the circuit court voted to rehear this case *en banc* on the issue of immunity, and, upon rehearing *en banc,* granted qualified immunity to the teacher and counselor involved in the search because, at the time of the search, the law related to searches in school to locate allegedly stolen money was not clearly established.[92]

Since *T.L.O.* did not include a strip search, and since lower courts are rendering conflicting decisions, we must await a Supreme Court ruling before we have uniform law on the strip search of students in schools.

Other searches purporting to apply the *T.L.O.* standards may or may not be upheld depending on the circumstances. For example, a Texas case upheld a search that led to the discovery of marijuana on a student although the initial search was based on a report that he was carrying a weapon.[93] But a "hunch" alone will not support a search. This was the case in Illinois, where a student's flashlight was searched on a "hunch" that it might contain drugs. The court held this unreasonable under the circumstances.[94] In sum, the facts of each situation must be carefully scrutinized to determine whether they might lead a reasonable administrator to suspect that an illegal substance or weapon is being hidden by the student.

Is Age a Relevant Consideration in Strip Searches?

Age is generally considered a relevant factor in the intrusiveness of a search. This was recognized by the U.S. Supreme Court in *T.L.O.* and was elaborated by the federal appeals court in *Cornfield ex rel. Lewis* v. *Consolidated High School District No. 230.*[95] In *Cornfield,* the court explained that the ages of 7 and 14 are important transitional periods in a child's development. At common law, children under age 7 were considered to have no criminal capacity; over age 14, they were treated as having the same criminal capacity as adults; between ages of 7 and 14, they were presumed to be incapable of committing crimes, although this presumption was rebuttable.

Thus, the *Cornfield* court was concerned about the impact a search might have on the student; how likely it was that the student would engage independently in criminal activity; and whether the student had the mental capacity to consent to a strip search. In light of its analysis, the *Cornfield* court would not allow a strip search of students under age 7; over age 14 such a search would likely be upheld if otherwise warranted; and between ages 7 and 14 it might be allowed, but only with great circumspection.

Cornfield involved a 16-year-old high school student who was spotted by a teacher outside the school building in violation of school rules. The teacher also noted that the student appeared "too well-endowed" and suspected that he was "crotching" drugs. This observation—along with reports of suspicious smells by the bus driver, the student's prior comments about drug use, some student reports, and other evidence—led school officials to ask the student to change into his gym clothes in the locker room while they observed him. No drugs were found on him. The court, applying the *T.L.O.* test, found the search to be reasonable as well as the least intrusive method under the circumstances.

By contrast, a Texas district court struck down a school rule requiring urinalysis for drugs as a condition for participation in any extracurricular activities.[96] In this case, there was no evidence presented that participants in extracurricular activities were more likely to use drugs than nonparticipants, or that testing would deter drug use.

Although the Supreme Court in *Vernonia* ruled specifically on the *suspicionless* search of *student athletes* (see p. 256), the Eighth Circuit Court decided in 1996 that the *general* student population could be searched when the school official had reason to believe that one or more weapons were brought to school.[97] This case arose in Arkansas and the circuit court holding indicates that more latitude is given to school officials to carry out searches without individualized suspicion when dangerous contraband might be involved than the earlier Supreme Court ruling that seemed to apply only to student athletes.

Can a Coach Compel a High School Student to Take a Pregnancy Test?

Probably not. A 17-year-old Pennsylvania high school student, Leah Gruenke, showed a variety of symptoms that led her swim coach to suspect she was pregnant. The coach, the guidance counselor, and the school nurse each had individual meetings with Leah, who denied she was pregnant and refused to divulge any information. Several of her teammates and their mothers also recommended to Leah that she take a pregnancy test. Ultimately, she took four tests, the first one of which came back positive, the others, negative.

After the first positive test, the coach sought a medical opinion about the safety for Leah and her baby to remain on the swim team. According to the physician, there was no medical reason to keep Leah off the team. Soon thereafter, Leah and her mother learned from a doctor that she was six months pregnant. Leah claims that after the delivery of the baby, the coach refused to speak to her, removed her from swim meets, and encouraged her teammates to alienate her.

Leah and her mother filed suit in a federal court,[98] claiming an illegal search, a violation of familial privacy, violation of the right of privacy regarding personal matters, violation of her free speech and association rights, and violation of state tort laws. As defense, the coach asserted qualified immunity, claiming that the laws related to these issues were not so clearly established that he knew or should have known what they were. The appeals court ruled that the right to refuse to submit to the pregnancy test was clearly established even though the Supreme Court has never ruled on this specific issue. An official will not be liable if the action was a reasonable one; thus the court must balance the individual's expectation of privacy and the government's interest. Clearly, the student had a valid interest in her privacy and could not be compelled to take a pregnancy test absent a legitimate health concern. Some circumstances might justify such testing, but it can't be justified merely by the coach's curiosity. The coach lacked medical expertise; thus his conduct was unreasonable.

Since the appeals court determined that the law was clearly established, the coach could not claim qualified immunity as a defense. It held that the disclosure of medical information was a violation of privacy. Even if Leah was forced to take the test, the results had to be kept confidential. Discussing the test results with other coaches and parents and having other students administer the test also infringed on Leah's privacy. The court ruled against Leah's claim of infringement of familiar integrity since the school still has certain powers over students under the *in loco parentis* doctrine and found the law not clearly established over this issue.

Thus, school personnel should not compel or pressure students to undergo pregnancy testing in the absence of legitimate health concerns and, even then, only with the cooperation of the parents.

Can Schools Create "Zero Tolerance" Policies to Keep Weapons, Drugs, or Alcohol Away from Schools?

Yes, they can. In light of the proliferation of illegal drugs, weapons of various types, bomb threats, and other violence in schools, state legislatures and school boards enacted a variety of laws and school policies to make schools safe. These various efforts are generally referred to as "zero tolerance" laws or policies, for the very first violation will lead to suspension or expulsion. Each such law or policy must be examined to determine what is forbidden and what the consequences of the violation will be.

A high school student in Pennsylvania wrote a note stating: "There is a bomb in this school—Bang, Bang!!" He left the note on a table in art class. He was first suspended and later expelled for making "terroristic threats." He and his parents went to court, claiming a violation of his rights to procedural due process.[99]

The student claimed the note was a joke for two girls in art class and that he forgot to discard it after class. When he was confronted and questioned by the assistant principal and a police officer, they informed him that the threatening note was compared to his handwriting and he was given an opportunity to explain the circumstances. According to this 2001 ruling, this was all the due process required for a 10-day suspension. The lack of *Miranda* warnings did not violate the student's Fifth Amendment rights since those warnings are not required in school disciplinary proceedings.

In a case that arose in Ohio, a plastic toy gun was seen, partially concealed, under the front seat of a student's car. When asked to go to the principal's office, the student became belligerent, hostile, and made veiled threats. There was an informal hearing and a suspension appeal hearing with notices signed by the student's mother. An expulsion recommendation was made primarily for his belligerent behavior. In court, the student claimed a violation of his due process rights and that the handbook prohibition on look-alike guns was unconstitutionally vague and overbroad.

The court found the handbook provision "that a student shall not handle or transmit any object that can be reasonably considered a weapon" not overly broad or vague. The informal hearing and appeal process also satisfied both the Constitution and the state code.[100]

Can the Police Search School Lockers or Students without Search Warrants?

No. In general, the same legal principles apply to police behavior in and out of schools. Nevertheless, school officials often cooperate with the police in warrantless searches. The question becomes whether evidence so gathered may be used in criminal proceedings against students.

The U.S. Supreme Court developed the *exclusionary rule,* whereby illegally obtained evidence may not be used in court. Cases have raised the question whether evidence obtained in locker searches through the cooperation of police and school officials falls within the exclusionary rule. So far, courts are divided on this question, with some courts excluding such evidence and others allowing it if school officials had at least reasonable suspicion concerning the student's locker.

An unusual case arose when police and school officials, with the aid of specially trained dogs, planned and conducted a search in the junior and senior high schools of Highland, Indiana. On a predetermined day, students were kept in their first-period classes for two and a half hours while a team of handlers led the dogs on a room-to-room inspection tour. Particular students singled out by the dogs were asked to empty their pockets and purses, and some of them were strip searched in the nurse's office. With this dragnet, 17 students were caught with illegal drugs. Of these, 12 withdrew from school voluntarily, 2 were suspended, and 3 were expelled. Five sets of parents whose children were strip searched went to court, though four of them withdrew before trial.

In the final analysis, the U.S. district court ruled that the strip searches were illegal, violating the Fourth Amendment right against unreasonable search and seizure.[101] The court did not consider a dog alert to be a reasonable suspicion sufficient to warrant a strip search. On the other hand, it saw nothing wrong with the use of dogs and with asking suspected students to empty their pockets or purses. The court ruled on the *in loco parentis* doctrine to uphold the action of the administrators and the school board in using the canine units in this way if the school officials felt they had reasonable suspicion of drug violations. On appeal, the Seventh Circuit Court of Appeals upheld the right of school officials to use dogs in an exploratory sniffing of students.[102] There were strong dissenting opinions in this case, followed by widespread criticism when the court ruled that the sniffing of students was not a "search." One important aspect of this case was a prior agreement between school officials and the police that illegal materials discovered during the search would not be used in any criminal investigations or proceedings.

Doberman pinschers and German shepherds were used in a drug-detection program involving the Goosecreek School District in Texas. The dogs, with the aid of trainers, sniffed students, lockers, and cars for the presence of drugs they were trained to recognize. The search yielded only a bottle of perfume, but some students filed suit, claiming that their right to be free from unreasonable searches had been violated. The federal appeals court held in *Horton* v. *Goosecreek Independent School District* that the use of trained dogs to sniff *objects,* such as cars or lockers, is not a search.[103] When objects and their odors occupy public space, a "public smell" is analogous to seeing something in "plain view." A dog's alerting its handler to a locker or car might be grounds for reasonable suspicion and thus enable school officials to check for contraband. The court, however, reached a different conclusion regarding the search of persons. Since a personal search is a more intrusive invasion of privacy, the court held that using dogs to sniff students was a search and that, before a body search could be conducted, school officials would have to have reasonable cause to believe that a *particular* student possessed drugs or other forbidden substances.

In *Goosecreek,* the Fifth Circuit Court rejected the reasoning of the Seventh Circuit Court, which saw nothing objectionable in the use of dogs to sniff students and did not consider it a search. Although the full Supreme Court has not yet decided a case involving the use of dogs to search students, Justice Brennan expressed a clear and strong personal view when he said, "I cannot agree that the...school officials' use of the trained police dogs did not constitute a search."[104]

Can Schools Conduct a General Search of All Students with the Aid of Metal Detectors?

Yes, if there has been a high rate of violence in the local schools, if the search is part of a plan to ensure student safety, and if the search is conducted in a uniform manner. So ruled the Superior Court of Pennsylvania in 1995, where the search revealed a Swiss-type folding knife in the possession of a youth on probation for a prior adjudication of delinquency.[105]

When the student wanted the evidence suppressed because there was no individualized suspicion for the search, the court relied on *T.L.O.* as a precedent. The U.S. Supreme Court in *T.L.O.* noted that "...the Fourth Amendment imposes no irreducible requirement of individualized suspicion." It concluded that various cases permitted administrative searches without individualized suspicion, "when the searches are conducted as a general regulatory scheme to ensure the public safety, rather than as part of a criminal investigation to secure evidence of a crime." This type of school search is similar to airport searches or courthouse security measures. On balance, the student's privacy interest is far outweighed by the security of the rest of the school and the student group.

Can a School System Require School Bus Drivers to Submit to a Routine Urine Test for Drugs?

Yes, if doing so is reasonable under the circumstances ruled a U.S. appeals court in the District of Columbia.[106] In this case, the school system instituted a routine, mandatory drug-testing policy for employees in the Transportation Branch. The program was instituted because of evidence of widespread drug use by employees whose main duty was the daily transportation of handicapped children to and from school. The court examined the program when it was challenged by an employee who was discharged when she tested positive for drug use. Applying the *T.L.O.* test, the court balanced the individual's expectancy of privacy against the reasonableness of the governmental action attempting to protect a public interest. On balance, the court upheld the requirement, since the system had a serious safety concern in the transportation of the students; the intrusion on employees' privacy was minimal because the drug testing was conducted as part of a routine, reasonable, annual medical examination; and the school system agreed to test its employees only in a manner that would validly detect the type of drug abuse with which it was legitimately concerned.

May Students Be Given a Urine Test to Detect or Prevent Drug Abuse?

As a general rule, no, but special circumstances may justify urine tests. Since schools seldom use such tests, there are few reported cases. One state court struck down a required yearly urine test as a violation of students' reasonable expectations of privacy.[107] On the other hand, the U.S. Supreme Court in *Vernonia School District* v. *Acton* upheld the policy of an Oregon school district prescribing a random urine-testing program as a requirement for participation in interscholastic athletics.[108] Testimony at the trial indicated that there was a significant rise in disciplinary problems in the school, much of it involving students who participated in interscholastic athletics. The disciplinary problems "had reached 'epidemic proportions'…fueled by alcohol and drug abuse as well as by the students' misperceptions about the drug culture."[109]

The drug-testing program was limited in scope, carefully carried out to protect privacy as much as possible, and the results were available only to the relevant administrators. Justice Scalia, writing for the majority, applied the balancing test and concluded that the compelling interest of the state in having a drug-free school environment and the safety of the students, particularly of the athletes, outweighed the very limited invasion of their privacy. While he recognized the students' right to privacy, Justice Scalia noted that "with regard to medical examinations and procedures…'students within the school environment have a lesser expectation of privacy than members of the population generally.'" Furthermore, privacy expectations are even less for student athletes. As one example, he cited that in locker rooms "an element of 'communal undress' [is] inherent in athletic participation."

While the Court upheld the urinalysis as a reasonable search under the circumstances, it made clear that such random searches must be justified by a compelling state interest and the facts of the particular situation.

Justices O'Connor, Stevens, and Souter dissented and argued that individualized suspicion should be required to justify such an intrusive search as urinalysis and that blanket or random searches have always been considered intolerable and unreasonable "under our Constitution."

Suspicionless Drug Testing

School boards have interpreted *Vernonia* in various ways. For example, the Anderson Community School Corporation passed a policy that required all students suspended for three or more days for fighting to take a drug test. Refusal to take the test would lead to further suspension or even expulsion. The school board reasoned that students who were fighting were likely to be substance abusers.

When James Willis refused to take the test after his suspension and received a second suspension, he filed suit. The district court upheld the policy as a reasonable one based on studies that showed a connection between substance abuse and violent behavior. The court of appeals, however, ruled otherwise, holding that the causal connection revealed by the studies was not strong enough and that the use of illegal substances might be manifested in various behaviors other than fighting. It distinguished this case from *Vernonia*, which involved student athletes who have lesser expectation of privacy than students in general.[110]

The same appeals court earlier upheld the *suspicionless* drug search (a random, unannounced urinalysis) of students before they could participate in any extracurricular programs or before they would be permitted to drive to or from school.[111] The district policy was developed after surveys disclosed drug and alcohol use by students to be higher than the state average. Positive results would not lead to disciplinary action, but to referral for drug counseling. Relying on *Vernonia*, the court ruled that "[we] find that the reasoning compelling drug testing of athletes also applies to testing students involved in extracurricular activities. Certainly, successful extracurricular activities require healthy students."

Although it is clear that athletes are used to less privacy than students participating in such extracurricular activities as the library club or chess club, nonetheless the appeals court used *Vernonia* as a precedent for ruling in this case, and the Supreme Court refused to review it.

In light of conflicting rulings on suspicionless urinalysis drug testing of public school students, the Supreme Court accepted a case for review. The Tenth Circuit Court of Appeals struck down as unconstitutional a school board policy requiring students who voluntarily wished to participate in nonathletic extracurricular activities to submit to random, suspicionless urinalysis drug testing.[112] There was no evidence of widespread drug use among the students in general or among students who participated in extracurricular activities. However, the Supreme Court, in a 5–4 decision, written by Justice Thomas, upheld the suspicionless search in *Board of Education* v. *Earls,* for all students engaged in extracurricular activities (*New York Times,* June 28, 2002).

Can Schools Forbid the Bringing of Weapons to School?

Yes, schools can forbid students from bringing knives, firearms, or other dangerous weapons to the campus. Furthermore, within reason, school officials may define what constitutes a weapon.

The Supreme Judicial Court of Massachusetts faced this issue in 1995 when a ninth-grade student brought to school a lipstick case containing a 1¼-inch pointed blade.[113] Pursuant to a state law, the Worcester School Committee adopted a policy on the possession or use of weapons that stated that any student found at a school or school-related event with a dangerous weapon may be expelled by the principal "…regardless of the size of the knife." Furthermore, the policy indicated that for its purposes "…a dangerous 'weapon' includes but is not limited to, a gun, knife (or other specified items)."

At the disciplinary hearing, evidence showed that the student had attempted to commit suicide three times, she had many unexcused absences, she was thought to be the victim of child abuse at home, and she had run away from home at least once. These facts led the principal to conclude that in his opinion, she was a threat to the safety of other students and school staff. All of the students were informed of the no-weapons rule through their handbooks and posters displayed around the school. Thus, the principal believed that the student had knowingly violated the weapons rule. When she was expelled for a year, she went to court.

The courts of Massachusetts ultimately upheld the expulsion because the laws of the state and the policy of the school committee empowered the principal to act as he did. In fact, explained the court, when the principal was convinced that the student might be a threat to others in the school, he no longer had any discretion but was compelled to expel her.

Widespread concern over school violence and weapons being brought to school led Congress to enact the Gun-Free School Zone Act of 1990.[114] However, the U.S. Supreme Court declared this law unconstitutional in 1995, in a 5–4 decision.[115] The Court ruled that the act was unconstitutional because it was an invalid exercise of federal authority under the commerce clause to control weapons on or near public school grounds. Under the U.S. Constitution, this matter should be handled by the states. While the 1990 act was being challenged in the courts, Congress enacted the Gun-Free School Act of 1994.[116] Under this act, schools that receive federal funds must have a written policy to expel for at least one year any student who brings a weapon to school. The superintendent, however, has the discretion to "modify such expulsion requirement…on a case by case basis."

Consistent with this view, most states have laws making it a crime to bring firearms to school and for minors to possess firearms, and empower school officials to exclude students whose presence constitutes a danger to other students or to school personnel.[117]

Concerned with the increasing presence of firearms in the schools, a Florida school district adopted a policy authorizing random hand-held metal detector searches of high school students. Students were informed that the searches would be conducted by an independent security firm. The search team would visit the school unannounced and select a classroom at random. The students would be segregated by gender and scanned in the presence of an administrator. If the metal detector so indicated, the student would be patted down. When a dangerous weapon was found, the campus police officer would arrest the student.

A gun was found on the defendant in a search pursuant the school policy. In the juvenile court proceedings that followed, he wanted to exclude the evidence, claiming the search was unlawful because it was a police search and it was not based on reasonable suspicion. While the trial court agreed with the student, the appeals court upheld the search, finding it reasonable for *school searches.* It applied a balancing test used by the U.S. Supreme Court in *Vernonia* and held that the school's interest in maintaining a safe learning environment outweighed the student's legitimate expectation of privacy.[118]

Courts give school administrators wide leeway to search when safety of students is concerned. For example, a federal district court upheld a warrantless "pat-down" search of sixth-grade students when a 13½-inch pizza knife was missing from the cafeteria. Students were first asked to come forward if they knew where the knife might be. When no one responded, officials conducted a pat-down search; males searched the boys and females the girls. (The knife was discovered in an empty pizza box in a dumpster behind the cafeteria.)

The search was simple, unobtrusive, and by officials of the same gender as the students. Since the safety of the students was urgent and compelling, the court held the simple search reasonable under the circumstances.[119]

In an interesting case from Alabama, a high school student was suspended and then placed in the long-term alternative school when an air rifle was found in plain view inside his locked car in the school parking lot.[120] The Code of Student Conduct called for disciplinary action for the "possession of any item which may be conceivably used as a weapon on a person or in a person's clothing, vehicle, possessions, locker, or items carried by that person."

Upon the principal's recommendation, the board of education placed the student in the long-term alternative school as punishment for violating the code. When he appealed the ruling to the juvenile court, the court ruled the code provision unconstitutional because it was too broad, vague, and ambiguous. Under its vague language, "one may conceive …that a sharpened pencil, a set of chemistry supplies, a baseball bat, and a tennis racket, for example, could be used as weapons." The state appeals court agreed. Furthermore, the student's due process rights were also violated when the board accepted the principal's recommendation without reaching an independent judgment pursuant to a hearing.

Thus, it is clear that school policies and rules related to weapons, just as other school rules, cannot be unreasonably broad, vague, or ambiguous.

Summary

This chapter presents the major dimensions of due process rights of teachers and students. It is clear that laws or policies that are arbitrary, capricious, unreasonable, or overly vague violate the due process clause of the Fourteenth Amendment. Lawyers and courts refer to these as "violations of substantive due process." There are also "procedural due process" rights based on the same amendment, which prohibits states from depriving anyone of "life, liberty or property' without fair procedures.

Tenured teachers have a "property' interest in their continuing contract, and any attempts to suspend or dismiss them must be carried out with full observance of fair procedures. Statutes usually specify the steps that are part of such procedures, and these must be meticulously followed. Although all teachers have a right to due process if they are dismissed *during* the term of their contract, probationary teachers do not have a property right in continuous employment; therefore, if their employment is not renewed, they may not claim the constitutional right to due process. Nevertheless, if the announced grounds for the nonrenewal are stigmatizing, if their reputation is damaged and thus their opportunities for further employment are diminished, due process must be observed so that the stigmatizing charges can be challenged. Probationary teachers also have a right to due process if the grounds for nonrenewal were constitutionally protected activities (e.g., controversial speech or unionizing activity).

If a teacher has a constitutional right to due process, the administrative hearing before the board must be orderly and fair, but it need not be formal and technical. Elements of a fair procedure include a written notice of the charges; a hearing before an impartial tribunal; an opportunity to present evidence and cross-examine witnesses; a right to representation; a written statement of the findings, conclusions, and recommendations; and the right to appeal. In addition to the constitutional right to due process, many states provide some due process by state law. Such laws must be followed scrupulously by school boards, and courts will enforce them strictly.

The U.S. Supreme Court has ruled that the right to due process applies also to students, since a suspension or expulsion affects their property or liberty interests, protected by the Fourteenth Amendment. The Court has ruled that even a short suspension requires some modicum of due process. But the courts do not want to turn schools into courtrooms, and they recognize the need for administrative authority and discretion. Therefore, a brief, informal process usually satisfies the law in cases where the punishment might be a short suspension. More serious infractions, ones that are likely to lead to long-term suspensions, entries in school records, or expulsions, require more meticulous due process. While no fixed formula for such process exists, it should include a written notice specifying the charges; a hearing at which the student should have an opportunity to respond to the charges, present evidence, cross-examine witnesses, and be represented by his or her parents or by counsel; a fair tribunal; a written statement of the findings and conclusions; and the right to appeal. A student who constitutes a danger to people or property may be removed from school immediately as long as due process procedures follow such removal as soon as practicable.

As a general rule, school discipline is a matter within the discretion of school authorities and local school boards. The practice of corporal punishment in public schools has been challenged. Twenty-seven states and the District of Columbia clearly prohibit corporal punishment. In addition, many school districts prohibit it through local policy. In states or school districts that allow corporal punishment, courts have upheld the legality of *reasonable* use of corporal punishment. Excessive brutal punishment is nowhere sanctioned by the law; if it is used, educators may be sued for money damages as well as be prosecuted for assault and battery. But even excessive punishment does not constitute "cruel and unusual punishment" under the Constitution, for the Supreme Court has ruled that the Eighth Amendment was intended to apply to "closed" institutions, like prisons, and not to schools. Two appeals courts ruled, however, that excessive corporal punishment may be a violation of substantive due process, protected by the Fourteenth Amendment.

School lockers may be searched by appropriate school officials if they have reasonable suspicion that unlawful or dangerous materials are hidden there. Similarly, the Supreme Court held that students' purses may be searched. The search of students' clothing, and "strip searches," are more invasive and therefore merit greater protection. While the Supreme Court has not ruled on such cases, and while lower courts are divided on the issue of strip searches, most lower courts indicate that a standard akin to "probable cause" must be used by educators, which means that they must have evidence from highly reliable sources that a particular student is hiding illegal or dangerous materials. As a general rule, the police need a search warrant before they can conduct locker searches in schools. Evidence gathered in warrantless searches, or without the student's consent, is excluded by some courts but allowed by others on the theory that school administrators may consent on behalf of the students. Many courts are concerned that such collaboration between administrators and the police undermines the relationship between administrators and students.

Trained dogs may be used to search lockers or cars, but students may be sniffed by search dogs only when there are reasonable grounds to suspect particular students. If a dog's reliability has been established, lockers and cars may be searched when the dog alerts a handler to them. However, a dog's alert is not sufficient to warrant a strip search of a student.

One appeals court has upheld a random urine analysis requirement for teachers. Also, at least one federal appeals court has upheld mandatory urine testing for drugs for employees involved in pupil transportation, when there was strong evidence of widespread drug use among such workers. The Supreme Court has upheld the random search or urinalysis of members of student athletic teams, even without individualized suspicion, when special circumstances indicate widespread drug use among athletes. In addition, at least one circuit court upheld such searches as a condition to participate in extracurricular activities and to drive to and from schools.

NOTES

1. *Wieman* v. *Updegraff*, 344 U.S. 183 (1952).

2. Courts and lawyers often distinguish *substantive* and *procedural* due process. Actions that are arbitrary, unreasonable, discriminatory, or based on vague rules are said to violate substantive due process; unfair procedures violate procedural due process. For most educators, such distinctions become needlessly technical.

3. *Wieman* v. *Updegraff, Id.*

4. *Board of Regents* v. *Roth*, 408 U.S. 564 (1972).

5. Although Roth was a college professor, the legal principles of this case apply equally to public elementary and secondary schools.

6. *Lombard* v. *Board of Education of City of New York*, 502 F.2d 631 (2d Cir. 1974); *Huntley* v. *North Carolina State Board of Education*, 493 F.2d 1016 (4th Cir. 1974); *McGhee* v. *Draper*, 564 F.2d 903 (10th Cir. 1977); *Perry* v. *Sindermann*, 408 U.S. 593 (1972).

7. *Hill* v. *Silsbee Independent School District, 933* F.Supp. 616 (E.D. Tex. 1996).

8. *Chandler* v. *Board of Educ. of City of Chicago, 92* F.Supp.2d. 760 (N.D.Ill. 2000).

9. *Winegar* v. *Des Moines Independent Community School District, 20* F.3d 895 (8th Cir. 1994).

10. *Gorden* v. *Nicoletti, 84* F.Supp.2d 304 (D.Conn. 2000).

11. *Slochower* v. *Board of Higher Education, 350* U.S. 551 (1956).

12. *Wieman* v. *Updegraff, 344* U.S. 183 (1952).

13. *Greminger* v. *Seaborne, 584* F.2d 275 (8th Cir. 1978).

14. *Miller* v. *Board of Education of the County of Lincoln, 450* F.Supp. 106 (S.D. W.Va. 1978).

15. *Mt. Healthy City School District Board of Education* v. *Doyle, 429* U.S. 274 (1977).

16. *Foreman* v. *Vermilion Parish School Board, 353* So.2d 471 (La. Ct. App. 1977).

17. *Guerra* v. *Roma Independent School District, 444* F.Supp. 812 (S.D. Tex. 1977).

18. *Roberts* v. *Lincoln County School District No. 1, 676* P.2d 577 (Wyo. 1984).

19. *Hortonville District Association* v. *Hortonville Education Association, 426* U.S. 482 (1976).

20. *Adams* v. *Professional Practices Commission, 524* P.2d 932 (Okla. 1974).

21. *Syquia* v. *Board of Education, 579* N.Y.S.2d 487 (App. Div. 1992).

22. *State ex rel. Curry* v. *Grand Valley Local Schools Board of Education, 375* N.E.2d 48 (Ohio 1978).

23. *Johnson* v. *Selma Board of Education, 356* So.2d 649 (Ala. 1978).

24. *Rafael* v. *Meramec Valley R-III Board of Education, 591* S.W.2d 309 (Mo. Ct. App. 1978).

25. *Cleveland Board of Education* v. *Loudermill—Parma Board of Education, 470* U.S. 532 (1985).

26. *Santiago deCastro* v. *Morales Medina, 943* F.2d 129 (1st Cir. 1991).

27. *Georgia Association of Educators* v. *Harris, 749* F.Supp. 1110 (N.D. Ga. 1990). The district court relied on *National Treasury* v. *Von Raab, 490* U.S. 656 (1989).

28. *Knox County Education Association* v. *Knox County Board of Education, 158* F.3d 361 (6th Cir. 1998).

29. *National Treasury Employees Union* v. *Von Raab, 489* U.S. 656 (1989).

30. *Hearn* v. *Savannah Bd. of Educ., 191* F.3d 1329 (11th Cir. 1999).

31. *Board of Education of County of Gilmer* v. *Chaddock, 398* S.E.2d 120 (W.Va. 1990).

32. *Jager* v. *Ramona Board of Education, 444* N.W.2d 21 (S.D. 1989).

33. *Rankin* v. *Independent School District No. 1–3, 876* F.2d 838 (10th Cir. 1989).

34. 419 U.S. 565 (1975).

35. *Dixon* v. *Alabama State Board of Education, 294* F.2d 150 (5th Cir. 1961).

36. *DeJesus* v. *Penberthy, 344* F.Supp. 70 (D. Conn. 1972).

37. *Smith* v. *Miller, 514* P.2d 377 (Kan. 1973).

38. *Tibbs* v. *Board of Education of Township of Franklin, 284* A.2d 179 (N.J. 1971).

39. *L.Q.A. by and Through Arrington* v. *Eberhart, 920* F.Supp. 1208 (M.D. Ala. 1996).

40. *Newsome* v. *Batavia Local School District, 842* F.2d 920 (6th Cir. 1988).

41. *Racine Unified School District* v. *Thompson, 321* N.W.2d 334 (Wis. Ct. App. 1982).

42. *Goldwyn* v. *Allen, 281* N.Y.S.2d 899 (Sup. Ct. 1967).

43. *Gabrilowitz* v. *Newman, 582* F.2d 100 (1st Cir. 1978).

44. 377 U.S. 201 (1966).

45. *Pollnow* v. *Glennon, 594* F.Supp. 220 (S.D. N.Y. 1984).

46. In the Interest of R.H. 791 A.2d 331 (Pa. 2002).

47. *Boynton* v. *Casey, 543* F.Supp. 995 (D. Me. 1982).

48. *Hardy* v. *University Interscholastic League, 759* F.2d 1233 (5th Cir. 1985).

49. *Zehner,* v. *Central Berkshire Regional School District, 921* F. Supp. 850 (D. Mass. 1996).

50. *Darby* v. *School Superintendent, 544* F.Supp. 428 (W.D. Mich. 1982).

51. *Myers* v. *Arcata Union High School District, 75* Cal. Rptr. 68 (1969).

52. *Sullivan* v. *Houston Independent School District, 333* F.Supp. 1149 (S.D. Tex. 1971).

53. *James P.* v. *Lemahieu, 84* F.Supp.2d 1113 (D. Hawaii 2000).

54. *Corporal Punishment Fact Sheet* (Columbus, OH: National Coalition to Abolish Corporal Punishment in Schools, 2000).

55. *Fredrickson* v. *Denver Public School District No. 1, 819* P.2d 1068 (Colo. Ct. App. 1991).

56. *Ingraham* v. *Wright, 430* U.S. 651 (1977).

57. *Commonwealth of Pennsylvania* v. *Douglass, 588* A.2d 53 (Pa. Super. Ct. 1991).

58. *Burton* v. *Kirby,* 775 S.W.2d 834 (Tex. Civ. App. 1989).
59. *Tomczik* v. *State Tenure Comm'n,* 438 N.W.2d 642 (Mich. Ct. App. 1989).
60. *Landi* v. *West Chester Area Sch. Dist.,* 343 A.2d 895 (Pa. Commw. Ct. 1976).
61. *Spacek* v. *Charles,* 928 SW.2d 88 (Tex. Ct. App. 1996).
62. *P.B.* v. *Koch,* 96 F.3d 1298 (9th Cir. 1996).
63. *Harris* v. *Tate County School District,* 882 F.Supp. 90 (N.D. Miss. 1995).
64. *Faye Elizabeth Hall et al.* v. *G. Garrison Tawney et al.,* 621 F.2d 607 (4th Cir. 1980).
65. *Garcia* v. *Miera,* 817 F.2d 650 (10th Cir. 1987).
66. *Doe* v. *Taylor Independent School District,* 975 F.2d 137 (5th Cir. 1992).
67. *Baker* v. *Owen,* 395 F.Supp. 294 (M.D. N.C. 1975).
68. *Wingfield* v. *Fort Bend Independent School District,* No. 72-H-232 (D.C. S.D. Tex. 1973).
69. *Howard* v. *Clark,* 299 N.Y.S.2d 65 (N.Y. Sup. Ct. 1969).
70. *Fremont Union High School District* v. *Santa Clara County Board of Education,* 286 Cal. Rptr. 915 (Ct. App. 1991).
71. *Carlino* v. *Gloucester City High Sch.,* 57 F.Supp.2d 1 (D.N.J. 1999).
72. *New Braunfels Independent School District* v. *Armke,* 658 SW.2d 330 (Tex. Ct. App. 1983).
73. *Katzman* v. *Cumberland Valley School District,* 479 A.2d 671 (Pa. Commw. Ct. 1984).
74. *State ex rel. Yarber* v. *McHenry,* 915 S.W.2d 325 (Mo. 1995).
75. *Spring Branch I.S.D.* v. *Stamos,* 695 S.W.2d 556 (Tex. 1985).
76. *People* v. *Overton,* 249 N.E.2d 366 (N.Y. 1969).
77. *New Jersey* v. *T.L.O.,* 469 U.S.325 (1985).
78. *Shamberg* v. *State of Alaska,* 762 P.2d 488 (Alaska Ct. App. 1988).
79. *In re Guy Dumas, a Minor,* 515 A.2d 984 (Pa. Super. Ct. 1986).
80. *Cales* v. *Howell Public Schools,* 635 F.Supp. 454 (E.D. Mich. 1985).
81. *State* v. *Brooks,* 718 P.2d 837 (Wash. 1986); *R.D.L.* v. *State,* 499 So.2d 31 (Fla. Dist. Ct. App. 1986).
82. *Cason* v. *Cook,* 810 F.2d 188 (8th Cir. 1987).
83. *Webb* v. *McCullough,* 828 F.2d 1151 (6th Cir. 1987).
84. *People* v. *Scott,* 358 N.Y.S.2d 403 (1974).
85. *Bellnier* v. *Lund,* 438 F.Supp.47 (N.D. N.Y. 1977).
86. *M.M.* v. *Anker,* 607 F.2d 588 (2d Cir. 1979).
87. *Williams by Williams* v. *Ellington,* 936 F.2d 881 (6th Cir. 1991).
88. Lawrence F. Rossow and Brenda L. Stubblefield, *Student Strip Search Upheld:* Williams by Williams v. Ellington, 75 EDUCA. L. REP. 723–731 (1992).
89. *Cornfield* v. *Consolidated High School District No. 230,* 991 F.2d 1316 (7th Cir. 1993).
90. *State ex rel. Galford* v. *Mark Anthony B.,* 433 S.E.2d 41 (W.Va. 1993).
91. *Jenkins by Hall* v. *Talladega City Board of Education,* 95 F.3d 1036 (11th Cir. 1996).
92. Affirmed on appeal, *Jenkins by Hall* v. *Tallageda City Board of Education,* 115 F.3d 821 (11th Cir. 1997).
93. *Wilcher* v. *State,* 876 S.W.2d 466 (Tex. Ct. App. 1994).
94. *People* v. *Dilworth,* 640 N.E. 2d 1009 (Ill. App. Ct. 1994).
95. *Cornfield* v. *Consolidated High School District No. 230,* 991F.2d 1316 (7th Cir. 1993).
96. *Brooks* v. *East Chambers Consolidated Independent School District,* 730 F.Supp. 759 (S.D. Tex. 1989).
97. *Thompson* v. *Carthage School District,* 87 F.3d 979 (8th Cir. 1996).
98. *Gruenke* v. *Seip,* 225 F.3d 290 (3rd Cir. 2000).
99. *Arthur A. ex rel. Brian A.* v. *Stroudsburg Area Sch. Dist.,* 141 F.Supp.2d 502 (M.D.Pa. 2001).
100. *Turner* v. *South-Western City Sch. Dist.,* 92 F.Supp.2s 757 (S.D.Ohio 1999).
101. *Doe* v. *Renfrow, Superintendent of Highland Town District,* 475 F.Supp. 1012 (N.D. Ind. 1979).
102. *Doe* v. *Renfrow,* 631 F.2d 91 (7th Cir. 1980), *cert. denied,* 451 U.S. 1022 (1981).
103. *Horton* v. *Goose Creek Independent School District,* 690 F.2d 470 (5th Cir. 1982), *cert. denied,* 463 U.S. 1207 (1983).
104. *Doe* v. *Renfrow,* 451 U.S. at 1028 (1981).
105. *In re F.B.,* 658 A.2d 1378 (Pa. Super. Ct. 1995); see also *Commonwealth of Pennsylvania* v. *Heron,* 680 A.2d 1176 (Pa. Super. Ct. 1996).

106. *Jones* v. *McKenzie*, 833 F.2d 335 (D.C. Cir. 1987).

107. *Odenheim* v. *Carlestadt-East Rutherford Regional School District,* 510 A.2d 709 (N.J. Super. Ct. Ch. Div. 1985).

108. *Vernonia School District 47J* v. *Acton,* 515 U.S. 646 (1995).

109. *Id.,* at 2395.

110. *Willis* v. *Anderson Community School Corp.,* 158 F.3d 415 (7th Cir. 1998).

111. *Todd* v. *Rush County Schools,* 139 F.3d 571 (7th Cir. 1998).

112. *Earls* v. *Board of Educ. of Indep. Sch. Dist. No. 92,* 242 F.3d 1264 (10th Cir. 2001).

113. *Doe* v. *Superintendent of Schools of Worcester,* 421 Mass. 117, 653 N.E.2d 1088 (1995).

114. 18 U.S.C. § 922 q(1)(A).

115. *United States* v. *Lopez,* 514 U.S. 549 (1995).

116. 20 U.S.C. § 3351.

117. See, e.g., MASS. GEN. L. ch. 71-37H (1994); VA. CODE ANN. § 18.2 (Michie 1994).

118. *State* v. *J.A.,* 679 So.2d 316 (Fla. Dist. Ct. App. 1996).

119. *Brousseau* v. *Town of Westerly,* 11 F.Supp.2d 177 (D.R.I. 1998).

120. *Dothan City Board of Education* v. *V.M.H.,* 660 So.2d 1328 (Ala. Civ. App. 1995).

13 How Free Is My Personal Life?

Overview

In the past, schools severely restricted many aspects of a teacher's personal life. The following excerpt from a teacher's contract illustrates some of the extraordinary restrictions in the 1920s.

> I promise to abstain from all dancing, immodest dressing, and any other conduct unbecoming a teacher and a lady.
>
> I promise not to go out with any young men except in so far as it may be necessary to stimulate Sunday school work.
>
> I promise not to fall in love, to become engaged or secretly married.
>
> I promise to sleep at least eight hours a night [and] to eat carefully...in order that I may be better able to render efficient service to my pupils.[1]

Even in the 1950s and 1960s, teachers who violated their community's moral standards usually resigned or were quickly dismissed. Few educators doubted that teachers could be fired for adultery, drunkenness, homosexual conduct, illegal drug use, committing a felony, or becoming pregnant while single. In recent years, however, community consensus about what constitutes immoral conduct has broken down. The concept of morality seems to vary according to time and place. As the California Supreme Court observed: "Today's morals may be tomorrow's ancient and absurd customs." Moreover, many educators believe that their personal behavior away from school is their own business and should be protected by their right to privacy. Yet many administrators argue that educators teach by example and thus should be adult role models for their students, conforming to the moral standards of the community. This chapter examines how courts have resolved this conflict between teacher freedom and community control. It focuses on three questions: What constitutes immoral or unprofessional conduct for teachers? When can teachers be punished for such behavior? Can schools concern themselves with other aspects of a teacher's personal life, such as age, weight, residency, or citizenship? Since the answers are often determined by state statutes and district policies that reflect changing social norms, the law on this topic may vary from state to state.

"Immoral" and "Unprofessional" Conduct

The *Morrison* Case[2]

In 1969, the California Supreme Court rejected the notion that teachers can automatically be dismissed for immoral behavior. The case involved Marc Morrison, who engaged in a brief homosexual relationship with another teacher. About a year later, the other teacher reported the incident to Morrison's superintendent. This disclosure led the board of education to revoke Morrison's teaching credentials on the grounds of immoral and unprofessional conduct. The board defended its action by saying that teachers should be models of good conduct, that state law requires teachers to impress on their pupils "principles of morality," that homosexual behavior is contrary to the moral standards of the people of California, and that the board of education is required to revoke a teacher's credentials for immoral conduct.

Despite these arguments, the California Supreme Court ruled in favor of Morrison. The court explained that it was dangerous to allow the terms "immoral" and "unprofessional" to be interpreted broadly. To many people, "immoral conduct" includes laziness, gluttony, selfishness, and cowardice. To others, "unprofessional conduct" for teachers includes signing controversial petitions, opposing majority opinions, and drinking alcoholic beverages. Therefore, unless these terms are defined carefully and narrowly, they could be applied to most teachers in the state. Furthermore, the court ruled that the board should not be able to dismiss an educator merely because it disapproved of his personal, private conduct unless the conduct is clearly related to his professional work. According to the court, when a teacher's job is not affected, his private behavior is his own business and should not be a basis for discipline.

But how can a board determine whether a teacher's behavior affects his or her job in such a way that he or she is unfit to teach? In making this decision, the court suggested that the board consider all the circumstances. Here there was no evidence that Morrison's conduct affected his teaching. There was no evidence that he "even considered any improper relationship with any student," that he "failed to teach the principles of morality," or that the single homosexual incident "affected his relationship with his co-workers." Therefore the court ruled against the board and concluded: "An individual can be removed from the teaching profession only upon a showing that his retention in the profession poses a significant danger of harm to either students, school employees, or others who might be affected by his actions as a teacher."

Morrison marked a change in the way many courts considered questions of teachers' "immoral" conduct. In the past, the fact that a teacher engaged in behavior a community considered immoral would have been enough to support the teacher's dismissal. After *Morrison,* other courts began to rule that teachers could not be dismissed simply because of such conduct unless there was evidence of a "nexus," or connection, between the conduct and the teacher's effectiveness. For example, in a 1996 Alabama case, several teachers challenged the state code that allows for the revocation of certificates for teachers who have been "guilty of immoral conduct." According to the judge, while these words may have had

> concrete meanings in simpler times, this court has serious doubts as to whether these terms currently provide fair warning as to the proscribed conduct.... There are simply too many good faith moral debates in our diverse multicultural society at this time to allow totally

subjective judgments about the meaning of the term "immoral conduct" to control the livelihood of our educators.[3]

Rather than declare the state law unconstitutionally vague, the court narrowed its construction to "cure its constitutional ill." Thus, as many courts have done since *Morrison,* the judge limited the statute so that a teacher's certificate can be revoked for immoral conduct only where there is a direct connection between the misconduct and the teacher's work.

When is the nexus or connection sufficient to dismiss a teacher? In answering this question, the state courts of Washington and California suggest that judges consider the following factors: the likelihood that the conduct will adversely affect students or teachers, the age and maturity of the students, the proximity or remoteness of the conduct, the teacher's motivation, extenuating or aggravating circumstances, and the likelihood of the conduct being repeated.[4]

Are There Statutory Ways to Limit the Ambiguity of the Term "Immorality"?

Yes. To avoid such ambiguity, state laws can define and limit the concept. In some states, statutes require proof of a connection between the immoral conduct and the education of students. In Wisconsin, for example, an administrative code states that a teacher's license may be revoked for immoral conduct "if there is clear and convincing evidence that the person engaged in the immoral conduct and there is a nexus between the immoral conduct and the health, welfare, safety or education of any pupil."[5]

In order to dismiss a teacher for immorality in Florida, state law requires that the school board prove that the teacher engaged in conduct that (a) is "inconsistent with the standards of public conscience and good morals" and (b) "was sufficiently notorious so as to disgrace the teaching profession *and* impair the teacher's service to the community."[6] The case of Florida teacher Richard McNeill illustrates how this statute is applied.

McNeill was terminated for immoral conduct following his arrest for touching an undercover officer in a sexually suggestive manner. But a hearing officer and state court found that there was no evidence that McNeill's effectiveness was impaired. Instead, there was "an outpouring of affection and support" for McNeill from 50 past and present students, parents, and co-workers "who lauded his performance as a parent, citizen and teacher" and testified that he "can continue to effectively perform his duties."[7] Since the evidence indicated that McNeill's conduct had no significant impact on the school and did not impair his effectiveness, he was reinstated.

However, another Florida court ruled differently in the case of teacher and coach Barrett Purvis. After participating in a fight at the Shark Attack nightclub, Purvis was terminated for "misconduct in office" for resisting arrest and lying under oath.[8] Purvis argued that he should not be dismissed since there was no direct testimony from administrators or parents to prove that his effectiveness was impaired. But the court found that Purvis' willingness to lie under oath did damage his effectiveness and credibility as a teacher. The court concluded that the decision concerning whether a teacher's misconduct is so serious as to impair his effectiveness does not always require "testimony of actual impairment from students or parents."

Is Discrimination against Homosexuals a Violation of Their Constitutional Rights?

Several federal courts have ruled that such discrimination violates the Equal Protection Clause of the Fourteenth Amendment. In Ohio, for example, Bruce Glover charged that the school board unconstitutionally failed to renew his teaching contract because of his sexual orientation. A federal judge agreed and held that homosexuals "are entitled to at least the same protection as any other identifiable group" that is discriminated against and that decisions based on "animus against homosexuals can never be a legitimate government purpose."[9] Since the reason for the board's decision was the teacher's sexual orientation, the judge reinstated Glover and compensated him for loss of salary, mental anguish, and attorney's fees.

In a recent Utah case, Wendy Weaver went to court after she was not reassigned as girls' volleyball coach because of her sexual orientation. The court ruled that the Equal Protection Clause prohibits public schools "from engaging in intentional discrimination—even on the basis of sexual orientation—absent some rational basis," and "irrational prejudice" cannot provide that rational basis.[10] Since the only reason the principal did not assign Weaver to the coaching job was the community's negative reaction and that reaction was based solely on her sexual orientation not on her coaching ability, the court ruled in favor of the teacher.

In a similar Kansas case, Vernon Jantz alleged that a principal violated his equal protection by not hiring him as a teacher because of his "homosexual tendencies." A federal court agreed and concluded that there is no rational basis for considering sexual orientation in this case since "homosexual orientation alone does not impair...the job of teaching public schools."[11]

Can a Teacher Be Dismissed for Homosexual Behavior?

This depends on a variety of circumstances, such as whether the conduct is criminal and public. In California, for example, the board of education revoked the teaching credentials of Thomas Sarac after he was convicted for making a "homosexual advance" to a plainclothes policeman at a public beach, and the court ruled in favor of the board. The California Supreme Court distinguished the *Sarac* ruling from the *Morrison* decision on the grounds that the circumstances were different. Unlike Morrison, Sarac pleaded guilty to a criminal charge arising from a public homosexual advances.[12] However, another California court reinstated a teacher arrested for lewd conduct in a restroom because the incident was isolated, it was unlikely to recur, and no criminal charges were filed.[13]

In Nebraska, a high school teacher was dismissed for making a homosexual advance to a salesman in the teachers' lounge. Although there was no direct evidence that the incident impaired the teacher's efficiency, a state court upheld the dismissal, reasoning that such sexual advances in school are "a clear departure from moral behavior and professional standards" and indicate "unfitness to teach."[14]

In Oregon a court upheld the dismissal of a teacher for homosexual conduct that was observed by undercover police and occurred in the rear of an adult bookstore.[15] According to the judge, engaging in sexual activity in a public place violates contemporary moral standards, and once the behavior became known among the parents of his pupils, "his ability to function as a teacher was severely impaired."

In a Wisconsin decision, a court upheld the revocation of Ray Thompson's teaching license because he had sexually assaulted two men.[16] Thompson argued that his behavior "could not adversely affect the educational process" because the community did not know about it. But, according to the court, the superintendent did not have to wait until Thompson's criminal behavior was discovered. "In an age of rapid mass communications," wrote the judge, "it is unrealistic to believe the public would forever remain ignorant of his conduct."

In a highly controversial 1977 decision, the Washington Supreme Court sustained the dismissal of James Gaylord even though his sexual behavior was not public. Gaylord, an excellent high school teacher, was fired after he was reported by a student whom he counseled and admitted to his vice principal that he was a homosexual.[17] The judge noted that "at least one student plus several administrators, teachers, and parents publicly objected to Gaylord remaining on the teaching staff" and they testified that his continued presence "would create problems." According to the court, this evidence supported the school's concern that the continued presence of Gaylord after he voluntarily became known as a homosexual would result in confusion, fear, and parental concern, which would impair his efficiency as a teacher.

Another controversial decision involved an Ohio guidance counselor who told a school secretary, the assistant principal, and several colleagues that she was bisexual and had a female lover.[18] When she was not rehired because of these and other comments, she sued, arguing that her speech should have been protected by the First Amendment. But a divided federal appeals court ruled that her statements about her sexual preferences were not protected because the First Amendment protects a teacher only when she speaks about matters of "public concern" and not about her "personal interests." (For related First Amendment cases, see chapter 3.)

Can Teachers Be Fired for Advocating Legalization of Homosexual Activity?

Probably not. In Oklahoma, a law was passed permitting teachers to be dismissed for public homosexual "conduct" or "activity." A federal appeals court upheld part of the law, punishing homosexual "activity" that is "indiscreet and not practiced in private."[19] But the prohibition against homosexual "conduct" was unconstitutional because it defined such conduct to include "advocating" homosexual activity in a way that could come to the attention of school children or employees. Thus a teacher could violate the law by appearing on television or before the legislature to urge repeal of an antisodomy statute. However, firing teachers for advocating legal or social change violates the First Amendment. Therefore such restrictions on teachers' rights are permitted only if the state proves they are "necessary" to prevent disruption or to ensure effective teaching, and the state proved neither. The U.S. Supreme Court reviewed this case and was evenly divided (since one of the justices did not vote). As a result, the appeals court decision stands.

Can Teachers Be Dismissed for Being Unwed Mothers?

Probably not. The trend of decisions is illustrated by a federal appeals court case involving a Mississippi rule that automatically disqualified school employees who were parents of illegitimate children.[20] Officials offered these reasons for the rule: Unwed parenthood is proof of immoral conduct, unwed parents are improper role models for students, and such teachers contribute to the problem of student pregnancy. In rejecting these reasons, the judge explained that "present immorality" does not necessarily follow from unwed parenthood. Under the school rule, a teacher "could live an impeccable life yet be barred as unfit for employment for an event...occurring at any time in the past." This policy, wrote the court,

> equates the single fact of the illegitimate birth with irredeemable moral disease. Such a presumption is not only patently absurd, it is mischievous and prejudicial, requiring those who administer the policy to investigate the parental status of school employees and prospective applicants. Where no stigma may have existed before, such inquisitions by over-zealous officialdom can rapidly create it.

The court also did not agree that unwed parents would be improper models. The judge doubted that students would seek information on the private family life of teachers and then try to emulate them. Moreover, the school district offered no evidence that the presence of unwed parents in school contributed to student pregnancy. Finally, the court noted that "unwed mothers only, not unwed fathers" were penalized by the policy. For these reasons, the court ruled that the policy violated the constitutional right to equal protection.

In an Illinois decision involving a teacher who was fired for being unmarried and pregnant and for deciding to raise her child as a single parent, a judge wrote: "Under the overwhelming weight of authority, it is beyond question that [the teacher] had a substantive due process right to conceive and raise her child out of wedlock without unwarranted...School Board intrusion."[21] Similarly, a federal district court opinion indicated that an unmarried Ohio teacher had a "constitutional privacy right to control her reproductive functions," which included "the right to become pregnant by artificial insemination."[22]

Are Students Likely to Emulate a Teacher's Immoral Conduct?

There is little agreement about this issue. One liberal California judge wrote that the fear that students will emulate immoral teacher conduct "becomes realistic only under two conditions: First, the teacher's conduct must be sufficiently notorious that the students know or are likely to learn of it. Second, the teacher must continue to model his past conduct."[23]

Can Teachers Be Dismissed for Immoral or Unprofessional Conduct Involving Students?

Yes. Although most courts will not allow teachers to be dismissed for immorality involving other consenting adults unless there is evidence that such conduct will negatively affect their teaching, judges are generally quite strict concerning immoral behavior involving students, especially in the area of sexual relations.

Joseph Stubblefield was a teacher in a California junior college. After teaching one night, he drove one of his female students to a deserted side street and parked. Later, a deputy sheriff discovered Stubblefield and the student involved in sexual activity. Stubblefield knocked down the deputy and drove away at speeds of 80 to 100 miles per hour. Because of these events, the teacher was dismissed for immoral conduct. Stubblefield argued that the evidence against him concerned only his out-of-school conduct. But a California appeals court wrote that "there are certain professions which impose upon persons attracted to them, responsibilities and limitations on freedom of action which do not exist in regard to other callings. Public officials such as…school teachers fall into such a category."[24] According to the court, Stubblefield's misconduct and the notoriety of his behavior were evidence of his unfitness to teach. In conclusion the court wrote: "The integrity of the educational system under which teachers wield considerable power in the grading of students and the granting or withholding of certificates and diplomas is clearly threatened when teachers become involved in relationships with students such as is indicated by the conduct here."

An Illinois court upheld the dismissal of a Peoria teacher because he was discovered partially undressed playing strip poker in his automobile with a female high school student.[25] In a Washington case, teacher Gary Denton was discharged after a high school student he had dated became pregnant. Denton admitted being the prospective father, but he claimed his discharge was improper because his girlfriend was not a student at his school and there was no evidence that their relationship had a negative impact on his teaching. The court ruled that no direct evidence is needed when the sexual misconduct involves "a teacher and a minor student."[26] Similarly, Brian Hamm was fired after police found a 14-year-old student at his home around midnight against the wishes of her parents. Hamm argued that her presence did not prove immorality. But a state court ruled that by disregarding the rights of the student's parents, Hamm's conduct and poor judgment rendered him unfit to teach.[27]

In New York, a state court upheld the dismissal of a tenured teacher, Bernard Weaver, for insubordination for refusing to obey an order to stop living with a 16-year-old former male student who was still attending school in the district.[28] Weaver had encouraged the student to leave home and assisted him (he "waited outside the student's house with a loaded gun") despite the mother's strong objections.

In Michigan, an appeals court upheld the firing of a tenured teacher because of an "unprofessional relationship" with one of her 17-year-old high school students.[29a] She had been warned to avoid "the appearance of impropriety" with male students, but the teacher visited the student's apartment several times (one time overnight) and allowed him to drive her car without a license. Although there was no proof that the teacher's conduct had an adverse effect on other students or teachers, the court ruled that her dismissal was supported by "competent, material, and substantial evidence." In a related Maine case, Kathleen Elvin, a divorced fourth-grade teacher, was fired for having sexual relations with a 15-year-old neighbor who baby-sat for her children. Although the neighbor had never been her student, the court agreed that Elvin "had proven unfit to teach," as was shown by her poor judgment in having a sexual relationship "with a young boy from a neighboring school," and because of public awareness of her conduct, which would "undermine her ability and her reputation in dealing with students and parents" and participating in the school's "program dealing with sexual abuse and exploitation of children."[29b]

Can a Teacher Be Dismissed for Sexual Conduct with a Student That Occurred Years Before?

Yes. In a Minnesota case, a principal was discharged for sexual abuse of a student that occurred 12 to 16 years earlier, when the student was in the first to fifth grades.[30] The superintendent learned of the incident from the former student when he became a father and was concerned for his own children. The principal argued that the remoteness of the alleged behavior denied him due process. A state court ruled, however, that the seriousness of the sexual contact with the student "required dismissal" even though it occurred years before.

Similarly, David Toney, a tenured teacher from Alaska, was fired when administrators learned that he had had a sexual relationship with a 15-year-old student in Idaho 12 years earlier. Toney argued that it was unfair to summarily dismiss him for conduct that occurred long before his employment. But the court labeled Toney's argument "nonsensical" because it would "immunize from dismissal" a teacher who had concealed his prior illegal and immoral conduct.[31] In addition, the court doubted whether conduct such as Toney's "could ever be too remote" to support a teacher's dismissal.

Can a Teacher Be Dismissed for Sexual Advances toward Students?

Yes. Cases indicate that courts also tend to be quite strict in this area. In an Alabama case, Montgomery teacher Howard Kilpatrick was discharged for immoral conduct because he made "sexual advances towards female students."[32] The teacher claimed that the term "immoral conduct" was unconstitutionally vague and could include innocuous activity. Although the judge acknowledged that the "ultimate reach" of the term "immorality" was not clear, he felt there was no problem about vagueness in this case. According to the judge, any teacher can be expected to know that sexual advances toward students "cannot be condoned in the classroom setting." In Colorado, a court upheld the firing of a high school teacher because of his "horseplay" with several female students on a field trip.[33] This consisted of tickling them all over their bodies and carrying on a vulgar and sexually suggestive dialogue. The teacher viewed his behavior as an attempt to act his "natural self to gain rapport" with his students. But the court, viewing his conduct as "sordid," ruled that it had "no legitimate professional purpose," and upheld his dismissal. Similarly, in a New York case, the court approved the discharge of a teacher for "intolerable behavior," which included kissing the girls in his sixth-grade class, patting them "on the behind," and permitting obscene jokes and profanity in his classroom.[34]

Can a Teacher Be Dismissed for Hugging or Kissing a Student?

Not necessarily. It depends on the teacher's intent, the circumstances, and the school policy. In Missouri, for example, Ronald Youngman, who taught for 20 years, approached a troubled, teary-eyed, 14-year-old male student and hugged him, rubbed his back, and kissed him on the neck. Evidence indicated that Youngman's actions were motivated "only by care and concern for the student's apparent distress." But the student interpreted the conduct as an offensive sexual advance, and Youngman was fired for immoral conduct. However, a state court wrote that "immoral conduct cannot properly be predicated solely on the student's reactions to the teacher's conduct."[35] According to the court, if a teacher's actions were for sexual gratification, he would be guilty of immoral conduct regardless of whether the student found it offensive or even solicited it. But where a teacher's actions are misconstrued by a student, his subjective reactions, even if they are the result of the teacher's poor judgment, "cannot transform well-intentioned conduct into an immoral act."

This is especially true when, as in this case, there is no school policy concerning physical contact with students.

Similarly, an Illinois court ruled in favor of a guidance counselor who was dismissed for hugging and stroking a fifth-grade girl while she sat on his knee. Experts disagreed about the wisdom of the counselor's conduct. However, a state court ruled that in this case it was not immoral for the counselor to hug "a crying, distraught ten-year-old child" or to permit her to sit on his knee while they discussed her school work and family situation.[36]

Can Teachers Be Punished for Talking to Their Students about Sex?

Sometimes. Talking about sex may subject a teacher to disciplinary action, especially when such talk is not related to the curriculum. In a recent Massachusetts case, a tenured teacher, Thomas Conward, was discharged for "unbecoming conduct" after he handed a female student a document entitled "Application for a Piece of Ass." The application consisted of a series of lewd questions written in the style of an employment form. Conward argued that his punishment violated his free speech rights. But the court disagreed and ruled that "indecent speech directed to students" was not protected by the First Amendment.[37]

In Wisconsin, a state court upheld the dismissal of a Milwaukee teacher because of a series of discussions about sex in his 12th-grade speech classes.[38] Specifically, he explained the operation of houses of prostitution and indicated which students were old enough to be admitted; he told stories about intercourse with a cow and about the size of a penis. The teacher argued that the speech curriculum was broad enough to include sex education, which was never specifically prohibited. But the court concluded that the teacher's discussions transcended the bounds "of propriety of the contemporary community" and constituted immoral conduct. And in a New York case, a tenured photography instructor was fired for showing his 11th- and 12th-grade students a "pornographic film that included scenes involving oral sex."[39]

On the other hand, a Mississippi teacher who merely answered a student's question about sex on one occasion was held not guilty of immoral behavior.[40] After several boys in an eighth-grade spelling class asked, "What is a queer?" she briefly discussed homosexuality. The judge concluded that such a discussion was "certainly not an act 'repulsive to the minimum standards of decency' required of public school teachers." In other cases where teachers have been dismissed for using objectionable language in the classroom, courts have sometimes ruled that their actions are protected by their right to freedom of speech under the First and Fourteenth Amendments. (For a detailed discussion of this issue, see chapter 9.)

Can a Teacher Become Overinvolved with a Student?

Yes, even if there is no sexual impropriety in the relationship. This occurred in Colorado when Drew Kerin, a fourth-grade teacher, became a "father substitute" for one of his students. For nine months, the mother allowed her son to stay with Kerin. However, when the mother wanted her son to live with her, Kerin began a custody battle over the boy. This led to extensive publicity, a community dispute about Kerin's behavior, and his dismissal. Kerin argued that his motivation was only to help the boy, there was nothing immoral in his relationship, and that he was an excellent teacher. While a hearing officer agreed that Kerin "set out with the best of intentions" to assist the student, he "crossed the line" and undertook inappropriate action when he sought custody against the wishes of the mother. Furthermore, wrote the hearing officer, Kerin "exploited his position as a teacher" to fulfill his emotional needs, and this constituted "just cause for termination."[41]

Can a Teacher Be Fired for Using Profanity or Abusive Language toward Students?

Yes. In Colorado, a music teacher took a troublesome student outside the high school and told him he was a "disgrace to the band," an "S.O.B.," and a "fucking asshole." As a result, the director was dismissed because he previously had been ordered not to use profanity in dealing with the students.[42] Similarly, a Pennsylvania foreign-language teacher was fired for calling a 14-year-old student a "slut" and implying that she was a prostitute. In upholding the dismissal, the court explained that school officials must be able to protect students from abusive language by teachers, which, in this case, was "totally inappropriate."[43]

In Omaha, a teacher was fired for calling black students "dumb niggers." According to the Nebraska Supreme Court, there may have been a time when it was thought appropriate to "refer to each other as 'kikes' or 'wops' or 'shanty Irish' or 'nigger.'" But, "thankfully, we have overcome that disgrace. And those who insist on making such words a part of their vocabulary must be labeled by the public as immoral."[44]

In a controversial Indiana case, a divided state appeals court even upheld the dismissal of a teacher for immorality because she was alleged to have said, "Fuck you" during class.[45] In a skeptical comment on the conflicting evidence, the court wrote: "The School Board chose to believe that a mature grade-school teacher with 12 years of experience and an unblemished record would stand in the middle of her fifth-grade art class and mindlessly utter a barracks-room obscenity in response to a student's question." Although other judges might have ruled differently, this court held that the board had adequate evidence to believe the students who testified against the teacher and that the harsh penalty was not an abuse of the board's discretion. In a dissenting opinion, Judge Canover wrote that the record revealed the absence of a fair hearing and "a mockery of justice." (This case illustrates the extreme reluctance of some judges to overturn the findings and judgment of a school board.)

Can Teachers Be Dismissed because of Rumors of Immoral Conduct?

No. If teachers are terminated for immoral conduct, such action should be based on fact, not rumor. This was the ruling in the case of Annabel Stoddard, a competent, divorced teacher whose contract was not renewed in a small, religious Wyoming community.[46] Despite the official written reasons given for her nonrenewal, the evidence indicated that the real reasons were because of "rumors that she was having an affair" and because she was unattractive and did not attend church regularly. As a result of this evidence, a federal appeals court ruled that the school officials were "motivated by constitutionally impermissible reasons" in not renewing her contract.

In a related 1996 case, "rumors ran rampant" through a Louisiana high school community concerning the sexual orientation and improper relationship between a teacher–coach and a student after a slumber party at Coach Gwendolyn Holt's home and a bus ride to a basketball game in which the student sat close to the coach.[47] As a result, Holt was dismissed for "failing to maintain an appropriate teacher–pupil relationship." Because no substantial evidence existed to support the charges, a Louisiana appeals court ruled that the dismissal was "arbitrary and an abuse of discretion," and it reinstated the coach with back pay.

Are There Other Reasons Teachers Have Been Dismissed on Grounds of Immoral or Unprofessional Conduct?

Yes. A tenured California elementary school teacher was dismissed after she was arrested by an undercover policeman for openly engaging in sexual activity with three men at a swingers' club party in Los Angeles. A state court upheld her dismissal because her conduct at the semipublic party reflected "a total lack of concern for privacy, decorum or preservation of her dignity and reputation" and indicated "a serious defect of moral character, normal prudence, and good common sense."[48]

In Ohio, a counselor who was also a wrestling coach was dismissed for telling a student to lie about his weight during a wrestling tournament. As a result, he resigned as coach, but he argued that this conduct should not affect his position as guidance counselor. The court disagreed, ruling that telling a student to lie and cheat was immorality that related directly to his performance as a teacher.[49] In a Pennsylvania decision, a court upheld the revocation of Regina Nanko's educator's certificate for immorality because she forged the signature of a superintendent on her application for a superintendent's certification.[50]

In Missouri, the state supreme court upheld the dismissal of a building trades teacher for immoral conduct because he permitted male students to "engage in sexual harassment" of the only female student in the class by repeatedly using obscene and sexually explicit language toward her, by displaying a "suggestive centerfold," and by using a plastic phallus to embarrass her.[51]

A New Jersey court upheld the dismissal of a male tenured music teacher, Paul Monroe Grossman, after he underwent "sex-reassignment" surgery[52] and became Paula Miriam Grossman, who began to live and dress as a woman. While there was conflicting testimony about Grossman's probable future effectiveness, the court supported her termination because of "potential psychological harm to students" if she were retained.

On the other hand, a Pennsylvania court ruled in favor of two teachers who were punished for engaging in a water fight with their students on the last day of school. Since administrators had clearly prohibited such behavior, the school board found the teachers guilty of immoral conduct and suspended them for 15 days. The judge, however, noted that immorality usually involves "sexual improprieties, stealing," or "illegal gambling." Therefore the court concluded that although the teachers' conduct in this case was "most inappropriate and an error in judgment," it was "not immoral."[53] And, in Iowa, a court ruled that an admission of adultery does not make a person automatically unfit to teach.[54] The case involved an excellent teacher whose certification was revoked after he was discovered committing adultery. The court ruled that this "isolated incident" was not grounds for revocation when there was no evidence to indicate it would adversely affect his teaching.

Does a School Have to Warn Teachers Before Dismissing Them for Immoral or Unprofessional Conduct?

Not if the misconduct is serious or a clear violation of professional ethics. Thus a Minnesota guidance counselor was discharged for a series of unprofessional incidents, including breaching the confidence of students (e.g., he disclosed an incest victim's confidences in a social setting to teachers who had no need for the information). The teacher argued that he should have been warned about his deficiencies and given an opportunity to remedy them. But the state court rejected his argument.[55] "It should not be necessary," wrote the judge, "to tell a counselor that his conduct is inappropriate when the conduct clearly violates [his] code of ethics."

Similarly, an Illinois high school teacher claimed that his discharge without prior warning for hugging and kissing two students and writing them letters about their physical attraction was improper. The court ruled that in a case such as this involving a teacher's immoral conduct with students, the behavior is self-evidently harmful, and no warning is needed to justify termination.[56]

Can a Teacher Be Dismissed for Allowing Students to Drink or Use Drugs at the Teacher's Home?

Yes. During Christmas vacation, two 16-year-old students asked teacher Archie Vivian if they could play pool at his house. There, they gave Vivian a bottle of whiskey as a Christmas gift. Although the teacher had only one drink, the girls helped themselves and finished the bottle. Vivian saw them do this and did not attempt to stop them. As a result, one of the girls became intoxicated and passed out, the incident became public, and the teacher was dismissed. Witnesses testified that Vivian (who had not been disciplined in 23 years of teaching) could soon overcome the adverse effects of this incident. In response, the judge wrote: "No doubt, Vivian can at some time in the future regain his ability to teach," but schools are not established to rehabilitate teachers.[57] In upholding Vivian's dismissal, the court concluded that the district "was entitled to a teacher who would be an effective role model and teacher on the date of his discharge, not the following day, or the following month."

In a related Kentucky case, two tenured teachers, Greg and Donnie Wood, were fired for allowing two 15-year-old students to participate in a marijuana smoking party in their home. The Wood brothers argued that they should not have been fired for "acts committed during off-duty hours, during the summer...and in the privacy of their own apartment." The court acknowledged that teachers should not be dismissed for every "private shortcoming that might come to the attention of the Board of Education."[58] However, in this case, the court held that smoking marijuana with two students was "serious misconduct of an immoral and criminal nature" and that there was a direct connection between the off-campus misconduct and the teachers' in-school role "as a moral example for the students."

Can a Teacher Be Dismissed for Lying?

It depends on the facts of the case. In Kentucky, a teacher called in sick in order to drive a coal truck to Ohio and later falsely swore that he was ill in order to collect sick leave for that day. As a result, a state court upheld his dismissal for conduct unbecoming a teacher.[59]

In California, however, a court reached a different result in the case of a teacher who was fired for calling in sick so she could attend a landing of the space shuttle.[60] The judge acknowledged that the teacher's behavior constituted unprofessional conduct for which she might have been suspended, but in view of the teacher's "previously unblemished record," the court agreed with a state commission on professional competence that dismissal was excessive punishment for her behavior. Similarly, Bruce Katz, an Ohio teacher, was fired for reporting he was sick when he took his family to Florida. But a court agreed with a referee that Katz should receive a lesser penalty because the board failed to consider the referee's recommendation, Katz's 13 years of competent service, and the "severe emotional pressure" he was under at the time he falsified his sick leave report.[61]

In another case concerning a teacher who was dismissed for dishonesty for misusing her sick leave, a court noted that "dishonest conduct may range from the smallest fib to the most flagrant lie."[62] Therefore, it ruled that "not every falsehood will constitute 'dishonesty' as a ground for dismissal." Instead, the court said that judges should weigh the seriousness of the dishonesty in each case and consider a number of factors, including the likelihood of its recurrence, extenuating or aggravating circumstances, motivation, the extent of publicity, its likely effect on students, and the proximity or remoteness of the conduct.

Will Courts Reverse Penalties against Teachers That Seem Harsh?

Not usually. Although courts are willing to overturn a school board's decision for constitutional or procedural reasons, most judges are reluctant to reverse a penalty imposed by a board because it seems harsh. In Colorado, for example, Patricia Blaine, a high school teacher and cheerleading coach, was dismissed for not stopping her cheerleaders from drinking beer in their motel room during a basketball tournament. Blaine admitted poor judgment but said she did not "make a scene and throw the beer away" because she wanted to keep the cheerleaders "safe, supervised, and in their rooms." Since Blaine failed to stop the drinking, a majority of the Colorado Supreme Court refused to hold that the dismissal "was such an unwarranted form of discipline as to constitute an abuse of school board discretion."[63] In a dissenting opinion, three justices emphasized that Blaine was "a concerned and well-intentioned, but inexperienced chaperone" who tried "a nonconfrontive approach" to control the cheerleaders during a night of widespread partying. Although the dissenters agreed that Blaine "erred in judgment," they concluded that her conduct "simply did not warrant the devastating sanction of dismissal."[64]

Similarly, in Alabama, Leroy Burton, a 29-year veteran teacher, was dismissed for "possession of firearms" on school grounds after he fired his pistol into the ground to scare four nonstudents who attacked him in a night school. Evidence indicated that Burton had a license to carry the pistol, that he injured no one, that violence was common at the school, and that he had unsuccessfully requested school security. Although the judges wrote that they were "troubled" by the dismissal of this "dedicated teacher," they felt required to affirm the dismissal because Burton had technically violated a school policy.[65]

In some cases, however, a penalty that seems relatively light in view of the seriousness of the offense is still challenged by the teacher. In New York, for example, a driver education and industrial arts teacher was convicted and jailed for negligent homicide in a widely publicized hit-and-run auto accident that killed a teenage biker. As a result, the teacher was suspended for two years. Even though he taught driving, the teacher argued that there was no connection between the accident and his ability to teach. But the court disagreed and concluded that "the adverse effect of this particular notorious conviction and sentence on a teacher's legitimate function" is 'self-evident.'"[66]

Criminal Conduct

Is Conviction for a Felony[67] Grounds for Dismissal?

Usually a teacher who is convicted of a serious crime, such as a felony, can be dismissed. This was the ruling of a Delaware court in the case of Leon Skripchuk, an outstanding industrial arts teacher.[68] After Skripchuk pleaded guilty to charges of theft and aggravated assault with a gun, he was dismissed for immorality. This was the only blemish in his long teaching career, and experts testified that it was "most unlikely" that he would ever again be involved in similar criminal conduct. But school officials testified that his conviction, which received widespread publicity, would make parents fearful and would impair his teaching effectiveness. In view of the seriousness of this crime, the court ruled that the teacher's actions were "unquestionably immoral" and his termination was reasonable. In a 1996 Missouri case, Donna Thomas, an "exemplary" ninth-grade English teacher, was dismissed for immoral conduct for shooting at her estranged husband's girlfriend.[69] Thomas argued that there was no connection between her personal marital conflicts and her teaching. But, according to the court, the teacher's use of violence to solve personal problems was likely to have an adverse affect on her "very impressionable" adolescent students "by confusing the violence-free message promoted by the school," by undermining her position as a role model and authority figure, and by presenting a "do as I say, not as I do" dilemma for her students.

On the other hand, a California court pointed out that not all felonies involve immoral behavior or crimes of such seriousness that by themselves they would be sufficient to justify dismissing a teacher.[70] This view was endorsed by the Washington Supreme Court in a case involving a teacher who was fired after being convicted of grand larceny for purchasing a stolen motorcycle.[71] The court ruled that a teacher should not be dismissed unless the school district shows that his criminal conduct "materially and substantially" affects his teaching. According to the court, "simply labeling an instructor as a convicted felon will not justify a discharge." This is especially true in this case, where the teacher might not have known the motorcycle was stolen when he bought it; where he received support from students, parents, and other teachers; and where the conviction had no adverse effect on his teaching.

Does Conviction for a Misdemeanor[72] Justify Dismissal?

Not usually. But it may if the misdemeanor constitutes a crime of moral turpitude or unprofessional conduct. For example, in Alaska, a tenured teacher was dismissed after being convicted of illegally diverting electricity from the power company to his home. The board characterized the teacher's crime as a "form of larceny or theft…involving moral turpitude." The Alaska Supreme Court agreed.[73] The court wrote: "The legislature, in enacting certain criminal statutes, has established minimum acceptable moral standards for the state as a whole. If a teacher cannot abide by these standards, his or her fitness as a teacher is necessarily called into question."

Similarly, in Minnesota, social studies teacher Donald Shelton was discharged for unprofessional conduct after being convicted for theft from a company he ran with two other teachers. Shelton made restitution and argued that he should not be fired because the conviction for this misdemeanor did not impair his teaching. However, the school board claimed that Shelton's fitness "was directly affected" because he teaches business ethics and "lost his credibility to teach such values." A state court agreed.[74] The judge added that, because of Shelton's theft from fellow teachers and the resulting animosity, his "continued presence in this small district will result in...an unsatisfactory learning environment."

In a 1996 Missouri decision, a teacher resigned after being arrested for indecent exposure. The following year, he was hired in a different district even after telling the principal about his misdemeanor. When the superintendent's office learned about the conviction, it fired the teacher for that conduct because it could "bring discredit upon the school system." The teacher argued that the school should not be able to fire him for conduct that he freely disclosed to the hiring principal. But the court disagreed because "the Board, not the principal, is the employing authority" and the principal did not report this information to the board.[75] Therefore, it was reasonable for the board to conclude that a person who behaved as he did "within a recent time frame, is unsuitable to serve as a teacher."

The outcome was different, however, when a black Tennessee band director was fired for unprofessional conduct after he was fined $25 for the misdemeanor of "possession of controlled substance" when police found two marijuana cigarettes in his pocket that he had taken from students earlier that day. Evidence indicated that the teacher was treated differently than two white teachers who had been charged with misdemeanors (shoplifting and driving under the influence of an intoxicant) but had not been fired. Because the school retained "guilty employees of one color while discharging those of another" in similar circumstances, the court found the school guilty of racial discrimination and awarded the teacher damages for his illegal discharge.[76]

Can a Teacher Be Dismissed If Arrested for Excessive Drinking?

Probably. California teacher Joseph Watson was denied a secondary teaching credential on grounds of immorality because of six convictions involving the use of alcohol. Although there was no proof that his convictions affected his teaching, the court ruled that the evidence amply demonstrated his unfitness to teach.[77] First, Watson's use of alcohol had gotten out of control and indicated that he did not have the proper attitude necessary for successfully counseling students away from the harmful effects of alcohol, as state law requires. Second, being arrested as a "public drunk" and for driving under the influence of alcohol set a poor example for high school students. Through his behavior, Watson had repeatedly jeopardized the welfare of his students and the public. Finally, the judge wrote: "I don't know what better evidence there could be of immorality than a series of criminal convictions."

In 1991, an Alabama court upheld the dismissal of a driver education teacher whose auto insurance was cancelled after he was arrested twice in thirteen months for driving under the influence of alcohol.[78] The teacher argued that he should have been reassigned to teach other students because he was certified in health and physical education, but the court was not persuaded. In Indiana, Mary Aaron was fired for stopping to drink beer on the way home from a field trip with students. Aaron claimed she was a victim of discrimination since a white teacher, Louis Martin, was only suspended for twice smelling of alcohol at school. However, a state court upheld Aaron's termination, since, unlike Martin, Aaron drank in front of students and then drove the students home—conduct which could have resulted in a criminal conviction.[79]

In a related Wyoming case, a state court upheld the dismissal of a teacher who was found drunk in school in front of his students and had to be removed from the class by other teachers.[80] Similarly, an Arizona court ruled that a teacher could be dismissed after she pleaded guilty to fighting and "disturbing the peace by being under the influence of intoxicants."[81]

A few courts seem more sympathetic to teachers whose excessive drinking is not linked directly to their classroom effectiveness. Thus a Florida judge ruled in favor of Sarah Clark, a tenured fifth-grade teacher, who was dismissed after a three-day summer "alcohol-related binge" that resulted in misdemeanor charges, probation, and rehabilitation.[82] The court reversed Clark's dismissal because her binge took place during the summer vacation, was not widely known, and did not impair her effectiveness. According to the judge, the evidence did not support terminating a teacher "who exhibited a human weakness to a few persons for a few days during a troubled time of her life." In Montana, another sympathetic court ruled in favor of a teacher who was discharged after pleading guilty to driving under the influence for the third time.[83] In overruling the school authorities, the court held that violations for driving under the influence of intoxicating liquor" are not in themselves "tantamount to immorality." To sustain the dismissal of such a teacher, the court required evidence that the convictions would affect the teacher's professional performance.

Is Shoplifting Sufficient Grounds for Dismissal?

Judges differ on this issue. Some believe conviction for shoplifting is a sufficient basis for dismissal; others hold that schools must prove that the crime impairs teacher effectiveness. A case illustrating this conflict involved Arlene Golden, a West Virginia guidance counselor, who was fined $100 for shoplifting at a local mall. Although there were mitigating circumstances indicating that the counselor was "totally distraught" at the time, the board dismissed her. But the West Virginia Supreme Court ruled in Golden's favor because there was no evidence that the counselor's conviction had any relationship to her professional effectiveness.[84] Since the only competent evidence was favorable to Golden, the court ruled that the board could not conclude she was unfit as a counselor. In a strong dissenting opinion that reflects the views of other courts, Judge Neely wrote: "What type of example does a confessed shoplifter set for impressionable teenagers?... I can hear the dialogue now in the guidance office of this particular counselor: 'Say Miss Golden, do you know a good fence for some clean, hot jewelry?' ... The result in this case is absurd."[85]

In a Pennsylvania shoplifting case, a state court upheld the right of a school board to dismiss a teacher for shoplifting on grounds of immorality. According to the court, immorality includes conduct that offends community morals and is "a bad example to the youth whose ideals a teacher is supposed to foster."[86] Clearly, wrote the court, "shoplifting falls squarely within this definition."

Should Conviction for a Serious Crime Preclude Future Employment as a Teacher?

Not necessarily. According to some courts, commission of a crime is not always sufficient to bar a person permanently from teaching. In considering this issue, the liberal California Supreme Court wrote that dismissal for illegal conduct is reasonable only under two conditions: (1) The teacher's conduct must be "sufficiently notorious" that students know or are likely to learn of it, and (2) "the teacher must continue to model his past conduct."[87] According to the court:

> The teacher who committed an indiscretion, paid the penalty, and now seeks to discourage his students from committing similar acts may well be a more effective supporter of legal and moral standards than the one who has never been found to violate those standards. Since these conditions will vary from case to case, proof that one has at some past time committed a crime should not in itself suffice to demonstrate that he is not now and never will be a suitable behavior model for his students.

A related New Mexico case involved Geronimo Garcia, a teacher who had been found guilty of sexual misconduct with his 13-year-old stepdaughter.[88] After completing his three-year probation, Garcia applied for renewal of his teaching certification. Medical testimony indicated that the teacher had been rehabilitated. But others testified that parents would feel uncomfortable with any teacher convicted of sexual misconduct with a minor. The court acknowledged that a person convicted of a crime such as this, which related to teaching of children, has the burden of showing he has been rehabilitated. Since the only competent evidence indicated that Garcia had been rehabilitated, the court ruled in his favor.[89]

Can Teachers Be Fired If There Is No Evidence Linking Their Crime and Their Job Performance?

Yes, in some states. For example, the Kansas Board of Education suspended Todd Hainline's teaching certificate because he committed a burglary. Hainline argued that there was no evidence that the burglary impaired his teaching. However, the Supreme Court of Kansas wrote that "teachers are role models for their students" and that one goal of education is "to instill respect for law."[90] Therefore the court ruled that there is "a presumption that the felonious conduct has sufficient relationship or nexus to Hainline's fitness to teach" to warrant his suspension. The court noted that these penalties did not apply just to teachers, that conviction of a felony such as burglary is grounds for revocation of a license to practice medicine or law, even if the felony is unrelated to the profession. Therefore the teaching profession, "with its great influence on young people," certainly "has no lesser justification for the discipline of a person within its ranks who has committed a felony." Hainline also argued that his right of privacy was violated by suspension of his certificate for conduct occurring outside of school, but the court responded that "there is no right of privacy involved in the commission of a burglary" because "felonies are public offenses." In a related Ohio case, Barbara Stelzer's teaching certificate was revoked after she was convicted for illegally receiving welfare benefits. Stelzer argued that there was no connection between the felony and her classroom effectiveness, but an Ohio appeals court ruled that "continued receipt of stolen property over a period of five years" constituted conduct unbecoming a teacher and a just cause for discharge.[91]

In a 2001 Minnesota case, a teacher argued that his license should not be suspended because of his arrest for indecent exposure since the arrest did not affect his teaching. But a state court ruled that the act of exposing one's self in "a *public* restroom, whether he is a homosexual or heterosexual" constitutes immoral conduct, and Minnesota law does not require a finding that a teacher is unfit to teach before disciplining him for such conduct.[92]

Can Teachers Be Suspended on the Basis of a Criminal Indictment?

Yes, if the alleged misconduct relates to their job as teacher (e.g., stealing school funds or molesting students). In Massachusetts, the state courts have broadly interpreted the concept of "misconduct in employment." In one case, a court sustained the suspension of a junior high school teacher after his indictment for "possession, with intent to distribute, cocaine."[93] There was no evidence that the teacher engaged in misconduct with school personnel or students. However, the judge reasoned that because of the teacher's position as role model, because of the increased use of drugs among students, and because his conduct was in "direct conflict with the message his teaching should impart," school officials should have discretion to consider the cocaine indictment to be "an indictment for misconduct in office." In a subsequent case, another Massachusetts court used the role model argument to sustain the suspension of two teachers who were indicted for welfare fraud of $32,000.[94]

Can Teachers Be Dismissed because of Criminal Charges against Them?

Not simply because of the charges or the publicity surrounding them. In Florida, after a teacher was arrested for possession of illegal marijuana and alcohol, the charges were dropped when it was found that both illegal substances belonged to his brother. Nevertheless, the teacher was dismissed because the school board believed his "effectiveness as a teacher has been impaired." But a state appeals court rejected this argument.[95] "Otherwise," wrote the judge, "whenever a teacher is accused of a crime and is subsequently exonerated with no evidence being presented to tie the teacher to the crime, the school board could, nevertheless, dismiss the teacher because the attendant publicity has impaired the teacher's effectiveness." Such a rule, concluded the court, "would be improper."

If Criminal Charges against a Teacher Are Dismissed, Can the Teacher Still Be Fired for the Behavior That Resulted in Those Charges?

Yes, and punishment by the school would not constitute double jeopardy.[96] In a Louisiana case, teacher Eric Dubuclet pleaded guilty to possession of marijuana and cocaine and was fired for immorality. After he successfully completed probation, the criminal proceedings against him were dismissed. Dubuclet then argued that because he was never convicted, he should not have been fired by the school. The court, however, ruled that even though the criminal charges were dismissed, Dubuclet could still be disciplined by his school. According to the court: "The statutory expungement of one's criminal record does not erase the fact that the party committed the act, nor does it erase the moral turpitude of his conduct."[97]

Similarly, acquittal of a criminal charge, such as selling drugs to students, does not prevent a school from dismissing a teacher on those grounds. To convict someone of a crime, the state must prove that the person is guilty "beyond a reasonable doubt." But to dismiss a teacher, a school board need show only "by a preponderance of the evidence" that the teacher engaged in immoral or criminal conduct that impaired his or her teaching. Thus an Alabama teacher who was arrested for possession of crack cocaine was dismissed even though he was not indicted or convicted of the crime.[98] In this decision, the teacher's dismissal for drug possession was upheld not because of his arrest, but because of independent evidence presented to the school board.

Can a Teacher Be Fired for Taking School Property of Relatively Little Value?

Yes. In a controversial Missouri decision, a state court upheld the dismissal of a tenured teacher–librarian who, during an eight-year period, took from the school a teapot, $20 from baseball gate receipts, and a set of books.[99] The court explained: "The taking of property belonging to another without consent, notwithstanding its return when confronted with such wrongdoing, breaches even the most relaxed standards of acceptable human behavior, particularly so with regard to those who occupy positions which bring them in close, daily contact with young persons of an impressionable age."

Can a Teacher Be Punished for Considering a Crime?

No. David Bogart, a Kansas teacher, was charged with possession of marijuana because of drugs his son kept in his room. Although Bogart was cleared of the charge, he was dismissed by the school committee for "conduct unbecoming an instructor." Before the committee, Bogart admitted that he considered trying to protect his son and taking the blame himself, although he did not. But a federal court held that this was not a lawful basis for dismissal.[100] "It is fortunate," wrote the court, "the state is not allowed to penalize its citizens for their thoughts, for it would be the rare and either mindless, supine, or super-saintly citizen who has not at some time contemplated and then rejected the illegal."

Can a Teacher Be Dismissed for the Use or Possession of Illegal Drugs?

It depends on the circumstances. Courts, for example, might not support the firing of a teacher solely because the teacher once was indicted for possessing a small amount of marijuana. But they would probably support a dismissal based on evidence of a widely publicized conviction combined with testimony indicating how the teacher's criminal behavior would undermine his or her effectiveness as a teacher. California courts have decided the following four cases on this question:

Arthur Comings' teacher's certificate was revoked based on evidence that he had been convicted for possession of marijuana. But at Comings' hearing, no evidence was presented indicating whether his conduct adversely affected students or fellow teachers, the likelihood of its recurrence, his motives, or other evidence concerning his unfitness to teach. Under these circumstances, the court held that there was not sufficient evidence to revoke Comings' certification.[101] The court said it was not ruling that marijuana offenders must be permitted to teach, only that they cannot be dismissed without adequate evidence of their unfitness.

In a later case, a California appeals court ruled that teacher Theodor Judge could not be discharged after being convicted for cultivating one marijuana plant.[102] The judge wrote that in this case, "a felony conviction, standing by itself, is not a ground for discipline in the absence of moral turpitude," and "marijuana-related offenses need not necessarily always be crimes of moral turpitude...measured by the morals of our day."

Barnet Brennan was the teaching principal of a California school when she wrote an affidavit in support of a friend who had been convicted of possessing marijuana. In the sworn statement, she said: "Marijuana is not harmful to my knowledge, because I have been using it since 1949 almost daily, with only beneficial results." Because Brennan's statement attracted wide publicity and her students learned of its content, she was dismissed. Brennan argued that there was no evidence that her statement had a negative effect on students. In this 1971 decision, the court responded that the school acted so promptly after learning of the affidavit that there was little time for such evidence to develop.[103] Here, said the court, there was "competent evidence" on the "likely" effect of Brennan's conduct on students. As one witness testified: "I would be inclined to believe that the pupil would be thinking, 'If my teacher can gain her ends by breaking the law, then I, too, can gain my ends by breaking the law!'"

In a related case, art teacher Selwyn Jones was fined for possessing marijuana while on a trip to Hawaii. His conduct was reported in the *San Francisco Chronicle* and reached the attention of Daly City school officials, who dismissed him. At a hearing, the vice principal testified that Jones's return to the school would adversely affect its art department, faculty, student body, and parents because many of these persons had expressed "disapproval" or "concern" at reinstating a teacher convicted of using marijuana. According to the vice principal, Jones's return "would be an example in opposition to the instructions we are giving to the students" concerning drug use; in fact, his return would "work against the total goals of our school." On the basis of this "substantial evidence" concerning Jones's fitness to teach, the court upheld his dismissal.[104]

Does Mental Illness Excuse a Teacher's Criminal Behavior?

Not necessarily. Mental illness might result in a teacher's being acquitted of criminal intent, but it might not protect the teacher's job. In an Iowa case, an elementary teacher, Kathleen Davies, was dismissed after being arrested for and admitting to shoplifting. Davies argued that her shoplifting was the result of a "mental illness/disability" caused by her medication and that it was unfair to dismiss her because of an illness she could not control.[105] But the court agreed with the school board's conclusion that "Davies' status as a role model was permanently impaired…with no hope of reconstruction" because of the small size of the district and the widespread knowledge of her crime.

In a related Missouri decision, a state court ruled that a lack of intent to commit an illegal or immoral act due to a mental illness might not protect a teacher.[106] The case involved Nancy Howard, who repeatedly initiated sexual contact with a student and other boys. Her psychiatrist said Howard's behavior was the result of a mental disorder or her medication and that she "lacked intent to commit any immoral act." But the court ruled it was not necessary to prove intent to revoke a teacher's license for immoral and illegal behavior where, as here, there was "grossly offensive and inherently harmful sexual conduct by a teacher practiced upon school-aged children."

Lifestyle

Does the Right to Privacy Protect Teachers' Personal Lives?

It might. In 1985 a federal appeals court ruled that a school could not refuse to renew a teacher's contract because of her pending divorce.[107] The nonrenewal decision was based on some parents' worry that too many divorcees were teaching in the school and on the superintendent's concern for the school's image in the community. While the court acknowledged that the school could deny reemployment for any legitimate reason, it could not take such action in violation of the teacher's "constitutional right to privacy." The court ruled that "matters relating to marriage and family relationships involve privacy rights that are constitutionally protected against unwarranted government interference." Thus a school cannot refuse to hire a teacher simply because of her "constitutionally protected decision to seek a divorce."

When Virginia teacher Pamela Ponton was forced to take a leave because she was pregnant and unmarried, she argued that this action violated her right to privacy. A federal judge agreed and ruled that the constitutional "right to privacy encompasses decisions regarding whether to have a child" and "protects the right to have a child out of wedlock."[108] The school board had argued that unmarried pregnant teachers set a bad example for the students. In rejecting this role model theory, the judge doubted "that students would have even been aware" that Ponton was unmarried, and even if they had, "the mere knowledge that the teacher had gotten pregnant out of wedlock would seem to have a fairly minimal impact on them." The court concluded that the school's interest "in support of the coerced leave of absence is, at best, very weak" and does not outweigh Ponton's constitutional right to privacy.

Can a Teacher Be Prohibited from Breastfeeding Her Child in School?

Not necessarily. In Orange County, Florida, Janice Dike, an elementary schoolteacher, challenged her principal's refusal to allow her to breastfeed her child in school. To avoid interference with her duties, Dike arranged to have her child brought to school during her duty-free lunch period, and she nursed the baby in a private room. However, the principal ordered her to stop because of a rule prohibiting teachers from bringing their children to work. A trial judge dismissed Dike's suit as "frivolous," but a federal appeals court disagreed.[109] The appeals court ruled that the U.S. Constitution "protects from undue state interference citizens' freedom of personal choice" in some areas of family life which the court described as "rights of personal privacy" or "fundamental personal liberties." According to the court, this right or liberty interest includes breastfeeding—"the most elemental form of parental care." The court's ruling does not mean that schools cannot restrict this protected liberty to prevent disruption or to ensure that teachers perform their duties. However, a school can interfere with this right only when it is clearly necessary to do so.

Can an Unmarried Teacher Be Dismissed for Living with Someone of the Opposite Sex?

It depends on the circumstances. Kathleen Sullivan, an elementary school teacher, began living with a male friend in a small, rural South Dakota town. When 140 residents petitioned for her dismissal because of her unwed cohabitation, Sullivan's principal asked her to change her living arrangement. Sullivan replied that whom she lived with was her business, not a school matter. As a result, Sullivan was fired because she violated local mores, was a "bad example" for her students, and would not get parental cooperation because of her improper conduct. Sullivan claimed that her dismissal violated her right to privacy.

Although a federal appeals court acknowledged that this case posed "very difficult constitutional issues," it ruled in favor of the school board.[110] First, it wrote that the scope and limits of the "newly evolving constitutional right to privacy" are not clear. Second, even if courts rule that the Constitution does protect a teacher's personal lifestyle, this ruling would not necessarily resolve a case such as this. A court would still have to balance the privacy interest of the teacher against the legitimate interest of the board in promoting the education of its students.

On the other hand, a Florida appeals court ruled that a single teacher could not be fired simply because she lived with a man.[111] The case involved a high school Spanish teacher who was dismissed because she lived with a boyfriend for a month and later spent the night with him on occasion. The school board alleged that such cohabitation showed that the teacher lacked good judgment and that she failed "to conform to the moral standards established by the vast majority of teachers" in the county, and that such conduct "reduces her effectiveness." Despite these allegations, there was no evidence that the cohabitation reduced her effectiveness, and there was substantial testimony that she was an excellent teacher. Moreover, her relationships were not common knowledge until the matter was publicized by the board. Under these circumstances, the court ruled that the private sexual relationships of a teacher are not "good cause" for termination "unless it is shown that such conduct adversely affects the ability to teach."

Can a Teacher Be Fired for Using Vulgar or "Obscene" Language Off Campus?

Probably not, although it may depend on where and with whom the language is used. In Ohio, a court protected a high school teacher in a case involving two offensive letters he had sent to a former student who had just graduated.[112] They were found by the student's mother, who was shocked by their language and gave them to the police. As a result, local newspapers wrote several stories about the letters. The prosecuting attorney said that they contained hardcore obscenity and that "a person who would write letters of this kind is not fit to be a school teacher." Subsequently the school board terminated the teacher's contract on grounds of immorality but a state court ruled in his favor. The letters, wrote the court, contain language that many adults would find "gross, vulgar, and offensive" and that some 18-year-old males would find "unsurprising and fairly routine." Moreover, there was no evidence that these letters adversely affected the school—except after public disclosure. And this, wrote the judge, "was the result not of any misconduct on [the teacher's] part, but of misconduct on the part of others." The court concluded that a teacher's private conduct is a proper concern of his employer only when it affects him as a teacher; "his private acts are his own business and may not be the basis of discipline" as long as his professional achievement is not affected.

Age, Citizenship, and Disability

Can Teachers Be Forced to Retire because of Their Age?

Not according to the federal Age Discrimination in Employment Act (ADEA), which has led to the virtual elimination of mandatory teacher retirement.

There are strong arguments on both sides of the compulsory retirement debate. Those who support mandatory retirement argue that it opens up employment for younger teachers, makes more places available for minorities, brings new energetic teachers with fresh ideas into the schools, reduces costs, eliminates the potentially ineffective, and facilitates personnel planning.

Opponents of mandatory retirement emphasize other points: (1) forced retirement based solely on age is arbitrary, and age alone is a poor indicator of ability; (2) mandatory retirement decreases life expectancy: therefore, the right to work as long as one can is basic to the right to survive; (3) forced retirement has relatively little effect on the recruiting of minorities or younger people; (4) it is a poor method for eliminating the incompetent; and (5) older workers are as good as younger co-workers with regard to "dependability, judgment, work quality, work volume, human relations [and] absenteeism."[113] On the basis of arguments such as these, Congress passed the ADEA "to promote employment of older persons based on their ability" and "to prohibit arbitrary age discrimination."[114]

In 1978, the ADEA applied only to individuals who were "at least 40 years of age but less than 70." In 1986, the act was amended to eliminate the age ceiling. As a result, it is now unlawful for schools to refuse to hire, to discharge, or to discriminate against any teacher on the basis of age with respect to compensation or conditions of employment. Thus a California teacher successfully challenged a state law that excluded individuals over 60 from eligibility for disability allowances as a violation of the ADEA.[115]

In 2000, the U.S. Supreme Court ruled, in *Kimel* v. *Florida Board of Regents,* that the states' Eleventh Amendment sovereign immunity prohibits individuals from suing states under the ADEA. However, the Court emphasized that citizens are still protected by "state age discrimination statutes, and may recover money damages from their state employers, in almost every state in the Union."[116] Furthermore, the federal government may still sue states to enforce the ADEA and individuals may sue states when the state waives its immunity, as it recently did in a California higher education case.[117] In addition, a citizen may sue under the ADEA "when the defendant is not the state itself but a 'lesser entity' such as a municipality"—a distinction that depends on each state's law.[118] Thus, in a 2001 Connecticut case, an art teacher was permitted to pursue his age discrimination claim under the ADEA against a local school board.[119] In sum, despite *Kimel,* many teachers will still be able to sue under the ADEA and almost all teachers will be protected by state age discrimination statutes.

How Can a Teacher Prove Age Discrimination?

Proving age discrimination involves a three-step process. First, the teacher must establish a *prima facie* case.[120] To establish such a case, teachers must show they were: (1) within the protected age group, (2) replaced by a younger worker, (3) discharged, and (4) performed their work satisfactorily. Second, if a *prima facie* case is established, the school must produce evidence of a nondiscriminatory reason for its action. Third, if such reasons are presented, the teacher must show that the school's reasons are not true, but are pretexts for age discrimination.

This process was illustrated by a 1997 decision involving John Schartz, a Kansas teacher who retired after a pretermination hearing.[121] The hearing was held after a series of students complained about his inappropriate sexual comments. Schartz alleged age discrimination and claimed he was forced to retire to protect his health insurance. The federal court ruled that Schartz established a *prima facie* case because he (1) was over age 40, (2) was replaced by a younger worker, (3) was "constructively discharged" (since he was given the choice between retirement and termination and therefore felt "compelled to retire"), and (4) had made "a minimum showing that his performance was satisfactory" during his 29 years. Next, the burden of proof shifted to the school, which presented reasons for terminating Schartz that had nothing to do with his age. Based on five documented student complaints during the previous year, administrators maintained that Schartz's job performance was unsatisfactory. Schartz countered with affidavits from nine teachers who retired during 10 previous years and also believed they were discriminated against because of their age. However, the court wrote that these "conclusory affidavits" concerning "perceived" discrimination were insufficient evidence to show that older teachers were treated differently than younger ones. Thus, the court ruled against Schartz because he failed to prove that the school's reasons for his termination were a pretext for age discrimination.

Can a Teacher Be Demoted because of Approaching Retirement?

No. In Illinois, two administrators were reclassified as teachers at lower salaries after they notified their superintendent of their plans to retire in two years. The district said the reclassification was based on its "concern about continuity." The educators, however, argued that this violated their rights under the Age Discrimination in Employment Act, and a federal court agreed.[122] To establish a violation of the ADEA, the plaintiff need not prove that age was the only factor motivating the employer, only that age was a "determining factor." Since the judge found that the district would not have reclassified the educators but for their intent to retire, and that such an action was "inexorably linked with age," the court concluded that the demotion violated the ADEA.

Does a School's Budget Problems Justify Hiring Only Younger Teachers?

No. The fact that a school district is suffering from tight budget constraints and that most young, inexperienced teachers can be hired at lower salaries than older, experienced teachers does not justify discriminating against a candidate because of age. This was the ruling of a federal appeals court in a Connecticut case in which a school selected a 25-year-old art teacher (over one who was 55 years old) in order to save money.[123] As the court explained, to classify employees "solely on the basis of age" for the purpose of cost savings in hiring, promotion, or termination perpetuates "the very discrimination at which the ADEA is directed."

Can Teachers Be Fired because of Obesity?

Probably not. Although weight may be a relevant factor in considering whether teachers can perform their jobs effectively, cases indicate that teachers cannot be fired solely because of obesity. Elizabeth Blodgett, a 42-year-old physical education teacher from California, was not rehired because her overweight condition allegedly rendered her "unfit for service." Blodgett was 5 feet 7 inches tall and weighed about 225 pounds. Although she was following a medical diet, her principal recommended she not be rehired because she was unable "to serve as a model of health and vigor" and was "restricted in her ability to perform or teach aspects of the physical education program [such as] modern dance, trampoline, gymnastics, and track and field."

Blodgett argued that obesity may justify discharging a teacher only when her weight "has impaired her ability to function effectively." Since the evidence in this case indicated she had been a successful teacher and coach, Blodgett felt that the school acted arbitrarily in refusing to rehire her. The court agreed.[124] As to her inability to serve as a "model of health," the court wrote: "Any requirement that the teachers embody all the qualities which they hope to instill in their students will be utterly impossible of fulfillment." As for a contention that the teacher set a bad example which her students might imitate, the court observed that "obesity, by its very nature, does not inspire emulation." Furthermore, there was extensive testimony that physical education teachers "need not excel at demonstration in order to perform their instructional duties competently and well." Since there was no evidence that Blodgett's weight had a negative effect on her teaching, the court ruled in her favor.

In a related New York case, Nancy Parolisi was denied a teaching license solely because she was overweight. Although she had established an excellent record during three terms of teaching, a board of examiner's physical fitness policy excluded candidates who were "extremely overweight or underweight." However, the court ruled that "obesity, standing alone, is not reasonably related to the ability to teach or to maintain discipline."[125] In another New York case, the commissioner of education ruled that school officials lacked authority to order a teacher to visit a doctor to develop "an appropriate weight loss program" and visit a dentist "to improve the condition and appearance of his teeth."[126]

Can Teachers Be Denied Certification because They Are Not Citizens?

Yes. Although several federal laws prohibit discrimination based on "national origin," the U.S. Supreme Court ruled that a state could prohibit individuals from becoming certified as public school teachers if they were not citizens or applicants for citizenship.[127]

The case involved two qualified New York teachers who applied for elementary certification but were turned down because they were not American citizens. In a 5–4 decision, Justice Powell noted that the distinction between alien and citizen is ordinarily irrelevant to private activity, but it is fundamental to certain state functions, especially teaching, which "goes to the heart of representative government." The Court emphasized that teachers "play a crucial part in developing students' attitude toward government and understanding of the role of citizens in our society." Moreover, a teacher "serves as a role model for his students, exerting a subtle but important influence over their perceptions and values." According to Justice Powell, all public school teachers, not just those who teach government or civics, may influence student attitudes toward the political process and a citizen's responsibilities. And schools "may regard all teachers as having an obligation to promote civic virtues" in their classes. Therefore the Court ruled that the state's citizenship requirements for teachers was rationally related "to a legitimate state interest."

Similarly, a federal appeals court upheld the authority of the Puerto Rican Department of Education to "unceremoniously" fire a qualified speech therapist because she was not a citizen as required by local law.[128]

Can Teachers Be Required to Reside in Their School District?

Most courts say yes. In 1972, the Cincinnati school board established a policy that required any employee hired after that year either to reside in the district or to agree to establish residency there within ninety days. Terry Wardwell, who was hired to teach, challenged the policy as discriminating against new teachers, because those already hired were permitted to live outside the district. But a federal appeals court held that there was a "rational basis" for the residency requirement.[129] Its reasonable purposes included employing teachers who are "deeply committed to an urban educational system," are less likely to engage in illegal strikes and more likely to help obtain passage of school taxes, and more likely to be involved in school and community activities and to understand the racial, social, and economic problems of the children they teach. The judge acknowledged that the rule's "limited applicability" to new teachers was "its most questionable feature." However, because the rule was designed to achieve a reasonable purpose, the court concluded that it was not unconstitutional solely "because it did not apply to all teachers."

A few courts have ruled against residency requirements. In a Kansas case, for example, a federal court held that a local residency requirement was "too crude" and arbitrary to meet its "avowed purpose."[130] The judge observed that the district offered "no proof that residents...are more effective teachers than nonresidents." However, as the Arkansas Supreme Court noted in a decision upholding residency requirements, "School boards are increasingly requiring employees to maintain residence within the school district and challenges have been rejected by a majority of federal and state courts."[131]

Can Teachers Be Denied Jobs because They Are Disabled?

No, not merely because of their disability. In 1973, Congress passed Section 504 of the Rehabilitation Act, which stated that "no otherwise qualified individual...shall, solely by reason of his handicap, be excluded from participation...or be subjected to discrimination under any program" receiving federal funds.[132] In many school situations, the question arises concerning what the statute means by an "otherwise qualified individual." In one case, a federal court explained that the term does not mean that disabled individuals must be hired despite their disability. Rather it prohibits the nonhiring of a disabled individual when the disability does not prevent that individual from performing the job.[133] (For related material on disabled students, see chapter 16.)

Can a Teacher Be Dismissed because of Extensive Absences Caused By an Illness?

The answer may depend on whether the illness continues to impair his or her teaching. In a New Hampshire case, Kenneth Dunlap's teaching contract was not renewed due to extensive absences.[134] Because of chronic asthma, Dunlap had missed an average of 22 school days per year over the previous six years. When Dunlap learned that his contract might not be renewed, he contacted a specialist, who prescribed a new treatment which the doctor asserted (without contradiction) would control Dunlap's asthma so that it would not continue to impair his teaching. Also Dunlap argued that the nonrenewal violated his rights under a state law prohibiting an employer from discharging an individual "because of [a] physical or mental handicap" that is "unrelated to a person's ability to perform a particular job."

However, the school board concluded that Dunlap's extensive absences clearly impaired his job performance. Dunlap responded that he had only a past record of impairment and that all of the medical testimony indicated that his illness did not then and probably would not in the future affect his ability to teach. Since the board presented no evidence that Dunlap's asthma caused his present teaching to be deficient or that it made "future deficient job performance probable," the court reinstated the teacher.

Can a Teacher Be Barred from Teaching because of Acquired Immunodeficiency Syndrome (AIDS)?

Probably not. After Vincent Chalk was diagnosed as having AIDS, the Orange County School Department transferred him to a nonteaching job. On the basis of extensive medical evidence, Chalk claimed that as a teacher, he posed no health risk to students or to other school staff. A federal appeals court agreed and ruled that Chalk's transfer violated his rights under Section 504 of the Rehabilitation Act, which prohibits discrimination against otherwise qualified handicapped people.[135]

The court acknowledged that "a person who poses a significant risk of communicating an infectious disease to others in the workplace will not be otherwise qualified." However, the judge emphasized that "there is *no* evidence" of "any appreciable risk of transmitting the AIDS virus under the circumstances likely to occur in the ordinary school setting." The court recognized that despite this medical opinion, there is widespread confusion about AIDS, and some people want to exclude anyone with the virus from the schools. The judge pointed out that the purpose of Section 504 was "to insure that handicapped individuals are not denied jobs or other benefits because of the prejudiced attitudes or ignorance of others." Therefore, since all medical evidence indicated that Chalk's illness was not communicable in the normal classroom, it ruled that he could not be barred from teaching because he had AIDS.

In addition, the U.S. Supreme Court has ruled that the Americans With Disabilities Act of 1990 protects individuals who test positive for human immunodeficiency syndrome (HIV) from the moment of infection, even when asymptomatic.[136] As a result, schools will have to make reasonable accommodations for such teachers unless there is a "credible scientific basis" for believing this would create a "direct threat" to others.[137] Whether a teacher's accommodation would create such a threat would depend on the specific facts of each case.

Summary

Most courts now hold that teachers cannot be dismissed for private conduct simply because it is contrary to the mores of a community. Thus the fact that a teacher had done something people often regard as immoral (e.g., smoking marijuana, committing adultery, engaging in homosexual activity, or using vulgar language) is not by itself sufficient grounds for dismissal in most states. For such a teacher to be dismissed, there must be substantial evidence that the alleged immorality is likely to have a negative effect on his or her teaching. As long as a teacher's competence is unaffected, most courts hold that private behavior is a teacher's own business. In addition, some judges are applying the new constitutional "right to privacy" to protect some aspects of a teacher's personal behavior.

On the other hand, courts usually uphold the dismissal of teachers whose unprofessional or immoral conduct becomes known through their own fault and, as a result, has a negative impact on their teaching effectiveness. They may be *suspended* because of a criminal indictment if the alleged crime relates to their job, but they may not be *dismissed* simply because of a serious criminal charge if they are not guilty. In cases of notoriously illegal or immoral behavior, some courts allow teachers to be fired even without evidence that the conduct impaired their teaching. For example, in cases involving armed assault, illegal drug use, or repeated convictions for drunk driving, some judges say that the negative impact of such behavior is obvious. Whether using profanity, hugging students, or committing a misdemeanor could result in dismissal probably would depend on the circumstances. Courts might consider the size, the sophistication, and the values of the community; the notoriety of the activity; the reaction of the students and parents; when the conduct took place; the teacher's motivations; whether it occurred in the community where the teacher is employed; and its impact on other teachers.

In cases of immoral conduct involving students, courts tend to be strict. Evidence of a single sexual relationship between a teacher and a student would probably sustain a teacher's dismissal even if the relationship occurred years before and even if no other students, teachers, or parents knew about it. Similarly, a teacher who made sexual advances toward students, told them to cheat, showed them pornographic films, smoked marijuana, drank excessively, or used obscene language with them would probably receive no protection from the courts. Teachers also could be disciplined for allowing students to drink or sexually harass others.

In addition to immoral behavior, schools also consider other aspects of teachers' private lives, such as age, weight, residency, and citizenship, when deciding whether to employ or rehire them. Under current federal law, it is illegal to discriminate against a teacher solely because of a disability or to compel such a teacher to retire. In addition, cases indicate that a teacher cannot be fired merely because of obesity. On the other hand, a state may refuse to hire teachers if they are not U.S. citizens or applicants for citizenship or if they refuse to live in the school district.

As the cases in this chapter indicate, the law concerning the removal of teachers for immoral or illegal conduct reflects the changing mores of our society. There are no recent U.S. Supreme Court opinions on the topic, and decisions in the state courts are sometimes inconsistent. Although teachers today have much more personal freedom than they did 50 years ago, they are still held to a higher standard of personal morality than most other professionals. Much depends on the circumstances of the case.[138] Nevertheless, most courts recognize that teachers should not be penalized for their private behavior unless it has a clear impact on their effectiveness as educators.

NOTES

1. T. Minehan, *The Teacher Goes Job-Hunting,* 124 *The Nation* 606 (1927).
2. *Morrison v. State Board of Education,* 461 P.2d 375 (Cal. 1969).

3. *Alford* v. *Ingram*, 931 F.Supp. 768, 771 (M.D. Ala. 1996).

4. *Hoagland* v. *Mount Vernon School District No. 320*, 623 P.2d 1156, 1160 (Wash. 1981).

5. Wis. Admin. Code § PI 3.04 (1989).

6. *McNeill* v. *Pinellas County School Board*, 678 So.2d 476 (Fla. App. 2 Dist. 1996).

7. *Id.*

8. *Purvis* v. *Marion County School Board*, 766 So. 2d 492 (Fla. App. 2000).

9. *Glover* v. *Williamsburg Local School District Board of Education*, 20 F.Supp.2d 1160 (S.D. Ohio 1998).

10. *Weaver* v. *Nebo School District*, 29 F.Supp.2d 1279 (D. Utah 1998). In addition, the court listed the laws of the District of Columbia and eleven states that prohibit discrimination based on sexual orientation. *Id.* Note 10.

11. *Jantz* v. *Muci*, 976 F.2d 623 (10th Cir. 1992). It is unclear whether a teacher could be terminated because of a homosexual marriage in those states that still criminalize sodomy. *Shahar* v. *Bowers*, 114 F.3d 1097 (11th Cir. 1997).

12. *Sarac* v. *State Board of Education*, 57 Cal. Rptr. 69 (1967).

13. *Board of Education of Long Beach Unified School District* v. *Jack M.*, 139 Cal. Rptr. 700 (Cal. 1977).

14. *Stephens* v. *Board of Education, School District No. 5*, 429 N.W.2d 722 (Neb. 1988).

15. *Ross* v. *Springfield School District No. 19*, 691 P.2d 509 (Or. Ct. App. 1984).

16. *Thompson* v. *Wisconsin Department of Public Instruction*, 541 N.W.2d 182 (Wis. Ct. App. 1995).

17. *Gaylord* v. *Tacoma School District No. 10*, 559 P.2d 1340 (Wash. 1977).

18. *Rowland* v. *Mad River Local School District, Montgomery County, Ohio*, 730 F.2d 444 (6th Cir. 1984).

19. *National Gay Task Force* v. *Board of Education of Oklahoma City*, 729 F.2d 1270 (10th Cir. 1984).

20. *Andrews* v. *Drew Municipal Separate School District*, 507 F.2d 611 (5th Cir. 1975).

21. *Eckmann* v. *Board of Education of Hawthorn School District*, 636 F.Supp. 1214 (N.D. Ill. 1986).

22. *Cameron* v. *Board of Education of Hillsboro Ohio School District*, 795 F.Supp. 228 (S.D. Ohio 1991).

23. *Board of the Education of Long Beach Unified School District* v. *Jack M.*, 139 Cal. Rptr. 700 (Cal. 1977).

24. *Board of Trustees of Compton Junior College District* v. *Stubblefield*, 94 Cal. Rptr. 318 (Cal. Ct. App. 1971).

25. *Yang* v. *Special Charter School District No. 150, Peoria County*, 296 N.E.2d 74 (Ill. 1973).

26. *Denton* v. *South Kitsap School District No. 402*, 516 P.2d 1080 (Wash. 1973).

27. *Hamm* v. *Poplar Bluff R-1 School District*, 955 S.W.2d 27 (Mo. App. S.D. 1997).

28. *Weaver* v. *Board of Education of Pine Plains Central School District*, 514 N.Y.S.2d 473 (N.Y. App. Div. 1987).

29a. *Clark* v. *Ann Arbor School District*, 344 N.W.2d 48 (Mich. Ct. App. 1983).

29b. *Elvin* v. *City of Waterville*, 573 A.2d 381 (Me. 1990).

30. *Fisher* v. *Independent School District No. 622*, 357 N.W.2d 152 (Minn. Ct. App. 1984).

31. *Toney* v. *Fairbanks North Star Borough School District*, 881 P.2d 1112 (Alaska 1994).

32. *Kilpatrick* v. *Wright*, 437 F.Supp. 397 (M.D. Ala. 1977).

33. *Weissman* v. *Board of Education of Jefferson County School District No. R-1*, 547 P.2d 1267 (Colo. 1976).

34. *Katz* v. *Ambach*, 472 N.Y.S.2d 492 (N.Y. App. Div. 1984).

35. *Youngman* v. *Doerhoff*, 890 S.W.2d 330 (Mo. Ct. App. 1994).

36. *Board of Education of Tonica Community High School District No. 360* v. *Sickley*, 479 N.E.2d 1142 (Ill. App. Ct. 1985).

37. *Conward* v. *Cambridge School Committee*, 171 F.3d 12 (1st Cir. 1999).

38. *State ex rel. Wasilewski* v. *Board of School Directors of Milwaukee*, 111 N.W.2d 198 (Wis. 1961).

39. *Shurgin* v. *Ambach*, 442 N.Y.S.2d 212 (N.Y. App. Div. 1981).

40. *United States* v. *Coffeeville Consolidated School District*, 365 F.Supp. 990 (N.D. Miss. 1973).

41. *Kerin* v. *Board of Education, Lamar School District*, 860 P.2d 574 (Colo. Ct. App. 1993).

42. *Ware* v. *Morgan County School District*, 748 P.2d 1295 (Colo. 1988).

43. *Bovino* v. *Board of School Directors of the Indiana Area School District*, 377 A.2d 1284 (Pa. 1977).

44. *Clarke* v. *Board of Education of the School District of Omaha*, 338 N.W.2d 272 (Neb. 1983).

45. *Fiscus* v. *Board of School Trustees Central School District of Greene County,* 509 N.E.2d 1137 (Ind. Ct. App. 1987).

46. *Stoddard* v. *School District No. 1, Lincoln County, Wyoming,* 590 F.2d 829 (10th Cir. 1979).

47. *Holt* v. *Rapides Parish School Board,* 685 So.2d 501 (La. App. 3d Cir. 1996).

48. *Pettit* v. *State Board of Education,* 513 P.2d 889 (Cal. 1973).

49. *Florian* v. *Highland Local School District Board of Education,* 570 F.Supp. 1358 (N.D. Ohio 1983).

50. *Nanko* v. *Department of Education,* 663 A.2d 312 (Pa. Commw. Ct. 1995).

51. *Ross* v. *Robb,* 662 S.W.2d 257 (Mo. 1983).

52. *In re Grossman,* 316 A.2d 39 (N.J. Super. Ct. App. Div. 1974).

53. *Everett Area School District* v. *Ault* 548 A.2d 1341 (Pa. Commw. Ct. 1988).

54. *Erb* v. *Iowa State Board of Public Instruction,* 216 N.W.2d 339 (Iowa 1974).

55. *Downie* v. *Independent School District No. 141,* 367 N.W.2d 913 (Minn. Ct. App. 1985).

56. *Board of Education* v. *Illinois State Board of Education,* 577 N.E.2d 900 (Ill. App. Ct. 5th Dist. 1991).

57. *Coupeville School District No. 204* v. *Vivian,* 677 P.2d 192 (Wash. Ct. App. 1984).

58. *Board of Education of Hopkins County* v. *Wood,* 717 S.W.2d 837 (Ky. 1986).

59. *Board of Education of Laurel County* v. *McCollum,* 721 S.W.2d 703 (Ky. 1986).

60. *Fontana Unified School District* v. *Burman,* 753 P.2d 689 (Cal. 1988).

61. *Katz* v. *Maple Heights City School District Board of Education,* 622 N.E.2d 1 (Ohio Ct. App. 8th Dist. 1993).

62. *Bassett Unified School District* v. *Commission on Professional Responsibility,* 247 Cal. Rptr. 865 (Ct. App. 1988).

63. *Blaine* v. *Moffat County School District,* 748 P.2d 1280 (Colo. 1988).

64. *Id.* at 1294.

65. *Burton* v. *Alabama State Tenure Commission,* 601 So.2d 113 (Ala. Civ. App. 1992).

66. *Ellis* v. *Ambach,* 508 N.Y.S.2d 624 (N.Y. App. Div. 1986).

67. Under federal law, a felony is a crime punishable for more than one year in prison.

68. *Skripchuk* v. *Austin,* 379 A.2d 1142 (Del. 1977).

69. *In re Thomas,* 926 S.W.2d 163 (Mo. Ct. App. E.D. 1996).

70. *Board of Trustees of Santa Maria Joint Union High School District* v. *Judge,* 123 Cal. Rptr. 830 (1975).

71. *Hoagland* v. *Mount Vernon School District No. 320,* 623 P.2d 1156 (Wash. 1981).

72. Misdemeanors are crimes punishable for less than one year in jail.

73. *Kenai Peninsula Borough Board of Education* v. *Brown,* 691 P.2d 1034 (Alaska 1984).

74. *In re Shelton,* 408 N.W.2d 594 (Minn. Ct. App. 1987).

75. *C.F.S.* v. *Mahan,* 934 S.W.2d 615 (Mo. Ct. App. E.D. 1996).

76. *Daniels* v. *City of Alco,* 732 F.Supp. 1467 (E.D. Tenn. 1990).

77. *Watson* v. *State Board of Education,* 99 Cal. Rptr. 468 (Cal. Ct. App. 1971).

78. *Alabama State Tenure Commission* v. *Lee County Board of Education,* 595 So.2d 476 (Ala. Civ. App. 1991).

79. *Dickson* v. *Aaron,* 667 N.E.2d 759 (Ind. App. 1996).

80. *Tracy* v. *School District No. 22, Sheridan County, Wyoming,* 243 P.2d 932 (Wyo. 1952).

81. *Williams* v. *School District No. 40 of Gila County,* 417 P.2d 376 (Ariz. 1966).

82. *Clark* v. *School Board of Lake County, Florida,* 596 So.2d 735 (Fla. Dist. Ct. App. 5th Dist. 1992).

83. *Lindgren* v. *Board of Trustees, High School District No. 1,* 558 P.2d 468 (Mont. 1976).

84. *Golden* v. *Board of Education of the County of Harrison,* 285 S.E.2d 665 (W.Va. 1981).

85. *Id.* at 670.

86. *Lesley* v. *Oxford Area School District,* 420 A.2d 764 (Pa. 1980).

87. *Board of Education of Long Beach Unified School District* v. *Jack M.,* 139 Cal. Rptr. 700 (Cal. 1977).

88. *Garcia* v. *State Board of Education,* 694 P.2d 1371 (N.M. Ct. App. 1984).

89. The court also noted that the state legislature intended "to encourage the rehabilitation of criminal offenders by removing barriers to their employment." *Id.*

90. *Hainline* v. *Bond,* 824 P.2d 959 (Kan. 1992).

91. *Stelzer* v. *State Board of Education,* 595 N.E.2d 489 (Ohio Ct. App. 3d Dist. 1991).
92. *Shaw* v. *Minnesota Board of Teaching,* 2001 Minn. App. LEXIS 609.
93. *Dupree* v. *School Committee of Boston,* 446 N.E.2d 1099 (Mass. App. Ct. 1983).
94. *Perryman* v. *School Committee of Boston,* 458 N.E.2d 748 (Mass. App. Ct. 1983).
95. *Baker* v. *School Board of Marion County,* 450 So.2d 1194 (Fla. App. Dist. Ct. 5th Dist. 1984).
96. Double jeopardy consists of being prosecuted twice for the same crime.
97. *Dubuclet* v. *Home Insurance Company,* 660 So.2d 67, 69 (La. Ct. App. 4th Cir. 1995).
98. *Stovall* v. *Huntsville City Board of Education,* 602 So.2d 407 (Ala. Civ. App. 1992).
99. *Kimble* v. *Worth County R-111 Board of Education,* 669 S.W.2d 949 (Mo. Ct. App. 1984).
100. *Bogart* v. *Unified School District No. 298 of Lincoln County, Kansas,* 432 F.Supp. 895 (D. Kan. 1977).
101. *Comings* v. *State Board of Education,* 100 Cal. Rptr. 73 (Cal. Ct. App. 1972).
102. *Board of Trustees of Santa Maria Joint Union High School District* v. *Judge,* 123 Cal. Rptr. 830 (Cal. Ct. App. 1975).
103. *Governing Board* v. *Brennan,* 95 Cal. Rptr. 712 (Cal. Ct. App. 1971).
104. *Jefferson Union High School District* v. *Jones,* 100 Cal. Rptr. 73 (Cal. Ct. App. 1972). Jones was decided together, with *Comings, supra* note 94.
105. *Board of Directors of the Lawton-Bronson Community School District* v. *Davies,* 489 N.W.2d 19 (Iowa 1992).
106. *Howard* v. *Missouri State Board of Education,* 913 S.W.2d 887 (Mo. Ct. App. S.D. 1995).
107. *Littlejohn* v. *Rose,* 768 F.2d 765 (6th Cir. 1985).
108. *Ponton* v. *Newport News School Board,* 632 F.Supp. 1056 (E.D. Va. 1986).
109. *Dike* v. *School Board of Orange County, Florida,* 650 F.2d 783 (5th Cir. 1981).
110. *Sullivan* v. *Meade Independent School District No. 101,* 530 F.2d 799 (8th Cir. 1976).
111. *Sherburne* v. *School Board of Suwannee County,* 455 So.2d 1057 (Fla. Dist. Ct. App. 1984).
112. *Jarvella* v. *Willoughby-East Lake* City School *District,* 233 N.E.2d 143 (Ohio 1967).
113. *Kuhar* v. *Greensburg-Salem School District,* 466 F.Supp. 806, 809 (W.D. Pa. 1979).
114. Age Discrimination in Employment Act, 29 U.S.C. § 621 (1986). The law also provides that mandatory retirement shall not be unlawful "where age is a bona fide occupational qualification." 29 U.S.C. § 623(f)(1) (1986).
115. *Smith* v. *Alum Rock Union School District,* 8 Cal. Rptr. 2d 399 (Cal. Ct. App. 1992).
116. *Kimel* v. *Florida Board of Regents,* 528 U.S. 62 (2000). A footnote on p. 91 of the decision lists the age discrimination laws in 48 states.
117. *Katz* v. *Regents of the University of California,* 229 F.3d 831 (9th Cir. 2000).
118. John Borkowski and Alexander Dreier, "The 1999–2000 Term of the United States Supreme Court and Its Impact on Public Schools," 148 *Ed. Law Rep.* 1, 19 (Dec. 21, 2000).
119. *Byrnie* v. *Town of Cromwell, Board of Education,* 243 F.3d 93 (2nd Cir. 2001).
120. A *prima facie* case is the evidence the plaintiff needs for the case to proceed and would enable the plaintiff to prevail unless contradicted by the defendant's evidence.
121. *Schartz* v. *United School District No. 512,* 953 F.Supp. 1208 (D. Kan 1997).
122. *Equal Employment Opportunity Commission* v. *Community Unified School District No. 9,* 642 F.Supp. 902 (S.D. Ill. 1986).
123. *Geller* v. *Markham,* 635 F.2d 1027 (2d Cir. 1980), *cert. denied,* 451 U.S. 945 (1981).
124. *Blodgett* v. *Board of Trustees, Tamalpais Union High School District,* 97 Cal. Rptr. 406 (Cal. Ct. App. 1971).
125. *Parolisi* v. *Board of Examiners of City of New York,* 285 N.Y. S.2d 936 (N.Y. Sup. Ct. 1967).
126. *Mermer* v. *Constantine,* 520 N.Y.S.2d 264 (N.Y. App. Div. 1987).
127. *Ambach* v. *Norwick,* 441 U.S. 68 (1979).
128. *Quintero de Quintero* v. *Aponto-Roque,* 974 F.2d 226 (1st Cir. 1992).
129. *Wardwell* v. *Board of Education of City School District of Cincinnati,* 529 F.2d 625 (6th Cir. 1976).
130. *Hanson* v. *Unified School District No. 500, Wyandotte County,* 364 F.Supp. 330 (D. Kan. 1973).
131. *McClelland* v. *Paris Public Schools,* 742 S.W.2d 907 (Ark. 1988). As the court noted, those challenging these requirements usually have the difficult burden of proving that they are "not rationally related to any legitimate objective." For more on this issue and a critique of the criteria used by courts in judging

these cases, see Bruce Beezer, *School Employees and Continuous Residency Policies: Is Competence Related to Immobility?* 41 EDUC. L. REP. 21 (1987).

132.   29 U.S.C.A. § 794 (1989).

133.   *Carmi* v. *Metropolitan St. Louis Sewer District,* 471 F.Supp. 119 (E.D. Mo. 1979).

134.   *Petition of Dunlap,* 604 A.2d 945 (N.H. 1991).

135.   *Chalk* v. *United States District Court,* 840 F.2d 701 (9th Cir. 1988).

136.   *Bradgon* v. *Abbott,* 524 U.S. 624 (1998).

137.   John Borkowski and Alexander Dreier, "The 1997–98 Term of the United States Supreme Court and Its Impact on Public Schools," 129 *Ed. Law Rep.* 887, 894-5 (1998).

138.   For more on this issue, see Todd R. DeMitchell, *Private Lives: Community Control* v. *Professional Autonomy,* 78 EDUC. L. REP. 187 (1993); Clifford P. Hooker, *Terminating Teachers and Revoking their Licensure for Conduct Beyond the Schoolhouse Gate,* 96 EDUC. L. REP. 1 (1994).

14 Are Teachers and Students Protected against Racial Discrimination?

Overview

Many scholarly studies have established that American culture, throughout its history, has been fraught with racism. There have been regional differences in the openness and intensity of racial discrimination, but rare indeed is the community that can claim to have been completely free from it. Even at the beginning of the twentieth century, blacks were "considered by many whites, North and South, to be depraved, comic, childlike, or debased persons."[1]

Schools, like other institutions in American culture, have reflected this widespread prejudice against blacks, Native Americans, Orientals, and Latinos. Many social forces have interacted to influence the schools, including the courts and the law. While no claim is made here that law is the most important force influencing attitudes toward different racial groups, it is recognized as one important influence on people in general and public schools in particular.

This chapter examines the impact of the courts and the law on racial discrimination against students and school personnel in the light of the U.S. Supreme Court ruling that segregation in schools is unconstitutional.

School Desegregation

Why Is Racial Segregation in Schools Unconstitutional?

The equal protection clause of the Fourteenth Amendment has been the major legal vehicle used to challenge various aspects of racial discrimination in public life. Section I specifies that "no State shall...deny to any person within its jurisdiction the equal protection of the laws." Early in the history of the amendment, it was determined that since public schools are state institutions, actions by public officials and employees are *state* actions. However, the famous case of *Plessy* v. *Ferguson*[2] established the principle that separate but equal facilities satisfy the equal protection clause of the amendment. Although *Plessy* involved public transportation facilities, the Supreme Court used it as precedent in a public school conflict in 1927.[3] Between *Plessy* in 1896 and the landmark case of *Brown* v. *Board of Education* in 1954, many lawsuits challenged the separate but equal doctrine, particularly in graduate and professional schools. Several such suits succeeded because it was not possible for the southern states engaged in segregated schooling to provide law schools or medical schools of equal quality in separate facilities for blacks and whites. These suits ultimately prepared the way for Linda Brown's successful legal action.

The Brown Case[4]

Linda Brown, an elementary school student in Topeka, Kansas, filed suit challenging a Kansas law that sanctioned the racially separate school she was attending. The district court found "that segregation in public education has a detrimental effect upon Negro children" but upheld the arrangement since schools for white children and black children "were substantially equal with respect to buildings, transportation, curricula, and educational qualifications of teachers." When Brown appealed to the U.S. Supreme Court, school officials argued that the Fourteenth Amendment was never meant to apply to the schools and that in any event, the *Plessy* principle of "separate but equal" should be followed and the Kansas law upheld.

Was the Fourteenth Amendment meant to apply to public schools? Chief Justice Earl Warren, writing for a unanimous Court, answered in the affirmative. He wrote that the amendment must be considered in the light of current facts and conditions and not those of 1868, when the amendment was adopted. Only by considering the importance of public schools in the middle of the 20th century could it be determined whether segregated schooling deprives students of equal protection of the law. Other judges and scholars have voiced the same conviction by asserting that the Constitution and its amendments stay alive by constant application to new conditions, lest they become mere "parchment under glass."

Courts do not follow precedents blindly, however. Changing conditions, as well as new knowledge generated by the sciences, may lead to the overruling of a precedent. This is precisely what happened in the *Brown* case.

The Court recognized that education has become

> perhaps the most important function of state and local governments.... It is the very foundation of good citizenship. Today it is a principal instrument in awakening the child to cultural values, in preparing him for later professional training, and in helping him to adjust normally to his environment. In these days, it is doubtful that any child may reasonably be expected to succeed in life if he is denied the opportunity of an education. Such an opportunity, where the state has undertaken to provide it, is a right which must be available to all on equal terms.

The Court then considered evidence offered by social scientists concerning the impact of segregation on school children and concluded that

> segregation...has a detrimental effect upon the colored children. The impact is greater when it has the sanction of the law; for the policy of separating the races is usually interpreted as denoting the inferiority of the Negro group. A sense of inferiority affects the motivation of the child to learn. Segregation with the sanction of law, therefore, has a tendency to retard the educational and mental development of Negro children and to deprive them of some of the benefits they would receive in a racially integrated school system.

Thus, in rejecting *Plessy* v. *Ferguson,* the Court concluded that "in the field of public education the doctrine of 'separate but equal' has no place. Separate educational facilities are inherently unequal."

How Soon Must Schools Desegregate?

Each community has its unique history of segregation, its unique traffic and residential pattern, and its own educational system, so the Court considered it unwise to pronounce one formula or timetable for desegregation applicable throughout the country. Instead, after hearing arguments on behalf of various possible remedies, the Court ordered that schools must desegregate "with all deliberate speed." Local school districts were to create desegregation plans, under the supervision of federal district courts, which are the courts closest to each locality. Thus school authorities were given the primary responsibility to solve local educational problems, but local courts were to decide whether the school officials acted in "good faith implementation of the governing constitutional principles." This decision is commonly known as *Brown II*.[5]

Are Parents Free to Choose Which Schools Their Children Will Attend?

No, not if their choices will perpetuate segregated schooling. This question arose after *Brown,* when various arrangements were created to delay and even avoid the mandate of the U.S. Supreme Court. Some localities even closed their public schools and then used public funds to support segregated private schools. Such subterfuge was ruled unconstitutional.[6]

The "freedom-of-choice" plan appealed to many parents and politicians. The plan gave individual families the choice of where to send their children to school, and it was quickly adopted in many communities and by many legislatures. One such plan was challenged in New Kent County, Virginia, where segregated schools existed under a law enacted in 1902. In the three years of operation of the freedom-of-choice plan, not a single white child chose to attend what had historically been the black school, and 85 percent of the black children continued to attend the all-black school. Eleven years after *Brown I* and ten years after *Brown II,* the dual system of schooling had not been eliminated.

The Supreme Court struck down the freedom-of-choice plan in this community as ineffective. In the words of the Court:

> Freedom-of-Choice" is not a Sacred Talisman; it is only a means to a constitutionally required end—the abolition of the system of segregation and its effects. If the means prove effective, it is acceptable, but if it fails to undo segregation, other means must be used to achieve this end. The school officials have the continuing duty to take whatever action may be necessary to create a "unitary, nonracial system.

A lower court gave a simple, pragmatic test for similar cases: "The only school desegregation plan that meets constitutional standards is one that works. "[7]

Must All One-Race Schools Be Eliminated?

Not necessarily. Geographic factors, population concentrations, location of schools, traffic patterns, and good-faith attempts to create a unitary school system must all be taken into consideration. The U.S. Supreme Court addressed this question in *Swann* v. *Charlotte-Mecklenburg Board of Education.* [8] The North Carolina schools in this case had adopted a desegregation plan that was being challenged during the 1968–1969 school year as inadequate. Chief Justice Burger, in writing for a unanimous Court, recognized that in large cities minority groups are often concentrated in one part of the city. In some situations, certain schools remain all or largely of one race until new schools can be built or the neighborhood changes. Thus the mere existence of such schools is not in itself proof of unconstitutional segregation. Nevertheless, the courts will carefully scrutinize such arrangements, and the presumption is against such schools. District officials have the burden of showing that single-race schools are genuinely nondiscriminatory.

The *Swann* case reached the Fourth Circuit Court[9] again in the year 2000, twenty-nine years after the ruling of the Supreme Court. Plaintiffs challenged the extent to which unitary status was achieved during all these years and the extent to which the desegregation criteria listed in *Green* have been satisfied (see page 303),[10] among several other actions by the school district. The court held that the original desegregation orders were still not fully satisfied and the district must continue its efforts under the continued supervision of the district court.

Can Racial Quotas be Used in Attempts to Desegregate Schools?

It depends on how such quotas are used. The U.S. Supreme Court ruled in *Swann* that "the constitutional command to desegregate schools does not mean that every school in every community must always reflect the racial composition of the school system as a whole." Thus, if a mathematical quota were used that required a particular percentage of racial mixing, the Court would disapprove. On the other hand, it is legitimate to use mathematical ratios as starting points or as general goals in efforts to achieve racial balance in a previously segregated school system.

Are There Limits to Using Buses for Desegregation?

Yes, in a general sense. Courts have recognized that "bus transportation has been an integral part of the public school system for years and was perhaps the single most important factor in the transition from the one-room school-house to the consolidated school." During the year (1965) that the *Swann* case went to court, 18 million public school children, or about 39 percent of the nation's enrollment, were bused to school. The U.S. Supreme Court has accepted bus transportation as an important tool of desegregation. Its use may be limited "when the time or distance of travel is so great as to either risk the health of the children or significantly impinge on the educational process." Furthermore, "it hardly needs stating that the limits on time of travel will vary with many factors, but probably with none more than the age of the students."

Can an Ethnic Group Be Exempt from Desegregation?

No. This was illustrated in San Francisco when Chinese parents brought suit to exclude their children from a citywide desegregation plan. The children attended neighborhood elementary schools that enrolled mostly Chinese American students. Parents valued this enrollment pattern, for it helped them maintain and perpetuate their subculture and the Chinese language. They expressed fear that a dispersal of Chinese American students, as part of an overall plan to achieve racial balance, would destroy their subculture and make it more difficult to teach their children the Chinese language. They also argued that San Francisco never had a dual school system so it need not create a unitary one. Moreover, claimed the parents, San Francisco had no rules or regulations segregating the races; district officials merely drew attendance lines to determine who goes to which school.

The district court ruled that if school officials draw attendance lines knowing that the lines maintain or heighten racial imbalance, their actions constitute officially imposed segregation and are therefore unconstitutional. The fact that San Francisco never had an official dual system is irrelevant. It developed such a system partly by the location of different racial groups and partly by the actions of school officials in arranging and rearranging attendance lines. While sympathetic to the concern of the parents, the court ruled that the Chinese American students must participate in the overall desegregation of the schools. Nevertheless, the court also supported efforts to develop bilingual classes for Chinese-speaking children, as well as courses that taught the "cultural background and heritages of various racial and ethnic groups."[11]

Is Unintentional Segregation against the Law?

No. Since the Fourteenth Amendment forbids the state from denying anyone the equal protection of the law, some actions by state officials must be identified as discriminatory action. In the early years of school desegregation, attention focused on southern states because they typically had laws that explicitly mandated or permitted segregated schooling. Such laws led courts to distinguish *de jure* and *de facto* segregation. *De jure* meant "by law"; *de facto* meant "as a matter of fact." The former was a violation of the Constitution; the latter was not.

As more cases were brought to court, in northern as well as southern communities, it became clear that segregation often occurs without explicit laws yet with the help of state, municipal, and school officials. Are such actions *de jure?* Yes, said the courts, for any action by governmental officials in the course of their duties is action "under color of the law." Examples of such official actions are the drawing of school district lines and attendance zones, zoning ordinances, creating housing and other residential restrictions, governmental support or insurance of home loans, and governmental enforcement of restrictive covenants in deeds to private property. All these practices had been used to create residential segregation and hence segregated schools. When the U.S. Supreme Court established these legal principles, it became clear that *de jure* segregation had occurred in virtually every city in the nation. School boards often contributed to such segregation without malice or bad faith but simply by being unaware of the consequences of their actions. Nonetheless, *their actions were intentional* in establishing district lines, attendance zones, location of new schools, hiring policies, and so forth.

This was illustrated in 1984 in San Jose, California, when a federal circuit court held that, considering the cumulative impact of all the evidence, there was segregative intent behind the policies and actions of the school board.[12] Among other actions, the board built new schools, rebuilt schools, used portable buildings, and closed schools in a manner that intensified racial imbalance. While the board's public pronouncements repeatedly declared its intentions to create a better racial balance, its actions, including its refusal to use busing to achieve integration while it bused one-third of its students for other purposes, maintained and even intensified segregation.

In 1979, the Supreme Court ruled once again, in cases involving Columbus and Dayton, Ohio, that intentional acts by school or other governmental officials were required for *de jure* segregation to be established.[13] If such acts occurred, the school district had the affirmative duty to eliminate all vestiges of segregation, even if the acts occurred years before. In Dayton, for example, the segregative acts occurred twenty years previously, but the city never completely overcame the effects of past segregation; therefore, said the Court, the duty to do so was never completely satisfied.

Can Courts Prevent the Transfer of Students That Would Cause Racial Imbalance?

Yes, ruled the Eleventh Circuit Court of Appeals in an Alabama case.[14] It held that courts could prohibit transfers to neighboring counties when such transfers would result in *de facto* segregation.

However, a request to transfer to a magnet school within the same school district could not be denied based on race. In a case that arose in Montgomery County, a request by a white student to transfer to a math and science magnet program was denied due to the "impact on diversity."[15] The court indicated that nonremedial racial balancing is unconstitutional and calls for the application of the "strict scrutiny" test. Where race is used as a criterion in such balancing or to achieve diversity, it must be justified by a compelling state interest and must be narrowly tailored to achieve its goal. Therefore, the court ordered that the student be allowed to transfer.

In a somewhat similar case, the West Irondequoit Central School District had an interdistrict transfer program that allowed only minority students to transfer from the city to the suburbs and only nonminority students to transfer from suburban schools to schools in the city.[16] When Brewer, a white student, requested a transfer, her request was denied solely because of her race. The court held that making race a complete bar to her participation in the transfer program was unconstitutional.

If Part of a School District Is Segregated, Must the Entire District Undergo Desegregation?

That depends on what portion of the school district is unconstitutionally segregated. The U.S. Supreme Court ruled in a case in Denver that if a substantial portion of the district is unlawfully segregated, the entire district must be involved in the remedy.[17] How much is a "substantial portion"? That depends on the circumstances; the district court closest to the facts is in the best position to determine whether the segregation is substantial enough to have an impact on the student composition in the entire district.

What If a Desegregated District Becomes Resegregated?

A community may desegregate its schools yet, as a result of population shifts and without any official action, resegregation may occur. Is there a duty to desegregate all over again? No, ruled the U.S. Supreme Court in a case from Pasadena, California.[18] Once the school district creates a "racially neutral system of student assignment," it does not have to readjust attendance zones when population shifts occur, because no official action caused the new imbalance. The new segregation is *de facto* and thus not unconstitutional.

After Achieving Unitary Status, May a School Board Modify Its Busing Plan?

Yes, ruled a federal appeals court in 1986 in a case involving the school system of Norfolk, Virginia.[19] Norfolk, pursuant to a court-approved desegregation plan that involved busing, achieved a unitary status and in 1975 received a court order recognizing this status.[20] Thereafter the school system stopped its busing, changed to a neighborhood plan, and shifted its sixth graders to middle schools, where busing continued. When plaintiffs challenged the end of elementary school busing, the courts ruled that in a unitary system, busing is a policy decision within the discretion of the school board as long as the board's intent in creating the policy was not racial discrimination.

In a similar case, involving the schools of Oklahoma City, another federal appeals court ruled otherwise.[21] Perhaps the conflicting holdings of these cases will be addressed by the U.S. Supreme Court in the future.

To further illustrate the complexity of school desegregation, we point to Topeka, Kansas, once again. There, on October 6, 1986, hearings opened in a case that is now called *Brown III*. Plaintiffs claimed that Topeka never fully complied with the order to establish a unitary, integrated school system. The defendant school district responded that it had complied with all court orders and legal requirements to desegregate and that the plaintiffs must prove that intentional state action caused the current segregation. The Tenth Circuit Court of Appeals found that Topeka still had not achieved unitary status. Until it does, ruled the court, the plaintiffs do not have to prove intentional conduct on the part of the school system to establish that current practices still reflect vestiges of the dual system. The burden of proof is on the school district to show that is has "eliminated all traces of past intentional segregation to the maximum feasible extent."[22]

When May a Desegregation Order Be Dissolved?

The U.S. Supreme Court addressed this question in *Board of Education of the Oklahoma City Public Schools* v. *Dowell,* a case that arose decades earlier, and handed down its decision in 1991.[23] The majority held that since desegregation orders were not meant to operate in perpetuity, the district court must determine whether the school system has complied in good faith and has, to the extent practicable, eliminated vestiges of past discrimination. The district court must examine not only student assignment, but also "…every facet of school operations …faculty, staff, transportation, extracurricular activities, and facilities" (criteria specified in *Green* v. *County School Board of New Kent County, Virginia,* in 1968).[24] In his dissent, Justice Marshall expressed his concern that the majority ignored the reemergence of one-race schools as vestiges of the earlier *de jure* segregation.

The Supreme Court addressed this issue again in *Freeman* v. *Pitts* in 1992 with the further question of whether a desegregation order can be incrementally dissolved.[25] The Court ruled in the affirmative, holding that federal judges have the power to relinquish control of desegregative orders and allow for "incremental withdrawal" of supervision of the schools. Among others, the judges should consider

> whether there has been full and satisfactory compliance with the decree in those aspects of the system where supervision is to be withdrawn; whether retention of judicial controls is necessary or practicable to achieve compliance with the decree in other facets of the school system; and whether the school district has demonstrated, to the public and to the parents and students of the once-disfavored race, its good-faith commitment to the whole of the Court's decree and to those provisions of the law and the Constitution that were the predicate for judicial intervention in the first instance.

The Court recognizes in both the *Dowell* and *Freeman* cases that while it has often used the terms "dual" and "unitary" schools, these have never been defined with precision, nor does the Court do so in these cases. In *Dowell,* it reiterated the importance of considering the six factors identified earlier in *Green,* namely, student, faculty, and staff assignments; transportation; extracurricular activities; and facilities. However, in *Freeman,* the Court mentions only four of these, thus indicating that there is no strict formula for solving these problems. It is clear that the Court values local control of public schools and intended federal supervision to be a temporary measure to remedy past discrimination. In the words of Chief Justice Rehnquist, school desegregation decrees "are not intended to operate in perpetuity." Socioeconomic changes alter the demography of schools, and the Court will not hold school boards responsible beyond good-faith efforts at meeting the *Green* criteria over a reasonable period of time. Thus judges have the power to remove desegregation orders in full or incrementally, depending on their assessment of the good-faith accomplishments of a particular school board. In 1995, the Denver school district went to court seeking to terminate judicial jurisdiction in its school desegregation case.[26] The Congress of Hispanic Educators and others opposed such a request, claiming that all that is possible has not been done for minority students in the district. After careful examination of the facts and relevant U.S. Supreme Court decisions, the district court concluded that earlier desegregation orders have been complied with and vestiges of past discrimination eliminated to the extent practicable. Therefore, the request to end continued court supervision was granted.

It is interesting to note that significant demographic changes occurred in Denver during the quarter of a century between the original *Keyes* case and this most recent one. The court noted that at the time the 1995 case was decided the mayor of Denver was black, his predecessor was Hispanic, the superintendent of schools was black, and the business and professional leadership multiracial. Thus, there was little danger that they would permit the public schools to deny minorities full participation.

In a recent case, the issue of dissolution of a desegregation order came up along with the use of racial quotas to enter a magnet school.[27] The district court, in its analysis, had high praise for the conscientious efforts of the Jefferson County Board of Education over a 25-year period to carry out the provisions of its desegregation decree. In light of the results of these good-faith efforts, the court dissolved the original decree. The school board, however, continued to use racial quotas to control enrollment in its magnet school. In this 2000 decision, the court ruled that such quotas violate the Equal Protection Clause of the Fourteenth Amendment.

The Commonwealth of Pennsylvania and a consolidated school district under federal court supervision for a desegregation order requested the court to lift the order and end the oversight since they achieved unitary status.[28] After thoroughly examining the evidence, the court held that the school district satisfied the criteria specified in the *Green* case and repeatedly approved by the Supreme Court. Thus, the unitary status was granted except in one respect. In the court's initial action, there were some ancillary remedies, including the detracking of the mathematics curriculum, which were not achieved. Thus, the court decided to retain supervision over curriculum, assessment, compensatory programs, and staff development. This case is a good example of the flexibility federal district courts have in their supervision of the process of desegregation.

Similarly, the administration of the Cleveland (Ohio) school system requested the federal district court to declare that they have achieved unitary status by satisfying all the requirements of a previously agreed-upon consent decree. The motion for declaration of unitary status was granted.[29] The original consent decree found that disparities in reading scores between African American students and other students were the results of an impermissible dual system. In this case, the court found socioeconomic factors to be the primary cause of the continuing disparities. Minority student absenteeism, high rates of dropout, suspension, and expulsion, as well as low academic achievement, were in no way attributable to actions of the administrators.

Can a Desegregation Plan for a City Cross District Lines to Include Suburbs?

Yes and no. This question has arisen in metropolitan areas where the core city, made up predominantly of racial minorities, is surrounded by suburbs that are predominantly white. In Detroit, for example, the city population (64 percent black, 36 percent white) made it impossible to achieve substantial desegregation within the city. Yet people living in Detroit's suburbs (81 percent white, 19 percent black) objected to a metropolitan area desegregation plan that would have included busing students across district lines.

Proponents of the "metropolitan plan" (also known as the "cross-district plan") argued that since education is a state function and the state only delegates its responsibility to local districts, Michigan had the obligation to desegregate Detroit's schools. Since many other governmental functions are performed on a regional rather than a citywide basis, there is no compelling reason why school desegregation should not be regionalized. District and appeals courts agreed, but the U.S. Supreme Court rejected this line of argument. In a close decision (5–4), the Court ruled that desegregation must take place within the city of Detroit because that is where the constitutional violation occurred: "the scope of the remedy is determined by the nature and extent of the constitutional violation."[30]

Chief Justice Burger noted, however, that "an interdistrict remedy might be in order where the racially discriminatory acts of one or more districts caused racial segregation in an adjacent district, or where district lines have been deliberately drawn on the basis of race." A case in Wilmington, Delaware, involved just such facts. When the evidence showed cross-district collaboration through official policies that created segregated schooling, and when it was clear that an interdistrict remedy was feasible, the federal district court ordered such a remedy, [31] and the Supreme Court affirmed this decision.

Three school districts were involved in a legal action that sought interdistrict remedy in the Little Rock, Arkansas, area in 1984.[32] The district court found that the three school districts engaged in racially discriminatory acts resulting in substantial interdistrict segregation. When a comprehensive examination of the entire situation indicated that these violations could be corrected only by a substantial interdistrict remedy, the court ordered a consolidated plan encompassing the three districts. The plan included a racial composition standard for each school (± 25 percent of the racial makeup of the student population); a uniform grade structure (K–6, 7–9, 10–12) "so as to enhance the ability of students to move about the district more freely"; a careful, court-supervised plan for busing; and a plan for magnet schools. The court, realizing the need for public support to achieve desegregation, required the school to hold "no less than three public meetings within their district for the purpose of explaining the…consolidation plan to their patrons and allowing constructive criticism." In sum, since the three districts collaborated to bring about unconstitutional segregation, they have an "affirmative obligation to eliminate segregation 'root and branch.'"

In Benton Harbor, Michigan, not only did the court order an interdistrict remedy for unconstitutional segregative acts engaged in by four school districts, but it also held the state of Michigan responsible for purposely violating both the U.S. and Michigan constitutions. As part of the remedy, the state was ordered to pay a substantial portion of the transportation costs entailed in the interdistrict remedy.[33]

By contrast, in a Cincinnati area school desegregation case, the court dismissed claims for an interdistrict remedy because there was not substantial evidence presented, only "unsubstantiated speculation" of interdistrict racial segregation.[34] And in a 1995 case that arose in Missouri, the U.S. Supreme Court ruled that the lower courts improperly ordered the state to provide funds for the Kansas City schools as part of a desegregation order designed to lure white students from surrounding districts.[35] The majority opinion in this (5–4) case, written by Chief Justice Rehnquist, shows a reluctance to link school segregation and residential segregation to a desegregation order. The majority opinion also indicated that federal trial courts should restore control of school systems to local and state authorities as soon as possible.

During 1999, the Missouri State Board of Education declared the School District of Kansas City to be unaccredited. When the school district went to court, the district court upheld the decision of the state board regarding the withdrawal of accreditation. However, on its own, the court also ruled that the district achieved unitary status, and would no longer be under a desegregation order.[36] On appeal, the circuit court reversed the lifting of the desegregation order because the district court proceeded on its own and the parties to the desegregation litigation never had a chance to be heard before the district court reached its decision.[37]

Do State Constitutions and Laws Relate to Desegregation?

Yes. Since the U.S. Constitution is the basic law of the land, no federal law, state constitution, or state law may contradict it. State constitutions, laws, and policies may go further than the federal Constitution, as long as they are not inconsistent with it. For example, several states, such as Connecticut, Illinois, New Jersey, and New York, have erased the *de jure—de facto* distinction by state law or policies of state boards of education and made them both illegal. Similarly, California eliminated the distinction by its state constitution.[38] (But see the next question and answer.)

The relevance of state constitutions is illustrated in the 1996 Connecticut Supreme Court decision in *Sheff* v. *O'Neill.*[39] In the Hartford area, suit was brought on behalf of public school children alleging denial of equal educational opportunities as a result of racial and ethnic segregation. When facts indicated that such segregation was *de facto* and the result of no official action or law, the defense wanted the case dismissed. Plaintiffs, however, claimed that their rights under the state constitution were violated, since it provided "both a right to a free public elementary and secondary education…and a right to protection from segregation."[40] The Connecticut Supreme Court agreed with the plaintiffs.

In its words:

We direct the legislature and the executive branch to put the search for appropriate remedial measures at the top of their respective agendas. We are confident that with energy and good will, appropriate remedies can be found and implemented in time to make a difference before another generation of children suffers the consequences of a segregated public school education.[41]

Thus, the court directed the legislative and executive branches to come up with some remedies, while retaining supervision over the case, whether the segregation was *de facto* or *de jure*.

Once a State Chooses to Do More to Desegregate Its Schools Than the Fourteenth Amendment Requires, May It Recede on Its Commitment?

Yes, ruled the U.S. Supreme Court in 1982 in a case involving the Los Angeles Unified School District.[42] In a previous ruling, the California Supreme Court held that the state constitution forbade both *de facto* and *de jure* segregation. Thereafter, in 1979, the voters of California ratified an amendment (Proposition I) to their constitution, which in effect repealed the state's antidiscrimination laws. The U.S. Supreme Court held that a simple repeal does not constitute an invalid racial discrimination and that the people of a state may experiment with different laws in addressing problems of a heterogeneous population. Thus it was proper for Californians to decide that the Fourteenth Amendment standards were more appropriate than standards repealed by Proposition I. In effect, the state went back to the requirement that intent to segregate must be proven to uphold a claim of unconstitutional action.

Very different results were reached in the state of Washington in regard to the so-called Seattle Plan for desegregation. This statewide initiative allowed students to go to schools outside their neighborhoods for various purposes (e.g., for special education, to avoid overcrowding, because of the lack of certain physical facilities) but *not* for purposes of achieving racial integration. In other words, there was to be extensive use of mandatory busing, but busing was permitted only for nonracial reasons. The U.S. Supreme Court struck down this initiative, which was clearly quite different from the simple repeal of a law as in the Los Angeles case discussed above.[43]

Can Private Schools Exclude Black Students?

No. Many private schools genuinely welcome students from all racial, ethnic, and religious groups, but some schools accept applications only from Caucasians or certain religious denominations. The First Amendment of the U.S. Constitution protects freedom of religion and thus the creation and maintenance of separate, private religious schools. No such protection is extended to racial prejudice, however. When black parents brought suit against a private school that denied admission to their children, the Supreme Court ruled in favor of the parents.[44]

Since no state action is involved when a private school denies admission, why did the Court rule for the parents? A federal law protects the equal right to enter into contracts,[45] and the Court ruled that this law prohibits private, commercially operated schools from denying admission to an applicant simply on the basis of race. Even private schools must submit to reasonable government regulation. The only exception is for a religious school where the religion itself forbids racially integrated schooling. However, as we explain below, such schools run the risk of losing their tax exemption.

In a highly controversial case, the Court reexamined this post—Civil War statute on contracts and significantly restricted its coverage.[46] The Court ruled in 1989 that this federal law does prohibit "racial discrimination in the making and enforcement of private contracts," but it does not address racial discrimination or harassment on the job. Legislative efforts were mounted to overcome the Court's ruling, and on November 21, 1991, President Bush signed into law the Civil Rights Act of 1991, which counters the Supreme Court's interpretation of § *1981,* making it applicable to postcontract formation employment issues, such as harassment and termination.

Sectarian private schools may lose their tax-exempt status if they engage in racial discrimination. The Supreme Court upheld the authority of the Internal Revenue Service (IRS) to deny tax-exempt status to Bob Jones University[47] The facts showed that while the university allowed blacks to enroll as students, it denied admission to those who engaged in or advocated interracial dating or marriage. The university argued that when the IRS denied its tax exemption, it violated the university's rights to free exercise of religion. The IRS, on the other hand, maintained that the tax code that grants exemptions applies only to institutions that are "charitable," are consistent with public interest, and are not at odds with the common conscience of the community. Since racial discrimination in education is contrary to public policy, institutions that practice it cannot be "charitable" within the intent of Congress as embodied in the relevant sections of the Internal Revenue Code.[48] The Supreme Court upheld the argument of the IRS that discrimination on the basis of racial association is a form of racial discrimination. In all likelihood, the same principles would apply to subcollegiate schools that engage in race discrimination.

What Is a Racially Hostile Educational Environment?

African American parents brought suit in federal court on behalf of their children, alleging that the school district of Tempe, Arizona, violated their equal protection rights and Title VI of the Civil Rights Act of 1964 (§601, 42 U.S.C.A. § 2000d).[49] Students in an English class were required to read classic literary works (*The Adventures of Huckleberry Finn,* by Mark Twain, and *A Rose for Emily,* a short story by William Faulkner) that allegedly contained "repeated use of profane, insulting, and racially derogatory terms." This, according to the parents, created a racially hostile environment in the school in violation of Title VI. We address the free speech issue in chapter 9, and here we discuss the claim of racially hostile educational environment.

The appeals court quoted the Department of Education's definition of a racially hostile environment "as one in which racial harassment is 'severe, pervasive or persistent so as to interfere with or limit the ability of an individual to participate in or benefit from the services, activities or privileges provided by the recipient.'" The facts of each case must be examined to determine whether such hostile environment exists. The race and age of the victim are important factors, yet the racist attacks need not be directed at the complainant to create the hostile environment. The students involved in this case were ninth graders, admittedly a very sensitive age. Fellow white students repeatedly called them "niggers," and the word was written on the walls of their school buildings. Yet the school authorities did nothing about the situation. The court noted that such harassment by fellow students, "that is tolerated or condoned in any way by adult authority figures is likely to have a far greater impact than similar behavior would on an adult." Since the school authorities allowed this situation to continue unchecked, after actual notice of it from parental complaint, the court found a violation of Title VI.

Racial Discrimination against Teachers and Staff

Does Brown *Apply to Teachers and Staff?*

Yes. While *Brown I* dealt with the general constitutional principles related to desegregation, the U.S. Supreme Court addressed the question of judicial remedy a year later in *Brown II*. Considering the appropriate remedies, the Court was mindful that the wide variety of local conditions would make a single monolithic order inappropriate. Therefore it generated several guiding principles. First, it required that school districts "make a prompt and reasonable start toward full compliance" with the ruling in *Brown I* and proceed "with all deliberate speed." Second, it gave the district courts supervisory responsibility to oversee school officials as they proceeded with good-faith implementation to desegregate the schools. The courts were to be "guided by equitable principles," a term that has traditionally meant "a practical flexibility in shaping remedies and by a facility for adjusting and reconciling public and private needs." Third, courts may consider "the physical condition of the school plant, the school transportation system, personnel," and other factors in supervising good-faith compliance.[50] Courts have relied heavily on *Brown II* in the breadth of their discretionary powers and in considering the role of teachers, administrators, and staff in efforts to desegregate schools.

Can Schools Still Delay Desegregation?

No. The Supreme Court's ruling in *Brown* was met with massive resistance, some blatant and some subtle, but schools were not desegregating. Therefore, fifteen years later, the Court declared that the doctrine of desegregating "with all deliberate speed" had run its course, and that schools may no longer operate a dual school system based on race or color but must "begin immediately to operate as unitary systems within which no person is to be effectively excluded from any school because of race or color."[51]

How Quickly Must Faculty and Staff Be Desegregated?

That depends on the local situation, including the racial composition of the teaching force and the staff, as well as the overall plan to desegregate in good faith. For example, in Montgomery County, Alabama, the district court required the immediate desegregation of "the substitute teachers, the student teachers, [and] the night faculties," since this could be accomplished without any administrative problems, but the desegregation of the regular faculties was ordered on a slower, more gradual basis. The U.S. Supreme Court approved the actions of the district court, saying that it had repeatedly recognized faculty and staff desegregation "to be an important aspect of the basic task of achieving a public school system wholly free from racial discrimination."[52]

Can Minorities Be Dismissed When Reductions Occur as a Result of Desegregation?

Yes, but only if objective criteria are used to make the reduction decisions. This question arose in many school districts that maintained a dual system, one for black students and the other for whites. There were many underenrolled classes, and small schools with administrators in charge of each school. When unitary school districts were being formed as a result of court-ordered desegregation, it became clear that many communities had been supporting a surplus of teachers and administrators as a price of segregation. As a result, when the schools were consolidated, many black educators lost their jobs. When some black educators in Mississippi challenged such practices, the courts generated some guiding principles.

In *Singleton* v. *Jackson Municipal Separate School District,* a school desegregation case that arose in Jackson, Mississippi, the U.S. Court of Appeals for the Fifth Circuit, ordered that principals, teachers, teacher aides, and staff who work with children be so assigned within the district that "in no case will the racial composition of a staff indicate that a school is intended for Negro students or white students."[53] Subsequent hiring should be conducted so that the racial composition of teachers and staff within each school reflects the racial composition in the entire school system. Moreover, if there is to be any reduction in the number of administrators, faculty, or staff, or if there are any demotions, members to be demoted or dismissed "must be selected on the basis of objective and reasonable and nondiscriminatory standards from among all the staff of the school district." If demotions or dismissals occur, no replacements may be made through the hiring or promoting of a person of a different race or national origin from that of the dismissed or demoted individual until each displaced staff member who is qualified has had an opportunity to fill the vacancy. This is the *Singleton* principle.

Where Do the Objective Criteria Used in Dismissals or Demotions Come From?

Such criteria must be developed by the school district. These nonracial objective criteria must be available for public inspection.

Do Faculty and Staff Have Access to the Evaluations?

Yes. This was a requirement in *Singleton,* and many subsequent courts, including the U.S. Supreme Court, have referred to the *Singleton* principles with approval.

What Is a Demotion?

Singleton held that a demotion is any reassignment that (1) leads to less pay or less responsibility, or (2) requires less skill than the previous assignment, or (3) requires a teacher to teach a subject or grade other than one for which the teacher is certified or for which he or she has had substantial experience within the previous five years.

Must Objective Criteria Always Be Used Before a Black Teacher Can Be Dismissed?

No, only when faculty reduction accompanies school desegregation. This question arose concerning Watts, a black teacher who taught for 25 years in the Tuscaloosa County school system in Alabama, 24 of those in all-black schools. When the schools were desegregated pursuant to a court order in 1970, she was transferred to a predominantly white school. According to the testimony presented at the trial, Watts had severe discipline problems, which she could not master. The school board suspended her a year later and held hearings with respect to her competence. She called no witnesses on her own behalf, nor did she cross-examine those who testified about her lack of competence.

When the hearings resulted in her dismissal for incompetence, she appealed to a state administrative commission, and when that agency upheld the decision of the school board, she went to court. The court held that the *Singleton* principle that requires the application of objective criteria before a teacher can be dismissed governs only reductions resulting from court-ordered conversion to a unitary system. In Watts's case, there was no faculty or staff reduction immediately before or following desegregation. Courts will be reluctant "to intrude upon the internal affairs of local school authorities in such matters as teacher competency." Thus if there is substantial evidence to support the board's finding of incompetence, courts will not substitute their judgment for that of the board. A federal appeals court upheld the dismissal of Watts.[54]

What Is Affirmative Action?

During the 1960s, there was widespread recognition that after about 200 years of racial discrimination it was not sufficient to merely prohibit discrimination. Under the leadership of President Lyndon B. Johnson, policies and programs were created to overcome inequities suffered by racial and ethnic minorities and women. The various forms of these policies and programs became known as "affirmative action." The Nixon administration expanded these programs by imposing goals for the inclusion of minorities in admissions and hiring and by specifying timetables for meeting such goals. While these programs have sought special assistance for veterans, the poor, the disabled, women, racial and ethnic minorities, and others, the greatest controversy arose concerning race-based affirmative action programs.

Can School Boards Hire by Race to Fill Vacancies?

Yes and no. In a school district undergoing court-ordered desegregation to overcome the results of past unconstitutional actions, the district court may order school officials to take race into account when filing vacancies. This happened in Boston, where the district court, as part of an overall plan of desegregation, ordered (1) the hiring of black and white teachers on a one-to-one basis until the percentage of black faculty reached 20 percent, (2) the creation of an affirmative action program to recruit black faculty until their proportion reached 25 percent of the faculty, (3) a coordinator of minority recruitment and a recruiting budget for 1975–1976 of no less than $120,000, and (4) periodic reports to the court on recruiting and hiring.[55]

The same question arose in Alabama when a school board's practice of filling "white vacancies" and "black vacancies" was challenged. The court ruled that if a school district is not involved in a desegregation process, and if there are no reductions, dismissals, or hirings in connection with such desegregation, then boards must seek the most qualified applicants, regardless of race.[56]

Can Schools Override Seniority and Tenure in Favor of Integration When Layoffs Are Necessary?

This depends on the situation. This question arose in Boston in 1982, in one of the series of lawsuits involving the desegregation of the city schools. Pursuant to the initial district court order in 1974 to desegregate the schools, a systematic effort was made to hire black faculty and administrators until they made up 20 percent of the work force. When massive layoffs threatened as a result of a budget crisis in 1981, questions arose concerning the validity of court orders to maintain the 20 percent proportion of minority educators when such action would override seniority and tenure rights of whites. The district court ordered maintenance of such ratios, and the circuit court of appeals affirmed this order.

The appeals court relied on principles laid down by the U.S. Supreme Court in 1977 in *Milliken* v. *Bradley,* where the Court said "the nature of the desegregation remedy is to be determined by the nature and scope of the constitutional violation."[57] Thus the appeals court upheld the order overriding seniority in favor of integration.[58]

In a similar case in Buffalo, New York, a court ordered a racial quota that superseded contractual and statutory rights. Evidence showed that the school system consistently hired a disproportionately small percentage of minority staff and assigned them to schools with large proportions of minority students. The court ordered the school system to hire black and white teachers on a one-to-one basis until the staff consisted of 21 percent black teachers in each tenure area; to maintain such ratio of black and white staff in each area in case of future layoffs; and to apply the same one-to-one hiring rule to any recall of laid-off, probationary, and permanent teachers. The appeals court up-held these requirements imposed by the district court in the face of proven past practices of discrimination.[59] It did indicate, however, that on the recall provision, the district court order was harsh in its treatment of laid-off, probationary, and permanent teachers, unless it was a "demonstrable necessity" that their rights be so impaired.

By contrast, the Sixth Circuit Court of Appeals struck down a quota system based on racial percentages that overrode contractual and statutory tenure rights in Kalamazoo, Michigan.[60] Pursuant to court orders, the schools there desegregated and made a good-faith effort over a 10-year period to remedy the effects of past discrimination. In the face of threatened layoffs, the district court imposed a quota to maintain the percentage of blacks hired. The appeals court held that a more flexible affirmative action plan with goals rather than quotas should be used. According to the court, seniority and tenure rights of teachers should be overridden only when it *is necessary* and not merely *reasonable* to "vindicate the rights of students." In this case, there was no evidence to prove such necessity.

In 1986, in *Wygant* v. *Jackson Board of Education,* the U.S. Supreme Court ruled on a voluntary plan in a Michigan school district calling for quotas in hiring, layoffs, and recalls.[61] The plan was included in a collective bargaining contract, binding on teachers, in which the board and the teachers agreed to a layoff plan designed to maintain the racial composition of the faculty, and whereby seniority provisions might in some instances be superseded. The federal appeals court had held the plan to be a reasonable means of remedying the chronic underrepresentation of minority teachers on the teaching force and therefore not a violation of the U.S. Constitution.[62]

Although previously the Supreme Court had not ruled on a public sector voluntary quota plan, it had ruled on a related matter in *United Steel Workers of America* v. *Weber* in 1979.[63] That case was brought under Title VII, and the Court ruled that Title VII does not forbid "private employers and unions from voluntarily agreeing upon bona fide affirmative action plans that accord racial preferences" designed to overcome racial problems in the work force. On appeal, the Supreme Court struck down the *Wygant* voluntary quota plan and concluded that the layoff provision violated the equal protection clause of the Fourteenth Amendment. The Court distinguished affirmative action from layoff plans, supporting the former but striking down the latter if racial classification is used, unless there is convincing evidence of prior racial discrimination in the particular school district. Since there was no such evidence presented in *Wygant,* the voluntarily bargained layoff plan that used racial classification to override seniority was declared unconstitutional.

Educators often use the role model theory to support affirmative action as well as racial preference in layoffs. In *Wygant,* the Court thought the argument based on this theory too weak to support a racially based layoff plan. It distinguished hiring goals from layoff plans, noting that the former "impose a diffuse burden" while the latter "impose the entire burden of achieving racial equality on particular individuals, often resulting in serious disruption of their lives. That burden is intrusive." Or, as the Court succinctly phrased it, "Denial of a future employment opportunity is not as intrusive as loss of an existing job."

In two related cases involving firefighters in Cleveland and sheet metal workers in New York City, the Court reiterated the constitutionality of affirmative action plans as a way of remedying past discrimination against minority groups when other approaches have not succeeded.[64]

Is Remedial Race-Conscious Affirmative Action Legal?

That depends on the circumstances. In a case that arose in Colorado during a reduction in force, the school district rehired a black social worker who had less seniority than a white social worker. The federal appeals court held this situation to be racial discrimination, for there was no evidence of past discrimination that would justify remedial race-conscious affirmative action.[65] To justify such affirmative action, there must have been "manifest imbalance" in a traditionally segregated job category. Furthermore, once such imbalance is demonstrated, the affirmative action plan must not "unnecessarily trammel" the rights of others.

Can Voluntary Affirmative Action Plans Be Agreed on between School Districts and Unions?

Yes, for such efforts are consistent with policies approved by Congress and the Office of the President as well as various decisions of the U.S. Supreme Court. However, even voluntary plans will be carefully scrutinized by the Court, for any official policy or action that takes race or ethnicity into account is suspect and must be justified by a compelling governmental interest. Thus, as we saw in *Wygant,* as well as in other cases,[66] voluntary raceconscious affirmative action plans will be upheld for hiring and/or promotion to overcome historic patterns of discrimination; layoff plans or plans that contradict seniority, however, have been struck down as too intrusive and hurtful of identifiable employees.

What Is the Current Status of Affirmative Action?

In recent decades, there has been increasing dissatisfaction expressed concerning the application and alleged misuses of affirmative action. In *Adarand Constructors, Inc.* v. *Pena,* the U.S. Supreme Court voted 5–4 that federal programs that award benefits on the basis of race must be subjected to searching judicial scrutiny and must be "narrowly tailored" to accomplish a "compelling governmental interest."[67] This standard, also called "strict scrutiny," has been applied to *state* affirmative action programs since 1989, when, in *City of Richmond*

v. *J. A. Croson,* the Court struck down a public works program wherein 30 percent of all contracts had to be reserved for minority-owned companies.[68] Justice O'Connor, writing for the majority, said that the constitutional guarantee of equal protection must mean the same thing at *all levels of government.* The majority opinion also makes it clear that this decision does not declare all affirmative action programs unconstitutional. In the words of the Court, "The unhappy persistence of both the practice and lingering effect of racial discrimination against minority groups in this country is an unfortunate reality, and government is not disqualified from acting in response to it."

Affirmative action has also become the subject of vigorous debates in the states. Governor Wilson of California ordered an end to all state affirmative action programs in May 1995, except those required by law or by a court decree. And, in 1996, Californians voted in a ballot initiative to end affirmative action in state hiring and in state-supported institutions of higher education.

After the schools of Boston underwent desegregation pursuant to a court order, the courts vacated all orders in the area of student assignment.[69] The Boston School Committee, however, decided to continue voluntarily a goal of 35 percent set-aside admission for black and Hispanic students for Boston Latin School, a highly prestigious academic high school. This voluntary affirmative admission plan was challenged on behalf of Julia A. McLaughlin, who alleged that the set-aside, an effort to achieve racial balance, violated her Fourteenth Amendment right to equal protection. The district court agreed and based its decision on several recent U.S. Supreme Court cases.

Judge Garrity relied on *Adarand*[70] in his assertion that "all racial classifications, imposed by whatever federal, state, or local governmental action, must be analyzed…under strict scrutiny." Furthermore, as the Court stated in *Wygant,* racial classification cannot be justified by general societal discrimination but only by prior discrimination "by the governmental unit involved before allowing limited use of racial classifications in order to remedy such discrimination."[71] And, under strict scrutiny, the racial classification must be "narrowly tailored" to serve "an identified compelling governmental interest."

Judge Garrity also discussed and rejected the idea that "educational diversity" is a compelling state interest sufficient to justify the 35 percent set-aside in favor of minorities. In this part of his analysis, the judge drew on *Hopwood* v. *State of Texas,* which rejected the idea that race and ethnicity can be taken into account to achieve diversity in the student group.[72] In sum, Judge Garrity granted the injunction ordering the school to admit Julia and not to use the set-aside as a way of achieving racial balance or diversity in a school that has already satisfied earlier court orders related to desegregation.

A similar case arose again in Boston some 10 years later. In the *Wessman* case, racial and ethnic criteria were used to achieve diversity in the highly prestigious Boston Latin School and two other "examination schools."[73] While the district court upheld the policy, the Court of Appeals for the First Circuit declared it a violation of the Equal Protection Clause. The court applied the strict scrutiny test and, while recognizing the good intentions behind the policy, the judge concluded that "noble ends cannot justify the deployment of constitutionally impermissible means." The court noted that, while diversity in a school population might be desirable, the school system failed to prove that diversity is a sufficiently compelling interest to withstand strict scrutiny. Furthermore, the court was not impressed by the statistical evidence presented in support of an argument concerning the amelioration of past discrimination. Thus, the policy was not narrowly tailored to rectify a specific harm.

A recent case in Virginia again struck down a weighted admission policy used to promote racial and socioeconomic diversity.[74] While earlier cases have upheld such a policy where the purpose was to overcome past discrimination, the purpose of the policy in this dispute was not to remedy past discrimination, but to achieve diversity. Since racial classification was involved in this case, the courts applied strict scrutiny, which requires that the government have a compelling interest it is trying to achieve and that its remedy or policy be narrowly tailored to achieve its end. To determine whether a policy is narrowly tailored, the court considered the following factors: "(1) the efficacy of alternative race-neutral policies, (2) the planned duration of the policy, (3) the relationship between the numerical goals and the percentage of minority group members in the relevant population or workforce, (4) the flexibility of the policy, including the provision of waivers if the goal cannot be met, and (5) the burden of the policy on innocent third parties."

The board itself was aware of alternative race-neutral policies available to achieve diversity. The duration of the policy was "for the 1999–2000 school year and thereafter," thus, it could continue in perpetuity. The court considered other aspects of the policy as well, including the future probability that young children may not meet the policy's diversity criteria and thus suffer its burden. In sum, the policy was declared unconstitutional.

Do School Boards Have the Authority to Achieve "Racial Balance" in the Teaching Force, as an Aspect of Affirmative Action?

The answer depends on the situation. Lawsuits have been brought under Title VII of the Civil Rights Act of 1964,[75] which was specifically enacted to end employment discrimination on the basis of race, color, religion, sex, or national origin and to remedy the consequences of prior discrimination.

In the township of Piscataway, New Jersey, the school board accepted the recommendation of its superintendent to reduce the teaching staff in the business department of the high school by one. There were two teachers of equal seniority in the department, both tenured, and both considered to be of equal quality. One of them, Sharon Taxman, was white and the other, Debra Williams, black. The board decided to lay off Taxman and retain Williams because Williams was the only minority teacher in the business department. Taxman challenged this action in court as a violation of Title VII as well as the laws of New Jersey. The District Court ruled in her favor, and the Third Circuit Court of Appeals agreed with its decision.[76]

Relying on earlier U.S. Supreme Court decisions, the appeals court ruled that the board's action was inconsistent with the intent of Title VII. The action had no remedial purpose because there was no racial imbalance in the teaching force as a whole in the high school. The board's stated purpose was to encourage diversity, which is nowhere included in Title VII. There was no underrepresentation of minorities on the teaching force, nor was the board's action aimed at remedying consequences of past discrimination. While the board's objective of achieving diversity was recognized by the court as a laudable educational objective, it cannot be used to justify the consideration of race in an employment decision.

Following the Supreme Court's decisions in *Weber*[77] and *Wygant,*[78] the appeals court also noted the important distinction in voluntary affirmative action plans between hiring and dismissals. Hiring goals impose a diffuse burden, while layoffs impose the entire burden of achieving racial equality on particular individuals. In sum, the court held that the goal of racial diversity is insufficient to satisfy Title VII's prohibition of race discrimination. This type of case is popularly referred to as "reverse discrimination" and is against the law.

A 1990 case held similarly that "…a layoff decision aimed at ensuring the employment of the district's only black administrator was 'outright racial balancing' in violation…" of the Supreme Court's ruling in *Weber*.[79] The Supreme Court accepted the Taxman case on appeal. However, the case was settled out of Court, thus the Court did not face the issue, and we will have to wait for an authoritative ruling.

In sum, the Supreme Court, like the country as a whole, is deeply divided on the question of the constitutionality and desirability of affirmative action. For now, however, all race-based policies at any governmental level must be submitted to "strict scrutiny," be "narrowly tailored," and advance a "compelling governmental interest." The achieving of racial balance for the sake of diversity is not justifiable under Title VII. However, affirmative action and racial balancing are justifiable pursuant to a court order to remedy an identified history of past discrimination and to eradicate the consequences of such discrimination. Such programs should include a timetable and proposed reevaluation plan to indicate that the action is intended to remedy past wrongs and will be dismantled when those wrongs are redressed.

School districts can create programs to assist "socially and economically disadvantaged" students as long as members of any race or ethnic group can apply for such programs. These can take the form of "magnet schools," "charter schools," or other creative efforts.

Must Principals Be Selected on a Nondiscriminatory Basis?

Yes, the selection of principals must be based on professional qualifications. If a school district is either reducing or increasing the number of its administrators and these changes are not in connection with desegregation, then objective criteria need not be used to select new administrators. If a black teacher claims nonpromotion to a principalship because of race, the burden of proof is on the teacher to support such a claim. Cases have held that such proof could be established by the claimant's showing a large reduction in the number of black administrators in a district that had no reduction in the percentage of white administrators. The burden of proof then falls on the school board to show that there were nondiscriminatory reasons for its actions.[80]

Can a Minority Counselor Be Demoted?

Yes, if there are adequate nonracial reasons for the demotion. In El Paso, Texas, Eduardo Molina, a Mexican American high school teacher, was appointed school counselor. After serving in that capacity for three years at two different schools, he was demoted to classroom teaching. Molina claimed that his demotion reflected his ethnic status and involvement in Mexican American affairs. The school district claimed that the demotion was based on his unsatisfactory performance as a counselor and his inability to get along with students, faculty, and other counselors. The court was satisfied with the evidence establishing Molina's unsatisfactory performance as a counselor. Even though there was also evidence of discrimination in the school system at large, in the opinion of the court there were sufficient nondiscriminatory reasons for demoting this particular individual.[81]

Can Teachers Be Transferred to Promote Desegration?

Courts tend to uphold such transfers as a way of promoting faculty desegregation. For example, when a white teacher in San Bernardino, California, went to court challenging a transfer based on her race, the court upheld the board's action.[82] According to the court, there was no violation of the Fourteenth Amendment because she continued teaching with the same position, salary, and benefits. Furthermore, she had no due process right to a hearing in connection with the transfer.

By contrast, a federal district court struck down a policy adopted by the Philadelphia schools that specified percentage quotas for the employment of blacks and the transfer of teachers on the basis of race. The court held the policy to violate Title VII of the Civil Rights Act of 1964.[83] In this school district, desegregation had been achieved to the satisfaction of federal law and there was no evidence that resegregation would occur. According to the court, "the involuntary transfer of a teacher from a particular school solely on the basis of race and the imposed restriction on the selection of a new school solely on the basis of race constitute racial discrimination with respect to the terms and conditions of employment."[84]

Thus it seems that school districts may consider race in the transfer of teachers to achieve desegregation. It is quite likely, however, that once desegregration is achieved, race should not be a key consideration in the transfer of teachers or in their choices among schools.

A different kind of case arose involving a white counselor in Flint, Michigan. There, a federal court held that there was no violation of the equal protection clause when a white counselor was demoted to classroom teacher. This action was part of the board of education's affirmative action program in light of a history of discrimination against blacks in the school system.[85]

Can a White Teacher Challenge Her Dismissal as Racial Discrimination?

Yes, ruled a federal court in a recent case in Tennessee. A white female elementary school teacher in a predominantly black school system was discharged and filed suit, alleging racial discrimination and retaliation for filing a complaint with the Equal Employment Opportunity Commission (EEOC).[86] The evidence showed that the principal was inconsistent in evaluations, made excessive unannounced visits to her classroom, reassigned her from fifth to first grade, required that her husband obtain a pass to enter the school, and failed to recommend her for tenure after finding her work satisfactory the preceding school year. All this evidence raised questions about the credibility of the principal and allowed the jury to infer retaliation. The jury awarded the teacher $137,017 in back pay and $1,000 in compensatory damages. The court deducted $3,000, the amount she earned in wages as a motel clerk after she was fired.

Must an Employee Prove Intentional Acts by the Employer to Prove Discrimination?

Yes, ruled the U.S. Supreme Court.[87] The requirement of the showing of intent to discriminate was highlighted by the Court once again in 1989 in *City of Richmond* v. *J. A. Croson,* involving a 30 percent "set-aside" plan for minority subcontractors. The Court ruled such a plan unconstitutional as violative of the equal protection clause, unless plaintiffs have proven that the city of Richmond has practiced racial discrimination against such subcontractors in the past. Furthermore, the Court also ruled in 1989 that the employee always bears the burden of proof in claims of discrimination and it is not enough merely to show statistical disparities in the racial composition of the work force.[88]

Can Objective Tests Be Used for Teacher Certification or Pay If They Disproportionately Fail More Minorities Than Whites?

Yes, if the tests are valid and reliable and are not used with the purpose and intent of discrimination against any race. In South Carolina, the National Teacher Examination (NTE) was used to screen people for certification. Candidates had to achieve a minimum score to be certified to teach in the state, and their pay levels were also determined by their scores. The use of the test was challenged because more blacks than whites failed to acquire the minimum score, and therefore a racial classification was allegedly created in violation of the Fourteenth Amendment as well as Title VII of the Civil Rights Act of 1964. The U.S. Supreme Court, after examining the NTE, concluded that the test was a well-developed instrument reasonably calculated to assess the presence or absence of knowledge.[89] It also found that the test was not created or used with the intent to discriminate; therefore its use was proper and legal.

In the same case, the Court held that using the NTE to determine the level of teachers' pay was reasonable and rationally connected to a legitimate state interest. A unitary pay system had been introduced in South Carolina together with the new basis for certification. The Court found that the reason for the new arrangement was the state's desire to use its limited resources to improve the quality of the teaching force "and to put whatever monetary incentives were available in the salary schedule to that task." Thus, finding no discriminatory intent in the use of the NTE for salary purposes, the Court upheld the state policy.

In 1996, a federal district court in California ruled on a case brought by a class of "African American, Latino and Asian" teachers pursuant to Title VII, challenging the use of tests as requirements for teacher certification. The tests focused on basic skills in reading, writing, and mathematics.[90] Title VII requires that the class of plaintiffs (race, sex, or ethnic group) have a selection rate of less than 80 percent in order to have a *prima facie* case of discrimination. If they succeed in this, the defendant must show that the test is a valid measure of job-related skills and that it has business justification for requiring those skills. After such showing, the plaintiffs may show an alternative selection device to the proficiency test.

The court ruled that the test was a reasonable requirement, relevant to the job of teaching, and the plaintiffs offered no alternative selection device. Furthermore, there was no evidence of intent to discriminate on the part of the defendants. The Ninth Circuit Court of Appeals affirmed the decision in a split vote with many partial dissents.

How Do Courts Determine Employment Discrimination—by the Racial Composition of the Schools or of the Larger Area?

The area, according to the U.S. Supreme Court. In a case in St. Louis County, Missouri, the school district suggested that the comparison be made between the teacher work force and the student population. The Court rejected this position and held that "a proper comparison was between the racial composition of [the] teaching staff and the racial composition of the qualified public school teacher population in the relevant labor market."[91]

Can Nepotism Constitute Racial Discrimination?

Yes, depending on the circumstances. A federal court of appeals held that nepotism can constitute racial discrimination where a school board's reliance on it in filling teaching vacancies had a disparate impact on minorities.[92] Nepotism, together with reliance on word-of-mouth hiring, had such an impact where the workplace was predominantly white. Thus the court granted an injunction against these practices.

Summary

Schools are the center of the storm as various interest groups attempt to put their ideas into practice and use the schools to attain their social goals. The meaning of the equal protection clause is generally agreed upon in bold outlines by the courts, even though many details and "legal wrinkles" still have to be ironed out. The major remaining tasks are those of implementation, to carry out the U.S. Supreme Court's clear pronouncement in the landmark *Brown* case that "in the field of public education the doctrine of 'separate but equal' has no place."

Brown I declared that segregated public schools are unconstitutional; *Brown II* ordered schools to desegregate "with all deliberate speed." Most communities resisted the Court's mandate. As legal challenges were mounted against the different forms of resistance to desegregation, courts tended to respect various plans to overcome historic patterns of racial separation as long as the plans were advanced in good faith and were likely to work.

Busing is a legitimate means by which schools may desegregate. Factors such as time and distance to be traveled must be considered in any plan for busing children, and the age of the children is a vital factor. Quotas may not be used as fixed requirements in attempts to achieve racially balanced schools, but they may be used as general goals in a previously segregated school system. In a school district undergoing desegregation, all racial groups must participate; no group may be exempt.

The Fourteenth Amendment prohibition against segregated schooling applies to the entire country and to all situations where official acts were involved in the creation or perpetuation of segregated schooling. Any intentional act that has a segregative impact is unconstitutional, however indirect or hidden the act may be. Not only must the laws of the state and the formal policies of a school district be examined to determine whether *de jure* segregation exists, but other officials actions must be looked at as well. These include the drawing of school attendance zones, zoning ordinances, residential restrictions, government support for housing and insurance, and all other actions used to create residential and therefore school segregation.

The Supreme Court has ruled that if a substantial portion of a city has been unlawfully segregated, the entire school district must be involved in the remedy. On the other hand, once a school district has undergone legitimate desegregation and, through ordinary events and without any official action, some resegregation occurs, the U.S. Constitution does not require a new effort to desegregate. Such a situation would be a *de facto* segregation and thus not unconstitutional.

Efforts to create metropolitan area desegregation plans have met with mixed results in the courts. If there is evidence to prove that officials of a city and its surrounding suburbs collaborated in the creation of a city heavily populated by racial minorities with suburbs largely populated by whites, a plan for interdistrict desegregation will be ordered. In the absence of such cooperation (or collusion), the district lines will be respected by the courts and the remedy will have to be restricted to the area in which the constitutional violation occurred.

In any effort to achieve desegregation, both federal and state laws must be consulted. All public schools must meet the minimum requirements of the national Constitution and the federal laws; state laws and constitutions may provide some remedies that go beyond the federal law. Private schools may not exclude students on the grounds of race. The Supreme Court ruled that federal law protects the equal right to enter into contracts, and thus a private nonsectarian school may not deny admission to an otherwise qualified applicant simply on the basis of race.

The general principles pronounced by the Court in *Brown I* and *II* apply to all aspects of schooling, including teachers and staff. Racial segregation is unconstitutional, and racial discrimination in all forms is illegal. This does not mean that race cannot be taken into account when teachers and staff are assigned. *Swann* makes a strong argument for the assignment of teachers and staff to enhance faculty desegregation and specifically rejects the notion that teachers must always be assigned on a "color-blind" basis. The implementation of desegregation is a complex and demanding task. As the Supreme Court said:

> There is no universal answer to complex problems of desegregation; there is obviously no one plan that will do the job in every case. The matter must be assessed in light of the circumstances present and the options available in each instance. It is incumbent upon the school board to establish that its proposed plan promises meaningful and immediate progress toward disestablishing state imposed segregation. It is incumbent upon the district court to weigh that claim in light of the facts at hand and in light of any alternatives which may be shown as feasible and more promising in their effectiveness.[93]

Desegregation with "all deliberate speed" has run its course, and schools must desegregate immediately. Nevertheless, courts still allow individual school districts reasonable time to achieve desegregation as long as they are proceeding in good faith. If, in the process of desegregation, a surplus of teachers, administrators, or staff appears, individuals to be dismissed or demoted must be selected on the basis of objective, reasonable, and nondiscriminatory criteria. In ordinary cases of reduction in force, or in dismissals based on incompetence, in the absence of desegregation, courts will allow school districts to follow their usual procedures. When a school district has substantially overcome the consequences of past discrimination and has achieved a "unitary" status, it may request the termination of court supervision. Such end to judicial supervision has been granted in several desegregated school systems.

If racial quotas are imposed by a court order as a remedy for past discrimination, such quotas may also be applied to layoffs in case of a budget crisis as well as to a program of recalls in order to maintain racial balance, even where seniority and tenure are superseded. In the absence of a court-ordered desegregation plan, when a collective bargaining agreement specifies quotas for layoffs and recalls that override seniority and tenure provisions, the plan will be upheld only if there is substantial evidence of prior racial discrimination in the particular school district. A voluntary layoff plan that includes racial classification may not override seniority or tenure in the absence of a history of discrimination in the particular governmental unit. On the other hand, affirmative action plans stating goals and hiring procedures that are aimed at overcoming a history of race discrimination and the consequences of such discrimination have been upheld by the Supreme Court. In the eyes of the law, the distinction between goals and quotas is important; the latter will be upheld only if temporary and either ordered by a court or adopted by a governmental unit with a history of substantial discrimination.

Objective tests may be used by public schools and state agencies in the process of certification, as well as in deciding where to place teachers on a salary scale, if the objective tests are reasonable, are relevant to the occupational tasks, and were not created with the intent to discriminate. The fact that the tests have a disproportionate negative impact on a racial or ethnic minority does not invalidate an otherwise acceptable test.

Affirmative action policies aimed at achieving diversity or racial balance have been declared unconstitutional if they use race as a criterion. Courts have held that neither "diversity" nor "racial balance" holds up under strict scrutiny or is sufficiently narrowly tailored to satisfy the compelling state interest test in order to pass constitutional muster.

Various school districts succeeded in their requests to have the courts lift their desegregation orders and thus supervision by the courts because evidence showed that they met the criteria set forth in the *Green* case.

In sum, the courts continue their efforts to apply the equal protection clause of the Fourteenth Amendment to the functioning of all school personnel. The problems change with changing times and conditions, but the principles of the *Brown I* and *II* are still alive and powerful in situations related to the racial integration of schools and school personnel.

NOTES

1. J. W. Peltason, 58 *Lonely Men: Southern Federal Judges and School Desegregation* (Urbana: University of Illinois Press, 1971).
2. *Plessy* v. *Ferguson,* 163 U.S. 537 (1896).
3. *Gong Lum* v. *Rice,* 275 U.S. 78 (1927).
4. *Brown* v. *Board of Education,* 347 U.S. 483 (1954).
5. *Brown* v. *Board of Education,* 349 U.S. 294 (1955).
6. *Griffin* v. *Prince Edward County,* 377 U.S. 218 (1964).
7. *United States* v. *Jefferson,* 372 F.2d 836 (5th Cir. 1966).
8. *Swann* v. *Charlotte–Mecklenburg Board of Education,* 402 U.S. 1 (1971).
9. *Belk* v. *Charlotte-Mecklenburg Bd. of Educ.,* 233 F.3d 232 (4th Cir. 2000).
10. See Note 24 *infra.*
11. *Lee* v. *Johnson,* 404 U.S. 1215 (1971).
12. *Diaz* v. *San Jose Unified School District,* 733 F.2d 660 (9th Cir. 1984).
13. *Columbus Board of Education* v. *Penick,* 443 U.S. 449 (1979); *Dayton Board of Education* v. *Brinkman,* 443 U.S. 526 (1979).

14. *United States* v. *Lowndes County Board of Education,* 878 F.2d 1301 (11th Cir.1989).

15. *Eisenberg* v. *Montgomery County Public Schools,* 197 F.3d 123 (4th Cir. 1999).

16. *Brewer* v. *West Irondequoit Cent. Sch. Dist.,* 32 F.Supp.2d 619 (W.D.N.Y. 1999).

17. *Keyes* v. *School District No. 1, Denver, Colorado,* 413 U.S. 189 (1973).

18. *Pasadena City Board of Education* v. *Spangler,* 427 U.S. 424 (1976).

19. *Riddick* v. *School Board of Norfolk,* 784 F.2d 521 (4th Cir. 1986).

20. Courts have used the designation "plural system" for segregated school districts and "unitary system" for those that have achieved satisfactory legal desegregation.

21. *Dowell* v. *Board of Education of the Oklahoma City Public Schools,* 795 F.2d 1516 (10th Cir. 1986).

22. *Brown* v. *Board of Education of Topeka,* 978 F.2d 585 (10th Cir. 1992).

23. *Board of Education* v. *Dowell,* 498 U.S. 237 (1991).

24. *Green* v. *County School Board,* 391 U.S. 430 (1968).

25. *Freeman* v. *Pitts,* 503 U.S. 467 (1992).

26. *Keyes* v. *Congress of Hispanic Educators,* 902 F.Supp. 1274 (D. Colo. 1995).

27. *Hampton* v. *Jefferson County Bd. of Educ.,* 102 F.Supp.2d 358 (W.D.Ky. 2000).

28. *Hoots* v. *Pennsylvania,* 118 F.Supp. 2d 577 (W.D. Pa. 2000).

29. *Reed* v. *Rhodes,* 1 F.Supp. 2d 705 (N.D. Ohio 1998).

30. *Milliken* v. *Bradley,* 418 U.S. 717 (1974).

31. *Evans* v. *Buchanan,* 393 F.Supp. 428 (D. Del. 1975).

32. *Little Rock School District* v. *Pulaski County Special District No. 1, et al.,* 597 F.Supp. 1220 (E.D. Ark. 1984).

33. *Berry* v. *School District of the City of Benton Harbor,* 564 F.Supp. 617 (W.D. Mich. 1983).

34. *Bronson* v. *Board of Education for the Cincinnati Public Schools,* 578 F.Supp. 1091 (S.D. Ohio 1984).

35. *Missouri* v. *Jenkins,* 515 U.S. 70 (1995).

36. *Jenkins* v. *School Dist. of Kansas City, Mo.,* 73 F.Supp. 2d 1058 (W.D. Mo. 1999).

37. *Jenkins* v. *Missouri,* 216 F.3d 720 (8th Cir. 2000).

38. *Crawford* v. *Board of Education in City of Los Angeles,* 551 P.2d 28 (Cal. 1976).

39. *Sheff* v. *O'Neill,* 678 A.2d 1267 (Conn. 1996).

40. *Id.* at 1280.

41. *Id.* at 1291.

42. *Crawford* v. *Board of Education,* 458 U.S. 527 (1982).

43. *Washington* v. *School District No. 1,* 458 U.S. 457 (1982).

44. *Runyon* v. *McCrary,* 427 U.S. 160 (1976).

45. 42 U.S.C. § 1981.

46. *Patterson* v. *McLean Credit Union,* 491 U.S. 164 (1989).

47. *Bob Jones University* v. *United States,* 461 U.S. 574 (1983).

48. I.R.C. § 501(c)(3) (1954).

49. *Monteiro* v. *Tempe Union High School Dist.,* 158 F.3d 1022 (9th Cir. 1998).

50. *Brown II, supra* note 5.

51. *Alexander* v. *Holmes County Board of Education,* 396 U.S. 19 (1969).

52. *United States* v. *Montgomery Board of Education,* 395 U.S. 225 (1969).

53. *Singleton* v. *Jackson Municipal Separate School District,* 419 F.2d 1211 (5th Cir. 1969).

54. *Lee* v. *Tuscaloosa County Board of Education,* 591 F.2d 324 (5th Cir. 1978).

55. *Morgan* v. *Kerrigan,* 509 F.2d 580 (1st Cir. 1974).

56. *Lee* v. *Conecuh County Board of Education,* 464 F.Supp. 333 (S.D. Ala. 1979).

57. *Milliken* v. *Bradley,* 433 U.S. 267 (1977).

58. *Morgan* v. *O'Bryant,* 671 F.2d 23 (1st Cir. 1982).

59. *Arthur* v. *Nyquist,* 712 F.2d 816 (2d Cir. 1983).

60. *Oliver* v. *Kalamazoo Board of Education,* 706 F.2d 757 (6th Cir. 1983).

61. *Wygant* v. *Jackson Board of Education,* 476 U.S. 267 (1986).

62. *Wygant* v. *Jackson Board of Education,* 746 F.2d 1152 (6th Cir. 1984).

63. *United Steelworkers* v. *Weber,* 443 U.S. 193 (1979).

64. *International Association of Firefighters* v. *City of Cleveland*, 478 U.S. 501 (1986) and *Local 28 of the Sheet Metal Workers' International Association et al.* v. *Equal Employment Opportunity Commission et. al.*, 478 U.S. 421 (1986).

65. *Cunico* v. *Pueblo School District No. 60*, 917 F.2d 431 (10th Cir. 1990).

66. *City of Cleveland, supra* note 64.

67. *Adarand Constructors* v. *Pena*, 515 U.S. 200 (1995).

68. *Richmond* v. *J. A. Croson Co.*, 488. U.S. 469 (1989).

69. *Morgan* v. *Nucci*, 831 F.2d 313 (1st Cir. 1987).

70. *Adarand, supra* note 67.

71. *Wygant* v. *Jackson Board of Education*, 476 U.S. 267 (1986).

72. *Hopwood* v. *Texas*, 78 F.3d 932 (5th Cir. 1996). Although *Hopwood* was a law school admission controversy, it reflects the growing rejection of race-conscious affirmative action to achieve "student diversity."

73. *Wessman* v. *Gittens*, 160 F.3d 790 (1st Cir. 1998).

74. *Tuttle* v. *Arlington County, Va., School Board*, 195 F.3d 698 (4th Cir. 1999).

75. 42 U.S.C.A. § 2000(e) et seq.

76. *Taxman* v. *Board of Education of Township of Piscataway*, 91 F.3d 1547 (3d Cir. 1996).

77. *Weber, supra* note 63.

78. *Wygant supra* note 62.

79. *Cunico* v. *Pueblo School District No. 60*, 917 F.2d 431 (10th Cir. 1990).

80. *Lee* v. *Conecuh County Board of Education*, 464 F.Supp. 333 (S.D. Ala. 1979).

81. *Molina* v. *El Paso Independent School District*, 583 F.2d 213 (5th Cir. 1978).

82. *Bolin* v. *San Bernardino City Unified School District*, 202 Cal. Rptr. 416 (Cal. App. 1984).

83. 42 U.S.C. § 2000(e) *et seq.*

84. *Kromnick* v. *School District of Philadelphia*, 555 F.Supp. 249 (E.D. Pa. 1983).

85. *Marsh* v. *Board of Education of City of Flint*, 581 F.Supp. 614 (E.D. Mich. 1984).

86. *Lyons* v. *Memphis Bd. of Educ.*, 6 F.Supp. 2d 734 (W.D. Tenn. 1998).

87. *Richmond* v. *J. A. Croson Co.*, 488 U.S. 469 (1989).

88. *Ward's Cove Packing Company, Inc.* v. *Antonio*, 490 U.S. 642 (1989).

89. *United States* v. *State of South Carolina*, 445 F.Supp. 1094 (D.S.C. 1977).

90. *Ass'n of Mexican-American Educators* v. *California*, 937 F.Supp. 1397 (N.D. Cal. 1996).

91. *Hazelwood* v. *United States*, 433 U.S. 299 (1977).

92. *Thomas* v. *Washington County School Board*, 915 F.2d 922 (4th Cir. 1990).

93. *Green* v. *County School Board*, 391 U.S. 430 (1968).

15 Are Teachers and Students Protected against Sex Discrimination?

Overview

In the past, both the culture at large and our schools functioned as if there were significant differences between males and females that should be reflected in schooling. Though some of these practices persist, many have been challenged. This chapter summarizes these challenges by examining questions regarding students and equal access to school sports, curricular exclusions, discriminatory admissions policies, and separate schools, and by examining questions related to married or pregnant students. This chapter also examines the court cases and legislation that have struck down school practices that discriminate against teachers in areas such as salary, promotions, and maternity leave policies. In addition, this chapter explores the recent explosive development in the law and governing regulations involving such issues as sexual harassment by faculty against students, by students against students, and in the form of same-gender harassment.

Sex Discrimination against Teachers

Employment Discrimination

Can Schools Pay Men More Than Women?

No. Under both the Equal Pay Act of 1963[1] and Title VII of the Civil Rights Act of 1964,[2] sex cannot be used as the basis of a pay disparity between individuals who perform substantially the same work.[3] A pay difference is permissible, however, if it is based on factors other than sex, such as experience or educational qualifications. Thus in a New York case, the court dismissed a claim that Title VII was violated where elementary school principals were paid less than high school principals, even though the latter tended to be largely male, while elementary principals were nearly all female.[4] The court explained that the mere fact that a lower-paid job was "traditionally female" is not enough to establish a Title VII violation: the critical question, rather, is whether any present violation exists. In examining the current situation, the court found that the salary difference was justified by factors other than sex, including the fact that the high school principal's job entailed greater responsibility and effort due to the size of the staff, physical plant, and student body, the larger budget, and other nonsex factors.

When Can Schools Pay Some Teachers More Than Others?

Schools may base their salaries on formal preparation and experience, and thus teachers may be placed on different steps of a schedule on the basis of those factors. Given objectively equal preparation and experience, some teachers may be paid more than others if such additional pay is based on merit or additional duties. These standards, however, must apply equally to men and women.

Can Coaches Receive Extra Pay?

Yes. Schools can create policies or negotiate extra-duty compensation to pay for extra duties, whether the duties involve coaching, drama, outdoor club, or others.

Can Male Coaches Receive More Pay Than Female Coaches?

The principle of equal pay for equivalent work has been difficult to apply in the area of coaching. Historically, significant disparities existed in favor of male coaches. While Title IX of the Education Amendments of 1972[5] has equalized some aspects of the funding of athletics, it has not been applied to coaching because Congress intended this particular law to apply to students and not to coaches.

   The federal Equal Pay Act of 1963 and similar state laws have been used to challenge unequal pay. In one such case, for example, female junior high school coaches brought suit when they were paid less than the male coaches in the same sports.[6] The court explained that under the Equal Pay Act, the female coaches could prevail only if they could show that their coaching jobs were substantially similar to the male coaches' jobs. Examining their respective duties, the court found that there were no significant differences between the male and female teams in terms of numbers of students, length of season, or number of practice sessions, and it concluded that the work of the male and female coaches was substantially similar and required the same skill, effort, and responsibility, except that the female track coach worked longer hours than the male coach. The court therefore awarded back pay to the female coaches.

   In a similar case, however, the court found that a salary difference (ranging from $50 to $580) was not a violation where different work hours were required for female volleyball coaches and male football coaches.[7] Note, however, that the Washington State government successfully turned back a legal challenge by female employees alleging not that they were paid unlawfully below their male colleagues performing the same jobs, but rather, were entitled to be paid at identical rates based upon the "comparable worth" of their respective jobs as compared to those performed by males.[8] The court there held that the Equal Pay Act required a strict comparison between male and female jobs in order to justify a finding of discriminatory wages, and that it would not engage in the speculative process of determining the relative value of different jobs within a particular government agency.

Does Coupling a Teaching Position with Coaching Constitute Sex Discrimination?

It may, depending on the circumstances. An interesting case arose in Arizona where the board of education required applicants for a teaching position in biology to have the ability to coach varsity football.[9] A female applicant who was not selected on the list of finalists for the position sued, claiming sex discrimination under Title VII, which prohibits discrimination in employment on the basis of race, color, religion, sex, and national origin. The term *discrimination* has been interpreted by the U.S. Supreme Court to include two different concepts:

> "Disparate treatment"…is the most easily understood type of discrimination The employer simply treats some people less favorably than others because of their race, religion, sex, or national origin. Proof of discriminatory motive is critical, although it can in some situations be inferred from the mere fact of differences in treatment…. Claims of disparate treatment may be distinguished from claims that stress "disparate impact." The latter involve employment practices that are facially neutral in their treatment of different groups but that in fact fall more harshly on one group than another and cannot be justified by business necessity. Proof of discriminatory motive…is not required under a disparate impact theory….[10]

A plaintiff bringing a charge of disparate treatment has the burden of proving each of the following: (1) that he or she belongs to the protected class; (2) that he or she applied and was qualified for the position; (3) that despite such qualifications, plaintiff was rejected; and (4) that after plaintiff's rejection, the position remained open and the employer continued to seek similarly qualified applicants.[11] Once the plaintiff has met the burden of proving a *prima facie* case—that is, has proven the above four elements, and thus is entitled to take his or her case to a jury empowered to determine if discrimination was the reason for the plaintiff's nonselection for the position—then the employer must establish a legitimate, nondiscriminatory reason for the actions taken. If the employer can do so, the plaintiff must then show the reason given by the employer was merely a pretext.[12]

In the Arizona case mentioned above, however, the teacher was not claiming "disparate treatment," but was using the theory of "disparate impact" to establish discrimination. In such a case, the plaintiff must show a causal connection between the employment practice and the differing treatment of a protected group. Most commonly, statistics are used to show that an employment practice disproportionately disadvantages women or men, such as a weight requirement for firefighters which tends to exclude women in greater numbers than men. Once the plaintiff has shown disparate impact, the employer then has the burden of proving "business necessity," that is, that the challenged employment practice is necessary for the safe and efficient operation of the business. There must be a compelling reason for the practice without acceptable alternatives to accomplish the same business goals.

When applying this standard, the Arizona court held that the school district presented no evidence that less discriminatory hiring practices had been attempted and failed, "and there was in fact substantial evidence that hiring alternatives were available and were not used." The Arizona court recognized that it might be possible for a school district "to show business necessity in the practice of coupling addendums (extra coaching assignments) and academic contracts." However, the burden of proving that was on the school district and in this case, it did not prove such necessity.

In a landmark 1989 decision, the U.S. Supreme Court ruled that employment decisions such as promotions and pay raises which are based in part upon sexual stereotypes constituted unlawful sex discrimination, even where legitimate reasons are also offered to support an employment decision.[13] In such so-called "mixed motive" cases, the courts will allow a female employee or applicant to demonstrate that the unlawful reason motivated the decision.

What Remedies Are Available under Title VII to Victims of Sex Discrimination in Employment?

Title VII authorizes courts to enjoin a defendant from engaging in unlawful employment practices and to order such relief as is appropriate, such as reinstatement and back pay. In addition, the Civil Rights Act of 1991 amended Title VII to allow both compensatory and punitive damages.[14] While governmental employers such as public school boards are exempt from liability for punitive damages, compensatory damages of up to $300,000 per victim depending upon the size of the employer's workforce are available for such damages as mental stress, humiliation, and somatic conditions caused by the discrimination. In a 2001 decision, the U.S. Supreme Court ruled that so-called "front pay," which is intended to compensate employees for lost wages from the time of a verdict through their reinstatement or court-ordered promotion, is a separately available remedy which is not capped by the statutory maximum on compensatory damages.[15]

Other more drastic remedies may be ordered by the courts under Title VII, including directing that a school district with a proven history of sex discrimination or sexual harassment institute written policies intended to eliminate discriminatory practices. Such orders are often incorporated into Consent Decrees, which require long-term court supervision over an employer's employment practices, including periodic reporting of its claims management practices regarding complaints of workplace sex discrimination and sexual harassment, as well as management and employee training.

Are There Remedies Available If School Districts Retaliate against Employees Who Make Claims of Sex Discrimination or Sexual Harassment?

Yes, there are. Section 704(a) of Title VII specifically prohibits employers from retaliating against employees because they have made claims or charges of discrimination or because they assisted others in doing so.[16] This does not mean that employees are only protected when they file formal complaints of discrimination with a federal or local agency, such as the EEOC. Filing an internal complaint within the school system is an equally protected act for which retaliation is strictly prohibited.[17] The courts have consistently ruled that, in order to prove an act of unlawful retaliation, an employee must show: (1) that he or she engaged in protected conduct, such as the filing of a charge or the making of a complaint; (2) that he or she suffered an adverse employment action; and (3) that the adverse action was taken (at least in part) because of the filing of the complaint.[18]

Can Gender Be a Relevant Factor in Selection of a School Counselor?

Yes, ruled the Montana Supreme Court.[19] The school in this case already had a male counselor, and in the search for a second counselor, males were excluded from consideration. The plaintiff challenged his exclusion, but the court ruled that gender in this situation was a bona fide occupational qualification (called a "BFOQ," and a permitted defense to discrimination claims under Title VII) because the position might call for special sensitivities in relationships with female students. Thus, in this instance, discrimination based on sex was reasonable.

Sex discrimination may appear in the selection or promotion process in other ways as well. For example, an unsuccessful applicant for promotion showed evidence of her outstanding credentials and excellent work record as well as the successful applicant's[20] poor work record, unprofessional and dishonest behavior, and intimate sexual relationship with a supervisor. The appeals court held that the evidence was sufficient to prove sex discrimination even though there was no "direct evidence of an explicit sexual relationship."[21] While this case involved nurses and a chief medical officer, the legal principles would be equally applicable to educators.

Marriage and Pregnancy

Can Teachers Be Dismissed for Getting Married?

Not public school teachers. Whatever rules of celibacy private schools may wish to impose on their teachers, public schools can no longer fire teachers for entering wedlock. This is not to say that teachers always had such a freedom. Historically many communities had contractual provisions forbidding marriage, which today would be struck down by the courts as being arbitrary,[22] against public policy, and a violation of the liberty provision of the Fourteenth Amendment, which has been construed as prohibiting local governments from interfering with the fundamental right to marry.[23]

Moreover, in many states such as Maryland,[24] there are specific statutes which prohibit discrimination on the basis of marital status.

Must Pregnant Teachers Take Specified Maternity Leaves?

No. Under the Pregnancy Discrimination Amendments of 1979 to the Civil Rights Act of 1964 ("PDA"), an employer may not single out pregnancy-related conditions for special procedures to determine an employee's ability to work. If an employee is temporarily unable to perform her job due to pregnancy, the employer must treat her the same as any other temporarily disabled employee; for example, by providing modified tasks or alternative assignments. Only if modifications are not feasible may schools require teachers to commence a leave without pay at some point during the pregnancy which is not compelled by the teacher's own physician. Whenever such a leave is taken, however, the teacher taking such leave is protected from losing her job by the provisions of the federal Family and Medical Leave Act of 1991 (FMLA).[25] Even before the enactment of these federal laws, the U.S. Supreme Court ruled that school boards could not require that maternity leave be taken at mandatory and fixed time periods without running afoul of the Fourteenth Amendment.[26]

In both the *LaFleur* case and cases decided under the Pregnancy Discrimination Amendments, a school policy that requires all pregnant teachers to begin leaves at the fourth or fifth month of pregnancy may be administratively convenient, but it conclusively presumes such women to be unfit to teach past those dates. Such presumption, particularly if unsupported by the individual employee's own doctor, is overly broad and unduly penalizes female teachers who bear children; therefore the policy is unconstitutional. A "return policy" that specifies any number of months or years after childbirth before the teacher may return to work is equally invalid, as it is arbitrary. However, under the FMLA, a teacher may be required to commence her maternity leave at least five weeks before the end of a school term and to remain on such leave until the end of the term in order not to disrupt the instructional program.[27]

The FMLA—which is enforced by the U.S. Department of Labor—generally requires state and local government employers[28] to provide up to 12 weeks of unpaid leave during any 12-month period for the birth or adoption of a child. Where married couples both work for the same employer, they may divide a total of 12 weeks' unpaid leave between the mother and father as they choose. Upon return from FMLA leave, an employee must be restored to his or her original job, or to an equivalent job with equivalent pay and benefits. Employees seeking to utilize benefits under the FMLA may be required to provide reasonable notice when the need is foreseeable, medical certifications supporting the need for the leave, and periodic reports during the leave regarding the employee's intent to return to work. Employees may also bring civil actions against an employer for violations to recover damages for lost wages and employment benefits, as well as reinstatement.

What Are Reasonable Requirements in a Maternity-Leave Policy?

School officials may require a written notice of intention to begin a pregnancy leave as well as a notice of intention of the date of return. They may also require a medical certificate attesting to the medical fitness of the teacher to continue or resume her work. This would amount to a complete individualization of maternity-leave practices. Under no circumstances may a teacher be terminated because of a pregnancy (whether she is married or unmarried or whether she becomes pregnant through artificial insemination or other unconventional means) under both the PDA, the FMLA, and local antidiscrimination laws which exist in most states.

Do Teachers on Maternity Leave Receive Disability and Other Employment Benefits?

Yes. Laws today generally require employers to treat pregnancy disability the same as any other disability. A Pennsylvania court held, for example, that discrimination based on pregnancy constitutes sex discrimination.[29] While this case was decided specifically under the Pennsylvania law, it reflects general principles applicable in other jurisdictions as well. The federal PDA requires employers to provide medical benefits for pregnancy-related conditions of employee's spouses, the same as are generally provided to spouses for other medical conditions.[30] The U.S. Supreme Court, however, has ruled that the PDA, while mandating equal treatment regardless of pregnancy, does not prohibit a state from requiring employers to give women unpaid pregnancy leave and then to reinstate them to their jobs, when other disabled employees are not given such "special treatment."[31] The Court found that such a state law does not compel employers to treat pregnant employees *better* than other disabled employees; it merely establishes benefits that employers must, at a minimum, provide to pregnant workers.

Can a School District Enter into a Collective Bargaining Agreement That Allows Female but Not Male Teachers to Take a Leave of Absence for Child Rearing?

No. The Third Circuit Court of Appeals held that a provision in a collective bargaining agreement that allows only female teachers to take a year's unpaid leave for child rearing violates Title VII.[32] The court noted that the U.S. Supreme Court had ruled that Title VII did not forbid limited preferential treatment of pregnant employees,[33] but it explained that those benefits were to cover only the period of "actual physical disability on account of pregnancy." Here, the leave of absence was available to females only, and there was no requirement of any related disability. The court thus found that the collective bargaining agreement violated Title VII and was void for any leave granted beyond the period of actual physical disability on account of pregnancy, childbirth, or related medical conditions.

Are Teachers Protected against Sexual Harassment?

Yes. Sexual harassment is sex discrimination prohibited by Title VII of the 1964 Civil Rights Act. Sexual harassment claims can also be brought under Title IX, and many states also have laws barring sex discrimination in the workplace. Most sexual harassment litigation in the workplace, however, has involved Title VII. The Equal Employment Opportunity Commission, the agency that administers Title VII, has issued guidelines that define sexual harassment as unwelcome sexual advances, requests for sexual favors, and other verbal or physical conduct of a sexual nature when (1) submission to such conduct is made either explicitly or implicitly a term or condition of one's employment, (2) submission to or rejection of such conduct is used as a basis for employment decisions, or (3) such conduct has the purpose or effect of substantially interfering with one's work performance or creating an intimidating, hostile, or offensive work environment.[34] In its first decision in a sexual harassment case,[35] the U.S. Supreme Court approved these guidelines and held that a claim of "hostile environment" sexual harassment is a form of sex discrimination actionable under Title VII.

The primary purpose of laws and regulations related to sexual harassment is to protect women in the workplace, since historically they were victims of widespread abuse, intimidation, and exploitation. Most often, such abuse came from supervisors and bosses who were in positions of power over rewards and promotions. In education, it was principals, supervisors, and other administrators who occupied these positions.

Historically, this kind of behavior was treated as immoral[36] or unprofessional conduct, and many administrators lost their jobs or were otherwise disciplined. Even today, it is most likely that actions against administrators guilty of immoral and unprofessional conduct will proceed on that basis (see chapter 13). However, it is clear that all educators, and not only administrators, are bound by the same principles. Teachers who harass their peers, secretaries, or even outside employees assigned to their school may be guilty of immoral or unprofessional conduct or sexual harassment. It is also clear that sexual advances or relations with students constitute such conduct (see chapter 13). An important distinction between students and adults is that minor students are legally incapable of consenting to such activities, whereas for behavior to constitute sexual harassment of adults, it must be *unwanted* sexual advances or other conduct. In short, genuinely consensual sexual behavior is not grounds for sexual harassment.[37] Whether the advances or verbal behavior was unwanted is a question of fact and must be determined by taking all relevant evidence into consideration.

The courts have ruled that employers are liable when employees engage in sexual harassment and the employer knew or should have known about the harassment but failed to take appropriate remedial action. Indeed, in two recently decided cases, the U.S. Supreme Court ruled that although Title VII allows the imposition of vicarious liability on employers for sexual harassment committed by their supervisors, where no adverse action is taken against the employee (such as discharge or demotion), the employer may be able to avoid liability by showing that it exercised reasonable care to prevent and promptly correct any sexual harassment when it came to the employer's attention, but that the employee unreasonably failed to invoke the procedures provided by the employer for rectifying and terminating such behavior.[38] Therefore, school districts can best protect themselves from liability by adopting policies that specifically prohibit sexual harassment and describe official complaint procedures.

In a 1993 decision, the U.S. Supreme Court held that a hostile work environment requires an objective standard—an environment that a reasonable person would find hostile or abusive—as well as the victims' subjective perception that the environment is abusive.[39] The Court explained that whether an environment is "hostile" can only be determined by looking at all the circumstances, including the frequency of the discriminatory conduct, its severity, and whether it is threatening or humiliating. The Court also held that the sexual harassment must be more than "merely offensive" conduct, yet it need not be so severe that it causes "tangible psychological injury."[40] On the other hand, where the conduct in question is limited to an occasional offensive utterance, with little more, the Supreme Court recently rejected a claim of "hostile environment" sexual harassment.[41] Thus, where a female personnel department employee complained that her male supervisor embarrassed and offended her by reading a sexually suggestive statement contained in a psychological report relating to a job applicant, the Supreme Court observed that: "Workplace conduct is not measured in isolation; instead, 'whether an environment is sufficiently hostile or abusive must be judged by looking at all the circumstances, including the frequency of the discriminatory conduct; its severity; whether it is physically threatening or humiliating, or a mere offensive utterance; or whether it unreasonably interferes with an employee's work performance.'"[42]

Is Same-Gender Sexual Harassment Actionable under Title VII?

Yes, according to the U.S. Supreme Court's ruling in *Oncale* v. *Sundowner Offshore Services, Inc.*[43] Joseph Oncale was an offshore oil rig worker who alleged that he was assaulted, touched, and threatened by three other men while working on a Gulf of Mexico oil rig. Oncale said that he twice reported the situation to his employer's highest-ranking representative on the job site, but no action was taken. He said that he feared that he "would be raped or forced to have sex."

In this case of first impression, the Supreme Court held that Title VII applies to same-sex harassment. In writing for a unanimous Court, Justice Scalia said that the severity of the harassment should be judged from the perspective of a reasonable person in the plaintiff's position, and to find a violation of Title VII, the behavior must create a hostile work environment for the victim. The Court cautioned that the statute does not reach ordinary socializing at work, nor does it turn Title VII into a general civility code for the American workplace. Where an employee is "exposed to disadvantageous terms or conditions of employment to which members of the opposite sex are not exposed," Title VII is violated, according to the Court in *Oncale,* regardless of whether those conditions are created by members of the same or the opposite sex.

Sex Discrimination against Students

School Sports

Must Girls and Boys Have Equal Access to School Sports?

This area of schooling is both complex and controversial. Because no simple answer is appropriate to this question, a variety of questions must be explored.

Can Girls Try Out for the Boy's Team?

That depends. Governing regulations promulgated under Title IX by the Office of Civil Rights of the U.S. Department of Education state as follows:

> No person shall, on the basis of sex, be excluded from participation in, be denied the benefits of, or be treated differently from another person or otherwise be discriminated against in any interscholastic, intercollegiate, club or intramural athletics offered by a recipient, and no recipient shall provide any such athletics separately on such basis.

> *Separate team.* Notwithstanding the requirements of [the above paragraph], a recipient may operate or sponsor separate teams for members of each sex where selection for such teams is based upon competitive skill or the activity involved is a contact sport. However, where a recipient operates or sponsors a team in a particular sport for members of one sex but operates or sponsors no such team for members of the other sex, and athletic opportunities for members of that sex have previously been limited, members of the excluded sex must be allowed to try out for the team offered unless the sport involved is a contact sport. For the purpose of this part, contact sports include boxing, wrestling, rugby, ice hockey, football, basketball and other sports the purpose or major activity of which involves bodily contact.[44]

In distinguishing between contact and noncontact sports, this regulatory interpretation of Title IX reflects the physiological differences between boys and girls in muscle mass, size of the heart, and construction of the pelvic area, which one court suggested "may, on the average, prevent the great majority of women from competing on an equal level with the great majority of males."[45] These differences permitted the courts to allow classifying students by sex in athletic competition and thus separating boys and girls without running afoul either of the Constitution or Title IX. Where a female student was denied the right to play competitive tennis on a boys' team—a plainly noncontact sport within the meaning of the Title IX regulations—the court found that her rights to equal protection and due process were violated.[46]

Other courts have also ruled that in noncontact sports, such as golf, swimming, and cross-country skiing, where no teams exist for girls, they may compete for positions on boys' teams. Where competitive teams are available for both boys and girls, most courts were satisfied with the provision of separate teams, even though the quality of competition tends to be higher for the boys.[47]

Once Even a Contact Sport Is Open to Students of the Opposite Sex, May Schools Discriminate by Gender?

No. In a case brought against Duke University, Heather Sue Mercer successfully challenged a federal district court's finding that the above-quoted regulation interpreting Title IX provided a blanket exemption for contact sports, and thus that the university did not discriminate against her during her participation in Duke's intercollegiate football program. In so ruling, the court held that "where a university has allowed a member of the opposite sex to try out for a single-sex team in a contact sport, the university is subject to Title IX and therefore prohibited from discriminating against that individual on the basis of his or her sex."[48]

Ms. Mercer, who had been an All-State kicker in high school, tried out for the Duke football team as a walk-on kicker—the only woman ever to try out for the team. Following a year of participation in conditioning drills and her winning kick in an intersquad scrimmage, the Duke kicking coach informed Ms. Mercer that she had made the team. She was listed as an official member of the team and appeared at all practices, although the following year she did not participate in any games. Yet she was then denied the right to attend summer football camp, was refused the right to dress for games or sit on the sidelines during games, and given fewer opportunities to participate in practices than other walk-on kickers, and eventually dropped from the team. Rather than try out for the team the following fall, Ms. Mercer filed a sex discrimination suit in federal court, alleging violations of Title IX, negligent misrepresentation, and breach of contract.

The district court dismissed her lawsuit, relying upon what it believed to be a blanket protection from Title IX liability where a school excludes a student's participation from a contact sports team comprised entirely of members of the opposite sex. However, the court of appeals disagreed, finding that once Duke University opened up its football tryouts to girls, it was obligated not to discriminate on the basis of their sex once they made the team. On remand, a jury in Raleigh, North Carolina awarded Ms. Mercer $2 million in damages for having been discriminated against as a member of the Duke varsity football team.

How Has Title IX Affected School Sports?

Congress made a significant impact on sex discrimination in schools by enacting Title IX of the Education Amendments of 1972.[49] This law provides that "no person in the United States shall on the basis of sex be excluded from participation, be denied the benefits of, or be subjected to discrimination under any education program or act or activity receiving Federal financial assistance." Title IX is relied upon in many situations to strike down discrimination against students based on sex because it is specifically aimed at such discrimination, whereas the clauses of the Fourteenth Amendment are more general and abstract.

Can Boys Try Out for the Girls' Team?

The courts have disagreed on how to interpret the equal protection clause to answer this question. Some courts have permitted separate girls' teams. For example, a New Hampshire court held that a high school boy could be prohibited from playing field hockey on a girls' team.[50] The court found that the athletic association had shown that it had several important objectives for its rule: encouraging the development of girls' sports, redressing the effects of past discrimination against girls' athletics, and providing as many opportunities as possible for girls to participate on an interscholastic level. The court then examined the exclusion policy to see if the policy was substantially related to achieving these objectives, concluding that it was. The court reasoned that it was a physiological fact that the boys would have an undue advantage competing against girls, and that, if permitted to play, could easily dominate such competition and displace girls from the teams. The policy thus made for fairer and better competition, promoting "participation in which girls, like boys, can learn to win and lose in a fair game."

Other courts have reached the opposite conclusion. In ruling that a high school boy could not be prohibited from playing on the girls' field hockey team, a federal district court found that the school district did not demonstrate that the policy was substantially related to its goal of maintaining opportunities for girls to participate in athletics.[51] Unlike the New Hampshire court, this court refused to rely on the general physical differences between girls and boys as a sufficient justification for its policy. The court explained that policies based on stereotypes "are not an appropriate way to reach even a laudable goal." Instead, the court looked at the actual evidence concerning the level of interest among boys in playing on the girls' team. Finding that only a few boys had even tried out for the team, the court concluded that the school's fears that boys would dominate the field hockey team were an insufficient justification for a policy that discriminates against boys in order to provide equal athletic opportunities for girls.

The courts and the U.S. Department of Education's Office of Civil Rights (OCR) have made it clear that Title IX requires that schools must offer girls and boys "substantially proportionate" playing opportunities. Thus, schools should ensure that girls and boys have relatively equal access to athletic facilities and equipment, that they receive the same level of coaching, and that they receive comparable uniforms and playing times. The OCR enforces Title IX by withholding federal funds to schools that are not in compliance.

The OCR has issued regulations interpreting Title IX that specifically allow separate teams for boys and girls where the selection for such teams is based on competitive skill or the activity involved is a contact sport. Contact sports include boxing, wrestling, rugby, ice hockey, football, basketball, and other sports "the purpose or major activity of which involves bodily contact."[52] The regulations add, however, that where a school sponsors a team in a particular sport for members of one sex but not for members of the other sex, and athletic opportunities for members of that sex have previously been limited, members of the excluded sex must be allowed to try out for the team offered unless the sport is a contact sport.

By requiring that both genders have equal access to athletics, Title IX has had a profound impact on the growth of girls' sports in high schools, and many believe it has led to U.S. domination in world-class events such as women's hockey and soccer. The number of girl athletes has increased from 294,000 in 1971 to 2.4 million in 1995, and from 32,000 female college athletes in 1975 to 170,000 such athletes in 2001. (The number of male athletes has remained about the same during this time, or approximately 3.6 million in K–12 sports programs.) OCR complaints now generally concern schools that give the boys' soccer team the first shot at equipment or that let the boys use the gym while sending the girls off campus to practice.

Litigation still occurs, especially concerning what sports are "contact sports," and thus a situation where a school can offer a single-sex team. One court has ruled that field hockey is a contact sport for purposes of Title IX,[53] while another has declined to so rule, explaining that according to the OCR regulations, the answer depends on whether "the major activity of field hockey involves bodily contact," and concluding that field hockey does not meet this test.[54]

Most Title IX lawsuits involve colleges and universities. Some colleges, for example, have eliminated some minor men's sports in order to meet the mandates of Title IX. In *Kelley* v. *Board of Trustees,* members of the men's swimming team brought a Title IX suit against the University of Illinois after the university terminated the men's swimming program but retained the women's swimming program.[55] The Seventh Circuit found that the percentage of women involved in athletics at the university continued to be substantially lower than the percentage of women enrolled at the school, and concluded that the university's decision not to terminate the women's swimming program was extremely prudent.

In a 1997 decision, however, the U.S. Supreme Court let stand a lower court ruling that Brown University was in violation of Title IX when it eliminated women's gymnastics and volleyball.[56] The *Brown* case attracted national attention because the university had seemed to offer a model athletic program, with seventeen varsity sports for women and sixteen sports for men, and because when Brown eliminated women's gymnastics and volleyball it also cut men's golf and water polo. Women, however, made up 51 percent of the student body and only 38 percent of the varsity athletes, and the court held that the university was still in violation of Title IX. The *Brown* case thus made clear that colleges and universities cannot deal with budgetary constraints by cutting women's sports.

What Effect Do State Equal Rights Amendments Have?

Although many states have added equal rights amendments (ERAs) to their constitutions, the legal meaning of such amendments is not yet clearly established. There is no uniformity among the states on what the amendments mean for co-educational athletic competition, and variations probably will persist from state to state because such provisions are interpreted by the courts of the respective states and not by the U.S. Supreme Court.

Under its state ERA, a Washington court ruled that girls are allowed to try out for the football team on an equal basis with boys.[57] A Pennsylvania court similarly ruled that under its state ERA, boys and girls may try out for all school teams, including those in contact sports.[58] Massachusetts also has an ERA and, consequently, when the Massachusetts legislature was considering enacting a law prohibiting girls from practicing with boys in contact sports, the advice of the state Supreme Court was sought.[59] The justices advised that such a law would be inconsistent with the state's ERA. However, they specifically declined to render an opinion as to whether such a law would be valid "if equal facilities were available for men and women in a particular sport which was available separately for each sex."

What Options Are Available to Victims of Sex Discrimination?

Students who believe that they are victims of sex discrimination may sue under the U.S. Constitution, Title IX, state ERAs, and other state laws. As a general rule, schools are under no obligation to provide interscholastic athletics. If they have such a program, however, it should be available on an equal basis for boys and girls. Some courts are satisfied with separate teams as long as similar coaching, support, and a competitive schedule are available for each sex. Others have ruled that all sports, even contact sports, must be equally available for boys and girls. Because state laws vary and state ERAs have been variously interpreted, when controversies arise it is very important to check the applicable state law as well as the prior opinions of federal courts for the region.

Can Some Courses in the Curriculum Be Restricted to Boys Only or Girls Only?

In general, no. Girls and boys must have equal access to the full curriculum without the imposition of stereotypic views of what girls and boys ought to be. The historic exclusion of girls from shop courses and boys from cooking or home economics is no longer legal, and laws such as the Carl D. Perkins Vocational Education Act[60] provide that schools should develop programs to eliminate sex bias and stereotyping in vocational education. Title IX, state laws, and local policies have erased any legal bases of such exclusions, though in some schools they are perpetuated through custom and informal pressures. Guidance counselors, teachers, parents, and others who advise students have important roles to play in this area, together with peer pressures that tend to be so important in secondary schools. While the law is clear in forbidding such restrictions, ingrained attitudes often perpetuate practices that force students into believing that some courses are for boys only and some for girls only. Nothing in the law prevents schools from separating boys and girls for instruction in highly sensitive areas, such as sex education.

Does Title IX Prohibit Sex Discrimination in All Aspects of a School's Education Program?

Title IX prohibits discrimination based on sex in connection with all education programs or activities at public or private schools that receive federal financial assistance. In *Grove City College* v. *Bell,* the U.S. Supreme Court narrowed the application of the law when it held that Title IX prohibited discrimination only in the particular program being funded, and not discrimination in the entire institution.[61] Congress's reaction was to overturn the Court's decision by enacting the Civil Rights Restoration Act of 1987.[62] This act amended Title IX, as well as other civil rights acts, to provide that a "program or activity" means all of the operations of an educational institution, regardless of the limited use of federal funds in any particular program or activity. In other words, a school that receives federal support only, for instance, its science and technology program may no longer discriminate on the basis of sex in its athletics or music departments.

Can Students Who Are Victims of Sexual Harassment Sue for Damages under Title IX?

Yes, ruled the U.S. Supreme Court in *Franklin* v. *Gwinnett County Public Schools.*[63] In that case, a female high school student claimed that her economics teacher at North Gwinnett High School had forced her to have sex with him. She filed a complaint with the Office of Civil Rights (OCR), alleging that she had been subjected to sexual discrimination in violation of Title IX. Following a six-month investigation, the OCR found the school system in violation of Title IX, but because of the school's assurances that it had taken affirmative actions to prevent any future violations, the OCR found the school system to be in compliance with Title IX and closed the investigation. (The economics teacher had since resigned, although no further action had been taken against him.) The student then argued that she was entitled to maintain her own suit for damages under Title IX, but a federal appeals court disagreed, ruling that victims of intentional sex bias may not collect compensatory damages under Title IX. On appeal, however, the U.S. Supreme Court disagreed, saying that Congress intended victims of sexual discrimination, including sexual harassment, to have all appropriate remedies available, including compensatory and punitive damages.

In *Gebser* v. *Lago Vista Independent School Board,*[64] an eighth grader, Alida Starr Gebser, had joined a book discussion group led by high school teacher Frank Waldrop, who made suggestive comments during the discussion groups and continued to do so when

Alida took a class of his her freshman year. The two began an intimate sexual relationship, which continued until her sophomore year when a police office discovered them having sexual intercourse in a car, Mr. Waldrop was arrested and terminated by the school board, and the State of Texas revoked his teaching license. When the Gebsers sued the school district under Title IX, the district contended that it had no knowledge of Mr. Waldrop's conduct, and therefore, was not liable. The Gebsers asked the Supreme Court to apply a Title VII standard, arguing either that the school district was strictly liable for the acts of its teacher or that it should be vicariously liable for acts committed by an "agent" of the district. The U.S. Supreme Court eventually upheld the lower courts' dismissal of the Gebsers' lawsuit, refusing to apply Title VII principles in the Title IX context.

In so ruling, the Court rejected agency principles which would bind the school board to the acts of its subordinates, such as teachers. Instead, the Court urged a much more narrow construction of Title IX, holding that it would "frustrate the purposes" of that statute to permit a damages recovery against a school district for a teacher's sexual harassment of a student unless the district had actual notice to a school district official. The Court thus concluded that an implied remedy for damages could only be inferred in the law where school officials have actual knowledge of the alleged discrimination and act with "deliberate indifference" in responding to such discrimination. Only where such actual knowledge is attributable to a school employee with authority to take corrective action, however, can such indifference be presumed and liability found. Applying this test to the facts in *Gebser,* the Court said that evidence of complaints made to the school principal about the teacher's inappropriate statements made in class did not constitute sufficient notice by a responsible school official of acts of sex discrimination and harassment. Accordingly, the lawsuit was dismissed.

Can Individual Teachers Be Found Liable for Violating a Student's Rights under Title IX?

Although one federal district court has held that Title IX creates a right of action directly against an individual,[65] *Gebser* leaves this ruling in doubt, as it focused attention solely upon the liability of a federal fund recipient under Title IX, which would be the school district and not individual teachers. Thus, students whose Title IX rights are violated must sue the school district.

Can Schools Be Liable under Title IX If Students Engage in Sexual Harassment against Other Students?

In *Davis* v. *Monroe County School District,*[66] the Supreme Court settled a long-simmering dispute in the federal appeals courts by defining under what conditions a school district may be liable for student–student peer sexual harassment. There, a fifth-grade female student, Lashonda Davis, had been subjected to a prolonged pattern of sexual harassment by a male classmate, which included lewd comments and inappropriate, unwelcome touching. When the behavior did not stop even after the child and her mother complained repeatedly to the classroom teacher, the mother spoke to the principal, who asked her why her daughter "was the only one complaining," and allegedly told the mother that he would have to "threaten" the offending student a bit harder. When a group of Lashonda's classmates asked to speak to the principal about the offending student's behavior, they were told that if the principal wanted to speak to the girls, he would call them.[67]

The Davis family filed suit against the board and certain board officials under Title IX, seeking monetary damages and insisting that even after over three months of harassment no discipline was imposed against the offending male student; indeed, Ms. Davis was not even permitted to change her seat so that she would not have to sit next to her alleged harasser. The lawsuit also alleged that the board of education lacked a written policy regarding peer–peer sexual harassment and that its personnel lacked any training in dealing with it. Reversing the lower courts' dismissal of the lawsuit, the U.S. Supreme Court sent the case to trial based upon the following stated principles:

As in *Gebser,* the Court rejected theories of liability based upon agency principles such as vicarious liability, noting that *Gebser* imposed liability on a school district where "the district itself intentionally acted in clear violation of Title IX by remaining deliberately indifferent to acts of teacher–student harassment of which it had actual knowledge."[68] The Court thus concluded that federal fund recipients could only be subjected to liability for damages where their own deliberate indifference resulted from an "official decision" not to remedy a violation of Title IX, thus effectively "causing" discrimination.[69] In short, the Court held, a school district must be found to have deliberately ignored pervasive acts of peer–peer sexual harassment in order to be found liable under Title IX. If a school district is able to demonstrate that its response to such harassment was not "clearly unreasonable," no liability will accrue. Moreover, the Court noted, damages for peer–peer harassment are only available where the behavior is so severe, pervasive, and objectively offensive that it denies its victims the equal access to education that Title IX is intended to protect.[70] Thus, such things as "simple acts of teasing and name calling" were not considered sufficient grounds for imposing monetary liability on a school district.[71]

Can Public Schools Provide Separate Schools for Boys and Girls?

The answer is unclear. In *United States* v. *Virginia,* the U.S. Supreme Court ruled that the Virginia Military Institute (VMI) could not deny admission to women.[72] The Court held that the VMI policy of limiting admission to male students violated the equal protection clause. Justice Ruth Bader Ginsburg found that Virginia failed to offer an "exceedingly persuasive justification" for its admission policy[73] She examined the state's two justifications for its policy: (1) single-sex education contributes to diversity in educational approaches, and (2) the admission of women to VMI would require modifying its unique adversative method of teaching. Turning to VMI's first justification, she traced the long history of sex discrimination at VMI, and concluded that VMI had not shown any serious interest in promoting diversity. Examining the second justification, Justice Ginsburg granted that admitting women would require some changes, but found that there was no proof that women could not succeed in such a program, and VMI could not justify its policy on overly broad assumptions about women. She ruled that the remedy for VMI's discrimination was not to create a separate program for women at Mary Baldwin College, as the Fourth Circuit had decided, but for "women seeking and fit for a VMI-quality education" to be offered nothing less.[74]

The majority in *United States* v. *Virginia* was careful to explain that its decision applies only to educational programs recognized as "unique,"[75] thus leading many schools to conclude that a separate but equal educational program for females might be constitutional if it truly provided equal educational opportunities. In that respect, this reasoning sounds much like that asserted in the South prior to the Supreme Court's landmark decision in

Brown v.Board of Education,[76] which struck down the notion of "seperate but equal" as a defense to racially segregated school systems and school programs. What is perhaps of even greater significance is the Court's adoption of what appears to be a new standard of review in equal protection cases. Traditionally, the Supreme Court has held that gender-based classifications must be "substantially related" to an "important governmental objective." Both Justice Rehnquist (concurring) and Justice Scalia (dissenting) questioned the majority's use of its "new" test, in the VMI lawsuit *i.e.*, whether the state could demonstrated an "exceedingly persuasive justification" for sex-segregated programs. Only future cases will reveal the extent to which the Court subjects gender-based classifications to a stricter standard of review.

Can Schools Compel Students to Attend Sex-Segregated Schools?

Probably not. In Hinds County, Mississippi, an entire school district was sex-segregated as part of a racial desegregation plan. A federal appeals court struck down this arrangement as a violation of the Equal Educational Opportunities Act of 1974.[77]

Can Schools Set Different Admission Standards for Boys and Girls?

No. Such practices violate the equal protection clause of the Fourteenth Amendment. A case arose in Boston where girls had to score 133 or above on a standardized test to gain entrance into Girls Latin School, compared with a minimum score of 120 for boys who wanted to enter Boys Latin School. Although the different scores were based on the different capacities of the two school buildings, the court struck down the arrangement as discriminatory.[78]

Admission policies or procedures based on sexual discrimination will be struck down if it is established that their intent is discriminatory. The First Circuit Court of Appeals so ruled in 1985 in a case that originated over ten years earlier when a young woman was denied admission to the Massachusetts Maritime Academy.[79] According to testimony, when she applied for admission, the director of admissions told her that she would be admitted only if she went to Sweden to undergo a sex change operation. These comments, together with other evidence, clearly established that discriminatory intent underlay admission policies. The academy claimed exemption from Title IX because it has traditionally and continually from its establishment had a policy of admitting students of only one sex. Title IX grants exemption in such cases, the academy urged.

However, the court held that this exemption applied only to legal action brought under Title IX, but not to action brought pursuant to the U.S. Constitution as denial of equal protection or under other federal laws that prohibit gender discrimination. Therefore, the discriminatory admission policies of the academy were held to be unconstitutional.

Can Schools Set Different Standards for Boys and Girls When Awarding Scholarships?

No. In a 1989 case, a federal court issued an injunction to prevent the state of New York from awarding merit scholarships solely on the basis of scores on the Scholastic Aptitude Test (SAT).[80] A group of female high school seniors challenged this practice as discriminatory under Title IX based on the fact that females scored lower on the SAT than did males—a statistic that has significantly changed since the 1980's, with girls scoring nearly as well as boys in both math and verbal sections of the test.[81] The court ruled, in a case of first impression, that the female students could prove discrimination under Title IX by showing disparate impact. Applying the traditional Title VII analysis of disparate impact—in which the court examines a facially neutral policy or practice to determine whether there is an overall unfavorable *effect* on a protected class of individuals, such as girls—the court found that the plaintiffs had established a *prima facie* case of discrimination, and therefore it shifted the burden to the state to establish a business necessity for relying solely on SAT scores. Determining that business necessity in the educational setting meant a "manifest relationship between the use of the SAT and the award of academic achievement in high school," the court held that the state had not met this burden. The court explained that the SAT was not designed to measure achievement and was never validated for that purpose. The court then ordered the state to discontinue use of the SAT for selecting 1989 scholarship winners and, instead, to use a combination of grades and SAT scores.

Can School Districts Provide Alternative Separate Schools for Pregnant Students?

Yes, as long as the alternative is a genuine option that students may choose. Several cities have provided such alternatives where the curriculum also reflects the special needs of the pregnant students.

Can a School Exclude a Student from the National Honor Society on the Basis of Pregnancy?

In a 1985 case, a federal district court ruled that a school district's dismissal of a pregnant student from the National Honor Society (NHS) was a violation of both Title IX and the equal protection clause of the Fourteenth Amendment.[82] However, in a 1990 decision the U.S. Court of Appeals for the Third Circuit upheld a school's dismissal of a pregnant high school student from the NHS, on the grounds that her engagement in premarital sex and resultant pregnancy constituted a "failure to uphold the high standards of leadership and character" required for NHS membership.[83] The court remanded the case, however, for the lower court to hear evidence that a male student who was a NHS member and who had impregnated his girlfriend was not dismissed from the NHS. Such evidence, the court explained, could be relevant to the state of mind of the faculty council and could shed light on whether its explanation for dismissing the female student was pretextual.

Can Married Students Be Required to Attend Adult School Instead of Regular Day School?

No. Many school districts used to force married and/or pregnant students out of school by requiring them to choose between no schooling or adult or correspondence courses. The school districts stated reasons such as (1) the presence of pregnant students encourages immoral behavior among students, (2) their presence encourages early marriages, (3) their presence encourages "sex talk" in schools, and (4) pregnant students suffer psychological harm in school. Despite these reasons, the courts protected the right of these students to continue attending regular schools.

Courts have not been impressed with the reasons stated above because no reliable evidence has been found to support them. In fact, evidence shows that pregnant students suffer more by exclusion than from attendance in regular day school. Moreover, the courts have pointed out that where state laws make public education available up to a certain age, students have a right to attend even if they are married and/or pregnant.[84]

Can Married Students Be Excluded from Extracurricular Activities?

In the past, courts upheld such exclusions. In a 1959 Texas case, for example, the Garland Public School in Texas had a policy that barred "married students or previously married students…from participating in athletic or other exhibitions" and from holding "class offices or other positions of honor."[85] When 16-year-old Jerry Kissick, Jr., a letterman in football, married a 15-year-old girl, he received notice from the school barring him from further athletic participation on the basis of the school policy. Kissick, who planned to earn a college scholarship with his football prowess, filed suit claiming that the school policy was unreasonable and discriminatory and that it violated his Fourteenth Amendment rights to due process and equal protection.

The court upheld the school policy, recognizing the earlier dominant view that "Boards of Education, rather than Courts, are charged with the important and difficult duty of operating the public schools…. The Court's duty, regardless of its personal views, is to uphold the Board's regulation unless it is generally viewed as being arbitrary and unreasonable." In effect, the court accepted the distinction between academic and extracurricular activities and upheld the right of school officials to control access to the latter.

The trend of recent decisions is more accurately reflected in *Davis* v. *Meek* from Ohio.[86] This case involved a similar policy: excluding married students from school-sponsored athletic and other extracurricular activities. When Davis challenged the policy in court, the policy was struck down. The court acknowledged the importance of extracurricular activities and considered exclusion from them to be a significant deprivation. The judge cited the Supreme Court's landmark *Tinker* decision in examining whether the school rule was necessary to maintain appropriate discipline or whether it was part of an "enclave of totalitarianism." Since Davis's marriage did not lead to any "material or substantial" interference with school discipline, the court ruled in his favor.

Schools are also prohibited, under Title IX, from discriminating against a student on the basis of pregnancy or childbirth. Schools may not bar pregnant students from any part of their education program or from any extracurricular program. Regulations implementing Title IX also provide that when a student returns to school after giving birth she must be allowed to return to the same academic and extracurricular status as before.

In sum, the current legal trend is to protect students' rights to participate in both curricular and extracurricular activities, whether the students remain single, get married, or become pregnant. School officials in making individual decisions may use health and safety considerations, but male and female students must be treated equally.

Summary

Changes in public attitudes, together with important court rulings and an expansive reading by the U.S. Supreme Court of Title IX of the Education Amendments of 1972, have led to greater sensitivity to sex discrimination and sexual harassment in public schools. It is no longer legal to pay men more than women for the same work, though differences in pay are still acceptable if based on material differences in workload and responsibilities. Males may not be given preference over females in administrative positions or in other job assignments. Federal legislation has prohibited compelling pregnant teachers to leave their jobs on some predetermined date; that is now a decision left entirely up to a woman and her physician. Federal and local legislation also prohibits sexual harassment of teachers by other members of the school community.

Sex discrimination and stereotyping in the school life of students have also been successfully challenged. It is no longer legally acceptable to exclude girls or boys from parts of the curriculum, though in practice, cultural pressures remain influential. Preferential treatment of boys in school athletics has spawned many lawsuits as well as OCR regulations intended to equalize access to sports for both boys and girls. Title IX and its regulations have opened the door largely to improving opportunities for girls to participate in competitive sports at all levels, and has been credited with the worldwide success of implementing girls' soccer and softball teams.

Several states have enacted equal rights amendments, which also must be considered in sex-related controversies in those particular states. There is no uniform interpretation of such amendments in the area of school sports. Some courts, for example, interpret state ERAs as mandating equal access even in contact sports, while courts in other states allow the separation of the sexes in such activities. At least one federal appeals court has construed Title IX as prohibiting a female athlete to be discriminated against as a member of an all-boys' contact sports team once she has been offered the opportunity to try out for the team.

Sexual harassment and sex abuse by teachers against students of the opposite sex have formed the basis for the imposition of monetary damages under Title IX, but only where school officials with the power to intervene have actual knowledge of such activities and display "deliberate indifference" by failing to take appropriate action. Similarly, where students are victimized by sexual harassment committed by their peers, a school district may have monetary liability where school officials have knowledge of the harassment, the harassment is sufficiently severe or pervasive as to deny victims equal access to education, and school officials remain deliberately indifferent to such conduct.

Different admissions standards for girls and boys to selective public schools are unconstitutional. Married and/or pregnant students may not be excluded from school, nor compelled to attend separate classes, separate schools, or evening classes. Similarly, courts now tend to protect the rights of such students to participate in extracurricular activities, though health and safety considerations may be used to exclude an individual from a particular activity—although only where the student's own physician (and not merely school officials) so determines.

In general, although some vestiges of inequality and stereotyping remain as a function of tradition and habit, significant strides have been made in recent years toward the eradication of sex discrimination in the public schools.

N O T E S

1. 29 U.S.C. § 1206 (2000).
2. 42 U.S.C. § 2000e (2000).

3. As early as 1940—long before either the Equal Pay Act or Title VII were enacted—the courts found that paying black teachers less than white teachers violated the Equal Protection clause of the Fourteenth Amendment of the U.S. Constitution. *Alston* v. *School Board of City of Norfolk,* 112 F.2d 992 (4th Cir. 1940). Given the Constitutional protection against discrimination by government based upon an individual's protected status, *including sex,* the *Alston* case offers a constitutional basis for compelling equal pay for men and women performing the same teaching duties.

4. *Siegel* v. *Board of Education of City School District of City of New York,* 713 F. Supp. 54 (E.D.N.Y. 1989).

5. 20 U.S.C. § 1681.

6. *EEOC* v. *Madison Community School District No. 12,* 818 F.2d 577 (7th Cir. 1987).

7. *McCullar* v. *Human Rights Commission,* 158 Ill. App. 3d 1011, 511 N.E.2d 1375 (1987).

8. *American Federation of State, County & Municipal Employees* v. *State of Washington,* 770 F.2d 1401 (9th Cir. 1985).

9. *Civil Rights Division* v. *Amphitheater Unified School District No. 10,* 680 P.2d 517 (Ariz. Ct. App. 1983).

10. *International Brotherhood of Teamsters* v. *United States,* 431 U.S. 324, 335, n.15 (1977).

11. *McDonnell Douglas Corporation* v. *Green,* 411 U.S. 792 (1973).

12. *Reeves* v. *Sanderson Plumbing Products,* 530 U.S. 133 (2000). *Reeves* held that where a court or jury chooses to disbelieve the employer's proffered reasons for making an employment decision, either is entitled to then infer that discrimination was the true reason for the decision, even in the absence of direct evidence of discriminatory intent.

13. *Price Waterhouse* v. *Hopkins,* 490 U.S. 228 (1989).

14. 42 U.S.C. § 1981a (2000).

15. *Pollard* v. *E. I. DuPont de Nemours & Co.,* 532 U.S. 843 (2001).

16. 42 U.S.C. § 2000e-3(a) (2000).

17. *Chappell* v. *Southern Maryland Hospital Center, Inc.,* 320 Md. 483, 578 A.2d 766 (1990).

18. *Thaddeus-X* v. *Blatter,* 175 F.3d 378 (6th Cir. 1999); *Von Gunten* v. *State of Maryland,* 243 F.3d 858 (4th Cir. 2001).

19. *Stone* v. *Belgrade School District No. 44,* 703 P.2d 136 (Mont. 1984).

20. *Gargiul* v. *Tompkins,* 704 F.2d 661 (2d Cir. 1983).

21. *King* v. *Palmer,* 778 F.2d 878 (D.C. Cir. 1985).

22. 42 U.S.C. § 2000e(k).

23. *Loving* v. *Virginia,* 388 U.S. 1 (1967), which struck down a state statute prohibiting interracial marriages.

24. Maryland Annotated Code, Article 49B, Section 12.

25. 42 U.S.C. § 2601 *et seq.*

26. *Cleveland Board of Education* v. *LaFleur,* 414 U.S. 632 (1974).

27. Section 108 of the Family and Medical Leave Act, 29 U.S.C. § 2618 (2000).

28. The law also applies to private-sector employers who employ 50 or more employees and who are engaged in commerce or any industry or activity affecting commerce.

29. *Dallastown Area School District* v. *Pennsylvania Human Relations Commission,* 460 A.2d 878 (Pa. Commw. Ct. 1983).

30. 42 U.S.C. § 2000e(k). *United Teachers–Los Angeles* v. *Board of Education of City of Los Angeles,* 712 F.2d 1349 (9th Cir. 1983).

31. *California Federal Savings & Loan Association* v. *Guerra,* 479 U.S. 272 (1987).

32. *Schafer* v. *Board of Public Education,* 903 F.2d 243 (3d Cir. 1990).

33. *California Federal Savings & Loan Association* v. *Guerra,* 479 U.S. 272 (1987).

34. 29 C.F.R. § 1604.11(a) (1980).

35. *Meritor Savings Bank* v. *Vinson,* 477 U.S. 57 (1986).

36. Indeed, in one recent Maryland case, the court characterized a supervisor's demands for sexual favors as a condition of employment as tantamount to prostitution. *Insignia Residential Corp.* v. *Ashton,* 755 A.2d 1080 (Md. 2000). The concept of supervisory solicitation of sex for employment benefits has been recognized as a form of behavior contrary to public policy, such that an employee's termination for

refusing to submit to sexual requests has been characterized by the courts as a tortious "wrongful discharge." *Monge* v. *Beebe Rubber Co.,* 114 N.H. 130, 316 A.2d 549 (1974).

37. See *Keppler* v. *Hinsdale Township High School District No. 86,* 715 F.Supp. 862 (N.D. Ill. 1989).

38. *Burlington Industries, Inc.* v. *Ellerth,* 524 U.S. 742 (1998); *Farragher* v. *City of Boca Raton,* 524 U.S. 775 (1998).

39. *Harris* v. *Forklift Systems, Inc.,* 510 U.S. 17 (1993).

40. *Id.*

41. *Clark County School District* v. *Breeden,* 532 U.S. 268, 121 S.Ct. 1508 (2001).

42. 121 S.Ct. at 1510, citing and quoting from *Farragher* v. *City of Boca Raton,* 524 U.S. 775, 787–788 (1998).

43. *Oncale* v. *Sundowner Offshore Services,* 523 U.S. 75 (1998).

44. 34 C.F.R. § 106.41(a), (b).

45. *Brenden* v. *Independent School District No. 742,* 342 F. Supp. 1224 (D. Minn. 1972).

46. *Id.*

47. See, for example, *Bucha* v. *Illinois High School Athletic Association,* 351 F. Supp. 69 (N.D. Ill. 1972); *O'Connor* v. *Board of Education,* 645 F.2d 578 (7th Cir. 1981).

48. *Mercer* v. *Duke University,* 190 F.3d 643 (4th Cir. 1999).

49. 20 U.S.C. § 1681.

50. *Gil* v. *New Hampshire Interscholastic Athletic Association,* No. 85-E-646, slip op. (N.H. Super. Ct., filed Nov. 8, 1985) (unpublished decision).

51. *Williams* v. *School District of Bethlehem,* 799 F.Supp. 513 (E.D. Pa. 1992).

52. 34 C.F.R. § 106.41 (b) (1990).

53. *Kleczek* v. *Rhode Island Interscholastic League,* 768 F.Supp. 951 (D.R.I. 1991).

54. *Williams* v. *School District of Bethlehem,* 998 F.2d 168 (3d Cir. 1993).

55. *Kelley* v. *Board of Trustees,* 35 F.3d 265 (7th Cir. 1994).

56. *Cohen* v. *Brown University,* 101 F.3d 155 (1st Cir. 1996), *cert. denied* 520 U.S. 1186 (1997).

57. *Darrin* v. *Gould,* 85 Wash.2d 859, 54 P.2d 882 (1975).

58. *Commonwealth ex rel. Paekel* v. *Pennsylvania Interscholastic Athletic Association,* 334 A.2d 839 (Pa. Commw. Ct. 1975).

59. *Opinion of the Justices re House Bill No. 6723,* Mass. Adv. Sh. 2728, Massachusetts Supreme Judicial Court (December 22, 1977).

60. 20 U.S.C. § 2301 (1988).

61. *Grove City College* v. *Bell,* 465 U.S. 555 (1984).

62. 20 U.S.C. § 1681 (1988).

63. *Franklin* v. *Gwinnett County Public Schools,* 503 U.S. 60, 112 S.Ct. 1028 (1992).

64. *Gebser* v. *Lago Vista Independent School District,* 524 U.S. 274, 118 S.Ct. 1989 (1998).

65. *Mennone* v. *Gordon,* 889 F.Supp. 53 (D. Conn. 1995).

66. *Davis* v. *Monroe County Board of Education,* 526 U.S. 629, 119 S.Ct. 1661 (1999).

67. *Davis* v. *Monroe County Board of Education,* 119 S.Ct. at 1667.

68. 119 S.Ct. at 1671.

69. *Id.*

70. *Id.* at 1675.

71. *Id.*

72. *United States* v. *Virginia,* 518 U.S. 515 (1996).

73. 116 S.Ct. at 2274.

74. 116 S.Ct. at 2287.

75. 116 S.Ct. at 2276.

76. *Brown* v. *Board of Education,* 347 U.S. 483 (1954).

77. *United States* v. *Hinds County,* 560 F.2d 619 (5th Cir. 1977).

78. *Bray* v. *Lee,* 337 F.Supp. 934 (D. Mass. 1972).

79. *United States* v. *Massachusetts Maritime Academy,* 762 F.2d 142 (1st Cir. 1985); see also *Mississippi University for Women* v. *Hogan,* 458 U.S. 718 (1982).

80. *Sharif* v. *New York State Education Department,* 709 F. Supp. 345 (S.D. N.Y. 1989).

81. "SAT Scores Hit Their Highest Point in 31 Years," found at abcnews.go.com/sections/us/DailyNews/sat000829.html (Aug. 29, 2001).

82. Unreported opinion (Case #823169, C.D. Ill. 1984), discussed in *Wort* v. *Vierling,* 778 F.2d 1233 (7th Cir. 1985).

83. *Pfeiffer* v. *School Board for Marion Center Area,* 917 F.2d 779 (3rd Cir.1990).

84. *Alvin Independent School District* v. *Cooper,* 404 S.W.2d 76 (Tex. 1966).

85. *Kissick* v. *Garland Independent School District,* 330 S.W.2d 708 (Tex. 1959).

86. *Davis* v. *Meek,* 344 F.Supp. 298 (N.D. Ohio 1972).

16 Are There Special Rights for Students with Disabilities and Non-English-Speaking Students?

Overview

In recent years, much public attention has focused on exceptional children and on children with limited English-speaking ability. Perceived inequalities in their education have been challenged in courts and debated by legislative bodies. As a result of court cases, legislation, and political activism, significant gains toward the achievement of equal educational opportunities have been registered by these groups. This chapter examines the major developments in each of these areas, first the issues related to students with special needs and then the emerging law related to bilingual and multicultural education.

Until recently, the compulsory education laws of most states made exceptions for children who were retarded, emotionally disturbed, deaf, blind, or otherwise disabled. For various reasons—most of them based on ignorance, prejudice, or finance—many parents kept these children out of school with the consent of local school officials and the sanction of state laws. When such children attended school, it was all too often in an aura of charity for which they and their parents were to be grateful.

Recent developments have brought substantial changes in attitudes toward those with disabilities and in laws related to their schooling. These changes are based in part on scientific evidence that has reliably established that all humans can learn and benefit from appropriate education and training. The changes are also due to the civil rights movements of the 1950s and 1960s, which reverberated throughout the American culture and stimulated the disabled to make their claims on the basis of right and not of charity.

Historically, the language in all U.S. public schools has been English. Children who spoke little or no English had no choice in the language of instruction and, typically, no special help to acquire the language. It was generally assumed that such children would pick up English through their daily interaction in and out of school, as well as through the efforts of kind-hearted teachers. Americanization, as expressed in the "melting pot" ideal, relied on English as the common language necessary for survival and success in school and in the worlds of commerce and industry.

Indeed, for millions of children, sons and daughters of immigrants and first-generation Americans, schools became important places for language acquisition and an important step up the mythical ladder of success in the new world. For countless others, however, schools were unfriendly places conducted in a strange tongue where too many teachers had little sympathy for non-English-speaking students. These students left school early and often became industrial workers and unskilled laborers in various segments of our economy. As immigration continued and "the melting pot refused to melt," serious questions began to surface about the rights of minorities whose mother tongue was other than English. They too had their consciousness raised by the civil rights movements in the latter half of the 20th century, and they began to organize and assert their rights and those of their school-age children.

Educating Students with Disabilities

Are the Rights of Children with Disabilities Based on the U.S. Constitution, Federal Legislation, or Both?

On both. Earlier challenges to excluding and misclassifying children with disabilities were based on the U.S. Constitution. These challenges (discussed below) helped raise public consciousness about the issue to the point where state and federal laws were enacted to ensure the schooling rights of *all* children. It is interesting to realize that a landmark case in school desegregation, *Brown* v. *Board of Education,*[1] was heavily relied upon to establish the right to education of all children and bring the federal government into an important role in public education. A key paragraph of *Brown,* often used by advocates of the rights of children with disabilities, recognizes the pervasive influence and importance of education in contemporary American life.

> Today, education is perhaps the most important function of state and local governments. Compulsory school attendance laws and the great expenditures for education both demonstrate our recognition of the importance of education to our democratic society. It is required in the performance of our most basic public responsibilities, even service in the armed forces. It is the very foundation of good citizenship. Today it is a principal instrument in awakening the child to cultural values, in preparing him for later professional training, and in helping him to adjust normally to his environment. In these days, it is doubtful that any child may reasonably be expected to succeed in life if he is denied the opportunity of an education. Such an opportunity, where the state has undertaken to provide it, is a right which must be made available to all on equal terms.

What Key Constitutional Provisions Are Related to the Rights of Children with Disabilities?

Historically, two kinds of practices worked to the educational disadvantage of children with disabilities: exclusion from school and misclassification. *Exclusion* occurs when a school-age child is denied access to schooling or is provided grossly inappropriate education. The term *functional exclusion* is also used to describe grossly inappropriate placement, as exemplified by the placement of retarded children in regular classes with no special assistance for the children or the teacher, or the placement of non-English-speaking children in an English-speaking school program without special assistance. *Misclassification* occurs when a child is erroneously assessed, placed, or tracked in a school program. Both exclusion and misclassification have been attacked on constitutional grounds.

The *PARC*[2] and *Mills*[3] Cases

Two important cases brought constitutional challenges on behalf of children with disabilities. One was brought by the Pennsylvania Association for Retarded Children (PARC), asserting violations of the equal protection and due process clauses of the U.S. Constitution. The case was resolved in a consent decree that incorporated the agreement of the parties to the suit. The second case, *Mills,* was also brought on behalf of retarded children in Washington, DC. The district court decided in favor of equal access to schooling for children with disabilities and noted that financial difficulties or other problems "certainly cannot be permitted to bear more heavily on the 'exceptional' or handicapped child than on the normal child."

The *PARC* and *Mills* cases established the constitutional basis for attacking the exclusion from schooling and misclassification of children with disabilities. They paved the way for the conviction that the equal protection and due process clauses protect the right of such children to access to public schools and free and appropriate education. They also opened the way for major federal legislation, setting nationwide standards for the education of these children and serving as the "blueprint" for Public Law No. 94-142.

What Major Federal Laws Establish the Rights of Children with Disabilities?

The most important federal laws related to the rights of students with disabilities are Public No. Law 94-142, or the Education of All Handicapped Children Act, enacted in 1975;[4] Section 504 of the Rehabilitation Act (RHA) of 1973; and the Americans with Disabilities Act (ADA), enacted in 1990.[5] These federal laws overshadow all other federal legislation related to educating the disabled. Section 504 of the RHA protects qualified individuals with handicaps excluded "*solely by reason* of her or his handicap" from participation in any program or activity receiving federal funds. This act applies to all schools, public or private, that receive federal funds and also to any disabled person, not just to students. By contrast, the ADA protects all qualified individuals with a disability who, *by reason* of such disability, are excluded from some benefit, service, or program of a public entity. Thus, while the wording of the two laws is similar, they are not identical. For example, persons with AIDS,[6] hepatitis B[7], and tuberculosis[8] have been found to qualify as "disabled" under one or more provisions of these laws. Public Law No. 94-142 makes certain federal funds available to schools that comply with its requirements. Section 504 would cut off *all* federal funds from schools that discriminate against the disabled. Thus the two laws have the same objectives, but Section 504 applies a broader sanction, the cutting off of funds, whereas Public Law No. 94-142 would only withhold funds under its allocation formula. Public Law No. 94-142 was named the Education of All Handicapped Children Act when it was enacted; later, it was renamed the Education of the Handicapped Act; now it is known as the Individuals with Disabilities Education Act (IDEA), which is how we refer to this law under its various titles.

Public Law No. 94-142

When Congress enacted Public Law No. 94-142 in 1975, it found that there were more than 8 million children with disabilities in the country and that over half of them were not receiving an appropriate education. Furthermore, approximately 1 million were completely excluded from the public schools. In the preamble of the act, Congress recognized these disturbing facts and stated that the main purpose of the act was to ensure that states provide all handicapped children with "a free appropriate public education and related services designed to meet their unique needs." While Congress recognized that education remains a state responsibility, it also acknowledged that federal assistance was necessary "to assure equal protection of the law."

The law now specifies that all disabled children between the ages of 3 and 21 must have "free appropriate public education." Since schooling is basically a state responsibility, however, Public Law No. 94-142 applies only to the ages covered by state laws. For example, if state law exempts children from ages 3 to 5 or from 18 to 21, the federal law cannot extend to those age groups. A 1986 amendment to the act, Public Law No. 99-457, extended the mandate to include infants and toddlers, and emphasizes minimizing (1) developmental delays seen in very young children, (2) the cost of education when they reach school age, and (3) the likelihood of institutionalization.

Who Are the Disabled?

Federal regulations define *children with disabilities* to include those who are mentally retarded, hard of hearing, deaf, speech impaired, visually handicapped, seriously emotionally disturbed, orthopedically impaired, other health impaired, deaf-blind, multihandicapped, or with specific learning disabilities and who, because of these impairments, need special education and related services. Regulations published in 1977 further define each of these terms.

Can Schools Require Parents to Pay for the Cost of Educating Children with Disabilities?

No. The law specifies that such education must be free. Since special education in public or private schools is often expensive, school officials have tried various ways to shift all or part of the cost on to the parents. Courts, however, have consistently held that public schools have the obligation to provide appropriate education, including testing, guidance, and other special and support services, at no cost to the parents. This principle holds whether the schooling is provided in public or private facilities. There is only one exception: When appropriate free public facilities are available for a particular child but the parents choose a private facility instead, they must bear the cost of the private education. There are also disagreements among public agencies about who should bear what costs with certain kinds of children with disabilities.

Attorney fees and costs must also be paid by the school district where parents had to go to court to remedy the inappropriate placement of their child. In fact, in an Oregon case decided in 2000, the schools were obligated to pay attorney fees when the parents were represented in at least three IEP (Individual Educational Plan) meetings by a lawyer.[9] The court of appeals ruled that the resolution proceedings were like due process hearings and, if the school district's arguments were accepted, "parents of disabled children would be forced to pursue the longer and more expensive due process procedure to recover their attorney fees." However, where the services of an attorney were used to place a student in a high school the parents preferred instead of another high school within the same school district, no attorney fees were allowed by the court. There were only minor differences in the makeup of the classes which did not constitute a "change in educational placement" sufficient to warrant reimbursement of attorney fees under the IDEA.[10]

What Is the Legal Meaning of "Appropriate" Education?

Public Law No. 94-142 and its regulations conceive of an "appropriate" education as one designed specifically to meet the unique needs of the particular child. Thus an individual educational program or plan (IEP) must be drawn up for each child under the law, and such plan is to be carried out in an appropriate educational setting.

It is not enough to provide "equal" access, in the sense of identical schooling for children with and without disabilities. Without special provisions and support services, students with disabilities might not gain anything from instruction, even though they are physically exposed to the same experiences as the other children. Such treatment is referred to as *functional exclusion* by courts and lawyers. One important case, *Fialkowski* v. *Shapp,* considered functional exclusion as similar to the placement of non-English-speaking students in ordinary classrooms without support services.[11] They "are certain to find their classroom experiences wholly incomprehensible and in no way meaningful." In *Fialkowski,* children with the mental abilities of preschoolers were placed in a program that emphasized reading and writing skills way beyond their abilities. This was held to be inappropriate placement and does not satisfy the law.

The requirements of appropriateness and the IEP are best considered as complementary notions. The IEP is a tailor-made plan that follows careful assessment and evaluation of a particular student's abilities and disabilities. Curricular plans and instructional approaches are based on such evaluation, and periodic assessments follow to ascertain progress and the continuing appropriateness of the plan. The education provided must be comparable to that offered the nondisabled, and the procedural safeguards are provided in order to keep parents informed and to solicit their participation in the appropriate placement of their children. Moreover, when state laws set higher standards for the education of exceptional children than those required by the Individuals with Disabilities Education Act (IDEA), the higher standards must be followed. Various courts have so ruled, including courts in New Jersey[12] and Massachusetts.[13]

The *Rowley* Case[14]

In 1982 the U.S. Supreme Court interpreted the phrase "free appropriate public education" guaranteed under Public Law No. 94-142. *Rowley* involved a hearing-impaired first-grade student "mainstreamed" in a regular first-grade classroom. She was assisted by a hearing aid, and her IEP included a speech therapist for three hours each week and a special tutor one hour a day. Her parents argued that under the law Amy Rowley was entitled to the services of a qualified sign-language interpreter in order to gain the maximum from her school experiences. School authorities pointed to Amy's successful progress, citing that she was performing "better than the average child in her classes," and, after repeated consultation, they denied the request.

When Amy's parents sued, the lower courts ruled in their favor, interpreting the law as requiring services to maximize each child's potential. However, on the final appeal, the U.S. Supreme Court disagreed. The Court noted that Amy was progressing satisfactorily and was receiving "personalized instruction and related services." Since all procedural requirements of the law were followed, and since Amy's education was "adequate," the Court held that the IDEA was not violated.

In an interesting contrast to *Rowley,* the West Virginia Supreme Court held that a deaf student, who received the services of a sign-language interpreter for her academic classes, was entitled to the services of a signer while participating in extracurricular activities, in this case the basketball team.[15] The court noted that the IDEA and its implementing regulations specifically mandate equal opportunities for participation in nonacademic and extracurricular activities as well as the academic programs of schools.

It is perfectly acceptable for states or local communities to provide for more services than those specified by federal law, as long as they do not provide fewer services. It appears that current federal law requires only that the IEP enable the particular student to *benefit* from schooling and that the procedural requirements of the IDEA be carefully observed.

Some states have set standards considerably above the federal floor. For example, North Carolina requires that opportunities be provided for students with disabilities to reach their "full potential commensurate with the opportunity given other children."[16]

This issue arose again in Michigan, where a state statute went beyond the IDEA and required that an IEP be "designed to develop the maximum potential" of the handicapped child.[17] In a lawsuit, a federal appeals court held that the school district was not required to provide the "best" education possible, but the interpretation of the standard was left in the "reasonable discretion of the state officials dependent upon the circumstances of the case." In effect, the appeals court accepted the *Rowley* standard and, after making certain that due process was satisfied, left the decision concerning educational methods and standards to the relevant state authorities who are more informed about education than federal judges. Similarly, Massachusetts provided for the "maximum possible development" of the child but changed this standard to "free and appropriate public education" effective as of January 1, 2002, the same as the federal law (Mass.G.L. c. 71B).

What Are the "Related Services" Required by the IDEA?

Rowley relied to a large extent on the IDEA requirement that schools provide "related services" needed for the appropriate education of children with disabilities. The act defines *related services* as

> transportation, and such developmental, corrective, and other support services (including speech pathology and audiology, psychological services, physical and occupational therapy, recreation, and medical and counseling services, except that such medical services shall be for diagnostic and evaluative purposes only) as may be required to assist the handicapped child to benefit from special education, and includes the early identification and assessment of handicapping conditions in children.[18]

"Related services" may include the use of an *assistive technology device,* defined as a piece of equipment used "to increase, maintain, or improve" the functional capabilities of children with disabilities, while *assistive technology service* assists the child in the use of assistive technology. Thus, a computer or a hearing aid would be an assistive technology device, while the teaching of a student to use them would be assistive technology service.

Because of the ambiguity of phrases such as "medical services" and because of the high cost of some services required to educate certain types of students with disabilities, there have been an inordinate number of cases litigated under the IDEA and under Section 504 of the Rehabilitation Act of 1973. To cite an extreme example, a 1984 federal appeals court granted a seriously emotionally disturbed student an educational placement under the IDEA costing $88,000 per year, in preference to the school board's choice of placement costing $55,000 per year;[19] the national average expenditure per student was approximately $3,000 during the same year. What "related services" schools must provide was central in the case of Amber Tatro, an eight-year-old girl.

The *Tatro* Case

Amber Tatro, born with spina bifida, suffered from orthopedic and speech impairments and a condition that prevented her from emptying her bladder voluntarily. She had to be catheterized every three to four hours to avoid injury to her kidneys. Is such periodic catheterization during school hours a "related service" or an excluded medical service? The school district drew up an IEP that was quite comprehensive except that it made no provision for school personnel to administer the "clean intermittent catheterization" (CIC). CIC is a simple procedure that can be learned in about an hour and requires about five minutes to administer.

The Supreme Court ruled that CIC is a related service because it makes it possible for the child to remain in school during the day, without which she could not be educated.[20] It is not significantly different from dispensing necessary medicine or administering emergency injections pursuant to medical authorization, which are also related services. Litigation concerning the meaning of "related services" and especially concerning the distinction between medical services that are excluded and school health services that are to be provided is likely to continue.

A federal court in New Jersey, for example, held that psychotherapy might be a related service within the context of the IDEA.[21] This ruling was upheld on appeal, with the court noting that since Congress specifically authorized psychological and counseling services under the IDEA, it must have intended to provide psychotherapy as well, particularly if they are the kinds of services that could be performed by qualified social workers, psychologists, or counselors. There is doubt about the inclusion of psychotherapy that could be provided only by a psychiatrist, whose services might be categorized as medical services.

Extensive in-school nursing services are not likely to be considered a related service under the IDEA. A Pennsylvania court so held in the case of a 7-year-old child named Bevin, whose severe multiple handicaps required constant care by a specially trained nurse.[22] Bevin had fetal face syndrome, was profoundly mentally handicapped, suffered from spastic quadriplegia and a seizure disorder, and was legally blind. She was fed and given medicine through a gastrostomy tube and breathed through a tracheostomy tube. Without a doubt, the services of a trained nurse were necessary to enable her to be in school, in a classroom with six disabled students, one teacher, and two aides. Nursing services cost $1,850 a month in 1984–1985, excluding close to $1,000 additional monthly expenses for Bevin outside school. The court concluded that neither the IDEA, its regulations, nor case law would include such extensive and expensive nursing care under related services.

A case focusing on "related services" was appealed to the U.S. Supreme Court, which handed down its decision in 1999.[23] Four-year-old Garret F. severed his spinal column in a motorcycle accident, which left him paralyzed from the neck down. His speech and mental capacities were not affected, but he is confined to a wheelchair that he operates with a puff and suck straw. With his various problems, he requires assistance throughout the school day. Relatives and a hired nurse attended to Garret's needs for several years, after which his parents requested the school district to pay for the services he needed. When the district refused the request, an administrative law judge, interpreting the IDEA, ruled that the services Garret required were "related services" and not "medical services." The district disagreed and went to court.

Ultimately, the courts, following *Tatro,* decided that the requested services were "supportive services," including the "one-on-one nursing services" throughout the school day. The Supreme Court agreed and rejected the district's argument that was based, in part, on the heavy financial burden. While acknowledging the burdensome cost, the Court noted that cost alone does not morph a "school health service" into a "medical service." This was a seven-to-two decision with Justices Thomas and Kennedy dissenting. They would overrule *Tatro* and hold such services to be "medical services" not intended to be covered under IDEA.

Another case further raised questions about the state's responsibility under the IDEA to educate children so severely and profoundly disabled as to raise doubts about their educability even at minimal levels.

The *Timothy W.* Case

In the case of *Timothy W.,* the federal district court in New Hampshire held that the school district was not required by law to provide special education for Timothy because the child "was not capable of benefiting from special education." The court of appeals reversed this decision.[24]

Timothy, born two months prematurely, suffered from a variety of serious problems from the time of his birth. As a result, he is multiply handicapped and severely mentally retarded to the point that some pediatricians testified that he "had no educational potential" and that parts of his brain were destroyed. The district court, ruling against special education for Timothy, held that "under New Hampshire law, an initial decision must be made concerning the ability of a handicapped child to benefit from special education before an entitlement to the education can exist." The appeals court rejected the criterion of "ability to benefit" and ruled that the wording of the IDEA is clear concerning zero reject, that is *all* children with disabilities are entitled to a free appropriate education. Furthermore, noted the court, Congress made its intent clear "that the most severely handicapped be given priority" under the act.

The case of *Timothy W.* was so extreme that it elicited comments, pro and con, from a variety of sources. Some argued that public school funds, particularly in times of limited resources, ought not to be used for children like Timothy, particularly since public schools lack the professional expertise to provide for such needs. Even those quite sympathetic to the needs of Timothy and his parents urged closer cooperation among relevant social service agencies and the schools, so that schools are not exclusively responsible for services beyond their competence and their resources. Further litigation will likely clarify schools' responsibilities in this complex area of "related services," and there are also political moves afoot to address the implicit policy questions through legislation.

Must a School District Administer Prescription Drugs to Disabled Students?

The answer depends on the circumstances. Pursuant to school district policy, schools administer a variety of drugs to students prescribed by private physicians and approved by parents. When a student's physician prescribed a dosage of Ritalin larger than the recommended daily dose listed in the *Physician's Desk Reference,* the school refused to administer the larger dose, pursuant to district policy. The parents sued, claiming violation of § 504 of the Rehabilitation Act and Title II of the Americans with Disabilities Act. The courts ruled that the school had provided reasonable accommodation under a facially neutral policy, for it was willing to have the parents give the larger dose at school or modify the student's schedule so that the Ritalin could be provided at home.[25]

What Are the Due Process Rights of Parents and Children under Public Law No. 94-142?

It was clear to Congress that in the past, parents were all too often left out of educational decisions that were crucial in the lives of their disabled children. The current law has changed that and requires at least the following:

1. Prior written notice must be given a reasonable time before any proposed change is implemented in the child's educational program, together with a written explanation of the procedures to be followed in effecting the change.
2. All notices must be written in "language understandable to the general public" and in the primary language of the parents. If the parents cannot read, the notices must be interpreted for them orally or by other means.
3. The testing of children must be nondiscriminatory in language, race, and culture.
4. There is a right to independent testing and evaluation, free or at low cost.
5. Parents must have access to the records relevant to the case and the right to have the records explained, to make copies, and to amend records they consider inaccurate, misleading, or an invasion of privacy; and the right to a hearing on the issue if the school refuses to amend the records.
6. Opportunity for a fair and impartial hearing must be conducted by the State Educational Agency (SEA) or local school district, *not* by the employee "involved in the education or care of the child." At any hearing, parents have the right to be represented by a lawyer or an individual trained in the problems of children with disabilities; the right to present evidence and to subpoena, confront, and cross-examine witnesses; and the right to obtain a transcript of the hearing and a written decision by the hearing officer. Parents may appeal the decision to the SEA and, if they are still not satisfied, may appeal the SEA ruling in court.

7. The student has a right to remain in current placement until the due process proceedings are completed. A child who is just beginning school may be enrolled until the proceedings determining proper placement are completed.

8. A "surrogate parent" will be appointed for children who are wards of the state or whose parents or guardians are unknown or unavailable.

9. The child's records are confidential. Parents and the student may restrict access to the records; they have a right to be informed before any information in the file is destroyed and a right to be told to whom information has been disclosed.

While further details are given in regulations interpreting the law, this list presents the main procedural safeguards.

A case involving a high school student in Danbury, Connecticut, illustrates the powerful due process protection afforded special-needs students by Public Law No. 94-142. School records indicated that Kathy Stuart had various academic deficiencies caused by learning disabilities and limited intelligence. When, as punishment for disruptive behavior, the school wanted to expel her, she went to court. The federal district court believed that Kathy was exactly the type of student intended to be protected by the federal law.[26] While it interpreted the law and its regulations to allow short-term suspensions or new placements of disruptive students with disabilities after due process, it prohibited their expulsion. As the court stated: "The expulsion of handicapped children not only jeopardizes their right to an education in the least restrictive environment, but is inconsistent with the procedures established by the Handicapped Act for changing the placement of disruptive children."

Can Students with Disabilities Be Suspended or Expelled from School?

Yes, but under the law some alternative educational placement must be found for the disabled student expelled from school. Such students may be subject to discipline like any other students *if* their misbehavior is not a manifestation of their disabling condition and *if* mandated procedures are followed.[27] Long-term suspension or expulsion, however, is considered a change in educational placement and is allowed only after procedures specified by law are followed.[28] As a last resort, the student would have a right to continue his or her education by being taught at home, or in some appropriate but more restrictive institution.

Procedures for Disciplining Children with Disabilities

Before a disabled child can be suspended for 10 or more days, the IEP team (the team that determined the individual educational plan) must meet to determine whether the misbehavior was a function of the disability. This is referred to as a *manifestation determination*. The IEP team also performs a *functional behavioral assessment*, that is, a determination of why the student engages in the behavior that impedes learning and how that behavior relates to the environment, and the formulation of a hypothesis regarding the conditions under which the behavior usually occurs and the probable consequences that serve to maintain it.

At a subsequent meeting, a *behavior intervention plan* must be developed by the IEP team, together with the student's regular teacher and any other qualified personnel. The team may recommend a change of placement (COP), which the parents may accept or challenge.[29]

A highly significant provision of the 1997 amendments to the IDEA provides legal protection for students not yet eligible for special education who are facing possible expulsion.[30] This provision allows parents of children not previously identified as disabled to request protection under IDEA by alleging that school personnel knew or should have known that the student had a disability before the misconduct occurred that triggered the disciplinary process. The school will be deemed to have such prior knowledge if:

1. the parents have expressed concern in writing to the school that their child needed special education and related services; or
2. the performance or behavior of the child shows the need for such services; or
3. the parents have requested an evaluation of the child; or
4. the child's teacher or other school personnel have expressed concern to the director of special education or other school personnel.[31]

If any of the foregoing conditions exist, the "stay-put" provision of IDEA mandates that the student not be expelled, but an IEP team determine the student's eligibility for special education and all its procedural protections.

The 1997 amendment makes the application of the "stay-put" provision of IDEA highly controversial and places a heavy burden on school administrators. Prior to the amendment, some courts cautioned about such hindsight opinion that might trigger the "stay-put" provision. As the Seventh Circuit Court of Appeals noted: "For a child not previously diagnosed as disabled, the statement of one social worker, teacher, or doctor, excusing the child's aberrant behavior because of some perceived problem should be considered insufficient to meet the standard of 'staying put.'"[32] The 1997 amendment makes the school's job more difficult by accepting a lower threshold of evidence.

Long-term suspension is the removal of students from their regular school placement for 10 days or more during the school year. Removal that exceeds the 10-day limit constitutes a change in placement. The Department of Education considers the 10-day cap to start anew following each change in placement in the absence of bad faith; that is, the routine changing of placement so that additional suspension days would be possible.[33] When the 10-day limit is likely to be exceeded, it is advisable to consult legal counsel, for Department of Education opinion is not federal law.

Some schools use in-school suspension as a disciplinary device. If formal records are kept of in-school suspension and parents are notified, such days must be added to the out-of-school suspension days in calculating the 10-day maximum under the IDEA.[34]

Can Students with Disabilities Whose Behavior Is Dangerous Be Given Long-Term Suspensions?

No, ruled the U.S. Supreme Court in 1988 in *Honig* v. *Doe*.[35] Doe, a 17-year-old special education student whose IEP explicitly recognized his propensity for aggressive acts, acted explosively when taunted by a fellow student. He "choked the student with sufficient force to leave abrasions" on the neck and "kicked out a school window" while being escorted to the principal's office afterward. When the school system proceeded with a summary long-term suspension, suit was filed on behalf of Doe. The issue before the Court was whether the IDEA implicitly contained a "dangerousness exception" to the "stay-put" provision. In the final analysis, the Court ruled that there is no such exception explicit or implicit in the

IDEA. In fact, the "stay-put provision was intended to remove the unilateral authority school officials traditionally exercised to exclude disabled students, particularly emotionally disabled students, from school." School officials, however, are not left hamstrung. A student who is dangerous to self or others may be temporarily suspended for up to 10 school days. During this "cooling-down" period, officials can initiate review of the IEP and work with the parents to agree on an interim placement. If the parents "of a truly dangerous child adamantly refuse to permit any change in placement, the 10-day respite gives schools officials an opportunity to involve the aid of the courts" to approve a new placement.

Thus the Court ruled that there is no "dangerousness exception" to the stay-put rule, but there are ways, consistent with the IDEA's due process provisions, to deal with disruptive or even dangerous students, to protect their rights while also protecting an orderly learning environment in the schools.

The IDEA was amended in 1997 to enable school officials to place a student with dangerous drugs or weapons in an "interim alternative setting" for 45 days. The amendment specifies the steps schools must follow to determine the dangerousness of the situation and states that the interim educational setting must allow the student to participate in the curriculum and continue to receive IEP services along with services to ensure the dangerous behavior does not recur.

Can a Student with a Disability Be Given Corporal Punishment?

Yes, if the state law and local policies allow corporal punishment of other students. In a case that arose in Texas, parents sued under federal law (42 U.S.C.A. § 1983), seeking damages for deprivation of their child's substantive due process rights when a school principal allegedly administered excessive corporal punishment to their special education child. The federal circuit court held that since the state law of Texas provides both civil and criminal remedies for excessive and unreasonable corporal punishment, the substantive due process provision of the federal Constitution does not apply and neither does § 1983.[36]

Must Educational Services Continue If a Disabled Student Was Properly Suspended or Expelled?

Courts disagree on this question. In an Illinois case, a 13-year-old boy with a learning disability was suspended for 10 days and later expelled for the possession of a pipe and marijuana at a school dance. A special education team concluded that there was no connection between his disability and the misconduct. The district court held that educational services were not required for students properly expelled or suspended for misbehavior unrelated to their disabilities.[37]

The Fourth Circuit Court of Appeals ruled otherwise in a Virginia case in 1996,[38] and the Seventh Circuit Court in an earlier case held that no such services were required.[39] Because courts disagree on this matter, the U.S. Supreme Court will eventually have to provide an authoritative ruling.

What Is the Least Restrictive Educational Alternative?

Historically, children with disabilities tended to be segregated from other students. Various reasons were advanced for such isolation, but in recent years, these reasons have been challenged and in most instances rejected. Current law requires that students with disabilities be educated in *the least restrictive alternative* program. In brief, this means that the child should be educated in a setting that deviates least from the regular program yet is appropriate for the particular child.

Courts have recognized that various educational arrangements, or "treatments," have been "restrictive" in the legal sense. For example, segregation of the disabled that further handicaps or stigmatizes them is restrictive in the eyes of the law. So is the use of medication for many children. If a child's ability to learn is aided through medication, that use might be justifiable; if the chemical treatment merely restrains a child for the convenience of the staff, that use is "restrictive."

Mattie T. v. *Holladay* capsulizes the provisions of the federal law regarding the least restrictive alternative educational placement of a child:

> The Bureau of Education for the Handicapped Guidelines establish, inter alia, two important steps to be taken by school districts…: (1) 'a variety of program alternatives (e.g., continuum of education services) must be available in every L.E.A. [local educational agency] to meet the varying needs of handicapped children' and (2) an individual determination of the appropriate program alternatives must be made for each child in conformance with the procedures of nondiscriminatory evaluations.[40]

The principle of least restrictive alternative educational placement is what is popularly referred to as *mainstreaming*. The law does not require that each child be mainstreamed, that is, fully integrated with the other students. Such placement is appropriate for some children; others might benefit more by spending part of the day mainstreamed and part of the day in special classes with specially prepared teachers. Students who cannot handle either arrangement may have to be in special classes all day, an arrangement preferable to separate special schools. Finally, such schools are preferable to home schooling, although home schooling is better than no schooling. This principle was confirmed in a 1988 case involving two hearing-impaired students, where acquiring oral language skills outweighed benefits to be acquired from mainstreaming.[41]

Disagreements concerning mainstreaming (now referred to as "inclusion") and "separation" continue to arise. In a 1994 case, for example, parents of a moderately mentally retarded student requested that she be full-time in a regular classroom.[42] School officials were willing to place her in regular education only for her nonacademic subjects and into special education classes for academic courses. When the parents claimed that such placement violated the least restrictive environment requirement of IDEA, the federal appeals court agreed.

The court used several criteria to determine the appropriateness of the student placement: (1) compare the benefits to the student of a placement in a segregated setting with the benefits of inclusion, supplemented with appropriate aides and services; (2) consider the nonacademic benefits of interaction with regular education students; (3) evaluate the effects of the inclusion on the regular classroom teacher and on the other students; and (4) consider the cost of the inclusion, or mainstreaming.

Can Home Instruction Satisfy the Law?

Yes, in certain circumstances. So ruled the Sixth Circuit Court in the case of an 11-year-old severely retarded, multidisabled Ohio girl.[43] Emily Thomas was legally blind and functioned at a one-month level developmentally. She had no self-help skills and required the use of a wheelchair as well as gastrostomy and tracheostomy tubes that required constant monitoring and suctioning. The parents and their physician recommended daily transportation of Emily to a small special education program, but following a two-tiered review process, the school authorities specified once-a-week homebound instruction.

The circuit court held that where the procedural requirements of the law were followed, and where the state has set up a two-tiered review process, federal courts are required to defer to the final decision of the state authorities. The law does not establish a general preference for in-school placement when it specifies the least restrictive environment. Depending on the individual case, homebound instruction, as in Emily's case, may be appropriate.

The parents of a home-schooled disabled child, however, might have to forego some benefits public school children receive. So ruled the federal courts when parents of a home-schooled disabled child requested subsidized speech therapy pursuant to the IDEA. The courts accepted the states' discretion to determine whether home-schooling that was exempted from the state's compulsory attendance requirement constituted an IDEA-qualifying private school.[44]

Is Private Schooling an Alternative Available under the Law?

Yes, if no appropriate public facilities are available that can effectively meet the needs of the particular student. Public funds must be used to pay for the child's education, including room and board and transportation, where necessary, at no extra costs to the parents. Parents must be careful, however, not to make a unilateral decision to place their child in a private school and hope to recover the costs from the local school district. They should follow the procedures specified in the IDEA. Before parents place a handicapped child into a private institution, they should consult with the public school. Furthermore, if they acted unilaterally, they should seek reimbursement within the time limit specified by state laws. Parents in a Connecticut case lost in their efforts to gain reimbursement in 2000 when they filed their claim approximately four years after they took unilateral action.[45] If they acted unilaterally, they will not recover their costs, except in two types of situations: (1) if the court finds that had they selected otherwise, the child's physical health would have been endangered; or (2) if educational officials "acted in bad faith" by denying them the procedures guaranteed by the IDEA.[46]

The law gives courts discretion in this matter, and the U.S. Supreme Court ruled in 1985 that parents may be reimbursed even if they chose to place their children unilaterally in disagreement with public officials if such placement is deemed to be the proper one through appeal procedures specified by the law. Without this possibility, reasoned the Court, the child of poor parents might have to spend years in an inappropriate educational placement awaiting the outcome of the case.

In 1993, the U.S. Supreme Court expanded its earlier holding and ruled in favor of parents from Florida who unilaterally placed their hearing-impaired child in a South Carolina private school. The parents were entitled to tuition reimbursement if the public placement in the home district violated the IDEA and the private school placement was proper under the act.[47] Also, a federal law, the Handicapped Children's Protection Act,[48] allows parents and children to sue for attorneys' fees if they prevailed in their IDEA litigation efforts.

Parents must be careful, however, before they unilaterally place their child into a private facility. Under the 1997 reauthorization of IDEA, a court may assess costs against the parents if it is determined that the school placement was appropriate, even though the parents disagreed with it.[49] The Fifth Circuit Court so held in a Texas Case involving a student with Attention Deficit Disorder and Tourette's Syndrome. The school district, after careful evaluation, prepared an IEP which considered both academic and special process. The parents approved the IEP as well as subsequent changes to it. Nevertheless, the parents moved the student to a private 24-hour residential treatment center and sued for reimbursement. The district court ruled in favor of the school district and assessed the costs against the parents. The Fifth Circuit Court agreed with the district court. Since the IDEA is silent on the matter of costs, the district court may interpret such silence as permission to impose costs in favor of the school district as a prevailing party.[50] In this case the parents had to pay almost $4000 in court costs.

Is Private Sectarian Schooling an Alternative Available under the Law?

That depends on the laws of the particular state as well as the specific services requested for the disabled student. In one case, for example, the parents enrolled their young deaf child, Matthew, in the Fredericksburg Christian School in Virginia and requested that the public schools provide him with a cued speech interpreter and reimburse them for expenses already incurred for such an interpreter. In this school, Christian teachings pervade the curriculum, woven into all subject matter, and biblical education and spoken prayers occur daily. The Fourth Circuit Court ruled that the laws of Virginia forbid public aid to sectarian education and found that the public schools stood ready to make appropriate education available to Matthew.[51] Furthermore, it held that the arrangement requested by the parents would be excessive entanglement between religion and education, violating one of the prongs of the *Lemon* test for separation of church and state in education. (But see the *Lamb's Chapel* case discussed in chapter 10.)

Similarly, a federal district court in a Louisiana case held in 1994 that a state statute allowing special education teachers to teach on the premises of parochial schools violated the establishment clause of the First Amendment.[52] However, in the same state, another federal district court mandated the provision of a sign-language interpreter for a hearing-impaired student attending a private, parochial school.[53] The student paid his own tuition, but IDEA required the provision of the interpreter.[54]

In *Doolittle,* the Idaho Supreme Court granted tuition reimbursement to the parents of a hearing-impaired student who had placed their child in a parochial school after the school district refused to help find an appropriate educational placement for him.[55] The court found that the district denied him a free, appropriate public education and awarded the parents reimbursement for tuition, attorneys' fees, costs, and prejudgment interest. Although the state constitution forbade the use of public funds for the costs of tuition and an interpreter in a parochial school, the court ruled that the IDEA preempted the state constitution where it conflicted with reimbursement provisions of the federal statute.

However, the IDEA does not require a public school district to provide all services that would be provided in a public school to a disabled student voluntarily attending a private school. A federal appeals court so held in the case of a 6-year-old wheelchair-bound student whose parents enrolled her in St. Mary's School.[56] The school district was already providing her speech therapy, occupational therapy, physical therapy, and transportation. The parents, in addition to these services, requested a full-time instructional assistant, which the school district refused. A federal appeals court held that the IDEA and its regulations do not mandate that public schools provide all the services for a disabled student voluntarily attending a private school that they would for similarly disabled public school students.

What If the Parents and the School Disagree Concerning the Placement of the Child?

The law is clear that such disagreements must be resolved through a fair procedure: "Disagreements between a parent and a public agency regarding the availability of a program appropriate for the child, and the question of financial responsibility, are subject to the due process procedure."[57] Under federal law, local schools also have the obligation to locate all children who might fit the criteria, specified by law, to receive services provided for the disabled. Courts have held that parents are not always in the best position to recognize that their children are not functioning well academically or that special support services are available to help with a particular disability. Parents may or may not be aware of due process provisions provided by law, nor have the expert advice available to schools. Therefore, particularly with respect to children already in school, the duty rests with the provider of services to identify children in need of special services. Several states have sought to extend to regular students similar rights to "appropriate educational programs" currently available to those with disabilities. For example, the Wisconsin legislature enacted laws in 1980 that give students and their parents a wide range of choices if they are dissatisfied with their assignment in public schools.[58]

Educators' discretion is respected by courts, as was illustrated in a case where school officials changed a disabled student's placement because they considered his psychosexual disorder and overt sexual behavior disruptive of the educational process and dangerous to the physical and emotional health of other students. On behalf of the student, it was argued that his placement could not be changed until after he had exhausted all administrative and judicial appeals. The federal courts ruled, however, that school officials have the discretion to change the placement when there is clear evidence that the student endangers himself or others or threatens to disrupt a safe school environment.[59]

What If There Is a Conflict between Appropriateness and the Least-Restrictive-Setting Requirement?

Various cases have recognized an inherent tension between the criteria of appropriateness and least restrictive setting. Simply put, for a particular student, the most appropriate program may not be available in the least restrictive setting, and the least restrictive setting may not have the most appropriate program. While the U.S. Supreme Court has never addressed this issue, various courts, including courts of appeal, have concluded that Congress intended "appropriateness" to be the primary criterion. The Eleventh Circuit Court explained in a 1991 case the factors to be considered when a mainstreaming issue arises.[60]

The first factor to be considered is whether satisfactory education can be provided with supplementary aids and services in the regular classroom. If it cannot, school officials must determine whether the alternative placement involves mainstreaming to the maximum extent appropriate for the student. Parents must be involved in this process, and schools may not make the placement decision unilaterally.

The child may be placed in the more restrictive environment, such as a self-contained special education class, only if the school determines that "significantly more progress" will be made there than in the regular classroom. In addition to academic benefits, schools must consider social, language, and behavior developments likely to occur through association with nondisabled peers.

The second factor in placement consideration is the effect that the child will have on the education of other children in the classroom. If the child's behavior is highly disruptive so as to "significantly impair" the education of others, the placement is inappropriate. The requirement of extra attention by the teacher is not in itself sufficient to meet this criterion.

The third factor is the cost. The fact that supplemental aids and services cost more than placement in a special class would not justify such placement. The additional cost must be of such magnitude as to "significantly impact" the education of other children in the district. If that were the case, then the placement would be inappropriate. It is important to note, however, that cost may be a consideration only when two or more appropriate programs are available.[61] Courts have allowed cost considerations in least-restrictive-environment issues, but not in determining appropriate programs.[62]

Can Children with Disabilities Ever Be Excluded from a School Activity?

Yes, if the school has substantial justification for the exclusion. Cases have arisen in which students who were wholly or partially blind in one eye were not allowed to participate in contact sports. The schools excluded them from participation because of the risk of injury to their sighted eye. Courts would not overturn the educators' decision because school officials had a reasonable basis to act as they did. To win such a case, students would have to show either that school officials had no reasonable grounds for their action or that the students would suffer irreparable harm by not having an opportunity to participate in the sport.[63] By contrast, a New Jersey school could not exclude Poole, a high school wrestler, from the team because he had only one kidney and he was "otherwise qualified." According to the court, "the purpose of Section 504 is to permit handicapped individuals to live life as fully as they are able, without paternalistic authority deciding that certain activities are too risky for them."[64]

The U.S. Supreme Court upheld the exclusion of a severely hearing-impaired student from a nursing program to which she applied.[65] The student sued under Section 504, which prohibits discrimination against "otherwise qualified handicapped" individuals. The Court found that the student was not "otherwise qualified" for "otherwise qualified [means] otherwise able to function sufficiently in the position sought in spite of the handicap, if proper training and facilities are suitable and available." The Court said that Section 504 does not "compel the college to undertake affirmative action that would dispense with the need for effective oral communication in the college's nursing program."

Thus it is clear that students with disabilities can be excluded from some school activities or programs, but only if sound educational grounds exist for such exclusion. Such grounds might relate to health and safety considerations or to requirements inherent in the program that the individual cannot meet without support services. However, each decision must be based on a case-by-case analysis of the student's disability and the nature of the school activity.

What Does the Law Require for Program "Accessibility"?

For some years, concerns have been expressed about the difficulties that certain persons with disabilities have experienced in gaining physical access to buildings. The Architectural Barriers Act of 1968 addressed some of these issues and incorporated certain standards to be applied in buildings "designed, constructed, or altered." A 1976 amendment to this act extended its application, but the most fundamental regulation of program accessibility is derived from Section 504, which provides that no qualified disabled person, "because facilities are inaccessible to or unusable by handicapped persons," shall be excluded from participation or otherwise be subjected to discrimination.

Under this law, schools and all other programs receiving federal assistance must make facilities and programs accessible through the use of ramps, sufficiently wide doors, elevators, accessible lavatory facilities, support services, and other modifications of existing facilities and programs that might be necessary. This does not mean that every *building* on a campus must be modified, but only that each *program* must be accessible. In their efforts to make programs accessible to the disabled, schools must take care that they do not segregate or isolate them from the other students. Much of this accessibility can be achieved through careful scheduling, relocating offices, making services available at alternate accessible sites, new construction, and the remodeling of existing facilities.

In addition to the federal law, many states have enacted laws against architectural barriers and on behalf of accessibility by the disabled. State laws cover public places and structures such as local parks, public toilets, elevators, stairs, doors, ramps, and sidewalks, that do not necessarily receive federal support and are thus beyond the reach of Section 504.

Must Schools Provide Year-Round Schooling for Children with Disabilities?

There is no clear, authoritative answer to this question. For certain children with disabilities, the summer break is too long and they regress educationally. This is particularly true for the severely retarded. Earlier cases applied the *regression-recoupment* standard.[66] The regression-recoupment standard considers the amount of regression, lost learning, suffered by a student during the summer months, together with the amount of time required to recoup those lost skills when school resumes in the fall. The court ruled that no extended school year (ESY) was required in this case because significant regression occurred with this student even with ESY. Other courts, applying the same test, ruled in favor of the extension as a way of providing individualized appropriate schooling.[67]

In a 1995 case, *Johnson* v. *Independent School District No. 4 of Bixby,* the Tenth Circuit Court of Appeals rejected the regression-recoupment standard in favor of a broader one:

> In addition to the degree of regression and the time necessary for recoupment, courts have considered…the degree of impairment and the ability of the child's parents to provide the educational structure at home, the child's rate of progress, his or her behavioral problems, the availability of alternative resources, the ability of the child to interact with nonhandicapped children, the areas of the child's curriculum which need continuous attention, and the child's vocational needs."[68]

Based on *Johnson,* a district court in Virginia ruled in 1993 in favor of ESY for an autistic 6-year-old.[69] So far neither courts nor Congress has determined how much regression is excessive or how much recoupment is satisfactory.

Do Children with AIDS Qualify for Special Education?

Having AIDS or testing positive for HIV is not grounds to exclude a child automatically from school. In fact, courts have ruled that children have a right and duty to attend school, and barring special complications, AIDS does not diminish this right. A federal district court so held, for example, when a parent group claimed that an emotionally disturbed child who tested positive for HIV should be excluded from school under the state's contagious disease law.[70] The court held that the child had a right to attend school under the IDEA, and barring special factors, positive testing for HIV alone is insufficient grounds for denying that right. A child may become eligible for special education if he or she becomes disabled as a result of AIDS,[71] but the child may not be qualified for special education in the early stages of the disease.

Section 504 must also be considered in these cases, since it has a broader definition of "handicapped" to include those who are "regarded as having an impairment."[72] In two cases involving young children infected with the AIDS virus as a result of blood transfusions, the courts considered the relevance of both the IDEA and Section 504. The first case involved a five-year-old boy who was excluded from school after a biting incident.[73] The court concluded that the child was "handicapped" under Section 504 and was "otherwise qualified" to attend school. After considering the best available medical evidence, the court concluded that any risk of transmitting the AIDS virus in connection with attending kindergarten is remote and cannot be used as a basis for excluding the child.

The second case, decided in 1988, involved a seven-year-old "trainable, mentally handicapped" (TMH) child with AIDS, who was not toilet trained, had a disease that can cause blood to appear in the saliva, and sucked her thumb. The federal court of appeals ruled that she had a right to special education and that the "remote theoretical possibility" of transmitting the virus was insufficient risk to exclude her from the TMH class. The federal appeals court sent the case back to the trial court to determine whether the child was "otherwise qualified" or could be made so through some reasonable accommodations as required by Section 504.[74]

Since the incidence of children with AIDS is increasing, we may expect further legal developments related to their right to education and their inclusion under the IDEA and Section 504.

Does the Americans with Disabilities Act Apply to Schools?

In some respects it does, but it does not alter existing law significantly. The act, known as the ADA, was signed into law on July 26, 1990.[75] While the ADA does not directly address educational policy issues, it includes some amendments to Section 504, one of which is relevant to schools. Section 510 of the act specifies that the term "individual with disability" excludes a person who is currently engaged in the illegal use of drugs and who is disabled solely because of drug or alcohol dependency. Schools may apply ordinary disciplinary policies to such students. However, if the student has some other disabling condition as well, schools must follow disciplinary procedures applicable to special-needs students.

Just as earlier legislation expressed clear preference for mainstreaming, the ADA specifies that services be provided in the most integrated settings. This preference has clear implications for vocational education. As the National Council on Disability reported to the president and the Congress of the United States:

> Workplace integration during school years can provide students with a clear understanding of what employers' expectations are and what a work experience is about, and can provide critical exposure to a range of jobs and career possibilities. Employers benefit by gaining an appreciation of what individuals with disabilities can offer, what their needs may be, and what their capabilities and potentials are. This process is instrumental for breaking down attitudinal barriers and stereotypes.[76]

In recent years, the ADA has also been used to challenge state athletic associations' age requirements as applied to students with disabilities. Many of these students are held back in schools when they are quite young, which makes them overage for athletic participation during their last year of high school. Such was the case of Leo Pottgen, who at the age of 19, found himself ineligible to compete on his high school baseball team. His suit under the ADA and Section 504, *Pottgen* v. *Missouri State High School Athletic Association,* was unsuccessful when the majority of the Eighth Circuit Court of Appeals found that he was not "otherwise qualified, due to his age, and that waiving the age requirement would constitute a fundamental alteration in the nature of the baseball program."[77] The chief judge wrote a strong dissent criticizing the majority for "mechanically" applying the athletic association's rule. He concluded that the rule could be reasonably modified without serious damage to the athletic program.

Another case that arose in Florida agreed with the dissenting judge. Dennis Johnson, a 19-year-old student with serious hearing loss, sought judicial help to enable him to play football and to wrestle. He wanted a waiver of the activities association's age eligibility requirement. The federal district court rejected the *Pottgen* decision and held that in this case waiving the age requirement is a "reasonable accommodation" which will not damage the goals of fairness and safety. "…[T]o assert that the age requirement is an absolute, unwaivable rule, is to place form over substance."[78] The court urged a case-by-case analysis as the proper way to decide in each particular case whether the age eligibility rule should be applied, or whether "reasonable accommodation" should be made in light of the handicapping condition, the particular sport activity, and the individual student's condition.

On appeal, the federal circuit court ruled that the case was moot because the seasons were over for both football and wrestling, the sports in which the student wanted to compete.[79] Since no case or controversy existed any longer between the student and the activities association, the case was dismissed.

A 1996 Pennsylvania case also upheld the rule, holding that the requested waiver was not a reasonable accommodation even though sports participation was included in the student's IEP.[80] The age rule was applied to all students in a nondiscriminatory manner, and the student was excluded because of his age and not his disability. In sum, courts are split; the majority of the cases apply the rules with equal force to all students regardless of disabilities.

Can "High-Stakes" Tests Be Used with Students with Disabilities?

In recent years, "high-stakes testing" became the popular term that refers to standardized tests that may have dramatic and direct consequences for individual students.[81] As more and more states and school districts began using such tests, questions arose about the legal legitimacy of using them with educationally disabled children. The legal challenges came pursuant to Section 504 of the Rehabilitation Act of 1973, the Americans with Disabilities Act (ADA), under IDEA, and under the Fourteenth Amendment of the U.S. Constitution.

The 1997 Amendment to IDEA requires state or local education agencies to develop guidelines to enable children with disabilities to participate in state or district assessments. Alternate assessments must also be available to students unable to participate in state or district assessments. The student's IEP must describe modifications made to enable the student to participate in the assessment. If, on the other hand, the IEP team decides that a student should not participate, it should state its reasons and how the student will be assessed.

Responding to the constitutional challenges using the due process clause, courts have held that, where students have had adequate notice of the graduation requirements (including the testing), long enough time to prepare for it, and the school curriculum adequately presented the contents of the tests, due process was satisfied.[82] Thus, in the absence of new legislation, "high-stakes testing," when used following the provisions of IDEA, giving sufficient notice and adequately presenting the relevant curriculum, does not violate the law even if some students with disabilities are thereby prevented from receiving a diploma.

Does the ADA Apply to School Employees?

Eva Dyer was employed as a *school psychologist* during the 1990–1991 school year. She was injured during the year in a fall that continued to bother her. Her contract was not renewed the following year, but she was rehired for the 1992–1993 year as an *assessment psychologist*. The position required a lot of travel to different schools, along with sitting while administering tests and while driving from school to school. Her doctor specified the length of time she should sit and/or drive, along with other restrictions. The school system was willing to accommodate her medical needs, but ultimately she wanted her previous position as a school psychologist. When this was refused, she resigned and filed suit under the ADA, claiming discrimination and lack of reasonable accommodation to her as a disabled worker.[83] The federal district court ruled against her, holding that the school district offered reasonable accommodation to her disability, but was under no legal obligation to offer her alternative employment or a new position when she was unable or unwilling to meet the demands of her present position.

Cases such as those described in this section should sensitize those involved in education-related matters to the main legal issues involved in educating handicapped students and teachers with disabilities. There is no substitute, however, for scrutinizing the law of your state as issues arise, because it is impossible in a brief chapter to present all the variations in lawsuits on this topic. Literally thousands of such suits are filed each year and the facts of the case, along with school board policies, state and federal laws, and related court cases, must be analyzed to conclude how the courts are likely to rule in any particular case.

Bilingual and Multicultural Education

Are There Federal Laws That Apply to the Schooling of Non-English-Speaking Children?

Yes, the most important among them are Title VI of the Civil Rights Act of 1964;[84] the Bilingual Education Act of 1974, amended in 1988;[85] and the Bilingual Education Act of 1994.[86] The most significant case in this area is *Lau* v. *Nichols.*

The *Lau* Case[87]

Among the thousands of Chinese American students attending public schools in San Francisco in 1970, approximately 3,000 spoke little or no English, and of these, close to 1,800 received no special services designed to meet their linguistic needs. That year, these students and their parents filed suit in a federal district court and claimed that their right to equal protection under the Fourteenth Amendment of the Constitution, as well as their rights under Title VI of the Civil Rights Act of 1964, were being denied by the public schools. The main issue was whether non-English-speaking students are denied an equal educational opportunity when taught in a language they cannot understand.

The district court considered Title VI and the Fourteenth Amendment together and concluded that the non-English-speaking children did not have any of their rights violated when "the same education [was] made available on the same terms and conditions to the other tens of thousands of students in the San Francisco Unified School District" as to these students. When the Ninth Circuit affirmed this ruling, the case was appealed to the U.S. Supreme Court. The Court ruled in favor of the students and their parents, basing its decision on Title VI and deliberately not ruling on constitutional grounds. (The Court will, as a general policy, avoid ruling on a constitutional issue if it can dispose of the case on statutory grounds.)[88]

The Supreme Court held that students who understand little or no English are denied equal opportunities when English is the sole medium of instruction and when there are no systematic efforts to teach that language to non-English-speaking students. "Under these state-imposed standards there is no equal treatment merely by providing students with the same facilities, textbooks, teachers, and curriculum; for students who do not understand English are effectively foreclosed from any meaningful education." The Court did not specify what schools should do for these students, for remedies are usually left to educators under the supervision of district court judges, who are more aware of local conditions. Various educational arrangements might satisfy the courts, including English as a Second Language (ESL), bilingual education, or a combination of both. In fact, disagreements over appropriate remedies have spawned further lawsuits as well as governmental regulations to guide school districts. The most important feature of any plan is its effectiveness.

Since *Lau,* several other cases based on Title VI have resulted in court orders requiring bilingual programs in schools.[89] These rulings, however, require such instruction only if children have limited English-speaking abilities. For example, when a group of Chicano school children claimed that their school programs were inappropriate because they were "oriented for middle-class, Anglo children...staffed with non-Chicano personnel who do not understand and cannot relate with Chicano students who are linguistically and culturally different," the courts rejected their claims.[90] The court found that the plaintiffs did not prove the necessary facts to show violation of either Title VI or the Fourteenth Amendment.

Similarly, children of Mexican American and Yaqui Indian origin went to court to compel the schools to provide bilingual-bicultural education.[91] They wanted not only bilingual education for students deficient in English but continuous instruction in English and in the children's native language, Spanish or Yaqui, from kindergarten through high school. The court ruled against them, holding that education, though important, is not a fundamental right under the Constitution. "Differences in the treatment of students in the educational process, which in themselves do not violate specific constitutional provisions, do not violate the…Equal Protection Clause if such differences are rationally related to legitimate state interests."

It is clear that the result reached in *Lau* is still good law today. As the Fifth Circuit Court said: "[T]he essential holding of *Lau*, i.e., that schools are not free to ignore the need of limited English speaking children for language assistance to enable them to participate in the instructional program of the district, has now been legislated by Congress, acting pursuant to its power to enforce the [equal protection clause of the] fourteenth amendment."[92]

Pursuant to the *Lau* decision, Congress enacted the Equal Educational Opportunities Act (EEOA), which states:

> No state shall deny equal opportunity to an individual on account of…race, color, sex, or national origin, by…the failure by an educational agency to take appropriate action to overcome language barriers that impede equal participation by its students in the instructional programs.[93]

The Fifth Circuit Court created a three-prong test in this (*Castaneda*) case (see note 92). The first prong required that, while no specific instructional program or method needs to be followed by the school district, the program that is followed must be based on sound educational theory. Second, the school district must recruit and train teachers to lead the instruction in bilingual classrooms. And, finally, there should be a carefully conceived assessment program to find out whether or not the district's program is achieving its goals. The same three-prong test was used by federal judges in the *Keyes*[94] case in Denver, Colorado, as well as *Teresa P.,* in Berkeley, California.[95]

What Are the Rights of Parents in These Issues?

The first bilingual education act became law in 1968; following *Lau*, Congress passed a second act in 1974, which is commonly referred to as the Bilingual Education Act. Among its various provisions, the law specifies that programs "of bilingual education shall be developed in consultation with parents of children of limited English-speaking ability, teachers, and, where applicable, secondary school students." It is clear that the law intends to integrate these students, whenever practicable, with English-speaking students and separate them for special instruction only when necessary. For example, they should attend regular classes in art, music, physical education, and other courses where language skills are not of central importance to instruction. The 1988 act reaffirms these principles, appropriated funds through 1993, and detailed the federal regulation relevant to bilingual education. Similarly, the 1994 act continues the philosophic and financial commitment of the federal government to improve educational opportunities for students with limited English proficiency.

Are There State Laws That Provide Special Instruction for Non-English-Speaking Students?

Yes, in some states. California, Connecticut, Illinois, Massachusetts, and Texas have laws related to bilingual education that predate *Lau* and federal legislation. It must be recognized that the federal law provides only transitional bilingual education and only for students of no or limited English proficiency ability. Thus schools are not required to provide any special instruction for students who benefit from instruction in English. Most state laws similarly provide only for transitional bilingual education, but states or local schools may, at their discretion, provide further instruction in the student's native language. States, however, may change their laws. For example, California voters adopted a referendum in 1998 amending the California Education Code to require that "all children in California public schools shall be taught English by being taught in English. In particular, this shall require that all children be placed in English language classrooms" (Cal. Educ. Code § 305). Bilingual education in California can only be used with children who obtain a waiver in accordance with procedures and criteria specified by law.

Do Federal Laws Apply to Students Who Speak "Black English"?

Yes, ruled a district court in Michigan.[96] Suit was filed by black students living in a low-income housing project located in an affluent section of Ann Arbor, near the University of Michigan. They claimed that their language, black English, was a distinct language different from standard English. They further claimed that they were denied equal educational opportunities because their language constituted a barrier to their learning and to using the written materials of the school, which were in standard English. The students alleged that Section 1703(f) of Title 20 of the U.S. Code was violated by the school. This statute provides: "No state shall deny equal educational opportunity to an individual on account of his or her race, color, sex, or national origin, by (f) the failure by an educational agency to take appropriate action to overcome language barriers that impede equal participation by its students in its instructional program."

Evidence showed that the school provided various services to students, including speech and language specialists, school psychologists, individualized instruction, and tutoring. Nevertheless, the court found that the teachers' lack of awareness and knowledge of black English, the home language of the children, was in part the reason for their not learning. Thus the school board was ordered to develop a plan whereby teachers would become aware of the language used in students' homes and in the community so that they might identify children who used the dialect and then be able to instruct them more effectively in standard English. The court did not require the creation of a bilingual program, nor did it require the teaching of black English. It did find that the teachers' lack of knowledge in this area denied students equal educational opportunities.

"Black English" made national news again in 1996 and 1997 when the Oakland, California, school board passed a resolution to treat it as a second language under the term "ebonics." The resolution described the language as "genetically based" and a "primary language" of many of its students, and wanted to request federal funds appropriated for bilingual programs.[97]

During the widespread controversy that followed, in California and nationwide, the Oakland school committee watered down its resolution but was still denied any bilingual education funds by Richard Riley, Secretary of Education, who stated: "Elevating black English to the status of a language is not the way to raise standards of achievement in our schools."[98] D. Thomas Sowell, a black economist, criticized the Oakland effort simply as a way of getting federal funds. He also explained that what is referred to as black English originated from an impoverished area of England, from which many white southerners came to America, and blasted "ebonics" as "pretentious nonsense."[99]

Summary

Until recently, children with disabilities were generally excluded from schooling and misclassified or improperly placed in educational programs. Case law as well as legislative enactments have changed this situation dramatically. While significant developments have occurred in some states through state legislation, the most powerful developments are embodied in Public Law No. 94-142, currently known as IDEA; in the ADA; and in Section 504 of the Rehabilitation Act of 1973. Together, these laws mandate that free and appropriate education, with all necessary support services, be available to all children and youth with disabilities in America. In fact, while the IDEA originally applied to children between the ages of 3 and 21, a 1986 amendment applied it to infants and toddlers as well; Section 504 and the ADA have no age limit and forbid discrimination against the disabled in any program or activity receiving federal support. To qualify for federal funds under the IDEA, states must comply with standards set forth by law, which include individual education plans, nondiscriminatory assessment, appropriate placement of children in the least restrictive educational alternative, periodic reevaluation, and full due process rights for parents as well as students.

When no appropriate public school placement is available for a particular child, the child may be placed in a private school at no extra cost to the parents. Thus it is clear that major strides have been made toward extending equal protection of the law and due process to all school-aged children with disabilities. This is not to say that all their educational and social problems have been resolved. Important obstacles still prevent their full functioning in our society. Some of these obstacles relate to social prejudices and others to the lack of professional knowledge and even trained personnel. Nevertheless, the legal standards and tools are substantially in place to help these students achieve their full human potential.

Significant strides have also been made to provide equal educational opportunities for children of limited English-speaking ability. These developments contrast dramatically with our historic attitude of "sink or swim" toward such students. Attempts to use the Fourteenth Amendment's equal protection clause on behalf of such students have not been successful. Title VI of the Civil Rights Act of 1964 was relied on by the U.S. Supreme Court in the landmark case of *Lau* v. *Nichols* to require transitional bilingual education for children who cannot benefit from instruction in English. *Lau* was followed by the Bilingual Education Acts of 1974, of 1988, and of 1994, which similarly mandate bilingual education for children of limited English-speaking ability. The law provides for parental participation in program planning, personnel preparation, and other support services. Several states have laws that further provide for bilingual education, some of which go beyond transitional, bilingual education and provide for maintenance instruction to help perpetuate the students' second language.

Despite the federal and state laws, transitional bilingual education remains controversial, even during the first decade of the 21st century. There is no general agreement on the best means and methods to achieve English proficiency for students with limited English-speaking ability.[100] In fact, the controversy extends beyond schooling and raises questions such as whether driver's license tests and any other official acts should be conducted in any language other than English. The most extreme position on this issue is expressed by those who, under the slogan of "English Only," wish to enact laws to carry out their educational and philosophic ideas. As of this writing, such proposals have been introduced in Congress, but no legislation has resulted from the efforts.

Thus it is clear that in recent years—in the years to come—both the Constitution and legislation have been used—and will continue to be used—to gain a significant degree of equality in education for students with disabilities and those with limited English proficiency.

NOTES

1. *Brown* v. *Board of Education,* 347 U.S. 483 (1954).
2. *Pennsylvania Association for Retarded Children* v. *Commonwealth of Pennsylvania,* 343 F.Supp. 279 (E.D. Pa. 1972).
3. *Mills* v. *Board of Education of the District of Columbia,* 348 F.Supp. 866 (D. D.C. 1972).
4. 20 U.S.C. §§ 1401, 1402, 1411–1420 (1970).
5. 29 U.S.C. § 794. Final regulations published at 42 Fed. Reg. 22676 (May 4, 1977) (codified at 45 C.F.R. 84). Section 504 is brief and to the point: "No otherwise qualified handicapped individual in the United States, as defined in section 7(6), shall, solely by reason of his handicap, be excluded from the participation in, be denied the benefits of, or be subjected to discrimination under any program or activity receiving Federal financial assistance."
6. *Doe* v. *Dolton Elementary Sch. Dist. No. 148,* 694 F.Supp. 440 (N.D. Ill. 1988); *Thomas* v. *Atascadero Unified Sch. Dist.,* 662 F.Supp. 376 (C.D.Cal. 1986).
7. *Jeffrey S. ex rel. Ernest S.* v. *State Bd. of Educ. of Ga.,* 896 F.2d 507 (11th Cir. 1990); *New York State Ass'n for Retarded Children* v. *Carey,* 466 F.Supp. 479 (E.D.N.Y. 1978).
8. *School Bd. of Nassau County, Fla.* v. *Arline,* 480 U.S. 273 (1987).
9. *Lucht* v. *Molalla River School District,* No. 99-35733 225 F.3d 1023 (9th Cir. 2000).
10. *D.S. ex rel. J.S.* v. *Lenape Regional High School,* 102 F.Supp.2d 540 (D.N.J. 2000).
11. *Fialkowski* v. *Shapp,* 405 F.Supp. 946 (E.D. Pa. 1975).
12. *Geis* v. *Board of Education of Parsippany-Troy Hills,* 589 F.Supp. 269 (D. N.J. 1984).
13. *David* v. *Dartmouth School Committee,* 615 F.Supp. 639 (D. Mass. 1984).
14. *Board of Education* v. *Rowley,* 458 U.S. 176 (1982).
15. *Lambert* v. *West Virginia State Board of Education,* 447 S.E.2d 901 (W.Va. 1994).
16. *Burke County Board of Education* v. *Denton,* 845 F.2d 973, 983 (4th Cir. 1990).
17. *Renner* v. *Board of Education of the Public Schools of the City of Ann Arbor,* 185 F.3d 635 (6th Cir. 1999).
18. 20 U.S.C. § 1401(17) 1982.
19. *Clevenger* v. *Oak Ridge School Board,* 744 F.2d 514 (6th Cir. 1984).
20. *Irving Independent School District* v. *Tatro,* 468 U.S. 883 (1984).
21. *T.G. and P.G.* v. *Board of Education,* 576 F.Supp. 420 (D. N.J. 1983).
22. *Bevin* v. *Wright,* 666 F.Supp. 71 (W.D. Pa. 1987).

23. *Cedar Rapids Community School District* v. *Garret F.,* 526 U.S. 66 (1999).

24. *Timothy W.* v. *Rochester, New Hampshire, School District,* 875 F.2d 954 (1989).

25. *DeBord* v. *Board of Educ. of Ferguson-Florissant Sch. Dist.,* 126 F.3d 1102 (8th Cir. 1997).

26. *Stuart* v. *Nappi,* 443 F.Supp. 1235 (D. Conn. 1978).

27. *S-I* v. *Turlington,* 635 F.2d 342 (5th Cir. 1981).

28. See *Sherry* v. *New York State Education Department,* 479 F.Supp. 1328 (W.D. N.Y. 1979); *Keelin* v. *Grubbs,* 682 F.2d 595 (6th Cir. 1982).

29. We wish to acknowledge the assistance of Atty. Karen Norlander of the N.Y. State Bar for interpreting these portions of the law relevant to disabled children.

30. 20 U.S.C. § 1415 (k)(8)(b).

31. *Id.*

32. *Rodiriecus L.* v. *Waukegan School Dist. No. 60,* 90 F.3d 249 (7th Cir. 1996).

33. *Rhys,* 18 IDELR 217 (OSEP 1991).

34. *Big Beaver Falls Area Sch. Dist.* v. *Jackson,* 624 A.2d 806 (Pa.Commw.Ct. 1993).

35. *Honig* v. *Doe,* 484 U.S. 305 (1988).

36. *Fee* v. *Herndon,* 900 F.2d 804 (5th Cir. 1990).

37. *Doe by Doe* v. *Board of Education of Oak Park River Forest High School District No. 200,* 24 IDELR 385 (N.D. Ill. 1996).

38. *Commonwealth of Virginia, Department of Education* v. *Riley,* 24 IDELR 278 (4th Cir. 1996).

39. *Metropolitan School District of Wayne Township, Marion County, Indiana* v. *Davila,* 969 F.2d 485 (7th Cir. 1992).

40. *T.* v. *Holladay,* 522 F.Supp. 72 (N.D. Miss. 1981).

41. *Visco* v. *School District of Pittsburgh,* 684 F.Supp. 1310 (W.D. Pa. 1988).

42. *Sacramento City Unified School District* v. *Holland,* 14 F.3d 1398 (9th Cir. 1994).

43. *Thomas* v. *Cincinnati Board of Education,* 918 F.2d 618 (6th Cir. 1990).

44. *Hooks* v. *Clark County Sch. Dist.,* 228 F.3d 1036 (9th Cir. 2000).

45. *Mr. & Mrs. D.* v. *Southington Bd. of Educ.,* 119 F.Supp.2d 105 (D.Conn. 2000).

46. *Anderson* v. *Thompson,* 658 F.2d 1205 (7th Cir. 1981).

47. *Burlington School Committee* v. *Department of Education, Commonwealth of Massachusetts,* 471 U.S. 359 (1985); *Carter* v. *Florence County School District Four,* 510 U.S. 7 (1993).

48. 20 U.S.C. § 1415(e)(4)B); *Williams* v. *Boston School Committee,* 709 F.Supp. 27 (D. Mass. 1989); Jean B. Arnold and Mark Chestnut, *Attorney Fees in Special Education Cases Under the Individuals with Disabilities Education Act,* 100 EDUC. L. REP. 497 (1995).

49. 20 U.S.C. 1400 *et seq.* (1997); *L.K. ex rel. J.H.* v. *Board of Education for Transylvania County,* 113 F.Supp.2d 856 (W.D. N.C. 2000).

50. *Cypress-Fairbanks Independent School District* v. *Michael F.,* 118 F.3d 245 (5th Cir. 1997).

51. *Goodall by Goodall* v. *Stafford County School Board,* 930 F.2d 363 (4th Cir. 1991).

52. *Holmes* v. *Cody,* 856 F.Supp. 1102 (E.D. La. 1994).

53. *Cefalu* v. *East Baton Rouge Parish School Board,* 907 F.Supp. 966 (M.D. La. 1995).

54. The Supreme Court ruled in *Mitchell* v. *Helms,* 530 U.S. 793 (2000), that, under the Elementary and Secondary Education Act (ESEA) of 1965, local educational agencies may lend materials and equipment to private schools, including religious schools, to implement "secular, neutral, and nonideological programs." (See chapter 10.)

55. *Doolittle by Doolittle* v. *Meridian Joint School District No. 2,* 24 IDELR 357 (Idaho 1996).

56. *K.R.* v. *Anderson Community School Corporation,* 81 F.3d 673 (7th Cir. 1996).

57. 45 C.F.R 121a403(b).

58. Reported in *NOLPE Notes,* October 1980, pp. 3–4.

59. *Jackson* v. *Franklin County School Board,* 765 F.2d 535 (5th Cir. 1985).

60. *Greer* v. *Rowe City School District,* 950 F.2d 688 (11th Cir. 1991).

61. *Clevenger* v. *Oak Ridge School Board,* 744 F.2d 514 (6th Cir. 1984).

62. See, e.g., *In re Smith,* 926 F.2d 1027 (11th Cir. 1991). *Board of Education* v. *Holland,* 786 F.Supp. 874 (E.D. Cal. 1992), also followed the criteria used in *Greer supra* note 58, and presents a useful explanation of coping with the issue of mainstreaming as well as its costs.

63. *Kampmeier* v. *Nyquist,* 553 F.2d 296 (2d Cir. 1977).

64. *Poole* v. *South Plainfield Board of Education,* 490 F.Supp 948 (D. N.J. 1980).

65. *Southeastern Community College* v. *Davis,* 442 U.S. 397 (1979).

66. *Rettig* v. *Kent City School District,* 539 F.Supp. 768 (N.D. Ohio 1981).

67. *Battle* v. *Pennsylvania,* 629 F.2d 269 (3d Cir. 1980).

68. *Johnson* v. *Independent School District,* 921 F.2d 1022 (10th Cir. 1990).

69. *Lawyer* v. *Chesterfield County School Board* 19 IDELR 904 (E.D. Va. 1993).

70. *Parents and Child, Code No. 870901W* v. *Group I/II/III/IV Defendants,* 676 F.Supp. 1072 (D.C.E.D. Oklahoma, 1987).

71. *District 27 Community School Board* v. *Board of Education of the City of New York,* 502 N.Y.S. 2d 325 (N.Y. Sup. Ct. 1986).

72. Section 504 of the Rehabilitation Act of 1973 and the IDEA both protect the rights of the disabled but are enforced by different agencies. Section 504 is broader in its coverage, since it also includes individuals addicted to alcohol or drugs. Furthermore, Section 504 extends civil rights protection beyond the school years and into the workplace as well.

73. *Thomas* v. *Atascadero Unified School District,* 662 F.Supp. 376 (C.D. Cal. 1986).

74. *Martinez* v. *School Board,* 861 F.2d 1502 (11th Cir. 1988).

75. 42 U.S.C. § 12101 (1990).

76. National Council on Disability, A Report to the President and the Congress of the United States— The Education of Students with Disabilities: Where Do We Stand? 43 (1989).

77. *Pottgen* v. *Missouri State High School Athletic Association,* 40 F.3d 926 (8th Cir. 1994).

78. *Johnson* v. *Florida High School Athletic Association,* 899 F.Supp. 579 (M.D. Fla. 1995).

79. *Johnson* v. *Florida High School Athletic Association, Inc.,* 25 IDELR 149 (11th Cir. 1996).

80. *Beatty by Beatty* v. *Pennsylvania Interscholastic Athletic Association,* 24 IDELR 1146 (W.D. Pa. 1996).

81. See J. Heubert and R. Hauser (eds.), *High Stakes Testing for Tracking, Promotion, and Graduation* (Washington, DC: National Academy Press, 1999).

82. *Board of Education of Northport-East Northport Union* v. *Ambach,* 457 N.E.2d 775 (N.Y. 1983); *Brookhart* v. *Illinois State Board of Education,* 697 F.2d 179 (7th Cir. 1983); *G.I. Forum* v. *Texas Educ. Agency,* 87 F.Supp.2d 667 (W.D. Texas 2000).

83. *Dyer* v. *Jefferson County School District R-1,* 905 F.Supp. 864 (D. Colo. 1995).

84. 42 U.S.C. § 2000d (1970).

85. 20 U.S.C. § 800b; 20 U.S.C. § 3281–3341 (1988).

86. 20 U.S.C. § 3420.

87. *Lau* v. *Nichols,* 414 U.S. 563 (1974).

88. Title VI of the Civil Rights Act of 1964 states: "No person in the United States, shall, on the grounds of race, color, or national origin, be excluded from participation in, be denied the benefits of, or be subjected to discrimination under any program or activity receiving federal financial assistance." (42 U.S.C. § 2000).

89. *Serna* v. *Portales Municipal Schools,* 499 F.2d 1147 (10th Cir. 1974); *Aspira* v. *Board of Education of City of New York,* 423 F.Supp. 647 (S.D. N.Y. 1976); *Rios* v. *Read,* 480 F.Supp. 14 (E.D. N.Y. 1978).

90. *Otero* v. *Mesa County Valley School District No. 51,* 408 F.Supp. 162 (D. Colo. 1975).

91. *Guadalupe Organization, Inc.* v. *Tempe Elementary School District No. 3,* 587 F.2d 1022 (9th Cir. 1978).

92. *Castenada* v. *Pickard,* 648 F.2d 989 (5th Cir. 1981).

93. 20 U.S.C. § 1703(f).

94. *Keyes* v. *School District No. 1,* 576 F.Supp. 1503 (D.Colo. 1983).

95. *Teresa P.* v. *Berkeley Unified School District,* 724 F.Supp. 698 (N.D. Cal. 1989).

96. *Martin Luther King, Jr., Elementary School Children* v. *Michigan Board of Education,* 473 F.Supp. 1371 (E.D. Mich. 1979).

97. See J. Leland and N. Joseph, "Hooked on Ebonics," *Newsweek,* January 13, 1997, at 78; R. L. Jones, "Not White, Just Right," *Newsweek,* February 10, 1997, at 12.

98. *Id.,* January 13, 1997.

99. D. T. Sowell, "Ebonics: Follow the Money," *Forbes,* January 27, 1997, at 48.

100. R. Porter, *Forked Tongue: The Politics of Bilingual Education* (New York: Basic Books, 1990).

17 Who Controls Student Records?

Overview

In 1974 Congress passed the Family Educational Rights and Privacy Act (also known as FERPA or the Buckley Amendment) to define who may and may not see student records. The law guarantees that parents have access to their children's school records; it also prohibits release of the records without parental permission, except to those who have a legitimate "right to know." Many administrators, teachers, and guidance counselors felt the act would cause more harm than good. Some teachers decided to put nothing critical in student records, fearing that any negative information could become the basis for a possible libel suit. Counselors were concerned that able students would be handicapped by a law that required nonconfidential recommendations, because they believed all such recommendations would tend to sound the same and consist simply of positive platitudes. And many administrators saw this law as another legislative intervention in the field of education, creating additional unnecessary procedures and paperwork and threatening to cut off federal funds for noncompliance. In view of these concerns, this chapter examines the reasons for the act, what the act does and does not require, and some of its consequences and controversies.

The Buckley Amendment

Why Did Congress Pass the Buckley Amendment?

Congress acted because of abuses in the use of student records, especially the tendency of schools to provide access to the records to outsiders but to deny access to students and their parents. The establishment of health, guidance, and psychological records on students was originally a progressive development. It enabled teachers, counselors, and administrators to have access to information about the "whole child," not just about grades and subjects studied. In subsequent years, many schools developed extensive records on each student. In New York City, for example, student records typically included a guidance record of the counselor's evaluations of aptitude; behavior and personality characteristics; disciplinary referral cards; recommendations for tracking; a teacher's anecdotal file on student behavior; and cards containing standardized test results, grades, and health information. These records usually were open to government inspectors, employers, and other nonschool personnel but not to parents.[1]

As the quantity of information grew, so did the abuses. One mother was told she had no right to see records that resulted in her son's being transferred to a class for the mentally retarded. A father, attending a routine parent–teacher conference, discovered in teachers' comments in this son's record that he was "strangely introspective" in the third grade, was "unnaturally interested in girls" in the fifth grade, and had developed "peculiar political ideas" by the time he was age 12.[2] Edward Van Allen, who was told by teachers that his son needed psychological treatment, had to get a judicial order to see all of the school's records on the boy.[3] During the 1960s, researchers found that the CIA and the FBI had complete access to student files in more than 60 percent of the school districts, while parents had access in only about 15 percent.[4]

A few years before the Buckley Amendment was passed, a group of prominent educators and lawyers reported these problems in school record keeping:

1. Pupils and their parents typically have little knowledge of what information about them is contained in school records or how it is used.
2. Policies for regulating access to records by nonschool personnel do not exist in most school systems.
3. The secrecy with which school records are usually maintained makes it difficult for parents to assess their accuracy, and formal procedures for challenging erroneous information generally do not exist.[5]

The report concluded that these deficiencies "constitute a serious threat to individual privacy in the United States." Although many state and local regulations to control misuse of student records were developed during the 1960s, they were neither uniform nor comprehensive. Because of these problems, Congress passed the Family Educational Rights and Privacy Act (FERPA), which also will be referred to as the Buckley Amendment.

What Are the Main Features of the Act?

The act contains five important features:

1. It requires school districts to inform parents of their rights under the act each year.
2. It guarantees parents the right to inspect and review the educational records of their children.
3. It establishes procedures through which parents can challenge the accuracy of student records.
4. It protects the confidentiality of student records by preventing disclosure of personally identifiable information to outsiders without prior parental consent.
5. It entitles parents to file complaints with the U.S. Department of Education concerning alleged failures to comply with the act.

The act, which has been amended seven times, applies to all public and private schools and educational agencies receiving federal education funds, either directly or indirectly.[6] Parents or guardians may assert their children's rights of access and consent until they become 18 years old or begin attending a postsecondary institution; after this, these rights will only be accorded to the student.

Right of Access

What Education Records Are Accessible Under the Act?

Education records include any information maintained by a school (or a person acting for a school) that is directly related to a current student regardless of whether the record is in handwriting, print, tape, film, microfilm, or computer file. The information may be in a teacher's or principal's desk as well as in an official student file and includes disciplinary as well as academic information. Regulations issued in 1996 now afford parents access to their children's records maintained by "state educational agencies" as well as records maintained by local school districts.[7] The act also protects material in student files received from outsiders such as consultants or parents. Thus, a federal court in Louisiana ruled in 2000 that a parent's critical letter to a teacher about her son was a FERPA record and should not have been made public.[8]

How Does the Act Guarantee Access to Parents and Students?

The Buckley Amendment states that no federal funds will be made available to any school that prevents parents from exercising "the right to inspect and review the education records of their children." This includes the right (1) to be informed about the kinds and location of education records maintained by the school and the officials responsible for them and (2) to receive an explanation or interpretation of the records if requested. Officials must comply with a parental request to inspect records "within a reasonable time, but in no case more than 45 days after the request." Either parent (including a noncustodial parent) has the right to inspect them, unless prohibited by court order. Although a school may not deny parental access to student records, it may for a legitimate reason deny a request for a copy of such records.

In a court case on this point, former students sued their college for not sending out certified copies of their transcripts because they had failed to repay their student loans.[9] The students claimed that the Buckley Amendment required the college to send out their records when they requested them. A federal court disagreed, ruling that the amendment was "for the inspection of records by students and their parents, not for the release of records to outside parties."[10]

Do "Education Records" Include Only Records Maintained by the School?

No. In New Hampshire, Theresa B. sued for access to her son Daniel's file that was in the possession of the school district's lawyer, who consulted with school officials about the boy's individual educational plan. The school gave Theresa access to Daniel's cumulative file, which contained all of the records the school maintained. But the lawyer refused her access to records that came from juvenile court proceedings, not from the school. The court, ruled that under FERPA, education records include not only records created and retained by the school but also information maintained "by a person acting for" a school.[11] According to the judge, since the school's attorney kept records related directly to Daniel, they are records that his mother should be able to review because "parents need access to such information in order to protect the interests of their child." Furthermore, it makes no difference whether the educational records were created by the school or by outsiders. "A parent," wrote the court, "has a right of access to all records," maintained by the district, whatever their source, unless they are subject to the exceptions noted below.

Do Parents Have the Right to See Teachers' Personal Notes about their Children?

No. The Buckley Amendment does not give parents the right to review the personal notes of teachers, counselors, and administrators if these records are used only as a "personal memory aid," are in their "sole possession," and are not revealed to any other individual except a substitute teacher.

What Other Records Are Not Accessible?

Students do not have the right to see records of a physician, psychologist, or other recognized professional used *only* in connection with their treatment. Parents have no right to see records of a law enforcement unit of the school maintained *solely* for police purposes; or job-related records of students who are employees of the school.

Can Students Waive Their Right of Access?

Yes. Individuals who are applicants for admission to postsecondary institutions may waive their right to inspect confidential letters of recommendation. Although institutions may not require such waivers "as a condition of admission," they may "request" them. These waivers must be signed by the individual students, regardless of age, rather than by their parents. Just as a college is not required to permit students to see these confidential recommendations, so it may also prohibit students from inspecting the financial statements of their parents.

How Does the Buckley Amendment Restrict Access to Outsiders?

The act requires that a school obtain "the written consent of the parent...before disclosing personally identifiable information from the education records of a student." The consent must be signed and dated and include the specific records to be disclosed and the purpose and the individual or group to whom the disclosure may be made. Schools must keep a file of all requests for access to a student's record; the file must indicate who made the request and the legitimate interests in seeking the information.

Can a Parent Who Has Custody of a Child Prohibit the Other Parent from Gaining Access to the Educational Records of Their Child?

No. In a New York case, Michike Page, who had legal custody of her son Eric, asked the school not to permit Eric's father to see their son's educational records.[12] In ruling that neither parent could be denied access to their son's records under FERPA, the judge wrote that despite "some inconvenience," schools should make educational information "available to both parents of every child fortunate enough to have two parents interested in his welfare."

Are There Exceptions to the Consent Requirement?

Yes, there are several. For example, prior consent is not required when education records are shared (1) with teachers and "other school officials" in the district who have "legitimate educational interests," (2) with officials of another school in which the student seeks to enroll (provided the parents are notified), (3) with persons for whom the information is necessary "to protect the health or safety of the student or other individuals," (4) pursuant to a subpoena issued by a court, and (5) in connection with financial aid for which a student has applied. FERPA requires each school district to adopt a policy specifying which school people have a "legitimate educational interest" in accessing student records. Furthermore, a federal court decision held that FERPA does not prohibit college police from disclosing student crime reports.[13] The trial court ruled that criminal reports are not protected because "such records relate in no way whatsoever to the type of records which FERPA expressly protects; i.e., records relating to individual student academic performance" and other educational matters. Similarly, a 1992 FERPA amendment stated that separate records by a school district's "law enforcement unit for the purpose of law enforcement" are not protected by the act.

Does FERPA Prohibit a School from Releasing a Teacher's College Transcript without the Teacher's Consent?

No. In Texas, a parent concerned about the quality of public education requested access to the academic records of a teacher under the state's Open Records Act. The teacher, Rebecca Holt, and the superintendent claimed that the disclosure of Holt's college transcript would violate her privacy rights under FERPA. But a federal appeals court disagreed.[14] It ruled that FERPA was intended to protect only student records, not the records of a school employee. Because Holt was a teacher and not a student, the judge ruled that her college transcript was not an educational record protected from disclosure by FERPA. However, a teacher's personnel file may be protected from public disclosure under the laws of some states.

Does the Buckley Amendment Require Schools to Restrict Distribution of Personal Student Information in School Newspapers?

It depends on the source of the information. In defending their seizure of a school newspaper that contained personal information about a student's suspension, school officials argued that the Buckley Amendment prevented schools from disclosing such information about their students. However, the court ruled that the act could not justify the seizure.[15] Although some of the information in the newspaper would fall within the act's protection "if the source of that information had been school records," the court wrote that "the Amendment cannot be deemed to extend to information which is derived from a source independent of school records."

In a related case, the University of North Carolina Law School argued that its official faculty meetings could not be open to the public because the meetings might concern the personally identifiable educational records of students, and any such disclosures would be inconsistent with the Buckley Amendment. The court ruled that the amendment does not prohibit open faculty meetings that might discuss student records, although it might penalize schools that have a regular practice of releasing such information.[16]

Can Courts Require Schools to Disclose Personal Information about Students without Their Parents' Permission?

Yes, under certain conditions. A case occurred in New York when a group of parents claimed that the schools failed to provide their children with adequate bilingual education.

As part of their suit, the parents asked a federal court to order the schools to provide the names, test results, class schedules, and other information about bilingual students who had English deficiencies. The school refused, claiming that the Buckley Amendment prohibited them from disclosing this information without parental consent. The court ruled that the school may disclose such "personally identifiable information" if it does so in compliance with a judicial order and if those seeking the order "demonstrate a genuine need for the information that outweighs the privacy interest of the student."[17] Since this information was essential to determine whether the suit was justified, the court ruled that a genuine need was shown.

The school also expressed concern about violating the act's requirement that the school notify all parents of the students involved before disclosure. Since several hundred students were potentially involved, the judge said that the school could meet this requirement by making "a reasonable effort" to notify the parents by publishing a notice in Spanish and in English in the local newspapers. The court explained that the act did not establish a school–student privilege analogous to an attorney–client privilege but merely sought to deter schools from releasing personal student information unless there were appropriate educational, medical, or legal reasons. The act, concluded the court, was certainly not intended "as a cloak" for allegedly discriminatory practices.

What Information about Students Can be Shared without Consent?

A school can disclose "directory information" from the education records of a student without requiring prior parental consent. Directory information includes such facts as a student's name, address, email address, phone number, date and place of birth, field of study, sports activities, dates of attendance, awards received, photograph,[18] and similar information. Before freely releasing such information, a school must try to notify parents of current students about what facts it regards as directory information and of the parents' right to refuse to permit the release of such information. It is the parents' obligation to notify the school in writing if they refuse. A school may release directory information about former students without first trying to notify them.

A school also has the discretion not to designate directory information. In a New York case, Francis Krauss asked Nassau Community College to give him the names and addresses of all students to be enrolled in the fall.[19] The school refused and Krauss sued, arguing that this was directory information that should be provided under the Buckley Amendment. The court noted that under FERPA, a school *may* disclose such information; however, in this case, the college chose not to include student names and addresses as directory information, and therefore its refusal to disclose such information did not violate the act. On the other hand, another New York court ruled that FERPA does not *prohibit* a school from giving parents of an injured student the names and addresses of all pupils taking gym at the time of the accident, since this was designated directory information and therefore not privileged under the act.[20]

In some situations, a school may be required to provide information about students even to outsiders. This occurred in a Missouri case in which a state appeals court ruled that a local district must disclose its students' names, addresses, and telephone listings, which were requested by a local teachers' association.[21] The court concluded that disclosure of the requested information under the state's Sunshine Law was not barred by FERPA, since it had been designated "directory information" by the school district. However, a 1992 federal decision indicated that a school's distribution of class rosters with students' social security numbers was a violation of FERPA.[22] In addition, it noted that the frequent practice of posting students' names and grades also violated the act.

Can Teachers Be Disciplined for Disclosing Confidential Information about Students?

Yes, whether the information is protected by FERPA or not. In Minnesota, James Downie, a tenured junior high school guidance counselor, was terminated for, among other things, breaching the confidentiality of students whom he counseled. In upholding the termination, the court wrote that sharing sensitive, confidential information with those who had no need to know was "the most serious of the charges against Downie and certainly the conduct which has the most potential for causing long-lasting harm to students."[23]

What About Confidential Information That Is Not Recorded?

FERPA does not cover and therefore does not prohibit disclosure of confidential information that is not recorded. However, the sharing of such information by a teacher with persons who have no need to know is usually unprofessional and unethical and might violate state privacy laws. Thus, such a disclosure would be a valid reason for disciplinary action. On the other hand, FERPA cannot be used as a defense by teachers or counselors for failure to report reasonable concerns about students who are abused and neglected or are suicidal.

Can School Officials Be Held Liable for Releasing Personally Identifiable Information about Students to the Press?

They might be if it is confidential information that was released without parental consent in clear violation of FERPA. This issue was discussed in a 1996 federal court decision concerning a Kentucky parent who sued the local school board for releasing information about her daughter's medical condition to a newspaper reporter.[24] The newspaper article referred to a "12-year-old female [hermaphrodite] with severe emotional and behavioral problems." The school board members said they were simply trying to explain why they needed to expend emergency funds to deal with the student's problems. They argued that the information was not personally identifiable because they did not use the student's name and because no one who did not already know the student would have learned her identity from the newspaper article. For these reasons, they asked the judge to issue a summary judgment in their favor. But Judge Coffman declined. Instead, he ruled that whether the disclosure by the board was personally identifiable is "an issue of fact that the jury must decide at trial."

Does FERPA Prevent Administrators from Sharing Critical Information about Students with Teachers?

No. An article on youth records, privacy rights, and public safety in *Education Weekly* described three criminal incidents by students in schools and suggested that the crimes might have been prevented if information in the students' records could have been shared.[25] The article implied that FERPA prevented the sharing of such information and that school administrators believed it even barred the release of students' names and addresses to police investigating the crimes. While some educators may believe these errors, the Buckley Amendment is not to blame. As noted above (and as the article failed to point out), the amendment does *not* prohibit administrators from sharing information with teachers who have legitimate educational interests in the information or with anyone for whom the information is necessary to protect the health and safety of students or teachers. In addition, FERPA was amended in 1994 to explicitly allow schools to share with any teacher or school official who has a legitimate interest in the student's behavior information about disciplinary action taken against the student for conduct "that posed a significant risk to the safety or well being" of a member of the school community.[26]

Furthermore, courts have supported local districts that shared important, relevant information about students among educators. In Illinois, for example, a federal judge ruled that a school board did not violate FERPA when it used a videotape of a disruptive student at a special education hearing without parental permission because the school officials at the hearing had a legitimate educational interest in the student.[27] In another case concerning a disruptive student, an Indiana school board was not held liable for revealing information from the student's record without parental consent to officials in the state department of education.[28] The parents argued that disclosures to people who were not employed by the school district violated their privacy rights. But the judge wrote, "A student does not have a legitimate expectation that information potentially related to his educational needs will not be available within the educational system."

Other Rights

Can Schools Destroy Student Records?

Yes. If state law does not determine how long student records must be kept, schools may destroy some or all of a student's educational record at any time, except where there is an outstanding request to inspect them.

Must Parents Be Informed of Their Rights under the Buckley Amendment?

Yes. Every school must give parents of all current students "annual notice" of their rights under the act, indicating where they can obtain copies of the school's policy for implementing and protecting these rights, and informing them of their "right to file complaints" for the school's failure to comply with the act. In addition, the act requires that elementary and secondary schools find a way to effectively notify parents of students whose primary language is not English.

Do Parents Have a Right to Challenge Their Children's Records?

Yes. If the parents of a student believe that a school record is "inaccurate or misleading or violates the privacy or other rights of the student," they may request that the school amend it. If the school refuses, it must so inform the parents and advise them of their rights to a hearing. The hearing may be conducted by anyone, including a school employee, "who does not have a direct interest" in its outcome. Parents must be given "a full and fair opportunity" to present their evidence and may be represented by counsel, at their own expense. The school must make its decision in writing "based solely on the evidence presented at the hearing," which must include the reasons and evidence to support its decision. The decision is final and there is no appeal. If, as a result of the hearing, the school decides the record was inaccurate or misleading, it must amend the record accordingly. But if the school decides that the information was correct, it must inform the parents of "the right to place in the education records of the student a statement commenting upon the information…and/or setting forth any reasons for disagreeing with the decision" of the school. Such explanation must be maintained by the school as part of the student's record; if the contested portion of the record is disclosed to anyone, the explanation must also be disclosed.

May Parents or Students Contest the Appropriateness of a Grade?

No. In a Texas case, a student challenged the grade he was assigned in a physics course and also the professor's grading process.[29] The federal appeals court held that FERPA did not give judges authority to rule on disputes about the wisdom of a teacher's grades. The judge wrote that Congress did not intend "to afford students a federal right…to challenge their teachers' or educational institutions' grading process." As the court explained, FERPA gave parents the right to challenge a misleading or improperly recorded grade, but they "could not…contest whether the teacher should have assigned a higher grade."

Does FERPA Prohibit Students from Grading Each Other's Classroom Work or Assignments?

No. ruled the U.S. Supreme Court in *Owasso* v. *Falvo*.[30] This 2002 case began in Tulsa, Oklahoma, when Kristja Falvo objected to the practice of her children's teacher who had students exchange papers, grade them, return them to the students who prepared them, and then ask the students to call out the scores which the teacher entered in a grade book. Mrs. Flavo asked the school to prohibit peer grading which embarrassed her children. When the school refused, she went to court and argued that the practice violated FERPA. A federal appeals court agreed, ruling that the grades marked by students on each other's work are education records protected by the statute. The Supreme Court, however, did not agree.

The High Court ruled that an assignment is not an education record as soon as it is graded by another student. In explaining why the justices did not want to prohibit peer grading, Justice Kennedy wrote:

> Correcting a classmate's work can be as much a part of the assignment as taking the test itself. It is a way to teach material again in a new context…. By explaining the answers to the class as the students correct the papers, the teacher not only reinforces the lesson but also discovers whether the students have understood the material.

If homework or class work were considered education records protected by FERPA, "this would impose substantial burdens on the teachers across the country," wrote the Court, since it would force instructors to correct daily student assignments and "would make it much more difficult for teachers to give students immediate guidance." The Court concluded that the grades on student papers are not covered under FERPA "at least until the teacher has collected them and recorded them in his or her grade book."

Are Special Education Students Entitled to Additional Rights?

Yes. In addition to their rights under FERPA, special education students have additional rights under the Individuals with Disabilities Education Act (IDEA). This is because special education services often involve the sharing of especially sensitive and personal information. Thus the IDEA requires that teachers and staff who use personally identifiable information must receive training on confidentiality requirements.[31] The IDEA also requires that schools notify parents when their children's special education records are no longer needed and that they destroy such records at the parents' request.[32] However, federal rules require schools to maintain IEPs and evaluations for at least three years to document compliance with IDEA. In addition, IDEA requires schools to provide parents with access to student records before any IEP meeting or special education hearing.

Legal Enforcement

Are There Any Procedures to Enforce the Buckley Amendment?

Yes. There are detailed federal regulations concerning enforcement. The Family Policy Compliance Office of the Department of Education has been established to "investigate, process, and review violations and complaints." After receiving written complaints regarding alleged violations, the office will notify the school and provide an opportunity to respond. After its investigation, the office will send its findings to the complainant and the school. If there has been a violation, the office will indicate the specific steps the school must take to be in compliance. If the school does not comply, a review board hearing will be held. If the review board determines "that compliance cannot be secured by voluntary means," federal education funds will be terminated. FERPA, however, does not provide individual citizens with a legal right to enforce the act through the courts. According to a federal appeals decision, "enforcement is solely in the hands" of the U.S. Department of Education.[33]

Thousands of complaints have been received by the Family Policy Compliance Office, and about 80 percent of them have been resolved informally through phone calls to the school districts. As of October 2001, there have been over 1,000 formal investigations.[34] No cases have yet been referred to the review board; thus federal funds have never been terminated for noncompliance.

In addition to enforcing FERPA, the Family Policy Compliance Office tries to help educators understand the act. Its staff will consult with teachers and administrators by letter or phone and will answer questions concerning the act, its regulations, and their interpretation and application in specific school districts.[35]

Can Parents Sue Schools for Violating Their FERPA Rights?

Yes, but not under FERPA. FERPA does not provide for an individual to sue a school district for violations; instead, it requires the Secretary of Education to enforce the act. However, several federal appeals courts have ruled that a parent can bring suit under Section 1983 of the federal civil rights laws, which allows individuals to sue government officials who violate their rights. (Individual liability under Section 1983 is also discussed in chapter

5.) In a New York case, a divorced father who had joint custody unsuccessfully tried for 11 months to get information from school officials about his children's educational progress.[36] Since FERPA does not prohibit a private suit under Section 1983, the court ruled that judges may award compensation to parents where their FERPA rights are clearly violated by public officials and where damages can be proved.

Furthermore, a 1992 federal decision held that students do not have to "exhaust the requirements in FERPA" before taking legal action against schools that do not comply with the act.[37] The trial court noted that requiring complainants to first exhaust their rights under the act would have the effect of "exhausting" them first. Thus, when public schools violate parents' FERPA rights, parents may either ask the Department of Education to enforce the act or they may sue the school officials directly under Section 1983 of the federal civil rights laws. However, winning a Section 1983 suit is not easy since parents must prove that the school's violation was intentional or reckless and pursuant to official custom or policy.

Can Parents Sue Schools for a Single Violation of FERPA?

Not on the basis of Section 1983 of the Civil Rights law. In Minnesota, Samuel Ackman initiated a Section 1983 suit, claiming that his high school violated his FERPA rights by disclosing confidential information about him. In a 1999 decision, a federal court agreed that FERPA "is enforceable through Section 1983 actions."[38] Nevertheless, the court dismissed Ackman's claim since he only alleged one instance where the school released his records without his parents' consent. The court explained that FERPA was adopted to address "systemic, not individual, violations." The judge concluded that "a solitary violation is insufficient to support a finding that the District has violated FERPA as a matter of policy or practice"—a finding that is required to support a Section 1983 suit.

In a related Utah case, parents of C. J. charged that the principal, in responding to harassment complaints against their son, disclosed to the complaining parents information about C. J. protected by FERPA. The court, however, ruled that the principal did not violate FERPA by explaining to concerned parents how he was responding to their complaints. Such an explanation, wrote the judge, did not constitute a "release of educational records" under FERPA.[39]

Can School Board Members Be Held Personally Liable for Violating FERPA?

Only if they knew or should have known they were violating a student's rights. This issue arose in a federal case involving a small South Dakota school district that raised taxes to send J. M., an autistic student, to a residential school in Connecticut. In a newspaper article about the tax increase, J. M. was identified by name and photograph. After J. M.'s parents received harassing phone calls, they sued the school board members for violating their FERPA right to confidentiality.[40]

The court noted that school board members may be held liable for conduct that violates "clearly established statutory or constitutional rights of which a reasonable person would have known."[41] But the judge also wrote that J. M.'s parents had already publicly disclosed in an open letter to school district voters, that they had an autistic son, and the release of board minutes about its expenditures for J. M. was done in compliance with state law. Under these circumstances, the court ruled that board members could not be held personally liable because "an objectively reasonable school board member would not know that the release of information regarding the cause of the increase in property taxes was a violation of the plaintiff's clearly established right to confidentiality."

What Have Been the Results of FERPA?

Initially schools were slow to comply with the statute. Federal regulations for implementation were not published until a year and a half after the act became law. But as hundreds of complaints have been filed with the Washington, D.C. enforcement office each year, information about the act has increased, and compliance has become more widespread.

According to some observers, two notable results of the Buckley Amendment have been the destruction of old records and the improvement of new ones. After the law was passed, many schools nationwide conducted "massive housecleanings" of records. Emptying school files of "undesirable material," wrote Lucy Knight, "remains the single most effective way for a school to attempt compliance with the Buckley Amendment."[42] Second, the quality of student records and the caliber of recommendations have "improved substantially" according to Chester Nolte. This improvement, wrote Professor Nolte, reflects the fact that under the act, teachers, principals, and counselors "must adhere to absolute truth, rather than opinion, when writing reports on individual students."[43]

Fears that teachers would be sued for libel if they wrote anything negative in student records have been greatly exaggerated. There is little chance of students' winning libel suits against teachers whose comments are based on first-hand observation, are accurate, and are educationally relevant. (For more on libel, see chapter 7.)

Four other areas of misunderstanding have regularly occurred concerning the act. First, many educators are still unaware that access applies to all student records, not just to the cumulative file. Second, many parents believe the act gives them the right to challenge the fairness of a student's grade. Although the act does allow parents to question whether a teacher's grade was recorded accurately, it does not allow them to challenge the reasonableness of the grade. Third, many administrators are not aware that the parental right to inspect and review the educational records of their children applies equally to noncustodial parents who do not live with their children (unless their access has been prohibited by a court order). Fourth, FERPA does not prohibit schools from sharing information about students who pose significant safety or health problems with any teacher who has a legitimate interest in the student.

Summary

Abuses in the use of student records led Congress to pass the Family Educational Rights and Privacy Act (the Buckley Amendment) in 1974. The act has several important features. First, it guarantees parents the right to inspect and review their children's educational records (excluding teachers' personal notes about students). Second, it limits access to student records by providing that such records cannot be released to outsiders without a parent's written consent. However, such consent is not required when the records are shared with teachers in the school who have a "legitimate educational interest" in the student, or when they are released pursuant to a court order. Third, the act gives parents the right to challenge recorded information that is "inaccurate, misleading, or otherwise in violation of privacy or other rights of students." It also gives parents the right to place an explanation in the record of any information with which they disagree. Students who apply to college may waive their right to inspect confidential letters of recommendation. When students become age 18 or begin attending a postsecondary institution, they assume their parents' rights under the act. Although the act has imposed additional administrative responsibilities on the schools, it has generally led to an improvement in the quality and accuracy of student records.[44]

NOTES

1. D. Divoky, "Cumulative Records: Assault on Privacy," *Learning Magazine, 2* (1) (September 1973): 18–23.

2. *Id.*

3. *Van Allen* v. *McCleary,* 211 N.Y.S.2d 501 (N.Y. Sup. Ct. 1961).

4. M. Stone, *Off the Record: The Emerging Right to Control One's School Files,* 5 N.Y.U. REV. L. & SOC. CHANGE, 39, 42 (1975).

5. *Divoky, supra* note 1, at 10.

6. The text of the act is in Title 20, Section 1232g of the *United States Code Annotated* (1996). Regulations for implementing the act are in the *Code of Federal Regulations* Title 34, Part 99. (1996) Quotations about the act in this chapter are from the *Code of Federal Regulations,* unless otherwise indicated.

7. The right of access is the only right parents are afforded at the state level (FERPA Final Regulations. November 21, 1996, *Federal Register.*)

8. *Warner* v. *St. Bernard Parish School District,* 99 F. Supp.2d 748 (E.D.La. 2000).

9. *Girardier* v. *Webster College,* 421 F.Supp. 45 (E.D. Mo. 1976).

10. On the other hand, where a student's debt for college loans has been legally discharged by a bankruptcy court, "schools could not withhold a transcript as a means of forcing collection of [such] a debt." *Johnson* v. *Edinboro State College,* 728 F.2d 163 (3d Cir. 1984).

11. *Belanger* v. *Nashua, New Hampshire, School District,* 856 F.Supp. 40 (D N.H. 1994).

12. *Page* v. *Rotterdam-Mohonasen Central School District,* 441 N.Y.S.2d 323 (N.Y. Sup. Ct. 1981).

13. *Bauer* v. *Kincaid,* 759 F.Supp. 575 (W.D. Mo. 1991).

14. *Klein Independent School District* v. *Mattox,* 830 F.2d 576 (5th Cir. 1987).

15. *Frasca* v. *Andrews,* 463 F.Supp. 1043 (E.D. N.Y. 1978).

16. *Student Bar Association Board of Governors* v. *Byrd,* 239 S.E.2d 415 (N.C. 1977).

17. *Rios* v. *Read,* 73 F.R.D. 589 (E.D. N.Y. 1977).

18. Added in the revised 2000 regulations. 65 *Fed. Reg.* 41852 (2000).

19. *Krauss* v. *Nassau Community College,* 469 N.Y.S.2d 553 (N.Y. Sup. Ct. 1983).

20. *Staub* v. *East Greenbush School District No. 1,* 491 N.Y.S.2d 87 (N.Y. Sup. Ct. 1985).

21. *Oregon County R-IV School District* v. *LeMon,* 739 SW.2d 553 (Mo. Ct. App. 1987).

22. *Krebs* v. *Rutgers,* 797 F.Supp. 1246 (D. N.J. 1992).

23. *Downie* v. *Independent School District No. 141,* 367 N.W.2d 913 (Minn. App. 1985).

24. *Doe* v. *Knox County Board of Education,* 918 F.Supp. 181 (E.D. Ky. 1996).

25. *Privacy Rights and Public Safety Concerns: Debate Stirs over Access to Youth Records,* EDUC. WEEKLY, June 21, 1989, at 1.

26. 20 U.S.C.A. § 1232g (h) (1997).

27. *M. R. by R. R.* v. *Lincolnwood Board of Education, District No. 74,* 843 F.Supp. 1236 (N.D. Ill, 1994), *aff'd,* 56 F.3d 67 (7th Cir. 1995).

28. *Norris by Norris* v. *Board of Education of Greenwood Community School Corporation,* 797 F.Supp. 1452 (S.D. Ind. 1992).

29. *Tarka* v. *Cunningham,* 917 F.2d 890 (5th Cir. 1990).

30. *Owasso Independent School District No. I-011* v. *Falvo,* 534 U.S. 426 (2002).

31. 34 C.F.R. § 300.572(c) (1992).

32. 34 C.F.R. § 300.573 (1992).

33. *Girardier* v. *Webster College,* 563 F.2d 1267 (8th Cir. 1977). However, the issue of whether FERPA provides individuals with the right to sue under § 983 is now before the U.S. Supreme Court.

34. Telephone interview with J. E. Smith, Program Assistant, Family Policy Compliance Office (September 17, 2001).

35. For copies of the regulations or a Model Policy Document for elementary and secondary schools, contact the Family Policy Compliance Office, U.S. Department of Education, 400 Maryland Avenue, S.W., Washington, D.C. 20202, or phone (202) 260-3887.

36. *Fay* v. *South Colonie Central School District,* 802 F.2d 21 (2d Cir. 1986).

37. *Krebs, supra* note 22, at 1257.

38. *Ackman* v. *Chisago Lakes Independent School District No. 2144,* 45 F.Supp.2d 664 (D.Minn. 1999).

39. *Jensen ex. rel. C. J.* v. *Reeves,* 45 F.Supp.2d 1265 (D. Utah 1999).

40. *Maynard* v. *Greater Hoyt School District No. 61–4,* 876 F.Supp. 1104 (D. S.D. 1995).

41. *Harlow* v. *Fitzgerald,* 457 U.S. 800 (1982).

42. L. Knight, "Facts About Mr. Buckley's Amendment," *Amer. Educ.,* June 1977, at 6.

43. M. C. Nolte, "Read This Before You Allow Sensitive Information To Be Released About Students, *American School Board Journal,* 38 (April 1977).

44. For an excellent update and overview, see D. S. Huefner and L. M. Daggett, "FERPA Update: Balancing Access to and Privacy of Student Records," 152 *Education Law Reporter,* 469 (June 2001).

18 Do Parents Have Choices in Educating Their Children?

Overview

Universal, publicly supported education is a uniquely American idea, one that has been borrowed by many other nations. On the basis of the conviction that an enlightened citizenry can best serve the needs of society, the states provide free schools for children and youth and require them to attend. Thus, since every state provides schools at public expense, schooling is a *right* provided not by the U.S. Constitution but by each state.

Furthermore, where attendance is compulsory, children and youth have a *duty* to attend school. All of the states have compulsory attendance laws, but the age of mandatory school attendance varies, beginning at ages 6, 7, or 8 and extending through ages 15 to 18, depending on the wording of the specific state statute.

With the rise of compulsory schooling came disagreements concerning the constitutionality of such compulsion and proposals for alternatives to the public schools. Laws requiring that children attend school have been uniformly sustained, and it is clear today that there is no constitutional provision violated by such a mandate.[1]

Nevertheless, specific questions continue to arise regarding such matters as conflicts between parents' rights and compulsory schooling, educational choice, home schooling, and parental objection to teaching materials or to the curriculum. This chapter examines how the issues of compulsory education and curriculum objections have been dealt with in state laws and in courts.

Compulsory Schooling and Parents' Rights

Must All Children Attend Public School?

In 1922, Oregon passed a law, effective September 1, 1926, requiring every parent or guardian of a child between the ages of 8 and 16 to send such child "to a public school for the period of time a public school shall be held during the current year." Failure to comply with the law was a misdemeanor. The Society of Sisters, a religious organization that maintained various schools in Oregon, challenged the state law, claiming it to be unconstitutional in that it took away property rights arbitrarily, in violation of the due process clause of the Fourteenth Amendment.

No questions were raised about the right of the state to require school attendance or to regulate all schools; what was questioned was the requirement that all children attend *public* schools. To this challenge, the U.S. Supreme Court in *Pierce* v. *Society of Sisters,* recognizing the basic right of parents and guardians "to direct the upbringing and education of children under their control," said:

> The fundamental theory of liberty upon which all governments in this Union repose excludes any general power of the state to standardize its children by forcing them to accept instruction from public teachers only. The child is not the mere creature of the state; those who nurture him and direct his destiny have the right, coupled with the high duty, to recognize and prepare him for additional obligations.[2]

Since *Pierce,* courts have uniformly held that a state's requirement that children attend school can be met through either public or private schools; furthermore, if the school is private, it may be either religious or secular.

Following the landmark *Pierce* decision, parental choice has been expanded through the decades by the use of charter schools, voucher plans, and the rise of home schooling as well as the availability of private schools, both religious and secular, and, of course, the free public school system.

What Are Charter Schools?

Because of widespread dissatisfaction with the quality of public education in recent decades, the National Commission of Excellence was created by the federal government to study the schools. In 1983, it published its report, *A Nation at Risk,* and warned that the public schools were creating a "rising tide of mediocrity that threatens our very future as a nation and a people."[3] Charter schools were among the various educational reforms designed to remedy the shortcomings of public schools. It was believed that charter schools would encourage competition, innovation, and create incentives to improve the schools. The federal government provided funds to support the charter school movement through several statutes.[4]

However, since schooling is a function of state governments, the laws and regulations that govern the establishment of charter schools vary from state to state, yet have certain features in common. Charter schools may not charge tuition but receive per pupil state aid dollars to support their activities. They must outline their mission and curriculum and undergo a review process to show that their program qualifies for charter school status. Thereafter, they enter into a contract to deliver the services to children who will elect to attend. These schools are evaluated to see whether they are meeting their stated goals. If they fail to meet the goals, they must develop an educational plan that explains how it will accomplish the goals of the charter. The sponsor may revoke the charter if the school continues to fail reaching the goals established in the charter.

Charter schools are autonomous or semiautonomous public schools created by a contract or charter between the school's organizers and a sponsor, either a state department of education or a school district. The creators of the schools are held accountable for achieving the educational goals and, in turn, the school is exempt from many restrictions that apply to traditional public schools. As of July, 2000, 36 states, the District of Columbia, and Puerto Rico have created charter schools.[5]

There is great variability in the availability and quality of charter schools. Depending on their location, the physical facilities, and racial/ethnic and socioeconomic composition of the student population, programs tend to vary, and it is the responsibility of the parents to decide whether to enroll their child in a particular school.

Do Voucher Plans Enhance Parental Choice?

Yes, they do, for low-income parents. Recent voucher plans were created to enable low-income families, dissatisfied with the quality of education their children are receiving in public schools, to enroll them in private schools. Public funds are used to issue "vouchers" or "certificates" to parents, which are endorsed to the private school where their children are enrolled. The value of the vouchers depends on the particular program and is usually related to the state aid per student during the particular school year.

The voucher plans of some states, such as Maine, prohibit the use of the vouchers in religious schools. Other plans, like those of Milwaukee, Wisconsin, and Cleveland, Ohio, allow their use in both religious and secular schools as long as students are not required to participate in religious activities. For a more thorough discussion of this topic, see chapter 10.

If Parents Have Religious Objections to Schooling, Can They Avoid Sending Their Children to School?

No. Nevertheless, a variation on this question led to a partial exemption from schooling for children of the Amish religion. Several Amish parents in Wisconsin decided not to send their 14- and 15-year-old children to school beyond the eighth grade, in violation of the state's compulsory attendance law. The parents claimed that high school attendance would be destructive of the children's religious beliefs and, ultimately, of the Amish way of life. The Amish way rejects material success, competition, intellectual and scientific accomplishment, self-distinction, and other values central to the curriculum and social climate in high schools. The parents further claimed that competition in classwork, sports, and peer pressure would alienate Amish children from their families and from their close-knit, co-operative, agrarian, religion-based lives.

The Amish did not object to elementary schooling, for they believed in the necessity of the 3 R's to read the Bible, to be good farmers and good citizens, and to be able to interact occasionally with non-Amish people. The U.S. Supreme Court, after considering the conflicting interests of the state of Wisconsin and the Amish, exempted the students from schooling beyond the eighth grade. The Court based its decision on the religious freedom clause of the First Amendment and in effect considered the Amish way of life as an acceptable alternative to formal secondary education. About its decision to protect the Amish, the Court wrote that "there can be no assumption that today's majority is 'right' and the Amish and others like them are 'wrong.' A way of life that is odd or even erratic but interferes with no rights or interest of others is not to be condemned because it is different."[6] (A related question appears in chapter 10, on pp. 186–187.)

Can Other Parents, Individually or in Groups, Avoid the Requirements of Compulsory Schooling?

No. The Amish case cannot be used as legal precedent for those who simply disagree with today's schools or who even form "religious" groups to gain exemption from schooling. As Justice Burger wrote:

> A way of life, however virtuous and admirable, may not be interposed as a barrier to reasonable state regulation of education if it is based on purely secular considerations.... It cannot

be overemphasized that we are not dealing with a way of life and mode of education by a group claiming to have recently discovered some "progressive" or more enlighted [sic] process for rearing children for modern life.[7]

Thus the law respects the rights of parents to guide the upbringing of their children by allowing parents to choose among existing schools or even set up new schools. At the same time, the compulsory laws of the states are upheld, mandating that all children go to some school.

Home Schooling

Under What Conditions Can Parents Educate Their Children at Home?

State laws that mandate school attendance for children usually provide for alternative ways of satisfying that requirement. The most common equivalent is private schooling that meets certain minimum state requirements related to health and safety, curriculum, and teacher qualification. Today, all states allow for alternatives to public schools as long as such alternatives are "equivalent" in scope and quality. Some states provide that alternatives to public schooling must meet the approval of the local superintendent of schools and/ or the school board. As for whether parents can educate their school-age children at home, in general the answer is yes if the requirements of their particular state statute are satisfied. In recent years, the number of children being home schooled has increased significantly, although the precise number is unknown because not all states collect such information. One estimate has placed the number for 1996–1997 at 1.23 million with a 15 percent per year increase since 1990.[8] Most parents who choose home schooling do so for religious reasons. State laws vary in their wording, and courts have interpreted these laws differently, so one must look carefully at the law of the individual state.

A typical state law requires that the alternative to public schooling include teaching "the branches of education taught to children of corresponding age and grade in public schools," that the education be "equivalent," and that some systematic reporting be made to the local school superintendent to enable the state to supervise the alternative schooling. Disagreements often arise concerning the meaning of "equivalent" education as well as the qualification of the parents to teach their children. Roughly speaking, courts can be characterized as bringing a liberal or a strict interpretation to such state statues.

All courts are more concerned with the requirement that the child be educated than with the specific form or place of that education. Some courts place the burden on the parent to prove that the home teaching is adequate and equivalent to that of the public schools, while others place the burden of proof on the state or school officials to show that the particular home schooling is not adequate. Where the burden of proof is placed is very important in a lawsuit, for the party that has the burden of proof must present the initial evidence to establish the claim it is making. If the initial evidence is insufficient, the case is dismissed; if it is sufficient, the other side must refute it in order to prevail. Which side has the burden of proof is usually indicated by the relevant state statute under which the suit is brought.

The *liberal* interpretation can be exemplified by an Illinois case in which parents were accused of violating the state compulsory education law by teaching their seven-year-old daughter at home. At the trial, evidence proved that her mother, "who had two years of college and some training in pedagogy and educational psychology," taught her at home for five hours each day and that the child could perform comparably with average third-grade students. Nevertheless, the laws of Illinois made no specific provision for home teaching, only for "private or parochial school where children were taught the branches of education taught to children of corresponding age and grade in public schools." The parents claimed that their daughter was attending a "private school" within the meaning of the state law, since she was receiving instruction comparable to that of the public school.

The Supreme Court of Illinois agreed with the parents, noting that the purpose of the law "is that all children shall be educated, not that they shall be educated in a particular manner or place."[9] The court was satisfied that the intent of the law in specifying "private school" as an alternative included the "place and nature of instruction" provided in this case. While wanting to protect children against educational deprivation, the law did not intend to punish conscientious parents. In the words of the Illinois court: "The law is not made to punish those who provide their children with instruction equal or superior to that obtainable in the public schools. It is made for the parent who fails or refuses to properly educate his child."

State courts using a *strict* interpretation of the law tend to emphasize that the requirement of equivalent instruction includes qualified and even certified teachers. Some states specify that certification is the evidence necessary to prove qualification for home teaching. California is one of these states, and the court of appeals there ruled that children enrolled in a correspondence course were not receiving equivalent instruction.[10]

In a case that arose in Maine in 1983, the court held that the state has the power to impose reasonable regulations for the duration and control of basic education.[11] When parents refused to submit their plans for home schooling to school authorities for approval, they were fined on the grounds that their children were habitually truant. Similarly a Kansas court found that home instruction that was unplanned and unscheduled, by a mother who was not certified or accredited, did not satisfy the state compulsory attendance law.[12]

Must State Laws Be Clear and Unambiguous?

Yes. The Georgia Supreme Court declared the state compulsory education law "unconstitutionally vague in that it failed to provide fair notice to persons of ordinary intelligence and to establish minimum guidelines to local officials as to what constitutes 'private school.'"[13] This case involved a family who were members of the Worldwide Church of God. The parents began teaching their children at home because they felt the public schools would have a disruptive influence on their children, and that they were of poor quality, unsafe, and immoral. The issue of freedom of religion was not addressed in the case. If, however, a state's statute requires that children attend only public or approved private schools, and if such laws are clear, specific, and unambiguous, courts will sustain them.[14]

Since earlier statutory language often failed because of vagueness, much of the recent legislative activity has aimed at clarifying statutory language. For example, Arkansas made its law clearer and more specific, requiring that students taught at home be given the same standardized tests as students in public schools. When parents challenged the law, a federal appeals court upheld it in 1988, indicating that this type of monitoring of student achievement was "the least restrictive system to assure its goal of adequately educating its citizens."[15] A similar conflict in Missouri over the vagueness of a state statute requiring "substantially equivalent" education led to a lawsuit, and the court held that a statute was too vague if "persons of common intelligence must necessarily guess at its meaning and differ as to its application."[16] As a consequence of this lawsuit, the Missouri statute was revised to cure the vagueness.[17]

Parents in Ohio challenged a statutory requirement that they seek approval of the local superintendent for their home education program, but the Ohio Supreme Court upheld the statute as one that "reasonably furthers the state's interest in the education of its citizens." Though some dissenting judges considered the statute vague in that it gives the superintendent "unbridled discretion to determine if a home-schooling teacher is qualified," the majority found no problem in this, and the U.S. Supreme Court declined to review the case.[18]

Compulsory school attendance laws that are so vague that they require school officials to clarify their meaning are unconstitutional under the Fourteenth Amendment's due process clause. In recent years, the laws of six states have been successfully challenged on the ground of vagueness (Georgia, Iowa, Michigan, Minnesota, Missouri, and Pennsylvania).[19] Such states can remedy the vagueness by amending their laws to make them clear or specific.

In a Michigan case, parents claimed the right to educate their children at home, as an exercise in religious freedom. State law required that students who did not attend public schools be taught by certified teachers. The court upheld the state law, ruling that the state's compelling interest in an educated citizenry outweighs the rights claimed by the parents. The Michigan Supreme Court, however, reversed the appeals court's decision and held that the DeJonges' First Amendment right to practice their religion superceded the state requirement that home schooling be conducted by a parent who is a certified teacher.[20] The court found that these parents had a sincerely held belief that God commanded them to educate their children without state certification. The court noted that the certification requirement imposes a loathsome dilemma upon these parents: violate the law of God to abide by the law of man, or commit a crime under the laws of man to remain faithful to God. Thus, the certification requirement presents an "irreconcilable conflict between the mandates of law and religious duty."[21] On the same day as this ruling was handed down, the Michigan Supreme Court upheld the state certification requirement for home schooling parents whose objection to the certification requirement was not based on religion.[22] The Virginia Supreme Court upheld the state's compulsory attendance law in the face of a challenge to exempt from attendance on religious grounds.[23] The court held that parents had the burden of proof to show that their request for nonattendance was based on religious beliefs, a burden they did not satisfy. In sum, home schooling based on parental claims of religious conviction may find protection in some states but not in others, and under some sets of facts but not others. Since the U.S. Supreme Court has never ruled directly on this issue, one must examine the case law of the particular state where the conflict arises.

In recent years, advocates of home schooling have succeeded in influencing many state legislatures to pass laws that accommodate their wishes. Thirty-one states have revised or adopted laws or regulations concerning home schooling since 1956, mostly in response to parents challenging existing laws in court actions or through lobbying. Most of the changes are favorable toward home schooling.

State statutes controlling home schooling can be grouped into four categories: (1) "explicit language" statutes, which explicitly permit home instruction; (2) "equivalency language" statutes, which require attendance in public schools or their "equivalent"; (3) "qualifies as private school" statutes, which permit private school attendance and allow home instruction to qualify as a private school; and (4) "silent language" statutes, where state laws are silent on the matter, leaving it entirely in the hands of courts, state departments of education, and local officials.[24]

What About the Social Development of Children Schooled at Home?

In an earlier case, a New Jersey court ruled that "equivalent" instruction requires that standard, approved teaching materials be used, that the parent doing the teaching have the necessary qualifications, and that the children have the full advantages supplied by the public schools, including free association with other children.[25] In this case, the home instruction was found not to be equivalent because the mother, though certified to teach in secondary schools, had not kept up with educational developments for the previous 20 years. Furthermore, the children's home school did not include opportunities for social interaction with others of their age.

The requirement that there be opportunities for social development is a difficult one for home schools to meet. And, in fact, most courts do not impose this requirement, for it effectively eliminates the alternative of home schooling. Courts have said that the inclusion of social development in deciding whether home schooling is equivalent would in effect eliminate "instruction elsewhere than at school." Group interaction and instruction in groups would constitute a *de facto* school, and if that is what the legislature intended, it should so specify. With this line of reasoning, most courts do not impose social interaction as a requirement for home schooling, and even in a later case in New Jersey, the court refused to follow the requirement imposed by the earlier decision in that state.[26]

Can the State Vest the Power of "Approval" of Home Schooling or Private Schools in School Boards?

Yes, ruled the First Circuit Court of Appeals, upholding a Massachusetts statute that gave local school boards such authority.[27] When a religious academy objected to the "approval" authority and wanted to substitute standardized testing in its place, the court found that the free exercise clause of the First Amendment is not violated by the reasonable regulation of private education and found the use of standardized testing insufficient to replace the authority of the school board.

What Constitutional and Statutory Grounds Are There for Home Schooling?

A trial court in Massachusetts faced the home schooling issue in 1978 in light of a state statute on compulsory attendance that exempted children who are "being otherwise instructed in a manner approved in advance by the superintendent or the school committee."[28] The court found both constitutional and statutory grounds to protect the right to home education. The constitutional grounds are derived from the right to privacy, which, though nowhere mentioned explicitly in the U.S. Constitution, is nonetheless an important right recognized by various decisions of the U.S. Supreme Court.

The Massachusetts court relied on the words of Justice Douglas, who expressed the following as a source of parents' rights:

> The Ninth Amendment obviously does not create federally enforceable rights. It merely says, "the enumeration in the Constitution of certain rights shall not be construed to deny or disparage others retained by the people." But a catalogue of these rights includes customary, traditional and time honored rights, amenities and privileges.... Many of them, in my view, come within the meaning of the term "liberty" as used in the Fourteenth Amendment... [one] is *freedom of choice in the basic decisions of one's life* respecting marriage, divorce, contraception, *and the education and upbringing of children.*[29]

In addition to the constitutional source of parents' rights, the trial court also noted that when the Massachusetts legislature revised its compulsory attendance law, it chose to retain the phrase "otherwise instructed." From this, the inference can be drawn that home education was intended to be maintained as an alternative available to parents. The court nonetheless recognized the interest of the state in an educated citizenry and thus wanted to preserve reasonable regulatory powers in the hands of school officials. In search of an appropriate balance between the rights of parents and the interests of the state, the judge ordered the school committee to consider the following in determining the adequacy of home instruction:

1. the competency of the teachers ("and though certification would not be required, the presence or absence of the requirements that would lead to certification may be considered");
2. the teaching of subjects required by law or regulation;
3. the "manner in which the subjects are taught so as to impart comparable knowledge as given in the local schools";
4. the "number of hours and days devoted to teaching";
5. the "adequacy of the texts, materials, methods, and programs being used"; and
6. the "availability of periodic tests and measurements of the child's educational growth."

School officials were *not* to consider the following factors in judging the adequacy of the home educational plan:

1. the parents' reasons for wanting to educate their child at home;
2. the lack of a curriculum identical to that of the school;
3. the lack of group experience; and
4. the possibility that this exemption may become a precedent for other cases.

Another Massachusetts case similarly upheld the state law authorizing local education officials to approve home schooling programs regarding curriculum, length of program, competency of the parent, content of instruction, and processes for the evaluation of progress.[30] The Massachusetts court, while upholding the power of the state to supervise home schooling, was also concerned with the protection of the liberty interests of the parents under the Fourteenth Amendment. Thus, it cautioned against the state dictating every detail of home schooling; it accepted the right of the school committee to examine the competency of parents to teach, while rejecting the requirement of certification or any requirement that the parents have a college or advanced academic degree. Periodic standardized testing of home-schooled children was also accepted by the court to ensure satisfactory progress toward minimum standards.

Do Home Schooled Students Have a Right to Participate in Extracurricular Activities?

This issue has arisen with increasing frequency in recent years as the number of home schoolers has increased. Since schooling is primarily a state responsibility, it is not surprising that no uniform law exists on this issue among the fifty states.

Home schooled students who have claimed a constitutional right to participate in school-based extracurricular activities have been generally unsuccessful. A good example of this is a 1995 New York case in which a 14-year-old home schooled student wanted to participate in the interscholastic sports program of the school district of her residence.[31] She was prevented from participating by a state board of education rule that provided that only students in regular attendance could participate in interscholastic sports. She went to court, claiming that her constitutional rights to due process and equal protection were violated.

The court ruled against her on the due process claim, holding that she had no property right to participate in interscholastic sports that would be protected by the due process clause. In ruling against her on the equal protection claim, the court said that "…absent a suspect classification or fundamental right claim, neither of which is advanced here, a regulation will withstand an equal protection challenge if it bears some rational relationship to a legitimate state purpose."

The commissioner of education cited several state objectives justifying the rule:

1. It promotes loyalty and school spirit that leads to cohesion of the student body, role models for other students if the student athlete has daily contact with the student population, and assists in maintaining academic standards for sport participation.
2. Sports have a quasi-curricular nature, since they may be accepted for credit toward physical education requirements.
3. It would lead to havoc if home schoolers could opt out of school programs in general yet selectively participate in athletics and then extend that ability to select courses of instruction as well.

In effect, the court considered participation on school sports teams a privilege not a right, with no clear reason why such privilege should be extended to those who do not attend the school.

Most courts have ruled consistently with the New York court, though there have been exceptions. An Arkansas case found a property interest in participation in extracurricular activities,[32] and the New Hampshire Supreme Court found a similar right under its state constitution.[33]

Since the overwhelming majority of cases addressing a federal constitutional right to extracurricular activities for home schoolers denied such a right, efforts have been directed at state legislation to enact laws specifically permitting participation. Such laws have been enacted in Iowa, Oregon, and Washington. Efforts are being made in other states to enact similar laws, but school districts and interscholastic athletic associations tend to oppose such laws, claiming that they would place undue hardship upon the administration of public schools.

It is claimed that most parents who home school their children would like to enroll them in public schools for extracurricular activities or for part time, in academic courses as well. Most school administrators object to this on grounds of administrative difficulties.[34]

In sum, whether a particular home teaching arrangement satisfies the law depends on the constitution and statutes of the particular state as well as the courts' interpretation of those state laws. It also tends to turn on whether the parent is qualified to teach, whether systematic instruction is given, how well the children are progressing in comparison with their age mates in public schools, and the adequacy of a reporting system supervised by a responsible school official.

Do Home Schooled Students Have a Right to Part-Time Enrollment in Public Schools?

They do not if there is a school board policy requiring full-time attendance, ruled the Eighth Circuit court in an Oklahoma case.[35] Because the State of Oklahoma reimbursed school districts only for students enrolled full time, one district school board created a policy denying the right to part-time attendance for home schooled students. The parents of Annie Swanson challenged this policy as a violation of her constitutional right to a free public education and her right to free exercise of religion.

The court acknowledged the parents' right to control the education and upbringing of their child but also recognized that this right is not absolute. They have no right to use the public schools at their pleasure and combine it with home schooling as they saw fit. The court also found no merit in the claim that their religious views required the use of the public school on a part-time basis. In sum, the school district violated no parental rights by requiring full-time enrollment.

The laws of the states vary on this issue and must be examined along with the policy of the district where the issue arises.

Is a Decision to Home School a Child Grounds for a Change in Custody?

No, ruled to Supreme Court of Oklahoma in 1997.[36] Lynn Martin was awarded custody of her two young sons in a 1989 divorce. In 1994, she gave up a well-paying job to educate her boys at home. Her ex-husband went to court to seek a change in custody, claiming that home schooling was against the best interest of the children, particularly since their mother had only a high school education.

The Oklahoma Supreme Court concluded that home schooling had no adverse effect on the children even though their mother had no formal schooling beyond high school. Education, held the court, is but one of many factors to consider in determining what is in the best interest of children. Furthermore, courts and judges should "not interfere with fundamental parental rights and interests in directing education and the religious upbringing of their children." It is up to the state legislature, explained the court, to enact laws related to the education of children. In Oklahoma, the legislature did not enact minimum standards for teaching and curriculum when it enacted the statutory right to home schooling. Oklahoma's home schooling statutes are unique among the 50 states in having no statutory minimal standards for home schooling.

Can States Supervise Home Schooling through Home Visits?

In a 1998 case, the highest court of Massachusetts held that the requirement of home visits violated state law where parents were willing to submit their curricular and teaching plans for review by school officials. The court noted that, while the school committee had authority to assess the progress of home schooled students, it could not "apply institutional standards to non-institutionalized settings."[37]

A similar case was filed by a Maryland mother and her daughter in federal court, claiming that the state statutory requirement for supervision violated their freedom of religion.[38] The state laws and regulations required, among other things, instruction in a list of specific subjects, a portfolio of instructional materials and examples of the student's work, and a signed consent form to observe the teaching and review the portfolio at a mutually agreeable time and place not more than three times a year. Consistent with earlier cases in other states, the district court upheld the Maryland statute as a reasonable exercise of state authority in the supervision of an important state interest, without placing any undue burden on plaintiff's exercise of her religion.

Although many cases and controversies arise related to home schooling, not all home schooling arrangements are controversial. For example, at least one school district in Virginia hired a Family Training Specialist to provide training for parents who home schooled their children.[39]

Objections to the Curriculum[40]

Can Parents Object to Certain Courses or Materials?

The answer depends on the grounds of the parental objection, the nature of the course or material to which the parent is objecting, and relevant state and constitutional laws. All parental objections to curriculum and instruction are based on two conflicting propositions. The first asserts that parents have the right to guide the upbringing of their children. The second proclaims that states and boards of education have the power to make and enforce reasonable regulations for the efficient and effective conduct of schools.

Every state has laws prescribing portions of the curriculum, and it is clear that legislatures can require children to study subjects that are "essential to good citizenship." Although what this phrase covers is often controversial, there have not been many cases challenging it. The most common objections to curriculum and instruction have had a religious basis. Perhaps the best-known issue is parental objection, on religious grounds, to the inclusion of theories of natural evolution in the school curriculum. When the Arkansas legislature forbade the teaching of evolution in the public schools of that state, the U.S. Supreme Court declared the state law unconstitutional as a violation of the establishment clause of the First Amendment.[41]

In recent years, several states have enacted laws requiring "equal time" for the teaching of creationism along with theories of evolution. Such laws have been struck down as violations of the establishment clause, for they tend to protect or advance particular religious beliefs.[42] (See also chapter 10.)

Can Children Be Exempt from Portions of the Curriculum to Which Their Parents Object on Religious Grounds?

Only if their parents have bona fide religious or moral objections. A California court so ruled in 1921, when parents objected, on religious grounds, to their children's participation in dancing, which was part of the school's physical education program. The court, ruling in favor of the parents, noted that beyond religious objections, parents may also have moral objections "which may concern the conscience of those who are not affiliated with any particular religious sect."[43]

More recently, objections have arisen concerning various sex education classes. For example, some New Jersey parents objected, on grounds of religion, to their children being required to take a course entitled "Human Sexuality." School board surveys indicated widespread citizen support for the program (70 percent approval), but the court indicated that issues such as this are not decided by majority vote.[44] "If majority vote were to govern in matters of religion and conscience, there would be no need for the First Amendment," wrote the judge. That amendment was adopted precisely to protect the small minority "who is sincere in a conscientious religious conviction." The Supreme Court of Hawaii[45] and the U.S. Court of Appeals for the Fourth Circuit[46] also ruled that parents' rights in general, or their religious freedom, are not violated simply by the inclusion in the curriculum of family life or sex education, as long as children of objecting parents may be excused from the instruction.

In 1987, a federal appeals court decided the highly controversial case *Mozert* v. *Hawkins Country Public Schools,* which arose in Tennessee.[47] Parents there objected to the use of the Holt, Rinehart, & Winston reading series, readers that were widely used nationwide. Parents claimed that the readers violated their constitutional rights "to the free exercise of their religion" because they taught values offensive to their religious beliefs. While the district court ruled in favor of the parents, a divided appeals court reversed the decision. The majority held that just because the readers contained some ideas objectionable to the parents on religious grounds, that fact "does not create an unconstitutional burden under the free exercise clause," since the students are not required to affirm or deny any religious beliefs. The books were used to teach reading as well as critical thinking, both legitimate purposes of schooling. Although the several judges who made up the majority could not agree on their exact reasoning, they upheld the school's position over parental objections. Crucial to the majority was a perception that accommodation to every parents' religious claim "will leave public education in shreds." Thus schools may select materials useful to achieve important educational goals even if some parents consider some of the materials objectionable on religious grounds. Courts will consider the importance of the educational goals and the nature of the materials used as well as the grounds of the objections. As long as students are not required to affirm or deny religious beliefs, courts are likely to protect schools' discretion in the use of curricular materials.

An interesting case arose in New York, where some parents objected on religious grounds to their children's receiving instruction regarding AIDS and alcohol and drug abuse. They claimed that according to their religion, such education was "evil." The trial court acknowledged that there may be some merit to the claims that a compulsory health curriculum that includes instruction about AIDS as well as substance abuse may impose a burden on some religious beliefs. However, such interests may be outweighed where a state has a compelling interest to achieve an overriding governmental purpose. The controversial health education curriculum in this case met such a test in the eyes of the court. However, the state's court of appeals reversed this decision and remanded the case to the trial court for a more complete determination of the facts and the application of the law to those facts.[48]

Can Parents Have Their Children Excused from Parts of the Curriculum for Reasons Other Than Religious or Moral Objections?

Yes, as long as the studies to be missed are not "essential for citizenship." A historic case on this issue arose in Nebraska in 1891.[49] It involved a father's objection to his daughter's studying rhetoric and his desire that she study grammar instead. After his wish was granted, he changed his mind and demanded that she not study grammar. When the school board expelled her, the Supreme Court of Nebraska ordered a reinstatement without the requirement that she study grammar. The court protected the parents' preference because the study of neither grammar nor rhetoric was considered to be essential for citizenship.

Similarly, in more recent years, the deputy attorney general of California supported the "good citizenship" standard under which "elementary mathematics could be required, although calculus could not; handwriting could be required, creative writing could not."[50] He further wrote that "when the state chooses to override a parent's wish, the burden is on the state to establish that in order to function effectively as a citizen, one must be versed in the subject to which the parents object." Thus parents could withdraw their children from a music class and have them take private music lessons instead. Local schools could not object to such parental decisions unless the state law required instruction in the particular subject.

Can Schools Require Certain Courses as Prerequisites for Graduation?

Yes, as long as their requirements are reasonable. Students who meet such requirements are entitled to their diplomas even if they violate a school rule, such as the requirement that they wear a cap and gown and attend graduation ceremonies. At least one court ruled that such a student has a right to the diploma but the school may exclude the student from participating in the graduating exercises.[51]

When a Home Schooled Student Enrolls in a Public School, Who Decides What Is the Appropriate Grade Placement?

There are no reported cases to help us answer this question. It is our opinion that courts would respect the judgment of educators in placing the student as long as they used reasonable methods to reach their decision. School board policy should guide the administrator, and board policy is likely to take into consideration such factors as the existence of an approved home schooling curriculum, the qualification of the home teacher, hours spent teaching, and supervision by school personnel. Standardized tests could also be used to help determine placement.

If the home schooled student received grades from the parent or other teacher, the public school does not have to accept those grades in calculating grade point averages for purposes of determining honors or class standing. There is a difference in accepting the work to satisfy credit requirements and accepting the grades assigned since, in assigning grades, teachers might make comparative judgments and use criterion- or norm-referenced grading according to their professional judgment or school policy. Courts are most likely to defer to the professional judgments of educators in this matter.

Can Parents Require a Local School System to Offer Certain Courses of Instruction, Use Particular Books or Materials, or Exclude Books or Materials?

No. Local school boards must offer courses of study required by state law, and they may not violate state and federal constitutional provisions. Within the boundaries of such laws, however, school boards have discretion to determine what courses will be taught, what books and materials will be used, the selection of personnel, and even the methods of instruction employed. Although the states have basic authority over the provision of public education, significant authority and responsibility have been delegated in almost all states to local school districts. Courts are reluctant to interfere with the discretion of local boards in the operation of public schools and will do so only in clear cases of arbitrary and unreasonable exercise of authority or violation of constitutional rights. In a celebrated case in West Virginia, for example, courts upheld the discretion of a local board in its choice of books, since parents could not show that such books were "subversive" or "maliciously written."[52]

Must Homeless Children Attend School?

Yes, they must under the state laws controlling compulsory school attendance. Furthermore, a federal law states that: "It is the policy of the Congress that (1) each state educational agency shall ensure that each child of a homeless individual and each homeless youth has equal access to the same free, appropriate public education, including public preschool education, as provided to other children and youth;..."[53] The law makes funds available to each state to create an office for the implementation and supervision of this policy. Funds are made available to school districts to implement the policy and to gather data on the education of homeless children, which data is to be reported every two years to a state co-ordinator, who in turn reports to the secretary of health and welfare. This law was first enacted in 1987 and has been amended several times.

Summary

Although the U.S. Constitution and federal laws neither mandate nor provide public schools, each of the fifty states makes publicly supported schools available for all children. State laws provide such schools, although the age of compulsory attendance varies from state to state.

State compulsory education laws generally have been upheld by the courts because important social interests are served by a well-educated citizenry. The state requirement that children attend school can be satisfied by attendance at public or private schools, and if private, at religious or secular schools. In general, states have the authority to supervise the quality of schooling in both public and private institutions, but they vary in the provision and rigor of such supervision.

In recent years, new developments expanded the range of choices parents have for the education of their children. The best known among these are charter schools and educational vouchers. Both of these arrangements are controlled by state law as well as school district policy, but they must not enhance racial segregation and must satisfy constitutional principles on church–state relationships.

State laws requiring children to attend school usually provide for alternative ways of meeting such requirements if the alternatives are "equivalent" to public schools. Home schooling has been ruled to satisfy such "equivalencies" as long as the parents or tutors are qualified, the time spent on instruction is comparable to time spent in schools, and the subjects taught cover the "common branches of knowledge" taught in public schools. In one case, involving a traditional Amish religious group, the courts exempted children from attendance beyond the eighth grade when evidence indicated that such attendance would be destructive to their religious beliefs and way of life. This kind of exemption would be very difficult for other groups to achieve.

Most courts have ruled that home schooled children have no constitutional right to participate in extracurricular activities. Currently, parents in some states are attempting to secure such rights through legislation.

Where state laws prescribe part of the curriculum, local school systems must follow such prescriptions. Beyond that, local boards have wide discretion over curriculum and instruction as well as book and material selection, personnel, and other aspects of schooling. Parents may exempt their children from parts of the curriculum that clearly conflict with their religious or moral values. They may also exempt their children from elective studies in order to substitute other, out-of-school experiences. Courses of study considered "essential for citizenship" may not be avoided by children, even if their parents object to them. Finally, local school officials may specify requirements for graduation as long as such requirements are reasonable and not arbitrary. Thus courts and the law attempt to maintain an appropriate balance between the needs of society and the rights of parents to guide the upbringing of their children.

NOTES

1. *Concerned Citizens for Neighborhood Schools, Inc.* v. *Board of Education of Chattanooga*, 379 F.Supp. 1233 (E.D. Tenn. 1974).

2. *Pierce* v. *Society of Sisters*, 268 U.S. 510 (1925).

3. D. P. Gardner, et al., *A Nation at Risk: The Imperative for Educational Reform. An Open Letter to the American People. A Report to the Nation and the Secretary of Education* (1983).

4. 20 *U.S.C.S.* § 5888; 20 *U.S.C.S.* § 8061–8067.

5. P. C. Green, *Preventing School Desegregation Decrees from Becoming Barriers to Charter School Innovation*, 144 *Ed.Law.Rep.* 15 (July 6, 2000).

6. *Wisconsin* v. *Yoder*, 406 U.S. 205 (1972).

7. *Id.*

8. R. D. Madsley, *Home Schools and the Law,* 127 *Ed. Law Rep.* 1 (2000).

9. *People* v. *Levisen,* 90 N.E.2d 213 (Ill. 1950).

10. *In re Shinn,* 16 Cal. Rptr. 165 (Cal. Ct. App. 1961).

11. *State* v. *McDonough,* 468 A.2d 977 (Me. 1983).

12. *In re Sawyer,* 672 P.2d 1093 (Kan. 1983).

13. *Roemhild* v. *State,* 308 S.E.2d 154 (Ga. 1983).

14. See *State* v. *Edgington,* 663 P.2d 374 (App. N.M. 1983).

15. *Murphy* v. *Arkansas,* 852 F.2d 1039 (8th Cir. 1988).

16. *Ellis* v. *O'Hara,* 612 F.Supp. 379 (D.C. Mo. 1985).

17. Mo. Ann. Stat. § 167. 031–167.071 (Vernon 1988).

18. *State* v. *Schmidt,* 505 N.E.2d 627 (Ohio 1987).

19. See L. M. Lukasik, *The Latest Home Education Challenge: The Relationship between Home Schools and Public Schools,* 74 N.C.L. Rev. 1930, note 110 (1996).

20. *Michigan* v. *DeJonge,* 501 NW.2d 127 (Mich. 1993).

21. *Id.* at 137.

22. *People* v. *Bennett,* 501 N.W.2d 106 (Mich. 1993).

23. *Johnson* v. *Prince William County School Board,* 404 S.E.2d 209 (Va. 1991).

24. For more on this topic, see S. Yastrow, "Home Instruction: A National Study of State Law," unpublished doctoral dissertation, Loyola University, Chicago, 1989.

25. *Knox* v. *O'Brien,* 72 A.2d 389 (N.J. 1950).

26. *State* v. *Massa,* 231 A.2d 252 (N.J. 1967).

27. *New Life Baptist Church Academy* v. *East Longmeadow,* 885 F.2d 940 (1st Cir. 1989).

28. *Perchemlides* v. *Frizzle,* No. 16641 (Mass. Super. November 13, 1978).

29. *Roe* v. *Wade,* 410 U.S. 113 (1973) (Emphasis added).

30. *Care and Protection of Charles,* 504 N.E.2d 592 (Mass. 1987).

31. *Broadstreet* v. *Sobol,* 630 N.Y.S.2d 486 (N.Y. Sup. Ct. 1995).

32. *Boyd* v. *Board of Directors of McGehee School District No. 17,* 612 F.Supp. 86 (D. Ark. 1985).

33. *Duffley* v. *H. H. Interscholastic Athletic Association,* 446 A.2d 462 (N.H. 1982).

34. See Lukasik, *supra* note 19.

35. *Swanson* v. *Guthrie Independent School District. No. 1–1,* 135 F.3d 694 (10th Cir. 1998).

36. *Martin* v. *Stephen,* 973 L.2d 92 (Okla. 1997).

37. *Brunella* v. *Lynn Public Schools,* 702 N.E. 2d 1182 (Mass. 1998).

38. *Battles* v. *Anne Arundel County Board of Education,* 904 F.Supp. 471 (D. Md. 1995).

39. *Thurston* v. *Roanoke City School District,* 26 F.Supp.2d 882 (W.D.Va. 1998).

40. This section is included in this chapter since being exempt from certain courses or materials is somewhat analogous to being exempt from attending school.

41. *Epperson* v. *State of Arkansas,* 393 U.S. 97 (1968).

42. *Edwards* v. *Aquillard,* 482 U.S. 578 (1987).

43. *Hardwick* v. *Board of Trustees,* 205 P. 49 (Cal. 1921).

44. *Valent* v. *New Jersey State Board of Education,* 274 A.2d 832 (N.J. 1971).

45. *Medeiros* v. *Kiyosaki,* 478 P.2d 314 (Hawaii 1970).

46. *Cornwell* v. *State Board of Education,* 428 F.2d 471 (4th Cir. 1970).

47. *Mozert* v. *Hawkins County Board of Education,* 827 F.2d 1058 (6th Cir. 1987).

48. *Ware* v. *Valley Stream High School District,* 551 N.Y.S.2d 167 (N.Y. 1989).

49. *State ex rel. Sheibley* v. *School District No. 1,* 48 N.W. 393 (Neb. 1891).

50. Joel S. Moskowitz, *Parental Rights and Responsibilities,* 50 Wash. L. Rev. 623 (1975).

51. *Valentine* v. *Independent School District,* 183 N.W. 434 (Iowa 1921).

52. *Williams* v. *Board of Education of County of Kanawha,* 388 F.Supp. 93 (S.D. W.Va. 1975).

53. 42 U.S.C. 11431 (1997).

19 When Can Schools Restrict Personal Appearance?

Overview

During the 1950s, teachers and students rarely questioned a school's dress and grooming codes. Had they thought of challenging these codes in court, they would have uniformly lost. Teachers were expected to be adult models of neatness and good taste and to conform to the dress and grooming standards of other professionals in the community. Generally they did. In the late 1960s, however, teachers began to challenge dress and grooming codes, and many school districts abandoned them. As a result, many teachers came to believe that such codes were unconstitutional. But this is far from true. An issue that seemed buried in the 1970s reemerged in the 1990s and the beginning of this century.

Controversy over student dress and grooming was especially intense in the 1960s. Long hair and unconventional clothes were among the hottest students' rights issues of the time, and in many communities they still are. Thus controversial student clothing, hats, and hairstyles continue to be important symbols of intergenerational and cross-cultural conflict.

Grooming controversies did not begin in the 1960s, however. Disputes about hair length have been taking place on this continent at least since 1649, when the magistrates of Portsmouth decried "the wearing of long hair, after the manner of ruffians" and declared their "dislike and detestation against wearing such long hair, as against a thing uncivil and unmanly."[1]

Unlike most constitutional controversies that bombard the courts, judges have been deeply divided over the question of grooming in the public schools. Although they are less divided about dress codes and school uniforms, the law concerning personal appearance still differs among the states. This chapter examines the constitutional and educational reasons underlying these differences and the current state of the law on the subject.

Grooming Standards for Teachers

Can Teachers Be Punished without Due Process for Violating a School's Grooming Code?

No. What constitutes due process in such cases was explained by a federal court in a Massachusetts controversy.[2] David Lucia, a teacher, grew a beard one winter vacation. This conflicted with an unwritten school policy explained to Lucia by the superintendent after the vacation. When Lucia failed to shave his beard following a meeting with the school committee, he was suspended because of "insubordination and improper example set by a teacher." He was not invited to a subsequent meeting at which the committee voted to dismiss him. He therefore took his case to court.

The court ruled that Lucia's freedom to wear a beard could not be taken from him without due process. The court noted several deficiencies in the procedure used to dismiss Lucia: Prior to this case, there was no announced policy against teachers wearing beards, and the committee did not indicate that failure to remove his beard would result in dismissal. After criticizing the committee's lack of due process, the court observed: "The American public school system, which has a basic responsibility for instilling in its students an appreciation of our democratic system, is a peculiarly appropriate place for the use of fundamentally fair procedures."

This case shows that a teacher cannot be lawfully dismissed for wearing a beard or sideburns unless (1) there is a clear school policy outlawing such grooming, (2) teachers are given adequate notice of the policy and the consequences of not adhering to it, and (3) teachers are given the right to request a hearing if specific facts are in dispute.

Have Courts Ruled That Teachers Have a Constitutional Right to Wear Beards and Sideburns?

Yes. In the case of a Pasadena schoolteacher, Paul Finot, a California appeals court explained why.[3] When Finot arrived at school wearing a recently grown beard, his principal asked him to shave it off. After he refused, the board of education transferred him to home teaching because he violated the teacher handbook requirement that teachers conform to acceptable standards of grooming and set an example for the students. (The student handbook prohibited beards and mustaches.) The administrators were concerned that Finot's beard might attract undue attention, interfere with education, and make the prohibition of beards for students more difficult to enforce.

The court was not persuaded. It ruled that Finot's right to wear a beard was guarded by two constitutional provisions. It was one of the liberties protected by the Fourteenth Amendment, and it was a form of symbolic expression protected by the First Amendment. The court noted that some people interpret a beard as a symbol of masculinity, authority, or wisdom; others see it as a symbol of nonconformity or rebellion. In either case, the court felt that such symbols "merit constitutional protection." Thus the state court ruled that beards on teachers "cannot constitutionally be banned from the classroom" unless the school can show that the beard had an adverse effect on the educational process.

Have Courts Ruled That Teachers Do Not Have a Constitutional Right to Wear Beards and Sideburns?

Yes. In the case of an Illinois math teacher, a federal appeals court explained why many judges do not believe teacher grooming is a major constitutional issue.[4] When Max Miller's contract was not renewed because of his beard and sideburns, he alleged that his rights were thereby violated. The judge acknowledged that he personally regarded "dress and hair style as matters of relatively trivial importance on any scale of values in appraising the qualifications of a teacher." He noted that, logically, "a teacher should be able to explain the Pythagorean theorem as well in a T-shirt as in a three-piece suit." But the judge doubted whether grooming choices are protected by the U.S. Constitution. Therefore he concluded that if a school board decided a "teacher's style of dress or plumage" had an adverse educational impact, there was "no doubt that the interest of the teacher is subordinate to the public interest."

In a related case upholding a school's antibeard policy for teachers, the Tennessee Supreme Court wrote:

> The grooming of one person is of concern not only to himself but to all others with whom he comes in contact; we have to look at each other whether we like it or not. It is for this reason that society sets certain limits upon the freedom of individuals to choose his own grooming.[5]

Is There a Trend of Decision in Teacher Grooming Cases?

Yes. Although there are few recent decisions on this issue, the trend of decisions is reflected in a ruling of the Fifth Circuit Court of Appeals.[6] The case involved a Louisiana district that applied its student antibeard rule to teachers. The court upheld the no-beard rule, explaining that grooming "may be regulated" if the regulation is reasonable. "In the high school environment," wrote the court, "a hair-style regulation is a reasonable means in furthering the school board's undeniable interest in teaching hygiene, instilling discipline, asserting authority, and compelling uniformity." On the other hand, a school rule would be unconstitutional if it was irrational and arbitrary.[7] Thus, in a related case, the Seventh Circuit Court struck down a rule prohibiting school bus drivers but not teachers from wearing mustaches.[8] The court concluded that this policy had no reasonable relationship "with a proper school purpose" and was "so irrational as to be arbitrary."

Is Grooming a Constitutional Right If It Reflects a Teacher's Racial or Ethnic Values and Beliefs?

Perhaps. Booker Peek, a black teacher from Florida, wore a goatee to show racial pride. Although Peek was a superior high school French teacher, he was not rehired because he refused repeated requests to remove his goatee. Peek called the action unconstitutional. The judge agreed.[9] According to the court. when a goatee is worn by a black man as an expression of his heritage, culture, and racial pride, its wearer "enjoys the protection of First Amendment rights." Thus it appeared that the decision not to recommend reappointment was racially motivated and tainted with "institutional racism," the effects of which were manifested in "an intolerance of ethnic diversity and racial pride."

Teachers' Clothing

Do Teachers Have a Constitutional Right to Dress As They Wish?

No. Even courts that recognize grooming as constitutionally protected may not rule the same way in matters of dress because judges usually feel that school regulations concerning dress are not as personal and that their impact is not as great. Therefore most teachers who challenge clothing regulations do not argue that they have a right to dress any way they wish; rather, they contend that the dress code is arbitrary, unreasonable, or discriminatory. Edward Blanchet used this argument after he was suspended for violating a Louisiana school board dress policy requiring that male teachers wear neckties.

The state appeals court wrote positively about Blanchet's sincerity, convictions, and character. It described him as "a dedicated and effective teacher, an assistant principal at his school, [and] a sober churchgoing family man." Nevertheless, the court ruled against him.[10] Since the purpose of the board's rule was to enhance the professional image of its teachers in the eyes of students and parents, and since there was some evidence supporting the rule, the court concluded that it could not find the necktie policy arbitrary or unreasonable.

In a related case, a 25-year-old high school French teacher was not rehired because she insisted on wearing short skirts. A federal appeals court observed that the teacher was terminated because her "image" was "overexposed."[11] Although the court had recognized grooming as a constitutional right, it refused to extend constitutional protection to clothing regulations, which the court felt involve less personal matters and affect teachers only during school hours.

Would a Teacher's Refusal to Conform to a School Dress Code Be Protected As a Form of Symbolic Expression?

Probably not. This was the argument used by Richard Brimley, an English teacher from East Hartford, Connecticut. Brimley wanted to present himself to his students as a person not tied to "establishment conformity," so he refused to comply with his school's dress code. That code required a coat and tie for male teachers. Brimley argued that an individual's appearance was protected by the First Amendment as a form of symbolic expression and academic freedom, which should give teachers wide discretion over teaching methods and style of clothing—especially when the teachers are neat and reasonable in their appearance. Moreover, he argued that a tie was no longer typical among other young professionals and that the requirement did not promote discipline, respect, or good grooming among students.

Two judges of a federal appeals court were persuaded by these arguments, but most were not.[12] On behalf of the majority, Judge Meskill wrote that federal courts should not overturn school rules that "appear foolish or unwise" unless they directly involve "basic constitutional values." Therefore, wrote Judge Meskill, "we are unwilling to expand the First Amendment protection to include a teacher's sartorial choice." If we bring "trivial activities" under constitutional protection, "we trivialize the Constitution." Thus teacher clothing is not constitutionally protected unless the clothing expresses a clear message that is understood by an observer.

Students' Grooming

Are Students Free to Wear Their Hair As They Wish?

About half of the U.S circuit courts of appeals answer yes. A typical case arose in Indiana's Wawasee High School, where a committee of students, teachers, and administrators developed a dress code "to insure the best possible overall appearance" of the student body. The code was adopted by a vote of the students, and they and their parents were notified of its provisions. Nevertheless, Greg Carpenter, with his parents' consent, violated the code's "long hair provision" and was punished. As a result, Greg's father sued on Greg's behalf to prohibit enforcement of the code's hair length regulations.[13]

The school board argued that because the code was adopted by a majority of the students, it was not an unreasonable interference with Greg's constitutional rights. But the Seventh Circuit Court of Appeals disagreed.[14] It held that "the right to wear one's hair at any length or in any desired manner is an ingredient of personal freedom protected by the United States Constitution." To limit that right, a school would have to bear a "substantial burden of justification." But the board presented no evidence that Greg's hair disrupted classroom decorum or interfered with other students. The school showed no reasonable relationship between the code and a significant educational purpose. Therefore the court concluded that the democratic process by which the code was adopted did not justify the denial of Greg's constitutional right to wear his hair as he chose. The U.S. Constitution, said the court, cannot be amended by majority vote.

What Other Arguments Support Student Grooming Rights?

Judges have used a variety of legal, educational, and philosophic arguments to uphold grooming as a constitutional right. Here are a few:

A personal liberty protected by the Fourteenth Amendment. In holding unconstitutional a Marlboro, Massachusetts, school policy forbidding "unusually long hair," the First Circuit Court of Appeals noted that the case involved the Fourteenth Amendment's protection of certain "uniquely personal aspects of one's life."[15] The court saw "no inherent reason why decency, decorum, or good conduct" requires a boy to wear his hair short. Nor, it concluded, does "compelled conformity to conventional standards of appearance seem a justifiable part of the educational process."

Symbolic speech protected by the First Amendment. Some courts argue that long hair is a form of symbolic speech by which the wearer conveys his individuality or rejection of conventional values and that it should therefore be protected under the First Amendment. According to one judge:

> A person shorn of the freedom to vary the length and style of his hair is forced against his will to hold himself out symbolically as a person holding ideas contrary, perhaps, to ideas he holds most dear. Forced dress, including forced hair style, humiliates the unwilling complier, forces him to submerge his individuality in the "undistracting" mass, and in general, smacks of the exaltation of organization over member, unit over component, and state over individual.[16]

In a related North Carolina case, a judge wrote that long hair is simply

> a harkening back to the fashion of earlier years. For example, many of the founding fathers, as well as General Grant and General Lee, wore their hair...in a style comparable to that adopted by the [student] plaintiffs. Although there exists no depiction of Jesus Christ, either reputedly or historically accurate, he has always been shown with hair at least the length of that of the plaintiffs.[17]

Thus the judge noted that none of these great men would have been permitted to attend high school if the disputed hair regulations were enforced.

A denial of equal protection. In an Indiana case, a high school principal said his grooming regulations were required for health and safety—that long hair could cause problems in the gym, swimming pool, and laboratories. But the Seventh Circuit Court of Appeals observed that girls engaged in similar activities wore long hair, yet only boys were required to wear short hair.[18] Since the principal offered no reason why health and safety regulations were not equally applicable to girls, the court concluded that the rules constituted "a denial of equal protection to male students" in violation of the Fourteenth Amendment.

A right to govern one's personal appearance. In striking down a St. Charles, Missouri dress code that prohibited long hair, the Eighth Circuit Court of Appeals wrote that each student possesses "a constitutionally protected right to govern his personal appearance while attending public high school," based on the due process clause of the Fourteenth Amendment. In a concurring opinion, one of the judges rejected the arguments given by school officials to defend their grooming regulations in these words:

> The gamut of rationalizations for justifying this restriction fails in light of reasoned analysis. When school authorities complain variously that such hair styles...make boys look like girls, that they promote confusion as to the use of restrooms, and that they destroy the students' moral fiber, then it is little wonder even moderate students complain of "getting uptight." In final analysis, I am satisfied a comprehensive school restriction on male student hair styles accomplishes little more than to project the prejudices and personal distastes of certain adults in authority on to the impressionable young student.[19]

Can Schools Restrict Student Grooming?

In about half the states, they can. A case in El Paso, Texas, illustrates the views of courts that hold that schools have the authority to restrict student hair length. In this case, the Fifth Circuit Court of Appeals considered and rejected the following arguments, which were presented by a high school junior, Chelsey Karr.[20]

Symbolic speech. Although some students wear long hair to convey a message, the court noted that many wear it simply as a matter of personal taste. Karr, for example, sued not because his hair symbolized anything but "because I like my hair long." Judge Morgan felt that it would be inappropriate and unworkable to have the U.S. Constitution protect a student who intends to convey a message by wearing long hair but not other students.

A protected liberty. The court pointed out that individual liberties may be "ranked in a spectrum of importance." At one end are the "great liberties," such as speech and religion specifically guaranteed in the Bill of Rights. At the other end are the "lesser liberties" that may be curtailed if the restrictions are related to a proper state activity. The court concluded that hair regulations are reasonably related to schooling, that they do not restrict any fundamental constitutional liberty, and that their interference is a "temporary and relatively inconsequential one." Judge Morgan observed that administrators "must daily make innumerable decisions which restrict student liberty," including the regulation of student parking, eating, and attendance. Students should not be able to force administrators to defend such restrictions in court when fundamental rights are not involved.

An unnecessary burden. The appeals court was disturbed by "the burden which has been placed on the federal courts by suits of this nature" by the number of days spent on trials and appeals. Judge Morgan noted that it was impossible for the courts to protect every citizen against every minor restriction on his or her liberty. Because of this burden and because these cases do not raise issues of "fundamental" importance, the court ruled that henceforth all such regulations would be presumed valid.

Have Ethnic Hair Styles Received Protection?

They have in one case where Native American students from Texas were suspended for wearing long hair in violation of their school's dress code. The students wore their hair long as an expression of their heritage and tribal religious practice. Although the Fifth Circuit Court of Appeals had ruled that grooming was not a constitutional right, the judge said that this case was different, since the hair regulations infringed on these students' rights. First, wearing long hair is deeply rooted in Native American religious belief; second, it is a "communicative activity" protected by the free speech clause.[21]

The school argued that the grooming restrictions were intended to maintain discipline, foster respect for authority, and project a good public image. Since the court found that there were "less restrictive, alternative means of achieving these goals," it prohibited the school from enforcing its hair restrictions against the Native Americans. According to the court, wearing long hair by these students is a "protected expressive activity" like the wearing of arm-bands in *Tinker*. Earlier, however, another federal court refused to strike down an Oklahoma school's grooming code that was used to punish a Native American for wearing traditional braids because it ruled that hair-length regulations do not "implicate basic constitutional values" and are a responsibility of the states, not the federal courts.[22]

Do the Principles That Apply to the Classroom Also Apply to Sports?

Usually. In an Alabama case, two black high school athletes challenged their coach's "clean-shaven" policy, which barred them from varsity football.[23] They argued that there was no rational connection between athletic performance and shaving and that shaving caused skin problems—especially among blacks. However, the judge upheld the shaving rule on the basis of the court's prior decision that "grooming regulations at the high school level do not deprive the plaintiffs of any constitutionally recognized rights" and that this policy was aimed "not at athletic performance, but at presenting the school in a favorable light." On the other hand, the court suggested that its decision might have been different if there was medical evidence that these specific students suffered skin problems from the shaving policy. Moreover, in states where grooming choice is a constitutional right, courts are likely to be critical of team grooming regulations that are *not* clearly related to athletic performance.

Grooming codes do not apply to non-school-related activities or beyond the school year. Thus an Ohio court ruled that the photograph of a long-haired student could not be banned from a high school yearbook even if the student violated the school's grooming code. The court reasoned that since the yearbook was distributed after graduation, the ban would not affect what occurred in school and therefore had no valid educational purpose.[24]

Why Has the U.S. Supreme Court Not Resolved the Grooming Conflict?

When federal appeals courts differ in their interpretation of the U.S. Constitution, the U.S. Supreme Court usually reviews the issue, renders a decision, and thus establishes a "uniform law of the land." But despite the sharp differences of opinion among federal courts concerning student grooming, the Supreme Court has on at least nine occasions declined to review the decisions on this issue. It did so because most Justices of the Court apparently did not believe the cases raised important constitutional questions of national significance. In rejecting an urgent appeal to the Supreme Court in one grooming case, Justice Black wrote: "The only thing about it that borders on the serious to me is the idea that anyone should think the Federal Constitution imposes on the United States courts the burden of supervising the length of hair that public school students should wear."[25] As long as the Supreme Court refuses to hear these cases, the law will continue to vary throughout the United States.

Can We Predict How the Various Federal Courts Might Rule on Grooming Cases?

Despite the many conflicts over grooming regulations, the law on this subject has become relatively clear, as Figure 19.1 indicates. Most U.S. circuit courts of appeals have ruled on this issue directly, and the others have indicated how they would probably rule.

What Is the Law in My State?

The federal appeals courts have decided that grooming is a constitutional right in the First Circuit (Maine, Massachusetts, New Hampshire, Rhode Island), the Fourth Circuit (Maryland, North Carolina, South Carolina, Virginia, West Virginia), the Seventh Circuit (Illinois, Indiana, Wisconsin), the Eighth Circuit (Arkansas, Iowa, Minnesota, Missouri, Nebraska, North Dakota, South Dakota), and probably the Second Circuit (Connecticut, New York, Vermont). In these states, courts will hold grooming regulations unconstitutional unless school officials present convincing evidence that they are fair, reasonable, and necessary to carry out a legitimate educational purpose.

In 1973, the Second Circuit clearly ruled that hair-length regulations raised "a substantial constitutional issue."[26] Although the U.S. Supreme Court overruled that decision as it applied to police,[27] the Second Circuit would probably reaffirm its decision as applied to students because of the important differences between regulating the appearance of students and of police and the refusal of the Supreme Court to rule on student hair cases.

The law is different in the Fifth Circuit (Louisiana, Mississippi, Texas), the Sixth Circuit (Kentucky, Michigan, Ohio, Tennessee), the Ninth Circuit (Alaska, Arizona, California, Hawaii, Idaho, Montana, Nevada, Oregon, Washington), the Tenth Circuit (Colorado, Kansas, New Mexico, Oklahoma, Utah, Wyoming), and the Eleventh Circuit (Alabama, Florida, Georgia). In these states, the circuit courts have decided that grooming is not a significant constitutional issue and that federal courts should not judge the wisdom of codes regulating hair length or style.

Although the Third Circuit (Delaware, New Jersey, Pennsylvania) held that civilian employees of the National Guard could challenge the Guard's hair-length regulations,[28] this court clearly ruled in 1975 that "the federal courts should not intrude" in the area of school regulation of student hair length and that it would no longer consider school grooming cases.[29]

The Washington, D.C. Court of Appeals has not ruled directly on the issue of school grooming regulations, but in a related case it indicated that it agreed with the U.S. Supreme Court and "sees no federal question in this area."[30]

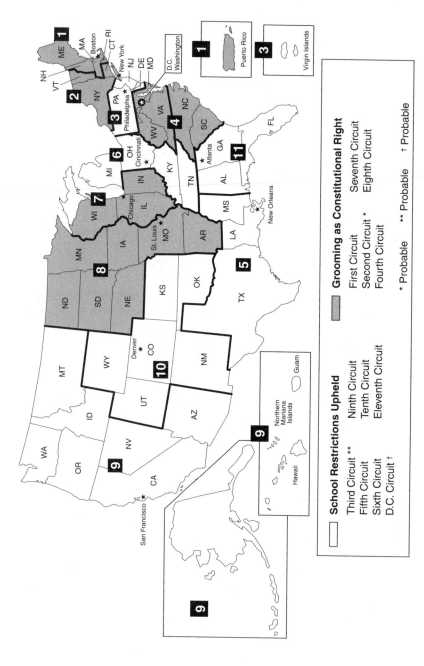

FIGURE 19.1 Circuit court rulings on grooming.

Source: 28 USCA, Section 41.

Can Grooming Rules Be Challenged Under State Law?

Yes. Although about half of the federal circuits have held that the U.S. Constitution does not protect student grooming, individuals who live in those circuits can still challenge grooming policies under their state's Equal Rights Amendment (ERA) or antidiscrimination statutes. However, there are sharp differences among state judges about these issues, and their conflicting perspectives are summarized in the recent cases discussed below.

Do Grooming Rules That Only Apply to Boys Violate State Equal Rights Amendments?

The differing answers to this question are illustrated in the case of Austin Barber, a high school senior, who challenged his district's dress code that prohibited boys from wearing hair below the collar or earrings. Barber argued that the code discriminated on the basis of gender in violation of the state's ERA. In 1995, a divided Texas Supreme Court ruled against Barber because it refused to use the state constitution "to micro-manage Texas high schools."[31] Without analyzing the evidence, the majority simply stated that "the state judiciary is less competent to deal with students' hair length" than the schools. The court concluded that Barber's claims are not "such an affront to his constitutional rights as to merit our intervention."

In contrast, one dissenting justice wrote that the school's grooming code clearly discriminates against male students. He concluded that our fundamental law should not permit such "baseless and irrational discrimination;" and our schools "should not teach it, condone it or engage in it, and our courts...should not—even passively and benignly— enforce it." Another dissenting justice wrote that the only lesson taught by this dress code "is that local school officials are free to make arbitrary distinctions based solely on gender." She concluded: "We can only hope that the school boards of Texas will show greater respect for individuals' rights under the ERA than this court has shown today."

Do State Antidiscrimination Laws Invalidate Grooming Rules That Apply to Boys and Not Girls?

Judicial disagreement about this issue is illustrated by the case of Zachariah Toungate, an eight-year-old student who was transferred to in-school suspension and isolated from all other students for four months for wearing a ponytail that extended below his collar.[32] Zachariah offered to pin his ponytail above his collar or tuck it inside his shirt. But the principal refused to deviate from the dress code and Zachariah's mother sued, arguing that the code violated the state's antidiscrimination law since it didn't apply to girls.

A state appeals court rejected the school's four justifications for its policy:

1. *It prevents gang activity.* In response, the court noted there was no evidence of any connection between hair style and gang activity in the district and no gang activity existed in Zachariah's school.
2. *The rule instills a sense of gender identity.* Witnesses testified that "boys should look like boys." This justification, wrote the judge, "is a perfect description of improper gender discrimination."
3. *The rule socializes students to community norms.* The court found this goal to be "counterproductive because it simply teaches a mindless conformity" in conflict with the community's tradition of tolerance and diversity.

4. *The rule is needed to maintain discipline and prevent disruption.* While the court agreed with the need for discipline, no witness explained why the grooming code was needed to achieve this goal, and there was no evidence that the many schools that have no hair-length rules have greater discipline problems.

However, a divided Texas Supreme Court overruled the appeals court. In a 1997 decision, it held that the state law that prohibits discrimination "because of sex" does not prohibit "grooming or dress codes that differentiate between males and females."[33] According to the court, grooming rules are not like illegal gender discrimination because they do not "elevate females over males any more than a requirement that females wear their skirts at a specified length elevates males over females." Furthermore, wrote the court, such restrictions "impose no barriers that operate to favor one sex over the other."

In her dissenting opinion, Judge Rose Specter criticized the superintendent for taking the position that "rules are rules, whether arbitrary or not and students must follow them." She concluded that such a rule "teaches intolerance" and is in conflict with the school's "asserted goal" of teaching an appreciation for human differences.

School Dress Codes

Can Schools Regulate Student Clothing?

Yes. All courts recognize that schools have authority to regulate student clothing; but not all dress codes are constitutional.[34] In New Hampshire, for example, a federal court held that a rule prohibiting the wearing of blue jeans or dungarees was unconstitutional.[35] The court rejected the argument that wearing jeans "detracts from discipline and a proper educational climate" because the school presented no evidence supporting this position. However, the judge wrote that a school "can and must...exclude persons who are unsanitary, obscenely or scantily clad." Good hygiene may require that dirty clothing be prohibited. And a school may prohibit scantily clad students "because it is obvious that the lack of proper covering, particularly with female students, might tend to distract other students" and disrupt the educational process. Furthermore, a North Carolina court held that a student was properly excluded from his graduation ceremony for violating a rule requiring men to wear "dress pants, as opposed to jeans" under their graduation gowns.[36]

Can Girls Be Prohibited from Wearing Slacks?

Not according to a New York court which ruled that school boards have the authority to regulate dress only for reasons of safety, order, and discipline.[37] Since the no-slacks rule "applies only to female students" and applies to every kind of slacks, "it [is] evident that what is being enforced is style or taste and not safety, order, or discipline." Similarly, an Idaho court ruled that an absolute prohibition against female students wearing "slacks, pant-suits, and culottes" was "unreasonable, capricious, and arbitrary" and had "no reasonable relationship" to the educational process.[38] However, a Kentucky appeals court refused to strike down a prohibition against girls wearing jeans because the judge felt that school dress code conflicts were not matters of constitutional importance.[39]

What Kinds of Clothing Regulations Would Probably Be Upheld by the Courts?

In the New York "slacks" case, Judge Meyer gave several examples. In the interest of safety, a school board can probably prohibit "the wearing of bell-bottomed slacks by students...who ride bikes to school." In the interest of discipline, a regulation against slacks that are "so skintight and, therefore, revealing as to provoke or distract students of the opposite sex" might be valid. And in the interest of order, a rule against slacks "to the bottom of which small bells have been attached" would be upheld. According to the judge, such regulations would be valid because they clearly relate to the school's "authorized concerns"; a flat prohibition against all slacks is invalid "precisely because it does not."[40]

In recent years, conflicts have arisen over comprehensive dress codes. Such a dispute arose in 1999 over Atherton High School's detailed code that limited what students could wear (e.g., no denim, hoods, spandex, logos, capri pants, or T-shirts) and how they could wear it (e.g., no bagging, sagging, or untucked shirts). And it required certain styles and colors of clothing. Several students who wanted to wear clothes of their choice claimed the code violated their First Amendment rights. A federal court acknowledged that the dress code "does reach expressive conduct." However, in its 2000 decision, the court wrote that schools can restrict such conduct if the regulation furthers an "important government interest" such as preventing conflict and the purpose of the code was not to suppress student speech.[41] "The court's role," concluded the judge, "should be to determine whether a reasonable basis existed for school officials' judgment, not to second guess or micromanage it."

Is Wearing Ethnic Clothing a Protected Form of Expression?

According to a federal court, wearing some ethnic clothing might be protected as nonverbal conduct if it meets a two-part test: (1) if there is an intention "to convey a particularized message" and (2) if there is "a great likelihood that the message would be understood" by observers.[42] This test was used in the case of Richard Bivens, a ninth-grade student at the Albuquerque, New Mexico Del Norte High School, who was suspended for violating the school's dress code against wearing "sagging pants." The school explained that sagging pants are associated with street gangs and "wannabes" who seek gang affiliation. However, Richard was neither a gang member nor an aspiring member. Moreover, he argued that the prohibition was an unconstitutional restriction on his freedom of expression because he wore sagging pants in the "hip-hop" style, "as a statement of his identity as a black youth" and "to express his links with black culture." But, the judge ruled against Richard. Although he met the court's first test by showing that wearing sagging pants was intended "to express his link with his black identity," he did not meet the second test because he failed to show that wearing the pants conveyed "an objectively recognizable message" that an observer would understand.

Does a "No Hats" Policy Violate Students' Free Speech Rights?

Not usually. In a Maryland secondary school, Shermia Isaacs was not allowed in school because she wore a headwrap in violation of the school's no hats policy. Since Shermia wore the headwrap to celebrate her cultural heritage, she argued that her nondisruptive head cover should be protected as a form of expression just as the Supreme Court protected students who wore armbands to protest against the Vietnam War. But a federal court disagreed.

Judge Motz explained that the Supreme Court's *Tinker* decision protected students' political speech ("which lies at the heart of the First Amendment") but specifically excluded clothing.[43] Furthermore, the judge noted with approval some of the school's reasons for banning hats which can: (1) increase horseplay and conflict in halls, (2) block teachers' views of students and the view of students behind the hat wearer, (3) allow students to hide drugs, cheat sheets, and other contraband, and (4) foster a less respectful learning climate.

Shermia argued that the rule was discriminatory since it permitted religious headcovering. But the judge wrote that courts give increased protection "for conduct implicating more than one Constitutional right" and this allowed schools "to protect religious speech more strictly than non-religious speech." Although Shermia's headwrap caused no disruption, the judge concluded that it would be "entirely unrealistic to ask school administrators…to decide on a hat-by-hat basis whether a particular hat poses sufficient danger of disruption." Thus, except for nondisruptive religious headcovering, courts are likely to uphold no hats rules.

Will Courts Rule the Same Way in Clothing Cases as in Hair Controversies?

Sometimes. Courts that do not protect a student's choice of hairstyle will probably not protect a student's choice of clothing unless it contains a message. But courts that *do* protect hairstyle may or may not protect student freedom in matters of dress. This is so because some judges believe that hair restrictions are more serious invasions of individual freedom since: (1) hairstyle is more fundamental to personal appearance, (2) hair restrictions have a long-term effect, and (3) hairstyles today usually do not involve issues of morality and distraction, as do some clothing styles. And even courts that protect both clothing and grooming give schools wider discretion to regulate clothing in the interests of health, safety, order, or discipline.

New Controversies: School Uniforms, Gang Clothing, and Message T-Shirts

During the 1990s, new conflicts about student dress codes emerged. In some large cities, such as Baltimore, Detroit, and Los Angeles, students, teachers, and parents developed stricter dress policies to decrease crime on campus and to minimize locker break-ins. Detroit's Mumford High School, for example, prohibited fancy clothing, including fur coats, gold jewelry, and certain name-brand trinkets. According to one observer, the goal of these policies is "to ban clothing that made kids look like wealthy drug merchants."[44] An article in *Newsweek* reported that stricter student dress codes "have spread from Texas to Alabama, Georgia and North Carolina."[45] Some of these codes cover everything from the length of pants and skirts and the wearing of undergarments to the prohibition of clothing associated with gang membership and the banning of T-shirts with vulgar words or symbols. A Los Angeles high school banned "baggy pants" to prevent students from smuggling weapons into school under their clothing.[46] As one attorney noted, "The pendulum is

swinging to conformity."[47] Also in the late 1990s, a number of states enacted laws to encourage local districts to require school uniforms. An indication of how courts are likely to respond to these new regulations may be found in the following recent cases.

Can Schools Require School Uniforms?

Generally, they can. During the 1999–2000 school year, a Louisiana school board required uniforms for all students. As a result, several parents claimed the requirement violated their children's First Amendment rights. The Fifth Circuit Court of Appeals (which had upheld any "reasonable" hair regulations) ruled that clothing restrictions should require higher justification than grooming regulations since some clothing functions as pure speech, as when a student's shirt has a message "supporting political candidates or important social issues," or where clothing symbolizes "ethnic heritage [or] religious beliefs," and where "the message is likely to be understood by those who view it."[48] Because choice of clothing is "personal expression that happens to occur on school premises," the level of scrutiny of dress codes should be higher than the reasonableness test. But, since a uniform policy is viewpoint neutral and is not intended to restrict a particular political opinion, the school need not demonstrate that the uniforms are required to prevent substantial disruption. Therefore, the Fifth Circuit applied an intermediate standard of review.

In this 2001 opinion, the court ruled that a uniform policy will be constitutional if it meets three requirements: It furthers a "substantial government interest" (in this case decreasing discipline problems); "the interest is unrelated to the suppression of student expression"; and "the incidental restrictions on First Amendment activities are no more than is necessary to facilitate that interest." Since the school board's uniform policy met these three requirements, the policy did not violate First Amendment Rights. (For more on student expression, see chapter 9.)

The parents also argued that requiring uniforms creates a financial burden that denies some students the right to a free education. The court also rejected this argument, since the cost of the uniform was no more "than the normal cost of a student's clothes" and uniforms are donated "to the less fortunate."

In a related Texas case, another federal court recently held that a school's uniform policy did not violate students' freedom of expression. According to this 2000 decision, even if the students intended to convey a message of individuality by not wearing the uniforms, it is unlikely that reasonable persons would have understood their message. "To an onlooker," wrote the judge, "a student wearing [prohibited] blue jeans and a T-shirt may be perceived as conveying 'I'm confident' or 'my other clothes are dirty' or any other conceivable message other than 'I'm an individual.'"[49] Thus, the wearing of prohibited clothing does not contain the essential elements of communication to be protected by the First Amendment. Therefore, the only question for the court is not whether uniforms are the best policy but only whether they are intended to accomplish a permissible objective. Since the policy was reasonably intended "to improve the learning climate," the court ruled that the goal was legitimate and the means were reasonable.

Similarly, an Arizona court ruled against two students who refused to comply with their school's uniform policy. One student wore a T-shirt with a U.S. flag and words stating "I support my country." The second wore a shirt with a picture of Jesus and a Bible, stating

"The School of Higher Learning." The school said it adopted the policy to increase security, foster school unity, eliminate label competition, ensure modest dress, and minimize costs. Based on this rationale, a state appeals court found the policy was constitutional since it was "reasonably related to legitimate pedagogical concerns."[50]

Can Schools Prohibit the Wearing of Earrings, Jewelry, or Other Symbols of Gang Membership?

Yes. Because Illinois students at Bremen High School were intimidated by gang members, the school banned all gang activities at school and the wearing of gang symbols including earrings, jewelry, and other emblems. But senior Darryl Olesen wore an earring to school because it "expressed his individuality" and was "attractive to young women."[51] As a result, he was suspended, and he challenged the earring ban as a violation of his freedom of expression and his right to equal protection (since the ban applied only to men). A federal court supported the school policy. Olesen's earring was not a protected form of expression, the judge wrote, because it did not "convey a particularized message" that "would be understood by those who viewed it." Unlike unconstitutional rules against long hair, there was a clear reason for this rule "directly related to the safety and well-being" of the students. Furthermore, the "gender-based classification" was not unconstitutional because it related to a legitimate government objective (curtailment of gang activity), and it was men, not women, who wore earrings to indicate gang membership.

Can Prohibitions of Gang Symbols Be Void for Vagueness?

Yes. In Iowa, West High School's rules stated that "Gang-related activities such as display of 'colors' [or] symbols...will not be tolerated." Pursuant to this rule, Brianna Stephenson was suspended after a counselor noticed a small cross tattooed between her thumb and index finger, which she had worn for 30 months as a form of self-expression. School officials considered the tattoo a gang symbol even though other students did not and Brianna was not involved with gangs. To avoid expulsion, she went through painful surgery to remove the tattoo. She then went to court, arguing that the gang rule should be held void for vagueness, and a federal appeals court agreed.

The court explained that a rule is void for vagueness when it forbids an act in terms so vague that "persons of common intelligence must necessarily guess at its meaning and differ as to its application," or when the rule allows for arbitrary or subjective enforcement. In this case, the school rule violates the vagueness doctrine because it does not define "gang activities," it "fails to provide adequate notice" about what conduct is prohibited, and "fails to offer clear guidance for those who apply it."[52]

A related Texas case involved two high school students who were prohibited from wearing rosaries as necklaces because school police believed the rosaries were gang-related apparel. The students were not members of a gang and wore the rosaries as religious symbols. Here, too, a federal judge ruled that the school's ban on gang apparel was void for vagueness. The school handbook defined gang-related apparel as "any attire" which is "gang related." Administrators argued that this "flexible" definition was necessary to provide them with the discretion they needed "to maintain order." However, the judge wrote that the school's ban on gang clothing is ambiguous, "reveals little about what conduct is prohibited," and provides "excessive discretion" to officials to define and decide what is prohibited.[53]

The court also held that the rosary is a religious symbol that cannot be prohibited unless schools have evidence that it causes substantial disruption. Although there was a prior incident of rosaries worn as "an alleged gang identifier," the judge wrote that this was insufficient evidence of actual or anticipated disruption to justify restricting these students' religious expression.

Are Male Earring Prohibitions Constitutional If Wearing the Earrings Is Not Associated with Gangs?

They might be. The conflicting judicial views on this question were included in a 1995 Indiana decision concerning Jimmy Hines, a fourth-grade student, who wore an earring to school in violation of a rule against wearing "jewelry or other attachments not consistent with community standards."[54] After being suspended for violating the rule, Jimmy's parents sued, arguing that the earring prohibition violated the U.S. Constitution because it was unreasonable and discriminatory.

The school presented several reasons for its rule, and the court rejected two of them. It found "no evidence…of a correlation between earrings and cults or homosexuality." In addition, the court rejected the school's safety concerns, since female students who are allowed to wear earrings avoid injury by removing them before gym. However, a majority of the judges felt that the following justifications for the strict policy were reasonable: (1) "It creates discipline [and] discourages rebellion against local community standards of dress," and (2) it creates a "positive educational environment." The majority also rejected Jimmy's sex discrimination argument because "the dress code prohibits all students from wearing jewelry inconsistent with community standards, without respect to gender."

In a detailed dissenting opinion, Judge Barteau emphasized that there is a "complete absence of evidence demonstrating a relationship between the ban on earrings" and the school's justifications or its educational objectives. The school in this case, wrote the judge, "seeks academic improvement by repressing students' constitutional rights, rather than attempting to achieve its objective through other activities that bear a positive correlation to student performance."

In a related Louisiana case, Brandon Cooper's mother allowed him to get his ear pierced because he improved his conduct. When Brandon was suspended from the third grade because school rules prohibited boys from wearing earrings, his mother sued, claiming that the gender-based rules violated the Equal Protection Clause. The principal explained that the reasons for the rule were to avoid disruption, foster "respect for authority and discipline," and to conform to community standards. A state appeals court agreed. Since it is not common for boys in Louisiana elementary classrooms to wear earrings, the court decided (apparently without evidence) that "the presence of one will surely cause a distraction."[55] Therefore, the court concluded that the gender-based rule was justified since it "furthers an important governmental objective"—it prohibits distraction through a dress code that reflects "the values of the community."

Can Students Be Prohibited from Wearing T-Shirts with Controversial Messages?

It depends on the message. In Idaho, Rod Gano, a senior at Twin Falls High School, was sent home for wearing a T-shirt with caricatures of three school administrators drinking alcoholic beverages and acting drunk. Rod argued that the school abridged his freedom of speech by disciplining him for wearing the T-shirt. But a federal court disagreed.[56] First, wrote the judge, Rod could not articulate any particular criticism or idea he was trying to convey by wearing the T-shirt. Therefore banning the shirt would not suppress any specific message. Second, the judge wrote that the T-shirt "falsely accuses the three administrators of committing a misdemeanor"—consuming alcohol on school property. Since the U.S. Supreme Court has upheld the authority of schools to discipline students for "lewd, inde-cent or offensive speech and conduct,"[57] that precedent applies to this case. Therefore Twin Falls administrators were acting within their authority when they disciplined Rod for wearing his "clearly offensive" T-shirt that falsely depicted the administrators in an alco-holic stupor.

Courts also have ruled that schools can ban T-shirts with sexual connotations even if they include a serious message. In one federal decision, a Virginia middle school student was suspended for wearing a shirt with the words "Drugs Suck!" The student said she wore the shirt to convey the message that "it is not right to use drugs." But the principal said the word "suck" had sexual connotations and could be disruptive. After hearing conflicting testimony about the meaning of the message, the court ruled that educators can protect young students from vulgar and offensive language on a T-shirt even if the shirt's message is laudable.[58]

Similarly, in a 1994 Massachusetts case, a federal judge upheld a policy prohibiting clothing that is "obscene, profane, vulgar, or lewd."[59] Under this policy, two students, Jef-frey and Jonathan Pyle, were prohibited from wearing T-shirts that said, "Co-ed Naked Band: Do It To The Rhythm" and "See Dick Drink. See Dick Drive. See Dick Die. Don't be a Dick." Administrators prohibited the first shirt because of its suggestive sexual slo-gan; the second, because of its "slang reference to male genitalia." Jeffrey wore the first shirt because his parents gave it to him since he played in the school band; Jonathan said the second shirt carried an important message. The court, however, ruled that schools can prohibit clothing with "vulgar" speech and "sexual innuendo" even if the message does not cause disruption. On the other hand, administrators permitted the brothers to wear a shirt depicting a marijuana leaf and the words "Legalize it" and another with "Co-ed Naked Gerbils: Some People Will Censor Anything" because the shirts contained political mes-sages and did not cause disruption.

The court struck down part of the school's dress code that broadly banned all cloth-ing that "harasses, threatens, intimidates, or demeans" certain groups. The judge applied the principles of *Tinker*[60] to this case and concluded that the First Amendment "does not permit official repression…of even odious ideas" and even when these ideas "may result in hurt feelings or a sense of being harassed." (For more discussion on *Tinker,* see chapter 9; sexual harassment issues are further discussed in chapter 15.) According to the court, edu-cators may teach tolerance and respect, but they may not "demand that students express agreement" with their values. Therefore, wrote the judge, schools "cannot silence non-vulgar, non-disruptive speech simply based on the viewpoint expressed."

In an Oklahoma T-shirt case, a high school student was prohibited from wearing a shirt with these words: "The best of the night's adventures are reserved for people with nothing planned." Administrators said the words came from a Bacardi Rum advertisement and therefore violated school policy prohibiting clothing that advertises alcoholic beverages. But a federal court ruled in favor of the student's freedom of expression. The judge explained that administrators who punish students for wearing controversial shirts violate the First Amendment unless they have evidence that "the T-shirt message would substantially disrupt…the work or discipline of the school or that it would infringe upon the rights of other students."[61]

Thus schools generally can prohibit students from wearing clothing with "lewd or indecent" words or gestures. This does not mean that administrators can prohibit all messages on clothing; words or symbols that clearly concern issues of public policy and are not disruptive or indecent are still protected by the First Amendment.

Can Schools Ban Team and College Clothing?

It depends on the facts of the case. In San Jacinto, California, the district dress code prohibited all students from wearing clothing bearing "writing, pictures or any other insignia" that identifies any college or professional sports team because of possible gang activity associated with such clothing. Elementary, middle, and high school students were disciplined for wearing UCLA, Chicago Bears, LA Lakers, and Dodgers clothing. Parents charged that the policy violated their children's freedom of expression.

The court ruled that schools may not abridge students' free speech rights "in the absence of facts which might reasonably have led school authorities to forecast substantial disruption."[62] Applying that principle to the facts of this case, the court held that there was "no justification for application of the restrictive dress code" to elementary students because the district "offered no proof at all of any gang presence at those schools." The district also failed to justify its restrictions at the middle school because there was only "negligible [gang] presence and no actual or threatened disruption." Although evidence about the high school situation was in conflict, the court permitted the restrictive policy because there was evidence of possible disruptive gang presence. The court, however, doubted that the dress code "will negate that presence and possible disruption" because "reliable testimony" indicated that "gang members do not wear university or sports clothing" and the prohibition has affected "only the regular kids who follow the rules."

Can Schools Regulate Student Dress at Off-Campus, Extracurricular Activities?

Yes. Warren Harper and his sister Florence attended their high school prom in elegant attire—of the opposite sex. Warren wore earrings, high heels, a dress, and a fur cape. Florence wore a black tuxedo and men's shoes. The principal was not amused and told the Harpers to change their clothes or leave; they refused and were escorted out by a police officer. They claimed that their constitutional rights were violated. The court disagreed, since it found that the school's dress code was "reasonably related to the valid educational purpose of teaching community values."[63] According to the judge, the code does not discriminate on the basis of sex (e.g., by allowing females, not males, to wear dresses) but simply "requires all students to dress in conformity with the accepted standards of the community." In addition, the judge indicated that these principles also would apply to transvestites, homosexuals, and others who wished to defy the code because of their nonconventional sexual orientation.

Summary

Some judges hold that teachers have a "constitutional liberty interest" in grooming, but this right is not fundamental. Therefore courts rule that grooming may be regulated by the schools and regulations will be struck down only if teachers prove that they are unreasonable. Administrative discretion is even greater regarding teacher attire. Courts have ruled that teachers do not have a constitutional right to dress as they please. Judges have even upheld the authority of administrators to discipline teachers for violating dress requirements the judges thought unwise or insignificant because it is assumed that all employers can establish some clothing regulations and because such restrictions on teacher freedom are relatively minor. Courts might protect certain nonconforming clothing under special circumstances—for example, a black teacher of African studies who wears a dashiki as a matter of academic freedom or racial pride. But it is doubtful that any court would protect a teacher who insisted on going to class in frayed jeans, sandals, and a T-shirt in violation of school policy.

As far as students are concerned, 9 of the 13 U.S. circuit courts of appeals have clearly ruled on the constitutional right of students to choose the length of their hair. Three other circuits have not ruled directly on this issue, but they have indicated how they likely would vote. Some circuits hold that grooming is a constitutional right; others disagree. The arguments used on each side are varied and vigorous, and no final decision establishing a national policy has been reached because the U.S. Supreme Court has refused to rule on the issue. However, even where federal courts have upheld grooming restrictions, students can challenge hair length rules under a state's constitution and statutes. But just like federal judges, state courts vary in this interpretation of their laws and the application of these laws to school grooming restrictions.

Most courts hold that student clothing styles are not protected by the U.S. Constitution. Moreover, some courts that protect student hair length reject students' claims to wear the clothing of their choice. Judges justify the distinction on the grounds that restrictions on hairstyle are more serious invasions of individual freedom; clothing can be changed after school, but if haircuts are required, the effect is more lasting. Recent court decisions tend to uphold the school's authority to ban T-shirts with sexual references as well as jewelry or clothing symbolizing gang membership. However, T-shirts with political messages are protected by the First Amendment, and some prohibitions of gang clothing have been held void because of vagueness.

There is not yet a single standard for reviewing school uniform policies. While courts have generally upheld school uniforms, some judges only require the policies to be reasonable, while others require that they further a "substantial government interest" unrelated to the suppression of student expression.

The questions raised by the controversies in this chapter may concern more than personal appearance; they often concern such fundamental legal and educational issues as: When should schools restrict student and teacher freedom? When should nonconformity be protected or punished? Educators cannot escape these difficult questions as they develop and enforce dress codes for students and teachers and search for an appropriate balance between freedom and conformity in the public schools.

NOTES

1. D. Goddy, *Rights and Freedoms of Public School Students* 25 (Topeka, KS: National Organization on Legal Problems in Education, 1971).

2. *Lucia* v. *Duggan*, 303 F.Supp. 112 (D. Mass. 1969).

3. *Finot* v. *Pasadena City Board of Education,* 58 Cal. Rptr. 520 (Ct. App. 1967).

4. *Miller* v. *School District No. 167, Cook County, Illinois,* 495 F.2d 658 (7th Cir. 1974); *modified, Pence* v. *Rosenquist,* 573 F.2d 395 (7th Cir. 1978).

5. *Morrison* v. *Hamilton Board of Education,* 494 S.W.2d 770 (Tenn. 1973).

6. *Domico* v. *Rapides Parish School Board,* 675 F.2d 100 (5th Cir. 1982).

7. The appeals court based its reasoning on a U.S. Supreme Court decision that upheld grooming restrictions on police but acknowledged a "liberty interest in freedom to choose [one's] own hairstyle." *Kelly* v. *Johnson,* 425 U.S. 238 (1976).

8. *Pence* v. *Rosenquist,* 573 F.2d 395 (7th Cir. 1978)

9. *Braxton* v. *Board of Public Instruction of Duval County, Florida,* 303 F.Supp. 958 (M.D. Fla. 1969).

10. *Blanchet* v. *Vermilion Parish School Board,* 220 So.2d 534 (La. 1969).

11. *Tardif* v. *Quinn,* 545 F.2d 761 (1st Cir. 1976).

12. *East Hartford Education Association* v. *Board of Education of the Town of East Hartford,* 562 F.2d 838 (2d Cir. 1977).

13. The code contained a consent provision that allowed noncompliance if, at the beginning of each semester, a parent appeared before the principal and gave written consent for the exception of his child. Greg's father decided not to seek an exception but to challenge the constitutionality of the code.

14. *Arnold* v. *Carpenter,* 459 F.2d 939 (7th Cir. 1972).

15. *Richards* v. *Thurston,* 424 F.2d 1281 (1st Cir. 1970).

16. *Karr* v. *Schmidt,* 460 F.2d 609 (5th Cir. 1972) (Wisdom, J., dissenting).

17. *Massie* v. *Henry,* 455 F.2d 779 (4th Cir. 1972).

18. *Crews* v. *Cloncs,* 432 F.2d 1259 (7th Cir. 1970).

19. *Bishop* v. *Colaw,* 450 F.2d 1069 (8th Cir. 1971).

20. *Karr* v. *Schmidt,* 460 F.2d 609 (5th Cir. 1972).

21. *Alabama and Coushatta Tribes* v. *Big Sandy Independent School District,* 817 F.Supp. 1319 (E.D. Tex. 1993).

22. *Hatch* v. *Goerke,* 502 F.2d 1189 (10th Cir. 1974).

23. *Davenport* v. *Randolph County Board of Education,* 730 F.2d 1395 (11th Cir. 1984).

24. *McClung* v. *Board of Education of City of Washington,* 346 N.E.2d 691 (Ohio 1976).

25. *Karr* v. *Schmidt,* 401 U.S. 1201 (1971).

26. *Dwen* v. *Barry,* 483 F.2d 1126 (2d Cir. 1973).

27. *Kelly* v. *Johnson,* 425 U.S. 238 (1976).

28. *Syrek* v. *Pennsylvania Air National Guard,* 537 F.2d 66 (3d Cir. 1976).

29. *Zeller* v. *Donegal School District Board of Education,* 517 F.2d 600 (3d Cir. 1975).

30. *Fagan* v. *National Cash Register Co.,* 481 F.2d 1115 (D.C. Cir. 1973).

31. *Barber* v. *Colorado Independent School District,* 901 S.W.2d 447 (Tex. 1995).

32. *Bastrop Board of Trustees* v. *Toungate,* 922 S.W.2d 650 (Tex. Ct. App. Austin 1996).

33. *Board of Trustees of Bastrop* v. *Toungate,* 958 S.W.2d 365 (Tex. 1997).

34. Students probably would be exempt from a requirement to wear standard gym clothing for religious reasons if they and/or their parents believed such clothing was "immodest" or "improper." But that would probably not exempt them from physical education requirements. *Moody* v. *Cronin,* 484 F.Supp. 270 (C.D. Ill. 1979).

35. *Bannister* v. *Paradis,* 316 F.Supp. 185 (D. N.H. 1970).

36. *Fowler* v. *Williamson,* 251 S.E.2d 889 (N.C. 1979).

37. *Scott* v. *Board of Education, Hicksville,* 305 N.Y.S.2d 601 (N.Y. Sup. Ct. 1969).

38. *Johnson* v. *Joint School District No. 60, Bigham County,* 508 P.2d 547 (Idaho 1973).

39. *Dunkerson* v. *Russell,* 502 S.W.2d 64 (Ky. 1973).

40. *Scott* v. *Board of Education, Hicksville,* 305 N.Y.S.2d 601 (N.Y. Sup. Ct. 1969).

41. *Long* v. *Board of Education of Jefferson County, Kentucky,* 121 F.Supp.2d 621 (W.D.Ky. 2000).

42. *Bivens by Green* v. *Albuquerque Public Schools,* 899 F.Supp. 556 (D. N.M. 1995). This test is based on the U.S. Supreme Court's flag-burning decision in *Texas* v. *Johnson,* 491 U.S. 397 (1989).

43. *Isaacs ex rel. Isaacs* v. *Board of Education of Howard County, Maryland,* 40 F.Supp.2d 335 (Md. 1999).

44. *Newsweek,* November 27, 1989, p. 79.

45. *Id.*

46. *Daily Hampshire Gazette,* December 14, 1993, p. 5.

47. *Newsweek, supra* note 44.

48. *Canady* v. *Bossier Parish School Board,* 240 F.3d 437 (5th Cir. 2001).

49. *Littlefield* v. *Forney Independent School District,* 108 F.Supp.2d 681 (N.D.Tex. 2000).

50. *Phoenix Elementary School District No. 1* v. *Green,* 943 P.2d 836 (Ariz.App.Div.2 1997).

51. *Olesen* v. *Board of Education of School District No. 228,* 676 F.Supp. 820 (N.D. Ill. 1987).

52. *Stephenson* v. *Davenport Community School District,* 110 F.3d 1303 (8th Cir. 1997).

53. *Chalifaux* v. *New Caney Independent School District,* 976 F.Supp. 659 (S.D.Tex. 1997).

54. *Hines* v. *Caston School Corporation,* 651 N.E.2d 330 (Ind. Ct. App. 1995).

55. *Jones* v. *W. T. Henning Elementary School,* 721 So.2d 530 (La.App.3 Cir. 1998).

56. *Gano* v. *School District 411 of Twin Falls County, Idaho,* 674 F.Supp. 796 (D. Id. 1987).

57. This was the holding in *Bethel School District No. 403* v. *Fraser,* 478 U.S. 675 (1986). See chapter 9 for more on the scope and limits of student freedom of expression.

58. *Broussard by Lord* v. *School Board of City of Norfolk,* 801 F.Supp. 1526 (E.D. Va. 1992).

59. *Pyle* v. *South Hadley School Committee,* 861 F.Supp. 157 (D. Mass. 1994). The Massachusetts Supreme Judicial Court ruled that under the state's Student Free Expression Law, students are allowed to wear the "Co-ed Naked" T-shirts because vulgar and suggestive messages are protected if they are not school-sponsored and are not legally obscene or libelous and cause no disruption. 667 N.E.2d 869 (Mass. 1996).

60. *Tinker* v. *Des Moines Independent School District,* 393 U.S. 503 (1969).

61. *McIntire* v. *Bethel School District,* 804 F.Supp. 1415 (W.D. Okla. 1992).

62. *Jeglin* v. *San Jacinto Unified School District,* 827 F.Supp. 1459 (C.D. Cal. 1993).

63. *Harper* v. *Edgewood Board of Education,* 655 F.Supp. 1353 (S.D. Ohio 1987).

20 What Issues Will Face the Courts in the Next Decade?

Overview

This chapter highlights controversial issues that have recently emerged or that continue to be high on the national agenda of educational and legal concerns: AIDS education and condom distribution; prohibitions on school computer usage; school choice; high-stakes student tests and teacher tests; compulsory community service; frivolous lawsuits; school uniforms and gang clothing; prohibitions on hate speech; protections for homosexual students and teachers; and funding for public education.

Control of the Internet

Computer Use and Free Speech

With the growing numbers of computers in elementary and secondary schools, many educators and parents worry about their use by students for pornographic, commercial, or other inappropriate purposes. Questions then arise about whether schools can restrict the use of the Internet or whether such restrictions might violate students' rights by arbitrarily denying them access to ideas or by punishing them for violating ambiguous school rules or for inappropriate use of their home computers.

Can Schools Legally Restrict Use of School Computers?

Yes, if the restrictions are related to legitimate educational purposes. Although there are no reported cases challenging school computer use policies, there are several non-school cases that appear relevant. In 1997, the U.S. Supreme Court struck down the federal Communications Decency Act that made it a crime to use a computer to transmit indecent material to someone under age 18.[1] The Court held that the Internet is entitled to First Amendment protection as books and newspapers are. The act was declared unconstitutional because of its vagueness and ambiguity and because it suppressed communications addressed to adults. But some of the key precedents that led the Court to strike down that criminal statute are not likely to apply to public school policies.

Two less recent Supreme Court cases dealing with school censorship may be more relevant. The first ruled that administrators may not remove controversial books from their school libraries to deny students access to ideas with which they disagree; they can, however, remove books that are educationally unsuitable, pervasively vulgar, or age inappropriate.[2] The second case allows educators to restrict the content and style of curricular-related student publications as long as the restrictions are related to "legitimate educational concerns."[3]

Although the analogy is not exact, students' use of the Internet might be considered similar to a curricular-related project or to the use of the school library. If so, schools presumably would be able to limit use of school computers if their limitations were related to legitimate educational purposes. Nevertheless, constitutional problems could arise if students are punished for "inappropriate" Internet use under school policies that are overbroad, vague, or ambiguous.

To protect against improper computer use, schools have several options. They can develop policies that allow computers to be used only for specific educational purposes. Policies also could prohibit such inappropriate uses as violations of copyright laws, harassment of students or staff, commercial purposes, and transmission or search for pornographic material. Furthermore, students could be required to sign an agreement stating that they understand the policy before receiving a password and computer account.

In addition, the Children's Internet Protection Act requires public schools to use filters that protect against access to obscene material and to child pornography. Schools can install software to filter the Worldwide Web by blocking sites known to harbor explicit sexual material, or they can subscribe to online services that offer similar control options. These are not foolproof, however, and talented teenagers might view such controls as challenges to be circumvented.

In sum, if school policies restricting Internet use are not arbitrary or ambiguous and are clearly related to legitimate educational purposes, they are likely to pass constitutional muster.

Can Schools Punish Students for Using Their Home Computers to Insult or Harass Students or Teachers?

It depends on the message and its consequences. In 1998, Brandon Beussink was a student at Missouri's Woodland High School when he created a controversial web page on his home computer. The home page used vulgar language and was highly critical of the school's teachers and administrators. After the principal learned about the web page, he suspended Brandon for 10 days, which resulted in his grades being lowered, in his failing classes, and in a federal lawsuit. The court ruled in Brandon's favor, holding that a school's need to maintain discipline does not outweigh a student's freedom of expression that causes no disruption. The judge concluded, "It is provocative and challenging speech, like Buessink's, which is most in need of the protections of the First Amendment."[4]

In a similar 2000 case, Nick Emmett, a high school student from Washington, posted a web page on the Internet he created at home, that included a fictional student obituary section. It also asked viewers to vote on "Who Should Die" and be featured in the next mock obituary. In the aftermath of the school shootings in Colorado and a news story about the web site's "hit list," the administration wanted to take no chances and placed Emmett on "emergency expulsion for intimidation, harassment [and] disruption to the educational process." However, the school had no evidence that the web page caused any disruption or that anyone felt intimidated. Ruling in Emmett's favor, the court noted that schools cannot prohibit distribution of student material "on the basis of undifferentiated fears of possible disturbances."[5] In a related 2001 decision, Paul Killion was suspended for emailing an insulting "TopTen" list about his school's athletic director.[6] In ruling for Killion (since the list caused no disruption), the court noted that a school's authority over off-campus speech is substantially more limited than over speech at school. Responding to the school's justification for its action, the judge wrote, "We cannot accept that the childish and boorish antics could impair the administrator's ability to discipline students and maintain control."

In contrast, a 2000 Pennsylvania decision upheld the expulsion of J. S., a middle school student who posted a website at home titled, "Teacher Sux" that was harassing and threatening to his algebra teacher. The website solicited $20 to pay a hit man to kill the teacher and contained a picture of her with her head cut off. As a result of viewing the site, the teacher suffered mentally and physically and was unable to continue teaching.[7] Unlike the cases noted above, the court ruled against the student since his website had a profoundly disruptive effect. In sum, the trend of recent court decisions indicates that students should not be punished for posting an offensive, insulting, or vulgar home page on the Internet unless it causes substantial disruption at school.

School Choice

During recent years, the concept of school choice has become quite popular with politicians and voters. Ex-president Clinton favored school choice within the public school system, while President Bush and Republican leaders argue that government funds should be used to expand parental choice of private as well as public schools.

Two major innovations make such choice available: charter schools and the voucher system. As indicated in chapter 18, charter schools creation is increasing rapidly, and there is every reason to believe that they will continue to proliferate. Some have also been eliminated due to fiscal irregularities or for failure to achieve their goals. However, there seems to be strong support for the movement, as evidenced by the U.S. Senate's amendment to its education bill in 2001 that would provide $525 million in aid of charter schools. We can expect legal challenges to charter schools under the establishment clause of the First Amendment and under the equal protection clause of the Fourteenth Amendment as well as pursuant to IDEA. Until now, none of these challenges have succeeded.[8]

The second major innovation expanding parental choice is the voucher system. Under this system, public funds are used to enable low-income families, dissatisfied with their children's public schools, to enroll them in private schools. The value of the vouchers, which parents can use toward the tuition and other costs of the private schools, usually relates to the state aid per student during the particular year.

State law and school district regulations prescribe the uses of the vouchers and some states, such as Maine, prohibit their use in religious schools. Others, like the ones in Milwaukee, Wisconsin, and Cleveland, Ohio, allow their use in both secular and religious schools as long as participation in religious activities is voluntary. The constitutionality of using vouchers for religious schools is now before the Supreme Court. For more on this issue, see chapter 10.

High-Stakes Testing

High-stakes testing has become the popular term that refers to the use of standardized tests that may lead to serious consequences. Depending on state laws and school district policies, they may be used for tracking students, for promotions, and for receiving of diplomas. Since many schools have used "social promotion" during the recent past, a change to high-stakes testing brought on significant failures in schools and widespread public protests.

Inevitably, these failures and protests resulted in lawsuits that challenged such testing on various grounds. Most of these cases were brought on behalf of children with disabilities and those with limited English (see chapter 16). Challenges were also mounted by racial and ethnic minorities under the Fourteenth Amendment's equal protection and due process clauses (see chapter 14).

Laws and regulations related to the testing of children with disabilities require that appropriate accommodations be made for their testing along with full due process provisions. The tests must be valid and reliable and they must assess the curricular content the children study. Similarly, standardized tests used with racial and ethnic minority students must be valid tests that are related to the curriculum taught to the children who must have had sufficient notice of the tests they will have to face. The tests and their administration must not be discriminatory, and the principles of due process must not be violated.

It is probable that many new lawsuits will be filed as high-stakes testing is applied in an ever-increasing number of school districts throughout the country. Even if all the legal requirements for such testing are satisfied, experience shows that children from poor families and neighborhoods will fail in greater numbers than those from affluent backgrounds. Thus, it is likely that political efforts will be used to avoid the dire consequences of high-stakes testing.

Teacher Testing

It is self-evident that good schools require competent teachers. There is no general agreement, however, on how best to select good candidates for teaching, how to educate them, and how to assess their competence for certification. During recent years, a movement arose to administer competency testing to candidates for certification and even for recertification at certain time intervals. Not surprisingly, this development led to rigorous disagreements and to a variety of legal challenges.

The most common of these challenges came under the due process clause of the Fourteenth Amendment, the equal protection clause of the Fourteenth Amendment, Title VII of the Civil Rights Act of 1964, as well as the federal laws protecting people with disabilities. Each of these challenges faces great difficulties if the competency test used by the state is a valid measure of the job-related knowledge and skill, if there is reasonable time to prepare for the test, and if it does not discriminate on the basis of race, national origin, religion, or gender. Furthermore, the testing procedures must make reasonable accommodations for teachers with handicaps.

If protected groups such as racial or ethnic minorities or women can show a disparate impact on their members as a consequence of the competency test, the employer must show that the selection criterion is job-related, that there is educational necessity for using it, and that there is no better alternative way to achieve its objective.

According to reliable predictions, the next decade will require that about two million new teachers enter the teaching profession. How to ensure that these will be competent teachers is a monumental challenge. Professional organizations as well as our courts will be involved in the complex efforts to ensure that only well-prepared teachers enter our classrooms, and competency testing is likely to play a significant part in these efforts.

Frivolous Lawsuits

To many educators, it sometimes appears as though disgruntled students and their parents can sue schools simply because they resent a teacher's critical judgment about their child or are angry about an administrator's disciplinary decision. Even when the plaintiff's case is dismissed, educators often feel as though they were victims of legal harassment because defendants often pay a high emotional and financial price to defend against a suit although they did nothing illegal. However, as the following cases illustrate, victims of such suits are not always without a remedy.

Can Lawyers and Parents Be Punished for Filing Frivolous Lawsuits?

Sometimes. In an extreme case, a New Jersey lawyer was fined $100,000 because of a pattern of frivolous suits against local teachers and administrators.[9] The case began when a high school student, Robert Giangrasso, threatened to punch a teacher in the head after she awakened him from sleeping while serving an in-school suspension. As a result of his threat, Robert was suspended for one day. Two years later, Attorney Edward Gaffney sued the teacher, assistant principal, superintendent, and school board charging that Robert had been suspended without due process. Since the court found that Robert had received two hearings before being suspended ("both of which were more than sufficient") and had admitted threatening to punch the teacher, the attorneys for the school charged that Gaffney's suit was frivolous and asked the court to impose sanctions on him under the *Federal Rules of Civil Procedure.*

Federal Rule 11 states that by filing a case in court, an attorney is certifying that "to the best of the person's knowledge" formed after a reasonable inquiry, the claims are warranted by law and that the allegations have "evidentiary support." If this rule is violated, the court may impose an "appropriate sanction" upon the attorney. In this case, the court agreed to impose a sanction against Gaffney because there was no basis in law or in fact for his suit. Robert not only admitted the charges against him, but he also received more process than was legally due. In addition, Gaffney had been previously sanctioned for filing a frivolous due process suit against the school. Since the evidence indicated that Gaffney "has abused the legal system to harass defendants" in this case and had been reprimanded in the past for unprofessional conduct, the judge imposed "extraordinary sanctions" against the attorney. The court not only fined Gaffney $100,000 to be paid to the defendants "to deter him from filing further frivolous suits," but also "permanently enjoined" him from filing any future complaints against the school.

A less extreme example occurred in a Texas case where Jonathan Shinn's parents sued their son's band teacher, Kenneth Wilbanks, and other school officials. The parents listed numerous complaints about Wilbanks' lack of leadership and professionalism that they charged "resulted in a poor year for the band and the infliction of severe emotional distress" upon their son. The trial court ruled that there was no legal basis for the Shinns' suit. Despite this, the parents appealed. The appeals court not only agreed with the trial court but also ruled that the parents' appeal was frivolous.[10] The court acknowledged that the parents were extremely dissatisfied with the band teacher, but emphasized the difference between debatable educational performance and illegal behavior. The court explained that "a constitutional violation does not occur every time someone feels they have been wronged or treated unfairly" in school. Since there was no legal basis for the appeal, the court required the parents to pay damages to the school consisting of "attorneys' fees and double costs" for pursuing this frivolous legal action.

In a 1999 New Jersey decision, a federal judge criticized parents and their attorney, Samuel Malat, for trivializing the law by filing a lawsuit that is both "silly and foolish" by invoking the Constitution to protect "the 'rights' of unruly high school seniors" who were prohibited from marching at their graduation after becoming drunk and disorderly on a class trip. Irate that such a controversy would lead to litigation, Judge Orlofsky wrote:

> One would have thought that the students and their parents would have been too embarrassed to seek the protection of a federal court over this tempest in a teapot. Instead they have shamelessly proceeded in this Court as if the fate of the Republic were at stake.[11]

While he declined to penalize the parents because they do not have the legal training "to understand the frivolousness and triviality of their claims," Judge Orlofsky repeatedly criticized Attorney Malat for failing to do "a few minutes of legal research" through which he "could easily have discovered" that his claims were "patently frivolous." To deter future similar conduct, the judge ordered the lawyer to attend two relevant continuing legal education courses and to pay a fine of $500.

AIDS Awareness and Condom Distribution

Over 30 states require AIDS education.[12] Yet the high level of sexual activity among teenagers and the continuing spread of AIDS have led an increasing number of school boards to consider alternative approaches to AIDS education and prevention. Among those alternatives are nonconventional AIDS awareness programs and the distribution of condoms in public schools. These alternatives often spark intense opposition from those who believe the programs violate their religious beliefs or parental rights. The following cases illustrate the legal arguments that opponents might use when schools institute nontraditional programs and how courts might resolve these controversies.

Can Schools Require Students to Participate in an AIDS Awareness Assembly?

Yes, according to a federal appeals court.[13] The case arose when students at Massachusetts's Chelmsford High School attended a mandatory schoolwide assembly which consisted of a 90-minute AIDS awareness program. The program included sexually explicit monologues and skits with students, and was presented by a consultant from Hot, Sexy, and Safer Productions, Inc.

Two 15-year-old students and their parents charged that the consultant used "profane, lewd, and lascivious language"; approved condom use "during promiscuous pre-marital sex"; and made repeated references to orgasms and male and female genitals. The parents complained that the presentation "humiliated and intimidated" their children and created a sexually hostile environment. Here are the parents' main legal arguments and the court's response.

The school violated parental privacy rights "to direct the upbringing of their children." The court acknowledged that the state cannot prevent a parent from choosing a specific educational program, whether it is religious or secular education at a private or public school. But this freedom, wrote the court, does *not* encompass a "constitutional right to dictate the curriculum," nor does it "encompass a broad-based right to restrict the flow of information in the public schools."

The program violated Title IX by creating a "sexually hostile environment." The court ruled that under U.S. Supreme Court precedent, the parents' allegations are clearly insufficient to establish the existence of an objectively abusive environment. This is because the offensive speech was not physically threatening or humiliating, not frequent (but "only a one-time exposure"), the plaintiff's children were not the direct object of any of the consultant's sexual comments, and "an objective person would understand that [the]... sexual commentary was intended to educate the students about the AIDS virus rather than to create a sexually hostile environment."

School policy requires parental permission as "a prerequisite to enrolling" in health courses dealing with human sexuality. The court ruled that the assembly was not a course in which students enrolled but rather a one-time, "random" event which was unlikely to be repeated without parental permission or an opt-out provision.

Although the court rejected each of the parents' arguments in the case, a compulsory AIDS education unit could not be required as part of a health course in the many school districts that have opt-out provisions for sex education.[14]

Is It Unconstitutional for Public Schools to Give Condoms to Students without Parental Consent?

Not according to a 1995 decision by the Massachusetts Supreme Judicial Court.[15] The case arose when the Falmouth school committee authorized the distribution of free condoms from the school nurse to all students in grades 7 to 12 who requested them. Parents challenged the program and argued that they have the right to be notified if their child requests a condom and to prohibit their child from obtaining one without their consent.

The court, however, explained that state action violates "parental liberty" rights only when it is "coercive or compulsory." In this case, the court found no coercion or compulsion because the students are not required to seek or accept condoms. Since parents are free to instruct their children not to participate, the program "does not supplant the parents' role" in their children's moral and religious development. Although the court recognized that the program may offend the moral and religious sensibilities of some parents, the judges ruled that "mere exposure to programs offered at school does not amount to unconstitutional interference with parental liberties."

The parents also maintained that the condom-availability program was coercive because it was implemented in the "compulsory setting" of the public school. They supported this argument by citing a state court opinion that struck down a similar program in the New York City public high schools.[16] In that 3–2 decision, the court explained that a New York law required parental consent for medical treatment, and the judges wrote that condom distribution is "clearly a health service for the prevention of disease" and "has absolutely nothing to do with education." The New York court concluded that condom distribution also violated the parents' rights to direct the upbringing of their children unless the program included an opt-out provision or parental consent.

The Massachusetts justices unanimously rejected the reasoning of the New York court. The Massachusetts court ruled that condom distribution was not a medical service requiring parental consent and that compulsory school attendance did not make the program coercive. The court concluded that "neither an opt-out provision nor parental notification is required by the Federal Constitution" and "parents have no right to tailor public school programs to meet their individual religious or moral preferences." As these conflicting judicial opinions indicate, no judicial consensus exists on whether condom distribution without parental consent violates state or federal law.

Controversial T-Shirts, Gang Clothing, and School Uniforms

In the 1970s, dress code controversies usually concerned the length of boys' hair and girls' skirts. In recent years, the focus shifted to offensive T-shirts, gang clothing, and school uniforms.

The range of controversial and creative T-shirts that students are wearing to school seems almost endless. And the courts that have ruled on T-shirt conflicts are divided on which constitutional principles apply. Those supporting administrative discretion to ban controversial shirts rely on the U.S. Supreme Court's comment in *Bethel* v. *Fraser* that educators "may determine that the essential lessons of civil, mature conduct cannot be conveyed in a school that tolerates lewd, indecent or offensive speech."[17] This was the reasoning used by judges to uphold the banning of the shirts that read "Co-ed Naked Band: Do It To The Rhythm" and "Drugs Suck."

In contrast, others say the U.S. Supreme Court decision in *Tinker* v. *Des Moines,* upholding student freedom of expression, protects message T-shirts. According to one federal judge, this ruling means that administrators who punish students for wearing controversial shirts violate the law unless they have evidence that "the T-shirt message would substantially disrupt…the work or discipline of the school or that it would infringe upon the rights of other students."[18] Legal disputes about the rights of students to wear controversial messages are likely to continue until a judicial consensus emerges about the scope and limits of student freedom in this area.

There are two other current dress code conflicts. The first concerns the wearing of gang symbols, especially in urban schools. Here, the courts will probably uphold the authority of administrators to ban earrings, jewelry, team jackets, or any other emblems of gang membership if the ban is directly related to student safety. However, some courts recently have struck down such prohibitions when schools could not produce any evidence of a link between wearing earrings or team clothing and gang activity, and some bans on gang attire have been held void because of vagueness. Second, an increasing number of public schools are beginning to experiment with required school uniforms for students. The U.S. Department of Education and many parents and school staff believe that uniforms can have a positive impact on the school climate, reduce clothing costs, reduce illegal efforts to obtain designer clothes, instill discipline, and help students concentrate on their work.[19] Some urban schools are also proposing uniforms as a way to protect students from wrongly being associated with gangs.[20] As such requirements expand, the conflict between the values of diversity and individualism versus the value of conformity to school dress codes is likely to intensify.[21] (For related cases, see chapter 9 on freedom of expression and chapter 19 on personal appearance.)

Prohibiting Hate Speech

An increasing number of schools are becoming concerned about the destructive impact of hateful speech, especially if it is directed to minorities or women. As a result, many districts have established policies that prohibit and punish speech that threatens, harasses, intimidates, or insults individuals on the basis of their race, religion, nationality, or gender. Proponents of these policies argue that they reduce verbal assaults that can lead to violence, they make students aware that hateful language can create a hostile learning environment, and they teach students in a multicultural environment that words can cause emotional injury. Opponents of such codes argue that they restrict First Amendment freedom of expression and that they are ineffective because codes do not stop hateful speech but merely drive it underground. Furthermore, they say, students who are punished for violating such codes often become First Amendment martyrs.

Are Hate Speech Codes in Public Schools Constitutional?

The answer may depend on whether the wording of those codes is narrow and clear. Federal courts have struck down a criminal hate speech law[22] and a college hate speech code.[23]

But it can be argued that decisions about colleges and criminal laws do not apply to public schools that have wide discretion to control student conduct, promote a safe environment, and teach manners of civility. Even if these decisions do apply to public schools, hate speech codes probably will still be upheld if they are "content neutral" and prohibit all "fighting words" (words that provoke violence or are intended to injure, not to convey an idea) and if they are narrowly worded to prohibit only threatening, intimidating, or harassing language, not controversial or unpopular ideas. (For more on student speech, see chapter 9.)

Protection of Homosexual Teachers and Students

Whether gay and lesbian teachers and students need legal protection continues to be divisive and unsettled, and the protection they receive varies with changing state and local law. At least 11 states (California, Connecticut, Hawaii, Maine, Massachusetts, Minnesota, New Jersey, New Hampshire, Rhode Island, Vermont, and Wisconsin) and the District of Columbia prohibit sexual orientation discrimination in employment.[24] Also more than 160 cities and counties prohibit such discrimination, including San Francisco, Chicago, Detroit, Baltimore, Philadelphia, New York City, and Washington, D.C.[25] In such cities and states, these laws should protect gay and lesbian teachers from being dismissed on grounds of immoral or unprofessional conduct. However, in some states, conservative groups have organized petition drives to repeal gay rights laws.[26] Thus the battles to pass and repeal anti-discrimination laws based on sexual orientation are likely to continue. Even in most states where no laws protect gay and lesbian teachers, recent federal decisions have held that they cannot be discriminated against because of their sexual orientation. Thus, in an Ohio education case, a judge wrote that homosexuals are entitled to "at least the same protection" as any other group. And, in a 1998 Utah case, a judge wrote that the Constitution's equal protection clause prohibits public schools from engaging in intentional discrimination "on the basis of sexual orientation." (For more on these cases, see chapter 13.)

Controversies about openly gay students continue in public high schools. In a Washington State school district, 400 parents signed a petition to ban teachers from discussing homosexuality or telling students about support groups for gays and lesbians.[27] In contrast, the Massachusetts Board of Education passed a series of recommendations to combat discrimination and promote Safe School Programs for gay and lesbian students.[28] These pioneering policies, endorsed by the state's Republican governor, not only prohibit harassment but also encourage teacher training about gay and lesbian issues and even encourage schools to establish support groups for gay and lesbian students and their families. And in 1996, a Wisconsin school district paid a gay high school student nearly $1 million after a federal jury found school officials liable for failing to protect him from abuse by his peers.[29]

In the past, some school administrators believed that gay, lesbian, and bisexual student organizations could be prohibited in the public schools. In recent years, however, hundreds of gay/straight alliance clubs have been organized in public schools across the country. And, in a series of decisions beginning in 1999, federal judges have ruled that, under the Equal Access Act, student clubs which focus on issues related to sexual orientation and homophobia must be able to use school facilities like all other extracurricular organizations. On the other hand, a few school boards have banned all extracurricular groups rather than allow a gay and lesbian club to form. Thus, despite the Equal Access Act, conflicts about lesbian and gay student organizations are likely to continue. (For more on student organizations, see chapter 11.)

Compulsory Community Service

In recent years, increasing numbers of schools have instituted mandatory community service programs. These have ranged from a statewide requirement in Maryland (calling for 75 hours of service before high school graduation) to district requirements (of 40 to 270 hours of service over four years) in communities as diverse as Long Beach, California; Washington, D.C.; Bethlehem, Pennsylvania; and Chapel Hill, North Carolina. The following 1996 case arose in Rye Neck, New York, when the district instituted a mandatory community service program as part of the high school curriculum.[30] Under the program, all students must complete 40 hours of community service and participate in classroom discussions about their service to earn their diplomas. Students may serve in a wide range of organizations but may not be paid for their service. Daniel Immediato and his parents challenged the program because they believed it violated their constitutional rights.

Is Compulsory Community Service Unconstitutional?

No. Although Daniel felt that voluntary charitable activities are admirable, he objected to the school's compulsory service program. First, he argued that mandatory service is a form of "involuntary servitude" prohibited by the Thirteenth Amendment. A federal appeals court noted that the constitutional ban on involuntary servitude was intended to cover "those forms of compulsory labor akin to African slavery," and therefore had "no trouble" concluding that this program was not unconstitutional because its purpose was educational, "not exploitative." The court imagined that there could be cases involving unconstitutional service programs, such as requiring students to wash their teachers' cars, paint their houses, and weed their gardens. But the Rye Neck program was not such a case.

Second, Daniel's parents argued that they had a constitutional responsibility for the upbringing of their children which included the right to exempt them from educational requirements to which they object. The judges acknowledged that the government may not "unreasonably" interfere with this parental right, but concluded that the community service program "easily meets the rational basis test" because the government has a compelling interest in teaching students "the value and habits of good citizenship and introducing them to their social responsibilities." Thus, the community service program "rationally furthers" this objective by exposing students to community needs and encouraging introspection about those needs and the ways that citizens can constructively respond to them. Since two other federal appeals courts have reached the same conclusion,[31] it appears that well-constructed, educational, compulsory community service programs rest on solid constitutional foundations despite repeated legal challenges.

Public Education Funding

The way public schools are funded in the United States varies widely. In some states, local school districts raise most of the costs through property taxes. In others, the state allocates most of the funds. The federal government contributes less than 10 percent. In some states, there is great inequality in the amount that is spent per pupil; poor districts might spend less than $2,500 per student while wealthy districts may spend more than $9,000. This situation raises the following question.

Is It Unconstitutional for a State to Allow Gross Disparities in the Amount Spent to Educate Each Student?

The answer depends on the state in which you live. In 1973, the U.S. Supreme Court ruled that the federal Constitution did not require states to fund their schools equally, since education is not a right under the federal Constitution.[32] However, education *is* a right under the laws of every state. Therefore, in dozens of states, citizens in poorer districts have brought suit asking that unequal education financing be declared illegal under their state law. The results have been mixed. Plaintiffs who challenged the traditional form of school funding have won in the state supreme courts in Alabama, Arizona, Arkansas, California, Connecticut, Kentucky, Massachusetts, Missouri, Montana, New Hampshire, New Jersey, North Carolina, Ohio, Tennessee, Texas, Vermont, Washington, West Virginia, and Wyoming. In contrast, plaintiffs have lost in Alaska, Colorado, Florida, Georgia, Idaho, Illinois, Maine, Maryland, Michigan, Minnesota, Nebraska, New York, North Dakota, Oklahoma, Oregon, Pennsylvania, Rhode Island, South Carolina, Virginia, and Wisconsin.[33]

There are at least two reasons for this disagreement among the state courts. First, the specific wording in state constitutions differs substantially. While one state may require "equal educational opportunity for all,"[34] others merely require "ample," "efficient," or "complete and uniform" public schools.[35] Second, many constitutional provisions concerning education are so vague and ambiguous that different judges have different interpretations even when the wording is similar. Since inequitable school funding continues to exist in most states, it is likely that poorer school districts will continue to bring suits challenging such inequities.

Conclusions

In some of the topics reviewed in this chapter, the law is clear. For example, mandatory community service does not violate the Thirteenth Amendment prohibition against involuntary servitude. On the other hand, the legality of hate speech codes and school choice plans may depend on the wording of the code or plan; the rights of gay and lesbian teachers and students may vary according to state law; and the constitutionality of T-shirt bans may depend on the wording of both the dress code and the shirt. In these and other areas, it is important to remember that state education laws and constitutions may differ significantly, that the law is constantly changing, and that teachers can influence its development and application in the school community.

N O T E S

1. *Reno* v. *ACLU,* 521 U.S. 844 (1997).
2. *Board of Education, Island Trees Union Free School District No. 26* v. *Pico,* 457 U.S. 853 (1982).
3. *Hazelwood School District* v. *Kuhlmeier,* 484 U.S. 260 (1988).
4. *Beussink* v. *Woodland R-IV School District,* 30 F.Supp.2d 1175 (E.D.Mo. 1998).
5. *Emmett* v. *Kent School District No. 415,* 92 F.Supp.2d 1088 (W.D.Wa. 2000).
6. *Killion* v. *Franklin Regional School District,* 136 F.Supp.2d 446 (W.D.Pa. 2001). For example, number 2 on Killion's insulting list reads, "Because of his extensive gut factor, the 'man' hasn't seen his own penis in over a decade." *Id.*
7. *J. S.* v. *Bethlehem Area School District,* 757 A.2d 412 (Pa.Commw. Ct. 2000). The website included abusive comments such as, "Fuck you Mrs. Fulmer. You are a stupid bitch." On March 13, 2001, an appeal was granted by the Pennsylvania Supreme Court.
8. See *Porter* v. *Klaghelz,* 19 F.Supp.2d 290 (D.N.J. 1998); *Daugherty* v. *Vanguard Charter Sch. Academy,* 116 F.Supp.2d 897 (W.D. Mich. 2000); *Thompson* v. *Board of the Special School Dist. No. 1,* 144 F.3d 574 (8th Cir. 1998).
9. *Giangrasso* v. *Kittatinny Regional High School Board of Education,* 865 F.Supp. 1133 (D. N.J. 1994). Gaffney also charged without evidence that school officials conspired to place Robert in a school for the emotionally disturbed.

10. *Shinn* v. *College Station Independent School District,* 96 F.3d 783 (5th Cir. 1996).

11. *Carlino* v. *Gloucester City High School,* 57 F.Supp.2d 1 (D.N.J. 1999).

12. E. C. Bjorklun, *Condom Distribution in the Public Schools: Is Parental Consent Required?* 91 EDUC. L. REP. 11 (1994).

13. *Brown* v. *Hot, Sexy and Safer Productions, Inc.,* 68 F.3d 525 (1st Cir. 1995).

14. Bjorklun at 11–12. However, such a required unit might be upheld against parental challenge in the minority of districts without opt-out laws because AIDS education might be defended as a compelling government interest to protect public health.

15. *Curtis* v. *School Committee of Falmouth,* 652 N.E.2d 580 (Mass. 1995).

16. *Alfonso* v. *Fernandez,* 606 N.Y.S.2d 259 (N.Y. App. Div. 1993).

17. *Bethel School District* v. *Fraser,* 478 U.S. 675 (1986).

18. *McIntire* v. *Bethel School District,* 804 F.Supp. 1415 (W.D. Okla. 1992).

19. MANUAL ON SCHOOL UNIFORMS, U.S. Department of Education, Washington D.C., March, 1996.

20. P. Murphy, *Restricting Gang Clothing in Public Schools,* 64 S. CAL. L. REV. 1321, 1326 (1991).

21. *Model Guidelines for the Wearing of Uniforms in Public Schools: Report of the Department of Education to the Governor and the General Assembly of Virginia,* ERIC Document 348760 (1992). This includes a survey of seven public school systems with school uniforms and a discussion of constitutional concerns.

22. *R.A.V.* v. *City of St. Paul,* 505 U.S. 377 (1992).

23. *Doe* v. *University of Michigan,* 721 F.Supp. 852 (E.D. Mich. 1989).

24. ACLU News Release, Media Relations Office, New York, New York, July 1997.

25. *Id.*

26. *Lesbian and Gay Rights Docket,* ACLU, N.Y. (1996) pp. 5–7.

27. Seattle Times, May 13, 1993, at 21.

28. On December 10, 1993, Massachusetts Governor William Weld signed into law a statute banning discrimination against gays in schools. In 2001, the Massachusetts Department of Education allocated $750,000 to support safe school programs for gay and lesbian students.

29. *Your School and the Law,* Vol. 27, Issue 20, October 24, 1997, p. 1.

30. *Immediato* v. *Rye Neck School District,* 73 F.3d 454 (2d Cir. 1996).

31. *Herndon by Herndon* v. *Chapel Hill-Carrboro Bd. of Educ.,* 89 F.3d 174 (4th Cir. 1996); *Steirer by Steirer* v. *Bethlehem Area School District,* 987 F.2d 989 (3d Cir. 1993).

32. *San Antonio Independent School District* v. *Rodriguez,* 411 U.S. 1 (1973).

33. P. Minorini and S. Sugarman, "School Finance Litigation in the Name of Educational Equity: Its Evolution, Impact, and Future," in *Equity and Adequacy in Education Finance,* National Research Council, 1999, pp. 34, 42–45.

34. Ky. Const. § 183.

35. See, e.g., Texas Const. art VII, § 1; Wash. Const. art. IX, § 1.

APPENDIX A

Selected Provisions of the U.S. Constitution

Article I

Section 8. [1] The Congress shall have Power To lay and collect Taxes, Duties, Imposts and Excises, to pay the Debts and provide for the common Defence and general Welfare of the United States;...

Article III

Section 1. The judicial Power of the United States, shall be vested in one supreme Court, and in such inferior Courts as the Congress may from time to time ordain and establish. The Judges, both of the supreme and inferior Courts, shall hold their Offices during good Behaviour, and shall, at stated Times, receive for their Services a Compensation, which shall not be diminished during their Continuance in Office....

Section 2. [1] The judicial Power shall extend to all Cases, in Law and Equity, arising under this Constitution, the Laws of the United States and Treaties made, or which shall be made, under their Authority;...to Controversies to which the United States shall be a Party;—to Controversies between two or more States;—between a State and Citizens of another State;—between Citizens of different States;—between Citizens of the same State claiming Lands under the Grants of different States, and between a State, or the Citizens thereof, and foreign States, Citizens or Subjects....

Article VI

[2] This Constitution, and the Laws of the United States which shall be made in Pursuance thereof; and all Treaties made, or which shall be made, under the Authority of the United States, shall be the supreme Law of the Land; and the Judges in every State shall be bound thereby, any Thing in the Constitution or Laws of any State to the Contrary notwithstanding.

Amendment I [1791]

Congress shall make no law respecting an establishment of religion, or prohibiting the free exercise thereof; or abridging the freedom of speech, or of the press; or the right of the people peaceably to assemble, and to petition the Government for a redress of grievances.

Amendment IV [1791]

The right of the people to be secure in their persons, houses, papers, and effects, against unreasonable searches and seizures, shall not be violated, and no Warrants shall issue, but upon probable cause, supported by Oath or affirmation. and particularly describing the place to be searched, and the persons or things to be seized.

Amendment V [1791]

No person shall be...compelled in any criminal case to be a witness against himself, nor be deprived of life, liberty, or property, without due process of law; nor shall private property be taken for public use, without just compensation.

Amendment VIII [1791]

Excessive bail shall not be required, nor excessive fines imposed, nor cruel and unusual punishments inflicted.

Amendment IX [1791]

The enumeration in the Constitution, of certain rights, shall not be construed to deny or disparage others retained by the people.

Amendment X [1791]

The powers not delegated to the United States by the Constitution, nor prohibited by it to the States, are reserved to the States respectively, or to the people.

Amendment XIV [1868]

Section 1. All persons born or naturalized in the United States, and subject to the jurisdiction thereof, are citizens of the United States and of the State wherein they reside. No State shall make or enforce any law which shall abridge the privileges or immunities of citizens of the United States; nor shall any State deprive any person of life, liberty, or property, without due process of law; nor deny to any person within its jurisdiction the equal protection of the laws.

APPENDIX B

Major Civil Rights Laws Affecting Schools

Overview of Major Federal Civil Rights Statutes Related to Elementary and Secondary Schools

Statute	Discrimination Prohibited	Interest Protected	Schools Covered
Individuals with Disabilities Education Act, 20 U.S.C. § 1400, *et seq.*	Individuals with disabilities	Education	All schools
Section 504 of the Rehabilitation Act of 1973, 29 U.S.C. § 794	Individuals with disabilities	Education, employment	Recipients of any federal financial assistance
Title IX of the Education Amendments of 1972, 42 U.S.C. § 1681, *et seq.*	Sex	Educational programs and activities	Recipients of any federal financial assistance
Age Discrimination in Employment Act, 29 U.S.C. § 621, *et seq.*	Employees who are 40 years of age or older	Employment benefits	Employers with 20 or more employees and state and local governments
Title VI of the Civil Rights Act of 1964, 42 U.S.C. § 2000d, *et seq.*	Race, color, or national origin	Benefits under federally aided programs	Recipients of federal financial assistance
Title VII of the Civil Rights Act of 1964, 42 U.S.C. 2000(e), *et seq.*	Race, color, religion, sex, or national origin	Employment benefits	All state and local governments

APPENDIX C

Other Legal Resources for Teachers

1. American Arbitration Association
   140 W. 51st Street
   New York, NY 10020
   (212) 484-4000

   A national association of business, trade, and educational associations and individuals. Conducts workshops, seminars, and conferences on arbitration and mediation. Publishes the *Arbitration Journal* and has a library of 15,000 volumes covering dispute resolution topics.

2. American Association of School Administrators
   1801 N. Moore Street
   Arlington, VA 22209
   (703) 528-0700

   A national organization with state chapters that is a professional association of school administrators. Produces materials including *The School Administrator.*

3. American Civil Liberties Union
   132 W. 43rd Street
   New York, NY 10036
   (212) 944-9800

   A national organization with both state and local chapters that "champions individual rights set forth in the United States Constitution." Activities include litigation, lobbying for civil rights legislation, and publication of materials on civil liberties issues. State and local chapters also conduct seminars and take test cases.

4. American Federation of Teachers
   555 New Jersey Avenue, N.W.
   Washington, DC 20001
   (202) 879-4400

   A national organization with local chapters that works with teachers in the areas of collective bargaining and employment rights. Engages in research and lobbying activities, offers technical assistance, and publishes materials including *American Teacher.*

5. National Association of Secondary School Principals
   1904 Association Drive
   Reston, VA 22091
   (703) 860-0200

   A national organization with state chapters that assist school administrators. Sponsors conferences and publishes materials including *Legal Memoranda* (five times a year).

6. National Education Association
   1201 16th Street, N.W.
   Washington, DC 20036
   (202) 833-4000

   A national organization with state and local chapters that is a professional association of elementary and secondary school teachers and administrators. Provides technical assistance and publishes materials including *NEA Today.*

7. Education Law Association
300 College Park
Dayton, Ohio 45469
(937) 229-3589

An organization that exchanges information on school law among lawyers, school board members, and others. Conducts seminars and publishes materials on school law, including a monthly newsletter and an annual update.

8. National School Boards Association
1680 Duke Street
Alexandria, VA 22314
(703) 838-6722.

A national clearinghouse for information relating to a variety of educational and legal issues concerning public schools.

9. State Department of Education

Each state department of education has a legal department that may provide publications or lists of state and local resources concerning education law.

SELECTED BIBLIOGRAPHY

Alexander, Kern, and M. David Alexander, *American Public School Law,* 3d ed. St. Paul, Minn.: West, 1992.

Bosmajian, Haig A., ed. *Academic Freedom.* New York: Neal Schuman Publishers, 1989.

Connolly, Jr., Walter B. *A Practical Guide to Title IX: Law, Principles, and Practices.* Washington, D.C.: National Association of College and University Attorneys, 1995.

Deskbook Encyclopedia of American School Law. Rosemont, Minn.: Data Research, Inc., 1996.

Education for the Handicapped Law Report. Alexandria, Va: CRR Publishing Company, 1987.

Fischer, Louis, and Gail Paulus Sorenson. *School Law for Counselors, Psychologists, and Social Workers,* 2d ed. New York: Longman, 1991.

Helm, Virginia. *What Educators Should Know about Copyright,* Fastback 233. Bloomington, Ind.: Phi Delta Kappa, 1986.

Hogan, John C. *The Schools, the Courts and the Public Interest,* 2d ed. Lexington, Mass.: Lexington Books, 1985.

Hudgins, H. C., Jr., and Richard Vacca, *Law and Education,* 4th ed. Charlottesville, Va.: Michie, 1995.

Imber, Michael, and Tyll van Geel, *Education Law.* McGraw Hill, New York, 1993.

Individuals with Disabilities Education Law Report. Salem, Mass.: LRP Publications, 1993.

Journal of Law and Education. Cincinnati, Ohio: Jefferson Law Book Company.

McCarthy, Martha, Nelda Cambron-McCabe, and Stephen Thomas, *Public School Law,* 4th ed. Allyn & Bacon, Boston, 1998.

Memin, Samuel. *Law and the Legal System: An Introduction,* 2d ed. Boston: Little, Brown, 1982.

Morris, Arval A. *The Constitution and American Education.* St. Paul, Minn.: West, 1980.

Nygaard, Gary, and Thomas H. Boone. *Law for Physical Educators and Coaches,* 2d ed. Columbus, Ohio: Publishing Horizons, 1989.

O'Neil, Robert M. *Classrooms in the Crossfire: The Rights and Interests of Students, Parents, Teachers, Administrators, Librarians and the Community.* Bloomington: Indiana University Press, 1981.

O'Reilly, Robert C., and Edward T. Green. *School Law for the 1990's.* Westport, Conn.: Greenwood Press, 1992.

Reutter, Edmund E., Jr. *The Law of Public Education,* 4th ed. Westbury, N.Y.: The Foundation Press, 1994.

Rothstein, Laura F. *Special Education Law.* New York: Longman, 1990.

Russo, Charles J., ed. *The Yearbook of Education Law, 1996.* Topeka, Kan.: National Organization on Legal Problems of Education, 1996.

Sametz, Lynn, and Caven S. Mcloughlin. *Educators, Children, and the Law.* Springfield, Ill.: C. C. Thomas, 1985.

Schimmel, David, and Louis Fischer. *The Rights of Parents.* Columbia, Md.: National Committee for Citizens in Education, 1987.

School Law News. Washington, D.C.: Capital Publications, Inc.

Valente, William D., and Christina Valente, *Law in the Schools,* 4th ed. Upper Saddle River, N.J.: Merrill, 1998.

West's Education Law Reporter. St. Paul, Minn.: West.

Wong, Glenn M. *Essentials of Amateur Sports Law.* Danvers, Mass.: Auburn House, 1988.

Yudof, Mark G., David L. Kirp, Tyll van Geel, and Betsy Levin. *Educational Policy and The Law,* 3d ed. Berkeley, Cal.: McCutchan Publishing Corp., 1992.

GLOSSARY

Administrative agency. Any branch or division of the government other than the judicial or legislative branches (such as the Social Security Administration, Veterans Administration, or the Department of Education).

Administrative law. Regulations and procedures that govern the operation of administrative agencies.

Adversary system. System of law in America whereby the truth is thought to be best revealed through a clash in the courtroom between opposite sides to a dispute.

Affidavit. A written statement sworn to before a person officially permitted by law to administer an oath.

Amicus curiae. "Friend of the court"; a person or organization allowed to appear in a lawsuit, to file arguments in the form of a brief supporting one side or other, even though not party to the dispute.

Answer. The first pleading by the defendant in a lawsuit. This statement sets forth the defendant's responses to the charges contained in the plaintiffs "complaint."

Appeal. Asking a higher court to review the actions of a lower court in order to correct mistakes or injustice.

Appellate court. A court having jurisdiction to review the actions of an inferior court (such as a trial court) but not having the power to hear a legal action initially.

Appellee. See *Defendant.*

Beyond a reasonable doubt. The level of proof required to convict a person of a crime. This is the highest level of proof required in any type of trial, in contrast to by *a fair preponderance of the evidence,* the level of proof in civil cases.

Bill of Rights. The first ten amendments to the U.S. Constitution.

Brief. A written summary or condensed statement of a case. Also a written statement prepared by one side in a lawsuit to explain its case to the judge.

By a fair preponderance of the evidence. The level of proof required in a civil case. This level is lower than that required in criminal cases.

Cause of action. Facts sufficient to allow a valid lawsuit to proceed.

Certiorari. A request for review of a lower court decision, which the higher court can refuse. Circumstan-

tial evidence. Evidence that indirectly proves a main fact in question. Such evidence is open to doubt, since it is inferential—for example, a student seen in the vicinity of the locker room at the time of a theft is the thief.

Civil case. Every lawsuit other than a criminal proceeding. Most civil cases involve a lawsuit brought by one person against another and usually concern money damages.

Class action. A lawsuit brought by one person on behalf of himself or herself and all other persons in the same situation: persons bringing such suits must meet certain statutory criteria and must follow certain notice procedures.

Code. A collection of laws. Most states have an education code containing all laws directly relevant to education.

Common law. Law made by judges (as opposed to law made by legislatures).

Compensatory damages. Damages that relate to the actual loss suffered by a plaintiff, such as loss of income.

Complaint. The first main paper filed in a civil lawsuit. It includes, among other things, a statement of the wrong or harm done to the plaintiff by the defendant and a request for specific help from the court. The defendant responds to the complaint by filing an "answer."

Criminal case. Cases involving crimes against the laws of the state; unlike in civil cases, the state is the prosecuting party.

De facto. In fact, actual; a situation that exists in fact whether or not it is lawful. *De facto* segregation is that which exists regardless of the law or the actions of civil authorities. Defamation. Injuring a person's character or reputation by false or malicious statements. This includes both *libel* and *slander.*

Defendant (appellee). The person against whom a legal action is brought. This legal action may be civil or criminal. At the appeal stage, the party against whom an appeal is taken is known as the *appellee.*

De jure. Of right, legitimate; lawful. *De* jure segregation is that which is sanctioned by law. De minimus. Small, unimportant; not worthy of concern.

Demurrer. The formal means by which one party to a lawsuit argues against the legal sufficiency of the other party's claim. A demurrer basically contends that even if all the facts that the other party alleges are true, they do not constitute a legal cause of action.

De novo. Completely new from the start; for example: a trial *de novo* is a completely new trial ordered by the trial judge or by an appeals court.

Dictum. A digression; a discussion of side points or unrelated points. Short for *obiter dictum;* plural is *dicta.*

Disclaimer. The refusal to accept certain types of responsibility. For example, a college catalogue may disclaim any responsibility for guaranteeing that the courses contained therein will actually be offered, since courses, programs, and instructors are likely to change without notice.

En banc. In the bench. The full panel of judges assigned to a court sit to hear a case, usually a case of special significance.

Equity. Fairness; the name of a type of court originating in England to handle legal problems when the existing laws did not cover some situations in which a person's rights were violated by another person. In the United States, civil courts have the powers of both law and equity. If only money is represented in a case, the court is acting as a law court and will give only monetary relief. If something other than money is requested—injunction, declaratory judgment, specific performance of a contractual agreement, etc.—then the court takes jurisdiction in equity and will grant a decree ordering acts to be done or not done. There is no jury in an equity case. Actions at law and suits in equity involve civil cases, not criminal.

Et al. "And others." When the words *et al.* are used in an opinion, the court is thereby indicating that there are unnamed parties, either plaintiffs or defendants, also before the court in the case.

Ex parte. With only one side present; an *ex parte* judicial proceeding involves only one party without notice to, or contestation by, any person adversely affected.

Ex post facto law. A law that retrospectively changes the legal consequences of an act that has already been performed. Article 1, section 10 of the U.S. Constitution forbids the passage of *ex post facto* laws.

Expunge. Blot out. For example, a court order requesting that a student's record be expunged of any refer-

ences to disciplinary action during such and such a time period means that the references are to be "wiped off the books."

Ex rel. On behalf of, when a case is titled *State ex rel. Doe v. Roe,* it means that the state is bringing a lawsuit against Roe on behalf of Doe.

Fiduciary. A relationship between persons in which one person acts for another in a position of trust.

Guardian ad litem. A guardian appointed by a court to represent a minor unable to represent him or herself.

Hearing. An oral proceeding before a court or quasi-judicial tribunal. Hearings that describe a process to ascertain facts and provide evidence are labeled "trial-like hearings" or simply "trials." Hearings that relate to a presentation of ideas as distinguished from facts and evidence are known as "arguments." The former occur in trial courts and the latter occur in appellate courts. The terms "trial," "trial-like hearing," "quasijudicial hearing," "evidentiary hearing," and "adjudicatory hearing" are all used by courts and have overlapping meanings. See *Trial.*

Hearsay. Secondhand evidence; facts not in the personal knowledge of the witness but a repetition of what others said that is used to prove the truth of what those others said. Hearsay is generally not allowed as evidence at a trial, although there are many exceptions.

Holding. The rule of law in a case; that part of the judge's written opinion that applies the law to the facts of the case and about which can be said "the case means no more and no less than this." A holding is the opposite of *dictum.*

In camera. "In chambers"; in a judge's private office; a hearing in court with all spectators excluded.

Incriminate. To involve in a crime, to cause to appear guilty.

Informed consent. A person's agreement to allow something to happen (such as being the subject of a research study) that is based on a full disclosure of facts needed to make the decision intelligently.

Injunction. A court order requiring someone to do something or refrain from taking some action.

In loco parentis. In place of the parent; acting as a parent with respect to the care, supervision, and discipline of a child.

In re. In the matter of. this is a prefix to the name of a case, often used when a child is involved. For example, "*In re John Jones*" might be the title of a child neglect proceeding though it is really against the parents.

Ipso facto. By the fact itself, by the mere fact that.

Judicial review. The power of a court to declare a statute unconstitutional; also the power to interpret the meaning of laws.

Jurisdiction. A court's authority to hear a case; also the geographical area within which a court has the right and power to operate. Original jurisdiction means that the court will be the first to hear the case; appellate jurisdiction means that the court reviews cases on appeal from lower court rulings.

Law. Basic rules of order as pronounced by a government. Common law refers to laws originating in custom or practice. Statute law refers to laws passed by legislatures and recorded in public documents. Case law are the pronouncements of courts.

Libel. Written defamation; published false and malicious written statements that injure a person's reputation.

Mandamus. A writ issued by a court commanding that some official duty be performed. Material. Important, going to the heart of the matter; for example, a material fact is one necessary to reach a decision.

Misrepresentation. A false statement; if knowingly made, misrepresentation may be illegal and result in punishment.

Mitigation. The reduction in a fine, penalty, sentence, or damages initially assessed or decreed against a defendant.

Moot. Abstract; not a real case involving a real dispute.

Motion. A request made by a lawyer that a judge take certain action, such as dismissing a case. Opinion. A judge's statement of the decision reached in a case.

Concurring opinion. Agrees with the majority opinion but gives different or added reasons for arriving at that opinion.

Dissenting opinion. Disagrees with the majority opinion.

Majority opinion. The opinion agreed on by more than half the judges or justices hearing a case, sometimes called the opinion of the court.

Ordinance. The term applied to a municipal corporation's legislative enactments.

Parens patriae. Parent of the country; The historical right of all governments to take care of persons under their jurisdiction, particularly minors and incapacitated persons.

Per curiam. An unsigned decision and opinion of a court, as distinguished from one signed by a judge.

Petitioner. One who initiates a proceeding and requests that some relief be granted on his or her behalf. A plaintiff. When the term *petitioner* is used, the one against whom the petitioner is complaining is referred to as the *respondent*.

Plaintiff. One who initiates a lawsuit; the party bringing suit.

Pleading. The process of making formal, written statements of each side of a case. First the plaintiff submits a paper with facts and claims: then the defendant submits a paper with facts and counterclaims; then the plaintiff responds: and so on until all issues and questions are clearly posed for a trial.

Political question. A question that the courts will not decide because it concerns a decision more properly made by another branch of government, such as the legislature.

Precedent. A court decision on a question of law that gives authority or direction on how to decide a similar question of law in a later case with similar facts.

Prima facie. Clear on the face of it; presumably, a fact that will be considered to be true unless disproved by contrary evidence. For example, a *prima facie* case is a case that will win unless the other side comes forward with evidence to dispute it.

Punitive damages. Money awarded to a person by a court that is over and above the damages actually sustained. Punitive damages are designed to serve as a deterrent to similar acts in the future.

Quasi judicial. The case-deciding function of an administrative agency.

Redress. To set right, remedy, make up for, remove the cause of a complaint or grievance.

Remand. Send back. A higher court may remand a case to a lower court with instructions to take some action in the case.

Res judicata. A thing decided. Thus if a court decides a case, the matter is settled and no new lawsuit on the same subject may be brought by the persons involved.

Respondent. One who makes an answer in a legal appellate proceeding. This term is frequently used in appellate and divorce cases rather than the more customary term, *defendant*.

Sectarian. Characteristic of a sect or religion.

Secular. Not specifically religious, ecclesiastical, or clerical; relating to the worldly or temporal.

Sine qua non. A thing or condition that is indispensable.

Slander. Oral defamation; the speaking of false and malicious words that injure another person's reputation, business, or property rights.

Sovereign immunity. The government's freedom from being sued for money damages without its consent.

Standing. A person's right to bring a lawsuit because he or she is directly affected by the issues raised.

Stare deeisis. "Let the decision stand'; a legal rule that when a court has decided a ease by applying a legal principle to a set of facts, that court should stick by that principle and apply it to all later cases with clearly similar facts unless there is a good reason not to. This rule helps promote predictability and reliability in judicial decision making and is inherent in the American legal system.

Statute of limitation. A statute that sets forth the time period within which litigation may be commenced in a particular cause of action.

Strict scrutiny. A stringent standard applied by the courts when a person's important constitutional right is restricted or denied by official action.

Tort. A civil wrong done by one person to another. For an act to be a tort, there must be: a legal duty owed by one person to another, a breach of that duty, and harm done as a direct result of the action.

Trial. A process occurring in a court whereby opposing parties present evidence, which is subject to cross-examination and rebuttal, pertaining to the matter in dispute.

Trial court. The court in which a case is originally tried, as distinct from higher courts to which the case might be appealed.

Ultra vires. Going beyond the specifically delegated authority to act; for example, a school board which is by law restricted from punishing students for behavior occurring wholly off campus might act *ultra vires* in punishing a student for behavior observed at a private weekend party.

Waiver. An intentional or uncoerced release of a known right.

INDEX